$11.95

HISTORY OF THE THEATRE

THE MINNESOTA Theatre Company's production of *The House of Atreus,* John Lewin's adaptation of Aeschylus' *Oresteia.* Shown here are Orestes, Electra, and Pylades. All roles were played by men. [Courtesy of Minnesota Theatre Company]

HISTORY

OF THE

THEATRE

OSCAR G. BROCKETT

Library of Congress Catalog Card Number: 68-18812
Printed in the United States of America.

Fourth printing . . . February, 1970

PREFACE

In this book, I have attempted to trace the development of the theatre from primitive times until 1967, when I completed the manuscript. I have placed major emphasis upon the theatre in Europe, where it has been cultivated most assiduously, and in America as an extension of the European tradition. Because of space limitations, I have treated the Oriental theatre only briefly and with an eye to its influence upon recent trends in the West.

The theatre is an extremely complex institution, for it encompasses playwriting, directing, acting, costume, makeup, scenery, lighting, properties, theatre architecture, machinery, special effects, management, audiences, and criticism. I have touched upon most of these aspects in this book, although the space devoted to each varies. For example, because drama has been discussed merely as one element in the total theatrical context, only the basic outlines of its development have been traced, for it would require a book of equal or greater scope to do the subject justice. The object has been to provide a chronological narrative of the theatre's development as an institution rather than an exhaustive treatment of any one part. Furthermore, since the theatre cannot be divorced from the many social forces which have shaped it, I have sought to provide an account not only of how the theatre developed but of why it took particular paths. Although I have included facts in abundance, my major concern has been with those practices which give each era its distinctive flavor, and those trends which influenced succeeding periods.

While history aims at recreating the past, it is seldom a purely factual study. The evidence, whether slight or copious, must always be interpreted. Thus, the scholarly reconstructions of theatrical practices in any period often vary widely. I have tried to alert the reader to important differences of opinion and to encourage him to read several accounts before accepting any as definitive.

A book of this scope obviously depends heavily upon the work of many scholars. It has been impossible for me to acknowledge each debt within the text, for to do so would double the length of the book. Instead, I have included bibliographies arranged according to chapters, both as an indication of the principal sources used and as a guide to further reading. Since the theatre can at times be best understood through a study of visual materials, I have also supplied many illustrations in each chapter both to clarify the text and to give a flavor of the theatre in that period.

I acknowledge the assistance of many persons in the preparation of this book. In addition to the many published works of established scholars, I am also indebted to countless students who have contributed to my knowledge in classes and seminars. More immediately, I have been aided by George Bryan in verifying facts, by Arthur Hopper, Jr. in locating appropriate illustrations, and by Audrey McClure, Betty Hawes, Linda Anderson, and Gloria Gresham in the preparation of the manuscript. I am grateful to the Office of Research and Advanced Studies, Indiana University, for financial support for part of this project. My indebtedness to individuals and publishers for permission to reprint copyrighted materials is acknowledged in the captions accompanying pictures. Above all, I am grateful to my wife, Lenyth Brockett, who, with her extensive experience in the theatre, has given continuing and invaluable assistance and counsel throughout the writing of this book.

Oscar G. Brockett
Bloomington, Indiana

CONTENTS

CONTENTS

ix

THE ORIGINS
OF THE THEATRE

*T*he basic elements of theatre and drama are found in every society no matter how primitive or advanced. They may be seen in the dances and ceremonies of primitive peoples, just as they can be found today in such diverse activities as religious services, political campaigns, parades, sports, and children's make-believe. But most of these activities are not intentionally theatrical, even though they may use such theatrical elements as spectacle, dialogue, or conflict. Thus, it is essential to distinguish between *the theatrical in daily life* and *the theatre as a form of art*. It would be impossible to construct a coherent history of all the theatrical elements found in mankind's diverse activities through the ages. This book, consequently, will be concerned with the theatre as an institution; its origins, and its subsequent development.

In exploring the beginnings of the theatre, it has been customary to use evidence drawn from primitive societies. Anthropologists of the late 19th and early 20th centuries argued that all cultures go through similar patterns of development, and consequently that a study of primitive groups which still exist can supply valuable clues to the origin of drama 2500 years ago. As a result most accounts of the beginnings of theatre and drama are based upon studies of modern primitive societies, although more recent anthropologists have seriously questioned this procedure.

The pattern of development which has been deduced from the study of primitive groups can only be summarized here. In the beginning, man gradually becomes aware of forces which appear to control his food supply and the other determinants of his existence. Having no understanding of natural causes, he attributes occurrences to supernatural forces and assigns human motivations, such as anger and jealousy, to them. Next, he begins to search for means by which he may win the favor of these powers. Over a period of time, he perceives a supposed connection between certain of his attempts and the desired ends. These acts are then refined and formalized into a ritual. At this early stage, rites are usually performed by the entire tribe, while the "audience" is the supernatural force.

Once a ritual is clearly established, the demand soon arises that it always be performed precisely and without deviation. A failure to achieve success in battle, hunt, or harvest is often attributed to the displeasure of the god because of some mistake made in the performance of the ritual. Since all members of the tribe cannot perform the ceremony properly, the most effective are chosen as representatives of the entire group. The rest now participate only at second hand. Thus, the tribe is divided into "actors" and "audience."

By this time stories or myths—which explain, illustrate, or idealize the rites—have usually appeared. Often they draw on real events or persons, although these may be considerably transformed in the stories. Frequently the myths include as characters those supernatural forces which the rites celebrate or hope to influence. Performers may then come to impersonate the mythical characters in the enactment of rituals or in accompanying celebrations.

As a tribe becomes more sophisticated, its conceptions of supernatural forces and of causal relationships change. As a result, some rites are abandoned or modified. The myths which have grown up around the rites may be retained, however, as a part of the tribe's oral tradition. At some later time, stories based on these myths may be acted out as a kind of primitive drama divorced from all ceremonial concerns. When this occurs, the first step has been taken toward the theatre as a specialized activity.

Many tribes never take this decisive step. In most primitive cultures performances remain parts of rituals and thus are utilitarian, being intended to bring about some practical goal. To primitive man, the crucial problem is to survive in a world which he understands only dimly, and which often appears hostile. Thus, when he wears a disguise and impersonates a god, it is not, as a rule, for the sake of giving pleasure but rather of gaining some material reward, such as an adequate supply of food or success in war. His rituals are as "scientific" as his knowledge permits, and probably seem no more theatrical to him than the use of fertilizers or contour farming do to us.

In those societies which have developed drama, the precise evolutionary stages are still obscure. One sign of the change can be seen in the introduction of comedy, which was late in appearing in ritual drama. Comedy requires a greater degree of objectivity than does serious drama, for it depends upon the ability to see deviations from norms as ridiculous rather than as serious threats to the welfare of the whole tribe. Other probable sources of an independent theatre can be found in those dances which are primarily rhythmical and gymnastic, and in imitations of animal movements and sounds, both of which, completely divorced from any utilitarian functions, are to be found among many primitive tribes. In these cases, it is the virtuosity and grace of the performers which are admired.

A very few primitive tribes—in Australia, the Philippines, and Africa—have evolved "pleasure plays" (that is, short dramas intended primarily as entertainment). Most of these plays, however, seem to have been motivated by the attempt to ward off evil by ridiculing unfriendly spirits, unsuccessful war or hunting tactics, or socially unacceptable behavior. Such works are interesting in part because of their very rarity. A single pleasure play seems to be the most that any primitive tribe can produce, and these dramas have become as fixed and traditional as rituals. In every case, they are inconsequential when compared with the drama of advanced societies.

Within primitive societies, dramatic ritual serves a number of purposes. First, it is intended to influence events through "sympathetic magic." One of the fundamental premises of primitive magic is that a desired effect—such as success in battle or adequate rainfall—can be achieved by acting it out. Many rituals of this kind are related to seasonal changes. Primitive man does not always perceive that the years recur in a fixed pattern. Therefore, he may feel it essential to enact rites to insure the return of spring and the continuance of fertility. At times he may resort to sexual orgies to induce fertility in the earth; at others, he stages ritual combats between the representatives of winter/death and spring/life, ending with the triumph of the latter.

Second, dramatic ritual may be used to educate. Since one mark of a primitive society is the absence of a written language, dramatic ritual serves as a means for passing on traditions. Many primitive tribes use initiation rites, some occupying only a few days but others extending over a period of years, to acquaint the young with sacred beliefs, taboos, mores, and history. Such rites are still common among Australian and African tribes and were traditional with American Indian tribes.

Third, dramatic ritual is often used to glorify—a supernatural power, a victory in a hunt or war, the tribal past, a hero, or a tribal totem (an animal, plant, or natural element with which a tribe thinks itself closely related). Fourth, ritual drama may entertain and give pleasure. Even in the most

A HOOP DANCE by American Indians of the Southwestern
United States. [From Theatre Arts (1929)]

serious ceremony there may be an element of pleasure which derives from
the spectacle, the repetition of a formal pattern, or the skillful performance.
The emphasis upon pleasure as an end in itself, however, is not usually
developed in primitive societies.

Although our specific goals may differ considerably from those of primitive man, the modern theatre still serves the last three purposes. Similarly,
ritual drama and theatre employ the same basic elements—music, dance,
speech, masks, costumes, performers, audience, and auditorium. In almost all
dramatic ritual, pantomimic dance with rhythmical and musical accompaniment is more fundamental than speech, which may nevertheless be used.
Masks and costumes are usual accessories, for most primitive people believe
that a spirit can be controlled by making a likeness of it or by assuming its
likeness. Masks and costumes, consequently, are means of embodying the god
to be propitiated, the animal to be killed, the event to be brought about.
Makeup—in the form of paint, ashes, or juices—may supplement masks and
costumes by covering parts of the body. There must also be "actors," highly
skilled and disciplined ones when no deviations in the ritual are permitted.
When rites have become fixed, the tribal elders, priests, or witch doctors may
exercise strict control over the performances and serve in a capacity comparable to that of a theatrical director.

An "acting area" and, if there are spectators, an "auditorium" are
needed. The most typical spatial arrangement for dramatic rituals is the
circular performance area surrounded by spectators. In other instances, as in
certain Australian ceremonies which use painted-bark or cloth panels as a
background, the audience sits or stands on three sides of the performance
area. Thus in dramatic ritual all of the basic elements of theatre are present,

MASKED FIGURE from Nigeria. The masks in this area are often covered with skin and are worn by medicine men or members of secret societies. The masks, representing ancestors, are hidden from the sight of women. [Courtesy Field Museum of Natural History]

and it is usually assumed that they were gradually transformed into an independent drama.

But the theory that drama evolved from ritual has not gone unchallenged. Many anthropologists have questioned the premise that all primitive societies follow the same developmental patterns, and thus have cast doubt on the validity of evidence drawn from modern primitive groups in explaining the appearance of drama in antiquity. Futhermore, the exclusive concern for ritualistic origins is overly simplistic. In the beginning ritual also included religion, art, philosophy, history, science, and all of man's attempts to cope with human experience, since he could not as yet distinguish among various kinds of knowledge. An advanced society is differentiated in large part from the primitive by the degree to which specialized knowledge and skills have emerged. As a primitive society enters a more advanced state, it separates ritual from history, science, and other concerns. Consequently, on the surface it might seem that theatre as a specialized activity would inevitably appear; but not all societies, even advanced ones, produced a drama. Why, then, have some emerging societies created a theatre while others have not? Furthermore, why does drama continue to be valued after it ceases to fulfill any immediately practical or ritualistic purpose?

A partial explanation is suggested by Aristotle's argument that man is by nature an imitative creature—that he takes pleasure in imitating persons, things, and actions, and in seeing imitations. Aristotle states that drama is an imitation of human deeds, feelings, and thoughts, and gives pleasure because it helps man to understand his world and organize his responses to it. Thus it can be both entertainment and a form of knowledge.

Even this, however, is not a complete explanation, for the "imitative instinct" does not necessarily lead to drama. At least two other conditions seem to be essential: first, the appearance of men who can organize the theatrical elements into an experience of a high order, and second, a society which can recognize the value of theatre and drama as independent specialized activities. Only then can the ever-present potentialities be realized.

It is for these reasons that the Greeks must be considered the primary inventors of theatre and drama, for, regardless of all antecedents, it was they who first recognized the possibilities which had existed for centuries.

Ritual Drama in Egypt and the Near East

As a background, it may be helpful to consider briefly some of the rituals which had appeared in Egypt and the Near East long before drama emerged in Greece. The Egyptians were the first people to evolve an advanced society, having developed a calendar in 4241 B.C. (the earliest date known in history) and a central government by 3400 B.C.

Much of our information about the Egyptians has survived because of their preoccupation with insuring the continuance of life and power after death. Since they conceived of afterlife as an extension of material existence, they sought to preserve the bodies of the dead and to surround them with the necessities and luxuries of life. They discovered embalming and built tombs, including the great pyramids, to protect the remains. It is against this background that the dramatic rituals of Egypt must be viewed, since practically all were related either to the pharaoh's power on earth or after death.

It is difficult to assess the place of dramatic ritual in Egyptian life, since scholars have been unable to agree on what the available texts represent. For example, hieroglyphics and scenes, depicting the trials through which the spirit must pass before being admitted to an honorable place in afterlife, appear on the walls of many pyramids. Most of the more than 50 surviving

"Pyramid Texts" date from about 2750 to about 2475 B.C., although certain passages were probably traditional by this time and may have originated a thousand years earlier. But what do the Pyramid Texts represent? Some scholars have argued that they are ritual dramas which were enacted by priests at regular intervals to insure the well-being of the dead pharaoh. This view is based principally on the presence of occasional dialogue and indications of action. But there is no concrete evidence that they were intended as drama, or even that they were ever performed. Consequently, equally reputable scholars have denied any connection between the Pyramid Texts and dramatic representation, pointing out that such nondramatic works as the Bible also contain passages in dialogue and indications of action.

Other contested texts relate to the coronation of pharaohs. One of the few remaining fragments has been interpreted by some scholars as a series of ritualistic scenes performed at various places in Egypt, the new ruler in this way symbolically taking possession of his kingdom. In this text, the pharaoh is associated with Horus, who in mythology succeeded his father, Osiris, as king. Contrarily, other scholars have noted that these "coronation plays" are probably no more "dramatic" than the ceremonies surrounding the coronation of rulers in modern times.

Another ritual, sometimes called the Memphite Drama, may have been performed each year on the first day of spring. It dates from about 2500 B.C. and tells of the death and resurrection of Osiris and the coronation of Horus. Some historians interpret this as a drama in which Horus, symbolizing the regenerated year spirit, was impersonated by the pharaoh.

The most important example of a possible ritual drama in Egypt is the "Abydos Passion Play," treating the death and resurrection of the god Osiris. Said to be the son of Geb (the earth) and Nut (the sky), Osiris succeeded his father as ruler and was married to his sister, Isis. His brother, Seth, jealous of his power, eventually killed him and buried parts of the body at various places in Egypt. Isis gathered the pieces of the body and, with the aid of Anubis, the jackal-god later to be the god of embalmment, revived Osiris. Since he was not allowed to return to earth, Osiris was buried at Abydos and went to dwell in the underworld, where he became the judge of souls. Isis bore a son, Horus, who fought with Seth and won back his father's kingdom. This myth, of very ancient origin, was the most popular in Egypt.

At Abydos, considered the most sacred spot in Egypt, a ritual relating to Osiris came to be performed annually perhaps as early as 2500 B.C. and continued to about 550 B.C. In spite of this long history, no part of the text remains. What we know of the ceremonies is deduced from the account of Ikhernofret, a participant sometime between 1887 and 1849 B.C., of what he did at one of the celebrations.

Again, however, scholars cannot agree upon the interpretation to be given Ikhernofret's account. Some have argued that the major events of

Osiris' life were reenacted with much spectacle (including battles, processions, and burial ceremonies), the principal roles being taken by priests while the people participated in mass scenes, each section of the play being performed in a different location. In some accounts, this ritual is regarded as one of the most elaborate dramatic spectacles ever staged. Other historians have vigorously objected to the designation of the ritual as a passion play and have denied that the life or death of Osiris was enacted. Rather they see the ritual as a commemoration of all the dead pharaohs, each of whom is symbolized in Osiris. They argue that the basic premise of the ritual was that Osiris is dead and that the ceremony consequently had the characteristics of a royal funeral.

In addition to the Egyptian dramatic rituals, those of the Near East should be noted. Canaanite, Hittite, and Babylonian texts have been discovered on clay tablets dating from the 15th to the 13th centuries, B.C. For the most part, they record rituals concerned with the seasonal pattern of birth, maturity, death, and rebirth. (Translations and discussion of these and the Egyptian texts can be found in Theodor Gaster's *Thespis*.)

Some historians have suggested direct influence from Egypt and the Near East on the development of Greek theatre and drama. The most important evidence for this is found in the account of Herodotus (*c.* 484– *c.* 425 B.C.), the Greek historian who visited Egypt about 450. He noted two performances there and suggested that Dionysus, the god in whose honor plays were presented in Greece, was a disguised version of Osiris. Although this account records interesting parallels, no direct connection between the Egyptian and Greek theatrical traditions can be established.

Even if we posit a direct influence, each should be given its proper credit. The Egyptians maintained an advanced civilization for about 3000 years (a period longer than that which separates us from the beginnings of Greek drama) and never progressed theatrically beyond the stage of ritual drama. Their failure, and that of the people of the Near East with almost as long a history, only serves to emphasize the enormous achievement of the Greeks.

THEATRE AND DRAMA IN ANCIENT GREECE

*T*he first decisive steps toward theatre and drama were taken in Greece in the 6th century, B.C.; during the following century drama reached a level of excellence seldom surpassed. Consequently, any treatment of the Greek theatre must give primary emphasis to the years between 500 and 400 B.C. A too-exclusive concern for the 5th century, however, has often obscured the fact that the Greeks maintained a theatre for almost 1000 years. Therefore, while emphasizing the 5th century, the following account will sketch the development of the whole. Unfortunately there is practically no point on which agreement exists, for the incontestable facts are few. Historians have filled in the gaps by suggesting patterns of origin and development which seem logically consistent with the scant facts. The resulting conjectures have led to many controversies, the most important of which will be noted.

The Origin of Tragedy

Much of what we know of the Greek theatre has been preserved because the Athenian state gradually gave official recognition and financial support to it. Thus, our first certain reference to drama is in 534 B.C., when a prize was established for the best tragedy presented at the City Dionysia. It seems likely, however, that drama existed, at least in embryonic form, before that time.

Although tradition credits Thespis, winner of the first contest, with the invention of drama, some ancient accounts place him as late as sixteenth in the line of tragic poets. This disparity is probably due to the original ambiguity of the term "tragedy," which means "goat song." This label is now usually traced to a time when the chorus danced either for a goat as a prize or around a goat which was then sacrificed. Since none of the suggested derivations, of which there are many, provide any clues to the origin of dramatic forms, it is necessary to turn to the dithyramb, which Aristotle called the forerunner of tragedy.

The dithyramb was a hymn or narrative song honoring Dionysus, the god in whose honor drama was later presented. Before the 7th century B.C., it probably consisted of an improvised story sung by a choral leader, to which was added a traditional refrain sung by the chorus. Arion (c. 625–585 B.C.) is usually credited with transforming the dithyramb into a literary composition, which probably means that he was the first to write hymns on well-defined, heroic subjects and to give them titles. Solon attributed the invention of tragedy to Arion; from other sources, we know that either Arion's singers were called *tragoidoi* or that their songs were called *tragikon drama*. Arion also introduced satyrs as a chorus and used musical accompaniment which may have been similar to that found later in tragedy. Arion's dithyrambs were entirely narrative and lyrical, however, no parts being acted.

Arion lived at Corinth on the Peloponnesian peninsula, the home of the Dorian Greeks, who later claimed to have invented tragedy. Although this claim is unjustified, the Dorians did develop to a high degree certain qualities in the dithyramb which were later emphasized in tragedy. This may explain why some ancient writers did not consider Thespis to be the first author of tragedy. In any case, it is clear that by 534 lyric poetry, choral singing and dancing, and heroic subject matter were already highly advanced. This may account for the rapid perfection of tragedy.

Aristotle states that tragedy developed out of the improvisations of the leaders of dithyrambs. Exactly how this came about, or over what period of time, no one knows, but the final step is now usually attributed to Thespis. His innovation probably consisted of adding a prologue and lines (spoken by an actor impersonating a character) to what had previously been a wholly narrative work sung and danced by a chorus.

Little is known of Thespis. It is possible that he first performed plays in Icaria, a subdivision of Attica, as early as 560 B.C. Horace, the Roman poet, states that Thespis traveled about on a wagon with his plays, which, if true, would indicate that he performed at other towns than Athens.

The beginnings of tragedy, thus, are obscure. When it was accorded official sanction in 534 the major formative step had been taken. At this time an association with Dionysus was also officially recognized, one which was to continue thereafter.

The City Dionysia in the 6th Century

The worship of Dionysus probably originated in the Near East and was introduced into Greece around the 13th century B.C. The new cult met with considerable resistance because of its ecstatic nature; its celebrations often involved intoxication, sexual orgy, and the rending and devouring of a sacrificial victim (frequently human); bands of frenzied women, called Maenads, ran wild through the country. In spite of resistance, Dionysus was gradually accepted throughout Greece. In some places he displaced other gods and absorbed their attributes. Gradually the orgiastic nature of Dionysian worship abated, and by the 6th century it had lost most of its ecstatic characteristics.

According to the myths, Dionysus was the son of Zeus, the greatest of Greek gods, and Semele, a mortal. Reared by satyrs (who are often associated with him in dithyrambs, drama, and art), he was killed, dismembered, and resurrected. As a god, he was associated with fertility, wine and revelry, while the events of his life connect him with the year-spirit found in other primitive religions—that is, the cycle of the seasons and the recurring pattern of birth, maturity, death, and rebirth. The most important function of Dionysian worship was to insure fertility: to guarantee the return of spring and the productivity of both human beings and the land and to secure ample harvests.

The Greeks honored each of their gods through one or more annual festivals. In Attica, of which Athens was the principal town, four festivals were held in honor of Dionysus, and it was at one of these—the City Dionysia—that drama was first presented. Although the City Dionysia was the last of the four festivals to be inaugurated, by the end of the 6th

BIRD COSTUMES worn in ritual dances. A vase painting from
the 6th century B.C. [From Dieterich, *Pulcinella* (1897)]

century it was by far the most important as a result of its reorganization in
534, the year in which tragedy was recognized.

The various changes in the City Dionysia are closely connected with
local political events. During the 7th and 6th centuries the government of
Athens was unstable, largely because of the rivalries between great families.
One of these, the Peisistratidae, came to power in 560, and it was Peisi-
stratus, a member of this family, who elevated the City Dionysia to a role of
prominence. When the Peisistratidae were overthrown in 510, the political
structure of the state was changed. A democracy was created, and, in order
to break up the family loyalties which had been at the root of past troubles,
all the inhabitants of Attica were divided into ten tribes based on geographical areas and composed of a cross section of classes.

The attempt to stimulate loyalty to the new tribes may account for the
inclusion of dithyrambic contests at the City Dionysia after about 509, in
which each tribe presented one dithyramb in competition for a prize.
Although dithyrambic contests may have been held earlier, they could not
have been organized on this principle; nothing is known of the earlier
arrangements.

Around 501, satyr plays were added to the contests of the City
Dionysia; after this time, each dramatist was required to present three
tragedies and one satyr play. Thus, by the time Aeschylus began to compete
around 499 B.C., the festival and many of its basic rules were well established.

In the period between Thespis and Aeschylus, only three dramatists
are known. Choerilus, who began writing between 523 and 520 and
continued into the 5th century, is said to have written 160 plays, to have

won 13 contests, and to have made unspecified innovations in costumes and masks. Pratinas wrote about 50 dramas, and was especially noted for his satyr plays, a form which he supposedly invented. Phrynichus (*fl.* 511–476), the first author known to have written on contemporary subjects, is said to have introduced female characters. He was also noted for the beauty of his choral lyrics and for the invention of new varieties of choral dance.

No examples of drama from the 6th century survive. The little we know suggests that experimentation with dramatic forms and conventions was common, that the lyrical and choral elements were dominant and highly developed, that all characters were played by a single actor, and that subject matter was drawn from mythology or, occasionally, from recent history.

Tragedy in the 5th Century

Our knowledge of Greek tragedy is based almost entirely on the work of three playwrights of the 5th century: Aeschylus, Sophocles, and Euripides. Historians usually assume that the surviving plays by these authors are representative, but it is perhaps well to remember that only 31 tragedies remain from the more than 1000 that were written between 500 and 400 B.C.

Although there is no typical Greek tragedy, certain recurring structural features can be outlined. Most of the plays begin with a *prologue* devoted primarily to an exposition of prior events. Next comes the *parodos*, or entrance of the chorus; if there is no prologue, the *parodos* begins the play. The *parodoi* of extant plays vary in length, from 20 to 200 lines, and serve to introduce the chorus, to give exposition, and to establish the proper mood. After the *parodos*, a series of episodes, varying in number from three to six and separated by choral songs (or *stasima*), develop the main action. The *exodus*, or concluding scene, includes the departure of all the characters and the chorus.

The point of attack in the plays is late—that is, they usually begin just prior to the climactic moment and dramatize only the last part of the story—thus requiring considerable exposition of prior events. The convention of keeping deaths and physical violence offstage, one that was not invariably observed, also led to the regular use of messengers to relate offstage action. In most of the plays, the time of the action is continuous, although there are notable exceptions, as in Aeschylus' *Eumenides*. Similarly, most of the tragedies occur in a single place, but again some works, such as Sophocles' *Ajax*, deviate from the usual pattern. The unity of action is also typical, although several of Euripides' plays do not develop through a series of causally related episodes.

All extant Greek tragedies are based upon myth or history. Each writer was free, however, to vary the stories and to invent motivations, seldom provided in the myths, for characters and events. Thus, though many dramatists might begin with the same basic story, each treatment varied considerably. Agathon, writing at the end of the 5th century, was the first to invent stories for tragedies, but his example was never widely followed.

Greek dramatists were very economical in their choice of events and character traits, using a few broad strokes rather than a multiplicity of details. They paid little attention to physical and sociological aspects of characterization, concentrating instead upon the psychological and ethical qualities of their personages.

The oldest surviving Greek plays are by Aeschylus (525–456), who began competing at the City Dionysia about 499. Although about 80 titles are known, only seven plays by Aeschylus have survived: *The Persians* (472), *Seven Against Thebes* (467), the *Oresteia,* a trilogy of plays made up of *Agamemnon, Libation Bearers* and *Eumenides* (458), *The Suppliants,* and *Prometheus Bound* (exact dates unknown but probably after 468). The major innovation attributed to Aeschylus is the introduction of the second actor. It is usually assumed that this occurred early in his career, but no date for it can be fixed. Since Sophocles introduced the third actor about 467, Aeschylus' late plays also frequently take advantage of this additional performer.

All of Aeschylus' extant plays, with the exception of *The Persians,* formed parts of trilogies (three plays based on a single story, or developing a common theme). That Aeschylus often needed three plays to encompass his tragic idea indicates his interests and method. The *Oresteia* (the only surviving Greek trilogy) shows the evolution of the concept of justice, with the impersonal power of the state eventually replacing the personal revenge which had previously created an endless chain of guilt. In this trilogy, Aeschylus dramatizes conflicting ideals as they are embodied in human situations, and, because he is able to reconcile them in a still higher principle, the action can be resolved happily. This pattern, found in several of his works, indicates that Aeschylus was interested in a different kind of tragedy than were Sophocles and Euripides.

Because Aeschylus embodies cosmic conflicts in his agents, his characters are sometimes said to be superhuman. They are usually given a limited number of traits, but these are incisive, powerful, and entirely appropriate to the actions they perform. Aeschylus is also said to be essentially a philosophical and religious dramatist. This should not obscure the fact that he is also the most theatrical of the Greek tragedians, for he uses the resources of the theatre to great advantage. His plays often call for spectacle on a monumental scale: second choruses and numerous attendants, chariots drawn by horses, picturesque and sometimes frightening mythological characters. He also makes considerable use of visual symbolism, unusual choral dances, and lavish costumes. If Aeschylus was somewhat more primitive in his dramatic technique than his successors, the grandeur of his conceptions has seldom been surpassed.

Sophocles (c. 496–06) is thought to have written over 120 plays, but only seven have survived: *Ajax* (between 450 and 440), *Antigone* (c. 441), *Oedipus Rex* (c. 430–25), *Philoctetes* (409), *Electra* (c. 418–10), *Trachiniae* (c. 413), and *Oedipus at Colonus* (406). A substantial portion of one satyr play, *The Trackers,* is also extant. Sophocles won 24 contests, the first in 468 when he defeated Aeschylus, and never placed lower than second. He is credited with the introduction of the third actor, with raising the number of the chorus from 12 to 15, and with the first use of scene painting.

Sophocles emphasized his characters more than Aeschylus, in whose plays the chorus is always of major significance. Sophocles' characters are complex and psychologically well-motivated. His protagonists, noble but not faultless men, are usually subjected to a terrible crisis leading to suffering and eventual self-recognition, as well as to the perception of a higher law which lies behind human events.

Sophocles is the most skillful of the Greek dramatists, his *Oedipus Rex* often being called the greatest of Greek tragedies. In his plays, exposition is carefully motivated, scenes are built through suspense to a climax, the action is clear and logical. His poetry has been universally admired for its beauty and clarity of expression. There are no elaborate visual effects, the impact depending almost entirely upon the force of the dramatic action itself.

Euripides (c. 480–c. 406) wrote about 90 plays, of which 18 have survived: *Alcestis* (438), *Medea* (431), *Hippolytus* (428), *Children of Heracles, Andromache, Hecuba, Heracles, Suppliants, Ion* (dates unknown, but probably between 430 and 415), *Trojan Women* (415), *Electra, Iphigenia in Tauris* (dates uncertain, but probably between 417 and 408), *Helen* (412), *Phoenician Women* (c. 409), *Orestes* (408), *Bacchae, Iphigenia in Aulis* (produced after Euripides' death), and *Cyclops,* a satyr play (date unknown). The relatively large number of extant plays by Euripides is explained by his enormous popularity in late Greek times, although he was little appreciated during his lifetime.

There are at least two reasons for the adverse judgment made on Euripides by his contemporaries: First, he questioned traditional values and myths, and consequently was accused of undermining the bases of society. Second, his dramatic method was not always clear. The unifying element in most of Euripides' plays is thought, and since his basic themes are not always easily grasped, the significance of the dramatic action is sometimes obscure. His techniques, growing out of this concern for thought,

15

often seem inadequate when compared with those of Sophocles. For example, many plays begin with a monologue-prologue baldly summarizing past events; the episodes are not always causally related and some may even appear superfluous; speeches often resemble forensic addresses; choral passages are at times only tenuously related to the dramatic action; and gods are frequently used to resolve conflicts and foretell the future. Thus, Euripides was thought dangerous because of his ideas and artistically inferior because of his dramatic techniques. But, if Euripides' techniques call attention to themselves and seem too theatrical, they are counterbalanced by realistic strokes in characterization, dialogue, and costuming.

Euripides began many practices which were developed more fully in the fourth century. He often turned to minor myths for his subjects or severely altered the major ones. His dramatic form ranges from tragedy through tragicomedy and melodrama. Such works as *Ion, Helen,* and *Iphigenia in Aulis* are often cited as signs that Greek tragedy was in the late fifth century already abandoning profundity for intrigue and startling reversals. As the stature of Euripides rose in later times, the sentimental and melodramatic aspects of his work were admired and imitated all too often.

The Satyr Play

The tragic dramatist also had to master one kind of comic writing, since he was required to supply a satyr play each time he competed at the City Dionysia. As with tragedy, little is known of the origin of the satyr play. Some historians have argued that it was the first form of drama and that gradually both tragedy and comedy emerged from it. More usually, however, Pratinas is credited with having invented this form sometime before 500 B.C.

Out of the hundreds of satyr plays, only one complete work has survived, Euripides' *Cyclops.* In addition, a large part of Sophocles' *The Trackers* and fragments of other plays are extant. Because of the limited evidence, it is difficult to generalize about the form.

The satyr play takes its name from the chorus, which was made up of the half-beast, half-human companions of Dionysus. The leader of the chorus was Silenus, the father of the satyrs. Sometimes the basic story of a satyr play was connected in theme or subject to the tragedies it accompanied, but more often it was on an entirely independent story. Essentially burlesque treatments of mythology, often ridiculing the gods or heroes and their adventures, the action took place in a rural setting and included vigorous dancing, boisterous action, and indecent language and gesture.

Vase painting from the late 5th century b.c. showing actors of a Satyr play. Note the masks and various kinds of garments. [From Baumeister, *Denkmaler des Klassichens Altertums* (1888)]

In structure, the plays resembled tragedy, being a series of episodes separated by choral odes. Language and meter deviated from those of tragedy toward the everyday and colloquial. Serving as afterpieces to the tragedies, the satyr plays provided a kind of comic relief from the serious plays which had gone before.

Greek Comedy in the 5th Century

Comedy was the last of the major dramatic forms to receive official recognition in Greece, not being admitted to the festivals until 487/6 B.C. Its history prior to that time is largely conjectural.

Aristotle says that comedy grew out of the improvisations of the leaders of phallic songs, but since there were many phallic ceremonies it is not clear which he had in mind. Some were performed by a dancing chorus, which at times might masquerade as animals, ride on animals, or carry an animal as a representative; there were also choruses of fat men, satyrs, and men on stilts. The rites often included a procession, which became the occasion for considerable byplay and mockery between participants and spectators. All of these elements have their parallels in later Greek comedy.

None of these phallic rites were dramatic, however, and the process by which they achieved comic form is unknown. As with tragedy, the Dorians claimed to have invented comedy, and Aristotle associates the decisive step with Epicharmus, who lived at Syracuse, a Dorian colony on the island of Sicily. Little more is known about Epicharmus than that he was certainly writing plays between the years 485 and 467 B.C. The few remaining fragments of his works give some clues about the characteristics of his comedy: some scenes have as many as three speakers, but there is no evidence of a chorus; elaborate word play, parody, "patter" speeches, and farcical situations are typical. The relationship of these plays to the comedies performed in Athens is unclear, since comedy had been recognized at the City Dionysia before the first known work of Epicharmus. A direct influence may have existed, nevertheless, since Epicharmus may have been writing long before our records begin, and since the nature of the first Athenian comedy is unknown.

Another possible source of Dorian influence on Athenian comedy is the mime, which supposedly appeared in Megara after 581 B.C. No mimes from this early period survive, but later ones are short satirical sketches usually based on common domestic situations or burlesqued versions of myths. The Athenians may have combined these with their own phallic choruses. Some of the dances found in Athenian comedy—such as the *kordax* and the *mothon*—also were Dorian in origin.

Regardless of its origin and early history, comedy was sufficiently developed in 487/6 to be accorded a place at the City Dionysia. It had probably been performed earlier without official sanction or financial aid. A few names of comic dramatists prior to Aristophanes have been recorded: Chionides, who supposedly won the first victory; Magnes, who won 11 victories with such plays as *Birds, Fig-Flies,* and *Frogs;* Ecphantides, who is thought to have written a more refined comedy than his predecessors; Cratinus (*fl.* 450–22), credited with 21 plays and thought to have been the first truly outstanding comic writer; Crates (*fl.* 449–25), who dropped personal satire, which had previously characterized comedy, in favor of more general subjects; Eupolis (*fl.* 429–11), Aristophanes' chief rival, noted for his witty satire and inventiveness.

All of the extant comedies of the 5th century, however, are the work of a single author, Aristophanes (*c.* 448–*c.* 380). He is thought to have written about 40 plays, of which eleven survive: *Acharnians* (425), *Knights* (424), *Clouds* (423), *Wasps* (422), *Peace* (421), *Birds* (414), *Lysistrata* (411), *Thesmophoriazusae* (411), *Frogs* (405), *Ecclesiazusae* (392/91), and *Plutus* (388). Although it is usual to treat Aristophanes' plays as typical of Old Comedy, as the drama of this period is called, it is unclear how his plays compare with those of his predecessors and contemporaries. Nevertheless, any generalizations about Old Comedy rest necessarily on Aristophanes' works.

Probably the most noteworthy characteristic of Aristophanic comedy is its commentary upon contemporary politics, society, and literature. The plays are organized around a ruling theme which is embodied in a rather farfetched "happy idea," such as a private peace with a warring power, or a sex strike to bring an end to war. Unlike tragedy, Old Comedy has an early point of attack, with practically all action shown on stage; consequently, there is little need for elaborate exposition. In order to show all important developments, time, often extending to weeks or months, is severely telescoped. Although the events of most Old Comedies could not occur in everyday life, the parallels with real events are abundantly clear, the fantastic exaggerations serving to point up the absurdity of their real-life counterparts. In addition to fantasy, farcical situations are common, and considerable emphasis is placed on the pleasures of eating, drinking, sex, wealth, and leisure. Coupled with these comic elements are some of the most beautiful lyrical passages in Greek literature.

Although there are many variants, the basic structural pattern of Old Comedy is simple. A Prologue establishes the mood and sets forth the "happy idea"; the chorus enters, and the debate, or *agon,* over the merits of the idea follows, ending in a decision to try the scheme. The *parabasis,* or choral ode in which the audience is addressed directly, divides the play into two parts. In it, some social or political problem is discussed and a line of action suggested. The second part of the play shows, in a series of loosely connected scenes, the results of adopting the happy idea. The final scene, or *kommos,* usually concludes with the reconciliation of all the characters and their exit to a feast or revels.

With the defeat of Athens in 404 B.C., political and social satire gradually disappeared from comedy and new types evolved. The quality of tragedy also declined after this time. The world's first great age of drama was over.

The Dramatic Festivals of the 5th Century

Although there were four annual festivals in honor of Dionysus even before drama was introduced, at only one—the City Dionysia—were plays presented prior to 442, almost 100 years after the first dramatic contest. At one festival, the Anthesteria, plays were never produced. By the late 5th century, drama was important at both the Lenaia and the Rural Dionysia, although the City Dionysia continued to command the greatest prestige. Drama was never a part of the festivals honoring other gods.

The City Dionysia, which celebrated the coming of Dionysus to Athens, was held at the end of March. Both a civic and religious festival, it was open to the whole Greek world and served as a showcase for Athenian wealth and culture. It was under the general supervision of the *archon eponymous,* the principal civil magistrate of Athens.

A few days before the festival, a *proagon* was held at which each poet appeared with his actors and announced the subject of his plays. After another preliminary event, the reenactment of Dionysus' coming to Athens, came the procession, which included public officials, the *choregoi* (sponsors of the plays), and many others, who carried gifts for the god or escorted sacrificial animals. This procession wound through much of Athens, stopped for dances at various altars, and ended with the presentation of offerings and the sacrifice of a bull at the altar of Dionysus.

Next came the dithyrambic contests. During the 5th century, ten 50-member choruses, one from each tribe, competed annually. Then came the plays. Each of three dramatists presented three tragedies and one satyr play, the works of one playwright occupying a whole day. After 487/6, each of five comic writers presented a single play (except during the Peloponnesian War, when the number of comedies was reduced to three). The comedies were probably all given on the day preceding the tragedies, but the precise arrangement is unknown. Until 449, prizes were offered only for the best plays; after this time a contest was also held for tragic acting. Two days after the festival, an assembly considered the conduct of the officials and received complaints of any misconduct.

The Lenaia was celebrated near the end of January, under the supervision of the *archon basileus,* the principal religious official of Athens. It has been suggested that originally the Lenaia was identical with the Rural Dionysia, and that its date and nature were changed only after Athens lost its rural character. No deme in Attica celebrated both the Lenaia and the Rural Dionysia, and the Lenaia was restricted to the city.

As the seas were considered unsafe in January, the Lenaia was primarily a local festival. Consequently, more freedom of expression was permitted, and the Lenaia came to be especially associated with comedy.

Dramatic activities were not officially recognized at the Lenaia until about 442, although plays may have been offered on an informal basis before that date. Although by the late 5th century the plays were being performed in the Theatre of Dionysus, it is unknown when they were transferred there. Dionysus was worshipped under a number of guises, each cult having its own sacred area, just as many Christian sects do today. The City Dionysia was presented in honor of Dionysus Eleutherios, and the Theatre of Dionysus was in his sacred precinct, while the Lenaia was held in honor of Dionysus Lenaios, the location of whose sanctuary is unknown. It is now assumed that there was a performance area in the Agora, or principal marketplace, and that the plays at the Lenaia were originally performed there. Some historians have suggested that the plays were transferred to the Theatre of Dionysus in 442, when they were given official support.

At first only contests for comic dramatists and actors were established, but in 432 others for tragic playwrights and actors were added. As at the City Dionysia, five comic writers competed each year (except during the Peloponnesian War), but only two tragic dramatists, offering two plays each, participated. Satyr plays and dithyrambs were not presented.

The Rural Dionysia was celebrated in December, though not necessarily on the same day in all demes. The principal feature of the festival was a procession in which a phallus was carried aloft on a pole, apparently with the purpose of insuring fertility at a time when the sun was at its weakest.

It is unclear when dramatic preformances became a part of this festival, and it is unlikely that all of the more than 100 demes included plays in their celebrations. In some, drama may have appeared before it was recognized at the Lenaia. It is certain that plays were being performed in a number of rural demes before the end of the 5th century, and the custom seems to have been widely adopted during the 4th century. Plato (*c.* 427–347 B.C.) wrote that in his time the Rural Dionysia was held on different days in different demes so that people might travel from one to the other to see the plays presented by troupes of traveling actors. The major demes connected with dramatic production were Piraeus (where

Euripides is said to have presented at least one play), Icaria, Salamis, and Eleusis. Many of the rural demes eventually built their own permanent theatres.

Most of our information about the Rural Dionysia dates from the 4th century or later. By that time actors were reviving works already produced elsewhere, but the source of plays presented in the 5th century is unknown. Possibly the Rural Dionysia served as a "try-out" theatre, as an outlet for plays not accepted for the City Dionysia or Lenaia, or as a place where works already seen in the city were revived.

The Rural Dionysia probably had little effect on the development of Greek drama, but its activities suggest the intense interest in drama during the period and show that the theatre was not confined to Athens.

Play Selection and Financing

Each author wishing to have his plays produced at a festival had to apply for a chorus to the *archon*. It is not known how this official chose the plays to be presented, but it has been suggested that each dramatist recited parts of his work. The choices of the next year's plays were made approximately one month after the end of a festival. Although this would leave about eleven months until performance, it is unknown how much of this time was actually used for rehearsals.

Beginning about 501, a large share of the expense of play production was borne by the *choregoi*, chosen by the *archon* from wealthy citizens who performed this duty in rotation as a part of their civic and religious responsibilities. The *choregus* (one was appointed for each author and for each dithyrambic chorus) paid the chorus members and their trainer, supplied costumes, and probably paid the musicians. In addition he may have supplied properties, supernumerary actors, and other persons or things, such as the second chorus required in some plays, not provided by the state. The responsibility of the state seems to have been restricted to supplying a theatre, prizes for authors, *choregoi,* and actors, and payments to actors and, possibly, to dramatists. Because he bore the major financial burden, a *choregus* could do much to help or hinder the playwright. Most seem to have been liberal, perhaps because the prize for the best work was awarded jointly to the author and *choregus*.

Nearly all tragic dramatists directed their own plays, but it was not unusual for comic playwrights to turn this task over to someone else. In Aeschylus' time, the author acted in his own plays, trained the chorus, invented the music and dances, and supervised every aspect of production.

Before the end of the Greek era, however, each area of production had been taken over by specialists.

Actors and Acting

Originally the actor and the dramatist were one, a situation which continued until Aeschylus introduced the second actor near the beginning of the 5th century. Playwrights continued to act in their own plays, nevertheless, until the time of Sophocles, who both abandoned this practice and introduced the third actor. It seems likely that when the contest for tragic actors was introduced around 449, the separation between actor and playwright was completed.

After 468, the number of actors available to each tragic playwright was fixed at three, although these might impersonate any number of characters. While this rule was softened somewhat by allowing supernumerary actors to assume nonspeaking roles or to speak a very limited number of lines, Sophocles' *Oedipus at Colonus* could be performed by three actors only if the same character were played by different actors in successive scenes. Although the peculiarity of the "three-actor convention" has led many scholars to question whether it was really observed, there seems to be sufficient evidence to verify it.

Comedy was subject to fewer restrictions. Most scenes could be acted by three actors, but at least one play by Aristophanes requires five. Since the restrictions were probably established to make the contests fair, those at the Lenaia may have differed from those at the City Dionysia.

Before the establishment of contests for actors about 449, each playwright probably selected his own cast, but after that time the leading actors were assigned by lot to the competing dramatists. The other actors were probably selected by the playwright and his leading actor. Although all of the actors were paid by the state, only the leading actor could compete for the prize, which might be awarded for a performance in a non-prize-winning play.

The Greeks seem to have placed considerable emphasis upon the voice, usually judging their actors by beauty of tone and adaptation to mood and character. Besides skill in speaking, the actor also had to sing, since the texts required three kinds of delivery: speaking, recitative, and singing. While the best actors attained high standards of vocal excellence, others apparently ranted and roared.

Facial expression was of no importance to the Greek actor, since he was always masked. In tragedy, gesture and movement appear to have been simplified and broadened. In comedy, everyday actions—running the gamut from the commonplace to the bizarre—were exaggerated for comic purposes.

Although acting style is always difficult to determine, many factors argue against a realistic ideal in 5th century Greece. First, the necessity for a single actor to play many roles suggests conventionalization. Second, the assumption of female roles by men argues against realism. Third, the use of song, recitative, choral passages, dance, and masks indicates considerable stylization. On the other hand, the extreme stylization of later periods was probably not typical of the 5th century. Both tragic and comic acting undoubtedly departed from the everyday—tragedy in the direction of idealization and comedy in the direction of burlesque—but the recognizably human element probably was maintained.

The Chorus

In the early tragedies the chorus was dominant, since there was only one actor, who left the stage often to change roles. In the plays of Aeschylus, although a second actor was available, the chorus was still given as many as one-half of the total lines, while in the *Suppliants* the chorus was the protagonist and in the *Eumenides* the antagonist. After Aeschylus the role of the chorus diminished progressively, however, and in the plays of Euripides it was often only tenuously involved in the dramatic action.

Historians disagree about the size of the tragic chorus. The traditional view holds that the number was originally 50, was reduced to 12 during the career of Aeschylus, and was raised to 15 at some later time by Sophocles. There is no clear evidence to support any of these figures. The idea of a 50-member chorus is deduced primarily from two sources. First, Aristotle states that tragedy developed from the improvisations of the leaders of dithyrambic choruses. On the basis of this assertion, some scholars have assumed that the tragic chorus was originally the same size as the dithyrambic. Unfortunately, no one knows how large the dithyrambic chorus was before its size was fixed at 50, probably around 509 B.C. Second, the chorus in Aeschylus' *Suppliants* is composed of the Daughters of Danaus, in mythology 50 in number. Aeschylus does not indicate how many there are. Furthermore, recently discovered evidence dates this play after Sophocles began to compete, and thus in the period when the chorus is thought to have numbered either 12 or 15. Consequently, there is reason to doubt whether the chorus ever had 50 members. The evidence to support a chorus of 12 is based primarily upon a 12-line choral passage in the *Agamemnon* which is seemingly divided among individual members of the chorus. The evidence for a chorus of 15 comes from statements by commentators who wrote several centuries later without citing any authority for the figure. Therefore, the size of the tragic chorus cannot be determined with certainty, although 15 has long been accepted as the probable number in the extant plays of Sophocles and Euripides. In Hellenistic times, the chorus diminished in size to as few as three members.

Some Greek tragedies require a second chorus, essentially mute though sometimes with a few lines. Aeschylus' *Suppliants* has a chorus of attendants on the Daughters of Danaus, while Euripides' *Hippolytus* has two quite distinct choruses. Sophocles seems not to have used this device.

The basic spatial arrangement of the tragic chorus was probably rectangular, as opposed to the essentially circular formations of the dithyramb. As a rule, the choral entry was a stately march, but occasionally members came in singly or in small groups from many directions. Most choral passages were sung and danced in unison, but at times the chorus was divided into two semi-choruses who performed in turn. Sometimes the chorus exchanged spoken dialogue with a character, and, in rare instances, individual members may have spoken single lines. As for acting, it is assumed that all members responded appropriately to the situations, but it is unknown how they were grouped during episodes or how their formations changed during choral odes.

Since satyr plays were presented in connection with tragedy, it seems probable that the basic conventions governing the tragic chorus applied to the satyr chorus as well. Being less serious than tragedy, the satyr play permitted many deviations toward comic effects.

The chorus of Old Comedy was composed of 24 members. Sometimes it was divided into two semi-choruses, as in *Lysistrata* where the two are of opposite sexes. As in tragedy, the basic choral formation was probably rectangular but arranged into four rows of six persons. Comedy seems to have enjoyed much more freedom than tragedy, and the kinds of entrances, dances, and uses of the chorus are more varied. The texts of the plays suggest that the chorus was extremely active throughout the performance.

The chorus in each dramatic form normally made its entrance after the prologue and remained until the end of the play. In a few instances, however, it is present at the opening of a play, and occasionally leaves and returns.

The chorus served several functions. First, it was an agent in the play; it gave advice, expressed opinions, asked questions, sometimes took an active part in the action. Second, it often established the ethical or social framework of the events and set up a standard against which the action might be judged. Third, it frequently served as an ideal spectator, reacting to the events and characters as the dramatist might hope the audience would do. Fourth, the chorus helped to set the overall mood of the play and of individual scenes, and to heighten dramatic effects. Fifth, it added movement, spectacle, song and dance, and thus contributed much to theatrical effectiveness. Sixth, it served an important rhythmical function, creating pauses or retardations during which the audience might reflect upon the events.

Music and Dance

Music was an integral part of Greek drama. It accompanied the passages of recitative and was an inseparable part of the choral odes. Only rarely was it used apart from words, and then only for special effects. In the beginning, the musical accompaniment was probably subordinated to insure that the words would be understood. By the time of Euripides, the accompaniment had become more elaborate, with trills of several notes prolonging single syllables of words. As a result, many verbal passages were unintelligible, and some critics suggest that this may be one reason for the decline in importance of choral odes.

The musical accompaniment for drama was played on a single flute, in tone resembling a modern oboe or clarinet, while other musical instruments, especially the lyre, were used occasionally for special effects. The flute player preceded the chorus into the orchestra, but his placement thereafter is unknown.

So little Greek music has survived that no accurate reconstruction is possible. The Greeks believed that music has ethical qualities, which suggests that they associated particular kinds of music with certain emotions or ideas. They recognized a large number of "modes," differing from each other in tonality and in sequence of intervals. The tones of the various modes were not always equal in value, however, some of the intervals being as small as quarter-tones. In quality, Greek music probably resembled oriental more than modern western music. The principal modes were the Dorian, Ionian, Phrygian, Aeolian, and Lydian, but there were many variations on these, such as Hypodorian or Myxolydian. Each had qualities which associated it with a particular range of feeling.

Like music, dance was considered to have ethical qualities. The Greeks defined dance as any expressive rhythmical movement; thus, for them, dance did not necessarily involve "footwork" at all, since gestures or pantomime might qualify as dance if they were rhythmical. Most Greek dance was mimetic (that is, expressive of a particular kind of character). In theatrical performances it seems to have been closely related to the words moment by moment through a set of symbolic gestures.

By the 4th century, the dances of tragedy had come to be called *emmeleia,* which signifies harmony, grace, and dignity. Within this general classification, however, there was much variety. The choral passages range through religious processions, wedding dances, Menaedic frenzies, and many other types, and the dances were probably modified to suit the individual choral odes.

The dances of comedy were less dignified and many were intentionally ridiculous. Often at the end of plays the chorus exited dancing wildly. Choral dances were adaptations of animal movements, religious ceremonies, victory celebrations, and countless other activities. The actors also performed dances which involved kicking the buttocks, slapping the chest or thighs, leaping, performing high kicks, spinning like a top, or beating other actors.

The basic dance of the satyr play was the *sikinnis,* which probably involved vigorous leaping, horseplay, and lewd pantomime. Often it burlesqued the tragic dances.

Costumes and Masks

In addition to movement and voice, the performance style of actors and chorus was influenced by costumes and masks. Several modern historians have argued that the standard costume for all tragic actors was a sleeved, highly-decorated tunic, usually full-length though sometimes shorter. This garment is said to be derived from the robes of the Dionysian priests and to indicate the actor's sacred and ceremonial function. The use of a standard garment, however, is far from established. Its presumed appearance is derived almost entirely from figures depicted on vase paint-

THE "ANDROMEDA" VASE, dating from the end of the 5th century, generally used as evidence concerning tragic costuming, although no connection with the theatre has been established. Note also that some figures are nude. [From Engelmann, *Archaologische Studien zu den Tragikern* (1900)]

ings, evidence which is open to doubt for several reasons: (1) most of the vases are later than the 5th century; (2) the relation of the vase paintings to actual theatrical practice is unclear; and (3) most important, other vase paintings, usually ignored by the supporters of the view outlined above, show actors in quite different costumes, while even the vases used to substantiate a standard costume show many deviations from it, including completely nude figures. Other evidence cited for a conventionalized robe is the statement of certain ancient commentators that Aeschylus established the tragic costume. Aristophanes' *Frogs*, however, merely credits Aeschylus with clothing tragic actors in more dignified garments than those worn by ordinary persons. Thus, though the sleeved, decorated tunic may have been used, there are many reasons for doubting whether it was typical.

The extant plays, a basic source of information, contain few references to costume: some indicate that characters are in mourning, for which black was the usual color; Death in Euripides' *Alcestis* is clothed in a black and "terrifying" garment; several of Euripides' characters wear rags and the protagonists of Sophocles' *Philoctetes* and *Oedipus at Colonus* comment on their worn clothing. Although these lines may merely be included to justify departures from standard practice, they indicate that costuming was not rigidly prescribed.

The plays also give some information about the dress of the chorus. In Aeschylus' *Suppliants* the point is made that the chorus is clothed in non-Greek garments, while in Sophocles' *Philoctetes* the opposite point is made. An oft-repeated account of the first performance of Aeschylus' *Eumenides* states that the Chorus of Furies was so frightening in appearance that several women miscarried. Other textual evidence suggests a wide variety of costumes. As a result, historians, even those who argue for a standardized costume for actors, have suggested that the dress of the chorus was determined by relatively realistic criteria, such as sex, age, nationality, and social status. Was there, then, one governing principle for costuming the chorus and a quite different one for the actors? Although this seems unlikely, it is not impossible, since the state presumably supplied the costumes for actors while the *choregoi* supplied those for the choruses. A uniform principle would seem more logical, nevertheless, and it is possible that unusual characters, such as foreigners, gods, and supernatural beings, were clothed in the sleeved, decorated tunics, for which there was no counterpart in native Greek dress, while the more familiar personages wore some variation on Greek garments.

In addition to the tunic (or *chiton*), both actors and chorus might wear a short cloak (*chlamys*) or a long one (*himation*). Symbolic properties might be carried by suppliants, priests, seers, and others. Staffs, walking sticks, swords and other accessories were added as needed.

Footwear also varied. The usual foot covering seems to have been a soft shoe or boot, often reaching to the calf. In later times this was called a *cothornus* and was given a thick sole, but neither the name nor the elevation seems to have been used in the 5th century. In the vase paintings, figures are shown in a wide variety of footwear, or barefoot.

Fortunately there is more agreement among scholars about comic costuming, although the available evidence is no more reliable than that for tragedy. Most agree that costumes were adapted from everyday Greek garments. For theatrical use, the *chiton* was frequently made too short and too tight so as to emphasize comic nudity. It was worn over flesh-colored "tights" which were often padded. The comic actor, but not the chorus, wore a *phallus*.

This costume, shown in practically all extant pictorial evidence, was probably that of the comic slaves and ridiculous old men. But the plays also depict young men, many of whom are ridiculed only slightly. Probably the comically grotesque costume was considerably modified for these characters. Similarly, there is a wide range of female characters. Apparently no attempt was made to emphasize female sexual attributes through costume. Since some comedies parodied scenes from well-known tragedies, it may be that tragic costume was sometimes burlesqued.

STATUETTE of an Old Comedy character. [From Robert, *Die Masken der Neueren Attischen Komoedie* (1911)]

Relatively little attention has been paid by historians to the costuming of satyr plays. Satyrs are usually depicted as wearing goatskin loincloths to which are attached the phallus in front and a horse-like tail in the rear. Other parts of the body are seemingly nude, which in the theatre would probably have been represented with a tight flesh-colored covering. The leader of the Chorus, Silenus, is depicted as wearing shaggy or fleecy "tights" under an animal-skin cloak. Since the characters in satyr plays are usually mythological personages, the costumes probably were somewhat ridiculous variations on tragic costumes.

All performers during the 5th century, with the probable exception of flute-players, wore masks. This practice seems to have evolved during the 6th century. In the rituals which predated tragedy, masks were sometimes but not always used. Consequently, Thespis had two traditions upon which to draw and, according to ancient commentators, he experimented with several kinds of disguises before adopting the mask. Tradition also records that Phrynichus was the first to introduce female masks, and that Aeschylus was the first to use painted masks. No masks used by actors have survived, since they were made of perishable linen, cork, or light-weight wood. Although in later periods the masks seem to have been considerably larger than the face, with exaggerated features, in the 5th century neither the size nor the expression seems to have been unduly large. Masks covered the entire head and thus included the appropriate hair styles, beards, and ornaments.

FRAGMENT OF A VASE from about 470 B.C. showing an actor's mask. This is the oldest extant visual evidence concerning theatrical masks. Note the garment on the right, supposedly also used in the theatre. [Courtesy of the American School of Classical Studies in Athens]

It is impossible to determine whether masks for tragedy were restricted to a few conventionalized types during the 5th century. Some historians have argued that they were, but others have suggested that experimentation was encouraged. The masks for the characters of a single play must have been sufficiently differentiated to make the frequent changes of roles readily apparent. On the other hand, chorus members in tragedy were always depicted as identical in appearance.

FRAGMENT OF A VASE from Tarentum showing a tragic actor holding a mask. Note the short fringed tunic and the tasselled boots. This fragment probably dates from the 4th century B.C. [Courtesy of Martin von Wagner Museum of the University of Wurzburg]

The masks for comedy were extremely varied. The choruses often represented birds, animals, or insects, which were identified by appropriate, though not necessarily realistic, masks. The masks for human characters often exaggerated attributes, such as baldness or ugliness, considered to be ridiculous. Although all the members of some choruses wore identical masks, others were individualized. When actors portrayed well-known Athenians, "portrait masks" were worn.

Members of the satyr chorus are usually depicted as snub-nosed, with dark, unkempt hair and beards, and pointed, horse-like ears. Sometimes they are shown as partially bald and at others they are given horns. Silenus was depicted with gray hair and beard. It is assumed that the actors wore masks similar to those used in tragedy.

31

The Theatre of Dionysus

The Theatre of Dionysus, by far the most important of the 5th century, also affected the production style. The oldest part of this theatre is the *orchestra* (or dancing place). Originally it was probably the only essential feature, since the audience sat or stood on the hillside to watch the choral performances which predated tragedy. Sometime during the 6th century a terrace was formed at the foot of the hill and on it a circular orchestra, about 66 feet in diameter, was laid out. An altar, or *thymele,* was placed in the center. With minor exceptions, the orchestra remained essentially unchanged until the Christian era.

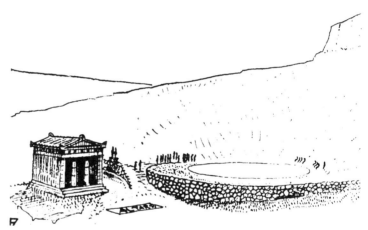

THE THEATRE OF DIONYSUS as it may have looked in the late 6th century B.C. From Fiechter's *Antike Griechische Theaterbauten.* [Courtesy Verlag W. Kohlhammer GmbH, Stuttgart]

The scene building, or *skene,* is probably of later origin than the orchestra. Since *skene* means "hut" or "tent," it has been suggested that the scene house developed out of some temporary structure intended originally as a dressing room but later incorporated into the action by some imaginative playwright. In seeking to date the *skene* as a scenic structure, most scholars turn to the extant plays, of which Aeschylus' *Oresteia,* produced in 458 B.C., is the first clearly to require a *skene.*

Since all parts of the early scene house have long since vanished, its appearance cannot be determined. Most attempts to reconstruct it are based upon later permanent structures. Some of the many possible arrangements are shown in the accompanying illustrations.

THREE RECONSTRUCTIONS showing possible appearances of the stage house of the Theatre of Dionysus in the 5th century, B.C. From Fiechter, *Antike Griechische Theaterbauten.* [Courtesy Verlag W. Kohlhammer GmbH, Stuttgart]

Extensive changes were made in the Theatre of Dionysus when the Odeion (or music hall) was built adjoining it in the 440's. At this time, the old curved retaining wall of the orchestra terrace was replaced with a straight one. On the side of this wall facing the auditorium were ten grooves. Most historians believe that these cuts were designed to hold the heavy wooden posts of the scene house. In addition, a stone-surfaced area jutted forward from the wall toward the orchestra. Although the purpose of this area is unknown, possibly it served as a foundation for certain theatrical machinery. These sketchy physical remains are all that survive of the 5th century structure.

It is usually assumed that a temporary scene house was erected for each festival; that its framework consisted of heavy timbers, some of which were inserted in the grooves found in the terrace wall; and that the scene house extended forward from the retaining wall toward the audience. The facilities required by the extant plays are one or more doors opening onto the principal acting area, and an upper level (either the roof or a platform in front of a second story) used primarily for the appearance of Gods. Most scholars believe that the scene house was similar in shape to the later stone structure (that is, a long rectangle with forward-projecting wings, or *paraskenia,* at each end). Since practically all of the extant plays of

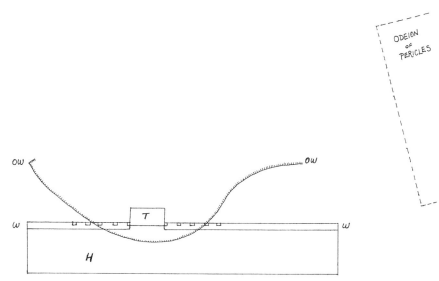

PLAN SHOWING CHANGES made in the Theatre of Dionysus in
the 440's. W—the new retaining wall with slots for timbers;
OW—original retaining wall; T—stone terrace at orchestra
level; H—the hall later built below the retaining wall.
[Drawing by Douglas Hubbell]

Aeschylus, Sophocles, Euripides, and Aristophanes were produced in the
Theatre of Dionysus before the erection of a permanent scene building,
they would have used the kind of *skene* described here. Although some
scholars have argued that a stone scene building was available by the late
5th century, most date the permanent *skene* from the 4th century and thus
after the era of the great drama.

Discussion of the *skene* leads inevitably to a consideration of scenic
practices, since it raises certain questions about the extent to which place
was suggested by the conventionalized facade of the scene house, and to
what extent the illusion of a specific place was attempted. Although the
problem cannot be settled, an examination of some possibilities can illuminate it.

The period prior to 458 (that is, before the existence of the scene
building can be clearly established) needs to be differentiated from later
times, since staging practices may have changed when the *skene* was introduced as a background. No play illustrates the problem during the early
period better than does Aeschylus' *Prometheus Bound,* in which the rugged
mountainous locale is supposedly engulfed in an earthquake during the
final scene. Some commentators have argued that in staging this play, a set
piece representing a mountain cliff was erected at the edge of the orchestra
terrace and that, during the earthquake, it was tipped over the embank-

ment. Others have countered that the whole performance was highly conventionalized, that the earthquake was conveyed merely by the lines, and that at the end of the play the actor playing Prometheus, who had been chained to the cliff, merely walked off. Still others have insisted that a fully-developed stage house, possibly disguised to represent the mountainous setting, served as the background. These various theories, none of which can be proven, illustrate some of the possible methods of staging the early plays.

It is usually assumed that after 458 all plays used the skene as a background, an assumption that may be incorrect since the building was temporary. Since most of the later tragedies are set before a temple or palace, a *skene* could have fulfilled the scenic demands of these plays. But what of those works which are set before caves (as are *Philoctetes* and many satyr plays), in groves of trees (*Oedipus at Colonus*), in army camps (*Ajax*), or places in which no buildings appear? The answers have been varied. Some historians have argued that a few stock sets, which could be changed from one play to the next, were used. Another group has argued for the use of a few symbolic properties (such as a shield to identify an army camp, or shells and rocks for a seashore, or a single tree for a grove). Still another group has suggested that the spoken lines were sufficient to indicate locale, and that the facade of the *skene* served as a conventionalized background for all plays.

This controversy is closely allied with another concerning scene painting, the invention of which Aristotle credits to Sophocles, while Vitruvius states that it originated in the time of Aeschylus. In attempting to reconcile these statements, the beginning of painted scenery is usually placed between 468 and 456, when the careers of Aeschylus and Sophocles overlapped. Vitruvius' description of the first scene painting suggests that it was an architectural design on a flat surface, which has been interpreted variously as meaning that an attempt was made to create the illusion of real architectural details or, conversely, that a previously undecorated surface was now given some schematic but nonillusionistic pattern.

The issue of conventionalization versus illusionism is an important one, for if illusion was attempted, then a single background could not have met the demands of all plays without changes of some kind. Thus, those who have argued for a degree of realism have also had to seek means whereby the appearance of the skene could have been altered. Two major devices have been suggested: *pinakes* (or painted panels similar to modern flats), and *periaktoi* (or triangular prisms with a different scene painted on each of the three sides). *Pinakes* supposedly could be attached to the scene building and changed as needed. Though the use of *pinakes* in the 5th century is well-documented, the practice of changing them for different plays is not, and it is possible that the painted panels were merely the face of the temporary skene used for all plays. *Periaktoi* were mounted on a central pivot and revolved to show the appropriate side. The use of this device during the 5th century has not been definitely established.

Since most plays are set in a single place, most of the suggested alterations in the *skene* would have occurred in the intervals between plays (three to five having been performed each day). On the other hand, some tragedies (such as Aeschylus' *Eumenides* and Sophocles' *Ajax*) change place internally, and many comedies have multiple settings. A number of devices for effecting these changes have been suggested. In some instances, the actors and chorus may merely have left the stage and returned, thus indicating a change in the place of the action. In some comedies, a trip around the orchestra accomplished the same result. It seems clear that in the comedies different doors or sections of the *skene* were used at times to represent widely separated places, a practice which may also have been used in the tragedies. If they were present, *periaktoi* could have been used to show internal changes of scene.

Enough has been said to demonstrate that the evidence concerning scenic practices in the 5th century is inconclusive. Nevertheless, it seems unlikely that illusionism was ever attempted to any marked degree. Although a fixed background may have served all plays, the use of a few symbolic properties or set pieces would not have been out of keeping with other Greek artistic conventions. The eventual erection of a permanent stone facade suggests that there was a steady movement toward a conventionalized background.

Inconclusive evidence has also led to disagreement as to whether the Theatre of Dionysus had a stage during the 5th century. Those who believe that there was none argue: (1) that the extant plays require the free mingling of actors and chorus, which a raised stage would have prevented; (2) that no extant plays require a stage; (3) that the choral performances which preceded plays did not use a stage and thus would have provided no precedent for one; (4) that during the 5th century no Greek word for stage existed, the term *logeion* dating from a later time after the stage was introduced; and (5) that there are no archeological remains of a stage from this period. On the other hand, those who favor a stage argue: (1) that all ancient commentators, though they admittedly lived much later, unanimously believed that there was a raised stage in the 5th century theatre; (2) that since every other innovation, such as the introduction of the second and third actors and of scene painting, was recorded, so drastic a change as the introduction of a stage would scarcely have gone unnoted; (3) that a number of extant plays indicate that actors are on a higher level, or go up to a higher level, than the orchestra; and (4) that the intermingling of actors and chorus is not often required, and that a low raised stage with steps to the orchestra would have accommodated such scenes.

The evidence cited on both sides is subject to opposing interpretations, but, on closer examination, the gulf between the two views is not so great as it might at first appear. Pickard-Cambridge, the most influential of recent opponents of the stage, is concerned primarily with refuting the idea of a high platform and admits the possibility of broad steps leading up to the *skene* or of a stage raised a foot or two. Arnott, the chief defender of the stage, suggests a platform approximately four feet high with steps to the orchestra. A reading of the plays clearly suggests the need for some raised areas, but whether these were temporary set pieces or a permanent platform is unclear. If a permanent platform was used, it lay between the *skene* and the orchestra, and presumably would have extended the full width of the stage house.

A limited amount of "machinery" was available for special effects in the 5th century. The most important devices were the *ekkyklema* and the *mechane*. The *ekkyklema* was a device for revealing tableaux, most often showing the bodies of characters killed offstage. This machine is thought to have been a platform which could be rolled out through the central doorway of the *skene,* although some ancient accounts state that it was revolved or turned, while others associated it with the upper story of the scene house or with the side doors.

The *mechane,* or crane, was used to show characters in flight or suspended above the earth. Occasionally characters are said to be in chariots or on the backs of birds, insects, or animals, while at other times the actor seems to have been suspended by a harness. The crane was probably situated so that an actor could be attached to it out of sight of the audience behind either the scene house or some part of an upper level, and then raised in the air and swung out over the acting area. It was most often used for the appearance of gods, but certain human characters in tragedy might require it (for example, Perseus on his flying horse). In comedy, it was often used to parody tragedy or to ridicule human pretensions. It is difficult to establish the use of the crane prior to about 430, but it may have been available much earlier. Its overuse in the last part of the century, especially by Euripides who often employed gods to resolve his plots, led to the term *deus ex machina* ("god from the machine") to describe any contrived ending.

Although stage properties were not numerous, they were essential elements. In many plays, characters sacrifice to a god or take refuge at an altar. Some scholars have argued that the altar in the center of the orchestra was used at these times; others have argued that, since this altar was dedicated to Dionysus, its use as a stage property would have been considered sacrilegious. Arnott suggests that there was a low structure in front of the central doorway which could be used either as an altar or tomb, as required. Other essential properties include chariots drawn by horses, biers for dead bodies, statues of various gods, torches and lamps to indicate night scenes. Furniture was rarely required in tragedy and was restricted to couches for persons too ill or weak to stand. On the other hand, both furniture and other common domestic articles were numerous in comedy. In neither comedy nor tragedy were properties used to create the illusion of reality, always serving rather to make some dramatic point. They were carried on and off stage as needed by the performers.

So far, only those elements relating to the acting areas and performers have been considered. But the auditorium and audience were equally important. In Greek theatres, the auditorium and the scene house always remained separate architectural units. Between them lay the orchestra and the *parodoi*, or entrances into the orchestra, at either end of the stage house. The *parodoi* were used principally by the chorus, although actors and even the audience might enter there as well.

The first *theatron* (or "seeing place") was the sloping hillside of the Acropolis. Stadium-like seating may have been erected as early as the 6th century, for the first major remodeling of the auditorium, shortly after 500, seems to have been caused by the collapse of wooden seats (though these may have been located elsewhere). At this time, the hillside was regraded to change the slope, and a series of terraces, on which were set up wooden brenches, probably was laid out. When the Odeion was built in the 440's, the slope was changed again and a number of supporting walls were added, although the seats probably continued to be temporary, since Aristophanes refers to them as *ikria*, a term normally reserved for wooden benches. Stone seats may have been gradually introduced, but the stone auditorium was not completed until some time between 338 and 326 B.C. A plan of the first permanent theatre is shown here.

It has been estimated that the auditorium seated from 14,000 to 17,000 persons. Nevertheless, only a small portion of the population could have attended the theatre at any one time, since in the second half of the 5th century Attica had about 200,000 residents. Thus, while the theatre may have been open to all, less than one-twentieth could have attended any given performance.

This may explain the introduction of tickets and an admission fee, although possibly fees were charged from the beginning. To equalize the opportunity to attend, around 450 Pericles established a theoric fund to provide tickets for the poor. He probably also regulated the price, although no definite record of admission costs before the late 4th century has been preserved. At that time, all seats not reserved by the state were sold at a uniform charge, the nominal sum of two obols. This money seems to have gone to the man who leased the theatre and was responsible for its upkeep.

Tickets admitted holders to a section of the theatre rather than to specific seats. It has been suggested that each of the tribes had its own section and that there was a special area for women. The central seat in the front row was reserved for the priest of Dionysus. Seats were also reserved for other priests and priestesses, for certain state officials, visiting ambassa-

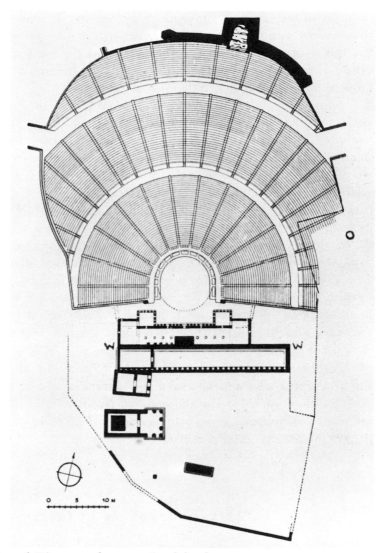

PLAN of the Theatre of Dionysus when completed in the
4th century B.C. The wall erected during the 440s is indicated by W–W. The square notches at the wall's front edge
represent the slots allegedly designed to hold the timbers of
the temporary stage house. O indicates the position of the
Odeion. [From Dörpfeld, *Griechische Theater* (1896)]

dors, and persons the state wished to honor. The audience was composed of
men, women, boys, and slaves. Officials were responsible for keeping order
and for checking tickets to see that their holders sat in the correct section.
Violence in the theatre was punishable by death.

Because of the number of plays presented, it is usually assumed that
performances lasted all day. Thus there must have been much coming and
going and considerable eating and drinking. The audience expressed its

opinions noisily and at times hissed actors off the stage. Tradition has it that Aeschylus once had to take refuge on the altar to escape the wrath of the spectators. Some ancient writers damned the audience as debased, but others praised it as discriminating. Probably the spectators represented a cross section of tastes, just as they did of society.

One of the high points of each festival was the awarding of prizes. Although not all of the procedures are clear, the following steps seem probable. Before the festival, a list of possible judges was drawn up from members of each of the ten tribes. All of the names from the same tribe were placed in a single urn, there being ten urns in all; these were then sealed and placed under guard until the beginning of the contest, when they were brought into the theatre and the *archon* drew one name from each urn. These men then served as judges for the contest. Each judge wrote out his verdict and placed it in an urn, from which the *archon* drew five. It was on the basis of these five that the winner was declared.

The nature of the prizes is unknown, but it may have included money. Certainly the honor was great, and the victorious *choregus* often erected a monument to commemorate the victory. State records were kept of the victories, and it is upon these that many ancient commentators drew in their accounts.

Although there are many unresolved questions about the theatre of the 5th century, we can be reasonably sure that it was a vigorous institution, in high repute with the general populace and with the civil and religious authorities. Drama was the most prized form of literature and the theatre the most popular of the arts.

Greek Drama after the 5th Century

After 400 B.C., tragedy declined in quality if not in quantity. Many writers no longer remembered, such as Theodectes, Astydamas, and Chaeremon, ranked at the forefront of dramatists in their day. Out of all the tragedies of this century, only one—*Rhesus*, formerly attributed to Euripides—has survived. Based on the tenth book of the *Iliad*, it is noteworthy primarily for simulating the atmosphere of nighttime.

During the 4th century, writers began to turn to the lesser myths, especially those of a slightly sensational nature. Forensic elements and melodramatic devices were also employed frequently. Some of the changes may have been due to Euripides' steadily increasing influence. Many of the earlier dramatists were still admired, and at least one old tragedy was enacted each year at the City Dionysia after about 341 B.C. Athens continued to be the center of tragic writing until about 300 B.C., when leadership passed to Alexandria. Although tragedy degenerated into an imitation of earlier plays, new works were written down to the 2nd century, A.D. Little is known of the satyr play after the 5th century. It must have declined in popularity, for beginning around 341 only one satyr play was produced each year.

On the other hand, comedy increased in popularity after the 5th century. Later commentators divided Greek comic writing into three periods: Old, dating from its origin to the defeat of Athens in 404 B.C.; Middle, from 404 until 336, when Alexander the Great came to power; and New, after 336. Middle Comedy is essentially a transitional type, moving away from personal invective and political and social satire to an increasing interest in contemporary life and manners or mythological burlesque. Although we know the names of about 50 writers of Middle Comedy and have numerous fragments, we cannot reconstruct a single play. The most famous authors were Antiphanes, Alexis, Anaxandrides, and Eubulus.

New Comedy differs drastically from Old Comedy. Although mythological subjects were still dramatized, the characteristic subject matter was the domestic affairs of the Athenian middle class. The immediate social and political problems were ignored in favor of the more universal topics of love affairs, money problems, and family life. Because of this trend toward generalization, the situations of New Comedy eventually became repetitious. Many plots depend upon concealed identity, coincidences, and recognitions. Often they involve a young man who seeks to marry a girl, frequently a slave about to be forced into prostitution, against the bitter opposition of his father; after many attempts to circumvent the father's wrath, a happy resolution is brought about by the discovery that the girl is the long-lost daughter of some wealthy Athenian. Thus the entire action is often based upon a misunderstanding, and its clearing up resolves the conflict. New Comedy was not restricted to this kind of plot; many were essentially character studies, and others were based upon mythological subjects.

The structure of New Comedy (a prologue, followed by a series of episodes separated by choral passages) was borrowed from tragedy, a change which some critics have attributed to the influence of Euripides, as they also have the popularity of such devices as long-lost children and recognition scenes. The choral passages were largely incidental, having little connection with the action. Furthermore, in many of the plays the chorus appeared onstage only during the interludes between episodes, although in others it was present throughout and played a more organic part in the plot. Many plays were partially serious because of the pathetic and moral element, although others were primarily farcical. The language reflected everyday usage, but extreme colloquialism was avoided and dialogue was still cast in poetic form.

41

A BAS-RELIEF from Naples of a scene from New Comedy: two old men at the left, the flute player in the center, and a youth and slave at the right. [From Robert, *Die Masken* (1911)]

Characters were gradually conventionalized into a restricted number of types. These were listed by Pollux, the Greek lexicographer of the 2d century, A.D., as follows: nine old men, four young. men, seven slaves, five young women, and various soldiers, parasites, and other types. Within these broad categories, each subtype had some distinctive quality, reflected in his mask and costume, which set him off from others in the same grouping (that is, there were nine types of old men, four types of young men, and so on).

Although the names of 64 writers of New Comedy are known and about 1400 plays of this type were probably produced, only one complete work, *The Grumbler* by Menander, survives. Menander (342–291 B.C.), who wrote more than 100 plays after 321, is by far the most important author of New Comedy. In addition to *The Grumbler,* a character portrait of an irascible old man, large fragments of *The Arbitration, The Girl from Samos,* and *The Shorn Girl,* and lesser fragments of about 85 other plays by Menander, are extant. Menander was celebrated for his varied and sympathetic characterization, his easy, natural style, his ability to adapt sentiments to character, and his ingenuity in constructing plots. In Rome, where his plays were frequently adapted, Menader's reputation was higher than that of any Greek author except Homer. Other important writers of New Comedy include Diphilus, Philemon, and Apollodorus. After the 3d century B.C., comedy began to decline just as tragedy had a century earlier. New Comedy was the last vital expression of drama in ancient Greece.

The Athenian Theatre in the 4th Century

Athens continued to be the major theatrical center through the 4th century B.C. As its vitality declined, changes were made in the festivals. At the City Dionysia, contests for the production of old plays were instituted in the last part of the 4th century, a practice which seems never to have been adopted at the Lenaia. The increased popularity of comedy was reflected in the institution of a contest for comic actors at the City Dionysia. A decline in personal wealth probably led to the discontinuance of *choregoi* at some time between 317 and 307, after which an elected official, the *agonothetes,* was given a state appropriation to finance all of the productions.

The 4th century also saw the increase of professionalism. By about 350 professional singer-dancers, who appeared in both comic and tragic choruses, were rehearsed by professional trainers. Acting grew in importance and tended to overshadow playwriting. As a result, around 350 the rules governing tragic actors at the City Dionysia were changed so as to require each of the three leading actors to appear in one play by each of the competing dramatists. A number of performers, among them Polus, Theodorus, Thettalus, Neoptolemus, Athenodorus, and Aristodemus, achieved far-reaching fame. By 300, well-known actors were touring the entire Greek world.

It is ironic that the permanent stone structure of the Theatre of Dionysus was not completed until around 325, when the Athenian theatre was already beginning to lose its privileged position. This completed structure is important nevertheless, for its archeological remains have served as the basis for most conjectures about the theatre in the 5th century. After 300 Athens was no longer in the forefront of developments, and its theatre building was soon considered old-fashioned. Sometime between the 3rd and 1st centuries B.C. it was remodeled along the more fashionable Hellenistic lines. Other extensive changes were made in the 1st century A.D., when the stage was extended forward over part of the orchestra to make it conform more nearly to the Roman ideal. After this time gladiatorial contests were sometimes staged in the orchestra, which was now fenced in with a stone barricade, and about the 4th century A.D. the orchestra was sealed so that water spectacles could be staged.

It is not clear when the dramatic contests ceased. The records of the City Dionysia continue until the 1st century A.D., while those of the Lenaia can be traced only until about 150 B.C. The Theatre of Dionysus continued to be used for various kinds of spectacles until the 6th century A.D., but after the 2d century A.D. the productions bore little resemblance to the great works of the 5th century B.C.

Aristotle and the Theatre

Although the Athenians displayed a lively interest in drama from the sixth century B.C. on, no theoretical treatises were written about it until the 4th century B.C., an age noted for its philosophers. Aristotle (384–22 B.C.), one of Athens' greatest thinkers, wrote by far the most influential Greek work on the theatre, the *Poetics* (*c*. 335–23). In addition to its discussion of literature in general and tragedy in particular, the *Poetics* contains in its early chapters the oldest surviving history of dramatic forms. In preparation for writing this work, Aristotle compiled a record of the plays and winners at the festivals, usually called the *didaskalia* (a term derived from "to teach" and used to refer to both the play texts and to the rehearsal of chorus and actors). This record was to be a major source of information for later historians in ancient times.

Aristotle has had enormous influence on critical theory, for his *Poetics* has been the foundation for practically all discussions of tragedy since the 16th century, when it became widely known. Because many of Aristotle's concepts are stated cryptically, the *Poetics* has been subjected to widely varying interpretations. Certainly it must be read with extreme care if it is to be understood.

In the *Poetics* Aristotle proposes six parts of drama—plot, character, thought, diction, music, and spectacle—as bases for analysis. He then discusses unity of action, probability in drama, the requirements of plot, characteristics of the tragic hero, problems of diction, and other topics. The ideas expressed in the *Poetics* have had incalculable influence on Western playwriting and criticism.

The Hellenistic Theatre

During the 4th century B.C., Philip of Macedon (382–36 B.C.) and his son, Alexander the Great (356–23 B.C.) extended their power over all of the Greek states, as well as throughout Asia Minor and northern Africa. As a result, the entire "civilized" world was gradually Hellenized, as Greek art and learning were absorbed by the conquered territories. Thus, the period following Alexander's assumption of power in 336 is usually called the Hellenistic Age. Pergamum, in Asia Minor, and Alexandria, in Egypt, gradually attained supremacy over Athens as centers of learning and culture. But most important, the theatre was cultivated throughout the Hellenized areas, where deviations from Athenian practice altered many of the older conventions.

The beginning of this great expansion can be seen in the victory festivals staged by Alexander, at one of which he is said to have assembled 3000 performers. Following Alexander's example, the occasions upon which plays might be presented were extended considerably and no longer confined to festivals honoring Dionysus.

The rapid expansion of festivals throughout the Greek world created a need for qualified performers at a time when professionalism was also increasing. One result was the formation of a guild for performers, the Artists of Dionysus. Although its date of origin is uncertain, it was recognized in an official decree of 277 B.C. and continued into the Christian era.

Members of the Artists of Dionysus included dramatic, epic, and lyric poets, actors of tragedy, comedy and satyr plays, oral readers, members of the chorus, trainers, musicians, and costumers—all of the personnel needed for the production of plays and recitations at festivals. Popular entertainers of other kinds were never admitted to this guild.

As the name of the guild suggests, the performers retained their old connection with Dionysus, even though they often produced plays for other occasions, and the head of the organization was usually a priest of Dionysus. Of the three major branches, the Athenian was probably the oldest and, for a long time, the most respected. A second branch, the Nemean and Isthmian guild, had its headquarters at Corinth, while the third major branch, the Ionian and Hellespontine guild, was based at Teos in Asia Minor. There may have been a fourth branch at Alexandria. As the theatre spread, each major branch established subdivisions throughout the areas over which it held jurisdiction.

A city apparently contracted with the nearest guild to produce plays at its festivals, the obligations of each party being clearly fixed by agreements. Because of the importance of the festivals and because the Hellenic world, following the death of Alexander, had dissolved into a number of small political divisions, the safety of the guild members was often guaranteed in international agreements, and they were immune from arrest and military service. Because they could move about freely, they sometimes served as ambassadors between states.

Before the end of the 4th century, theatres were being constructed at various places outside of Athens. Between the middle of the 4th century and the 1st century B.C. the Hellenistic theatre structure evolved, important examples of which are found at Priene, Oropus, Ephesus, Delos, Epidaurus, Oeniadae, Sicyon, Pergamum, Corinth, and Alexandria.

Although the basic features of the Hellenistic theatre are reasonably well established, their date and place of origin are much disputed. Some scholars argue that the drastic changes from the earlier plan were made as early as the late 4th century, while others date them from the 2nd century B.C. The theatres at Priene, Epidaurus, and Alexandria have been cited as the first of the new type. The evidence is hopelessly confused, mainly because archeologists cannot agree upon the dates of the original structures or of the various remodelings to which all were subjected. The details of this controversy are unimportant here; it is sufficient to note that the new structural features may have been present from the beginning of the Hellenistic age or may have evolved over a period of 200 years. Almost all scholars agree that the Hellenistic theatre was fully developed by about 150 B.C.

Probably the most important innovation was the high raised stage. Varying in height from eight to thirteen feet, it was sometimes as much as 120 feet long, although its depth was only from eight to thirteen feet. Since *paraskenia*, or side wings of the scene house, were eliminated, this long narrow platform was open at both ends. In some theatres, ramps parallel to the *parodoi* led up to the stage; in others, steps to the orchestra were provided at the ends of the stage; in still others, the stage could be entered only from the stage house. The front edge of the stage was supported by the *proskenion*, or facade of the first story, while the second story of the scene house, or *episkenion*, rose at the back edge of the stage. Often these two stories were approximately equal in height. In some theatres the orchestra continued to be a complete circle, but in many the *proskenion* extended a few feet into the circle. The auditorium underwent no significant changes.

This basic arrangement raises many questions about staging. Was the orchestra used for the performance of those old plays requiring a large chorus, while the raised stage served for newer plays in which the chorus was small and incidental? Or did the actors use the stage and the chorus the orchestra? Was the upper stage used at first only for gods or special scenes, later becoming the usual acting area for all scenes? Was the orchestra merely a vestigial structural feature no longer serving any function? Both affirmative and negative answers have been advanced for each of these questions, none of which can be answered with certainty.

Many problems also arise in relation to scenic practices. For example, in the early Hellenistic theatre the *proskenion* was composed of pillars spaced several feet apart; often these pillars were notched so as to hold painted panels (or *pinakes*). In many theatres dated after the second century B.C., however, the pillars are no longer notched. On this basis, some historians have argued that as long as performances occurred in the orchestra a scenic background had to be provided; whereas later, when all action

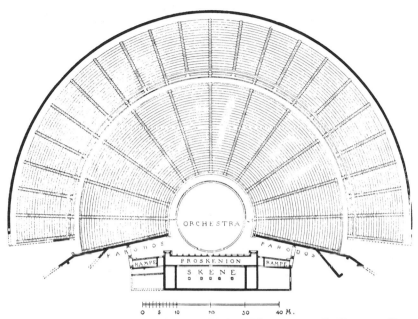

PLAN of the Theatre at Epidaurus. [From Dörpfeld, *Griechische Theater* (1896)]

THE REMAINS of the Hellenistic theatre at Epidaurus.

was transferred to the stage, the *proskenion* became merely an open colonnade, since *pinakes* were no longer needed on the orchestra level.

More drastic changes were made in the facade of the second story. During the 2nd century B.C., the *episkenion*, which probably had from one to three doors originally, was converted into a series of sizable openings, or *thyromata,* varying in number from three to seven. These *thyromata,*

47

THE HELLENISTIC THEATRE at Eretria. The upper view shows
an early phase in the stage building's development, while
the lower shows fully developed *thyromata*. [From Fiechter,
Antike Griechische Theaterbauten]

averaging about ten to twelve feet in width and as high as the roof would
allow, were separated from each other by narrow upright supports. Thus,
on the upper level there was now a long shallow forestage backed by a
rear stage as deep or deeper than the main stage.

This change is usually associated with the decline of the chorus and the
increased use of the high platform for the entire action, since the *thyromata*
provided more depth for playing. Some scholars have assumed that *thyromata* also permitted greater illusion in the scenic background, and have
suggested that each opening served as a miniature proscenium arch behind
which individual settings could be erected. Such theories (as well as all
others about the *thyromata*) are entirely conjectural.

Vitruvius, writing of the Greek theatre in the 1st century B.C., describes the facade as providing spaces for the *periaktoi*. Possibly *periaktoi*
were set up in *thyromata*. Vitruvius also indicates three kinds of backgrounds: one each for tragedy, comedy, and satyr plays. Though some
historians have interpreted this passage as an indication of illusionistic
pinakes, it seems more likely that conventionalized scenes mounted on the
periaktoi were considered sufficient.

Tragic costumes and masks changed considerably after the 5th century.
Although the progressive changes cannot be dated, it is reasonably clear
that by the 1st century B.C. the tragic actor was padded, wore thick-soled
boots (the *cothornus*), and a high headdress (the *onkos*) to increase his
apparent size. The facial features of the masks were also enlarged and

exaggerated. In other words, the tragic actor was now made larger than life and his overall appearance was distorted and conventionalized. Pollux, writing in the 2nd century A.D., lists 28 basic masks, supposedly covering the categories of tragic characters: six old men, eight young men, eight women, six servants. In addition, he enumerates unusual masks, such as that for Argos with his many eyes.

In New Comedy, costume, although somewhat conventionalized, approximated that of ordinary life. The basic garment was the *exomis*, a plain white tunic unseamed on the left side. Over this, old men wore a long white cloak (or *himation*), while young men wore a red or purple *himation*, and parasites a black or gray *himation*. Slaves wore a short white cloak over the *exomis*. Old women were dressed in green or light blue; priestesses wore white, as did young women.

TERRACOTTA FIGURE of a youth in New Comedy. [From Robert, *Die Masken der Neueren Attischen Komoedie* (1911)]

Pollux lists 44 masks for New Comedy: nine old men, four young men, seven slaves, three old women, five young women, seven courtesans, two maidservants, one rustic, two soldiers, one flatterer, and three parasites. Thus, it would appear that the character types of comedy were considerably more extensive than those of tragedy. Although most masks were realistic, caricature was used in those for slaves, certain old men, and ridiculous types. Most slaves had red hair, while courtesans usually had yellow.

STATUETTE supposedly representing a figure in New Comedy. [From Robert, *Die Masken der Neueren Attischen Komoedie* (1911)]

HEAD, supposedly representing the "Golden Courtesan" of New Comedy. [From Robert, *Die Masken der Neueren Attischen Komoedie* (1911)]

Although the Greek theatre continued until after 500 A.D., its vitality declined rapidly after the 1st century B.C. Beginning in the 2nd century B.C., the Romans gradually gained power over all of the Eastern Mediterranean and, although the Greek ideals persisted for a time, Roman practices eventually dominated. After the 1st century A.D., most of the older theatres were remodeled to conform more nearly to the Roman ideal, the resulting style usually being called Greco-Roman. Many purely Roman theatres were also erected.

The Greek Mimes

As regular drama declined, mime grew in importance. This form, which probably originated in Megara in the 6th century B.C., was at least as old as comedy and tragedy, but since it was not accorded official recognition at festivals until very late, little of its early history has been preserved. The mime was often coupled with such popular entertainments as juggling and acrobatics, and there may have been small troupes of professional mimes (the term was applied interchangeably to both plays and performers) as early as the 5th century B.C. The mime, therefore, was probably the first purely professional theatrical form and the first to use women.

Although the Greek colonies of southern Italy and Sicily appear to have favored the mime in the 5th century, it was not until Hellenistic times that it flourished throughout the Eastern Mediterranean. After 300 B.C., mime performers appeared increasingly at festivals, although they were never admitted to the Artists of Dionysus. The vogue for mimes is reflected in the rise of a school of "literary mime" writers at Alexandria and in southern Italy around 300–250 B.C. Eight mimes by Herodas, who lived in Alexandria in the first half of the 3rd century, still survive. These are short (usually no more than 100 lines), relatively subtle and realistic scenes from daily life.

In southern Italy the mimes were called *phlyakes*. Rhinthon, who lived at Tarentum in the first half of the 3rd century, is said to have formalized the type. Thirty-eight plays are attributed to him, most of them *hilarotragodiai*, or burlesques of tragedy, of which only a few fragments survive. Although mimes were popular throughout the Hellenic world, *phlyakes* have received most attention from scholars because of a series of vase paintings from southern Italy which are believed to depict scenes from this theatrical form. These vases have now been redated at 400–325 B.C., about a century before any known *phlyakes* plays, but they are still called *phlyakes* vases, even though their connection with mime performances is unclear and the scenes they depict may be from Middle Comedy. The

51

SCENE FROM A PHLYAKES VASE. Note the portico, steps, raised stage, and costumes. [From Baumeister, *Denkmaler des Klassischen Altertums,* Vol. II (1889)]

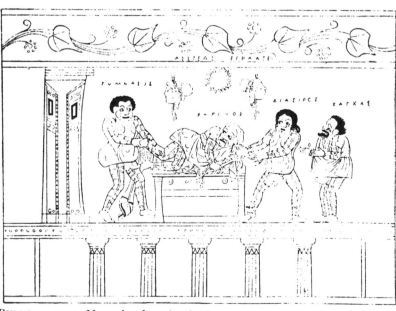

SCENE FROM A PHLYAKES VASE. Note the door in the background and the columns supporting the stage. [From Baumeister, *Denkmaler des Klassischen Altertums* (1889)]

characters wear padded "tights," short chitons, and the phallus. The subjects range from mythological burlesque (the adventures of Heracles is a favorite) to daily life. Lovemaking, gluttony, beatings, thievery, and trickery are popular motifs.

Probably of greater interest, however, is the representation of the stage. A raised platform, varying in height, rests on posts or decorative columns, between which draperies or painted panels are shown. Steps, often in use by the actors, lead up from the ground level to the stage, the back ground of which varies: a portico and door, columns and decorative motifs, a window or gallery higher than the stage level. Trees, altars, thrones, chests, and tables appear among the properties. Some scholars have interpreted the paintings as evidence of a temporary stage which could be erected as needed by traveling troupes; others have suggested that the vases show the permanent stages, which have merely been simplified because of the limited space and the conventions of vase painting.

Regardless of the interpretation of the vases, it is clear that the theatre flourished in southern Italy and that it was there, in the 3rd century B.C., that the Romans first encountered the more advanced Greek culture. From this time, historical interest shifts to Rome, where Greek forms and practices were adopted, transformed, and transmitted to other areas and to later times.

ROMAN
THEATRE
AND DRAMA

*R*ome was founded in the 8th century B.C. but did not begin its rise to world power until the 3d century. As it expanded and came into contact with other civilizations, it appropriated many of their arts and diversions. Thus, in 240 B.C. it imported Greek comedy and tragedy from southern Italy. This was not the beginning of Roman theatrical activity, however, for it had begun long before under Etruscan influence.

Pre-Greek Influences on the Theatre

Between the 6th and 4th centuries B.C., Etruria was stronger and culturally more advanced than neighboring Rome, which it dominated for many years. Music and dance flourished among the Etruscans and were featured at festivals, along with boxing, wrestling, chariot races, and gladiatorial contests.

The origin of the Roman theatre owes much to Etruria. Horace states that it is to be found in the Fescennine Verses, a term now thought to be derived from Fescennium, a town on the Etrurian border. These compositions were only crudely dramatic, consisting of improvised dialogue, abusive and often obscene, exchanged by masked clowns at harvest and wedding celebrations.

Livy (59 B.C.–17 A.D.), the Roman historian, does not mention the Fescennine Verses, but dates the first theatrical production in Rome at 364 B.C., when musical and dancing performers were imported from Etruria in an effort to appease the gods, at a time when plague was ravishing the city. Some time later, amateur performers combined music and dance with improvised dialogue scenes. Livy goes on to say that this new form was later acted by professional performers, or *histriones* (from the Etruscan word, *ister,* meaning dancer or actor).

It was also an Etruscan ruler of Rome, the elder Tarquin (616–579 B.C.), who established the *ludi Romani* (the festival at which Greek drama was later presented) with its chariot races, boxing contests, and other entertainments. Since Etruscan tomb paintings show "grandstands" for spectators at such festivals, stadium-like seating was probably used in Rome long before the Greek theatre was known and may have influenced the structure of the early Roman theatres.

Still another dramatic form, the Atellan farce, predated the importation of Greek comedy and tragedy to Rome. Since the *fabula Atellana* takes its name from the town of Atella (near what is now Naples), many scholars have argued that it probably evolved from the Greek mimes of southern Italy. By the time the Romans came into close contact with the Oscan territories in which Atella was located, near the end of the 4th century B.C., a crude drama had already developed there. This Atellan farce was probably imported to Rome during the first half of the 3rd century, for by 275 B.C. the Romans were undisputed masters of the Oscan region. Little is known of the early Atellan farce. It was probably short, largely improvised, and based on domestic situations or mythological burlesque. Type characters, each with his own fixed costume and mask, seem to have been featured.

During the first Punic War (264–41 B.C.), the Romans became acquainted with the Greek dramatic performances of southern Italy and Sicily, and it was from these areas that regular comedy and tragedy were imported to Rome in 240 B.C. By this time, various kinds of entertainment (music, dance, farce, chariot races, boxing, and gladiatorial contests) were already well-established at Roman festivals, and regular drama was merely added to them. The mingling of these diverse elements and the competition for popularity among them are the principal sources of the circus-like atmosphere of the Roman theatre. The triumph of minor entertainments over regular drama during the 1st century B.C. also marked the triumph of the Etruscan heritage over the Greek.

Roman Festivals

All public theatrical performances in Rome were given at festivals, or *ludi,* the majority being official state religious celebrations in honor of various gods. Other festivals were given on special occasions, such as major victories in war, the dedication of public buildings or monuments, the funerals of important personages, or when a private individual wished to curry favor with the people.

The oldest of the official festivals was the *ludi Romani,* given in honor of Jupiter each September. Established in the 6th century B.C., it added theatrical performances in 364 and regular comedy and tragedy in 240 B.C. The popularity of Greek plays soon led to their inclusion at other festivals, five of which were of special importance: the *ludi Florales,* given in April in honor of Flora, instituted in 238 and made an annual celebration in 173; the *ludi plebeii,* given in November in honor of Jupiter, inaugurated not later than 220 B.C., with plays introduced not later than 200; the *ludi Apollinares,* held in July in honor of Apollo, begun in 212, and with theatrical performances from about 179 B.C.; the *ludi Megalenses,* given in April in honor of the Great Mother, instituted in 204, and with theatrical productions by 194 B.C.; and the *ludi Cereales,* given in April in honor of Ceres, established by 202 B.C.

It is extremely difficult to estimate how many days were devoted to plays each year, since the number of special celebrations varied yearly and the annual festivals were sometimes repeated. *Instauratio,* or the repetition of an entire festival, including the plays, was required whenever there was some irregularity. That *instauratio* was not uncommon is shown by the repetition of the *ludi Romani* in eleven of the years between 214 and 200 B.C. and of the *ludi Plebeii* seven times in one year.

Although the precise number of performances in any given year cannot be determined, there was a steady increase from 240 B.C. on. Probably only one day was set aside for theatrical productions in the beginning, but by 200 B.C. the number had grown to between four and eleven, by 190 to between seven and seventeen, by 150 to about 25, and by the beginning of the Christian era to about 40. In 354 A.D. the number had increased to 100. These figures do not include the occasional festivals, the additional performances required by *instauratio,* or the days reserved for other entertainments, such as chariot races and gladiatorial contests, for which 75 days were set aside in 354 A.D. In addition to the public festivals, there may have been private indoor performances, as well as unofficial public performances by traveling troupes.

Drama Under the Romans

Rome remained a Republic until 27 B.C., when Augustus was crowned Emperor. Although drama had already declined markedly, there is a significant difference between the theatre under the Republic, the period of the best Roman drama, and that of the Empire, which was devoted almost altogether to the minor forms. Of the more than 800 years which the history of the Roman theatre encompasses, those between 240 and 75 B.C. are of most importance because of their level of achievement.

Livius Andronicus (*fl.* 240–04 B.C.) is considered the founder of Roman literature. The comedies and tragedies which he translated and adapted (beginning in 240) were the first literary works in Latin. Little is known of him. Some scholars believe that he was a slave, while others suggest that he was expressly imported from Tarentum (in the Greek territories of southern Italy) to produce plays. The first native-born dramatist was Gnaeus Naevius (*c.* 270–*c.* 201 B.C.), who began writing about 235. He excelled at comedy, although like Andronicus, who was best at tragedy, he wrote both types. Naevius did much to naturalize the drama by introducing many Roman allusions into the Greek originals, and by writing plays on Roman stories as well. By the time Andronicus and Naevius died, drama was well-established in Rome. Since each of their successors tended to specialize in a single form, the development of tragedy and comedy will be considered separately.

Although Roman tragedy is treated condescendingly today, it was highly regarded by Roman critics and audiences. Nevertheless, only three writers between 200 B.C. and 75 B.C. are known: Quintus Ennius (239–169), Marcus Pacuvius (*c.* 220–*c.* 130), and Lucius Accius (170–*c.* 86). It is difficult to generalize about this early tragedy, since no plays survive. Judging from fragments, titles, and contemporary comments, the majority of the plays were adapted from Greek originals (*fabula crepidata*), while a smaller number were based on Roman subjects (*fabula praetexta*). They probably did not depart structurally in any important way from Greek tragedy, but bolder effects (such as extremes of virtue and vice, of horror and noble deeds, melodramatic plots, and rhetorical or spectacular display) seem to have been favored.

Although tragedy was regularly performed into the Christian era, there seem to have been no new plays written for production after the *Thyestes* of Varius Rufus was seen at a festival in 29 B.C. celebrating the

57

A SCENE FROM ROMAN TRAGEDY. A wall painting in Pompeii of the 1st century A.D. or earlier. [From Dieterich, *Pulcinella* (1897)]

victory of Actium. On the other hand, closet dramas, such as Ovid's (43 B.C.–*c.* 17 A.D.) *Medea,* appeared, and scenes from tragedies were recited at banquets.

The only Roman tragedies which have survived are from this later period. Of these, all but one are by Seneca. Lucius Anneaus Seneca (5/4 B.C.–65 A.D.) was born in Spain and educated in Rome, where he became famous for his works on rhetoric and philosophy. Having been Nero's tutor, he was one of the most influential men in Rome after Nero became Emperor in 54 A.D., but lost his power and committed suicide in 65.

Nine plays by Seneca survive: *The Trojan Women, Medea, Oedipus, Phaedra, Thyestes, Hercules on Oeta, The Mad Hercules, The Phoenician Women,* and *Agamemnon.* All are adaptations of Greek originals. Although it seems unlikely that Seneca's plays were presented on the public stage, they were destined to become a major influence on Renaissance tragedy. Consequently, their characteristics are of interest. First, Seneca's plays are divided into five episodes, separated by choral interludes only loosely related to the action. In the Renaissance, the five-act form became standard, while the chorus, though reduced to a single character, often commented on the action. Second, Seneca's elaborate speeches, often resembling forensic addresses, were imitated by later writers. Third, Seneca's interest in moral philosophy, reflected in his plays through sensational deeds which illustrate the evils of unrestrained emotion and in *sententiae* (or brief generalizations, resembling proverbs, about human behavior), is paralleled in Renaissance drama by the use of horrifying examples of evil behavior and moralizing ruminations on the human condition. Fourth, Seneca's scenes of violence and horror (in *Oedipus,* Joscasta rips open her womb, and in *Thyestes,* the bodies of children are served at a banquet), were imitated by later writers. Fifth, Seneca's preoccupation with magic, death, and the close connection between the human and superhuman worlds paralleled a major interest of the Renaissance. Sixth, Seneca's creation of characters who are dominated by a single obsessive motive, such as revenge, which drives them to their doom, provided Renaissance dramatists valuable lessons in establishing psychological motivations and unifying characterizations. Seventh, many of Seneca's technical devices, such as soliloquies, asides, and confidantes, were seized upon by later authors.

Octavia, sometimes mistakenly attributed to Seneca, is the sole surviving example of the *fabula praetexta,* or tragedy on Roman themes. Of little merit, it deals with the death of Nero's wife, and in it Seneca appears as a character.

Because comedy was more popular than tragedy in Rome, the names of many comic writers have come down to us. Of these, two—Plautus and Terence—are of principal interest since they are the authors of the only surviving comedies. Plautus (*c.* 254–*c.* 184 B.C.) was the first important successor to Livius Andronicus and Naevius in comedy. His popularity was so great that, after his death, as many as 130 plays came to be attributed to him. In seeking to resolve the question of authorship, the Roman scholar Varro (116–27 B.C.) divided the plays into those which were certainly by Plautus, those which were doubtful, and those which were spurious. In the first group he placed 21 works, all of which have survived: *The Comedy of Asses, The Merchant, The Braggart Warrior, The Casket, Pot of Gold, Stichus, Pseudolus, Curculio, Bacchides, Casina, Amphitryon, The Captives, Epidicus, The Menaechmi, The Haunted House, The Persian, The Carthaginian, Rope, Trinummus, Truculentus,* and *Vidularia.* Few of the plays can be dated with certainty, although all are thought to have been written between 205 and 184. All are based on Greek New Comedies but, since none of the models survive, it is impossible to estimate the extent of Plautus' originality. He added many Roman allusions, was much admired for his Latin dialogue, the variety of his poetic meters, and for his jokes. Although his comic writing has a very wide range, he is best known for the farcical elements in his plays.

Publius Terentius Afer (195 or 185–159 B.C.) is said to have been born in Carthage, brought to Rome as a slave when a boy, educated, and freed. He wrote six plays, all of which have survived: *Andria* (166), *Mother-in-Law* (165), *Self-Tormentor* (163), *Eunuch* (161), *Phormio* (161), and *The Brothers* (160). Terence's plots are more complicated than those of his predecessors for he combined stories from more than one Greek original, a practice for which he was severely attacked. The chief interest in his works, however, does not lie in intrigue but in character, and the double plots often merely provide him with opportunities for showing

A BAS RELIEF allegedly showing a scene
from Roman comedy. [From Dörpfeld,
Griechische Theater (1896)]

contrasts in human behavior. His sympathetic treatment of characters
moves his plays toward romantic or sentimental comedy. He also sought for
consistency, and consequently avoided the insertion of Roman allusions
into the Greek plots. His language is that of everyday polite conversation,
without the great metrical variety of Plautus' plays. Although more conscious of artistic principles, Terence never achieved the popularity accorded Plautus.

Of the other comic writers, the most important was Caecilius Statius
(*c.* 219–168 B.C.), the principal dramatist in the years between Plautus and
Terence and considered by many Roman critics as the greatest of all comic
authors. Unfortunately, none of his plays survive. His work is thought to
have combined characteristics of both Plautus' and Terence's plays and to
form a transition between them. Other comic writers were Marcus Atilius,
Aquilius, Lucius Lanuvinus, and Sextus Turpilius (d. 103 B.C.). Turpilius
is the last known writer of *fabula palliata* (comedy on Greek materials), although these earlier plays continued to be produced for some time.

As with tragedy, it is customary to distinguish comedies based on
Greek originals from those on Roman materials (*fabula togata*). No plays

SCENE FROM ROMAN COMEDY. A wall painting in Pompeii.
[From Dieterich, *Pulcinella* (1897)]

of the latter type have survived and only three authors—Titinius, Afranius, and Atta—are known to have written in this form. Except in subject matter, the *fabula togata* seems to have differed in no important respect from the *fabula palliata;* they never attained the popularity of the Greek adaptations.

Comedy ceased to be a vital form after about 100 B.C. Nevertheless, the works of Plautus and Terence survived through the Dark Ages, perhaps because they were read as models of spoken Latin. Since critics turned to them once more during the Renaissance as the foremost examples of comic drama, their characteristics are of special interest. All of the plays are adaptations from Greek New Comedy. It is usually assumed that Plautus and Terence departed little from the structure of the originals and that changes were confined to details. One of the principal deviations is the elimination of the chorus, with the result that the plays are not divided into episodes (the division into acts was made by later editors). An important addition is the musical accompaniment of dialogue, a feature which may derive from the Etruscan inheritance. In Plautus' plays about two-thirds, and in Terence's about one-half, of the lines were accompanied by music.

In subject matter, plot devices, and characters, Roman comedy seems to have differed little from New Comedy. (See the discussion in Chapter II.) All of the action takes place in the street, with the result that many offstage events must be narrated and scenes which logically should occur inside are placed out of doors. Eavesdropping is common and many complications turn on overheard conversations.

After about 100 B.C. vitality in dramatic composition passed to minor forms, especially to the Atellan farce and the mime. Probably both had been brought to Rome before regular comedy and tragedy were imported. Little is known of their early history, however, for they remained nonliterary types until the 1st century B.C. At about the time when the major forms began to decline, the *fabula Atellana* and the mime were first written down.

Pomponius and Novius (writing between 100 and 75 B.C.) are credited with making the Atellan farce literary. At this time, the *fabulae Atellanae* seem to have been short, perhaps 300–400 lines, and to have served as *exodia,* or afterpieces, to regular drama. The Atellana emphasized rural settings, characters, and speech, while its subject matter most often was cheating, gluttony, fighting, or sexual exploits. Its rustic atmosphere and its use as an afterpiece led many Romans to associate it with the satyr play, and references to the latter form in Rome may in actuality be to the Atellan farce.

Four stock characters appeared in the *fabula Atellana:* Bucco, a vivacious, boisterous braggart; Pappus, a comic old man; Maccus, a gluttonous fool; and Dossenus, a hunchback of frightening appearance. Probably standardized costumes were worn by these figures; consequently, many historians have traced the similar conventions of the Italian *commedia dell'arte* of the 16th century back to the Atellan farce. The peak of popularity for the *fabula Atellana* was reached during the 1st century B.C., after which its place was increasingly usurped by the mime.

The first clear reference to the mime, or *fabula riciniata,* is found in Rome in 211 B.C., although it may have been performed much earlier. It was associated especially with the *ludi Florales,* the festival most popular with the common people. Like the Atellana, it was transformed into a literary type in the 1st century B.C. Decimus Laberius (106–43 B.C.) and his contemporary, Publius Syrus, are usually credited with this development. During the Christian era, the mime appears to have reverted to a nonliterary type, although its popularity increased until it virtually drove all other forms from the stage. Under the Empire, it became increasingly elaborate, spectacular, and obscene. Adultery was a stock theme, and Heliogabalus (Emperor, 218–22 A.D.) ordered that sexual acts be realistically portrayed on stage. Violence and cruelty also abounded, and Domitian (Emperor, 81–96 A.D.) had a real crucifixion inserted into one play. Since the Christian sacraments were also frequent subjects of ridicule, it is not surprising that the church condemned the theatre in general. The mime continued to flourish, nevertheless, until the closing of the theatres in the sixth century A.D.

Under the Empire, a new dramatic type, the pantomime (or *fabula saltica*) was introduced. Created in 22 B.C. by Pylades and Bathyllus, it was considered so distinctively Roman that in Greek it was called the "Italian dance." Pantomime required only one actor-dancer, who assumed all of the roles in a plot normally taken from mythology or history. A chorus sang the libretto, and an orchestra of flutes, pipes, and cymbals accompanied the performance. Characteristically, pantomime was serious, but there were also comic works, a type in which Bathyllus specialized. The comic variety

STATUETTE of a mime actor, or perhaps Dossenus of the *fabula Atellana*. [From Dieterich, *Pulcinella* (1897)]

soon declined, but the serious pantomine usurped the position formerly held by tragedy and was especially admired by more sophisticated theatregoers.

In addition to drama, other kinds of entertainment flourished under the Empire. Sham sea battles, or *naumachia*, were introduced in 46 B.C. They were held in theatres only when no other place was available, amphitheatres or lakes being more usual sites. The most famous *naumachia* is that of 52 A.D., held on the Fucine Lake with a cast of 19,000, many of them prisoners or condemned criminals. At times, the orchestras of theatres were flooded for water ballets or other aquatic entertainments on a less massive scale. Gladiatorial contests, animal baitings, rope dancing, and other nondramatic spectacles were also staged in the theatres.

Production Arrangements

The state festivals were under the management of magistrates, who received a grant to cover expenses. The magistrates themselves frequently supplied additional funds, since a well-received festival reflected honor on

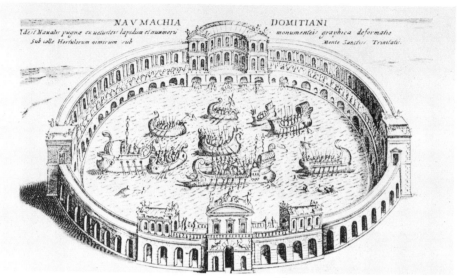

A *naumachia;* reconstruction made in the Renaissance. [From Laumann, *La Machinerie au Théâtre* (1897)]

them. For the *ludi scaenici* (or theatrical portions of the festivals), the magistrates contracted with the managers (*domini*) of acting troupes (*grex*) to produce the plays. The leader of each troupe probably bought plays directly from authors and arranged for music, properties, and costumes. The plays may have been performed before the magistrates prior to public viewing, both for purposes of censorship and to insure a high quality of performance. It is not clear whether any public notice of plays was given under the Republic, but during the Empire posters listed the various attractions.

Several companies normally presented plays at a festival. Each received a basic fee, but additional prizes or payments were made to companies, individual actors, and authors who especially pleased the audience. Occasional references are found to claques and attempted bribery of audiences and officials in awarding favors. During the Empire, rulers exerted considerable power over the plays, and often granted or withheld favors to actors. Ordinarily, however, it was the popular audience who most influenced theatrical performances. Each play was given without intermissions. Even the intervals between plays were usually filled with incidental entertainment or short mimes; consequently, performances were continuous throughout each day devoted to *ludi scaenici.*

Admission was always free and all classes attended. Plautus refers to nurses and children, slaves, prostitutes, magistrates' attendants, and women, and indicates that there was considerable jostling for places. In some periods, special seats in the orchestra were reserved for the Senators. Some tickets dating from the Empire have survived, but is not clear whether these were for the privileged few for whom seats were reserved, or whether they were used merely to prevent overcrowding in the theatre. It seems likely that, for the most part, seats were occupied on the "first come, first served" basis.

The theatres seated thousands of persons. The capacity of the early temporary structures is unknown, but the first permanent theatre is said to have seated 40,000. Even then, only a fraction of Rome's population could be accommodated in the theatre at once, for Rome grew in size from about 215,000 persons in 200 B.C. to about 1,000,000 during the Empire. Ordinarily, all of the plays for a festival were presented in the same theatre, but for one elaborate celebration in 17 B.C., three different theatres were used continuously for three consecutive days and nights.

Spectators were interested primarily in entertainment, and though special officials maintained order, the audience was free to come and go during a performance. Furthermore, other attractions competed for the audience's favor. The first two productions of Terence's *Mother-in-Law* were failures, because at the first the audience left to see a rope dancer, and at the second to watch gladiators. Spectators might also leave to buy food and drink, which were sold just outside the theatre.

The audience seems to have been quick to express praise and condemnation, and, since its response determined whether a troupe received additional payments, its favor was constantly sought. Many commentators have blamed the decline of the Roman theatre on catering to the increasingly debased taste of the common people.

The Roman Theatre Structure

The first permanent theatre building in Rome was not constructed until 55 B.C., almost 200 years after the beginning of regular drama, and over 100 years after the last surviving comedy was written. Consequently, as in Greece, the permanent structures date from a considerably later time than the period of significant dramatic writing.

In the 3rd century B.C., there were several precedents upon which the Romans could have built: (1) the Etruscan, (2) the *fabula Atellana*, (3) the mime, and (4) the Greek. Which of these, if any, they chose is unknown. It seems likely that Livius Andronicus would have adapted the Hellenistic structure for his plays, since he was most familiar with it. On the other hand, since many types of entertainment were given and a new temporary structure was supposedly erected for each festival, considerable experimentation would have been possible.

The problem is complicated by the relationship between theatrical performances and religious rites. Unlike the early Greeks, the Romans presented plays in honor of many gods, each of whom had his own sacred precinct in which it was considered unsuitable to dedicate offerings to any other god. Hanson, in *Roman Theater-Temples*, concludes that "all sites for *ludi scaenici* which can be located with certainty or probability before the erection of a permanent theatre in Rome are not only connected with a temple but are further specified as in front of a temple." He also suggests that performances were always given "in sight of the god" to whom they were dedicated, and that consequently the stage was erected facing the temple, where the image of the god was set up to view the performances.

The first permanent theatre in Rome had a temple dedicated to Venus at the top of the auditorium. Many historians have seen this as a sly trick to overcome the objections of the Senate to building a permanent theatre. Although this interpretation may be correct, it is equally possible that Pompey was following a tradition. On the other hand, there was always a group in Rome who objected to theatrical performances. Some historians

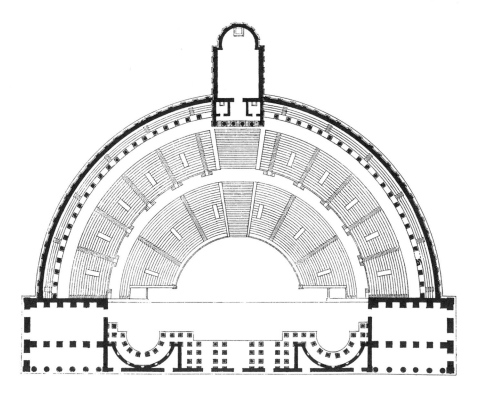

PLAN of the Theatre of Pompey. Note the temple of Venus at the top. [From Streit, *Das Theater* (1903)]

believe that it was as a concession to this group that no permanent theatres were erected prior to 55 B.C. Again, however, it may be that, before this time, the Senate thought it unwise to build a theatre dedicated to one god, unless they were to honor equally the other gods to whom plays were dedicated, and that it was too costly to build several. This may explain why the permanent theatres which were begun in 179, 174, and 155 B.C. were abandoned. Perhaps under the Empire, the claims of many gods could be met by placing in the theatre altars dedicated to them, and by bringing the effigy of the one being honored into the theatre during his festival. Regardless of the reasons for the change from temporary to permanent structures, the distinctions between them should be noted.

If we assume that there were at least five festivals each year, and that for each a temporary structure was erected and dismantled, then well over 500 would have been required prior to 55 B.C. It seems improbable that they were uniform in size or design. Their general characteristics are at best conjectural, and attempted reconstructions usually make the early structures merely flimsier and somewhat simpler versions of the later stone theatres. Disagreements among historians about the details of the temporary theatres center around such matters as the elaborateness of the stage background, the size of the stage, and the extent to which seating was provided for the audience, none of which can be resolved.

The structures appear to have become progressively more sumptuous and detailed. In 99 B.C. Claudius Pulcher, a magistrate, is said to have erected a theatre with such realistically painted details that birds tried to perch on them. Pliny (23–79 A.D.) states that Marcus Aemilius Scaurus built a theatre in 58 B.C. with a stage of three stories, the first of marble, the second of glass, and the third of gilded wood; the whole being decorated with 360 columns and 3000 bronze statues, while the auditorium accommodated 80,000 persons. Pliny also states that in 50 B.C., Gaius Scribonius Curio built two theatres back to back, each on a pivot; while the audience remained seated, the two parts were supposedly revolved to form an amphitheatre. Although modern historians seriously question their reliability, Pliny's accounts are indicative of structures sufficiently unusual and sumptuous to have become legendary by Pliny's time.

Considering the elaborateness of these temporary theatres, it is not surprising that Pompey was allowed to erect a permanent theatre in 55 B.C. Before the end of the century, two others had been built in Rome: the theatre of Balbus in 13 B.C., and the theatre of Marcellus in 11 B.C. Temporary structures continued to be used both in Rome and elsewhere for some time, but they gradually gave way to permanent buildings.

The theatres of the Empire are sufficiently similar in design to allow generalizations about their basic characteristics. Typically they were built on level ground, rather than on a slope as were the Greek theatres. Corridors and stairways around and beneath the auditorium allowed an efficient flow of spectators. When theatres utilized natural slopes, corridors were cut into the hillsides. A number of vertical aisles divided the auditorium (or *cavea*) into sections, while at least one broad aisle about half way up the slope and a covered portico at the top permitted horizontal movement.

A RECONSTRUCTION of the Roman theatre at Ostia, built between 30 and 12 B.C. [From D'Espouy, *Fragments d'Architecture Antique* (1901)]

The stage house (or *scaena*) and the auditorium were joined to form a single architectural unit. The passages corresponding to the *parodoi* were roofed over to provide corridors (or *vomitoria*) into the orchestra and auditorium. Over each there was a box reserved for the magistrates who had supervised the festival, or the Emperor and other important persons. The orchestra, an exact half-circle, was used most frequently for seating privileged groups, although at times it accommodated dancing, animal fights, gladiatorial contests, or water ballets.

The stage (or *pulpitum*) was raised about five feet, and its front placed on the diameter of the orchestra circle. In theatres built before 100 A.D., a slot was provided for the curtain near the front edge of the stage; after the 2d century, when other means of handling the curtain were developed, the slots were filled in. The size of the stage was determined by that of the theatre, but most were very large by modern standards, being from 20 to 40 feet in depth and from 100 to more than 300 in length.

There were from three to five doors in the rear wall, and at least one door in the wings (or *versurae*) which enclosed the ends of the stage.

The facade (or *scaenae frons*) of the stage house was decorated with columns, niches, porticos, and statues, and was often painted or gilded. The stage was covered by a roof which probably improved acoustics and protected the elaborate *scaenae frons*. Most of the early permanent theatres probably had straight facades; but after the 2d century A.D., curved niches, forming deep vestibules and alcoves, were usual. This later arrangement cut into the backstage space until often little more than a corridor remained. Dressing rooms and other work space were housed in the side wings. Trap doors in the stage floor were common, and in some theatres a peephole vantage point, probably for the stage manager's use, was provided at one side of the stage.

The Romans were concerned for the comfort of audiences. Under the Empire a system of air conditioning, based on air blowing over streams of water, was perfected. To protect the audience from the sun, an awning (or *velum*) was introduced around 70 B.C. Attached to masts set in two rows of corbels, or supporting projections, the awning was operated by sailors stationed on the roof of the colonnade which surrounded the auditorium. Frequently the surface of the awning was painted; Nero had himself depicted there as the Sun God seated in a chariot.

Under the Roman Empire about 125 permanent theatres were built. Among the most important were those at Ostia (in Italy) built between 30 and 12 B.C.; Arles (in France) perhaps as early as 46 B.C.; Orange (in France) 1st or 2nd century A.D.; Merida (in Spain) 18 B.C.; Timgad, Djemila, Dugga (all in North Africa) between 138 and 192 A.D.; Sabratha (North Africa), *c.* 200 A.D.; Aspendus (in southern Asia Minor) 161–180 A.D.; and Athens, 161 A.D.

A few purely Roman theatres were built in Greek areas of the Empire, but the usual practice was to remodel the existing Greek structures along Roman lines. In some, the *thyromata* were replaced by a Roman *scaenae frons;* many retained the high stage, but others lowered it to five feet. To increase the depth, the Greek stage was often extended forward into the orchestra as much as 20 feet. Since many of the Greek structures had no side wings, an extra door was often placed in the rear facade at the extreme ends to give a total of five to seven doors.

Most of the major Roman cities in Western Europe had amphitheatres as well, where gladiatorial contests, animal fights, water battles, and similar nontheatrical events were usually staged. Where there was no amphitheatre, such events were housed in the theatre. As the Greek territories never favored violent spectacles, few amphitheatres were built there. Nontheatrical entertainment was given only occasionally, and primarily for the benefit of resident Romans.

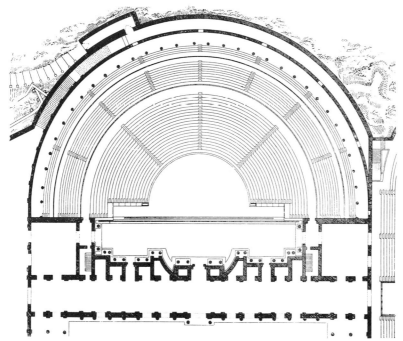

PLAN of the Theatre at Orange. [From Durm, *Handbuch der Architektur* (1905)]

Scenery

The basic scenic background in the Roman theatre was the *scaenae frons.* In comedy, this facade was treated as a series of houses opening onto a city street, represented by the stage. In tragedy, the facade normally became a palace or temple. Although some plays are set in the country or other open places, there was probably little attempt to change the visual appearance of the stage from one play to another. As the Prologue of *The Menaechmi* says: "This city is Epidamnus during the performance of this play; when another play is performed it will become another city." The audience probably depended primarily upon the dramatists' words to locate the action.

There are, notwithstanding, a number of problems relating to the scenic background. One concerns the amount and kind of three-dimensional detail required by the plays of Plautus and Terence, some scholars arguing for numerous porticos, alcoves, or similar architectural features, with others maintaining that all details were painted. The question has arisen largely because of the many scenes in the comedies involving eaves-

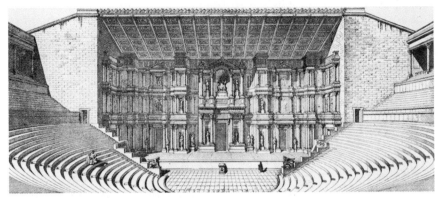

RECONSTRUCTED VIEW of the Theatre at Orange.
[From Durm, *Handbuch der Architektur* (1905)]

dropping or the failure of one character to see others who are on stage at the same time. One group of historians has insisted that three-dimensional structures would have been necessary to stage the scenes convincingly, while another insists that the conventions of the Roman stage permitted characters to see each other or not as the dramatic situation dictated.

Closely connected with this problem is another involving interiors. Since a few scenes in the comedies depict banquets or other actions which would ordinarily occur indoors, some scholars have argued that such scenes were staged in porches or vestibules in front of doors, so as to give a more convincing sense of an interior. Others have insisted that none of these scenes occur indoors, and that it is only the influence of modern realism that has led historians to such conjectures. Neither of these arguments can be resolved, although it seems likely that convention was stronger than realism in the time of Plautus and Terence. On the other hand, judging from the permanent structures, it is probable that the facade did become increasingly elaborate, although for other reasons.

The doors of the *scaenae frons* are of considerable scenic importance, since each may represent a different house, and since they are referred to so frequently by the characters. In the comedies, doors attract the attention of the actors by squeaking; characters beat on them and lock or unlock them. In tragedy, all of the doors in the *scaenae frons* were probably treated as entrances to the same building; some ancient commentators state that the central doorway was reserved for the principal personage, while the side doors were used by the lesser characters. The doors into the *versurae* may also have had conventionalized uses, one being understood to lead to the forum, and the other to the harbor or country.

For the most part, *periaktoi* seem to have been the chief means of differentiating place. Vitruvius, writing about 15 B.C., states: "The scaena itself displays the following scheme. In the center are double doors decorated like those of a royal palace. At the right and left are the doors of the guest chambers. Beyond are the spaces provided for the decoration—places that the Greeks call *periaktoi,* because in these places are triangular pieces of machinery which revolve, each having three decorated faces." As to what was painted on the *periaktoi,* Vitruvius adds: "There are three kinds of scenes, one called the tragic, second, the comic, third, the satyric. Their decorations are different and unlike each other in scheme. Tragic scenes are delineated with columns, pediments, statues, and other objects suited to kings; comic scenes exhibit private dwellings, with balconies and views representing rows of windows, after the manner of ordinary dwellings; satyric scenes are decorated with trees, caverns, mountains, and other rustic objects delineated in landscape style." The meaning of this passage has been the subject of endless debate. The most sensible interpretation seems to be that the decoration for each type of play was conventionalized and painted on *periaktoi* placed near each end of the stage. In any case, the *periaktoi* could not have covered more than a very small portion of the *scaenae frons,* most of which remained visible.

Most discussions of the stage background concentrate on the requirements of regular drama, but the permanent theatres were built after the minor dramatic forms came to the fore and placed a greater emphasis on spectacle. One change is to be seen in the introduction of two kinds of curtains: the *auleum,* or front curtain, and a background curtain, or *siparium.* The *auleum* may have been used as early as 133 B.C., but was certainly available by 56 B.C. Originally, it was lowered into a slot at the front of the stage by means of a series of telescoped poles. Extending the poles upward to their full height raised the curtain, while the reverse process lowered it. After the 2nd century A.D., the curtain was suspended from overhead and raised by ropes. The front curtain allowed the sudden revelation of a scene or the concealment of a striking tableau. Before its introduction, all characters had to be brought on at the beginning and gotten offstage at the end. After its introduction, dramatists seem to have capitalized on the surprises and striking effects it made possible.

The *siparium* probably came into the theatre with the mime. Originally a small curtain, it may have been hung at the rear of a platform to serve both as background and as masking of the offstage space. Entrances were probably made through slits in it. As the mime grew in importance, the *siparium* increased in size and was often hung against the *scaenae frons* in the manner of a backdrop. Nothing is known, however, of the scenes painted on these curtains or precisely how they were related to the facade. There appear to have been simultaneous and contradictory trends toward more elaborate curtains and more elaborate permanent facades.

Although intricate machinery is seldom mentioned in ancient accounts, scenic marvels could be achieved. Apuleius (2nd century A.D.), in his novel *Metamorphoses,* describes a spectacular production at Corinth. Although the account is both satirical and fictional, it is probably based upon contemporary practices. He tells first of a dance in the orchestra while the stage is concealed by the *auleum.* Suddenly the stage curtain is removed to reveal a towering mountain, with shrubs, trees, a stream, grazing goats, and a shepherd. There follows an entertainment based on the story of Paris' judgment on the beauty of Hera, Athena, and Aphrodite. At the end, a fountain of wine springs from the top of the mountain, and the entire structure sinks into the stage. Apuleius gives no details about the size of the mountain. Probably most of the many dances he records were performed on the stage floor. But even after allowances are made, such a spectacle would have required complex stage machinery. In the absence of other accounts, however, it is impossible to say to what extent Apuleius is describing typical practices.

Even if scenery were not always elaborate, spectacular effects were achieved through the use of large numbers of supernumeraries in dances, battles, and processions. The trend toward mass effects had begun as early as the 1st century B.C., when Cicero states that, at the dedication of the Theatre of Pompey in 52 B.C., 600 mules crossed the stage in one play, and 3000 bowls were displayed in another. The frequency of such productions increased under the Empire, when realism of spectacle and sensationalism seem to have been the guiding principles of the theatre.

Actors and Acting

The usual term for actors in Rome was *histriones,* although *cantores* (or declaimers) was also used. At first a clear distinction was made between the actors of regular drama and the performer of mimes (the *mimus* or *saltator*), who was considered to be inferior. In late Rome, however, the term *histriones* came to be applied to all actors. Except in mime troupes, women did not appear on the stage.

The social status of the Roman actor has been much disputed. Some historians have suggested that actors were slaves owned by company managers. While this may have been true in some troupes, it was not always so. Roscius, the most famous of Roman actors, was certainly never a slave and was eventually raised to the nobility. Similarly, Aesopus, a contemporary of

Roscius, was a member of the Optimate, a group who, because of its wealth, influence, and ability, exercised considerable control over public affairs. In the early years many actors were also members of the *collegium poetarum,* an association of writers and actors founded in 207 B.C. Records show honors being paid to members of this association which could be given only to men with full civil rights. On the other hand, mime actors seem always to have been considered inferior, and many of them probably were slaves. As the mimes increased in importance, the number of slave actors may also have increased. It seems likely, therefore, that the social status of the actor varied considerably, although the majority always ranked low.

There were probably some professional performers in Rome prior to the introduction of comedy and tragedy in 240 B.C. Although Livius Andronicus acted in his own plays, succeeding dramatists seldom followed his practice. There was no such intimate connection between playwriting and performance as there had been in early Greece.

The production of plays seems to have passed early into the hands of professional managers. Although there apparently were no restrictions on the number of actors on the Roman stage, the extant plays could have been performed by a company of five or six actors, if doubling was practiced and supernumeraries used occasionally. Troupes may have been much larger, however, for there is no information about their size. The names of only a few actors from the early period have survived. Plautus refers to Pellio as an actor in one of his plays, and Lucius Ambivius Turpio was the actor-manager for all of Terence's plays.

In the 1st century B.C., the emphasis shifted to the "star" performer as the regular drama declined. Scenes calculated to display the talents of an actor were substituted for entire plays. Pantomime featured a single dancer, and in the mime one performer was almost always starred, even though a large number of supernumeraries might be used for spectacular effects. Many of the actors amassed fortunes. Under the Empire, leading actors had followings not unlike those of a modern movie star, and in the 6th century A.D., Theodora, a mime actress, married Justinian, Emperor of the Eastern Roman Empire. Many of the most popular performers were tightrope dancers, trapeze artists, jugglers, sword-swallowers, fire-eaters, and dancers.

Acting style probably varied according to the dramatic form. In regular comedy and tragedy, actors wore masks and declaimed many of their lines to the accompaniment of a flute. The female roles were played by men, and there was probably much doubling. Since the theatres often seated as many as 40,000 persons, gestures and movements were probably enlarged. All of these factors would indicate an acting style considerably removed from realism. On the other hand, the Roman teachers of oratory often suggested actors as suitable models for the public speaker to imitate. Consequently, stylization in acting was probably not extreme.

For the most part, actors seem to have specialized in one type of drama, although Andronicus and Roscius departed from the usual practice by performing in both comedy and tragedy. It is often stated that Andronicus separated singing and speaking and that, after his time, musical passages were sung by another performer while the actor mimed the scene. This idea seems to derive from a single anecdote about one occasion upon which Andronicus lost his voice as a result of giving many encores. Most scholars now point out that the close connection between musical and spoken passages in the works of Plautus and Terence would make it difficult to divide the lines between a singer and an actor. That encores of well-received passages were often given, however, implies much about the Roman approach to acting.

In the mimes, masks were not worn, and facial expression was more important than in other forms. Through much of its history, the mime was in part improvised, and consequently required a talent for the invention of dialogue, business, and movement. Mime actors were selected for their physical beauty or comic ugliness. In the 2nd century B.C., the companies were probably very small, with perhaps no more than three or four members; but under the Empire they included as many as 60 entertainers, although some of these were tightrope dancers, tumblers, and jugglers. For the great spectacles, many supernumeraries were added.

In pantomime, the emphasis was upon the solo performer. Noted for their handsomeness and athletic qualities, these actors depended entirely upon gesture and movement to portray a series of characters and situations. Many were renowned for the subtlety and complexity of their portrayals, at a time when the mimes were becoming increasingly obvious and exaggerated in their playing.

In addition to the public performers, there may have been a number of private troupes in late Rome. These were probably composed of slaves kept by rich men to provide entertainment for their households and friends.

Masks and Costumes

Until recently, historians accepted as true a statement by a writer of the 4th century A.D. that Roscius, seeking to hide his squint, introduced the mask into the Roman theatre in the 1st century B.C. Newer studies, however, have discovered many references to masks long before Roscius' time and have concluded that they were used from the beginning of the Roman theatre. There is much evidence to support this conclusion. All of the areas of major influence on Rome—Etruria, Greece, southern Italy—had used masks in their entertainments, and it seems unlikely that the Romans would have rejected a standard part of Greek comedy and tragedy, of the Atellan farce, and of Etruscan dances. The use of masks would also have made the doubling of roles much easier, as well as simplifying the problem of casting characters of identical appearance, as in Plautus' *Menaechmi* and *Amphitryon*.

Masks were made of linen and, with the attached wig, formed a complete covering for the head. Since it is usually assumed that Roman masks resembled those used in the Hellenistic theatre, Pollux' list of masks (see Chapter II) has served as the basis for most discussions. Other sources are illustrated manuscripts, dating from the 4th or 5th century A.D., of Terence's plays showing the masks of each play.

MASKS for Terence's *Andria,* as shown in a manuscript of the 4th century A.D. [From Robert, *Die Masken der Neueren Attischen Komoedie* (1911)]

The masks for pantomime had closed mouths. Lucian, writing in the 2nd century A.D., describes them as being much more natural than those for tragedy, which were then much exaggerated. Quintilian, writing in the 1st century A.D., refers to masks with one cheerful and one serious side, apparently an attempt to indicate a change of emotion without a change of mask. Mime actors did not wear masks, and, as mime increased in popularity under the Empire, the use of masks in the theatre became less common.

Costumes varied with the type of play. Comedy based on Greek life (the *fabula palliata*) followed the costuming conventions of New Comedy (see Chapter II), for which everyday Athenian dress was adapted. Similar principles governed the costumes for comedies based on Roman life (the *fabula togata*), with Roman garments substituted for Greek. In this case, the Roman tunic was the usual garment and over this the cloak, or *toga,* was worn.

The costume for tragedy was also based upon Greek practice. The *fabula crepidata* (or tragedies on Greek themes) probably followed the conventions of the Hellenistic theatre (described in Chapter II), although some scholars have suggested that it was Roman influence which led to the

IVORY STATUETTE showing a tragic actor of about the 2nd century A.D. Note the distorted mask, high headdress, and thick-soled boots. Some scholars believe this figure represents a Greek actor of the Hellenistic period, but it is more likely Roman. [From *Monumenti Inediti* (1879)]

extreme stylization of dress in late Greek tragedy. Regardless of the direction of influence, it is likely that Greek and Roman tragic costumes were similar. For the *fabula praetexta* (or tragedies on Roman materials), costumes probably followed the conventions of the *fabula crepidata,* except

77

that Roman garments were used. The toga with a purple border (the *toga praetexta*) was sufficiently typical that the dramatic form took its name from it.

It is usually assumed that each of the four stock characters of the *fabula Atellana* had his own standardized mask and costume, which remained the same from one play to another. Since most of the other characters were rustics, their costumes were probably exaggerated versions of country dress. Some of the known titles of Atellan farces refer to doctors, musicians, painters, fortune tellers, and fishermen, each of whom may have been indicated by costume.

The pantomime performer wore a long tunic and cloak which allowed freedom of movement. As a subtle variation on tragedy, his costume probably was a less exaggerated version of tragic dress. Nothing is known of the costume for comic pantomime, the popularity of which was short-lived.

Mime actors wore the tunic as a basic garment, while their most distinctive accessory was the *ricinium*, or hood, frequently used as a disguise. Some mime characters, probably the fools, wore the *centunuculus*, or patchwork jacket, and had shaven heads. Others represented fashionable and sophisticated men and women, and, like modern film stars, were dressed lavishly in the latest fashions.

Music

Although the Romans did not value music highly, it was used more extensively in Roman than in Greek plays. Up to two-thirds of the lines of Plautus' plays were accompanied by music, and it figured only slightly less prominently in the work of other authors.

As with Greek music, we know little of the Roman modes. The accompaniment used in the theatre seems to have been composed by each troupe's own flute player, although probably he merely played suitable mood music. One reference from the 1st century B.C. suggests that the accompaniment was so conventionalized that the audience could tell what kind of character was to appear by listening to the music. Thus, it may have resembled the more trite musical scores for motion pictures. That the musician was valued, however, is indicated by records which list his name immediately after that of the principal actor.

The music for plays was performed on a "flute" with two pipes, each about 20 inches long, which was bound to the performer's head so as to leave his hands free to work the stops. The flute player was on stage throughout the performances and supposedly moved about to accompany first one character and then another.

The musical element in pantomime was more elaborate than that for regular drama, requiring an orchestra of flutes, pipes, cymbals, and other percussion instruments. It is also likely that the music for mimes became more extensive during the late Empire as the performances became more spectacular and ornate.

The Decline of the Theatre

In terms of numbers of performances, theatres, and spectacular display, the Roman theatre reached its apogee during the 4th century A.D. Although it continued as a publicly supported institution for another two hundred years, it had already encountered difficulties which were eventually to overwhelm it.

One source of opposition was the rising Christian church. At first the new sect was very weak, and, as it came to popular attention, met considerable opposition on political as well as religious grounds. Its adherents refused to place allegiance to the state above the dictates of religious teachings, and their insistence that other gods were false went counter to the Roman tradition of accepting all gods in the desire to offend none. Consequently, the Romans were willing to accept the Hebrew god as another deity but were unwilling to abandon all others. The intractability of the Christians resulted in the decision of the Emperor to stamp out the new religion as a subversive element in the state.

In spite of persecution, the power of Christianity gradually increased. Constantine (Emperor, 324–37) first made Christianity lawful, while Theodosius I (Emperor of the Eastern Empire, 379–95) made the profession of any religion other than Christianity a crime. From the 4th century on, some of the excesses of the theatre abated, but no ruler, even those who were Christians, thought it wise to forbid theatrical performances.

The theatre was a favorite target of the Christians for at least three reasons. First, it had always been associated with the festivals of pagan gods. Second, the licentiousness of the mimes offended the moral sense of the church leaders. Third, the mimes often ridiculed such Christian practices as baptism and the sacrament of bread and wine. As a result, the break between church and theatre was inevitable. Tertullian (c. 150–c. 220 A.D.), the North African theologian, denounced the theatre in his *De Spectaculis,* arguing that Christians forswore the theatre when they were baptized. From about 300 A.D. on, the church councils sought to dissuade Christians from attending performances, and in 398 the Council of Carthage decreed excommunication for anyone who went to the theatre rather than to church on holy days. Actors were forbidden the sacraments of the church unless they forswore their profession, a decree not rescinded in many places until the 18th century.

Church opposition, however, seems to have had little effect on the Roman theatre; alone, it perhaps would never have succeeded in prohibiting performances. Ironically, it was the pagan tribes who accomplished what the Christians had been unable to do. By 400 A.D. the barbarians from the north and east were making considerable inroads into Roman territories, and by 476 A.D. had twice sacked Rome itself. Wherever possible, the theatres were rebuilt and theatrical performances resumed. Although the barbarians despised the theatre, Theodoric (the Ostrogoth who ruled over Italy from 493 to 526) found it politically expedient to finance entertainments, and under his rule the Theatre of Pompey was repaired. His successors continued his policies. The last definite record of a performance in Rome is found in a letter written in 533 A.D. The theatre does not seem to have survived the Lombard invasion of 568, after which state recognition and support of the theatre was abandoned.

The Eastern Roman Empire, with its capital at Constantinople, survived, however, and the theatre continued there for some time. But by 692 A.D. the church was sufficiently strong that the Trullan Council passed a resolution designed to forbid all mimes, theatres, and other spectacles. Although the effectiveness of this decree has been questioned, historians usually let it mark the end of the ancient theatre, both the Greek and Roman.

Our knowledge of the theatre in the centuries which follow is shadowy at best. The institution which had attained such glory under the Greeks and Romans was now an outcast surviving, if at all, on the fringes of legality. Ironically, it was under the protection of the church that it began slowly to reemerge in the 10th century. But another four hundred years would have to pass before the greatness of the classical achievement would be once more appreciated and imitated.

THEATRE AND
DRAMA IN
THE MIDDLE AGES

*I*n the centuries which followed the disintegration of the Roman Empire, the theatre returned to a state almost as primitive as that out of which it had emerged in the 6th century B.C. For 400 years it was once more reduced to ritual-drama, supplemented occasionally by professional entertainment. Beginning in the 10th century, however, the theatre slowly revived, building gradually to the great secular drama of the 16th century.

The Dark Ages

It is often stated that the theatre in Western Europe ceased to exist after the fall of Rome in the 6th century A.D., but this assertion must be qualified. Official recognition and support of performances were withdrawn, the theatre structures ceased to be used, and educated men devoted their energies to a church which sought to stamp out all pagan pastimes, including drama. Consequently, the theatre existed, if at all, on a much-reduced scale and as a semi-legitimate activity. Actors were anathematized by church councils and Christians were urged to avoid them.

In spite of church opposition, however, it is clear from numerous references that *mimi, histriones,* and *ioculatores* were common in Europe between the 6th and 10th centuries. Some historians interpret these references as clear evidence that small itinerant companies of professional actors persisted throughout the Dark Ages. Others, however, insist that these Latin terms merely refer to entertainers such as the *jongleurs,* who sang songs and told stories, jugglers, and exhibitors of trained animals. Consequently, although all agree that there were professional performers, not all believe that there were theatrical troupes.

Another controversy centers around the theatre in Constantinople. Although the Trullan Synod of 692 sought to end all performances, some scholars believe that it was not successful. Again, the evidence is slight, but there are some convincing indications of a continuing theatrical tradition. In addition to the pagan mimes, a few Christian plays were written in Byzantium, some of which may have been performed. It is possible, therefore, that the Byzantine theatre provided an example upon which Western Europe built, although no direct links have yet been uncovered.

In seeking the sources of the Western revival of drama, scholars have also turned to those pagan rituals which survived despite the growing power of Christianity. Spring fertility rites were performed throughout Europe, and midwinter ceremonies designed to revive the waning sun were almost as common. These and other celebrations made use of such theatrical elements as music, dance, masks, costumes, and impersonation. Some historians have argued that the church introduced many of its dramatic ceremonies in order to combat the appeal of the pagan rites.

There are, then, a number of possible sources for the theatrical revival: the Roman mime tradition; the *jongleurs* and other individual performers; the Byzantine secular mimes; the Byzantine religious drama; and pagan rituals. Direct evidence is lacking to connect any of these with the church's adoption of drama in the 10th century, although any of them could have been a significant cause.

Liturgical Drama

Regardless of influences, it is the church which is normally credited with the revival of drama. The first true dramatic episode performed in the church dates from the last half of the 10th century. But this innovation had a number of antecedents which can be traced through the preceding centuries.

At this time the church had two kinds of services, the Mass and Hours. The Mass was divided into two parts: the introduction, and the sacrament of bread and wine. The introduction was largely devotional, including readings from the Bible, prayers, sermons, and psalms, and was variable from day to day according to the church calendar. The second part, the sacrament, varied little, being the central act of church worship. The importance of the Mass discouraged innovations; consequently, few dramatic episodes were ever attached to it, although some scholars have argued that the Mass itself is a drama.

Far more significant in the revival of drama were the services of the Hours, for these included no indispensable act. Since they were variable, the Hours could accommodate drama more easily, and it was here that most of the playlets were performed. By the 10th century there were eight Hours services each day: Matins, Lauds, Prime, Terce, Sext, Nones, Vespers, and Compline. Since lay Christians could not attend nine church services daily, the Hours were associated primarily with religious orders in cathedrals, collegiate churches, and monasteries where the drama first flourished.

The church calendar also provided an incentive to drama because it commemorated particular Biblical events on specific days of the year. By the 10th century a number of theatrical elements had been incorporated into these annual celebrations. Palm Sunday was usually observed with an elaborate procession, including a figure riding on an ass, from outside the city to the church. On Good Friday a cross was often wrapped in burial clothes and placed in a symbolic tomb, from which it was raised on Easter Sunday. Similar ceremonies commemorated other events of the church year.

Symbolic objects and actions—church vestments, altars, tombs, censers, and the pantomime of the priests—constantly recalled the essentially dramatic events which underlie Christian ritual. Certain emblems had also come to be associated with specific Biblical characters, such as "the keys of the kingdom" of Saint Peter and the dove of the Virgin Mary, making them easy to identify.

A type of dialogue existed in the church's antiphonal songs, the parts of which were divided between two groups or between an individual and a group. These choral portions of the Mass had been relatively standardized by the end of the 6th century, when they were arranged according to the church calendar in the *Antiphonarium* of Pope Gregory the Great.

All of these circumstances provided numerous possibilities for drama, but it was not until the 9th century that changing conditions prompted the crucial step. At this time, a new sense of the church's significance led to the erection of splendid buildings and the extension of church services, with more costly vestments, magnificent processions, and more elaborate music.

Most important, tropes, which were to develop into playlets, were introduced.

Tropes, or interpolations into an existing text, first took the form of lengthened musical passages, originally of the final syllable of the "Allelulia." Eventually this extended melody became so elaborate that words were added, one syllable for each note, as an aid to memory. Although the origin of this practice is obscure, it was perfected at the monastery at St. Gall under Notker Balbulus (*c.* 840–912). Tropes were soon used in most choral passages of the Mass.

It is from an Easter trope that the birth of drama is usually traced. The oldest extant text, dating from about 925, follows in its entirety:

> *Angel:* Whom seek ye in the tomb, O Christians?
> *The Three Marys:* Jesus of Nazareth, the crucified,
>   O Heavenly Beings.
> *Angel:* He is not here, he is risen as he foretold.
>   Go and announce that he is risen from the tomb.

This text, found in the introductory portion of the Mass, was probably merely antiphonal and did not involve actors impersonating the characters.

The step into true drama was soon taken. The earliest extant playlet, complete with directions for its performance, is found in the *Regularis Concordia* compiled between 965 and 975 by St. Ethelwold, Bishop of Winchester (England). Although it is usually assumed that St. Ethelwold was merely adopting practices already familiar on the continent, this cannot be established. It is clear, nevertheless, that by the last half of the 10th century dramatic episodes had found their way into the church liturgy.

Liturgical drama originated and flourished in the Benedictine monasteries, especially those at Limoges and Fleury (in France), St. Gall (in Switzerland), Richenau (in Germany), and Ripall (in Spain). For three hundred years, it developed entirely within the church. Not until the end of the 13th century were plays performed out of doors, and even after that time they remained a part of church services in many areas, persisting as late as 1865 in Spain.

Liturgical drama spread as far east as Russia, and from Scandinavia to Italy. The most prolific areas were France and Germany. In Italy the opposition of the papacy kept the plays few in number, while in Spain the Moorish occupation hampered their spread, except in the northeastern part which had been liberated about 800.

The length and complexity of liturgical plays differed considerably from one area to another. Of the extant works, some of the simplest date from the 15th century, whereas some of the most elaborate had been written by the 11th century. Consequently, no clear pattern of development can be traced. Although it is frequently assumed that the plays grew

THE THREE MARYS at the tomb. Title page of the *Concordia Regularis of St. Ethelwold*. [Courtesy Trustees of the British Museum]

by the gradual addition of new episodes, this is not necessarily true, for complex plays may have been written as soon as the desirability of dramatization was accepted.

The oldest and most numerous of existing plays are those which deal with the visit of the three Marys to the tomb of Christ; more than 400 have been discovered. The most elaborate Easter dramas date from the 13th century. One of these, found at Klosterneuberg, includes the following episodes: after the burial of Christ, Jewish high priests ask Pilate to set a watch over the tomb; Pilate agrees and the priests lead Roman soldiers to the tomb and give them money; while the soldiers are keeping guard, an Angel appears and strikes them to the ground; the Marys stop at a perfume-seller's stall to purchase ointments and then proceed to the tomb, where they discover that Christ has risen; the soldiers revive and report the news to the priests, who bribe them to declare that the body has been stolen; Mary Magdalen reports the news to Peter and John, who rush to the tomb; Mary Magdalen meets Christ disguised as a gardener; Christ is led by two Angels to the gates of Hell, which he forces open to free the imprisoned souls; the Marys and apostles proclaim the resurrection of Christ. In spite of the numerous events, there are only about 200 lines of dialogue. It is a long play, nevertheless, in comparison with most liturgical dramas.

The crucifixion was rarely dramatized, and only three plays on this subject have survived. Two of these are recorded in the *Carmina Burana,* a 13th century manuscript-collection of plays and poems discovered at the monastery of Benediktbeuern in Germany. The longest treats several events in the life of Christ and ends with the crucifixion, the point at which most Easter plays begin.

Next to Easter, the Christmas season prompted the greatest number of dramas. Few, however, treat the nativity itself; those which do are simple. On the other hand, there are many plays about the Three Kings (performed on January 6), some of which include Herod's rage and his massacre of the children. A few separate plays also dramatize the "slaughter of the Innocents," commemorated on December 28.

Another popular drama of the Christmas season was the Prophets Play. Unlike other liturgical plays, it was derived from a non-Biblical source, a sermon of the 5th or 6th century (inaccurately attributed to St. Augustine throughout the Middle Ages) which sought to convict the Jews of error in their dealing with Christ by summoning their own prophets. The witnesses were called one by one, each speaking his prophecy concerning Christ. The number of characters varied from two to twenty-eight, and in some plays such pagan figures as Virgil and the Sybil appeared. Most of the plays of the Christmas season were short and associated with particular days of the church calendar. Only one surviving work, found in the *Carmina Burana,* unites all of the episodes of the Christmas story into a single drama.

Although the Easter and Christmas plays are by far the most numerous, other events were dramatized: the raising of Lazarus, the conversion of St. Paul, the Wise and Foolish Virgins, Pentecost, Isaac and Rebecca, Joseph and his Brethren, Daniel and the Lion's Den, and various events in the life of the Virgin Mary. The most elaborate play of all is the *Antichrist,* dating from the 12th century. Based upon the prediction that before the second coming of Christ a deceiver will appear and attempt to subvert Christ's mission, its scenes are set at places ranging over the known world, while battles and similar complex episodes are so numerous that some scholars have questioned whether it was ever performed.

The Staging of Liturgical Drama

A number of staging conventions which evolved in the church were to continue in use throughout the Medieval period. The playing area had two basic components: small scenic structures (variously called mansions, *sedes, loci,* or *domi*) and a generalized acting area (the *platea,* playne, or place). The mansions served to locate the scene and to house any properties required. But, since the action could not be performed in the limited area of the typically-small mansions, the actors used as much of the adjacent space (the *platea*) as they needed, the same area often being required for several scenes. A series of mansions was arranged around the neutral playing space, and the performers moved from one to another as the action demanded.

THE INTERIOR of Saint Benoit-sur-Loire. The entry to the crypt can be glimpsed behind the bench at the left.

In the 10th to 13th centuries, church architecture was less elaborate than in the succeeding Gothic period. As yet there was typically no screen which divided the choir from the nave, and thus the mansions could easily be placed anywhere in the church. The earliest plays required only one mansion and a small *platea* in the choir, but the more complex plays used many mansions and spread into the nave. The individual mansions varied considerably in size and complexity. Often an altar represented the tomb of Christ. In other churches, however, imitations of the "true sepulchre" in Jerusalem, large enough for several persons to enter, were a permanent part of church furnishings. A few mansions housed elaborate and numerous properties, especially those for the Last Supper, Nebuchadnezzar's fiery furnace, Daniel in the lion's den, and the kitchen of Isaac and Rebecca.

Some mansions had curtains so that characters or objects might be revealed at the right moment or concealed at the end of an episode. The choir loft might be used to represent high places or Heaven, while the crypt often served for low places or Hell. Elementary flying machinery was also used at times to pull the star ahead of the Three Kings, to raise a figure representing Christ on Ascension Day, or to lower a dove for the Annunciation or flames at Pentecost.

Costumes, for the most part, were church vestments, to which might be added realistic or symbolic accessories. Female characters usually wore dalmatics, the hoods of which covered the head. Angels were signified by wings added to church vestments. The prophets and the Three Kings were sometimes given elaborate nonclerical garments in an attempt to distinguish them more realistically from other characters, although historical accuracy was not attempted. Symbolic emblems, identifying specific personages, were often carried.

The actors were members of the clergy or choir boys in most cases, although in the 13th century some roles may have been taken by wandering scholars or schoolboys. Much of our knowledge about the staging of plays comes from the rather detailed prescriptions contained in the church manuals of the period. In these, more space is often taken up with stage directions, especially those concerning movement, pantomime, and tone of voice, than with lines of dialogue. As long as the plays were written in Latin and performed in the church, the majority of lines were chanted rather than spoken, and the acting in general was probably more schematic than realistic.

The Feast of Fools and the Feast of the Boy Bishop

Although most of the performances in the church were probably serious and devotional, an element of buffoonery may have crept into some plays associated with Christmas. During this season a number of days were assigned to the minor clergy, who conducted the church services, staged processions through the town, and often collected gifts or exacted payments. St. Stephen's Day (December 26) was given over to the deacons; the Feast of the Holy Innocents (December 28) to the choir boys; and the Feast of the Circumcision (January 1), or alternatively January 6 or 13, to the subdeacons.

Of these festivals, two became especially prominent: the subdeacons' revelries, commonly called the Feast of Fools; and the choir boys' celebrations, usually designated the Feast of the Boy Bishop. The Feast of Fools was more elaborate, perhaps because the adult clergy were more difficult to discipline than the boys. The appeal of these festivals lay in the inversion of status, which allowed the lesser clergy to ridicule their superiors and the routine of church life. Although such practices may not have been typical, at times the celebrants rang the church bells improperly, sang out of tune, wore strange garments and masks, and used puddings, sausages, or old shoes as censers. The Feast of Fools was presided over by a "bishop fool," while the choir boys elected a "boy bishop." It is not clear when these festivals began, but both were well established by the end of the 12th century, and efforts to suppress them were unsuccessful until the 16th century.

The celebrations were accompanied by much revelry, the Feast of Fools being noted for its license. Sometimes plays were staged as a part of the festivities, and a certain amount of burlesque and comedy may have come into the liturgical plays in this manner. Extensive development of comic episodes, however, had to await the removal of the plays from the church.

The Removal of Plays from the Church

The performance of plays outside the church probably began in the 12th century, although the first certain instance occurred in 1204. It is difficult to determine why the performances were moved. Some scholars have suggested that church officials were opposed to the drama because of its interference with services and because of the growing buffoonery of the Feast of Fools. Others have argued that the plays had developed as far as they could indoors, and that they were moved so as to allow them more scope. Regardless of the reasons, the years between 1200 and 1350 saw the transition from liturgical drama to elaborate outdoor plays divorced from church services.

There is little evidence upon which to base an account of the transitional period, for few plays or records have survived, perhaps because the plays were no longer an integral part of church services and had not yet been taken over by other groups. Nevertheless, between 1200 and 1350 a number of important changes occurred. First, plays came to be staged primarily during the spring and summer months because of the weather. From the 14th century the favorite time was Corpus Christi, a festival first conceived by Pope Urban IV in 1264 and celebrated almost everywhere by 1350. The festival, observed on the Thursday following Trinity Sunday, may vary from May 23 to June 24. Since the redemptive power of the consecrated bread and wine, which this festival celebrates, symbolizes the whole scheme of salvation, Biblical events from any part of the church calendar could be attached to it without anachronism. Furthermore, Corpus Christi was one of many attempts to make the church more meaningful to the ordinary man; therefore, civic dignitaries, representatives of the trade guilds, and other persons were included in the procession which escorted the Host through the town. Many scholars see in this the beginning of the layman's involvement in church celebrations, which would end in his taking over the staging of religious plays.

Other favorite times for the presentation of plays were Easter and Whitsuntide (seven weeks after Easter). Most cities had a patron saint, whose holy day might also be chosen as the occasion for dramatic performances. In addition, elaborate productions were sometimes given in gratitude for deliverance from a plague, drought, or other disaster.

Second, the performance on a single occasion of a number of plays which had formerly been spread throughout the church year led gradually to the formation of cycles of plays, or "cosmic" dramas, treating events from the Creation to the Last Judgment. These, in turn, made new demands on staging at a time when removal from the church had eliminated the restrictions imposed by church architecture. Consequently, many diverse staging arrangements evolved.

Another important change came in the substitution of the vernacular tongues for Latin. A few of the liturgical dramas had contained some vernacular passages, but these were not extensive until the plays moved outside the church. Even then many of the plays were at first written in a mixture of Latin and everyday speech. One of the most interesting of transitional dramas, the 12th or 13th century *Play of Adam* (with episodes treating the Fall, Cain and Abel, and the Prophets) uses French in the dialogue of the first two parts, while stage directions are given in Latin. In the *Prophets Play*, however, the individual prophecies are spoken in Latin and then repeated in a French paraphrase. The mixture of Latin and the vernacular gradually gave way by 1350 to plays entirely in everyday language. This change is important for several reasons: it introduced spoken rather than chanted dialogue; it marked a turning away from an international to national drama; and it facilitated the use of nonclerical actors.

By the last half of the 14th century, lengthy cycles of plays produced by laymen had replaced the liturgical drama as the focus of theatrical interest. Between 1350 and 1550, the Medieval theatre reached the peak of its development. Most of the surviving information dates from the 15th and, especially, the 16th centuries.

The Vernacular Religious Drama

Although about 125 different towns in the British Isles produced plays at some time during the Middle Ages, only a few texts survive. Most of the extant works are parts of the cycles staged in four towns: York (48 plays),

Chester (24), Wakefield (sometimes called the Towneley Plays, 32) and Lincoln (usually called the *Ludus Coventriae* or N——town Plays and only recently assigned to Lincoln, 42). It is often assumed that these four cycles typify English practice, but such cosmic dramas can be clearly established in only twelve towns. It is certain that many cities never developed cycles, remaining content with less ambitious plays.

The existing cycles, all dating from about 1375, were performed until the mid-16th century. During these 175 years, individual plays were rewritten, new ones added, and others dropped. Consequently, the parts of a single cycle vary widely in date of composition, as well as in quality. The surviving texts record the cycles as they existed near the end of their history. In addition to the cycles, ten other plays in English and three in Cornish have survived.

A much larger number of plays from France are extant. They range from short works to those requiring 25 or more days to perform. Rather than covering material from the Creation to the Last Judgment, as did most of the English cycles, the French plays are usually more restricted in time. The favorite subject is the death and resurrection of Christ. Numerous religious plays were also staged in Germany and Spain. In Italy no long cycle of plays developed, and few of any kind have survived. Elsewhere in Europe, religious drama was less extensively performed, although there is scarcely any country in which it remained unknown.

While the length and scope of the dramas varied widely, all dealt with the same basic subject matter: God's ordering of existence as revealed in the Bible, the Apocrypha, legends about Biblical figures and saints, writings of the Church fathers, and collections of sermons. Consequently, regardless of where they were written, the Medieval plays have many common characteristics.

They seldom observe a clear-cut, cause-to-effect relationship among incidents. The plays are episodic, and there is no attempt to connect the parts of a cycle. This loose structure probably did not offend the Medieval audience, who believed that events occur because God wills them. The dramas display no sense of history, and Biblical characters often refer to things which happened long after their own times. Again, however, time and place were of little consequence to Medieval audiences, for temporal existence was seen as a short preface to eternity, and the telescoping of past events only served to make the dramatic characters contemporaries of the audience and to reenforce the message of the plays.

The dramas combine stylization with realism. They are written in verse, action is schematized, characterization is minimal, and the settings only sufficient to establish the place of action. On the other hand, some incidents, especially those dealing with miraculous occurrences, are presented in almost naturalistic detail. These serve two purposes: they establish the relevance to Medieval times, and they seek to reenforce faith through a convincing realism.

SCENES from the Valenciennes Passion Play, 1547. [From the manuscript drawings made by Hubert Cailleau. Courtesy Bibliothèque Nationale, Paris]

In spite of their essentially religious purpose, many plays contain extended comic scenes, usually involving devils, villains, or buffoons. Most of the comic episodes depend upon the juxtaposition of reality with the ideal, of human failings with Divine commandments, of the fashionable with the eternal, and thus remain relevant to the plays' didactic purposes.

Production Arrangements

Before the end of the 14th century, the production of plays had in most places passed out of the immediate control of the church, although the scripts were still approved by church officials and were performed at religious festivals. Thus, though the church gave up its direct participation, it kept a watchful eye on the contents of the plays and their presentation.

Producing organizations in the late Middle Ages were of many kinds. On the continent, religious guilds, or confraternities, were the usual producers. The members of these groups, which began to appear about 1300, were mostly laymen, although many also were clergymen. Dedicated to the worship of a particular saint, the guilds undertook charitable deeds and presented plays as acts of devotion.

Although in England confraternities also frequently produced plays, the trade guilds assumed much of this responsibility in the towns of northern England. While the trade guilds were primarily designed to protect the interests of craftsmen, they retained many religious connections; each helped to support a chapel, each had a chaplain and a patron saint. Like the confraternities, the guilds also undertook charitable deeds and presented plays as their contribution to religious festivals.

In other producing arrangements, responsibility might be assumed by the town, the clergy, an individual, jointly by town and clergy, or by a temporary society formed for the express purpose of presenting a play. Thus, arrangements differed widely, but usually involved many persons working together. For the most part, the church was content with a passive role. In every case, however, its right to approve the scripts was probably understood.

The complex motives and production arrangements are best summed up at Lucerne, where a passion play was presented at regular intervals for more than a century. Here the play was said to serve the purposes of honoring God, edifying man, and glorifying the city. The division of authority is revealed in the procedures: the proposal that the play be given came from the Brotherhood of the Crown of Thorns; after ratification by the city council, a public proclamation was made from the pulpit; the production was then placed under the supervision of a committee appointed jointly by the Brotherhood and the city council, while the church reserved the right to approve the script.

The delegation of responsibilities and the methods of financing productions depended upon the type of organization. In northern England, the town council and trade guilds shared the responsibilities. The council decided whether performances would be given in a particular year; it assigned the plays to individual guilds, held the approved copy of the script and demanded faithful adherence to it; it specified fines for those guilds that did not produce their plays or performed them badly; and it chose the playing places.

The majority of the work and expense fell to the guilds. The plays were supposedly assigned on the basis of appropriateness: dramas about Noah were given variously to the shipwrights, watermen, and fishers, while the plays about the Three Kings were assigned to the goldsmiths, those showing the Last Supper to the bakers, and so on. Each guild was then responsible for providing a pageant wagon, scenery, costumes, properties, special effects, actors, and supervisors. Two small or poor guilds might be given a joint assignment. Since the plays were performed in sequence, and each was a self-contained unit, little effort at coordinating the entire cycle was required.

On the fixed stages of the continent, all episodes were performed on the same platform, and the entire cycle came under the direction of one man or a small committee. Double casting could be used efficiently, crowd scenes were possible, and the fixed stage encouraged the development of elaborate scenery and special effects. This unification of effort, however, often led to complex financial arrangements. Sometimes a city corporation might make a grant; often those cast in the play were required to pay a fee and to furnish their own costumes and properties; sometimes the local chapter of clergy might provide part of the money. In many instances, admission was charged and salvaged materials were sold after the performances as a means of recovering expenses. At Valenciennes in 1547, where a cooperative society was formed to produce a play, the members raised the money and shared the considerable profits.

The Director

Such complex productions required careful organization, for the handling of casts that sometimes included as many as 300 actors, of complex special effects, and of large sums of money could not be left to chance. Consequently, the director (or stage manager, or pageant master) was of considerable importance.

The staging of plays was handled differently in various locales. In the guilds of northern England, the wardens of the companies were responsible to the town council for the proper staging of the plays; they controlled finances and paid all bills. The wardens seldom did the actual work of play production, however, and normally hired or appointed someone else to this post. Often this position was given to a member of the guild, but in some instances a "pageant master" was put under contract for a number of years at an annual salary. For example, at Coventry in 1454 the Smiths contracted for a period of twelve years with Thomas Colclow, who was to supply everything needed except the wagon and costumes. The pageant master secured actors, arranged rehearsals, and took charge of every phase of production. In addition, he supplied men to drive the wagon from one location to another and to control the crowds during performances.

The directors of the continental plays needed even more skills, since an entire cycle was often under the direction of one man. As a rule, a committee of supervisors was appointed, often with as many as twelve members, but they usually delegated their authority to one person or to a very few. At Lucerne in 1583 the committee turned over all details to the city clerk, Renward Cysat. At Mons in 1501, four actor-managers, each with one assistant, were employed to stage the play. Some directors became sufficiently famous to be sought by many towns. Jean Bouchet, after staging a cycle at Poitiers in 1508, was still in demand as late as 1532. In Spain, Lope de Rueda, a professional actor-manager, was put under contract by the city of Vallodolid in 1552 to serve as pageant master for the Corpus Christi festivities.

The Medieval director's duties were outlined by Jean Bouchet: he must oversee the erection of a stage and the placement of scenery and machines; he must find persons to build and paint scenery and to construct seating for the audience; he must insure that goods delivered are of the proper amount and quality; he must cast and rehearse the actors; he must discipline the actors and set a system of fines for infringement of rules; he may act some roles himself; he must assign persons to take money at the entrances; he must address the audience at the beginning of the play and after each intermission, give a resumé of the previous happenings, and promise greater marvels in the portions yet to come. Although not all directors had to cope with so many problems, many did. Consequently, the men given such positions had to be versed in every aspect of theatrical production.

Some historians have argued that the director was always on stage during performances, following the actors about whispering their lines and giving directions. This theory, which seems most unlikely, is based almost entirely upon one anecdote of doubtful authenticity and a painting showing a scene from a play about St. Apollonia in which a figure with a book and staff stands in the middle of the stage. Some scholars identify this figure as the stage manager, although there seems no good reason to assume that he is not a character in the play. Considering the emphasis in the period on the learning of lines and the fines levied on negligent actors, it seems improbable that actors depended upon the stage manager for their lines. On the other hand, the director or an assistant was probably in a position to give cues to actors and machinists, and to prompt in an emergency.

A few detailed promptbooks from this period still survive. The two most readily available are from Mons in 1501 and Lucerne in 1583. In them, nothing is left to chance; every detail has been prepared and recorded. They are the work of men who were stage directors in the modern sense.

Actors and Acting

The number of actors varied considerably. In the guild cycles of northern England, many of the individual plays include no more than five to ten characters. Thus the needs of each guild would not have been great, although the total number of actors in the entire cycle was considerable. On the continent, casting was more complicated. *The Acts of the Apostles*, staged at Bourges in 1536, included 494 roles distributed among 300 actors. Plays of so large a scope date from the 16th century and seem to mark a considerable increase in number of roles over earlier works.

The majority, perhaps all, of the actors were amateurs drawn from the local population. Only in a few cases can we tell how they were selected. At York in 1476, the city council decreed that four of "the most cunning, discreet, and able players within this city" were to audition all persons who wished to act. No one was to appear in more than two plays. These provisions seem to indicate that guilds did not confine casting to their own

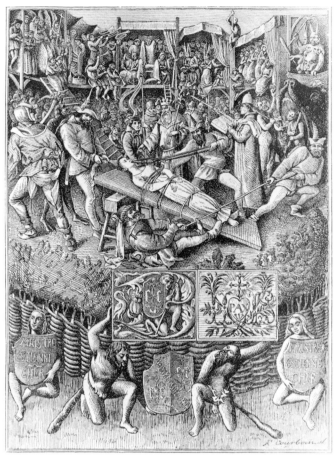

SCENE FROM A MEDIEVAL PLAY showing the martyrdom of St. Apollonia (c. 1460). The figure with the book is thought by some to be the stage manager. Engraving after the original miniature by Fouquet. [From Bapst, *Essai sur l'Histoire du Théâtre* (1893)]

members, and that actors might perform for two different guilds. At Seurre in 1496, the Mayor, assisted by three other persons, cast the play. In 1540, heralds rode through the streets of Paris appealing for volunteers. At Lucerne in 1583, requests were made from the pulpit that all those interested in acting register with the City Clerk, who then chose the cast with the aid of a committee. In those instances in which plays were repeated, a person might play the same role for many years.

The majority of actors were chosen from the merchant or working classes, although members of the clergy and nobility appeared at times. Most were men or boys, but in France women and girls appeared occasionally. Doubling was a common practice. At Valenciennes in 1547 the more than 100 roles were assigned to 72 actors, and at Mons in 1501 about 350 roles were cast with approximately 150 players. On the other hand, sometimes a single role required more than one actor, as when a character grew from childhood to adulthood. For scenes of violence, such as beheadings and burnings at the stake, realistic effigies were substituted.

The good faith and discipline of the actors were insured by a number of devices. At Lucerne in 1583, each person was allowed 14 days in which to decide if he wished to accept a role; once committed, he was bound by oath to continue. At Valenciennes in 1547, each actor was required to take an oath before a notary, in which he agreed to appear on the days of performance. Other provisions of the Valenciennes agreement are also revealing: each actor was required to accept the roles assigned to him and to attend rehearsals at the specified times; each agreed not to meddle in affairs of the supervisory committee or to grumble against their decisions. There was also a schedule of fines for missing rehearsals or for other infringements of rules. Agreements from other towns indicate that jealousies, bickerings, and resignations were common, and that producers had learned by the 16th century to guard against them.

The time devoted to rehearsals was not great by modern standards. Although the play given at Mons in 1501 required four full days to perform, there were only about 48 rehearsals. For the individual cycle plays of England, two to five rehearsals were considered sufficient.

Something of the overall process can be inferred from the detailed records preserved from Lucerne in 1583, when the play required 24 hours of performance time. Before the first rehearsals, a general meeting of the entire cast was held; the script was divided into 12 units for rehearsal; in addition to the regularly scheduled meetings, actors were urged to arrange other opportunities for working together privately; when the action presented unusual problems, extra rehearsals were called; changes in dialogue, action, and properties were frequently made during the preparatory period. Although the performances were given out-of-doors, rehearsals were held in a large hall. About 80 days elapsed from the first rehearsal to performance, but the total number of rehearsals is unclear.

The sponsoring organization usually supplied the actors with food and drink at rehearsals. If participants had to miss work, someone was paid to replace them. This expense usually fell to the actor, but if he was too poor, the producing group paid the necessary amount.

It is uncertain whether dress rehearsals were usual. Each episode was probably prepared separately; but some plays were so long, such as the one at Bourges in 1536 which required 40 days to perform, that a dress rehearsal in the modern sense would have been impossible. On the other hand, at Romans in 1509, the dress rehearsal revealed that the playing time was much too long and extensive cutting was done. At Valenciennes in 1547, in a production taking up the afternoons of 25 days, the actors were required to appear at 7 A.M. each morning for what was obviously a rehearsal of that day's episodes.

For the long plays given on the continent, actors assembled as a group on performance days and then went in procession to the theatre. Upon arrival, they marched around the playing area before taking their places inside or near the appropriate mansions. In many instances, the actors remained visible throughout the performances, coming forward when needed and retiring to their places when a scene was completed. At Lucerne, elaborate plans were made so that the actors might slip away to change costumes and to eat during the twelve-hour performances. At Valenciennes, the players agreed not to leave the stage during the performances without permission and to accept whatever food and drink might be passed to them there. At the end of the day's performance, the actors returned in procession to the place of assembly, where they were often served a banquet.

In the cycle plays of England, each episode was mounted on its own wagon and was repeated at designated places in the town. Thus, procession and performance were alternated.

Undoubtedly the quality of the acting varied considerably. Many contemporary references are lavish in praise of certain actors, but there are as many condemnations of other performers. Voice seems to have been valued above all else. When the plays left the church, chanting was abandoned and delivery began to resemble everyday speech. Since characters in the extant plays are developed with little subtlety, they would not have required great versatility of the actors. Most characters are types and are given a few clear-cut actions and emotions, such as adoration, joy, anger, or grief. Serious characters are usually restrained, but the comic roles allow much scope for improvisation and pantomime.

The attempts to achieve realism in certain scenes exposed actors to many dangers. At Metz in 1437, the actor playing Judas almost died while being hanged; at Seurre in 1496, Satan's costume caught on fire, and actors elsewhere in Hell scenes were often injured by the cannons and other devices used to create noise, fire, and smoke.

By the 16th century, there were a number of actors sufficiently skilled to be employed as coaches as well as to play roles themselves. The extent to which professionalism had arrived is a matter of controversy. Although the majority of players were clearly amateurs, a few were paid well for performing, although even they had other regular trades. Considering the attitude of the church toward professional performers, it is probable that the producers of plays did not consider any of their actors to be professionals.

Costumes

Most characters were dressed in garments such as their counterparts in Medieval life would have worn. Roman soldiers were given Medieval armor, and Jewish high priests wore the robes of Catholic prelates. Many of the Biblical characters closely associated with orthodox Christianity, though historically Jews, were dressed in clerical garb, while other Jews normally wore clothing associated with the Medieval Jew. God was costumed as an Emperor or Pope, and angels wore church robes to which wings were attached. Any important character, human or divine, might carry an identifying emblem; the Archangel Michael, for instance, always wielded a flaming sword. The costumes for the devils were the most imaginative, resembling great birds of prey, monsters with animal heads, or creatures with scales, tails, horns, or claws.

In most instances, actors had to supply their own costumes, unless these differed markedly from those available in daily life. Consequently, the records of producing organizations show payments only for such exceptional garments as those for devils or effigies. Actors often incurred heavy expenses, especially when playing wealthy personages. Double casting increased the outlay, particularly in the 16th century, when costumes, even for lower-class characters, came to be made of rich fabrics. Occasionally, as at Chalons-sur-Marne in 1507, nonparticipating wealthy citizens were required to buy costumes for actors unable to furnish their own. Other sources of supply include the clergy, who loaned or rented garments; producing organizations, which sometimes rented their costumes to other groups; and, rarely, an individual who contracted to outfit an entire production.

Because each actor usually supplied his own costume, supervision was needed. At Lucerne, the director gave each performer a detailed description of the appropriate dress for his character, and it is likely that similar procedures were followed elsewhere. Many of these practices extended to hand properties as well. Unless an item was not readily available, it was supplied by the actor who used it. Unusual articles were made at the expense of the producers.

The Stages

The stages upon which the plays were performed after the drama left the church might be either movable or fixed. The movable stage was most fully developed in England and Spain, while the fixed platform was more characteristic elsewhere. Both types, however, were in use throughout Europe.

Because most of the cycles of England were mounted on pageant wagons, the movable stage is usually treated as typical of English practices. Each play in a cycle was mounted on a wagon, and on the days of performance all were presented in succession at a number of different places in the town. No clear description of an English pageant wagon has survived.

RECONSTRUCTION of a Medieval English pageant wagon. [From Sharp, *A Dissertation on the Pageants or Dramatic Mysteries . . .* (1825)]

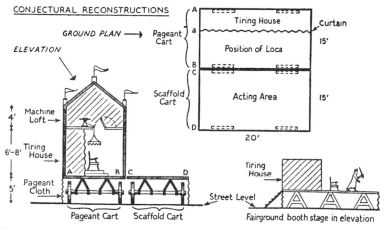

A RECONSTRUCTION of the English pageant wagon and playing arrangement. [From Wickham, *Early English Stages,* Courtesy Columbia University Press]

Most modern discussions are based upon the account given by David Rogers in *A Breviarye, or Some Few Recollections of the City of Chester* (a manuscript of the late 16th or early 17th century). Rogers states that the pageant wagons "were a big scaffold with two rooms, a higher and a lower, upon four wheels. In the lower they appareled themselves, and in the higher room they played." (Another surviving version of this account states that the wagons had six wheels.) This description would seem to indicate a two-storied structure, the lower part serving as a dressing room and the upper as the stage.

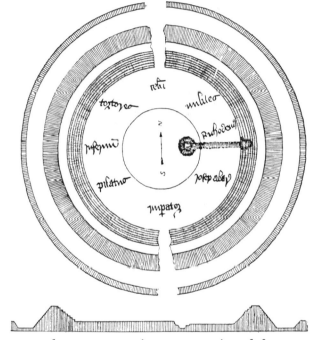

PLAN and section of the Cornish round at Perranzabulo. [From Albright, *The Shakespearian Stage* (1909)]

Roger's account, long accepted as accurate, is now questioned for two principal reasons. First, it is not certain that Rogers ever saw the plays performed. Second, the wagons as he described them would be extremely cumbersome. They would have been at least 15 feet tall (allowing for the wagon wheels, the dressing room space, and the scenery on the top level), but relatively narrow, since they had to be moved through alley-like streets. With the top level divided between the mansions and the playing space, the actors would have had to perform on a narrow ledge about nine feet above the street. Considering that a play such as the Chester cycle's "Last Judgment" depicts Heaven, Earth, and Hell, and includes more than 20 characters, this arrangement seems impractical. For these and other reasons, Glynne Wickham in his *Early English Stages* has argued that the pageant wagon was a one-leveled structure taken up entirely by the mansions and "off-stage" space. The wagon served, he suggests, merely to provide a scenic background and dressing rooms, while the acting took place on a platform alongside which the wagon was drawn up. From stage directions, we also

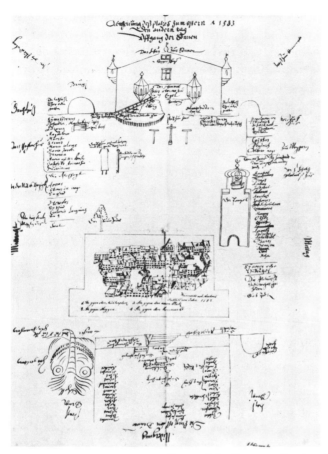

PLAN of the Lucerne Passion Play, second day. At the top is shown the Heaven mansion and at bottom left Hell. A sketch of the square in which the play was performed has been superimposed on the center of the plan. [From Leibing, *Die Inscenirung des zweitatigen Luzernes Osterspiels* (1869)]

know that characters sometimes played on the street level. While Wickham's theory cannot be proven, it is a more persuasive solution to problems of staging than those offered in earlier accounts.

The pageant wagons were not necessarily uniform in size or design. Since a guild always performed the same play, its wagon could be built to meet its special requirements. In those rare instances when the same wagon was used by more than one guild, the scenic needs of the plays mounted on that wagon are very similar.

"Processional" staging was not confined to England, but extended to Belgium, the Netherlands, and France, and was especially popular in Spain. It is not clear when wagons were first used in Spain, but they were clearly present by 1555, were typical by the 17th century, and continued in use until religious plays were finally abandoned in 1765. Here usage conforms rather closely to the pattern suggested by Wickham. At each playing place in the town, a platform was available. The wagons, or *carros,* on which the scenery was mounted, were pulled up alongside these platforms, which served as the acting area. Two to four wagons were required to mount one play.

Fixed stages, however, were in wider use than wagons. At Bourges and Rome, the ancient amphitheatres were used. In Cornwall, circular earthen embankments enclosing areas up to 120 feet in diameter provided similar playing arrangements. Sometimes stages were set up in cemeteries adjoining churches. Courtyards of private residences (as at Valenciennes in 1547) or of monasteries (as at Romans in 1509) were used. Most typical were the stages set up in large public squares, as at Mons in 1501 and Lucerne in 1583.

The actor-audience relationship varied considerably. In the amphitheatres, the audience may have viewed the plays from all four sides. At Lucerne, it occupied three sides, while at Mons it viewed the stage from the front only.

Most typically the stage was a long rectangular platform set against a building or row of houses, but sometimes it extended down the middle of a square. Occasionally there was no platform as such, the mansions being placed directly on the ground. The size of the stages varied. At Autun in 1516 the platform was about 200 feet long, while at Romans in 1509 it was 120 feet long and 60 feet wide. At Lucerne, the playing space was irregular in shape, being about 125 feet long, and varying in width from 80 to 60 feet.

Not all stages were out-of-doors. The Confrérie de la Passion in Paris played for more than 100 years at the Hôpital de la Trinité, where the stage was about 40 feet wide. Other indoor theatres were used elsewhere.

Scenery

As in the church, the playing space had two basic parts, the mansions and the *platea.* As before, the place of a scene was established by relating it to a mansion, and this locale was then extended to include as much of the adjoining stage space as was required for performing the action. This convention was observed regardless of the type of stage.

As many as three different mansions might be mounted on a single pageant wagon. While the scenic investiture of an individual wagon was limited, that for an entire cycle was considerable, often amounting to more than 100 mansions.

The fixed stages probably appeared more impressive than the movable, because on the former all of the scenery was visible simultaneously. This convention was somewhat modified, however, by other practices. Because of their scope, many of the plays were divided into parts (or *journées*), separated by intermissions varying in length from 1 to 24 hours. During these intervals, mansions were changed as needed; furthermore, the same mansion might represent more than one location. Consequently, it is difficult to know how many mansions were actually used to depict the places named in a script. In the play presented at Lucerne in 1583, about 70 different locales are indicated, but the number of mansions seems to have been only 32.

The scenic complexity of a production might vary daily. For a passion play at Arras in the early 15th century, the number of mansions required by each of the four *journées* ranged from 8 to 15. Other plays might require 20 or more mansions for a single *journée*. The identity of the mansions was not assumed to be self-evident. Typically, the director appeared before each *journée* and indicated, along with other information, what each mansion represented. At times, labels were placed above mansions as well.

The two mansions most often present were Heaven and Hell. Characteristically, Heaven was placed at one end of the platform and Hell at the other. Between these poles, which symbolized man's dual nature and the choices which faced him, the earthly scenes were set. Since these were both the most important and permanent structures, not being replaced each day, they were also the most complex.

Of all the mansions, Heaven is the most difficult to reconstruct from the available evidence, for it seems to have impressed audiences with its splendor and magnificence, qualities not always evident in the surviving pictures. In the 15th and 16th centuries, it was usually raised above the level of the other mansions. As a rule, it was supported structurally by an "earthly paradise" (the Garden of Eden), or a room placed below it at stage level. The size of Heaven was probably large, for it often accommodated many persons. At Rouen in 1474, God was accompanied by Peace, Mercy, Justice, Truth, and nine orders of angels. Sometimes Heaven included a series of intricately contrived turning spheres, and the whole was often gilded and brightly lighted with concealed torches to give the effect that golden light was emanating from it. In some instances, Heaven could open and close, and often machinery permitted angels to "fly" between Heaven and Earth, although stairs, either visible or concealed, were used in less elaborate productions. Above all, Heaven was made as inviting and awe-inspiring as possible.

Conversely, Hell was made as terrifying as possible. Just as Heaven was raised above the level of the stage, some portions of Hell were lower. Sometimes Hell was treated as a fortified town, an especially effective device in

THE STAGE of the Valenciennes Passion Play, 1547. This arrangement served for only one day, but Heaven and Hell remained throughout. [Courtesy Bibliothèque Nationale, Paris]

those productions in which Christ forces open the gates to Hell to free the captive souls within. Hell was frequently divided into four parts: the Limbo of Biblical prophets and others who, according to Medieval doctrine, were forced to languish there until Christ's redemptive power freed them; the Limbo of infants; Purgatory; and the pit of Hell, usually placed below stage level. The entrance to Hell was at other times represented by the head of a monster (the "Hell mouth") that seemed to swallow those who entered there. Fire, smoke, noise, and the cries of the damned issued from Hell, and from it devils sallied forth to seize sinners and thrust them into eternal damnation.

The mansions representing earthly places were less elaborately depicted, although the complexity varied with dramatic need. Many were equipped with curtains which could be drawn to conceal or reveal interior scenes. The structures were of many sizes and shapes. Some were hexagonal, others were square or rectangular. Some were elevated a few steps above the stage floor. Often they were furnished with beds, tables, benches, altars, or thrones. Sometimes, as at Mons in 1501, they were lavishly outfitted with tapestries borrowed from wealthy families and churches.

At the rear of the stage, a curtain representing the sky, and sometimes showing the sun, moon, and stars, was often hung. Clouds were frequently used to conceal the overhead flying equipment and other devices for special effects. The stage was unframed, and one place flowed into another. Encompassing Heaven, Earth, and Hell, the Medieval stage symbolized the entire universe.

Although a number of persons were required to build and paint the settings, few records of them have survived. Sometimes master artists were imported for the occasion, as at Mons in 1501. At Romans in 1509, the carpenters began work about four and one-half months prior to the performance. At Lucerne, the director of the play supervised the labor of city-employed workmen, who built the mansions, and of skilled artists, who painted the mansions, curtains, and effigies. Many other persons were required to operate the scenic effects during performances.

Special Effects

Most of the naturalistic touches in Medieval productions stemmed from special effects. These grew in number and complexity during the 15th and 16th centuries, when many scenes were added to take advantage of the machinists' abilities to contrive seemingly miraculous events.

Many special effects involved "flying." The fixed stages often were set against buildings, on the top of which pulleys and windlasses could be installed and concealed with painted clouds or sky cloths. Additional flying machinery was concealed within the Heaven mansion. Using such devices, Angels passed between Heaven and Earth; Lucifer lifted Christ to the top of the temple (sometimes a distance of 40 feet) ; the souls released from Limbo rose up to Heaven; and devils and fire-spitting monsters flew about the stage. In some instances, platforms were disguised as clouds, which could be raised and lowered to transport characters.

Other effects depended upon devices operated from beneath the stage. Trap doors permitted sudden appearances, disappearances, and the skillful substitution of effigies for live actors in scenes of violence. In such episodes as the feeding of the multitudes through the miracle of the loaves and fishes, the baskets could be replenished from underneath the stage. Concealed mechanisms allowed the fig tree cursed by Christ to wither, and fountains to spring up at magical touch.

Water was important in many plays. One of the most notable examples is the flood, for which at Mons in 1501 sufficient water was stored in wine-barrels on the roofs of adjoining houses to produce a continuous rain of five minutes. Other scenes involving water included Christ walking on the sea and the apostles pulling in their nets.

In the frequent executions and scenes of torture, effigies were usually substituted for live actors. In a production showing Barnabas burned at the stake, an effigy was filled with bones and animal entrails to give a properly realistic smell. In another, showing the decapitation of St. Paul, the head bounced three times, and at each spot a well flowed; one with milk, one with blood, and the third with water.

Many animals were required. While some could be live, others had to be impersonated by actors or by effigies. Lions kneeled to St. Denis and tigers to St. Andrew; dragons, wolves, and other wild or fanciful creatures appeared. In one play, tigers sprang up out of the earth and pursued the apostles until turned into sheep. The Serpent appeared in the Garden of Eden to tempt Eve.

Transformation scenes were popular. Moses' staff changed into a snake, Lot's wife into a pillar of salt, water into wine. Light also was a special effect. It sometimes surrounded God, Christ, and the saints. Normally, this was achieved by reflecting the rays of concealed torches off gilded or highly polished surfaces. Sometimes a change from light to darkness was indicated by substituting a painted cloth depicting the sun for another showing the moon and stars. In a few plays, buildings were burned. For these, wicker structures covered with cloth were actually set on fire.

Some special effects required by Medieval plays would baffle modern technicians. It is clear that considerable skill and ingenuity were needed. Thus, it is not surprising that by the 16th century accomplished machinists were in great demand. At Mons in 1501, two directors of "secrets" (as special effects were called) were imported from Chauny; for a Passion play at Vienna in the 16th century, eight master machinists were employed. These men were aided by numerous assistants who operated the effects during performance. At Mons, 17 were required for the Hell scenes alone.

During the 16th century, the machinist was second only to the director in importance. He made detailed cue sheets and planned the operation of the effects as carefully as the director planned other parts of the production. The ultimate success of the plays depended much upon his skills.

Music

Music was prominent in most Medieval productions. Frequently it was played until the actors were ready to begin. During the plays, a chorus of angels (composed of choir boys), usually visible in the Heaven mansion, sang hymns. Angels played fanfares on trumpets to introduce God's proclamations, and the transitions between scenes might be bridged with instrumental or vocal music. Most plays included a number of songs, ranging from popular secular tunes sung by individual actors to religious hymns sung by groups. The names and contents of songs, however, are seldom indicated in the scripts. While singing was usually by choir boys or actors, instrumental music was played by professionals. At least 40 minstrels were hired at Chelmsford in 1562, and 156 musicians were employed at Lucerne in 1571. The musicians also kept the populace amused during the intermissions and in the evenings.

Audiences and Auditoriums

In most places, plays were not given every year. Even where the cycles were established, the interval between productions ranged from two to ten years. Some of the most elaborate performances were never repeated. In those years when plays were to be given, preparations extended over a period of months, while the days of playing were declared holidays.

Prior to performances, various devices acquainted the public with forthcoming events. Invitations were usually sent to all the surrounding towns, posters were set up at the city gates, and a few days before the performance a procession, often with actors in costume, went about the town. On the days of performance, a herald rode through the city sounding a trumpet and summoning people to the play. The audiences were drawn from all classes and from both local and neighboring areas. In some places work was forbidden during the hours of performance, and special guards were set to protect homes and businesses against robbery.

The provisions made for spectators varied widely. In those parts of England where pageant wagons were used, a number of different playing places were established. At York there were 12 to 15, at Beverley 6. In most towns, performances lasted for several days. At Chester three days were required, and while York allotted only one, performances there began at 4:30 A.M.

Spectators were probably admitted free to the English plays, for the only certain instance of fees being collected is found at Leicester in 1477. It has been suggested, however, that at York charges may have been made by the persons who controlled the playing places. The first two performances were given at the church and town hall and were probably free, but the other playing places were assigned according to bids received. It is possible, therefore, that successful bidders erected some kind of barrier and charged admission. Distinguished citizens probably watched from the windows of surrounding houses; scaffold seating may have been erected for lesser personages, and the lower orders stood. These details are entirely conjectural, however, for there is no concrete evidence about how audiences were handled.

When a fixed stage was used, all spectators had to be accommodated in one place. Structures such as Roman amphitheatres or the Cornish "rounds" provided ready-made seating; but in courtyards or city squares, temporary auditoriums had to be improvised. In some instances, arrangements not unlike those that became typical of later professional theatres were used. At Romans in 1509, standing room was available near the stage; back of this was scaffold seating surmounted by a series of 84 boxes. At Vienna in 1560, private boxes could be rented for the entire performance. At Lucerne, scaffold seating surrounded three sides of the playing area, and the owners of adjacent houses probably rented space in their rooms and on the rooftops.

For many of the municipally-sponsored productions, entrance fees were not charged. On the other hand, some productions were intended to make money. At Valenciennes in 1547, the members of the producing organization divided the profits. Muncipalities also sometimes charged fees in order to recover their investment. Except when fees were charged, it is difficult to estimate attendance. If the available figures are typical, attendance was large. At Reims in 1490, 5616 persons paid admissions; at Romans in 1509, 4780 attended the first day, 4420 the second, and 4947 the third.

The hours of performance varied. In some cases, plays began about 7 A.M., ran until 11, allowed an hour's intermission, and then continued until about 6 P.M. In others, plays were presented in a series of afternoon performances; in still others, a production might proceed uninterrupted for as long as 12 hours. Often spectators began to take their places as early as 4 A.M., for usually seats were not reserved, except for officials, clergy, and important visitors. Sometimes children, elderly persons, and pregnant women were forbidden entry. A barrier of some kind (a ditch, a fence, or water) was used to prevent the audience from getting too near the stage. Guards were posted at night to protect the stage and its furnishings.

It is clear that by the 16th century the producers of plays had learned to cope with many problems. Although most were amateurs, they had achieved a high level of technical excellence as well as considerable sophistication in organizing and producing plays of great scope.

Secular Dramatic Forms

Alongside the religious stage, a less elaborate secular theatre slowly arose. With roots in such antecedents as pagan rituals, mimes, the stories and songs of *jongleurs,* and the activities of professional entertainers of all sorts, the secular theatre may be part of a tradition reaching back to Rome. Nevertheless, no records of secular drama can be found prior to the 13th century, about the time that the religious plays were being moved out-of-doors.

The oldest extant secular drama, *The Play of Adam, or the Bower,* was written by Adam de la Halle of Arras in 1262. It mingles satirical scenes about the residents of Arras with such folk elements as fairies and supernatural occurrences. Folk materials are even more evident in Adam's other work, *The Play of Robin and Marion* (c. 1283), a pastoral tale of the wooing of a shepherdess by a knight, the objections of her shepherd lover, and the eventual resolution of the conflict, followed by dances and games.

Farce also began to appear during the 13th century. The oldest, *The Boy and the Blind Man,* written in a Flemish dialect, shows how a masterless rogue deceives a blind man through ventriloquism, then robs and beats him. The cynical tone which is typical of Medieval farce is already fully developed in this work.

Examples of secular drama become more frequent after 1300. A number of short plays and farces of the 14th century from the Netherlands, Germany, and France have survived. But as with the religious drama, the majority of extant works were written after 1400. The secular entertainments of the 15th and 16th centuries were of many types: farces, moralities, plays of the Chambers of Rhetoric, interludes, mummings and disguisings, tournaments, and royal entries.

Farce

If the religious plays treat the triumph of virtue within an eternal order, the farces show imperfect man within the social order. Marital infidelity, quarreling, cheating, hypocrisy, and other failings of mankind are depicted. The clever man, even if a sinner, is usually the hero; the persons he dupes deserve their fates because they are stupid or gullible. Sentiment is almost totally absent.

There are no extant English farces before the 16th century, but numerous earlier French and German works have survived. Although the plays from these two countries vary considerably in subject matter, they are similar in tone and form. Most of the farces are short (no longer than a few hundred lines), are written in verse, and place considerable emphasis on sex and bodily excretions. The characters are few in number; no complicated exposition is required, and the action develops rapidly and simply.

The best of the French farces is *Pierre Patelin* (c. 1470), which tells how a lawyer tricks a merchant out of a piece of cloth and is in turn cheated out of his fee by a supposedly stupid peasant, whom he has defended on a charge of stealing sheep. The play was so popular in France that it had gone through 30 editions by 1600. Most of the other French farces are merely dramatized anecdotes.

In Germany, farces were usually called "shrovetide plays." Most of those which have survived come from Nuremberg, one of the principal intellectual and commercial centers of Germany. Here the plays seem to

CARNIVAL CELEBRATION in Germany in 1617 [From *Stuttgart Festival Book* (1617)]

have grown out of the apprentices' revelries (or *Schembartlaufen*) during the carnival preceding Lent. Most of the shrovetide plays are crude, but those by Hans Sachs (1494–1576) are of a higher quality.

Sachs was a shoemaker and a mastersinger, an art cultivated by the German trade guilds. As a singer he traveled widely and learned much about the poetry and drama of other areas. He was the author of 198 dramatic works, of which he classified only 64 as "shrovetide" plays. Nevertheless, his other dramas are of slight value and his reputation rests almost entirely upon the farces. One of his best works is *The Wandering Scholar and Exorcist,* in which a student convinces a man that he can call up the Devil, whom he forces a priest to impersonate as a price for concealing an illicit relationship with the man's wife; all three of the other characters bestow money on the student, the man as a reward for his skill in exorcism, the priest and the wife as bribes to insure his silence.

With a company of amateur actors drawn from his fellow tradesmen, Sachs presented plays twice a week between Twelfth Night and Lent each year. His work marked the culmination of the Medieval secular drama in Germany and established a foundation upon which a strong national drama might have been built, had not political and religious wars interfered.

In England, farce first developed within the religious plays. *The Second Shepherds Play* of the Wakefield cycle, for example, includes a fully-developed farce as part of a longer work. As an independent form, however, farce did not emerge until the 16th century in the work of John Heywood (*c.* 1497–*c.* 1580), whose most famous play, *Johan Johan* (1533) tells the story of a henpecked husband who, when ridiculed by his wife and her lover, a priest, drives them both from the house, only to worry about what they may be doing elsewhere.

111

In France, two variations on the farce—*sotties* and *sermons joyeux*—became popular. Both may have appeared because of the church's attempts to suppress the Feast of Fools, many features of which were taken over in the 15th century by secular guilds or "companies of fools" called *sociétés joyeuses*. In some places the celebrations were taken over by the *basoches,* or society of lawyers, as one of their social activities. At other times, student groups staged a "festival of fools." The date of the celebration was moved from the Christmas season to Mardi Gras, May Day, or to the summer months.

Although the entertainments took many forms, the most characteristic were the *sottie* and *sermon joyeuse.* The latter was a burlesque sermon, while the *sottie* was a farce in which all of the characters were fools. Often the *sotties* were only thinly disguised political, social, or religious satires. The characters wore variations on the fool's traditional parti-colored garments, including a hood with ass's ears or a cock's comb. In Paris the *sotties* were made famous by the Basoche du Palais and les Enfants sans Souci. The most celebrated plays were written by Pierre Gringoire (1475–c. 1539), notably *The Prince of Fools* (1512), a satire on the quarrel between Louis XII and Pope Julius II.

The farces required only simple scenery, rarely using more than two mansions. The basic conventions did not differ from those of the religious plays.

The Morality Play

The morality play is the secular form closest in tone to the cycle plays. These didactic dramas first appeared in the 14th century as religious plays, but they were gradually secularized and became one of the principal links between the religious and the professional stages.

The origin of the morality play can be traced to a number of influences. First, the "Pater Noster" prayers, which were divided into seven petitions, each relating to the seven cardinal virtues and seven deadly sins, had established a framework of continual struggle between good and evil to possess man's soul. Second, the popular outdoor preachers, in applying Biblical teachings to the problems of daily living, also adopted the concept of the seven virtues and deadly sins as a scheme for depicting the choices required of men. Third, literature, both religious and secular, had popularized allegory. One of the most influential of Medieval works was the *Romance of the Rose,* a 13th-century love story which included such characters as Slander, Danger, and Fair Welcome. Fourth, Christianity had become increasingly concerned with death and afterlife and men were constantly admonished to "think upon their last ending." In the visual arts, death's heads, skeletons, and similar devices were prominent; in drama this theme was epitomized in "The Dance of Death," in which Death summons representatives of all ranks and professions, from the Pope to the lowest of peasants, in a demonstration that death is the lot of all mankind.

The immediate dramatic ancestors of the moralities are probably the Pater Noster plays performed at York, Lincoln, Beverley, and elsewhere, although these continued long after morality plays were well developed. Many of the Pater Noster plays were presented by municipalities and trade guilds under the same general arrangements as those used for the religious cycles. At Beverley in 1469 there were eight pageant wagons, seven of which transported plays about the seven deadly sins. Since no Pater Noster plays have survived, their precise relationship to the moralities cannot be determined. As a distinct form, the morality play flourished between about 1400 and 1550. Although examples are found in France, it developed principally in England.

The oldest extant morality is a fragment of *The Pride of Life* (c. 1400), in which the King of Life displays an overweening pride from which he cannot be dissuaded. No doubt the lost portions showed his humiliation and repentance. The later plays fall into two basic categories: those that deal with a limited problem, and those that treat the whole of man's life. Of the first type, *Everyman* (c. 1500) is the best-known. It tells of Everyman's receiving Death's summons, his struggle to escape, and his final resignation to necessity. In seeking companions for his journey, Everyman is deserted by his former friends, such as Kindred, Goods, and Fellowship, while Good Deeds alone goes with him.

Of the second type, only one complete example, *The Castle of Perseverance* (c. 1425), has survived. It depicts Mankind's progress from birth to death and judgment on his soul. The play is long, more than 3600 lines, and includes 36 characters. The manuscript gives some information about its performance. In a Prologue, two heralds outline the action and declare that the play will be presented "on the green," beginning at 9 A.M. one week following the announcement. A diagram of the suggested playing arrangements is also included. It shows a circular area, concerning which it states: "This is the water about the place, if any ditch be made where it shall be played, or else let it be strongly barred all about." Five mansions are placed around the perimeter, while Mankind's mansion is set in the center of the circle. It is usually assumed that the water or fence served to control a paying audience and that the play was intended for production by professional actors.

Another play of the second variety is *Mankind* (c. 1470), only a part of which survives. It may originally have been a completely serious work which was later altered to include comic interludes and a number of songs

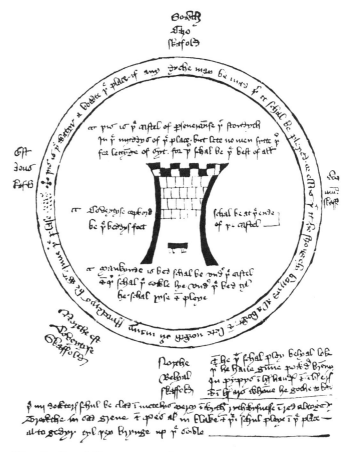

PLAN of the mansions for *The Castle of Perseverance*. In
the middle is the tower for Mankind. The circles represent
the ditch or fence enclosing the performance area. [From
the Early English Text Society edition]

and dances. It is interrupted to permit the actors to collect money from the
audience. The number of roles is only seven, and no scenery or complex
properties are required. Thus *Mankind* shows how the morality play was
adapted to the needs of professional players, and its purely didactic tone
altered in an attempt to attract a paying audience.

In the 16th century the morality underwent still other changes as its
moral intention was expanded to incorporate more clearly secular subjects.
One new direction is exemplified in John Skelton's (*c.* 1460–1529) *Magnificence* (*c.* 1516), which describes the splendor appropriate to a ruler.
Another direction is seen in the use of the morality as a weapon in the
religious controversies which swept England in the 16th century. Among
the best of these plays is John Bale's (1495–1563) *King John* (1538),
which shows the English ruler holding out against the evil forces of the
Pope. Here historical personages and events are integrated with the alle-

gorical figures and ethical struggles typical of the older morality plays. Bale's drama is often considered to be one of the major steps toward a serious secular drama, and a forerunner of the English chronicle plays.

Still another change came with the introduction of classical subjects and characters under the humanistic influence of Renaissance learning. This resulted in a shift toward educational, informative, and philosophical interests, as exemplified in such works as Henry Medwall's *Nature* (*c.* 1500) and John Rastell's *The Four Elements* (*c.* 1518) .

All of the strains of the morality can be found throughout the 16th century, the earlier type continuing in such works as George Wapull's *Tide Tarrieth for No Man* (1576) and T. Lupton's *All for Money* (1578) long after the newer variations had become common. As the morality was secularized during the 16th century, however, the distinctions which had separated it from the interlude vanished.

The morality plays were probably performed by amateurs at first, but gradually were taken over by professionals. In staging, the basic conventions of the religious stage were followed, although the requirements were less extensive. The introduction of allegory in the moralities, however, added another kind of costume to those previously in use, since abstractions such as Mercy, Kindred, and Good Deeds had seldom been seen in the cycle plays. The dress of allegorical figures was often very imaginative. Fame had eyes, ears, and tongues painted on her costume, while Vanity was covered with feathers of many hues, and Wealth wore a garment decorated with gold and silver coins. In the plays of religious controversy, each side drew on the allegorical tradition by dressing its adherents as the Virtues and its opponents as the Deadly Sins. Such figures as Flattery and Ignorance were often costumed as priests of the opposing religion.

As dramas, the moralities mark the gradual evolution from the emphasis upon Biblical characters and events, typical of the cycles, to men in their everyday surroundings. They pave the way for the more purely human preoccupations of the succeeding period.

Chambers of Rhetoric

Closely related to the moralities are the plays performed by the Chambers of Rhetoric in the Low Countries. Originating in the 14th century, these societies were concerned with poetry, music, and drama. By the 16th century practically every town in the Netherlands had at least one Chamber, while Ghent had five.

Competitions among guilds were being held by 1413 and were especially popular in the period from 1493 to 1570. Typically a question was

posed, to which the various Chambers composed an answer in the form of
an allegorical drama. These plays were the major dramatic works of the
Low Countries, since religious drama did not flourish there.

Although some of the plays were produced indoors, more typically
they were given out-of-doors on a stage which anticipated many features of
the Elizabethan public theatre. At the back of a large platform, a fixed
facade was erected. At the stage level there were normally three openings
which could be closed with curtains or opened to reveal interior scenes. A
second level included similar openings, while on the third level there was a
throne for the figure being honored (such as Wisdom, Lady Rhetoric, or
the Virgin). At the end of the contest, this figure was often flown to the
stage level to distribute the prizes.

The productions became increasingly lavish. The peak was probably
reached in 1561 at a contest in Antwerp which lasted for one month. The
nine competing societies made elaborate processional entries into the city
using a total of 23 triumphal chariots and 197 pageant wagons. Plays were
given over a period of 15 days, and the city spent about 100,000 guilders in
addition to the sums provided by the competing societies.

Until 1539 many of the plays had theological messages, but the Protestant leanings of the Chambers led to a demand that all dramas be explicitly

RHETORIC STAGE used at Antwerp in 1561. A contempo-
rary engraving.

approved by Catholic church officials. As a result, dramatists turned increasingly to secular subjects. After 1625 the Chambers declined rapidly, as the professional theatre gained in popularity in Holland.

Interludes

"Interlude" is an imprecise term, since it was at various times applied to almost every type of play presented in the Middle Ages. Today it is used to designate the plays first presented indoors as a part of the entertainments of rulers, nobility, or rich merchants. The name probably derives from the practice of presenting plays between the parts of some other event, such as between the courses of a banquet. The interlude might be of any type: religious, moral, farcical, historical. Since it was often given in crowded banquet halls, the interlude used little scenery and few characters. Like the morality play, it was associated with the rise of the professional actor.

Minstrels had been the most usual professional entertainers since the 11th century. By the end of the 13th century they were especially popular with the clergy and nobility of Europe, and, with the rise of the merchant class during the 14th century, they took up residence in the larger towns. By 1350 many nobles were retaining their own troupes. During the 15th century, minstrels began to specialize as actors, musicians, or fools. By the end of that century, "minstrel" was applied only to musicians, for acting was now recognized as a separate profession.

Since actors were more assured of a livelihood if attached to a noble household, many troupes became servants to great lords. Richard III maintained a troupe of actors after about 1450, Henry VII had a company of six actors in 1483, and Henry VIII had eight actors attached to his household. Probably many similar troupes existed by 1500. Most were permitted to tour under the name of their patrons when their services were not required at home. When they toured, they presented their credentials to the mayor of a town, gave a performance before him and the aldermen, and, if approved, then gave other performances for the general public in the town hall, an inn, or "on the green." In spite of their rising importance, however, professional players remained secondary to amateur performers until religious drama declined during the last half of the 16th century. That professional actors were only beginning to appear in the late 15th century may explain why there are so few interludes prior to 1500. The oldest extant English play of this type, *Fulgens and Lucrece* by Henry Medwall, dates from 1497. Examples from the 16th century are numerous.

The typical place for performing interludes was the "great hall" of a noble residence. These large rooms were constructed after a standard pattern: at one end was a raised platform for the nobleman, his family, and close friends; at the opposite end was the "screen," a wall which separated the banqueting hall from the kitchen; this screen usually had two or three doors and above it a gallery for the musicians; down the two sides of the room, and sometimes in the center, were other tables for less favored guests. Such an arrangement would have been typical when performances were given at banquets. On other occasions, the tables might be replaced by scaffold seating for the spectators.

A MUMMERS' PLAY at Haddon Hall, Derbyshire. Note the hall screen surmounted by a balcony. [From Nash, *The Mansions of England in the Olden Time* (1849)]

The basic scenic background was the "screen," with each of its doors representing a separate mansion. If the hall had a musician's gallery, it was incorporated into the action. At court, elaborate mansions might be built, but in other households the screen seems to have sufficed. There is little evidence of a raised stage until after 1550, the actors performing on the floor of the hall. The acting space was often small and the audience frequently encroached upon it, as the lines of some plays attest.

Most of the interludes were written for small troupes. The title page of Phillip's *Patient Grissell* states that it may be played by eight persons; the printed versions of Lewis Wager's *Mary Magdalene* and *Wealth and Health* are said to be suitable for a company of four; and the title page of Preston's *Cambises* shows the distribution of the 38 roles among eight actors.

TOURNAMENTS, MUMMINGS, DISGUISINGS

Tournaments, Mummings and Disguisings

Alongside the interludes, other courtly entertainments grew up around tournaments, mummings and disguisings. Tournaments began in the 10th century as a means of training knights in warfare. Because of the number of deaths, reforms were introduced during the 13th century, and by 1300 dramatic elements had begun to creep in. The knights now fought to capture such allegorical places as the Castle of Love, scenically represented and peopled with appropriate characters.

A FRENCH TOURNAMENT of the 16th century. [From a contemporary engraving]

Spectators were carefully segregated according to sex and rank in the two-tiered galleries which surrounded the field of combat, or "stage." Around this field were placed the elaborate mansion-like structures which established the allegorical framework of the tournament. Mountains, castles, woods, fountains, ships, and chapels were favorite emblems. For the most part, tournaments took over the visual symbols of the religious plays and applied them to such secular themes as courtly love.

Tournaments were principally noble or royal entertainments; some were international events for which heralds were sent to foreign courts with challenges. In addition to the combats, there were elaborate processions, and in the evenings interludes or other theatrical entertainments were presented. Many of these indoor celebrations were closely related to mummings and disguisings.

Although by 1500 mummings and disguisings were principally court entertainments, they had their origins in such pagan ceremonies as sword and Morris dances. The sword dance may have been military in origin, but by the 14th century minstrels were performing it at weddings and other festivities. Sometimes it was called "the dance of the buffoons" for it usually included one or more comic dancers. In the similar Morris dance, the participants wore bells, and some blackened their faces (Morris may be a corruption of Moorish). A Morris troupe often included a clown, a fool, a hobby horse, and a man dressed as Maid Marion. At times a dragon appeared, and St. George was eventually introduced as the slayer of the dragon.

Out of these beginnings came the "mummers' play," performed during the Christmas season with Father Christmas as "presenter." In the plays, at least one character is always killed in combat, after which a doctor arrives and brings the dead back to life through some grotesque device. Dances and songs were included in most performances. The "mummers' plays" were so called because of their association with "mumming and disguising."

At the Christmas or carnival season, groups of costumed and masked revellers went from house to house presenting plays or pantomimes. Most of the groups took up a collection, but others used the occasion to offer gifts to influential nobles or to the king. Because some revellers used their masks as covers for criminal behavior, mumming was suppressed in the 14th and 15th centuries. Eventually all that remained was a type of courtly entertainment out of which the English masques and Italian *intermezzi* developed.

These courtly "disguisings" (or in Italy, *mascherata*) might be given for any special occasion. They were performed at the banquets following tournaments, for visits of royalty, for weddings, and on a variety of other occasions. The first record of a courtly entertainment with elaborate scenic structures dates from 1377, when Charles V of France entertained the Emperor Charles IV. In England, disguisings were very popular under Henry VII (reigned 1485–1509) and Henry VIII (reigned 1509–47). The scenic units were usually mounted on wheels so that they might be brought into a hall between the courses of a banquet and removed for dancing which followed. Thus, they were somewhat similar to the pageant wagons used for religious cycles. The playlets were largely pantomimic, with major emphasis on spectacle and ingenious allegorical compliments to the persons honored.

A characteristic feature of these entertainments was the conclusion in a dance. In England, performers did not originally mingle with the audience, but, beginning in 1513, the dancers chose partners from among the spectators. Since this practice was borrowed from the Italian courts, the productions after this time were called "masques after the manner of Italy." In the masques, courtiers were the actors, while professional minstrels provided the music and songs. Since elaborate scenery and costumes were used, masques were far more costly to produce than interludes. In 1495, Henry VII spent only 13 pounds for a "disguising," but by the time of Elizabeth I (reigned 1558–1603), the cost often mounted to 400 pounds. Henry VIII was especially fond of court entertainments and in 1527 had a House of Revels built in which to stage them. In 1545, in order to centralize control over court entertainments, an Office of Revels was created. Under Elizabeth, the authority of this Office was to be extended to cover all professional acting troupes in England.

The most extensive uses of court entertainments occurred in Italy during the 16th and 17th centuries and in England between 1603 and 1642. As integral parts of the Renaissance theatre, these will be discussed in later chapters.

Royal Entries and Street Pageants

Theatrical productions also came to be incorporated in the street pageants given by municipalities in honor of coronations, royal weddings, military victories, or visiting rulers. These celebrations followed a basic pattern: civic officials and representatives of the clergy and trade guilds met the person being honored at a prearranged place outside the city; they then escorted him along a carefully planned route through the town to the cathedral for a religious service, after which he was taken to his place of residence. It was an occasion upon which the city could demonstrate its loyalty or respect.

At first there was merely a procession, but gradually plays were added. These may have appeared as early as 1236, but were definitely present by 1298, when the city of London honored Edward I's victory over the Scots. In Paris the first clear record of plays is found in 1313, when Edward II visited France. Gradually royal entries spread throughout Europe. Although they still persist in a modified form, they declined after the 17th century as occasions for dramatic performances.

The addition of plays to the entries came at about the same time that the religious dramas were moved outside the church, and in the early years the plays presented at the street pageants were almost identical with those given at religious festivals. Beginning in the 15th century, the plays produced for royal entries became increasingly allegorical or historical. These later works might be elaborate compliments to the visitor, but they

121

were often veiled lectures on a ruler's duty to his subjects. Since they exploited the Bible, history, mythology, and allegory, the plays might resemble religious dramas, moralities, tournament plays, disguisings, or serious interludes.

SCENE staged for the royal entry of Charles V into Bruges, 1514. King Solomon's court is shown. [From Bapst's *Essai sur l'Histoire du Théâtre* (1893)]

In the beginning only a single play was performed, but by the mid-15th century there might be six or more. Each play was a complete work, but all were connected by a common theme. In England during the 16th and 17th centuries, the best dramatists of the day (Nicholas Udall, John Lyly, Ben Jonson, Thomas Dekker, John Webster, and others) were commissioned to write them.

Each play was presented on a separate stage; the procession halted at each place to view the performance and then moved on to the next. The primary audience was the visitor and his party. The city's populace lined the route, stood on housetops or watched from windows; for them, the attraction was the procession and the opportunity to see the visitor. The stages erected for the plays varied in size and complexity. Many were multi-storied. In equipment and conventions, they were similar in all important respects to those of other dramatic types in the period.

Throughout Europe the planning and financing of the pageants were undertaken jointly by the city council and trade guilds. For example, at the

One of the triumphal arches erected in London for the entry of James I in 1603. [From Nichols, *The Progresses . . . of King James the First* (1828)]

entry of Katharine of Aragon into London in 1501, each play was assigned to a city alderman. He engaged workmen, obtained actors, and supervised all arrangements. The money was raised through taxes levied upon the citizens. This method, or some variation on it, was typical.

The Decline and Transformation of Medieval Drama

During the 600 years in which it flourished, the Medieval drama became increasingly complex and diverse. From the simple religious tropes and popular entertainments of the 10th century, it flowered into the great cycles, civic and court pageants, and secular plays of the mid-16th century. In spite of its vitality, new forces were soon to transform it.

Probably the most far-reaching change grew out of the religious controversies which swept Europe during the 16th century. In England,

Henry VIII's break with the Church of Rome in the 1530's resulted in such continuous religious and civil strife that Elizabeth, upon coming to the throne in 1558, forbade all religious plays in an attempt to still the conflict. Although not immediately successful, Elizabeth's edict silenced the cycles, except for rare instances, after the 1570's.

Parallel movements occurred in other countries. In the Netherlands, production of religious plays without the prior sanction of church officials was forbidden in 1539, with the result that religious subject matter was generally abandoned. The many Protestant secessions led the Catholic church to convene the Council of Trent (1545–63) to cope with the issues. One of the results was the almost universal withdrawal of church sanction from religious plays. Production of the plays had virtually ceased in Italy by 1547, and in 1548 they were forbidden in Paris. In some Germanic areas they continued into the 17th century, but in most of Europe the religious drama had been abandoned by 1600. Only in Spain, where the Inquisition had established its unquestioned control over theology, did they continue.

The abandonment of religious subject matter led to other changes. First, dramatists had to turn to secular subjects. The recently renewed interest in Classical learning supplied them with both new material and new conceptions of dramatic form. The blending of Classical with Medieval influences did much to create the great secular drama of the Renaissance. Second, the turning away from religious subject matter destroyed the last remaining basis for an international drama. Henceforth, each country developed its own national interests and characteristic style. Third, when the religious cycles were forbidden, the active support of the clergy, town councils, and merchant class, who had previously sanctioned and financed the most elaborate theatrical performances, was withdrawn. These groups made a clear distinction between the productions of amateurs motivated by religious and civic pride and the work of professional actors seeking to entertain for pay. The church had never rescinded the condemnation of the professional theatre pronounced in Roman times, and the censure was now reiterated. In Greece, Rome, and Medieval Europe the theatre had existed, in its most characteristic form, as an activity sponsored by governmental and religious authorities. Now it had to wage a fight for recognition apart from its political and religious uses. In its early struggles, it was sustained by noblemen and rulers who continued the system of patronage which had grown up in Medieval times. Under this protection, the professional theatre gradually established itself throughout Europe, although in some countries the process was not to be completed for more than 200 years.

5

THE
ITALIAN
RENAISSANCE

*L*ong before the Medieval drama declined, new conceptions of dramatic form and theatrical production had already taken shape. Beginning during the 14th century, they had spread throughout Europe by 1650 and continued to dominate practice until the 19th century. This chapter will trace the evolution of the new movements in Italy, from whence they were transmitted to other countries.

The Rise of a New Drama

The primary impetus for change came from that revival of interest in classical learning which began somewhat tentatively in the 14th century and accelerated after 1450. Its effects on the theatre were gradual, for the staging of classically-inspired plays did not begin until about 1470, while major developments had to wait until the 16th century.

The study of Roman drama had never been completely out of favor, although Seneca's tragedies were read principally as illustrations of moral lessons or of rhetorical display, while the comedies of Plautus and Terence were valued as models of oral style. During the 14th century, however, the dramatic values of the plays began to be appreciated, and soon imitations of the Latin originals appeared. The earliest Italian tragedy, Albertino Mussato's *Eccerinus* (c. 1315), uses a modified Senecan form to convey Christian doctrine, but in *Achilles* (c. 1390) by Antonio Laschi, classical form and subject are blended. Frequently called the first Renaissance tragedy, *Achilles* was followed by other similar Latin plays during the 15th century. Comedy also began to appear during the 14th century, the oldest known example being Pier Paolo Vergerio's *Paulus* (1390), a satire on contemporary student life. During the 15th century, a number of the leading Humanists wrote comedies, although none produced plays of lasting interest.

All of the early comedies and tragedies were written in Latin, and it was not until the early 16th century that a vernacular drama appeared. By that time, other events had accelerated the classical influence: in 1429, twelve of Plautus' lost plays were rediscovered; in 1453, the fall of Constantinople brought many scholars and the manuscripts of Greek plays to Italy; in 1465, the introduction of printing into Italy made the wide dissemination of classical texts possible, and between 1472 and 1518, all of the known Greek and Roman plays were published. At the same time, interest in classical drama, which until the late 15th century had been confined principally to scholars, spread to the courts of the many Italian states. After 1475, rulers began to patronize dramatists and to finance productions of Roman plays or modern imitations. The desire to make the plays more accessible to the courtly readers and spectators probably provided the major impetus to the writing of plays in Italian.

The vernacular drama was launched in 1508 with a production at the court of Ferrara of *La Cassaria* by Lodovico Ariosto (1474–1533). In this comedy, a favorite Roman plot, the uniting of lovers following the discovery that the girl is the long-lost child of a rich father, is given a contemporary Italian setting. Ariosto went on to write other plays, including *I Suppositi, The Necromancer, The Students,* and *La Lena.* The further development of vernacular comedy was much influenced by Bernard Dovizi da Bibbiena's *La Calandria* (1513), with its successful blending of Roman and contemporary elements. Based upon Plautus' *Menaechmi,* Bibbiena's play uses twins of different sexes and reunites them only after a complicated intrigue based upon disguises and illicit love affairs. His combination of traditional and contemporary materials served as a model for those who came later. Another significant trend is exemplified in Niccolo Machiavelli's (1469–1527) *La Mandragola* (*c.* 1513–20), in which the subject matter is original, but the form borrowed from Latin comedy. Showing the cuckolding of an overly-credulous husband, the play is similar in tone to Medieval farce.

By 1540 a native comedy was well-established in Italy. Although few of the dramatists are now remembered, they were the first in Europe to master the techniques of Latin comedy and to adapt them to contemporary taste. After 1575 their plays were read with increasing frequency in France and England and exerted considerable influence on the emerging drama of those countries.

The first important vernacular tragedy was *Sofonisba* (1515) by Giangiorgio Trissino (1478–1550). Following the example of the Greek tragedians, Trissino used a chorus of fifteen and avoided the division into acts. In his deliberate attempt to counteract the all-pervasive influence of Seneca, Trissino launched the century-long battle between the "Grecians" and the "Romans," which was won by the latter primarily because of Cinthio's popularity. Giambattista Giraldi Cinthio's (1504–73) *Orbecche* (1541), a tale of revenge in the Senecan manner, was the first vernacular tragedy to be produced on the stage. After writing two other tragedies, *Dido* and *Cleopatra*, Cinthio turned to serious plays with happy endings because they were more pleasing to audiences. As a result, his late plays,

SCENE from Guarini's *The Faithful Shepherd*. [From the Venice edition, 1602]

127

although essentially melodramas, influenced most of the writers who followed, even those who avoided the happy resolution. None of Cinthio's successors achieved his popularity, but many were admired both at home and abroad and did much to reestablish the tragic mode which had languished since Roman times.

In addition to comedy and tragedy, a pastoral drama developed, perhaps out of an interest in the satyr plays of antiquity. In the Renaissance, however, the boisterous and licentious world of the Greek satyrs was transformed into an idyllic society of shepherds, shepherdesses, nymphs, and refined satyrs. The principal theme was love, which usually triumphed over the many obstacles placed in its path. Although the first pastoral appeared in 1471, the principal popularity of the form came during the late 16th century, especially with Torquato Tasso's *Aminta* (1581) and Giambattista Guarini's *The Faithful Shepherd* (1590), both of which were admired and imitated throughout Europe.

The Neo-Classical Ideal

Dramatic practice was paralleled by an intense interest in critical theory, which by 1570 had been reduced to those "neo-classical" principles which were to dominate European literature until the late 18th century. Most critical writing of the 16th century drew heavily upon two classical treatises, Horace's *Art of Poetry* and Aristotle's *Poetics*. While Horace's work had never been ignored, the *Poetics* was little known prior to 1498, when it was published in a Latin translation. In 1548 the first commentary on Aristotle's treatise, that by Robertello, appeared, and in 1549 an Italian translation of the *Poetics* was published. After 1550, interest in criticism accelerated. Horatian and Aristotelean precepts were fused with Renaissance conceptions to form a distinctive set of principles most clearly set forth in the work of Antonio Minturno (?–1574), Julius Caesar Scaliger (1484–1558), and Lodovico Castelvetro (1501–71).

In neo-classical doctrine, the fundamental demand was for verisimilitude, "the appearance of truth." This complex concept is a fusion of three fundamental parts: reality, morality, and generality. The desire for reality required that the dramatist confine his subjects to events which could happen in real life. In practice, fantasy and supernatural events were eliminated unless they were integral parts of a traditional myth or Biblical story, and even in these instances were minimized. Furthermore, such conventions as the soliloquy and chorus were discouraged on the grounds that it is unnatural for characters to speak aloud while alone, or to discuss private matters in the presence of a group of people such as the chorus. To replace these devices, each main character came to be given a trusted companion, or *confidant,* to whom he could reveal his innermost secrets. Violence was placed offstage because of the difficulty in making it convincing.

This demand for faithfulness to reality was considerably modified by the insistence that drama must teach moral lessons. Consequently, the dramatist was asked not merely to copy life but to reveal its ideal moral patterns. Since God was thought to be both omnipotent and just, the pattern should show wickedness punished and good rewarded. Those instances in which justice seemingly does not prevail were explained as a part of God's plan, which is often beyond human comprehension but in which justice is inevitable. Such apparent aberrations were, therefore, not considered suitable subjects for drama, which should depict that ultimate truth which is inseparable from morality and justice.

Both reality and morality were further modified by the principle of abstraction or generality as the key to truth. Rather than seeking truth in the welter of peripheral details, the neoclassicist sought it in those attributes which are shared by all phenomena included in a particular category. Those characteristics which are variable were considered to be accidental and therefore not an essential part of truth. Thus, the truth was defined as those norms which are discoverable through the rational and systematic examination of phenomena, whether natural or man-made. Since these norms were considered the highest form of truth, which remains unchanged regardless of the period or locale, rational men were expected to accept them as the basis for literary creation and critical judgment.

This conception of verisimilitude led to many lesser principles. The idea that truth is to be found in "norms" was extended to every aspect of dramatic composition. Drama itself was reduced to two basic types, comedy and tragedy, with others labeled inferior because they are "mixed forms." Consequently, purity of type was urged.

Comedy and tragedy each had its own normative patterns. Comedy was said to draw its characters from the middle or lower classes; to base its stories on domestic and private affairs; to have happy endings; and to imitate the style of everyday speech. Tragedy was said to draw its characters from kings and nobility; to base its stories on history or mythology; to have unhappy endings; and to employ a lofty and poetic style. These distinctions include several departures from Greek practice, but the most significant is that which substitutes social rank of characters for moral qualities.

The concept of norms also extended to characterization, since the dramatist was expected to write about permanent aspects of human nature rather than those peculiar to one time and place. In establishing norms, all humanity was categorized according to age, rank, sex, and profession, and the attributes of each was specified. As a result, the dramas tended to show "type" characters who prosper if they observe the proper "decorum" and who are punished when they deviate from it.

All plays were said to have as their main functions teaching and pleasing. Although the didactic ideal was often stated in classical times, it was not given primary emphasis until the Humanists of the Renaissance found it necessary to justify literature at a time when learning was moving away from purely theological concerns. As a result, for the neo-classicist pleasure was always secondary to instruction. Comedy was expected to ridicule behavior which should be avoided, while tragedy was to show the horrifying results of mistakes and misdeeds.

The "three unities" of action, time, and place were also established during the 16th century. Unified action had been an ideal since Greek times, but unity of time was first advocated around 1543 and unity of place in 1570. It was Castelvetro who in 1570 first stated all three as essential rules. He argued that since an audience knows that it has been in the theatre for only a few hours, it cannot be convinced that long periods of time have elapsed. Likewise, since the audience knows that it has been in only one place, it cannot accept any change of locale. After this time, most critics demanded that a play have a single plot, take place in 24 hours or less, and be confined to one place, although the latter rule was often extended to include additional places if they could be easily reached without violating the 24-hour rule. The division into five acts was also considered essential to regular drama. Horace had first stated this rule in Roman times, and it was adopted in the Renaissance as a norm of drama.

Although many of the neo-classical principles now seem arbitrary and restrictive, they were accepted as reasonable and desirable in the years between 1550 and 1750. As the neo-classical ideal took shape in Italy, drama became increasingly "regular." Although some plays deviated from the rules, most of these were denounced as inferior and unworthy of serious consideration.

During the 16th century the neo-classical rules were little known outside of educated circles, and the plays written in accordance with them did not reach large audiences. Both tragedy and pastoral, even with educated groups, met a mixed reception, while the popularity of comedy, which was produced primarily at court, depended in large part on the *intermezzi* inserted between the acts.

Intermezzi and Operas

Intermezzi were descended from the *mascherata* and other entertainments given at banquets or on special occasions. They were first coupled with comedies in the late 15th century. *Intermezzi* appealed especially to the love for spectacle and their popularity increased as the neo-classical demand for unity of place restricted regular drama to single settings. Scenery, costumes, lights, special effects, music, and dance were the principal appeals of *intermezzi,* for dialogue was used only when explanation of the allegorical plots was essential. Since theatrical entertainments were given at court primarily on such special occasions as betrothals, weddings, births, and visits of royalty, the *intermezzi* permitted elaborate compliments to be mingled with the regular comedies.

As the five-act form became typical of drama, four *intermezzi* were performed between the acts. At first this interruption with allegorical spectacle was opposed, but by the 1570's the *intermezzi* had become more popular than the plays. Originally, the various *intermezzi* seen on a single occasion had no connection with each other or with the play they accompanied. Gradually, however, they were related both to each other and to the theme of the main drama, and by the late 16th century were often loosely-organized four-act works performed during the breaks of a five-act play. Critics were fond of likening them to the choral interludes of ancient comedy.

Since the *intermezzi* depended upon spectacle, they motivated many experiments with scenery. Furthermore, the need to change settings rapidly for the alternating segments of plays and *intermezzi* encouraged the development of new devices for shifting scenery. In the 17th century, the *intermezzi* were gradually absorbed into opera, although for a time they were performed between the acts of this new form as they had been with comedy. By 1650, they had virtually disappeared.

It was opera which was destined to become the most popular dramatic form in Italy. During the Renaissance, Italy had many "academies," or associations of men with common intellectual or artistic interests, and it was out of one of these, the Camerata of Florence, that opera came. Members of the Camerata, who were concerned with Greek music and its relation to drama, sought to create plays similar to ancient Greek tragedies. Their first full-length work, and the first "opera," was *Dafne* (1597), with text by Ottavio Rinuccini and Giulio Caccini and music by Jacopo **Peri**. The dialogue and choral passages were recited or chanted to a musical accompaniment which served merely to enhance the dramatic effectiveness of the dialogue. From this simple beginning, opera evolved.

The first great operatic composer was Claudio Monteverde (1567–1643), whose *Orfeo* (1607) enlarged the role of instrumental music and began the shift in interest from dramatic to musical values. Other composers continued these trends. Until 1637, however, opera remained principally an entertainment of the courts and academies. In that year, the opening of an opera house in Venice made the form available to the general public for the first time. So successful was this venture that between 1640 and 1700 four opera houses operated regularly in Venice, a city of about 140,000 population. From Venice, opera spread throughout Italy and then to the rest of Europe. As a popular entertainment, it underwent several significant changes. The melodious songs, or arias, increased in number as the passages of recitative and choral songs declined. Happy endings became typical, and all of the scenic wonders of the court *intermezzi* were incorporated and elaborated. Consequently, when opera was imported into other countries, so also were Italian scenic practices.

The Development of New Scenic Practices

Although the interest in classical drama began in the 14th century, no plays were performed until about 1468, when the Roman Academy began its experiments. By 1471 the court at Ferrara was presenting plays, and soon other academies and courts were competing for preeminence in lavish and "authentic" staging. By the early 16th century, plays were considered suitable entertainments for almost all court celebrations and were being presented frequently for members and guests by academies devoted to the study of drama.

The production of plays was first motivated by interest in Vitruvius' treatise on Roman architecture. Rediscovered in 1414 and printed in 1486, by 1500 *De Architectura* had assumed the authoritative position in architecture and staging that Aristotle's *Poetics* was to have in literature. Since the early producers desired to follow authentic Roman practices, they turned to Vitruvius for information about the auditorium and stage, scenery for tragedy, comedy, and satyr drama, and for justification of productions financed by rulers and wealthy citizens. But Vitruvius' many hints were easily misinterpreted, since no diagrams or illustrations accompanied the verbal descriptions. This ambiguity prompted many commentaries and critical editions which sought to clarify Vitruvius' account. Of these, the editions by Jocundus (1511) and Philander (1544) were especially influential.

When members of the Roman Academy began staging plays around 1468, it was to Vitruvius that they turned for guidance. Under the direction of Pomponius Laetus (1425–98), they sought to reconstruct the ancient theatre and applied the results in their productions of plays. Young men from all over Europe came to study with Laetus and took many of his ideas back to their native lands.

It is possible that Laetus, working from Vitruvius' description, utilized a stage similar to that shown in late-15th-century illustrated editions of Terence's plays. In these, a continuous facade, either straight or angled, is divided into a series of curtained openings, each of which represents the house of a different character. The first edition of Terence's plays to show this stage was that by Godocus Badius, a Fleming who had studied with Laetus, printed at Lyon in 1493. It was copied by the Venetian edition of 1511 and similar treatments were common after this time. Some scholars have argued that during the 16th century this "Terence Stage" was in use throughout Europe, especially in schools, although others have denied that it was ever widespread.

SCENE from Terence's *Adelphi*. Note the many doors, with the names of characters above them, an arrangement characteristic of the "Terence stage." [From the edition of Terence's plays published at Lyon in 1493]

Even if Laetus and others did employ a background of this type, their practice was soon modified by the addition of perspective painting, which was to have an influence even greater than that of Vitruvius. Although perspective developed over a long period, its principles were first systematized by Filippo Brunelleschi (1377–1446), a Florentine artist whose paintings demonstrated how all objects seen from a fixed eye-point could be drawn so as to maintain mathematically precise spatial relationships. But it was Leon Battista Alberti's *Della Pittura* (1435), the first treatise on the subject, which disseminated practical directions for making perspective drawings. Alberti's understanding of perspective was limited, however, for with his method all objects had to be drawn as parallel to the picture plane. It was not until the time of Leonardo da Vinci (d. 1519) that space was seen to be spherical, curving away from the viewer in all directions. Even then, techniques for transferring objects so perceived to the various flat surfaces of a stage setting had not yet been devised, and many of the later developments in scene design were possible only after much experimentation.

It is difficult now to appreciate the fascination that perspective drawing exerted. To the Renaissance mind, it seemed almost magical in its ability to manipulate illusion. Consequently, since scenery was usually designed by the leading painters and architects of the day, it is not surprising that perspective should soon find its way into the theatre. Although perspective settings may have been used as early as the 1480's, the first certain example is Pellegrino da San Daniele's setting for Ariosto's *La Cassaria* at Ferrara in 1508. In it, individual houses were placed in front of a painted backdrop. This arrangement, which was to be typical for many years, owed much to Vitruvius. First, it was inspired by his descriptions of settings: "Tragic scenes are delineated with columns, pediments, statues, and other objects suited to kings; comic scenes exhibit private dwellings, with balconies and views representing rows of windows after the manner of ordinary dwellings; satyric scenes are decorated with trees, caverns, mountains, and other rustic objects delineated in landscape style." Second, it embodied another Renaissance interest derived from Vitruvius, "the ideal city." The overall purpose of *De Architectura,* of which the discussion of the theatre is a very small part, is to provide a guide for the laying out of towns. Consequently, in designing stage settings, Renaissance artists tended to depict in the tragic scene the royal and ceremonial section of an ideal city, and in the comic scene the area occupied by the citizens.

The theatrical practices of the early 16th century are summed up in Sebastiano Serlio's (1475–1554) *Architettura* (1545), the first Renaissance work on the subject. Serlio was heavily indebted to other artists, especially Baldassare Peruzzi (1481–1537), with whom he had studied and who, according to Vasari, was the foremost developer of perspective settings. Serlio's book is valuable because it describes typical practices of the time. Since it was circulated throughout Europe, it was one of the principal disseminators of Italian ideas abroad. Furthermore, after 1547 Serlio's perspective sketches of the tragic, comic, and satyric scenes were often reprinted in editions of Vitruvius' *De Architectura,* a practice which hastened the assimilation of Vitruvian concepts into perspective settings.

In *Architettura,* Serlio takes it for granted that theatres will be set up in already existing rooms, for in his day the halls of state in palaces had become the usual places for staging plays. Thus, he fits Vitruvius' semi-circular auditorium into a rectangular space by constructing stadium-like seating around an orchestra, used to seat the ruler and his attendants. The stage is raised to the eye level of the ruler and the perspective scenery is designed to be seen from his chair. The front portion of the stage floor is level, since it is intended for the actors. Back of this, the floor slopes upward at a sharp angle, so as to increase the illusion of distance. All scenery is placed on this raked portion.

Serlio provides illustrations of the three Vitruvian scenes, which he

SERLIO'S SETTING for tragedy. [From *The Second Book of Architecture* (1545)]

SERLIO'S SETTING for comedy. [From *The Second Book of Architecture* (1545)]

considers adequate to meet all needs. Although the settings differ in appearance, all have the same basic floor plan. Each requires four sets of wings, the first three angled and the fourth flat, and a perspective backdrop. The downstage wings have many three-dimensional details, and some have open arcades or galleries. Although Serlio mentions no framing device, the downstage houses probably extended to the walls of the hall, while a valance probably limited the overhead view so as to preserve the illusion.

Such "architectural" settings were not designed to be changed during a performance. When *intermezzi* were performed, pageant wagons were usually drawn into the theatre in front of the stage, or portable set pieces were carried onto the platform. The growing interest in spectacle, however, created a demand for means of changing the settings.

SERLIO'S SETTING for pastoral drama. [From *The Second Book of Architecture* (1545)]

A CROSS-SECTION of Serlio's hall stage. [From *The Second Book of Architecture* (1545)]

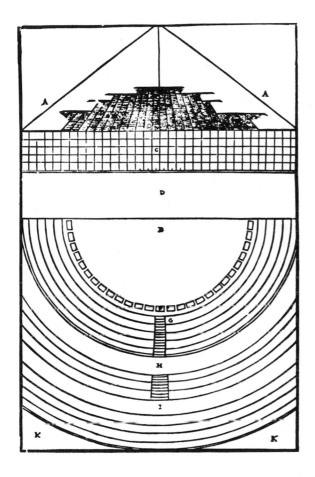

GROUND PLAN of Serlio's hall stage. [From *The Second Book of Architecture* (1545)]

The solution first adopted was derived from discussions of *periaktoi* found in the treatises by Vitruvius and Pollux. The earliest known use of *periaktoi* in the Renaissance is that by Aristotile da San Gallo (1481–1551) for a theatre at Castro in 1543. They were in use at Florence by 1569, and Vignola in his *Le Due Regola della Prospettiva Practica* (1583) recommends structures with from two to six sides for changing scenes.

Nicola Sabbattini's (1574–1654) *Manual for Constructing Theatrical Scenes and Machines* (1638), a major source of information about 17th century practices, lists three principal methods of changing scenery. One uses *periaktoi,* while the other two are clumsy devices for changing the angled wings. In the first, new wings are maneuvered around those already there, and in the second, painted canvas is pulled quickly around the wings to conceal the previously-visible surfaces. In addition, Sabbattini explains how to change the flat wings used near the back of the stage by sliding them in grooves or turning them like pages in a book. All of these devices indi-

137

cate a considerable simplification of Serlio's wings, for painted details have replaced the formerly three-dimensional ones.

The ultimate solution to scene shifting required that all angled wings be replaced with flat wings. This change, however, had to await new developments in perspective drawing. Throughout the 16th century, the angled wings had been painted in position on stage. To determine the proper proportions, a cord was run from the vanishing point to the flats. Drawing was then simple, for the two faces of each wing were treated as different sides of a single structure, one parallel to the picture plane and the other at right angles to it. On flat wings, however, all details had to be painted on a single surface parallel to the picture plane. The problems of transferring a perspective picture to a series of flat wings were not adequately solved until the appearance of Guido Ubaldus' *Perspectivae libri sex* in 1600. The first application of Ubaldus' principles to settings composed entirely of flat wings was probably made by Giovanni Aleotti (1546–1636) at Ferrara in 1606. By 1650, the new practice had almost completely outmoded the angled wings.

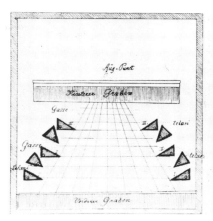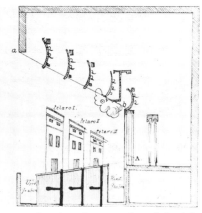

PLAN AND SECTION showing the use of *periaktoi,* bow-shaped borders, and a rear pit for special effects. Plan by Joseph Furttenbach. [From *Die Theater Weins* (1899)]

With the change to flat wings, any number of settings could be easily shifted. At each wing position as many flats were set up, one immediately behind the other, as there were settings. Changes were then accomplished simply by withdrawing the visible wings to reveal another set immediately behind. To support the flats and to permit their easy movement on and offstage, grooves were installed on the stage floor and overhead. The back scene was normally painted on two flats, or "shutters," which met at the center of the stage, although cloths which could be rolled up were sometimes used.

Until about 1650 most scenes, following ancient practice, showed exteriors; consequently, the overhead masking was painted to represent the sky or clouds. Sometimes an unbroken canvas was mounted above the entire setting, but as flying machinery became common, bow-shaped hanging borders were hung above each set of wings. When interior settings were introduced, the borders were painted to represent ceilings, beams, domes, or other appropriate details.

In the early 17th century, then, the three basic elements of every setting were the side wings, back shutters, and overhead borders, and it had become an accepted practice to change all of these simultaneously. At first, many stage hands were utilized to make quick changes, but even then the results were not always entirely satisfactory, since it was difficult to synchronize the movements of so many persons.

The final significant step was taken by Giacomo Torelli (1608–78), who perfected the chariot-and-pole system of scene shifting at the Teatro Novissimo in Venice between 1641 and 1645. Torelli cut slots through the stage floor to allow upright supports, or "poles," to pass through. These poles, on which the flats were mounted, were attached below the stage to "chariots" mounted on casters which ran in tracks parallel to the front of the stage. Thus, as the chariots rolled toward the center of the stage they carried flats into view, while the opposite movement took them out of sight. By means of an elaborate system of ropes, pulleys, and winches, every part of a setting could be changed by turning a single winch. This innovation, which at first seemed almost magical, was later adopted almost universally on the continent, where it became the standard method of shifting scenery until the late 19th century. Only in England, Holland, and America was the older and simpler groove system continued.

Following the acceptance of the flat wing, the visual conventions of stage settings also changed. So long as angled wings had predominated, each wing usually represented a separate building, a tradition which persisted for a time with flat wings. This convention, however, did not lend itself to creating an effect of grandeur. Consequently, as the taste for immensity grew during the 17th century, the former series of buildings gave way to a sequence of columns, porticos, or other architectural features, all of which were treated as parts of a single structure. This change increased both the unity and the apparent size of stage settings.

Since scenic design was long an adjunct of architecture or painting, many of Italy's finest artists designed scenery in the years between 1475 and 1650. Because they and their students moved about frequently, essentially the same scenic traditions were current throughout Italy. The prestige to be gained through lavish productions encouraged many rulers, notably those of Ferrara, Mantua, Urbino, Milan, and Rome, to patronize the theatre. Scenic grandeur was especially highly developed under the De'-Medicis at Florence, where Bernardo Buontalenti (1536–1608), Giulio

SCENE from the ballet *La Liberazione di Tirreno,* given in Florence in 1616. The setting is by Giulio Parigi. [From a contemporary engraving]

Parigi (*c.* 1570–1635), and Alfonso Parigi (d. 1656) contrived some of the greatest spectacles of the day. From Giulio Parigi, Inigo Jones learned much that he applied to the 17th century English masques, and in Florence Joseph Furttenbach (1591–1667) absorbed the ideas on staging which he made available in Germany through his books *Architectura Civilis* (1628), *Architectura Recreationis* (1640), and *Mannhaffter Kunstspiegel* (1663).

With the opening of the Venetian public opera houses, scenic splendor was made available to the general public for the first time since the Medieval religious plays. From opera it spread to the other dramatic forms of the public playhouses.

Development of Theatre Architecture

In spite of the great interest in theatrical production after 1470, plays were presented by courts and academies only on special occasions. Therefore, the need for a permanent theatre was slow in arising. Many of the early productions were given out-of-doors in courtyards or gardens, but during the 16th century banqueting halls or other large rooms became the typical sites. These temporary theatres were usually arranged in the manner described by Serlio.

Although a few permanent structures may have been built earlier (an allegedly permanent theatre at Ferrara burned in 1532), the oldest surviving Renaissance theatre is the Teatro Olimpico, built between 1580 and 1584 by the Olympic Academy of Vicenza. Founded in 1555 to study Greek drama, this academy had previously used temporary stages for its occasional productions. When the members decided to build a permanent theatre, Andrea Palladio (1518–80), eminent architect, student of Vitruvius and of Roman ruins, and a member of the Academy, undertook to reproduce a classical theatre inside a preexisting building. In the Teatro Olimpico, semi-elliptical seating curves around a small orchestra. The rectangular stage is enclosed at the back and ends by a facade decorated with pillars, niches, statues, and bas-reliefs. Five openings pierce the facade, one at either end and three at the back. The overall effect is that of a miniature Roman theatre brought indoors. Palladio died before the theatre was completed, and for the opening production in 1585, Sophocles' *Oedipus Rex*, Vincenzo Scamozzi (1552–1616) placed street scenes, built in perspective, behind each of the stage openings to create the impression that the stage is a city square into which a number of streets lead. Each spectator has a view down at least one of the streets. These vistas still remain as permanent parts of the stage.

The Teatro Olimpico was not, however, in the main line of development, which is better represented by the small theatre built by Scamozzi at

INTERIOR OF THE TEATRO OLIMPICO as it appears today.

Sabbionetta in 1588. Here a complete theatre building was designed as a unit, although the interior was still essentially Serlio's plan given permanent form. Semi-circular seating faces a stage without a proscenium arch, upon which angled wings are used for settings. As one of the few surviving Renaissance theatres, it is of considerable importance in showing the evolution of theatre architecture.

The prototype of the modern stage is that of the Teatro Farnese at Parma, completed in 1618, since it is the first surviving structure with a permanent proscenium arch. The origins of the proscenium arch are obscure. Some scholars have suggested that the doorways of the Roman or "Terence" stages were gradually enlarged to permit playing scenes inside the openings, with the eventual merging of all into a single arch. Others have argued for a similar evolution out of the triumphal arches used in street pageants. Still others believe that the proscenium frame was borrowed from perspective painting, which often surrounded a central view with architectural side units much as Serlio later did his stage settings.

Any or all of these practices may have contributed to the proscenium arch, which was adopted to fill a need first clearly felt in the Renaissance. In the Medieval theatre, Heaven, Hell, and Earth were shown simultaneously, since space was treated as unbounded and infinite. In the Renaissance, artists sought to depict only those objects which could be seen from one fixed point; space, therefore, was treated as finite, and a framing device was needed to restrict the view of the audience. The proscenium arch, then, helped both to create the illusion of reality and to mask the mechanisms upon which illusion depended.

The proscenium came into use only gradually. In the early 16th century settings, the first pair of wings and an overhead valance provided sufficient masking. As the desire to change settings increased, so did the need for downstage masking to conceal the changes. For a time, the first set of angle wings were neutralized so as to blend with the various settings; in some temporary theatres, an appropriate proscenium arch was erected for each new production. But in permanent theatres the desirability of a permanent framing device became clear, especially after the flat wing was adopted. Consequently, after 1618 the architectural proscenium arch triumphed.

The usefulness of the arch was not restricted to the front of the stage, however, and the Teatro Farnese (as well as many later theatres) had two additional frames further back on the stage. This feature encouraged the use of settings of varying depths, since the openings made it easy to increase or restrict the stage space. The concept of internal arches increased in importance as the desire for grandeur and size of setting grew. The opening between the last set of wings then came to serve as a second frame behind which a deep perspective vista could be placed. Barriers were sometimes erected to prevent actors from moving too near the perspective backdrops and thereby destroying the illusion of distance, but stages of great depth were also built with increasing frequency to permit scenes of true immensity. Down to the 20th century, theatres often had rooms back of the stage which could be used to increase the depth of scenes.

Although the stage of the Teatro Farnese was the prototype of those which followed during the next 250 years, its auditorium was still that of a conventional court theatre. In it, U-shaped, stadium-like seating surrounded a large open space which could be used for dancing or flooded for water spectacles. The prototype of the later auditorium, therefore, is not to be found at court but rather in the public theatres.

During the second half of the 16th century, the professional theatre began its rise in Italy. The first record of a public theatre building is found in 1565 at Venice. By the early 17th century, a number of public theatres existed, although none was very elaborate. The major innovations came with the introduction of opera in 1637. Venice was the logical place for the public theatre to develop, for it was the only Italian state not ruled by a monarch. Since its wealth depended upon commerce, there was a strong middle class capable of supporting a public theatre.

An ITALIAN PUBLIC THEATRE of the early 17th century. [From Bapst's *Essai sur l'Histoire du Théâtre* (1893)]

The auditorium of the Venetian public opera house was arranged so as to encourage attendance by all classes while permitting relative privacy for those who wished it. The San Cassiano, the first to be built, had five balconies each with 31 boxes. The first two levels, the most expensive, were patronized by the wealthier classes; the upper three were used by persons of lesser rank and wealth; the open area on the ground floor (the pit or *parterre*) attracted the lower classes or those to whom propriety was unimportant. The arrangement of tiers, one above the other, permitted large numbers of persons to be accommodated in a restricted space. The success of the San Cassiano was so great that by 1641 there were three others, and from Venice the public performance of opera, and its attendant auditorium design, spread to other cities in Italy and throughout Europe.

While the Venetian theatres popularized the "box, pit, and gallery" auditorium, they were not the first examples of it, for many of the theatres erected for the religious plays of the Middle Ages had employed this arrangement, and less elaborate versions were used by the public theatres of Paris, London, and Madrid before opera houses were opened in Venice. Nevertheless, the prestige of opera gave approval to the pattern which was to dominate auditorium design until the end of the 19th century. Furthermore, since the Venetian opera houses also incorporated the proscenium arch, elaborate machines, and perspective scenery, they were the first public theatres to include all of the standard features of the picture-frame stage.

Machinery and Special Effects

Much of the wonder inspired by the productions at courts and academies resulted from special effects. Building upon Medieval practice, the Renaissance machinists arranged seemingly magical transformations, making gods, monsters, and mythological creatures appear on the sea, in the air, on land, in Heaven, and in Hades. Pagan deities replaced Biblical characters, and classical authority for special effects was sought in Pollux' list of machines and Aristotle's inclusion of spectacle as one of the six basic parts of drama. Even those plays which observed the unity of place often introduced spectacle to reduce the austerity imposed by a single setting. Typically, however, elaborate special effects were associated with *intermezzi* or opera.

Much of the spectacle depended upon machinery for "flying." Gods appeared frequently to resolve the dramatic action, and these and other mythological characters were suspended above the stage in chariots, on clouds, or on the backs of animals or birds. From one to fifty figures might be shown in "the glory" of a brightly lighted paradise formed of clouds. To achieve these effects, appropriately shaped figures, such as chariots, horses, or clouds, were made of wood and canvas and then painted. Since the overhead space was limited in theatres of this period, beams and fulcrums at the sides of the stage were used for much of the flying. Some structures were hinged so that they might be collapsed within the overhead space.

SCENE BY TORELLI for *The Marriage of Thetis* (1654) showing a "glory" and action on three different levels: the stage,
an intermediate zone, and in the heavens. [From *Scene e
Machine Preparate all Nozze di Teti* (1654)]

Ingenious riggings were invented for moving objects up and down stage
while they were suspended in the air. In many productions, transformations were masked by clouds which engulfed the stage; in these, shaped and
painted cloths and flats were lowered from above and moved on from the
sides.

Other effects depended upon trap doors in the stage floor. Since in the
temporary theatres the platform was elevated only four to six feet, the
working space was restricted. Nevertheless, the effects were elaborate:
mountains, rocks, trees, and other objects rose and sank; characters suddenly appeared or disappeared; objects and persons were transformed by
means of substitutions from beneath the stage. Figures were painted on
cloth, attached to sticks, and slowly elevated through a slit to create the
effect of ghosts rising through the floor. Fire and smoke were common.
Sabbattini describes a torch and container of resin by means of which
flames seem to rise out of the earth and a scheme for placing fire in front
and back of actors to create the effect of dancing amid flames.

The popularity of sea scenes led to several devices for simulating
waves. In one, painted cloth was moved up and down by means of cords
attached to its under side; in another, a series of profile pieces shaped like
waves were moved up and down; in a third, a series of shaped cylinders
were turned to give the effect of movement. By combining these methods

with appropriate painting, changes from calm to storm, from darkness to light, and other conditions could be simulated.

Ships, whales, and dolphins moved through the waves. To create the proper illusion, miniatures were usually mounted on poles and operated from beneath the stage. When the ships had to accommodate a number of people, they were pulled across the stage by means of concealed ropes. An *intermezzo* at Florence in 1589 showed a shell bearing Amphitrite, accompanied by dolphins and Tritons; then a ship bearing 20 men sailed across the stage, while a watchman in the crow's nest sang a song and a dolphin danced in the waves below.

Sometimes spectacles demanded that walls, fortified castles, or other buildings collapse. In these instances, the scenery was built in sections and secured with bars, the removal of which caused the structures to fall.

Sound was also important. Thunder was created by rolling cannon balls or stones down a rough channel; wind was simulated by whirling thin pieces of wood through the air. Music was played during the scene shifts and to disguise unwanted noises. It also accompanied the numerous songs and dances and much of the action of the essentially pantomimic *intermezzi*.

The front curtain might also be considered a special effect, since it was used to conceal the scenic wonders and to increase amazement when they were suddenly revealed. It was used only to begin performances and never served to divide them into acts. At first, the curtain was dropped but, since this created too many hazards, the roll curtain was eventually adopted.

Although plays were the most usual entertainments, they were by no means the only ones, for the Italians courts revived many of the spectacles of the Roman Empire and continued others from the Middle Ages. Equestrian shows, naval and water displays, street revels, processions, and dances were common. In Florence in 1566, a street pageant, *Mascherata della Genealogie degli Dei,* required 21 pageant wagons and 392 costumes for the mythological figures. *The Battle of the Argonauts* was staged on the Arno River in Florence in 1608, and the wedding celebrations of Ferdinando I in 1589 included three weeks of plays, *intermezzi,* naval battles, animal baitings, religious processions, and tournaments.

Stage Lighting

When performances moved indoors, stage lighting became an important element of theatrical production for the first time. Although some of the Medieval courtly entertainments had been performed indoors, it was not until the 16th century that indoor productions were common. At that time, techniques for lighting the auditorium and the stage had to be devised.

The available illuminants were candles and oil lamps. Candles were preferred for the auditorium because they smoked less and had a more pleasant odor than oil. Usually the auditorium was lighted by chandeliers hung just in front of the stage, illuminating both the auditorium and a portion of the platform.

The downstage acting area was also lighted by footlights, often mounted behind a parapet placed a short distance in front of the stage. Sabbattini states that the smoke from footlights and chandeliers often created a haze, and other writers comment upon the heat and fumes. The stage lights were usually concealed behind overhead or side masking pieces. Here oil lamps were usual and several were placed in evenly-spaced rings attached to vertical poles behind the proscenium and each of the wings. Others were mounted on horizontal battens back of the valance and borders. To increase efficiency, reflectors made from tinsel, mica, or polished basins were placed behind the lamps. At least three methods of darkening the stage were used: lamps were extinguished (although this was awkward if the lights had to brighten again); open cylinders were suspended above the lamps and lowered over them to darken the stage or raised to brighten it; or all lamps might be mounted on rotating poles which could turn them either toward or away from the stage. When exceptionally bright light was required, some scenic device such as a cloud, shell, or

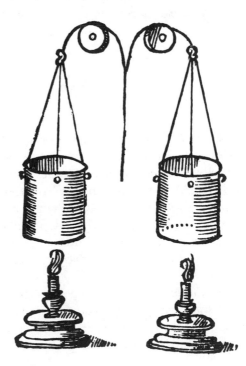

DEVICE FOR DIMMING CANDLES. [From Sabbattini's *Manual for Constructing Theatrical Scenes and Machines* (1638)]

147

grotto was equipped with a downstage rim behind which lamps could be concealed and directed toward persons inside the structure.

Sometimes the sun, moon, or lightning was shown. At Florence in 1539, San Gallo filled a crystal sphere with water and lighted it from behind with candles to form a sun which rose at the beginning of the play, moved across the sky, and set as the action closed. The moon was represented in a similar fashion. Bolts of lightning were made from jagged pieces of wood covered with tinsel. Occasionally attempts were made to color the light by placing containers filled with tinted liquids between the lamps and the stage. Since this reduced intensity markedly, it was normally reserved for such decorative devices as jewelled windows or festive lights on top of buildings.

Since the intensity of lamps and candles was so limited, the provision of an adequate level of illumination had to take precedence over the other functions of stage lighting. Nevertheless, Renaissance theorists formulated several artistic principles similar to those advocated in modern times. Leone di Somi (1527–92) argued that tragedy benefits from a lower level of illumination than that needed for comedy, and both he and Angelo Ingegneri (c. 1550–c. 1613) stated that the stage will appear brighter if it can be contrasted with a darkened auditorium. Sabbattini suggested that lighting the stage primarily from one side gives a more pleasing effect than even lighting from the front. For the most part, however, the Renaissance artist had to depend upon general illumination, for he had only limited control over color, distribution, and intensity. Nevertheless, he mastered most of the techniques which were to be typical until the late 18th century.

Commedia dell'Arte

The productions at courts and academies were given for aristocratic audiences on special occasions. The plays were usually written by court poets, while the scenery and costumes were designed by the court architects or painters. Acting was done by courtiers, and music supplied by court musicians. Thus, in spite of the high visual quality of the productions and their influence on later theatrical practice, they were essentially amateur performances. The development of a professional theatre for the general populace, on the other hand, was due primarily to performers of *commedia dell'arte*.

Commedia dell'arte (comedy of professional players), *commedia all'improviso* (improvised comedy), and *commedia a soggetto* (comedy developed from a plot, theme, or subject) are terms used to distinguish the plays performed by professional troupes from the *commedia erudita* (or learned comedy) presented by the amateur actors at courts and academies. It is not known when the *commedia dell'arte* came into being. The first clear records of it are found soon after 1550, but it may have existed long before that time. Several theories have been advanced to explain the origin of *commedia dell'arte*. One school seeks to trace it from the Atellan farce of Rome as preserved by wandering mimes during the Middle Ages. The principal evidence for this view is the similarity of stock characters in the two forms. A variation on this theory traces the *commedia* from troupes of Byzantine mimes who supposedly fled to the West when Constantinople fell in 1453. Other scholars have argued that it evolved out of improvisations on the comedies of Plautus and Terence. Still others have traced it to the Italian farce of the early 16th century.

SCENE from an Italian comedy of the early 17th century.
[From Rasi, *I Comici Italiana* (1895–1905)]

Farce had appeared in Italy, as elsewhere, during the late Middle Ages, but its most extensive development came between 1500 and 1550, when it was especially popular with the general public; after this time, it declined as *commedia dell'arte* rose in esteem. It reached its height in Venice in the work of Angelo Beolco (1502–42), who began writing and acting around 1520. Disliking the *commedia erudita*, he turned for inspiration to the simple life and natural speech of northern Italy. Many of his plays center around the peasant Ruzzante, a role played by Beolco. The continuance of Ruzzante through several plays has been cited as a forerunner of the *commedia's* use of stock characters.

None of the theories about the origin of *commedia dell'arte* can be established or refuted. Probably many influences contributed to its development. Regardless of its source, before 1600 it had spread throughout Europe, where it was a typical and popular form of entertainment until about 1750.

The two fundamental characteristics of *commedia dell'arte* were improvisation and stock characters. The actors worked from a plot outline, on the basis of which they improvised dialogue and action. Each performer always played the same character with its fixed attributes and costume.

The earliest clear reference to improvisational playing is found in 1568, but if new at that time, it soon became standard. Historians have disagreed over the extent to which improvisation was used in performances. Certainly, several factors worked to reduce it. Each actor usually played the same character throughout his career, and this practice must have encouraged the repetition of lines and business which had been well-received by audiences. Many bits of comic business, or *lazzi*, were sufficiently standardized to be indicated in plot outlines as "the hat *lazzi*," the "*lazzi* of fear," and so on. Prologues, as well as the rhymed couplets used to close scenes, were probably memorized, and the actors playing the fashionable young lovers were encouraged to keep notebooks filled with appropriate sentiments copied from poetry and popular literature. Consequently, most of the actors probably stored up lines and action which they repeated frequently. On the other hand, no actor could be sure what the others would say or do and thus he had to concentrate upon the unfolding action. As a result, performances must have had an air of spontaneity.

The scenarios were refined over a period of time and passed down from one troupe to another. More than 700 have been preserved, the oldest being the 50 published by Flaminio Scala (*fl.* 1600–21) in 1611. By far the greatest number of scripts were comic, although a few were serious and many were melodramatic. The popularity of the troupes, however, rested primarily upon comedies revolving around love and intrigue, disguises, and cross-purposes. The *commedia* actors also performed occasionally in written plays, of which more than 30 scripts have survived.

Although the fixed characters varied from one troupe to another, they may be divided into two general categories: the straight and the exaggerated. The straight roles were those of the young lovers, who served as a norm against which the peculiarities of other characters were seen. They were depicted as witty, handsome, well-educated young men and women; they dressed in the fashionable garments of the day and, unlike the other characters, were not masked. Each company had one or two pairs of lovers. The young man, the *innamorato* or *amoroso*, was often opposed in his love affairs by his elderly father. The young woman, or *innamorata*, was a sophisticated young lady, often courted by both young and old men.

The "character" roles can be divided into masters and servants. Of the masters, three types recurred most frequently: the Capitano, Pantalone, and Dottore. Originally the Capitano was one of the lovers and unexaggerated in his manners and dress. Eventually, however, he was transformed into a braggart and coward who boasted of his great prowess in love and battle, only to be completely discredited in both. The sword, cape, and feathered headdress were standard features of his costume, though the degree of stylization varied considerably. He was often given such fanciful names as Spavento da Vall'Inferno, Coccodrillo, Rinocorente, or Matamoros. Most frequently he figured in the action as an unwelcome suitor to one of the young women, and his discomfiture was often a highpoint of the comedy.

THE CAPITANO of the *commedia dell'arte*. [From Maurice Sand, *Masques et Bouffons* (1859)]

Pantalone was always an elderly merchant. He spoke in a Venetian dialect, was fond of proverbs, and in spite of his age, often posed as a young man and courted one of the young women. His traditional costume included a tight-fitting red vest, red breeches and stockings, soft slippers, a black, ankle-length coat, a soft brimless cap, from which trailed wisps of hair, a brown mask with a large hooked nose and straggling gray beard.

Dottore was usually Pantalone's friend and, like Pantalone, held an established place in society. He was a pedant, usually a Doctor of Laws, who spoke in a Bolognese dialect interlarded with Latin words and phrases. He loved to show off his spurious learning, but was often tricked by others because of his extreme credulousness. His dress was the academic cap and gown, and as this changed from one period to another, so did the Dottore's costume. A tyrant in his own household, he was a jealous husband and a demanding father.

The most varied of all the *commedia* types were the servants, or *zanni*. Most scripts required at least two, one clever and the other stupid, but the number might vary from one to four. They usually figured prominently in the intrigues, and their machinations kept the plots moving as they sought to help or thwart their masters. Most of the servants were male, but there might be one or more maids, or *fantesca*, who served the *innamorata*. Typically young, coarsely witty, and always ready for an intrigue, they carried on their own love affairs with the male servants. Occasionally, they were older and might be the hostess of an inn, wife to a servant, or the object of an old man's affection.

Of the *zanni*, Harlequin or Arlecchino was by far the most popular after the mid-17th century, although he did not figure prominently in the early scripts. He was a mixture of cunning and stupidity, accomplished ac-

Scene from a *commedia* play. [From Lambranzi's *Nuova e Curiosa Scuola de Balli Theatrali* (1716)]

robat and dancer. He was usually at the center of any intrigue. His costume underwent many changes. Originally he wore a suit with many irregularly placed patches, which gradually assumed the diamond-shaped red, blue, and green pattern. On his shaven head Harlequin wore a rakish hat above a black mask, and at his side he carried a wooden sword, or "slapstick," which figured prominently in the many fights and beatings of the *commedia*. Other common names for this character are Truffaldino and Trivellino.

Harlequin's most frequent companion was a cruel, libidinous, cynically-witty servant who went by a variety of names. He was often called Brighella in the 18th century, when his mask had a hooked nose and moustache, and his trousers and jacket were ornamented with green braid. Other variations on this character included Buffetto, Flautino, Scapino, and Mezzetino.

Scaramouche, another popular character, varied considerably in his attributes, sometimes resembling Harlequin, at others Brighella or the Capitano. Pulcinella was always a Neapolitan, but his function in the plays varied. Sometimes he was a servant, at others the host of an inn or a merchant. He was a mixture of foolishness and shrewdness, villainy and love, wit and dullness. He had an enormous hooked nose, a humpback, and wore a long pointed cap. He was the ancestor of the English puppet character, Punch. Many other servants and incidental characters are listed in the scripts, for each troupe tended to develop its own variations on the common types.

In size, the troupes averaged ten to twelve members, of which seven or eight were men and three or four women. A typical troupe included two sets of lovers, a servant girl, a *capitano,* two *zanni,* and two old men (Pantalone and Dottore), but this pattern might be augmented or reduced according to the financial state of the group.

Productions were supervised by the leader or most respected member of a troupe. It was his responsibility to explain the characters, clarify the action, enumerate the *lazzi,* and acquire the properties needed. Although it is not clear whether the plays were really rehearsed, pains were taken to see that each actor understood what was expected of him.

Most companies were organized on a sharing plan, members being responsible for the expenses and dividing the profits, although some of the younger actors may have been salaried until they were taken into full membership. They traveled constantly, and at each new town had to petition for the right to perform, a favor not always granted. Usually they hired large rooms in which to play, but they also improvised stages out of doors and performed on the elaborate court stages. Their adaptability was one secret of their success. When perspective settings and elaborate effects were available, the troupes used them, but they could perform just as easily with no scenery at all.

The *commedia* was most vigorous between 1550 and 1650, the period

SCENE from a *commedia* play. [From E. Gherardi's *Le Théâtre Italien*. 11th ed. (1741)]

of the most famous troupes. The history of the various companies is often difficult to trace because of scanty records, the frequent mergers and separations, and the similarity of names adopted by the troupes.

The first company of note was Alberto Ganassa's troupe which played in such diverse places as Mantua, Ferrara, Paris, and Madrid between 1568 and 1583. Its fame, however, was far exceeded by the Gelosi ("zealous") which performed between 1569 and 1604. The outstanding members of the Gelosi were Francesco Andreini (1548–1624), originally an *innamoroto* and later a Capitano, and his wife, Isabella (1562–1604), the most renowned *innamorata* of her day and a poet as well. Joining the company in 1583, they soon became its leaders and made it fashionable throughout Italy and France. They performed at the elaborate wedding celebrations in Florence for Ferdinando I in 1589 and were invited to France by Henri IV. The troupe disbanded upon the death of Isabella in 1604.

COMMEDIA DELL'ARTE figures. [From Jacques Callot's *Balli di Sfessania*.]

The Confidenti troupe performed between 1574 and 1621. Like others, it traveled widely, appearing throughout Italy, Spain, and France. Its many fine actors included Flaminio Scala, who published the first collection of *commedia* scripts. Because of internal bickering, it declined considerably in quality after 1610. The Desiosi ("desirous") company played between 1580 and 1595. In spite of references to its high quality, little is known of its work. The Accesi ("flashing" or "inspired") troupe performed between 1590 and the 1630's, although its best work was done between 1600 and 1609 under the leadership of Pier Maria Cecchini

(1575–1645), who played Fritellino. For a time, leadership was shared with Tristano Martinelli (c. 1557–1630), the first famous Arlecchino. The Accesi played in Italy, France, Austria, and Germany. The Fideli ("faithful") company was active from about 1598 until the 1640's. Its principal actors were Giambattista Andreini (c. 1578–1654), son of Francesco and Isabella Andreini, and his wife Virginia (1583–c. 1627/30). They made at least four trips to France and played as far north as Prague.

In addition to these important troupes, the Dukes of Mantua patronized companies throughout the 17th century, and the most important troupes between 1650 and 1700 were those attached to the courts of Parma and Modena. The *commedia dell'arte* continued until about 1750, but never regained the prestige it commanded between 1550 and 1650. Although it was always most popular in Italy, France was a second home, and troupes often traveled in Spain, Germany, Austria, and England. Wherever they went, they influenced the native actors and writers.

By 1650 Italy had evolved the dramatic types, critical principles, and theatrical practices which were to dominate the European theatre for the next 150 years. The neo classical ideal, classically-inspired comedy and tragedy, opera, *commedia dell'arte,* theatre architecture, perspective scenery, indoor lighting techniques, complex special effects and stage machinery—all of these were to find their way to other counties, where they would be assimilated and adapted to local needs.

THE ENGLISH
THEATRE
FROM 1558 TO 1642

*T*he years between Elizabeth's accession to the throne in 1558 and the closing of the theatres by Parliament in 1642 saw the emergence of a theatre so excellent that it is still considered one of the world's great achievements. Unlike Italy, England developed a vernacular drama of superior quality performed by professional troupes for both popular and aristocratic audiences. Consequently, there was no sharp division between the court and public stages. The English theatre developed its own distinctive traits by mingling traditions inherited from the Middle Ages with ideals of the emerging Renaissance.

The Transitional Drama

The great English plays written after 1585 were rooted in two earlier developments: the Medieval-like interludes performed by professional actors, and the classically-inspired plays written at schools, universities, and Inns of Court. Although the two types occasionally used common subjects and techniques, they developed along essentially different lines until well-educated men began to write for the public stage and to fuse them into a single and vital stream.

In 1558, the interlude was associated principally with the professional troupes. Aiming to attract a wide audience, the actors mingled elements of popular entertainment with subject matter drawn from many sources. Historical materials were exploited with increasing frequency as interest in the national past grew. Biblical stories were chosen for their romantic qualities, as in *Godly Queen Hester* (*c.* 1561) and *King Darius* (*c.* 1565). Foreign novels and chivalric tales were adapted in such plays as *Calisto and Melibea,* based upon a Spanish work. Classical myths were mingled with English historical and low-comedy figures in *Thersites* (1537) and *Horestes* (1567). The popular tradition is probably best summed up in Thomas Preston's (1537–98) *A Lamentable Tragedy Mixed Full of Pleasant Mirth, Containing the Life of Cambises, King of Persia, from the Beginning of His Kingdom, Unto his Death, His one Good Deed of Execution, after that Many Wicked Deeds and Tyrannous Murders, Committed by and Through Him, and Last of All, His Odious Death by God's Justice Appointed* (*c.* 1561). Although the play is set in Persia, many of the characters are mythological (Cupid and Venus), allegorical (Shame, Diligence, Trial, and Proof), or English (Hob, Lob, and Marian-May-Be-Good). It freely mingles the comic and the serious, ranges over a considerable period of time, and changes place with bewildering rapidity. The numerous bloody deeds, such as beheadings, flayings, and murders, are all shown on stage. As one of the most popular plays of the day, *Cambises* reveals much about the tastes of that audience which made a public theatre feasible. It also illustrates the need for dramatists capable of unifying the diverse elements of the interlude.

While the interlude was modifying the Medieval tradition, interest in classical drama was growing in the schools and universities. As in other countries, the plays of Plautus, Terence, and Seneca had long been studied for nondramatic values, but it was not until the 16th century that the English universities and schools performed plays. Beginning at Cambridge about 1520, the practice was adopted at Eton about 1525, at St. Paul's about 1527, and at Oxford about 1535. Other important schools which presented plays include Westminster, Winchester, and the Merchant Taylors. Until about 1580, the plays were either Roman or close imitations. Many were performed in Latin, although some were given in English. The audiences were composed of students and invited guests.

Of the school dramas, two are outstanding: *Ralph Roister Doister* and *Gammer Gurton's Needle*. Both are written in English but follow closely the techniques of Roman comedy. *Ralph Roister Doister* (*c.* 1534–41) was written by Nicholas Udall (1505–56), Headmaster of Eton from 1534 to 1541, and at Westminster in 1555–56. Heavily indebted to Plautus' *Braggart Warrior,* Udall's play demonstrates a command of dramatic construction far in advance of its time. *Gammer Gurton's Needle* by "Mr. S.," acted at Cambridge between 1552 and 1563, fuses subject matter and characters similar to those of Medieval farce with the techniques of Roman comedy.

After 1580, interest at the schools shifted from classical drama to plays based on English history or imported from Italy. By 1600, the influence of the schools had waned. Although with few exceptions the school dramas were of slight value, they did familiarize students with plays of other times and places, and with effective dramatic techniques. When school-educated writers began to work for the professional troupes, they put their lessons to good use.

Closely allied with the schools and universities were the Inns of Court: Gray's Inn, Lincoln's Inn, the Inner Temple, and the Middle Temple. Principally places of residence and training for lawyers, the Inns admitted young men, primarily recent graduates of Oxford and Cambridge, for further education. These wealthy and aristocratic students were taught music, dancing, and other graces, which were practiced in part through the presentation of plays. Most performances came during the Christmas "revels," which extended over a period of four weeks, but the Inns also gave many elaborate entertainments to honor their members, or on such special occasions as a royal visit, or births and marriages in noble families. The audiences were aristocratic, well-educated, and abreast of the latest fashions in drama, both at home and abroad.

The first English tragedy, *Ferrex and Porrex, or Gorboduc,* written by two students, Thomas Sackville and Thomas Norton, was presented by the Inner Temple in 1561. The subject, chosen from the legendary history of England, was treated in a pseudo-Senecan manner. Although the play now seems weak, it made such a deep impression on educated men of the time that it had been printed five times by 1590. In comparison with earlier serious plays, it marked an enormous advance. The Inns also did much to popularize contemporary Italian drama. In 1566, Gray's Inn presented George Gascoigne and Francis Kinwelmarsh's *Jocasta,* a translation of Lodovico Dolce's *Giocasta* (1559), and Gascoigne's *The Supposes,* a translation of Ariosto's *I Suppositi*. Other plays given at the Inns show the contemporary interest in Italian novels and English history.

The University Wits

The interludes and the aristocratic drama began to merge in the 1580's largely because a group of educated men, commonly called "the University Wits," turned to writing for the public stage. Of these, the most important were Thomas Kyd, Christopher Marlowe, John Lyly, and Robert Greene.

Thomas Kyd (1558–94) is remembered primarily for *The Spanish Tragedy* (*c.* 1587), the most popular play of the 16th century. Its reception established the vogue for tragedy, previously given almost entirely for aristocratic audiences. In telling his sensational story of murder and revenge, Kyd places all of the important events on stage. But while the play ranges freely through time and place, it uses such Senecan devices as ghosts, the chorus, soliloquies, confidantes, and the division into five acts. Most important perhaps, Kyd demonstrates how to construct a well-articulated plot so as to create a rapid, clear, and absorbing action. Although lacking in depth of characterization or thought, *The Spanish Tragedy* is a remarkable advance over preceding plays.

Christopher Marlowe (1564–93), after a classical education at Cambridge, wrote a number of plays for the public theatre, including *Tamburlaine*, Parts 1 and 2 (1587–88), *Doctor Faustus* (*c.* 1588), and *Edward II* (*c.* 1592). The focus in Marlowe's plays is on the protagonists, around whom episodic stories are organized to illuminate their complex motivations. *Edward II* was especially important in the development of the chronicle play, for with it Marlowe demonstrated how to construct a coherent story out of diverse historical events by rearranging, telescoping, and altering them to create a sense of causal relationships. Above all, Marlowe was a great poet and did more than any of Shakespeare's predecessors to perfect blank verse as a medium of drama.

John Lyly (*c.* 1554–1606) wrote primarily for boys' companies catering to aristocratic audiences. His most characteristic works are pastoral comedies which mingle classical mythology with English subjects. His is a fairy-tale world in which troubles vanish at the wave of a magic wand. All but one of Lyly's plays were written in the carefully-balanced, refined, and somewhat artificial prose for which he is famous. Among his characteristic works are *Campaspe* (1584), *Endimion* (*c.* 1588), and *Love's Metamorphosis* (*c.* 1590). These delicate pastoral works established the tradition upon which Shakespeare built *As You Like It* and *A Midsummer Night's Dream*.

Robert Greene (1558–92) also wrote pastoral and romantic comedies, but his works are more varied than Lyly's, since he crowds many diverse elements into a single play. In his *Friar Bacon and Friar Bungay* (c. 1589) and *James IV* (c. 1591), stories of love and pastoral adventures are mingled with historical materials. Greene is especially noted for his charming and resourceful heroines, who, after wandering in disguise through a series of temptations, are rewarded in the fulfillment of their fondest desires.

By 1590, several dramatists who bridged the gap between the learned and popular audiences had appeared. Their successful blending of classical and Medieval devices with compelling stories drawn from many sources established the foundations upon which Shakespeare built.

Shakespeare and His Contemporaries

William Shakespeare (1564–1616) is probably the greatest dramatist of all time. As a playwright, actor, and shareholder in acting troupes and theatre buildings, he was directly involved in more aspects of the theatre than any other writer of his time.

Shakespeare is credited with 38 plays, some of which were written in part by others. Although difficult to date precisely, the plays have been given the following chronology by E. K. Chambers: *Henry VI*, Parts 2 and 3 (1590–91), *Henry VI*, Part 1 (1591–92), *Richard III* (1592–93), *Comedy of Errors* (1592–93), *Titus Andronicus* (1593–94), *Taming of the Shrew* (1593–94), *Two Gentlemen of Verona* (1594–95), *Love's Labour's Lost* (1594–95), *Romeo and Juliet* (1594–95), *Richard II* (1595–96), *A Midsummer Night's Dream* (1595–96), *King John* (1596–97), *The Merchant of Venice* (1596–97), *Henry IV*, Parts 1 and 2 (1597–98), *Much Ado About Nothing* (1598–99), *Henry V* (1598–99), *Julius Caesar* (1599–1600), *As You Like It* (1599–1600), *Twelfth Night* (1599–1600), *Hamlet* (1600–01), *The Merry Wives of Windsor* (1600–01), *Troilus and Cressida* (1601–02), *All's Well that Ends Well* (1602–03), *Measure for Measure* (1604–05), *Othello* (1604–05), *King Lear* (1605–06), *Macbeth* (1605–06), *Antony and Cleopatra* (1606–07), *Coriolanus* (1607–08), *Timon of Athens* (1607–08), *Pericles* (1608–09), *Cymbeline* (1609–10), *A Winter's Tale* (1610–11), *The Tempest* (1611–12), *Henry VIII* (1612–13), and *Two Noble Kinsmen* (1612–13).

It is impossible to do Shakespeare justice in a short space, for no playwright's work has been more fully studied and praised. Thus, only a few characteristics of his dramaturgy can be reviewed here. Shakespeare borrowed stories from many sources, but always reworked them until they became distinctively his own. Typically, a number of plots are interwoven, at first proceeding somewhat independently but coming closer together as the denouement approaches, so that the resolution of one leads to that of the others. He ranges freely through time and place, creating a sense of a fully developed life behind the scenes. His large casts are composed of well-rounded, complex characters, into each of whom Shakespeare seems to have entered sympathetically, with the result that all appear to be living individuals rather than mere stage figures. No playwright uses language so effectively. His poetic and figurative dialogue not only creates specific emotions, moods, and ideas, but endows them with the quality of being events representative of universal human experience. Shakespeare was by far the most comprehensive dramatist of his day. He attempted almost all of the popular dramatic types and subjects of the time, and in each instance gave them their most perfect expression.

In his own day, nevertheless, Shakespeare's critical reputation was lower than that of Jonson or Beaumont and Fletcher. His fame began to increase in the late 17th century, but did not reach its peak until the Romantic era. Like most of his contemporaries, Shakespeare gave little thought to preserving his plays and their survival is due in large part to the desire of Henry Condell and John Heminges to preserve the memory of their fellow-actor by publishing 36 of the plays in the First Folio of 1623.

After Shakespeare, Ben Jonson (1572–1637) is usually considered the finest Elizabethan playwright. An actor for a time, he began writing plays in the mid-1590's, and by 1600 was considered the leader of those authors who favored conscious artistry in writing. More than any other dramatist, he turned attention to the classical precepts and sought to temper the excesses of English dramaturgy through greater concern for regularity. He attracted the favorable attention of the court, for which he wrote more masques than any other dramatist, and his acceptance of a royal pension in 1616 made him the first "poet laureate" of England. His preparation of his collected works in 1616 marks an important turning point in the English attitude toward drama, which had previously been looked upon much as television scripts are today. In many ways, therefore, Jonson was the most influential writer of his time.

Of his plays, the comedies, especially *Every Man in His Humour* (1598), *Volpone* (1606), *The Alchemist* (1610), and *Bartholomew Fair* (1614), are now best known. The scope of these works is limited, for Jonson, concerned primarily with reforming human behavior, concentrated upon the foibles of contemporary types. Jonson's comedy is often described as realistic and "corrective" since the characters are supposedly based upon direct observation and are castigated for their shortcomings. Because Jonson does not arouse sympathy for his characters, the plays appear more harshly moralistic than Shakespeare's. Jonson is also credited with popularizing the "comedy of humours." Since classical times it had been assumed that there were four bodily "humours," blood, phlegm, and yellow and black bile, and that health depended upon a proper balance among them. In Elizabethan times, this medical concept was extended to human psychology. Jonson in particular attributed eccentricities of behavior to an imbalance of humours and created a wide range of character types based upon this scheme. Although the self-conscious use of humours waned after 1603, it continued as one basis for characterization until about 1700. Jonson also wrote two tragedies, *Sejanus* (1603) and *Catiline* (1611), both of which were among the most respected plays of the century (although they failed in the theatre).

Shakespeare and Jonson were surrounded by a host of less-celebrated figures. Among the more important of these were George Chapman, John Marston, Thomas Dekker, Thomas Heywood, Thomas Middleton, and Cyril Tourneur. George Chapman (*c.* 1560–1634) wrote plays between 1595 and 1613, concentrating at first on comedy in the vein of Jonson, and then on tragedy in the manner of Marlowe. In such plays as *May Day* (*c.* 1600) and *Sir Giles Goosecap* (1603), he mingled satirical and romantic elements with "humours" psychology to produce a moral comedy less biting than Jonson's. His most famous tragedies, *Bussy D'Ambois* (*c.* 1604) and *The Revenge of Bussy D'Ambois* (*c.* 1610), center around strong men of action who are doomed to defeat.

John Marston (1576–1634) wrote his plays between 1599 and 1609. His preoccupation with man's imperfections is reflected in such comedies as *Histriomastix* and *What You Will,* and such serious plays as *Antonio and Mellida* and *The Malcontent.* In all of his works he lashes out at a world in which men have substituted their own desires for the Christian virtues, but he is most successful dramatically in *The Malcontent,* in which the discontent of the central character motivates the attack more effectively than in the other plays. Marston's violent and original imagery influenced many of his successors.

Thomas Dekker (*c.* 1572–*c.* 1632) was generally content to please the popular audience. He wrote a vast number of plays, on many of which he collaborated with other leading dramatists of the day. Dekker tended to see humanity as essentially good and drew moral issues in broad strokes. His most famous work, *The Shoemaker's Holiday* (1599), depicts the unsophisticated world of apprentices and tradesmen, emphasizing only its pleasant aspects, in the story of an industrious tradesman who becomes Lord Mayor of London. Like many of Dekker's plays, it appears to much better advantage on the stage than on the printed page.

Thomas Heywood (*c.* 1574–1641), like Dekker essentially a popular dramatist, claimed to have had a hand in more than 220 plays. He was especially good at arousing the pathetic emotions, but seldom rose to those of tragedy. Today he is remembered primarily for *A Woman Killed with Kindness* (1603), which capitalized on the current vogue for plays about actual murders or other deeds of violence. Rather than basing his play on a specific case, however, Heywood captures the essence of the type in this story of a woman who, on the point of murdering her husband, repents and later dies of contrition because he treats her with kindness after her confession.

Thomas Middleton (1580–1627) covered a range of moods and subjects second only to Shakespeare's in diversity. Like Shakespeare, he could enter into all characters and situations, but unlike Shakespeare, Middleton was often lacking in strong feeling or original insight. His early works are comedies, such as *The Family of Love, Michaelmas Term,* and *A Chaste Maid in Cheapside.* The last is especially noteworthy for its inventiveness, verbal wit, and vivid presentation of London life. Middleton came late to tragedy. With William Rowley (c. 1558–1625) he wrote *The Changeling* (1622) and *The Spanish Gypsy* (1623); his other tragic works include *The Game of Chess* (1624) and *Women Beware Women* (1625). In his serious plays, Middleton tends to show the destruction of a potentially great person through gradual corruption, but since his characters do not progress significantly in self-discovery, the tragic effect is blunted.

Cyril Tourneur (1570/80–1625/26) is unique among the dramatists of his time in seemingly accepting the world as inherently evil. In his three major plays, *The Revenger's Tragedy* (c. 1606), *The Atheist's Tragedy* (1611), and *The Nobleman* (1611–12), he achieves a complete unity of mood through his handling of imagery, character, and events, but the overall effect is one of loathing and horror of life itself.

The plays of Shakespeare and his contemporaries display many technical similarities. Almost all use an early point of attack and follow a chronological organization, making little use of retrospection or of "messenger" scenes, since all important episodes are shown onstage. Since they were written for a nonillusionistic stage, they are essentially placeless, although the locale is always specified in the dialogue when it is important to the action. The major emphasis is placed upon the development of an action, in the pursuit of which time and place may shift rapidly. Tone also may vary frequently from serious to comic. Most of the plays are shaped in part by the belief in a moral order under which man is free to make his own choices, but for which he is ultimately responsible to forces greater than himself. Although less obviously than in Medieval drama, the characters are still caught in a struggle between good and evil. Much of this moral tone is established through poetic imagery, soliloquies and *sententiae,* although the lesser writers resort to the straightforward statement of moral lessons. In most plays, the short scene is the basic structural unit.

Jacobean and Caroline Dramatists

Critics are agreed that a significant change in English drama began around 1610. In part the shift was one of subject matter, for the preoccupation with penetrating questions about man's nature and achievements abated in favor of interesting stories told for their own sakes. Thrills and excitement took precedence over significant insights or complex characterization. As tragicomedy increased in popularity, happy endings were contrived for otherwise serious plays, while the pathetic or sensational tended to replace the more genuinely tragic emotions.

At the same time, technical skill increased. The playwrights handled exposition more adroitly, compressed the action into fewer episodes, built complications to startling climaxes, and alternated quiet with tumultuous scenes. As a result, the plays of this later period are more skillfully written than those before 1610, but are often lacking in profundity. Of the many dramatists who worked between 1610 and 1642 the most important are Francis Beaumont, John Fletcher, Philip Massinger, John Webster, John Ford, and James Shirley.

By far the most successful of the new dramatists was John Fletcher (1579–1625), whose name is inextricably joined with that of Francis Beaumont (c. 1584–1616) because of the collection of about 50 plays published in 1647 and 1679 attributed to their joint authorship. Although they actually collaborated on few of these works, they did produce between 1608 and 1613 such works as *The Maid's Tragedy, Philaster,* and *A King and No King,* which did much to establish the tone and techniques of later drama. In many ways, *A King and No King* is typical of new directions, for in it a brother and sister are caught up in an apparently incestuous love, a problem which is resolved by the discovery that they are not related.

After Beaumont's retirement, Fletcher continued to work alone and with others, including Shakespeare, Rowley, and Philip Massinger, and probably replaced Shakespeare as principal dramatist for the King's Men. He was one of the most successful playwrights of his day, for he knew how to shape everything toward dramatic effectiveness. His dialogue was especially admired by aristocratic theatregoers, for it epitomized the way they would like to speak. During the Restoration, Fletcher's plays were more frequently performed than those of either Shakespeare or Jonson. In later periods his *The Scornful Lady* (1616), *The Chances* (1617), *The Spanish Curate* (1622), *A Wife for a Month* (1624), and *Rule a Wife and Have a Wife* (1624) were especially popular.

Philip Massinger (1583–1639/40) often collaborated with Fletcher and revised many of Fletcher's plays after his death. Consequently, it is difficult to separate their work. After 1625, Massinger became chief dramatist to the King's Men, supplying about two plays a year. Of all his works, *A New Way to Pay Old Debts* (1621/22) is by far the best known, because the role of Sir Giles Overreach, running the gamut from darkest villainy to madness and death, was a favorite with later actors.

John Webster (c. 1580–c. 1630) wrote many plays in collaboration with Dekker, Heywood, Middleton, Rowley, and others, but is remembered chiefly for *The White Devil* (1609–12) and *The Duchess of Malfi* (1613/14),

165

the Jacobean tragedies that rank closest to Shakespeare's in modern estimation. Webster's plays are flawed, however, by the obscurity of the
action, which is always secondary to characterization. Because his protagonists are surrounded by corruption and do not themselves achieve any
deep new insights, Webster's plays lack that sense of affirmation found in
Shakespeare's tragedies. Thus, in spite of well-drawn characters and powerful dramatic poetry, they manage only to raise important issues without
suggesting any answers.

The plays of John Ford (1586–c. 1639) are usually cited as exempli-
fying the decadence which characterized Caroline drama, since 'Tis Pity
She's a Whore (1629–33) treats with apparent sympathy a love affair
between brother and sister. Other significant plays among the 17 attributed to Ford are The Lover's Melancholy (c. 1628) and The Broken
Heart (c. 1627–31). Scarcely noted in his own day, Ford is now admired for
his treatment of essentially good characters caught in abnormal situations.
His practice of illuminating evil by associating it with ordinary human
beings has made Ford of special interest to modern critics.

James Shirley's (1596–1666) work is often said to be a precursor of
Restoration drama. His comedies, Hyde Park (1632) and The Lady of
Pleasure (1635), depict the manners and fashions of aristocratic London
society. Shirley himself considered his best work to be The Cardinal
(1641), a tragedy similar to The Duchess of Maifi.

Many other writers might be cited, but these serve to show the trends
toward greater polish and sophistication, and the decline in profundity.
With the closing of the theatres in 1642, further developments were postponed. England was never again to attain the heights reached between 1585
and 1642.

Government Regulation of the Theatre

The development of playwriting as a profession was made possible by
the emergence of a public theatre which constantly required new plays. In
turn, the stability of the theatre depended upon governmental regulations.
Since the attitude of the crown was always more favorable to professional
actors than was that of local governments, the growth of the theatre
paralleled the central government's assumption of authority over performances.

When Elizabeth came to the throne in 1558, any gentleman could
maintain a troupe of actors. Since they were usually permitted to tour when
not needed at home, actors were not always closely supervised and many
companies had no legal status, depending rather upon the chaotic condi-

tions to conceal their false claims to noble patronage. By performing partisan plays, the troupes had also aggravated the religious controversies which had shaken England since Henry VIII's break with Rome. Elizabeth took a number of steps to end the religious and political divisions. In 1559 she banned the performance of unlicensed works, forbade plays on religious or political subjects, and made local officials responsible for all public performances in their towns.

Since these regulations were not entirely effective, new measures were taken in the 1570's. The religious cycles, which had persisted in a few places, were now systematically suppressed. As a result, the secular drama of the professional troupes was soon the only theatrical entertainment available to the general public. At the same time, the actors were brought under closer supervision. In 1572, it was declared illegal for any nobleman below the rank of baron to maintain a troupe. Other companies could perform by obtaining a license from two Justices of the Peace, but since this license was good only in the locality where the Justices resided, a new license had to be secured in each town if the troupes toured. On the other hand, the law specifically absolved licensed actors from charges of vagabondage, the indictment which had previously been used against them. The overall effect of the law was to reduce the number of troupes but to extend firm legal sanctions to licensed companies.

The authority of the crown was extended much further in 1574 when the Master of Revels, an official of the royal household, was made the licenser of all plays and acting companies. Technically, this move gave the crown complete control over the theatre, and any troupe licensed by it had a clear legal right to perform anywhere in the kingdom. Many local officials, however, believed that the crown was usurping authority which should reside with them, since they were responsible for health, conduct, and morals in their communities. Consequently, during the next 30 years local governments found many ways of evading the licenses held by actors. The most usual reasons used in refusing permission to perform were the danger of plague, the rowdiness of crowds, and the drawing of persons from work or religious services. Even those towns which had supported the religious cycles resisted professional performers, and without crown support, actors would have had little chance of survival.

The crown had gained sufficient power by 1604 that Parliament in that year took away the right of noblemen to maintain troupes. After this time, all companies were licensed to members of the royal family. The new patents also specified the theatres in which troupes were to play, a provision which London officials seem to have accepted. Until 1608 all of the permanent theatres of London were outside the city limits, but after the crown assumed the right to specify playing places, companies began to move into the city, where, by 1642, at least five theatre buildings had been erected. The act of 1604 also deprived all provincial troupes of legal status. Although some continued for a time, the overall effect was to concentrate the theatre in London, except during times of plague, when the troupes made provincial tours.

The supervision of the theatre was delegated to the Master of Revels, who collected such handsome fees for his services that the office became a coveted one. Before the theatres were closed in 1642, he was receiving two pounds for each play licensed, besides three pounds a month and two annual benefit performances from each theatre. Sir Henry Herbert estimated that his income from this office was 4000 pounds per year, an enormous sum for the time.

Acting Troupes

Although there were many acting troupes in England before the 1570's, little is known of them. Between 1558 and 1574 at least 20 different troupes played at court. In these early years the actors were probably paid a fixed yearly sum by their patrons and allowed to give public performances to earn additional money. Since the number of days upon which they could play varied with the place and season of the year, the actors led an uncertain existence. During the 1570's, with the new governmental decrees, conditions became more favorable. The legal right to perform daily under crown sanction probably stimulated the building of permanent theatres and the assembling of larger companies.

The first important troupe was the Earl of Leicester's Men, licensed in 1574 under the leadership of James Burbage (1530–97), the builder of the first theatre. In 1583, the Master of Revels chose from the existing troupes the 12 best actors to form the Queen's Men, the leading company until 1593. At the end of the plague of 1592–93, two companies emerged as dominant: the Lord Admiral's Men, under the leadership of Edward Alleyn and with the financial backing of Philip Henslowe; and the Lord Chamberlain's Men, a cooperative venture of the Burbage family and the leading actors of the company. When James I came to the throne, the latter company was chosen to become the King's Men, a title which it retained until 1642. Between 1604 and 1611 there were three adult troupes, and after that time four. Occasionally these were reconstituted or amalgamated, but all remained under the patronage of some member of the royal family. The more important troupes were Queen Anne's Men (1603–19), Prince Henry's Men (1603–12), Palsgrave's Men (1612–31), Prince Charles' Men (1631–42), Lady Elizabeth's Men (1611–32), and Queen Henrietta's Men (1625–42).

Royal patronage increased in other ways after 1603. Elizabeth had seen an average of about five professional productions each year, for which she paid a standard fee of ten pounds. Although the Stuart kings paid the same basic fee, James I saw an average of 17 and Charles I of 25 productions each year. Each actor in the royal companies was paid a yearly retaining fee of five pounds and given allowances for food, light, and fuel. Occasionally the troupes were also given additional sums to buy new costumes or to tide them over during times when playing was impossible. The actors were called upon to help out with the court masques and to perform on special state occasions. Most court performances by the professional troupes were given in the evening so as not to interfere with public performances. Thus, the troupes benefited considerably from their attachments to the royal household. Since the plays given at court were usually those played for the general public, there was not that sharp division between the court and public theatres which characterized the Italian stage. On the other hand, some critics have suggested that catering to court tastes led to the decline of English drama.

Most of the acting companies in the years between 1558 and 1642 were organized on the sharing plan, under which financial risks and profits were divided among the members. The number of sharers varied, for not all actors were shareholders. Originally the sharing system was probably used as a means of raising capital, but it later became a way of rewarding valuable members of the company and insuring their continued service by including them in the management. Additional incentives were offered in some companies by making actors "householders," or part owners of the theatre building. Generous payments were also made to shareholders upon retirement after a specified period of service.

It is difficult to estimate the income of a sharing actor, for financial practices were complex. After each performance, the shareholders divided the money left after meeting all expenses, which included payments to authors, "hired men," and the fund out of which the "common stock" of costumes, properties, and other materials was purchased. In a court suit of 1635, one witness stated that shareholders in the King's Men earned about 180 pounds annually, although the actors themselves estimated their earnings at 50 pounds. Even the latter figure, however, is about twice the amount earned by skilled workers. Undoubtedly the King's Men was the most affluent company, but so long as performances were not interrupted by forced closures, the major actors in all companies were probably well off.

The shareholders formed a self-governing, democratic body, selecting and producing the plays given by the company. Each shareholder probably had some specific responsibility, such as business management, supervising properties or costumes, or writing plays.

More than half the members of each troupe were "hired men" employed under a two-year contract at a salary equivalent to that earned by a skilled laborer. In addition to acting, the hired men also served as stage managers, wardrobe keepers, prompters, and musicians, although they might also be required to appear on stage at times. The size of companies ranged from about 10 to 25 persons; consequently, double casting was essential to fill all the roles.

The company was further augmented by boys apprenticed to well-established adult actors. It is normally assumed that they played all of the women's roles, although this is by no means certain. Older women, especially the comic ones, may have been played by men. Little is known about the apprentices. The age of beginning has been estimated as from six to fourteen years, and that of termination from 18 to 21. The apprentices lived with their masters, who trained, fed, and clothed them. The masters were paid for their services by the company. Some of the apprentices went on to become adult actors, but many followed other professions upon reaching maturity.

Most troupes sought to acquire a permanent home, and after 1603 most succeeded in doing so. Before that time and during forced closures, many troupes had to tour. Troupes often went bankrupt during closures, or survived only by selling their stock of plays or mortgaging their wardrobes.

Touring entailed many problems, for outside of London there were no permanent theatres. Thus, though a troupe might have a license to perform, it could be denied the right to play on the grounds that there was no suitable place, that the danger of plague was too great, or for other reasons. Upon arriving in a town, a company presented its credentials to the mayor, who usually requested a performance before the council and other important persons. If they were pleased, they rewarded the actors with a payment out of the council's funds and authorized additional public performances. Often these were given in the city hall, but if refused its use, the troupe might perform in an inn or some other place. In some cities actors were welcomed, but in others they were paid not to perform. A number of troupes went to the continent during closures, and it is from these English troupes that the professional theatre in Germany descended.

Since companies both in and out of London changed their bills daily, they needed a sizable repertory. Plays were retained as long as they drew audiences and might be revised when they declined in popularity. The demand for new works made companies seek liaisons with dependable dramatists, many of whom worked under contract. Until about 1603 the average payment for a play was six pounds, but by 1613 the price had risen to ten or twelve pounds. After about 1610, in addition to his fee, a playwright was often given all of the receipts beyond a certain amount at the second performance. By the 1630's, a few writers were being paid a weekly salary plus one benefit performance for each play he supplied the company.

Once the playwright's fees had been paid, the play belonged to the troupe. Since there were no copyright laws, however, companies had no means of maintaining exclusive performance rights except by keeping plays out of the hands of others. The more popular works were often pirated by printers, and troupes sometimes sold publication rights during times of financial stress.

Every play had to be submitted to the Master of Revels for licensing before performance. The principal result was the prohibition of passages thought to be morally or politically objectionable. The company seems to have had only one copy of the play. In it, the "prompt book," were made all of the notes relating to performance: cues for sound, music, and special effects; entrances and exits; notations about properties. Actors were merely given "sides," which included only their own lines and cues.

Probably one of the shareholders rehearsed each play with the aid of the author, whose attendance was required, although his responsibilities are unclear. As a rule, a playwright knew in advance for which troupe he was writing and could adapt his work to the size of the company and to the skills of individual actors.

The prompter ("bookholder" or "bookkeeper") was responsible for running performances, as well as for making up the actors' sides and lists of the necessary properties, costumes, and music. During performances a "plot," or skeletal outline of the action (indicating entrances, exits, properties, music, the names of players to be called, and similar information) was hung up backstage for quick reference. Seven of these plots have survived.

Each company had elaborate rules of conduct and fines for their infringement. For example, in 1614 Lady Elizabeth's Men agreed upon this schedule of fines: one shilling for lateness to rehearsals; three shillings for lateness to performance; ten shillings for being intoxicated during a performance; twenty shillings for missing a performance; and forty pounds for taking company property.

The names of many actors between 1558 and 1642 are known, but few performers achieved lasting renown. Richard Tarleton (? –1588), a member of the Queen's Men and an accomplished comic and musical performer, was the first English actor to win a wide following. The first great actor was Edward Alleyn (1566–1626), who created Marlowe's Faustus, Tamburlaine, and Barabbas, and Kyd's Heironimo. He gave up acting about 1604, but continued in management with his father-in-law, Philip Henslowe. Other members of the Admiral's Men were John Singer, Richard Jones, Thomas Towne, Martin Slater, Edward Juby, Thomas Downton, and Samuel Rowley.

The members of the Lord Chamberlain's Men gained more lasting fame because Shakespeare was one of their fellow players. The leading performer was Richard Burbage (*c.* 1567–1619), who created such roles as Richard III, Hamlet, Lear, and Othello, and was generally acknowledged the greatest actor of his age. Other members of the company included William Kempe (? –*c.* 1603), noted for his low comedy acting and jigs; Augustine Philips (? –1605); Henry Condell (? –1627); John Heminges (1556–1630), the business manager; William Sly (? –1608); Thomas Pope (? –1604); Robert Armin (*c.* 1568–1615), a celebrated clown; John Lowin (*c.* 1567–*c.* 1659), noted for his Falstaff and Henry VIII; Joseph Taylor (*c.* 1585–1652), who replaced Burbage when he died in 1619; and Nathan Field (1587–1620), considered by many as second only to Burbage.

In addition to the adult companies, there were a number of children's troupes. In the 16th century these were made up almost entirely of choir boys at court chapels or cathedrals. The boys were given a good education, and it was under the guise of training that masters exploited their students' talents by staging plays and charging admission. Following a scandal in the early 17th century, the use of choir boys declined, although other school boys continued in the companies. The children's companies were especially popular from about 1576 to 1584, and from 1600 to about 1610. By far the best of these troupes was the Chapel Boys (after 1604, the Queen's Revels) between 1600 and 1608, although they continued until about 1617. The finest dramatists of the day, with the exception of Shakespeare, wrote for this company, which catered to a more educated and sophisticated audience than did the adult troupes. The decline of children's companies may be explained in part by the adult troupes' acquisition of both theatres and plays which had formerly been associated with the boys.

The acting style of the Elizabethan performer can only be guessed at. Some scholars have labeled it "formal" and others "realistic." Some of the conditions which suggest a "formal" style are the performance of female roles by male actors; the nonrealistic style of the plays; the conventionalized stage background; and the large repertory, which would have made detailed characterizations difficult. Arguments for a relatively realistic style include Shakespeare's "advice to the players" in *Hamlet;* contemporary references to the convincing characterizations given by such actors as Burbage; the emphasis upon contemporary life and manners in the comedies; the truthfulness of human psychology portrayed in the serious plays; and the closeness of audience to actors during performances. Judging by contemporary accounts, many actors moved audiences with the power and "truth" of their playing, but this tells little about their style, for what is considered "truth in acting" varies markedly from one period to another. The most that one can say is that the better actors adapted well to contemporary conceptions of artistic truth.

The Public Theatres

In 1576 the first permanent theatres in England were opened. One, The Theatre, was an open-air structure designed for a general public; the other, the first Blackfriars, was remodeled from rooms in a former monastery for an aristocratic audience. It is customary to call structures of the first type "public," and those of the second "private" theatres. Both types were in use until 1642, and after 1610 the same companies might use both according to the time of the year. Nevertheless, they will be discussed separately.

By the 1570's there were two well-established traditions in staging: the outdoor and the indoor. The religious cycles, street pageants, tournaments, and morality plays had been given out-of-doors, and the companies attached to noble houses often played outside when on tour. On the other hand, mummings, disguisings, interludes, and special entertainments were normally given indoors, and the touring players often performed in town halls, manor houses, or inns. Consequently, there were many precedents upon which the Elizabethan troupes could draw when building permanent theatres.

The unroofed public theatres are usually traced from two sources, innyards and gaming arenas. It is certain that many troupes played in inns both before and after permanent theatres were built, and that at least six inns in London were used as theatres. The usual reconstructions of innyard theatres show a booth-like stage set up at one side of a courtyard, while raised galleries provide seating and the ground level serves as standing room. The permanent structures are then said to be a formalization of this arrangement. Recently a few scholars have questioned the widespread use of innyards for playing, arguing that troupes normally played indoors. The principal arguments for indoor playing are that the use of the yards would have seriously disrupted the inn's normal activities, and that actors chose to play inside whenever they could. Certainly, all of the London inns known to have been used by actors were "carrier" inns (that is, they catered to drivers of wagons carrying goods to and from London). If wagons arrived at irregular intervals, closing off the yard would probably have interfered with this business. On the other hand, admission fees and the increase in tavern sales may have been sufficiently profitable that the innkeeper abandoned the carrier trade or forbade drivers to arrive during playing hours. Although many of the performances at inns may have been indoors, especially

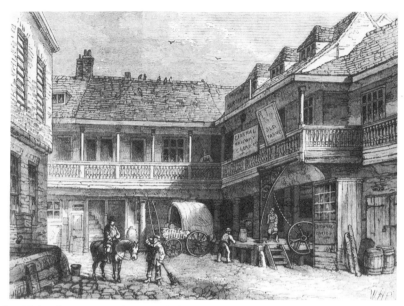

THE YARD of the Tabard Inn, London. This sketch was made just before the inn was destroyed in the 19th century. Supposedly the yard had remained unchanged since the time of Elizabeth I. Although the Tabard was probably not used for plays, it illustrates the arrangement of the innyard in Elizabethan times. [From Thornbury, *Old and New London*]

during the winter months, some were certainly outdoors and could well have supplied an example for the permanent structures.

The arenas used for bull or bear baiting and wrestling or fencing have also been cited as possible prototypes for the unroofed structures. Some scholars have argued that the theatres were formed merely by setting up a removable booth stage in an arena which could be used for other purposes when not needed for plays. Such an argument depends upon the belief that baiting rings with multileveled galleries for spectators existed before 1576. That such was the case, however, is open to considerable doubt, for much of the evidence upon which this view rested is now known to have been forged, while a close examination of the map-views of London will show that the baiting rings depicted in them are corral-like enclosures, rather than galleried structures. Thus, it is questionable that The Theatre was influenced by baiting or fencing rings.

Another possible source, less frequently cited, are the illustrations published in editions of Terence's works. Some of these show open-air, galleried, circular structures labeled *"Theatrum."* Since the troupes were in the service of aristocratic and educated patrons, these illustrations may have come to their attention. Perhaps this explains why Burbage called his

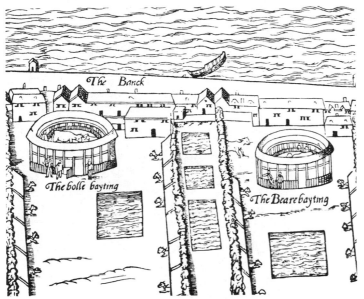

A PORTION of the Agas map of London (the sketches were made between 1569 and 1590 but not printed until 1631). Note that the bull- and bear-baiting rings appear to be more nearly corrals than three-tiered galleried structures.

building The Theatre, a term not in common use at that time and certainly not normally applied to an amphitheatrical or round structure such as The Theatre supposedly was.

The stage itself is thought to have been derived from such diverse sources as the pageant wagons and fixed platforms of the religious plays, and the booth stages of traveling players. The facade seems to have much in common with the "screen" found in manor halls. Thus, the possible influences on the public theatres are numerous, but no direct connection with any can be established.

The first permanent theatre was built by James Burbage in 1576 in Shoreditch, just outside the northern limits of London. It is usually assumed that the site was chosen to escape the London authorities, who frequently forbade performances within the city. The selection may also have been influenced by the lack of available land in the city and the fact that Shoreditch was a popular recreational area. Burbage's decision to build a permanent theatre was revolutionary and indicates a faith which was amply justified.

His success prompted others to follow his example, and at least nine public playhouses, not counting remodelings and reconstructions, were built before 1642: The Theatre (1576–97), The Curtain (1577–c. 1627), Newington Butts (c. 1579–c. 1599), The Rose (1587–c. 1606), The Swan

THE THEATRE as depicted in the edition of Terence's plays printed at Lyons in 1493. Note its several sides, galleries, and the label "Theatrum." A possible source for Burbage's The Theatre (1576).

(c. 1595–c. 1632), The Globe (1599–1613, 1614–44), The Fortune (1600–21, 1621–61), The Red Bull (1605–63), and The Hope (1613–17). All were built outside the city limits, either in the northern suburbs or on the south bank of the Thames River. All but one was constructed between 1576 and 1605, and thus they predate the crown's assumption of the right to specify playing places for troupes and the adult companies' practice of acquiring "private" theatres. After 1610 they came to be used principally as summer houses, secondary in importance to the private theatres used during the winter months. The most important of the public theatres were The Theatre and The Globe (because of their use by Shakespeare's company), and The Rose and The Fortune (operated by Edward Alleyn and Philip Henslowe).

Undoubtedly The Globe and The Fortune marked a considerable advance in design over The Theatre and The Rose. Some scholars have argued that all theatres prior to the Globe were multi-purpose structures with removable stages, because the theatre was too precarious a venture to justify buildings not easily adaptable to other uses. They suggest that the Globe, with its permanent stage, established the pattern adopted by subsequent theatres. Although it is impossible to establish that such a change occurred, it does seem likely that the public theatres were not uniform in design. Nevertheless, it is helpful to describe, insofar as possible, the typical features of the public playhouses.

Although the theatres varied in shape (circular, octagonal, square), the purpose was unvaried: to surround a playing area in such a way as to accommodate a large number of spectators. Most theatres had three-roofed galleries, one above the other, surrounding the yard. At least some parts of one gallery were divided into private boxes or "Lords' rooms." The other galleries, equipped with benches for seats, were undivided. The galleries enclosed a large open area, or "yard." This was probably paved and may have sloped toward the stage to aid viewing.

The overall size of the buildings probably varied. The dimensions of only one theatre, The Fortune, are known. It was 80 feet square on the outside, while the yard was 55 feet square. Since the stage extended well into the yard in all theatres, no spectator was far removed from the performers. At The Fortune the stage was 27½ feet deep by 43 feet wide. This would have left an additional 27½ feet in front of the platform, but only six feet on either side for spectators standing in the yard. The size and shape of the stage may have differed in other theatres, especially in those that were round or octagonal, but it is usually assumed that the platform jutted well into the yard and was viewed from three sides. A few scholars have argued that the galleries extended completely around the structure and that the action, therefore, was seen from four sides. The stage was raised four to six feet to improve the view for standing spectators and provide understage space for trapdoors and special effects.

The stage in most, perhaps all, theatres was sheltered by a roof, commonly called "the shadow" or "the heavens," which served two purposes: protection from the weather and housing for machinery and special effects. From it, thrones and other properties were lowered, and within its attic space such sound effects as thunder, alarum bells, and cannonades were operated. In some instances, the sky, sun, moon, and signs of the zodiac were painted on the underside of the "heavens." In most theatres the stage roof was supported by two posts which rose from the front of the platform, but at The Hope the "heavens" were cantilevered so that the stage could be removed.

The rear of the stage was bounded by a multileveled facade. On the stage level, two large doors served as entrances and as passageways through which heavy properties and set pieces could be moved. These doors were probably the most essential part of the background because of their frequent and varied use. Changes of place were often indicated by the exit of characters through one door, followed by an entry through the other. Usually the doors were unlocalized, but at times they were used to represent houses, gates, castles, or other structures. There was also a space for discoveries on this level. While the doors may have served this function, it is more usual to locate the "discovery" space between the doors. J. C. Adams has called this area the "inner below" or "study," and has depicted it as a miniature proscenium stage with a front curtain. He argues that it was used in staging interior scenes and that heavy properties were set there and then revealed by drawing the curtain. This view has been challenged by C. Walter Hodges and others. Hodges suggests that the rear stage was a "pavilion," jutting forward rather than receding into the facade. He argues that the restricted sightlines of Adams' inner stage would make it impractical, whereas the pavilion would be open on three sides. George Reynolds has suggested that the discovery space may have been raised a few steps above the main stage. Such an arrangement would solve the difficulties raised by those scripts which require characters to go from one level to another in full view of the audience, even though there seems to have been no visible stairway connecting the second story with the main stage.

Scholars also disagree about the permanency of the discovery space. Adams would make it an architectural feature of the building, while Hodges and others depict it as removable. The latter theory has been adopted in part because the only surviving picture of a public theatre, a sketch made of The Swan in 1596, shows a blank space between the two doors of the facade. Furthermore, Reynolds insists that some plays require additional discovery spaces and suggests that structures similar to Medieval mansions may have been erected on the stage as required.

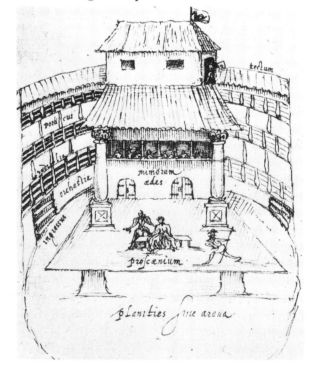

THE INTERIOR VIEW of The Swan in 1596. This is the only surviving contemporary pictorial evidence concerning theatre architecture. The original drawing by Johannes de Witt has not survived. This is a copy made by Arend van Buchell. [From Bapst's *Essai sur l'Histoire du Théâtre*, (1893)]

178

Another controversy centers around the use of the discovery space. Adams argues that numerous scenes were performed in it and that most large properties were set there. Other scholars believe that the discovery space was used only to locate scenes, after which most of the action took place on the main stage. According to this view, the discovery space would need only to be large enough to conceal such articles as a bed or table and chairs. Reynolds and Bernard Beckerman have shown that most properties were carried on stage in full view of the audience and have suggested that the discovery space was only rarely used.

Thus, historians agree that there was a discovery space in the public theatres, and most would place it between the two doors. On the other hand, they disagree about its size and use. The available evidence is insufficient for settling the controversy.

Similarly, scholars agree that there was a playing area on the second level of the facade, but disagree about its features. Almost all agree in placing openings above the two stage doors. These were allegedly used as windows, balconies, battlements, or other high places. Between these was a larger space. Adams depicts a narrow railed area at its front, called the "tarras," and back of it a curtained area, the "inner above," corresponding to the "inner below." Hodges argues that the upper stage was the top of a pavilion. The drawing of The Swan merely shows an open gallery.

Historians agree that some scenes were played on the second level, but disagree about the number and type. One popular theory about Elizabethan staging suggests a regular alternation of scenes between main stage, rear stage, and upper stage. Others, however, hold that practically all scenes were played on the main stage, other areas being used only rarely. These conflicting views are reflected in all attempts to reconstruct the upper stage, since the facilities shown there are those thought essential for staging particular kinds of scenes.

The stage facade may also have had a third level, although evidence to establish it is sketchy. Usually called the "musicians' gallery" because of its supposed use, it may have served occasionally for scenes requiring very high places. Reconstructions of the backstage area, or "tiring house," differ widely in the amount of space they reserve for production facilities. In some, barely more than a corridor is shown offstage, and in virtually none are allowances made for housing wardrobes, furniture, properties, and other equipment. Some companies owned adjoining structures which may have been used for storage and dressing rooms. In general, however, historians have devoted little attention to the spaces required for production.

It has been usual to depict the public theatres as somewhat crude, half-timbered structures, although all contemporary accounts speak of them as costly and sumptuous. DeWitt, describing The Swan in 1596, reports that the columns supporting the stage roof were painted to resemble marble. Thus, though the structures were made primarily of wood and plaster, they

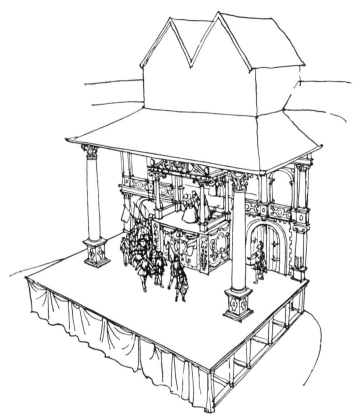

C. W. HODGES' RECONSTRUCTION of the Elizabethan stage
showing a pavilion at the rear. From Hodges' *The Globe
Restored* [Courtesy Mr. Hodges]

may have been painted to simulate other materials. It seems likely that they
became more elaborate as the troupes became more prosperous. The later
description of Elizabethan theatres as crude were written by admirers of the
Italianate stage, to whom the neglect of illusionism was a sign of naiveté
and simplicity.

Since few of the acting companies had sufficient capital to build their
own theatres, most borrowed money or rented theatres from speculators.
When Burbage built The Theatre, he borrowed money from John Brayne,
a grocer who had earlier invested in a playhouse at the Red Lion Inn.
Other speculators included Francis Langley, builder of The Swan, and
Aaron Holland, chief investor in The Red Bull. Most important and
successful of all, however, was Philip Henslowe, builder of The Rose, The
Fortune, and The Hope. Henslowe not only built theatres, but often
loaned money to the companies who played in them, and his surviving
records of financial transactions contain the principal evidence about the

J. C. ADAM'S RECONSTRUCTION of The Globe. [Courtesy Folger Library]

operation of Elizabethan theatres. The pattern of ownership began to change in 1598, when the Burbages made Shakespeare and four other actors part owners of The Globe. The success of this arrangement led to its adoption at The Curtain, The Fortune, The Red Bull, and at some private theatres.

The owners, or "householders," were responsible for the upkeep of the building, payment of the rent on the land occupied by the building, and the salaries of the men who collected entrance fees. Although arrangements may have varied from one theatre to another, The Globe's division of receipts is usually taken as typical: the actors received all admissions to the yard, while gallery fees were divided evenly between the actors and the householders. Additional money came from renting the theatre to amateur actors, fencers, tumblers, and miscellaneous entertainers, and from the sale of various articles in the auditorium during performances. A major source of revenue for most theatres was a taphouse which dispensed beer, ale, and wine. The householders, and sometimes the actors, shared this additional income.

The Private Theatres

Although historians have usually treated the public theatres as typical, it is likely that more performances were given indoors than outdoors in the years between 1558 and 1642. Many of the indoor productions were staged in manor houses, town halls, inns, or at court, but it is those at "private" theatres which are of major interest.

Many explanations have been offered for applying the term "private" to theatres open to the public. None is entirely satisfactory, but deviations from conditions at the public theatres help to clarify the usage: the theatres were roofed; they accommodated less than one-half as many spectators; they charged considerably higher admission; they provided seats for all spectators; and they were lighted by candles. Other distinctions, based on location and troupes, may be of even greater importance. All of the early private theatres were located in the "liberties" of London. These areas—the principal ones were Blackfriars and Whitefriars—had originally belonged to monastic orders, but had been confiscated by the crown when the orders were dissolved in 1539. Although much of the property was later ceded to private individuals, the crown retained jurisdiction over the areas until 1608. Thus, while surrounded by the city of London, the liberties were not under its control. Furthermore, within the liberties the first theatres were set up in private dwellings, which were exempted from injunctions against playing. Perhaps most important of all, until 1608 the private theatres were used by children, who were technically amateurs and free from the stigma attached to professional actors. The most sophisticated playwrights, such as Lyly, Jonson, Chapman, and Marston, preferred to write for the boys' companies. Generally, then, the private theatres were more refined, exclusive, and expensive than their outdoor counterparts.

The first private theatre, the first Blackfriars, was erected in 1576, the same year in which The Theatre was built. At that time the boys' companies were still preferred by courtly and aristocratic audiences, perhaps because the adult companies had not yet attracted outstanding dramatists. Before 1576 the boys had usually given only one or two performances of each play; it was probably the desire to extend the runs to tap the relatively large audience of sophisticated Londoners that the Blackfriars theatre was built.

Since Blackfriars was one of the most fashionable residential areas, it was a logical choice for Richard Farrant, choirmaster of the Chapel Royal at Windsor, when he planned a theatre. In leasing the property, he stated that it would be used in teaching the children prior to their appearances before the Queen; no mention was made of public performances. Farrant's concealment of his real intentions led to a series of lawsuits which put an end to the theatre in 1584. By that time, a number of different combinations of boys from various choir schools had performed there under a series of managements, Farrant having died in 1580. Although boys' companies continued to play elsewhere, no other "private" theatre existed until 1596.

By far the most important private theatre was the second Blackfriars, built in 1596 by James Burbage, whose lease on the site of The Theatre was due to expire in 1597. Though Burbage converted the newly acquired buildings into a playhouse, the residents of Blackfriars secured an injunction against its use by an adult company. When Burbage died in 1597, he willed the Blackfriars to his son Richard, who later built The Globe. In 1600, Burbage leased the Blackfriars for 21 years to Henry Evans, who, in alliance with the master of the Chapel Royal, opened the theatre with a boys' company. In 1604, after the accession of James I, this troupe was given the title "Children of the Revels of the Queen." Between 1600 and 1608, the Blackfriars troupe was one of the most popular and successful in London, seriously challenging the adult companies. The willingness of the residents of Blackfriars to accept a boys' company after rejecting an adult group says much about the disparity in attitude toward them.

In spite of their popularity, the Children of the Revels were frequently in trouble, most often for performing plays considered politically offensive. James I ordered the troupe disbanded in 1608, as a result of which Burbage regained possession of Blackfriars.

When the King's displeasure with the boys cooled, they were permitted to resume performances. They now moved into a theatre which had been erected in Whitefriars about 1606 for another boys' company. They played there until 1614, and then moved into a new theatre in Blackfriars, Porter's Hall, even though they had been forbidden to do so. Probably because of this defiance, the troupe was disbanded in 1617, and no more boys' companies were seen in London until 1637–42, when Christopher and William Beeston ran a training company for youngsters usually referred to as Beeston's Boys.

The private theatres were used exclusively by boys until 1610. After this time, the popularity of the children faded and the private theatres passed into the hands of the adult troupes. The first important change came with Burbage's reassumption of the Blackfriars lease in 1608. James I now authorized the King's Men to play there, although due to plague they did not begin until 1610. Their success led Christopher Beeston in 1616 to convert a cockpit into a private theatre. Burned shortly afterward, it was rebuilt as The Phoenix. Occupied successively by Queen Anne's Men, the Prince's Men, Lady Elizabeth's Men, Queen Henrietta's Men, and Beeston's Boys, it continued in use until the Restoration. The Salisbury Court Theatre, built in 1629, was used by the King's Revels, Prince Charles' Men, and the Queen's Men. Altogether, at least six private theatres were built between 1576 and 1642.

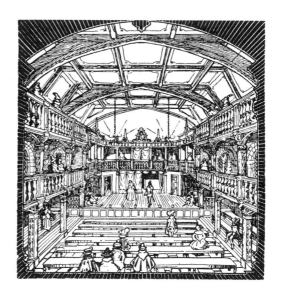

A RECONSTRUCTION of the interior of the Second Blackfriar's Theatre. Drawing by J. H. Farrar. [Courtesy the Architect to the Greater London Council]

The private theatres eventually became the primary homes of the adult troupes. The King's Men played from mid-October to mid-May at the Blackfriars, and for the remaining five months at the Globe. Since the Blackfriars brought the company about two and one-half times more income at each performance than The Globe, it is not surprising that the company preferred playing at the indoor theatre. As other private theatres were built, the public playhouses declined in importance, although they were still regularly used in summer.

There is even less evidence about the features of the private than of the public theatres. In terms of prestige and length of service, the second Blackfriars is by far the most important and has been the subject of most extensive inquiry. Irwin Smith's *Shakespeare's Blackfriars Playhouse*, the most complete study of a private theatre, locates the second Blackfriars in a room measuring 101 feet by 46 feet, of which he assigns 35 feet to the tiring house, leaving for the auditorium and stage a space measuring 66 by 46 feet. Other scholars have thought the last dimensions, mentioned in a contemporary law suit, to be those of the entire theatre.

It is certain that the theatre had galleries, the estimated number varying from one to three, that there were some private boxes which could be locked, and that there were seats in the pit. Using the eye level of a person seated in the pit, Smith has estimated the height of the stage at three feet. His reconstruction of the stage facade is derived from J. C. Adams' study of The Globe and is open to the same objections. Although they may differ about details, most scholars agree that the stage background in the private theatres was similar in all important respects to that of the public playhouses.

The estimated dimensions of the main stage at the Blackfriars range from 20 by 41 feet to 25 by 46 feet. Thus, the measurements were probably only slightly smaller than those of The Fortune (27½ by 43 feet). Most scholars, however, assume that, with the exception of those seated on the stage, all spectators viewed the action from the front. Neverthless, the stage was still open, having neither a proscenium nor a front curtain. Essentially, then, the private theatres differed little from the public in their basic features. The conventions of staging were probably much the same in both, since companies moved freely from one to the other.

Scenery, Properties, and Special Effects

Although it is usually assumed that the stage facade provided the background for all plays, scenic practices are by no means clear. The principal sources of information are the play scripts, the accounts of the Master of Revels, and Henslowe's papers.

A number of scholars have analyzed the plays for scenic requirements, but their results conflict because they begin with different premises. One group assumes that the players relied primarily upon "spoken decor," that places are mentioned only when dramatically relevant and because they are not physically represented. Thus, the imaginary decor suggested by dialogue is said to substitute for real scenery. Another group assumes that the audience would expect things described by the dialogue to be suggested by some scenic piece. Probably neither of these views is correct, for Reynolds' study of staging at The Red Bull concludes that the troupes were very inconsistent in their practices, varying according to available means rather than following a consistent theory. Nevertheless, all scholars agree that if scenic devices were used, they resembled Medieval mansions more than Italian illusionistic settings.

Reynolds states that the following items were at times represented on stage: trees, thrones, beds, scaffolds, barriers and lists, wells and springs, altars, prison bars, tombs, racks, tents, arbors, caves, tables, chairs, and benches. An inventory of 1598 preserved in Henslowe's papers lists similar articles: three trees, three rocks (two of which are "mossy banks"), two tombs, two steeples with bells, a Hell-mouth, a pair of stairs, Phaeton's chariot, a cage, a painted cloth showing the city of Rome, a stable, a wooden canopy, a bedstead, and other miscellaneous items. This list could be extended considerably by referring to other entries in Henslowe's diaries.

The Master of Revels' accounts of the late 16th century record items used for performances at court. When professional troupes played before the Queen, the Revels office prepared a hall and supplied the necessary scenery. The items listed in the accounts include rocks, mountains, battlements, trees, and houses, all of which suggest that Medieval-like mansions were in use. Numerous hangings, cloths, and curtains are also mentioned, but the majority of these were used to decorate the hall. Although staging at court was probably more elaborate than in the public theatres, the differences between them are unclear.

From the available evidence, however, it seems probable that scenic practices were adapted from Medieval conventions. The large platform was essentially a *platea*, the identity of which could be altered by several devices. Most often treated as a neutral place, it could be localized either by the dialogue or by the use of set pieces, such as trees, arbors, tents, altars, tombs, prison bars, beds, and thrones. Some scenic devices were so cumbersome that they were set on the main stage, where they remained throughout the performance, ignored except when relevant to the action. Other heavy pieces were revealed in the discovery space. Smaller articles were brought on and off stage by servants as needed. Reynolds suggests that the number of set pieces employed in each play depended both upon the company's stock and the sequence of scenes, for the troupes suited their practice more to convenience than to principle. Neither audiences nor actors seem to have been bothered by inconsistencies.

The theatres retained and stored all scenic pieces, most of which could be used in a number of plays. There seems to have been no systematic attempt to increase the stock, articles being added at random. Thus, Henslowe's accounts show no regular payments to painters or carpenters. The scene stock was looked after by a "stage keeper," who was also responsible for the scenery, properties, and sound of each production.

Emphasis on spectacle increased after 1603 as the influence of the court grew. Professional troupes appeared at court on an average of 17 to 25 times yearly between 1603 and 1642, and individual actors were called upon to perform speaking roles in the masques and to aid in their staging. Thus, the actors could hardly have escaped knowledge of the Italianate conventions of the court masques.

The boys' companies began to emphasize masque-like elements around 1605, and the adult troupes continued this trend when they took over the private theatres. The results were evident primarily in the more elaborate set pieces, the increased use of special effects, music, and dance, and the more gorgeous costumes; there was no attempt to copy the perspective settings. The flying of actors became common, and classical figures replaced the Medieval ones in the allegorical scenes derived from masques. The direction of change may be seen by comparing an early work by Shakespeare, such as *A Midsummer Night's Dream*, with a late work, such as *The Tempest*.

Music had played a large part in theatrical production from the beginning. Incidental songs were inserted into many plays, and most performances concluded with a "jig" or some other entertainment involving music and dance. Trumpets sounded flourishes before entrances or to introduce proclamations, drums aided the battle scenes, and background music accompanied many episodes. The children's troupes offered concerts, up to one hour in length, before performances, a practice taken over by the adult troupes when they moved to the private theatres. Dance had a similar history. In the early days, it was designed to appeal primarily to the popular audiences, but became more sophisticated as the influence of aristocratic audiences increased.

Costumes

Probably the most important element of spectacle was costume. Not only was the actor the center of attention, but the processions, pantomimes, and masques introduced into many plays emphasized elaborate dress.

The conventions of costuming between 1558 and 1642 differed little from those of the Medieval period. The majority of characters were dressed in contemporary garments like those worn by real persons of similar rank, sex, and profession. Other kinds of costumes, which were used sparingly, fall into five categories: (1) "ancient," or out-of-style clothing, used to indicate unfashionableness, or, occasionally, to suggest another period; (2) "antique," consisting of drapery or greaves added to contemporary garments, used for certain classical figures; (3) fanciful garments, used for ghosts, witches, fairies, gods, and allegorical characters; (4) traditional costumes, associated with a few specific characters such as Robin Hood, Henry V, Tamburlaine, Falstaff, and Richard III; and (5) national or racial costumes, used to set off Turks, Indians, Jews, and Spaniards. Although some of these costumes were conventionalized representations of past periods, they were not historically accurate. With rare exceptions, even the "history plays" were costumed in Elizabethan dress.

Since costumes were seen at close range, the companies used appropriate materials and fashions insofar as their finances permitted. Contemporary accounts mention the costliness and elegance of the players' costumes. Henslowe's papers record numerous loans for the purchase of costumes,

A SKETCH allegedly made in 1595 of a scene from Shakespeare's *Titus Andronicus*. Some scholars argue that this is a 19th century forgery. [Courtesy Marquess of Bath]

such as seven pounds for "a doublet of white satin laid thick with gold lace" and nineteen pounds for a cloak.

The troupes bought most of their costumes. Sometimes noblemen gave them garments, and frequently servants who had been willed their masters' clothing sold it to the actors. Occasionally the royal family made grants to the troupes to replenish their wardrobes. Since the actors relied heavily upon costumes, the acquisition and maintenance of a sizable wardrobe was important. Each company probably employed a tailor to keep the garments in good repair and to make new ones.

Audiences

The permissible playing days varied until 1574, when the right to perform daily was established by royal decree. James I later forbade playing on Sundays, but with this exception daily performances were permitted until 1642. In actuality, the number was considerably reduced by forced closures in times of plague, official mourning, religious observances, and unseasonable weather. It has been estimated that about 214 days a year were used for performances during the early 17th century.

Numerous devices were used to advertise plays. Posters were being set up in London as early as 1563, and handbills were in use in the 17th century. Occasionally a procession with drums and trumpets was employed, although this device was more typically used by touring companies. Flags were flown from the roof of the theatres on days of performance, and announcements of coming attractions were made from the stage.

The seating capacity of the public theatres was large. Contemporary estimates give 3000 as the capacity, but modern scholars suggest 1500 to

2500. The private theatres probably seated about 500. Usually two or more theatres were open in London, whose population was about 160,000. One historian has estimated that the theatres normally played to half-filled houses.

To hold the interest of the relatively small theatre-going public, the companies changed bills daily and added new plays regularly. Henslowe's accounts for 1592–1603 show that the Admiral's Men produced a new play about every two and one-half weeks. In the 1590's a new play was performed once and then placed in the repertory, rotating with others; on an average, a play was performed only ten times. Before 1642, however, many plays had been given several consecutive performances as an initial run. The record of nine performances was set by Middleton's *The Game of Chess* (1624–25). The number of plays in the active repertory also increased from about 30 in 1600 to about 45 in 1640.

The usual starting time was 2 P.M., so that spectators might return home before nightfall. The theatres had no box office, tickets, programs, or reserved seats. "Gatherers" collected money at the entrances to each of the three principal divisions of the house: pit, public galleries, and private boxes. The plays were performed without intermissions at the public theatres, although musical interludes might separate the acts at the private playhouses. Wine, beer, ale, nuts, apples, cards, tobacco, and playbooks were for sale in the theatre.

The public theatres catered to all classes. The pit, or "yard" for standing patrons was used primarily by the lower classes; the galleries with benches were patronized especially by the middle class; while the private boxes were called "lords' rooms." In the late 16th century, admission to the yard was one penny, to the galleries two pennies, and to the private boxes three pennies. During the 17th century these prices rose to two pennies for general admission, while private boxes sometimes cost as much as 20 pennies. Thus, at the public theatres the basic admission remained low, but the price of more desirable places increased considerably. At the private theatres, the lowest admission fee was six pennies, while a private box might run as high as 46. Consequently, in spite of their much smaller capacities, the private theatres regularly earned more money than the public playhouses. Prices were raised on special occasions and were often doubled for premieres of new plays, attendance at which was much in vogue. By the end of the 16th century, a few spectators were being allowed to sit on the stage. As stage stools gained in prestige, the lords' rooms fell increasingly to prostitutes and others.

Some scholars have argued that after 1610 audiences were divided into the sophisticated spectators of the private theatres and the less refined frequenters of the public playhouses. To this alleged trend, they attribute the drama's decline in vitality. If it existed, it did not lessen the popularity of the theatre, which continued unabated until the playhouses were forceably closed.

The Court Masques

In addition to the public performances, those at court were also numerous. Most of the plays were presented by professional troupes. Although they might make use of scenery and costumes from the Master of Revels' stock, the actors probably deviated little from the conventions followed in the public playhouses. The court masques, on the other hand, introduced Italian ideals of staging into England and began that trend toward the proscenium-arch theatre which was to end in the abandonment of the facade stage after 1660.

Although masques had been popular at the court of Henry VIII, they were rarely given during the reign of Elizabeth except by the Inns of Court. When James I came to the throne, however, they were revived and given productions of ever-increasing splendor. Under James I (reigned 1603–25) an average of one masque each year was performed, and under Charles I two, one at Twelfth Night and the other at Mardi Gras. The Carolinian masques were usually planned as pairs, one given by the King and gentlemen, the other by the Queen and ladies of the court. Other masques were produced by the Inns of Court, usually in honor of the royal family, an important visitor, or on a special occasion.

Great sums of money were lavished on masques. In 1618, James I spent 4000 pounds on a single production, considerably more than he paid for all the professional performances given at court during his entire reign. The most expensive of all masques, however, was given jointly by the four Inns of Court in 1634 to demonstrate their loyalty following an attack upon the theatre, and indirectly upon the crown, in *Histriomastix* by William Prynne, a member of Lincoln's Inn. Written by James Shirley and with scenery by Inigo Jones, *The Triumph of Peace* cost 21,000 pounds. One of the participants, Bulstrode Whitlocke, preserved an account of this masque so complete that it can be reconstructed in all important details.

Considering the rewards in both money and prestige, it is not surprising that the major dramatists of the period wrote masques. Among these were Marston, Chapman, Beaumont, Middleton, Daniel, Milton, and Davenant. The majority of masques, however, were written by Ben Jonson and designed by Inigo Jones. Jonson's objection to the dominance of spectacle led to a break with Jones in 1631, and his replacement by other authors.

The masque was similar in all important respects to the Italian *intermezzo,* being an allegorical story designed to honor a particular person or occasion through a fanciful comparison with mythological characters or situations. The text established a context for the elaborate spectacle. The speaking and singing roles were assumed by professional court musicians, while comic roles were played by professional actors. The major emphasis, however, was upon the courtier-dancers. This division of roles tells much about the current attitudes toward actors: the courtiers refused to speak lines, because they wished to maintain their amateur—and unsullied—status. Since they were the principal performers, nonetheless, the masques used a minimum of dialogue.

Embedded in the allegorical plot were usually three "grand masquing dances": the entry dance; the main dance, which included going down into the hall to dance with selected spectators; and the "going out" dance. Many social dances of the period were incorporated, but elaborate symbolic formations were often choreographed by the court dancing masters.

The dancers were all of one sex, except in the occasional "double masques," which employed equally balanced groups of men and of women. Each dancer was usually accompanied by a "torchbearer" (that is, the carrier of a candelabra) when the dancing took place in the auditorium. The torchbearers, usually young noblemen or children, often performed a special dance. In 1608, Jonson invented the "anti-masque" to contrast with the main story. In it, humorous or grotesque characters and dances, always performed by professionals, were introduced. It also provided ample opportunity for the scenic designer to contrive striking transformations from ugliness to beauty.

The characters of the masques were usually either allegorical or mythological. The women might be goddesses, nymphs, queens, "The Beauties," or "The Graces." The men might be gods, ancient heroes, Signs of the Zodiac, "Sons of Peace, Love, and Justice," or representatives of various countries. The torchbearers might represent fiery spirits, Indians, Oceanae, or "antique" Britons. The anti-masques featured satyrs, drunkards, gypsies, sailors, beggars, fools, and baboons or other animals.

The majority of masques were staged in the Banqueting Hall at Whitehall Palace until 1637, when Charles I had a "great new masquing room" built. All of the temporary theatres followed a similar arrangement. Tiers of seats were set up along the sides and across the back of the hall. The royal dais was placed well back in the auditorium so as to provide the best view of the stage and to leave room for the dancers. Steps connected the hall with the stage.

The stage varied in size, the average being about 40 feet wide by 28 feet deep. It was raised about six feet above the hall and sloped upward toward the rear. A flat area was provided at the front for the performers, although they might occasionally go further back on the stage to that area reserved principally for scenic wonders.

The scenery, costumes, and special effects for most of the masques were by Inigo Jones (1573–1652), the first important English scene designer.

Born in London, Jones went to Italy about 1600 to study, after which he worked for a time at the court of Denmark before returning to England around 1604. He designed his first masque for James I in 1605. He may have visited Italy again in 1607–08, and certainly did in 1613–15. In 1615, he was appointed Surveyor of His Majesty's Works, a post which he held until dismissed in 1643 by the Puritans.

COSTUME by Inigo Jones for a Fiery Spirit in *The Temple of Love* (1635). Devonshire Collection Chatsworth. [Reproduced by permission of the Trustees of the Chatsworth Settlement]

Jones was thoroughly familiar with Italian artistic movements. At the court of Florence, he studied the work of Guilio Parigi. His surviving copy of Palladio's treatise on architecture contains notes comparing Palladio's ideas with those of Serlio, Scamozzi, Vignola, and others. As the leading English architect and designer, Jones was the most influential artist of his day. At his death, he willed his papers to his pupil and assistant, John Webb, who was to become a leading architect and scene designer of the Restoration. Since William Davenant, one of the principal theatre managers of the Restoration, had written several of the last masques designed by Jones, and since Webb worked closely with Davenant after 1656, Jones also exerted considerable influence on Restoration scene design. To Jones, more than any other artist, can be attributed the naturalization of the Italian ideal in England.

Jones' innovations were not all evident in his early designs, for some of the most important did not appear until 1640. Thus, it is helpful to examine the evolution of Jones' techniques. The nature of his contributions can be seen by comparing them with the last masque presented before he began his work at the Stuart court. In 1604, Samuel Daniels' *The Vision of Twelve Goddesses* used the "dispersed decor" (that is, mansion-like structures scattered around the hall) which had been typical of Tudor masques. A new era began, therefore, when in 1605, for Jonson's *The Masque of Blackness,* Jones erected a stage at one end of the hall and placed all of the scenery on it. Furthermore, instead of mansions, he employed a perspective setting of angled wings and backscene, suddenly revealed by the dropping of a front curtain.

Between 1605 and 1610, Jones made other innovations. In 1606, for *The Masque of Hymen,* the principle of the *periaktoi* was used in the creation of a globe with no visible axle, which revolved to reveal eight dancers seated inside a "mine of several metals." In the same production, Jones suspended eight dancers in a cloud machine which moved from upstage to downstage. In 1608, for *The Hue and Cry After Cupid,* Jones made his first-known use of the prosecenium arch and of scenery which parted in the middle to reveal another scene behind it. In the *Masque of Oberon* (1610), two sets of shutters were worked in grooves to reveal three successive scenes. Throughout the rest of his association with Jonson, Jones merely reused the same basic technical devices.

INIGO JONES' SETTING from Act V of Davenant's *Salmacida Spolia* (1640). Devonshire Collection Chatsworth. [Reproduced by permission of the Trustees of the Chatsworth Settlement]

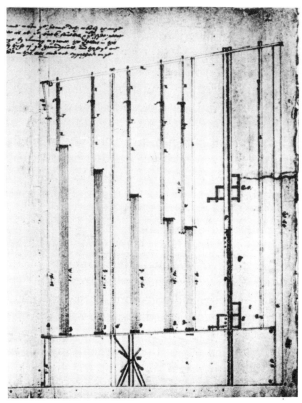

INIGO JONES' SECTIONAL PLAN for *Salmacida Spolia*. [Courtesy Trustees of the British Museum]

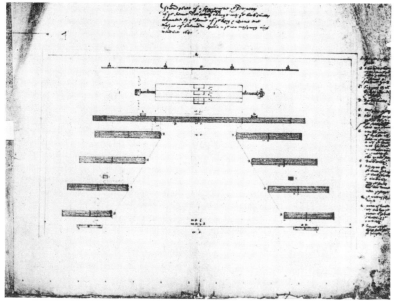

INIGO JONES' FLOOR PLAN for *Salmacida Spolia*. [Courtesy Trustees of the British Museum]

194

In the 1630's, however, he introduced other innovations. Perhaps most important, he abandoned angled wings for flat wings. This change may have been made as early as 1634 for *Coelum Britannicum,* but certainly was made for *The Temple of Love* (1635) by Davenant. Jones' experiments culminated in 1640 in his settings for the last court masque, *Salmacida Spolia* by Davenant. For it, four sets of flat wings and several back shutters were set in grooves to permit rapid changes of setting. Except for the chariot-and-pole system of scene shifting, Jones had introduced all of the major Italian developments into England before 1642. When the theatres were reopened in 1660, his practices triumphed over those of the public theatres.

The extravagances of the court masques contributed significantly to the antipathy of the Puritans toward the stage, which increased markedly during the reign of Charles I. Because all of the acting troupes were licensed to members of the royal family, the theatre came to be associated with the Cavalier party as factions were formed before the civil war. In 1642, Parliament used the war as an excuse for closing all theatres for five years. When that time expired, the Puritans were in control of the government and the closure was declared permanent. Thus ended one of the most brilliant and productive periods the theatre has ever known.

THE SPANISH
THEATRE
FROM 1500 TO 1700

L ike England, Spain had developed a theatre and drama of stature before 1600. So productive was the century between 1580 and 1680 that it is commonly called the *Siglo de Oro,* or Golden Age, of Spanish drama. Although influenced by Classical and Italian ideals, the Spanish theatre developed along quite independent lines. Its isolation from the rest of Europe, however, had by the end of the 17th century led to a stagnation from which it has never fully recovered.

The Religious Drama

Many influences on the theatre can be traced to the long Moorish occupation of Spain. Although northeastern Spain had been liberated about 800 A.D., the reconquest was not completed until the late 15th century during the reign of Ferdinand and Isabella, crowned rulers of the "united kingdoms" in 1479. During the following century Spain became the most powerful country in the world. At the same time, steps were taken which profoundly affected the future of its theatre. Many of these grew directly out of the desire to re-Christianize Spain. Under Ferdinand and Isabella, the Jews were expelled, and the Inquisition was given the task of weeding out heresy.

Close ties with Italy continued until about 1550, and in these years many of the new Italian artistic ideals were disseminated in Spain. After 1550, however, Spain rapidly became the most "Catholic" country in Europe, and by 1600 was effectively insulated from outside influences. A reaction against Italian literature had begun by 1590, and thereafter Spanish drama developed along strictly national lines. At first this probably contributed to the theatre's vitality, but insularity had by 1680 led to repetitiousness and decline.

Because of the Moorish occupation, religious drama was extensively developed during the Middle Ages only in northeastern Spain. As the territories were recovered, plays were introduced in many areas as a device of religious teaching. Perhaps because of the church's firm control over its content, Spain's religious drama grew in importance at the very time that it was being suppressed in other countries. Until the 16th century, the Spanish religious plays were similar to those performed elsewhere; after 1550, they assumed distinctive traits which they retained until performances were prohibited in 1765. During the 16th century the plays became closely associated with Corpus Christi, a festival which emphasizes the power of the church's sacraments. It is probably for this reason that the plays were called *autos sacramentales*.

The *auto sacramentale* combined characteristics of the morality and cycle plays. In it, human and supernatural characters mingled with such allegorical figures as Sin, Grace, Pleasure, Grief, and Beauty. Stories could be drawn from any source, even completely secular ones, so long as they illustrated the efficacy of the sacraments and the validity of church dogma.

Although production arrangements varied somewhat from one area to another, those in Madrid were sufficiently typical to stand for all. Until 1550 trade guilds were responsible for staging the plays, but at some time between 1551 and 1558 the City Council assumed control. Professional troupes were now employed to produce the plays, which were written by Spain's finest dramatists. Thus, after the mid-16th century the connection between the public and religious stages was to be close.

By the end of the 16th century, production procedures had assumed the pattern which was to be followed thereafter except for minor changes. Three *autos* were given each year until 1592, after which four were presented annually until 1647, when the number was reduced to two. The plays were sometimes new and sometimes old, except between 1647 and 1681, when all those given in Madrid were new and written by one author,

A RECONSTRUCTION by Richard Southern of an *auto sacra-mentale* in the Plaza Mayor, Madrid. It is based upon a ground plan drawn in 1644. Note the two *carros* alongside a platform and the box-like seating provided for the City Council and the Council of Castile. [Reprinted from *Le Lieu Théâtrale à la Renaissance*. [Courtesy Centre National de la Recherche Scientifique, Paris]

Calderón. The plays were performed by a single company until 1592, after which two companies were employed. The troupes were chosen during Lent. In addition to being paid a sizable fee, these companies were awarded exclusive rights to give public performances in Madrid between Easter and Corpus Christi. After Corpus Christi, the actors also toured the *autos* to neighboring towns and performed them in the public theatres of Madrid as well. Thus, there were many incentives for the actors to participate in the festivals.

The plays were mounted on *carros,* or wagons, supplied by the city, which also furnished everything else needed for the productions except the costumes and hand properties. Two *carros* were used for each play until 1647, when the number was increased to four. The two-storied *carros* were made of wooden frames covered with painted canvas and equipped according to instructions supplied by the dramatists. There is little information about the size of the wagons until the 1690's, when they were about 16 feet long by 36 feet tall. The facade of the upper story was often hinged so that it might open to reveal something within. Scenic devices might also rise out of the lower story, and many of the wagons included machinery for flying actors or objects. The *carros* served as entrances to the stage and as dressing rooms for the actors.

Until 1647 a portable stage, another wagon, accompanied the *carros* as an acting area. After 1647, when four wagons began to be used for each play, fixed platforms were erected at each playing place, since the portable stages were no longer large enough. Two *carros* were now drawn up at the back and one at either end of the stage, which was bare but equipped with trapdoors for special effects. The awkwardness of taking away the four *carros* used for one *auto* and bringing in four others for the next play led in 1692 to arranging all eight wagons around the platform throughout the performance. In the 1690's, the acting area was about 45 to 50 feet long by 36 feet deep.

Between eight and twenty days before Corpus Christi the actors were required to give a preview performance before the City Council. In some towns, the first official performance was given inside the cathedral. By the early 17th century this practice had largely been discontinued, although in many places the first performance was still given just outside the church. There is no evidence that the plays were ever performed inside the churches of Madrid; by the early 17th century even the performance in front of the church had been discontinued. Nevertheless, the *carros* were still included in the procession of the Host through the streets, and the plays remained an accepted part of the festival.

The City Council specified the playing places, often so many that the performances extended over several days. After 1600, the first performance was usually given before the King in a palace courtyard. The plays were then presented in the square before the City Hall, on one day for the Council of Castile (the most powerful of governmental groups), and on the next for the City Council. Several other state councils were also entitled to special showings and at least two performances were given for the general public. The *carros* were pulled from place to place by bullocks with gilded horns.

In addition to the *autos*, the actors also performed short farcical interludes and dances. Other performers were employed by the City to carry large carnival figures of giants and dragons about the streets and to perform the traditional dances. When the *autos* were forbidden in 1765, the reasons given were the predominance of the carnival spirit, the objectionable content of the farces and dances, and the undesirability of having religious plays performed by actors of questionable morality. All of these complaints had been voiced since the 16th century, however, and other reasons must have been equally important. Certainly interest had been declining since the death of Calderón in 1681, after which the *autos* became merely imitative of older works. The general loss of interest is probably also indicated by the abandonment of processional staging in 1705, after which the *autos* were performed only in the public theatres. Regardless of the reason for their decline and prohibition, *autos* were an important adjunct to the professional stage for more than 200 years.

The Beginnings of a Secular Drama

From about 1470 until 1550 the connections between Spain and Italy were close, and in these years the awakening interest in classical learning found its way into Spanish intellectual circles. A university was founded at Alcala de Henares in 1508 to encourage the study of Latin, Greek, and Hebrew. This study soon led to an interest in classical drama, and during the 16th century many Latin and Greek works were translated into Spanish. The introduction of printing into Spain in 1473 accelerated the dissemination of new ideas.

By 1500 a secular drama had begun to emerge. Perhaps the most important early work is *The Comedy of Calisto and Melibea,* first published in 1499. A novel in dialogue rather than a true play, the edition of 1499 consisted of 16 acts, which were increased to 21 in the edition of 1502. Usually attributed to Fernando de Rojas (*c.* 1465–*c.* 1541), it may contain some parts by other writers. Although *Calisto and Melibea* was not performed, it was widely read and influenced later writers through its examples of lifelike characters and situations created entirely by dialogue. Especially famous were the low-life scenes portraying La Celestina, the go-between in the love affair of Calisto and Melibea.

Juan del Encina (1469–1529) is often called the founder of Spanish drama, since his early works predate *Calisto and Melibea.* After studying with the great Spanish Humanist, Nebrija, Encina turned to writing "eclogues" in the manner of the Italian pastoral drama. His early plays, dating from the 1490's, are still essentially religious, and it was not until he went to live in Italy that he turned to more purely secular works, such as *The Eclogue of Placida and Victoriano* (1513). His relatively simple plays were the first Spanish secular dramas to be performed. Bartolemé de Torres Naharro (*c.* 1480–*c.* 1530) at first imitated Encina's work but went on to write much more sophisticated farces and comedies. Like Encina, he lived for a time in Italy, where his plays were performed before being published in Spain in 1517 under the title *Propolladia.* The structure of Naharro's plays is primitive, for without the prologues the action of many would be unintelligible. His fluent verse and topical satire, however, won him a wide reading public. Gil Vincente (*c.* 1465–*c.* 1539) wrote primarily for the Portuguese court, but many of his plays were in Spanish. He was superior to his contemporaries because of his considerable lyrical gift, great range, comic sense, and spontaneity.

In addition to these native works, Italian plays were being performed with Italianate scenery at the Spanish court by 1548. All of the early secular drama in Spain was aimed at an aristocratic audience, and its influence on the professional theatre was negligible. Nevertheless, these plays established a foundation which later Spanish dramatists recognized as the source of their own practices.

The Early Professional Theatre in Spain

As in other countries, the origin of professional players is obscure. As early as 1454 actors were being paid to perform at Corpus Christi; in 1539, six men were employed to perform farces at the Cathedral in Toledo; in 1529, 1535, and 1538 Italian companies appeared in Spain. Not until the 1540's, however, are notices concerning professional actors common. Although most of these relate to Corpus Christi festivities, it is clear that by 1550 a number of troupes existed.

The first important figure of the Spanish professional theatre is Lope de Rueda (c. 1510–c. 1565), of whom the first notice is found in 1542, when he appeared in religious plays at Seville. By 1551 he was sufficiently well-known to be summoned by the governors of Vallodolid, then the capital, to perform before Philip II. From 1552 until 1558, Rueda was employed there at an annual salary of 4000 maravedis to supervise the Corpus Christi festivities. In addition, he performed frequently at court and toured widely. Rueda was also the first important dramatist whose plays were produced for popular audiences. A number of his works, including *The Frauds, Medora, Armelina,* and *Eufemia,* have survived. In their earthy humor, they resemble Medieval farces. Fools and simpletons (roles which Rueda played) are the most developed characters, and the dialogue is picturesque.

Cervantes states that Rueda's stage consisted of four or five boards set on benches backed with a blanket, while his costumes were "four white sheepskins trimmed with gilded leather." This statement has often been accepted as an accurate description of the professional theatre during Rueda's time. Even a cursory examination of contemporary records, however, will show that Cervantes oversimplified the situation, not surprisingly since he was recalling after 50 years a performance which he had seen as a boy. Rueda's contracts required him to supply costumes of silk and velvet for Corpus Christi productions and it seems unlikely that he did not use them at other times, especially for his numerous court appearances. Probably Cervantes saw one of Rueda's clownish comedies, for which sheepskins would have been appropriate.

No permanent theatres existed during Rueda's lifetime. Sometimes he acted in courtyards, sometimes indoors, sometimes in city squares, sometimes at court. Like his English and Italian counterparts, he adapted to many conditions. Although Rueda is now almost universally considered the founder of the Spanish professional theatre, in actuality he was merely the most successful performer of his day. Nevertheless, it is his work which epitomizes the early years.

The popularity of the theatre mushroomed in the 1570's. Actors were welcomed throughout the country and permanent theatres began to appear. The major theatrical centers were Madrid, the capital of Spain after 1560, and Seville, but Barcelona, Valencia, Granada, Cordoba, and other cities also boasted troupes.

Although the demand for new plays increased rapidly after Rueda's death, no writer of importance appeared until about 1590, when Lope de Vega began to write regularly for the stage. Between 1565 and 1590 the plays were contrived primarily by the directors of theatrical companies, which led to the continuing designation of managers as *autores de comedias*. In these years, two authors achieved a measure of fame. Juan de la Cueva (1550–1610), working in Seville, was one of the first dramatists to draw on Spanish history in plays such as *The Seven Children of Lara*. He also wrote on classical subjects and on themes from everyday life. Miguel de Cervantes (1547–1616), remembered principally for *Don Quixote,* also wrote about 30 plays, of which 16 survive. Of these, the best are *The Siege of Numancia,* about a Roman attack on a Spanish town; *The Traffic of Argel,* concerning men captured by Algerian pirates; and *The Fortunate Ruffian,* a play of contemporary Spanish life. Cervantes' plays, most of which were written between 1580 and 1600, came to seem stilted after Lope de Vega's works appeared.

By the end of the 16th century, several dramatic types had become popular. Since Spanish terminology is unique, a brief summary will facilitate later discussions. *Comedia* is used to describe any full-length play, whether serious or comic; most are divided into three acts, for the five-act form was never widely adopted in Spain. *Comedias* are of two major kinds: *capa y espada,* or "cape and sword," a name derived from the popular dress of gentlemen of minor ranks about whom the plays revolve; and *teatro, ruido* ("noise"), or *cuerpo* ("corpse"), terms applied to plays in which rulers, nobles, mythological characters, or saints are involved in actions set in remote places or periods. Until about 1615, every performance began with a *loa* ("compliment") or prologue, either a monologue or a short dramatic sketch designed to gain the good will of the audience. The *loa* usually included singing and dancing. Although it declined in popularity after 1615, the *loa* was not abandoned for many years. *Entreméses* ("interludes"), or short topical sketches, were performed in the intervals between the acts of plays. Some were sung, others were spoken, and still others mingled speech and song. Around 1650, the term *sainete* came into use for many short farces which earlier would have been called *entreméses*. Most Spanish dramatists wrote all of these forms.

Lope de Vega and His Contemporaries

By far the most prolific Spanish playwright was Lope Félix de Vega Carpio (1562–1635), whose personal life was as flamboyant as the plays he wrote. He was a member of the Spanish Armada, secretary to a nobleman, participant in many business affairs, and, after 1614, a priest. In spite of his many activities, he declared in 1609 that he had written 483 *comedias*. Estimates of his total output run as high as 1800 plays, of which more than 450 have survived. Some were written in a couple of days, and near the end of his life he was regularly turning out two plays a week.

It is difficult to assess the quality of Lope's work because of its quantity. Nevertheless, some broad generalizations are possible. Above all, his plays are notable for clearly defined actions which arouse and maintain suspense. Many works revolve around the conflicting claims of love and honor, a theme which Lope popularized and bequeathed to all succeeding Spanish drama. Since he disliked unhappy endings, Lope usually found means for resolving conflicts happily. His characters include representatives of practically every rank and condition of mankind, into all of which Lope entered sympathetically. The female roles are among his best, and he extended the scope of the *gracioso,* or simpleton, a standard character in the plays of the day. Lope's dialogue is natural, lively, and appropriate; it ranges through many verse forms, for Spanish dramatists never developed an equivalent to English blank verse. In spite of Lope's achievements, however, he cannot be ranked with Shakespeare, to whom he is often compared. He never penetrates deeply into human nature, and the darker side of life is always glossed over in happy endings. Although the plays produce many surprises, they offer few new insights; they celebrate the variety of life without exploring its significance.

Lope was by far the most popular writer of his age. To modern audiences, his most appealing work is *Fuente Ovejuna* (*The Sheep Well, c.* 1614), in which a tyrannous feudal lord is killed by villagers, who refuse to confess even under torture and are saved by the intervention of the King. Many critics have seen revolutionary sentiments in the play, although it is more likely that Lope was praising the King for abolishing the feudal system. Among the best of Lope's lighter "cape-and-sword" plays are *The Gardener's Dog* (c. 1615), *Madrid Steel* (1603), and *A Certainty for a Doubt* (c. 1625).

Although Lope is now acknowledged as the foremost Spanish playwright of his time, he was surrounded by a host of lesser figures. The most important of these were Guillén de Castro, Tirso de Molina, and Juan Ruiz de Alarcón. Guillén de Castro (1569–1631), a friend and follower of Lope, wrote a number of plays but is now remembered almost entirely for his *Las Mocedades del Cid* (*The Youthful Adventures of the Cid*), which was to serve as the basis for Corneille's *Le Cid*. Tirso de Molina (*c.* 1584–1648), a friar who gave up writing for the stage in 1625 following a rebuke from the Council of Castile, is said to have written about 400 plays, of which 80 survive. Of these, by far the most famous is *El Burlador de Sevilla* (*The Trickster of Seville*), the first dramatic treatment of the Don Juan story. Juan Ruiz de Alarcón (*c.* 1581–1639) was born in Mexico and educated in Spain, where he worked for the government. Alarcón wrote 30 plays, in which he sought perfect finish at a time when other dramatists were noted for their facility. His best plays center around court life in Madrid. The finest is *La Verdad Sospechosa* (*The Suspicious Truth,* 1628), which explores the complications arising from the inability of a young man to tell the truth. In his plays, Alarcón makes characterization and subtle moral sentiments the bases of his dramatic actions.

Calderón and His Contemporaries

Before Lope de Vega died, his preeminence had been challenged by another writer, Calderón, who was to be ranked above Lope by many critics. Unlike Lope and his contemporaries, who were associated principally with the public theatres, Calderón and the best dramatists of his time wrote primarily for the court theatre. In this shift, many historians have seen a major cause for the decline of Spanish drama after 1650.

Pedro Calderón de la Barca (1600–81), the son of a court official, received a university education, after which he entered the service of a nobleman. In 1651, after a series of personal disasters, Calderón became a priest, although he continued to write *autos sacramentales* for the city of Madrid and occasional plays for the court. Of his approximately 200 plays, about 100 have survived, of which 80 are *autos*.

Calderón wrote practically all of his best secular plays between 1622 and 1640. These fall into two major categories: the "cape and sword" comedies, such as *The Phantom Lady* (1629), which depend on happily resolved love intrigues and misunderstandings; and the serious plays, many of which explore jealousy and honor. Of the latter type, the most famous is *The Physician to His Own Honor* (1635), a sympathetic treatment of a man who, in order to preserve his honor, manages to kill his wife in a manner that avoids scandal.

Calderón's most famous secular play, *Life is a Dream* (*c.* 1636), is a philosophical allegory about the human situation and the mystery of life. The main character, Segismundo, a prince by birth, is reared in anonymity, taken to court while unconscious, and returned to his former state after being found unworthy; afterward, he believes that the interlude at court was a dream. In the chaotic years following 1640, when Catalonia and Portugal revolted against Spain, Calderón wrote only one outstanding *comedia, The Mayor of Zalamea* (*c.* 1642), the story of a peasant who seeks revenge for the violation of his daughter by an army officer. After 1652, all of Calderón's secular plays were written on demand for the court. They are short and light, often based on classical myths, with choral passages and much of the dialogue set to music. Because so many of them were performed at the royal hunting lodge, La Zarzuela, this type of musical comedy, which became one of the most popular of Spanish dramatic forms, was called the *zarzuela.*

Above all, Calderón is noted for his *autos sacramentales,* for he perfected the form. In his *autos,* Calderón effectively embodies Catholic dogma in symbolic stories told in lyrical dialogue of great beauty. Although he had written *autos* from the beginning of his career, he turned to them especially after 1647, writing two each year until his death. He was the author of all those presented in Madrid between 1647 and 1681. Nevertheless, his finest *autos, Devotion to the Cross* (1633) and *The Great World Theatre* (*c.* 1645), were written before he became a priest.

Of Calderón's contemporaries, two—Rojas Zorilla and Moreto—stand out. Francisco de Rojas Zorilla (1607–*c.* 1648) lived chiefly in Madrid, where he held a position at court and wrote primarily for the royal theatre. His best-known work, *Del Rey abajo ninguno* (*All Equal Below the King*), tells the story of a nobleman who is forgiven by the king for killing a man who sought to seduce his wife. In light comedy, Rojas Zorilla broke new ground with such works as *The Boobies' Sport* and *What Women Are,* in which a variety of pompous characters replace the traditional *gracioso* as the principal source of humor. Unfortunately, since Rojas Zorilla had no real followers, his breaks with tradition had little effect in Spain. His plays were greatly admired in France, however, and were adapted by Scarron, Thomas Corneille, and LeSage.

Augustín Moreto (1618–69) was born in Madrid and spent most of his life at court, for which he principally wrote. His best-known play is *Scorn for Scorn,* which served as the basis for Molière's *La Princesse d'Élide.* It tells the story of a woman who scorns all her lovers, only to be captured by one who pretends to scorn her. Moreto's delicate poetry, elegant and subtle wit, and interesting character portraits won him a wide following among aristocratic audiences. Most of his plays are adaptations of *comedias* by Lope de Vega and others.

The output of the Golden Age was phenomenal, for by 1700 an estimated 30,000 plays had been written. In quantity and vigor, the drama of Spain is comparable to that of England between 1585 and 1642. On the other hand, its failure to probe deeply into man's destiny, and its preoccupation with a narrow code of honor are limitations which make it inferior to the best English work. Nevertheless, many of the plays were widely known and imitated outside of Spain, and at home they established a lasting standard.

The Corrales

Although after 1625 the court attracted many of the finest dramatists, the majority of plays continued, as before, to be presented in the public theatres, or *corrales* (so called because they were originally adapted from existing courtyards). The *corrales* were at first under the direct control of confraternities like those which had presented religious plays throughout Europe during the Middle Ages. In Madrid, the public theatres were controlled by three charitable organizations. Of these, the Cofradía de la Pasión y Sangre de Jesucristo, founded in 1565 to feed and clothe the poor and to support a hospital, was the first to be granted the privilege of operating a theatre as a means of raising money. By 1568 it had opened a theatre in the Calle del Sol and soon added two others. In 1574, the Cofradía de la Soledad de Nuestra Señora, founded in 1567, petitioned to have one of the existing theatres placed under its control, a move which led to a sharing of revenues and expenses by the two Cofradías. In 1583, the General Hospital of Madrid was also given a share in the revenues. These three organizations controlled the public theatres of Madrid until 1615. Similar arrangements were used in Barcelona, Zaragosa, Burgos, Vallodolid, Valencia, and Seville. Thus, the theatre was viewed as a means of raising money for charity, an attitude which saved it from closure on many occasions.

A new phase in the career of the theatres began in 1615, when the City of Madrid was ordered to pay the hospitals an annual subsidy, from which it could subtract a sum equal to the revenue which the *cofradías* received from the theatres. After this time, the *cofradías* gave up direct control over theatrical management and leased the theatres to entrepreneurs, normally for four-year periods. In 1638, ownership of the *corrales* passed to the City and two commissioners were appointed to oversee their operation, although the theatres continued to be leased as before. Despite some alterations in the system during the 18th century, the theatres were to finance charities until the mid-19th century. At no time during the Golden Age did the actors control the *corrales*, which were occupied merely for short-term engagements under contracts with the theatres' lessees.

At first the *corrales* were temporary, at least five different ones being used in Madrid during the 1570's. The desirability of permanent theatres soon became evident, however, and the Corral de la Cruz, the first perma-

A 19TH CENTURY RECONSTRUCTION of the Corral del Príncipe.
This sketch was made in 1888 to illustrate Ricardo Supel-
veda's *El Corral de la Pacheca* and is inaccurate in many
details, although it manages to give a flavor of the interior.
Unfortunately no visual evidence relating to the *corrales*
can be found until the 18th century.

nent theatre in Spain, was opened in Madrid in 1579. It was followed by
the Corral del Príncipe in 1583. After 1585 these were to be the only public
theatres for drama in Madrid until the 19th century. Permanent theatres
were also built in other cities.

Although the *corrales* were by no means uniform in design, they had
many common features. Almost all were built around a square or rectangular courtyard. The only exception seems to have been the oval-shaped
Corral de la Montería, built in Seville in 1626. In most, the courtyards
were unroofed until the 18th century, but a few were covered during the
17th. When roofs were added, a row of windows just under the eaves provided light.

The large central courtyard, or *patio*, was occupied primarily by
standing spectators, although by the end of the 17th century a few semi-
circular rows of benches, or *luneta*, had been set up near the stage. A raised
and roofed platform equipped with benches (the *gradas*) extended along
the side walls of the *patio*. At the rear of the *patio*, the *alojería*, or tavern,
occupied the ground floor, while above it was the gallery for women, the
cazuela or *corredor de las mugeres*. Above the *cazuela* were two other
galleries, the first divided into boxes and assigned to the City of Madrid and
the Council of Castile, while the upper, the Tertulia, was undivided and
used primarily by clergymen and intellectuals. The side walls of the courtyard were taken up by boxes, or *aposentos*, which were in reality rooms in

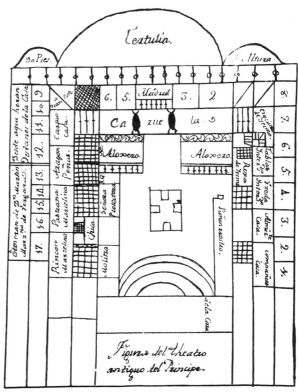

A ROUGH PLAN of the Corral del Príncipe made about 1730.
The stage is shown at the bottom, while the walls are
drawn as if the various levels were side by side. [From a
plan published in Milan in 1881]

the surrounding houses from which the occupants could watch the plays
from windows, typically covered with latticework or iron grilles. The third
floor boxes were often called *desvánes* (attics) because of their location at
the top of the buildings. On the first level, the *aposentos* were fronted by
the *gradas,* while an open and railed gallery fronted the *aposentos* on the
second level. Since the theatres in Madrid were converted from already
existing courtyards, some of the *aposentos* were located in houses which
were either rented or privately owned by persons having no connection
with the theatre. In these cases, the occupants were required to pay a yearly
fee for the use of the *aposentos* or to permit access to the *aposentos* through
their houses.

Many of the theatres outside of Madrid deviated from the usual
pattern. In some the *aposentos* were replaced by open galleries divided into
compartments like those later used in the Italian public opera houses;
others had one row of *aposentos,* above which were open galleries. Nevertheless, the basic arrangement—an enclosed courtyard—was the same everywhere.

The theatres had several entrances; at each there were two money takers, since two entrance fees were paid, one to the theatre lessee and one to the charities. Of the combined total, about three-fifths went to the lessee and actors. The entrance fee entitled women to sit in the *cazuela* and men to stand in the *patio*. Additional fees were collected from the men if they wished to sit in the *aposentos, gradas,* or galleries. Some of the *aposentos* were entered from the *patio,* but others were reached by passing through private houses. Many were rented permanently. The strict segregation of men and women was enforced by policemen. Women were forbidden in the *patio,* and men and women could occupy the same *aposento* only if they were known to be closely related.

Until the 1580's performances were confined to Sundays and feast days. In 1579, Alberto Ganassa's visiting *commedia dell'arte* troupe was permitted to play on a weekday, a privilege soon extended to Spanish companies. By the 17th century performances were allowed daily except Saturday. Sunday was always considered the best day, because of the larger potential audience. The theatrical season began in September and continued until Lent. All theatres were closed from Ash Wednesday until after Easter, when a new season extended until July, at which time the theatres were closed for the summer months. The theatres might also be closed during periods of official mourning, plagues, or war. It has been estimated that about 198 days each year were available for performances.

During the fall and winter season, performances began at 2 P.M., and during the spring season at 4 P.M. They were required to end at least one hour before nightfall. The daily bill began with music, singing and dancing; the *loa,* or prologue, was followed by another dance; then came the *comedia,* the acts of which were separated by *entreméses;* a dance concluded the performance.

Spectators, especially those in the patio and *cazuela,* were often noisy. The *mosqueteros* in the courtyard were usually the most unruly, but the women sometimes threw fruit at the actors, and both men and women carried such noisemakers as whistles, rattles, and keys. They were equally voluble in approval, which they demonstrated by applauding and shouting "Victor!" Articles such as fruit, wafers, and ale were sold throughout performances.

Acting Companies

It is difficult to estimate the number of acting companies between 1550 and 1680, for many lasted only a single season, and mergers or separations were frequent. The number increased so rapidly after permanent theatres were built that the government sought to regulate them. In 1603, the crown restricted the right to perform to eight companies; in 1615, the number was raised to twelve. Such regulations seem to have been ignored, however, for records show that many additional companies played during those years.

Companies were of two kinds: sharing troupes (*compañías de parte*) and salaried actors working for a manager. Contracts usually ran for one or two years. The size of companies varied considerably. Augustín de Rojas Villandrando's *Entertaining Journey* (1604) describes troupes ranging in size from the single performer, who recited monologues or scenes from plays, to those with 16 members and a repertory of 60 plays. Between 1610 and 1640, the period of the theatre's greatest popularity, the average company consisted of 16 to 20 actors. The troupes included both men and women. In addition, there were usually a few minors serving apprenticeships.

Since most troupes preferred to play in Madrid or Seville, other cities sometimes had to employ agents to secure companies for their theatres. Even in Madrid, however, no troupe remained in the same theatre very long and almost all toured. Traveling was time-consuming and costly. In 1586, it took one company 13 days to travel the 270 miles between Madrid and Seville. The mode of transportation, depending upon the company's finances, ranged from walking to using carts, pack animals, and coaches. Contracts often specified allowances for travel, as well as the type of lodging and food to be provided on the road.

Before performances could be given, a company had to obtain a license, which was usually granted only after civic officials had viewed a free performance. In addition, each play had to be licensed separately. After 1600 all plays were subject to censorship, and a dramatist could be excommunicated if he did not comply with recommendations. Since there were no copyright laws, a play could be performed by any company that could obtain a copy and a license.

Before 1590, many playwrights were attached to troupes as actors. After 1590, such close connections were unusual, and plays were bought outright for fees which varied according to the author's reputation. At the height of his career, Lope de Vega received about 500 reals for each play, at a time when an actor's average annual salary was about 6000 reals. This disparity in income may explain why dramatists were so prolific. By the 1650's, the payment had gone up to about 800 reals for works by the best writers.

Payments to companies varied widely. Usually a troupe was given a fixed sum for each performance, and to this a percentage of the receipts was sometimes added for long engagements. Occasionally companies were paid entirely through a fixed percentage of receipts. If a company had to travel a long distance to keep an engagement, it might receive additional payments to defray expenses.

For *autos,* the companies received relatively high fees, since they were required to furnish expensive costumes. In addition, the troupes selected to perform *autos* were given exclusive performance rights in the town between Easter and Corpus Christi. After the festival, the *autos* were often presented in the public theatres. The city governments also hired actors to give free performances on special occasions.

Little is known of individual companies, although the names of many managers have survived. Among the most famous were Alonso Riquelme (*fl.* 1602–21), Christobal Ortiz (*fl.* 1613–26), Roque de Figueroa (*fl.* 1623–50), and Antonio de Rueda (*fl.* 1628–62). In addition to the Spanish troupes, Italian *commedia dell'arte* companies frequently visited Spain during the last quarter of the 16th century. Among the most famous of these were the troupes of Alberto Ganassa (1574–84), Maximiliano Milanino (1581), and Tristano Martinelli (1587–88).

Actors and Acting

The position of the professional performer in Spain was ambiguous. Since Roman times actors had been forbidden the sacraments of the church, and Alfonso X (1221–84) had declared that all actors were to be branded infamous. These strictures were not officially removed in Spain until the 20th century. During the Golden Age the usual attitude was one of tolerance, however, so long as actors did not perform plays which contradicted church teachings; certainly many actors were married and buried in the church. Furthermore, they were employed by city officials to produce the *autos* given at Corpus Christi celebrations.

Nevertheless, many churchmen were opposed to the theatre, especially to the use of professional actors in religious plays. On many occasions, they petitioned the king to ban the public theatre and, in a few instances, were successful for short periods of time. Fortunately, the actors had strong allies in city officials, whose local charities depended upon the theatre for their funds. Consequently, closures were brief. The objections, however, did lead to closer supervision of the theatre.

A major source of dissatisfaction was the actress. Professional female performers in Spain can be traced back as far as the 15th century, and by Lope de Rueda's time, they were included in acting troupes. Nevertheless, most women's roles were played by boys or men until 1587, when women were first licensed to appear on the stage. Churchmen secured a royal decree banning actresses in 1596, but it seems never to have been enforced. After a bitter controversy in 1598–99, the royal council declared that no actresses were to perform unless their husbands or fathers were in the company, and that neither sex might appear in the dress of the other. Further attempts to still criticism probably lie behind the decree of 1608, which stated that only actors were to go backstage, forbade friars to attend the theatre, and banned the presentation of secular plays in churches or religious houses. Strict censorship was established over the plays, and in 1615 was extended to dancing, which had given rise to many complaints.

Dance played an important role in both the *comedias* and the *autos.* Most actresses danced as well as acted, and the contracts of many actors specified that they must dance and sing. Many complaints against the theatre cited the *zarabanda,* introduced about 1588, as licentious and voluptuous. In addition, *bayles,* dances accompanied by couplets, were considered morally questionable by many persons. After the decree of 1615, dances became more sedate.

In 1631 the actors were allowed to form a guild similar to those of other recognized trades. Called the Cofradía de la Novena, it still exists and is open to all theatrical personnel. It did much to raise the social status of the actor.

The names of more than 2000 actors of the Golden Age are known. Most were recruited from the common people, although occasionally members of the minor aristocracy went on the stage. Unfortunately, little is known about idnividual performers. Damien Arias de Penafiel (*fl.* 1617–43), with his "pure, clear voice, vivacious manner, and excellent memory," was universally regarded as the finest actor of his time. Other outstanding performers included Nicolas de los Rios (*fl.* 1570–1610), Antonio de Villega (*fl.* 1592–1613), Juan de Morales de Medrano (*fl.* 1595–1634), Alonso de Olmedo (*fl.* 1600–51), and Cosme Perez (*c.* 1585–1673), the most famous comic actor of the age. Jusepa Vaca (*fl.* 1602–34) was the most celebrated actress. Others included Juana de Villalba (*fl.* 1595–1619), Maria de Cordoba (*fl.* 1617–43), María Calderón (*fl.* 1623–35), and Maria de Riquelme (*fl.* 1620–44).

In his *Entertaining Journey,* Rojas Villandrando describes the actor's life around 1600: the performer must rise early and study his roles from 5 until 9 A.M., after which he attends rehearsals until noon; after eating, he goes to the theatre to perform, completing his work about 7 P.M.; after this, he may still be called by officials or noblemen to perform at night. Under Philip IV (reigned 1621–65), the actors were much in demand at court, and Philip's practice of sending for companies on such short notice that they had to cancel public performances is sometimes cited as a reason for the public's loss of interest in the theatre.

The actors were usually paid after each performance. The sharing companies divided the receipts after all expenses were subtracted. Salaried actors were paid by the day, and since the number of performances might vary widely from one year and troupe to another, it is difficult to calculate the average income. One historian has estimated it at about 6000 reals per year, a rather liberal sum for the time. Most salaries were supplemented by a daily maintenance allowance, and additional payments might be made for traveling expenses and costumes. Thus, though the actor did not rank high in the social scale, he was in many ways better off than his French contemporaries, who were denied religious rights, or the English actors who were always at odds with the civic authorities.

Costumes

The costume practices of the Spanish stage were similar to those of England during the same period. Contemporary clothing served in most cases, although historical and legendary figures were sometimes differentiated by outmoded or fanciful dress. Moors, toward whom the Spaniards felt a special antipathy, were always clearly distinguished from other characters.

Many actors owned their own costumes. Although a sharing company owned a common wardrobe, many actors acquired their own stage dress. Actors' contracts often specified allowances for costumes; managers were responsible for the wardrobes of apprentices.

In most cases, actors seem to have dressed as lavishly as finances permitted. As early as 1534, Charles V issued a decree against extravagant dress on the stage, and government regulations recurred throughout the Golden Age. In 1653 actresses were forbidden to wear strange headdresses, decolleté necklines, wide hooped skirts, or dresses not reaching to the floor. In addition, they were restricted to one costume for each play unless the scripts clearly demanded a change.

Records of extravagance are numerous. In 1589, an actor paid 1100 reals and in 1619 another paid 2400 reals for a single costume, sums equivalent to about one-third of an actor's average annual income. No doubt the minor performers were less richly dressed. The actor's wardrobe was considered his greatest financial asset, for it helped him secure employment and could be pawned in bad times.

The costumes for *autos* were probably more lavish than those used in the public theatres, for contracts usually specified costumes of silk and velvet. Often the actors petitioned civic officials for additional funds to pay for unexpectedly expensive garments, and their requests were frequently granted. In addition, towns voted special prizes to companies or actors who had distinguished themselves either through acting or costuming.

The Stage and Scenery

Like the costuming, the stage and scenery of the Spanish public theatre were in many ways similar to those of England. The stage was a raised platform without a proscenium arch or front curtain, bounded at the back by a permanent facade. Since the *gradas* and second-level galleries extended up to the facade, the action was normally viewed from three sides, although most of the spectators sat or stood in front of the stage. Railings separated the *gradas* from the acting area.

The stage at the Corral del Príncipe was about 28 feet wide by 23 feet deep, not including the semicircular projection at the front, which was about five feet deep at the center. Although the dimensions of the Corral de la Cruz are uncertain, its stage was probably about 26 feet wide by 29 feet deep, with a semicircular extension at the front. The open platform was backed by a facade of two levels. Two pillars divided the lower level into three openings, those at the sides serving as entrances, while the larger central space was used primarily for "discoveries." This discovery space was about nine feet deep. The second level, essentially a gallery, could be used in a variety of ways, but normally represented towers, city walls, or hills. At times, discoveries were also made there by drawing the curtains. It was possible to go from the lower to the upper level in full view of the audience, but it is not clear how this was managed.

For the most part, staging conventions were simple and resembled those of the Elizabethan theatre. An exit and reentry was sufficient to mark a change of place. In addition, three different kinds of scenic background might be used. First, the facade sometimes served. Second, the curtains, which concealed the facade, were used when the locale was unimportant. They were drawn aside to reveal portions of the facade or scenic pieces set up in the discovery space when localization of the action was required. Third, Medieval-like mansions were sometimes set up on the main stage. Surviving scripts clearly show that scenic pieces were used at times to represent gardens, fountains, rocks, trees, forts, and castles. Sometimes they are specified when not strictly required by the action, while in other instances the spectators are requested to imagine some place not shown. It seems likely that practice was inconsistent and was guided more by the availability of scenic pieces than by any conscious theory of stage decoration. On the other hand, as spectacle increased after 1650, painted flats and practicable windows and doors began to be set into the facade in lieu of curtains. Except in rare instances, however, there was no attempt to use perspective painting. The stage was equipped with several trapdoors, while the roof over the stage housed machinery for flying, which was increasingly popular after 1650. Essentially, however, scenic practices changed little during the course of the Golden Age.

Court Entertainments

Although court entertainments like those found elsewhere in Europe had been seen in Spain since the 13th century, it was not until the reign of Philip III (1598–1621) that theatrical performances were given regularly at court. Philip's queen was especially fond of the theatre, and both professional productions and masques performed by courtiers were frequent until her death in 1611.

The court theatre reached its height during the reign of Philip IV (1621–65), who between 1623 and 1653 saw about 300 different plays at court. Although Italianate scenery had been used occasionally since the 16th century, it was not until Cosme Lotti (?–1643) was imported from Florence in 1626 that it became usual. Until the 1630's most of the court entertainments were staged in a large hall at the Alcázar or in the gardens at Aranjuez; after 1633 the new palace, the Buen Retiro, became the center of court entertainments. After the opening of Buen Retiro, performances by courtiers declined rapidly and most productions thereafter were acted by professional troupes.

Many lavish outdoor productions were staged on the palace grounds. One of the most famous of these was Calderón's *Love the Best Enchantment* (1635), for which Lotti built a floating stage on a lake. The special effects included a shipwreck, a triumphal chariot drawn across the water by dolphins, and the destruction of Circe's palace. The whole was lit by 3000 lanterns and the King and his retinue watched from gondolas. In 1636, the three acts of Calderón's *The Three Great Prodigies* were given on three separate stages, each act being performed by a different professional troupe. In addition, there were many lavish masquerades, tournaments, and machine plays. For a carnival in 1637 Lotti designed huge wheeled structures measuring 22 feet in width, 32 feet in length, and 46 feet in height.

In 1640 a permanent theatre, the Coliseo, was constructed by Lotti in the Buen Retiro. This theatre seems to have resembled the public *corrales*, for it had a *patio*, three levels of *aposentos*, and a *cazuela*. The royal box was situated above the *cazuela*. On the other hand, the Coliseo was roofed and probably had a proscenium arch, the first in Spain, although this is by no means certain. The Coliseo was also frequently open to the public, which paid the same entrance fees as at the public *corrales*, and the same percentage of the receipts was given to the charities. The plays were performed by troupes which normally performed in the *corrales,* and the scenic demands for most of the plays were similar to those written for the public theatres. Other plays, however, were spectacular pieces which required Italianate scenery and special effects. Sometimes private court performances preceded those open to the public, and more intimate entertainments were usually given in another room in the palace.

The 1640's saw a marked decline in theatrical activities, both at court and in the public theatres. The Catalan and Portuguese rebellions of 1640 ushered in a period of uncertainty, and, following the deaths of Lotti in 1643 and of the Queen in 1644, court theatricals virtually came to an end. Between 1646 and 1651 the public theatres were closed as well.

By 1650, Philip had remarried and had settled many of his political problems; consequently, the Coliseo was reopened to the public in 1651, the same year in which the public theatres were permitted to resume performances. Another Italian designer, Baccio del Bianco, was imported in 1652, and the use of spectacular scenery increased markedly thereafter. Court performances were frequent until Philip's death in 1665. They were resumed about 1670 and the old practices were continued. In these years, a Spaniard, José Caudi, replaced the Italians to become the first native scene designer of note. After the death of Carlos II in 1700, the court theatre declined rapidly.

Although productions were given at regular intervals from the 1620's until the end of the century, the court never employed a company of its

SCENE FROM A PLAY at the Spanish court about 1680. [Courtesy Bibliothèque National, Paris]

own. Rather, actors were summoned from the public theatres of Madrid to rehearse and perform plays. Although the actors were well paid, the public theatres were often forced to cancel performances on short notice and to remain closed for some time. Some historians attribute much of the public's loss of interest in the theatre to this practice.

By the late 17th century, the financial resources of Spain were virtually exhausted and Spain's political power was rapidly declining. The great dramatic impulse was also over, for after the death of Calderón in 1681, new writers sought merely to recapture the past glory instead of exploring new paths. As a consequence, one of the most vital and productive periods the theatre has known was clearly over by 1700.

THE THEATRE
IN FRANCE
FROM 1548 TO 1700

*I*n France, which had been the major center for Medieval drama, the prohibition of religious plays after 1548 was a heavy blow. Although professional troupes sought to replace the amateurs, the development of a strong secular theatre was inhibited at first by religious and political strife. Consequently, it was not until the 1630's that a vigorous drama emerged. By 1700 the French theatre was the most admired in Europe, and did much to confirm the ideals of neo-classicism and the Italianate stage.

The Public Stage in Paris before 1595

In 1548 the Confrèrie de la Passion was the only group authorized to perform in Paris. Organized in 1402 to produce religious drama, it had in 1518 been granted a monopoly destined to continue for 160 years. Since the

15th century, the Confrèrie had presented its occasional productions in a large hall at the Hôpital de la Trinité. Forced to move in 1539, it settled in the Hôtel de Flandres until that building was torn down in 1543. In 1548, after a series of relocations, the Confrèrie began construction of a new building, the first permanent public theatre since Roman times. Because it was located on land formerly owned by the Dukes of Burgundy, the theatre was called the Hôtel de Bourgogne. Before the theatre could be completed, religious plays were banned, but the Confrèrie's monopoly over theatrical production in Paris was reconfirmed. Thus, while the traditional justification for the group's productions—the presentation of devotional dramas—had been removed, the Confrèrie was given complete control over the secular theatre.

Few records of performances between 1548 and 1575 have survived. The Confrèrie probably played at irregular intervals, but its popularity waned with its new repertory, principally farces. Consequently, it began to rent its theatre to other troupes. By this time, a number of professional companies had developed outside of Paris, possibly as offshoots of the confraternities formed to produce religious plays. Professional groups were performing at Rouen by 1556, at Amiens by 1559, at Dijon by 1577, and at Agen by 1585. Few played in Paris because of the Confrèrie's monopoly. Outside of Paris, however, where no monopolies existed, conditions were more favorable. In 1578 the troupe of Agnan Sarat and Pierre Dubuc leased the Hôtel de Bourgogne, the first record of this practice; after this time, the theatre was occupied increasingly by visiting companies. All actors performing in Paris, whether at the Hôtel de Bourgogne or elsewhere, had to pay fees to the Confrèrie.

Further development of the French theatre was impeded by religious controversies. Civil war raged intermittently after about 1560. It reached a climax when the assassination of Henri III in 1589 brought Henri of Navarre, a Huguenot, to the throne. Although Henri IV embraced Catholicism, he was unable to enter Paris until 1594, and peace was not fully restored until 1600. Soon after the theatre reopened about 1595, the Confrèrie had given up the production of plays, and thereafter restricted its role to that of landlord and exacter of fees from the troupes which came to Paris.

Neo-Classical Drama in the 16th Century

By 1595, an embryonic neo-classical drama had appeared in schools and at court. The pattern of its development in France was similar to that in other countries, for it began in the late 15th century with the study of Roman plays, continued with Latin imitations of classical works in the early 16th century, and progressed to plays in French after 1550. During the second phase, Ravisius Textor wrote a number of Latin *Dialogi* which were performed by students at the University of Paris between 1501 and 1524; in 1536, Roilletus published three Latin tragedies which had been acted by his students in Paris. At the College of Guienne in Bordeaux, Latin plays by George Buchanan and Muretus were produced between 1539 and 1545. Around 1540, classical plays and critical treatises began to be translated into French. Plays by Sophocles, Euripides, Aristophanes, Seneca, Plautus, and Terence and critical works by Aristotle and Horace had appeared before 1550. Recent Italian plays also were translated, and Italian commentaries on Aristotle's *Poetics* soon followed. Italian influence increased markedly after 1548, when Henri II married Catherine de'Medici.

The third phase was initiated by the Pléiade, an association of writers and critics who sought to develop French as the medium for a literature modeled on classical works. They formulated rules of grammar and prosody, enriched the language by inventing new words, and illustrated their ideals in their own works. Of necessity, the Pléiade addressed itself primarily to the educated classes. In 1552, a member of the Pléiade, Etienne Jodelle (1523–73), wrote both the first neo-classical tragedy, *Cléopatre captive,* and the first neo-classical comedy, *Eugène,* in French. *Cléopatre,* first acted before Henri II with Jodelle in the title role, is essentially narrative, since most of the action has occurred before the play begins. *Eugène* utilizes the conventions of Roman comedy in telling a story similar to those of Medieval farce. Following Jodelle's example, a number of authors wrote plays for courtly or university audiences, although the majority of works probably remained unperformed.

By 1572, when Jean de la Taille published a preface advocating the three unities, the neo-classical ideal had been fully set forth in France, and most of the scholastic dramatists were following these precepts in their writing. By far the best of these playwrights was Robert Garnier (*c.* 1535–*c.* 1600), who wrote eight tragedies between 1568 and 1583. Although most of Garnier's plays are composed of scenes adapted from Euripides or Seneca, they are almost devoid of dramatic action, for Garnier restricted himself primarily to relating the suffering of his protagonists. Nevertheless, his plays were widely read and admired.

Garnier's most popular, though least characteristic work is *Bradamante* (1582), a tragicomedy about a girl who can marry only that man who has overcome her in battle. It is indicative of changes which came over French scholastic drama after 1580, under the influence of novels and the popular theatre. For example, Beaubreuil's *Regulus* (1582) ignores the unity of time and places several battles on stage. In his preface, furthermore, Beaubreuil launched a vigorous attack on the unities. Although a few other writers departed from the neo-classical mode, no outstanding dramatist appeared to follow their lead. Under the impact of the civil war after 1589, the school drama declined. Future developments were to depend entirely upon professional playwrights.

The Public Theatre from 1595 to 1625

When theatrical activities resumed in 1595, French drama was still of little consequence. The neo-classical dramatists had catered to aristocratic audiences but had failed to produce any plays of lasting interest. Although a few of the learned dramas had been presented in the public theatres, the usual popular fare was farce, much of which was improvised under the influence of the *commedia dell'arte* troupes, which had played in Paris between 1572 and 1588 and were to return frequently after 1599.

These conditions began to change only with the appearance about 1597 of France's first professional playwright, Alexandre Hardy (c. 1572–1632). During the next 35 years, Hardy wrote about 500 plays, of which only 34 have survived. Working for a popular audience, Hardy adapted his plays to its tastes. Thus, although he used such neo-classical devices as the five-act form, poetic dialogue, ghosts, messengers, and the chorus, he did not permit theoretical considerations to interfere with his primary aim of telling an interesting story. He seldom observed the unities of time and place, and he put all important episodes, no matter how violent, on stage. At first he wrote tragedies, but since these did not please, he turned to tragicomedy and pastoral.

Although Hardy never achieved greatness, his accomplishment was considerable. Coming to the theatre when farce reigned, he paved the way for tragedy with his tragicomedies and for comedy with his pastorals. His success encouraged other writers to turn to the stage. Not until after 1625, however, did any plays equal Hardy's in merit or popularity.

Hardy's early work was done primarily for Valleran LeComte (*fl.* 1592–1613), the first important French theatrical manager. Although a number of itinerant companies played in Paris after 1595, the arrival of Valleran in 1598 marks the first attempt to provide production of high quality. By this time, Valleran was already well-established, having performed since 1592 in major provincial cities. In 1598 his troupe was already being called Les Comédiens du roi ("The King's Players"), probably because it had performed before Henri IV. The title, however, carried with it no special privileges or subsidy. Between 1598 and 1612, Valleran's was the most important company in Paris, although, like its competitors, it also toured elsewhere, for as yet no company was able to establish permanent headquarters in the capital.

221

THE THEATRE IN FRANCE FROM 1548 TO 1700

In the early 17th century, acting companies were bound together by two- or three-year contracts. All were organized on the sharing plan, under which profits were divided after each performance. The manager normally received two shares, while lesser actors might be allotted less than a full share. Companies ranged in size from eight to twelve members, sometimes supplemented by "hired men" and apprentices. By 1607, women were included in the companies. Although acting gained steadily in popularity between 1595 and 1625, the social and religious stigma attached to it led most performers to assume stage names when they went into the theatre.

In spite of the efforts of Valleran and Hardy, farce continued to be the most popular dramatic form. Between 1610 and 1625, the most famous actors in Paris were the farce players, Turlupin, Gaultier-Garguille, and Gros-Guillaume. Turlupin, acted by Henri LeGrand (c. 1587–c. 1637), who used the name Belleville in serious roles, was a rascally servant similar to Brighella of the *commedia dell'arte*. Gaultier-Garguille, acted by Hugues Gueru (c. 1573–1633), who played as Fleschelles in serious drama, was a tall, thin, bow-legged creature who could contort his body like a marionette. Gros-Guillaume, acted by Robert Guérin (c. 1554–c. 1634), who used the name LaFleur in serious roles, had a flour-whitened face and an obese body, emphasized by a belt above and below his enormous stomach. The practice of playing fixed characters with stock costumes and makeup suggests the closeness of French farce of this period to *commedia dell'arte,* a similarity which may have extended to improvisational playing. Associated for a time with Valleran's troupe, Turlupin, Gaultier-Garguille, and Gros-Guillaume were the principal performers of the Hôtel de Bourgogne after Valleran left Paris in 1612, and it is they who were probably most responsible for building up a theatre-going public.

The usual place for performances between 1595 and 1625 was the Hôtel de Bourgogne, since it was the only permanent theatre in Paris. Although it was used from 1548 until 1783, the dimensions of this building are uncertain. The land acquired by the Confrèrie in 1548 measured 101 by 108 feet, but part of this was sold before the theatre was built. One group of historians believes that the theatre was erected on a lot measuring about 42 by 108 feet, while another argues that it was 60 by 108 feet. Consequently, estimates of the theatre's width vary by almost 20 feet. Although it is difficult to choose between the claims, the overall dimensions of the Hôtel de Bourgogne were probably about 40 feet in width by 105 feet in length.

Around the halls of the auditorium ran two or three galleries, at least one of which was divided into boxes or loges. Above the loges facing the stage rose an undivided gallery (the amphitheatre or *paradis*). The first floor was taken up entirely by the pit, or *parterre,* in which there were no permanent seats, with the possible exception of a bench along the side walls. The total capacity of the auditorium was about 1600.

The stage was raised five or six feet above the pit. Although there was

La chambre de l'Hôtel de Bourgogne, d'après la gravure d'Abraham Bosse, vers 1630.

FARCE SCENE at the Hotel de Bourgogne about 1630. On stage are Turlupin, Gaultier-Garguille, and Gros-Guillaume. Note the sentry-like boxes at either side of the stage. [From Houssaye's *La Comédie Française*, 1880]

no proscenium arch, the side galleries, which extended to the stage, created a frame. The stage occupied the full width of the building, but the visible space was probably no wider than 25 feet. The depth of the stage is unknown, estimates ranging from 17 to 35 feet.

Although the Confrèrie probably used Medieval mansions on this stage, the little that is known of scenic practices before 1625 can be summarized briefly: the Confrèrie may have owned scenery which it rented with the theatre; Valleran's records show that he sometimes paid painters for scenic pieces; Hardy's extant plays require from three to seven locations, probably represented by separate mansions arranged around the periphery of the stage as they were in the 1630's; the few extant illustrations of farces show a stage with a compartment on either side, and either a cloth or doors at the back. Since all of the troupes were itinerant, none probably attempted elaborate settings.

Not all troupes performed at the Hôtel de Bourgogne, although the Confrèrie collected a fee each day from all troupes appearing in Paris. For those who did not play at the Bourgogne, the usual choice was a tennis court. Since the Middle Ages, tennis (or *jeu de paume*) had been a favorite European game, and by the 16th century many courts were enclosed and roofed. Estimates of the number in Paris range from 250 to 1800. By 1600, the measurements of tennis courts were standardized at about 90 by 30 feet. Thus, they did not differ markedly in size from the Hôtel de Bourgogne. A number of features recommended their use as theatres: the presence of a gallery along one side or end; the large open floor space; the row of windows just below the roof which provided ample light. To convert a tennis court into a theatre, therefore, required merely the addition of a platform, an operation so simple that it was often done for a single performance. For more permanent conversions, the galleries were extended around the other walls and divided into boxes. Throughout Europe, the tennis court became the first choice of actors seeking buildings to convert into theatres.

In Paris, performances were given two or three times a week. By 1600, posters were being used to advertise productions, and announcements were made from the stage. The starting time varied, but official regulations required that performances end sufficiently early that spectators might reach home before dark. Because the starting time was indefinite and spectators came early to secure good places, each company employed a "prologuist" to entertain the audience until the performance began. Bruscambrille (*fl.* 1610–34) was famous in this role. The daily bill usually consisted of a long play followed by a farce, although an entire program might be made up of short plays. Music was a part of all performances.

The audience was drawn from all classes, but prior to 1625 was largely undiscriminating in its search for entertainment. Many spectators wore swords or daggers, and fights in the pit were common. Probably there was much jostling and moving about by the 1000 persons who might stand in the pit throughout a performance. The confusion was increased by the sale of food, drink, and other articles.

By 1625, the professional theatre had established a rather precarious foothold in Paris. Although still crude in comparison with those of England, Spain, or Italy, the French theatre was soon to undergo changes which would raise it above all others in critical estimation.

The Theatre at the French Court Before 1625

The court theatre followed a path roughly parallel to the public theatres, for though many tentative steps had been taken toward the Italian ideal, no strong trend had been established by 1625. Vitruvius' treatise was well-known after 1500, but, unlike the Italians, the French did not try to apply it to the theatre. The "Terence Stage," first depicted in the edition published at Lyons in 1493, may possibly have been adopted at schools and court for performances of classically-inspired plays.

Italian ideals made their first impact in the 1540's. In 1542, Charles Estienne's preface to Terence's *Andria* discussed the use of *periaktoi;* between 1541 and 1554, Serlio worked in France, where his treatise on stage practice was published in 1545; in 1548, perspective scenery was used for the first time in France for Andrea Nannoccio's production of

Bibiena's *La Calandria* at Lyons celebrating the wedding of Henri II and Catherine de'Medici. In spite of these promising beginnings, no new developments followed immediately. Nothing is known of the court staging of scholastic dramas after 1552, or of the *commedia dell'arte* performances between 1572 and 1588.

After 1570, the *ballet de cour,* a form similar to Italian *intermezzi* and English masques, came into prominence at court. Uniting poetry, music and dance in an allegorical story designed to reflect favorably upon a person or occasion, most of the ballets were composed by Balthasar de Beaujoyeulx. His most famous work is the *Ballet Comique de la Reine* (1581), based on the myth of Circe. Settings for the *ballets de cour* were medieval, however, for they used a number of mansions dispersed throughout the hall. Most of the ballets were staged at the Louvre in the Salle du Petit Bourbon, which was to become one of the important court theatres of the 17th century. This hall measured about 49 feet in width by 177 feet in length, with an apse extending another 44 feet. The king and courtiers sat in the apse, while other spectators occupied two superimposed balconies extending around the side walls.

It was not until *Alcine* in 1610 that the court ballets began to use unified settings in the Italian manner. During the next ten years, largely due to the importation of such designers as Tomaso Francini, most of the Italian scenic developments were seen at the French court. At first, painted

Le Ballet de la Reine.

Ballet Comique de la Reine given at the Petit Bourbon in 1581. Note the dispersed decor and the placement of the audience. [From Papst, *Essai sur l'Histoire du Théâtre* (1893)]

cloths, which could be dropped to reveal others behind, were used, but in 1617, for *The Deliverance of Renaud,* the angled-wing was introduced. By 1620, perspective scenery, unified settings, the raked stage, and scene shifting had all been used. After 1620, however, the court ceased to produce ballets, and the naturalization of the Italian ideal was postponed until the 1640's.

The New Drama, 1625–36

In the years immediately after 1625, a new era in the French theatre began. It resulted from several factors: a group of well-educated and technically-proficient playwrights appeared; the audience came to prefer the new drama to the earlier farces; the neo-classical ideal was reintroduced; and professional troupes gained a firm foothold in Paris.

Of the dramatists who appeared around 1625, four were of special importance: Jean de Mairet, Pierre du Ryer, Jean de Rotrou, and Pierre Corneille. Jean de Mairet (1604–86) came to Paris in 1625, the year in which his first play, *Chryséide and Arimand,* a tragicomedy, was performed. In 1626 he turned to writing pastorals, which he helped to popularize through such works as *Sylvie* (1628) and *La Sylvanire* (1631). Soon recognized as the leading dramatist of his day, he confirmed his reputation with *Sophonisba* (1634), the first tragedy of the new age to observe the neo-classical rules. It revived interest in tragedy which had been dormant since the first years of the century. Although Mairet's reputation has suffered because of his intemperate attack upon Corneille's *Le Cid,* he was as successful and often more highly regarded than Corneille in his own day, and probably did more than any other writer to set the drama on its new path before he retired in 1640.

Pierre du Ryer (*c.* 1600–58), a well-educated government official, wrote prolifically in an attempt to overcome his perennial poverty. His early works were either irregular tragicomedies, such as *Clitophon* (*c.* 1629) and *Argenis and Poliarque* (1631), or farce vehicles for Gros-Guillaume. After coming under Mairet's influence about 1634, he turned to tragedy in the neo-classical mode. Of these later works, the best is *Scévole* (1644), which remained in the repertory for more than a century. Along with Mairet and Corneille, du Ryer established tragedy as a popular form.

Jean de Rotrou (1609–50) began writing plays in 1628, and eventually succeeded Hardy as principal dramatist to the Hôtel de Bourgogne. Through Rotrou's adaptations of Spanish drama, the theme of love versus honor became a staple of the French stage. Interested primarily in rapid and absorbing actions, Rotrou failed to create characters of depth. Consequently, his plays now seem shallow, although in their day they did much to extend public interest in drama and offered Corneille his severest competition.

Despite the accomplishments of his contemporaries, Pierre Corneille (1606–84) is now usually credited with establishing the neo-classical mode in France. Born in Rouen and educated for the law, he began to write plays after seeing the Montdory-LeNoir troupe perform. The result was *Mélite* (1629), a comedy unlike either farce or pastoral, the major comic forms of the time. Consequently, *Mélite* is often said to have set French comedy on a new path, in which the intrigues and misunderstandings of lovers replaced the former emphasis upon comic servants. Until 1636, most of Corneille's plays were comedies and, though much admired, they served only to establish his reputation as a promising writer.

Le Cid (1636–37) marked the turning point in Corneille's career and in French drama, for it precipitated a battle destined to clarify the conflict between the old and new ideals. Based upon Guillén de Castro's *Las Mocedades del Cid,* a play in six acts treating events occurring over many years and in many places, Corneille's play compresses the events into five acts, 24 hours, and four locations in a single town. Revolving around the theme of love versus honor, the action forces both the hero, Roderigue, and the heroine, Chimène, to choose between their love for each other and their duty to their parents. Although an enormous popular success, it was attacked by several critics, including Mairet and Georges de Scudéry (1601–67), another leading playwright.

The issues were several. While the unity of time had been observed, verisimilitude had been strained by crowding so many incidents into one day. Furthermore, Chimène's apparent agreement to marry Roderigue, who has killed her father less than 24 hours earlier, violated the neo-classical notion of decorum. The play did not fit any recognized dramatic type: it resembled tragicomedy in the number and variety of incidents, in the perils overcome by the hero, and in the happy ending; it resembled pastoral in the love story; and it resembled tragedy in its narrative and lyrical passages. The bitterness of the controversy prompted Cardinal Richelieu to request a verdict on the play from the newly-formed French Academy. The results were destined to focus public attention on the neo-classical ideal.

The Neo-Classical Ideal in France

Interest in the neo-classical ideal, which had been dormant since about 1590, began to revive again in the late 1620's as political conditions grew more settled. Following the death of Henri IV in 1610, France had gone through another period of unrest, for Louis XIII was only nine years old when he came to the throne. It was not until the 1620's that the king was able to wrest authority from those who had ruled in his name. With the aid of such men as Cardinal Richelieu (1586–1642), a member of the King's Council after 1624 and Chief Minister after 1629, he brought stability to the country and established a strong central government.

Between 1629 and 1642, Richelieu used his position to encourage the development of French literature and the arts. To him, greatness lay in pursuing the Italian ideals of writing and staging. Through financial support, he encouraged those authors who accepted neo-classicism, and in his palace he built the first Italianate theatre in France. He also urged the formation of the French Academy as an arbiter of literary taste.

The French Academy originated in 1629 when a small group began meeting to discuss literature. Richelieu urged them to form an organization modeled after the Italian academies. In 1636 they somewhat reluctantly did as he wished, and in 1637 received a charter, under which the Academy still operates. Membership is restricted to 40, presumably the most eminent literary figures of the time. The Academy took as its primary task the study and codification of French language and style.

It was to this newly-formed group that Richelieu referred *Le Cid*. Its judgment, written principally by its leader, Jean Chapelain, was contained in *Les Sentiments de l'Académie sur Le Cid* (1638). In it, Chapelain praised *Le Cid* insofar as it adhered to neo-classical doctrine and censured it for all deviations. He also restated the neo-classical ideal and urged its universal adoption. Although neoclassicism had already been adopted by Mairet and others, it was not to become dominant until the 1640's. Chapelain's arguments were reenforced by such later works as *Theatrical Practice* (1657) by the Abbé D'Augibnac (1604-76) and *The Art of Poetry* (1674) by Nicolas Boileau-Despreaux (1636–1711).

French Drama, 1640–60

Although Corneille later embraced neo-classical doctrine, he was stung by the reactions to *Le Cid* and wrote no more plays until 1640. Between 1640 and 1644, however, he produced the works now considered most characteristic of his style: *Horace* (1640), *Cinna* (1640), *Polyeucte* (1642–43), and *The Death of Pompey* (1643). Each centers around a hero of indomitable will who chooses death rather than dishonor. Since Corneille's protagonists are never in doubt about their goals, they often appear one-sided; never divided within themselves, they are revealed in a series of episodes showing their reactions to some external opposition. Consequently, Corneille's characters are simple, but his plots complex. Beginning with *Rodogune* (1644), Corneille's stories became so involved that many are difficult to follow. This trend toward complexity was general until Racine's simplicity brought a reaction in the 1660's. While Corneille is the most celebrated tragedian of the 1640's, other writers, such as du Ryer and Rotrou, were also productive in these years.

Corneille set the standard in comedy as well. *The Liar* (1643), adapted from Alarçon's *The Suspicious Truth,* is regarded the finest French comedy before Molière. Only one other comic writer, Paul Scarron (1610–60), challenged Corneille's supremacy. Scarron paved the way for Molière by combining the comedy of intrigue, in which Corneille excelled, with farce, notably in *Jodelet, ou le maître-valet* (1643) and *Jodelet souffleté* (1645) both written especially for the farce-player, Jodelet. In *L'Écolier de Salamanque* (1654), Scarron introduced the character Crispin, who became so popular that other dramatists incorporated him into their plays. Scarron's novel, *Le Roman Comique* (1651), which depicts the life of touring actors, is also noteworthy.

The vigor of the 1640's was followed in the 1650's by a decline. Tragedy lost its appeal and, after the failure of *Pertharite* in 1652, Corneille gave up writing for many years. The decline can be attributed in part to another civil war which lasted from 1648 to 1652. Hostilities developed out of the nobility's attempts to reassert rights taken from them by Richelieu. Under Richelieu's successor, Cardinal Mazarin, who ruled France in the name of the child-king, Louis XIV, the grievances came to a head after the nobles formed La Fronde ("the sling"). As a result of the war, the power of the nobility was completely broken; those of the highest rank were forced to live at court where they could be watched. All authority was to remain concentrated in the crown until the Revolution. The civil war of 1648–52 was followed by a war in Spain until 1660. When Mazarin died in 1661, Louis XIV became the real ruler of France. In the years that followed, French drama flowered as France's political prestige grew.

Acting Companies, 1625–60

The new vigor in playwriting between 1625 and 1660 was paralleled by the increasing stability of acting companies. In contrast with the preceding period, from 1625 to 1680 the Hôtel de Bourgogne housed only one troupe. By 1629, a second company had settled in Paris, and at least two theatres were open thereafter.

The Bourgogne's troupe was descended from Valleran's; it at first included a number of his actors and used the same title, Comédiens du roi.

Until their deaths in the 1630's, Turlupin, Gaultier-Garguille, and Gros-Guillaume were in the company. Its leader and most important actor, however, was Bellerose (Pierre le Messier, *c.* 1592–1670), who had begun as an apprentice in Valleran's company in 1609. After Valleran's death about 1613, Bellerose had toured with the remnants of the troupe until they returned to Paris in the early 1620's and amalgamated with the farce players at the Hôtel de Bourgogne. Bellerose was a fine actor in both comedy and tragedy. He brought dignity to the theatre just as the new drama was achieving greater subtlety and the taste for farce was declining. Noted for his natural style, he was nevertheless accused of affectation. His supremacy in the troupe remained unchallenged until his retirement in 1647.

The Comédiens du roi soon had a rival in the troupe headed by Montdory (Guillaume des Gilleberts, 1594–1654) and Charles LeNoir (*fl.* 1610–37). Montdory began his career about 1612 in Valleran's company, and, upon Valleran's death, joined the Prince of Orange's Players, with whom he remained for many years. In the late 1620's, he formed a company with Charles LeNoir, another actor-manager who had performed in Paris intermittently since 1610. After touring the provinces, they returned to Paris in 1629, bringing with them Corneille's first play, *Mélite*. They performed in a number of temporary theatres before settling in 1634 in a converted tennis court, the Théâtre du Marais, the first serious rival to the Hôtel de Bourgogne.

With his preference for the new drama, Montdory won the favor of Cardinal Richelieu, who awarded him a pension in 1634. In addition to *Le Cid,* many of the other outstanding plays of the 1630's were first played by Montdory. Sometimes called the first great French actor, Montdory was at his best in the roles of tragic heroes. Although a declamatory actor, he was capable of great emotion and brought conviction to all his parts. Under Montdory's leadership, the Marais became the leading theatre of Paris, a position which it was to hold until 1647. Unfortunately, Montdory suffered a partial paralysis in 1637 and was forced to retire.

Montdory was replaced at the Marais by Floridor (Josias de Soulas, 1608–72), an aristocrat who had played in a touring company for many years. Upon Montdory's retirement, he joined the Marais troupe as its leading actor until 1647, when he went to the Bourgogne to replace Bellerose. After Floridor's departure, the Marais declined, for Corneille and other leading dramatists now gave their plays to the Bourgogne. Floridor continued as the leading actor of Paris until his retirement in 1671.

Floridor shared tragic roles with Montfleury (Zacharie Jacob, 1600–67), who had joined the Bourgogne company in 1639 and risen rapidly to a position second only to that of Bellerose. Although he was enormously fat and employed a pompous delivery, he had a large following.

The farce tradition was continued by Jodelet and Guillot-Gorju.

Jodelet (Julien Bedeau, *c.* 1600–60) was a member of Montdory's troupe until ordered by Louis XIII to transfer to the Bourgogne in 1634. In the early 1640's he returned to the Marais, where he was so popular that a number of dramatists wrote plays especially for him. In 1659 he joined Molière, who created some roles especially for him, although Jodelet's death in 1660 made their association brief. Playing with a flour-whitened face in the manner of Gros-Guillaume, Jodelet was especially noted as the comic valet, a role which he raised to great popularity. Guillot-Gorju (Bertrand Hardouin de St. Jacques, 1600–48) joined the Bourgogne troupe in 1633, upon the death of Gaultier-Garguille. In the role of the ridiculous doctor, he was famous for his witty repartee. He retired in 1641 to practice medicine, which he had studied prior to going on the stage.

These leading actors were surrounded by numerous lesser figures. After 1647, the Bourgogne troupe gained the ascendancy which it was to maintain until 1680. Meanwhile, the Marais, in an attempt to retain its popularity, turned increasingly to spectacle. Under the management of Laroque (Pierre Regnault Petit-Jean, *c.* 1595–1676), it fought a losing battle from 1647 to 1673.

Both the financial and social position of the actor improved between 1625 and 1660. As Richelieu and others began to patronize the Marais troupe in the 1630's, Louis XIII granted the Comédiens du roi a subsidy, which by 1641 amounted to 1200 livres annually. All major troupes after this time received governmental assistance. Concern for the actor's dignity also appeared around 1630. Gougenot's *La Comédie des Comédiens* (*c.* 1631), a play depicting a rehearsal, defends actors from the charge of immorality, and Georges de Scudéry's play of the same title, performed in 1632, takes the same position. Scudéry argues that actors, like the members of other professions, vary and that each should be judged on his merits. Scudéry also lists as qualifications of the good actor appropriate facial expression, impressive bearing, unconstrained movement, absence of extravagant posturing and provincial accent, a good memory, and sound judgment.

In 1641, Louis XIII sought to remove the stigma attached to acting by issuing a decree stating his desire that "the actors' profession . . . not be considered worthy of blame nor prejudicial to their reputation in society." Although it abolished certain legal restrictions, this decree did not alter the church's denial of its sacraments to actors.

The Public Theatres, 1625–60

The major public theatres of Paris between 1625 and 1660 were the Hôtel de Bourgogne and the Théâtre du Marais. Presumably the appearance of the Bourgogne remained relatively unchanged from 1548 until

1647, when, by order of the King's Council, it was remodeled, probably in order to compete more effectively with the Marais.

Almost nothing is known of the first Théâtre du Marais, which was converted from a tennis court in 1634. When it burned in 1644, it was replaced immediately with a more elaborate structure which remained in use until 1673. The new Marais measured about 115 feet in length, 38 feet in width, and 52 feet in height. The pit, for standing spectators, was 61 feet by 36 feet; the side walls had three galleries, the first two divided into boxes, the third given over to the *paradis;* at the rear of the auditorium, the first gallery was divided into boxes, while above it rose the amphitheatre with its stadium-like seating. The capacity of the auditorium was about 1500 persons.

The stage, raised about six feet above the parterre, sloped up toward the back. It occupied the full width of the building and had a proscenium

Scene from *Martyre de Sainte Catharine* by Jean Puget de la Serre, produced at the Hotel de Bourgogone in the early 1640s, perhaps showing the *théâtre supérieure* in use. In this play the basic structure remained fixed, while the view behind the central doorway and on the upper level were changed for each act. [From the original edition of the play]

opening 25 feet wide. There was also a *théâtre supérieure,* or second stage, raised 13 feet above the main platform on 10 pillars. Semicircular, it curved upstage six feet at its center. Although documents clearly establish that the Marais had a *théâtre supérieure,* scholars differ in their estimates of its size and placement. The reconstruction by Deierkauf-Holsboer begins the second stage only six feet from the front edge of the main platform and makes the lower stage only 12 feet deep at its center. Bjurstrom, on the other hand, suggests that the lower stage was 29 feet deep at its center. Bjurstrom's reconstruction seems more logical, especially in light of the Marais' emphasis upon spectacle. On the other hand, much of the spectacle may have depended upon the upper stage. Since it might represent the "heavens," flying objects could rest on it in back of clouds used to conceal the platform. It is clear from many scripts, however, that not all flying was handled in this manner, and some scholars have questioned whether it was ever the usual method. Disagreement also exists about the use made of the second stage, some arguing that it was essential to almost every play, while others state that it was rarely employed. Although its precise use cannot be established, the *théâtre supérieure* was unquestionably available at both the Marais and the Bourgogne, although in the latter theatre it may have been removable.

The desire to compete with the new Marais probably motivated the remodeling of the Bourgogne in 1647. The imprecise contract still exists. It specifies that the stage is to be about 45 feet deep and "as wide as the building" (about 40 feet). The floor was raked upward toward the back and beams were installed at the front, probably to accommodate a curtain and to form a proscenium arch, neither of which apparently were used earlier. The stage opening was about 25 feet wide. In the auditorium, the galleries were curved into a U-shape so as to eliminate the former sharp angles. In spite of the remodeling, the Bourgogne remained the Parisian theatre least concerned with spectacle.

Scenic Practices of the Public Theatres, 1625–60

The scenic practices of the early 1630's are well-documented in *Le Mémoire de Mahelot, Laurent, et d'Autres Décorateurs . . . .,* one of the most valuable theatrical records of the 17th century. It is divided into three parts, each relating to widely separated years. The first part ends in 1635. Some scholars assume that it summarizes only the season of 1634–35, while others argue that it records usage from about 1622 to 1635. It consists of 71 notices (that is, summaries of the scenic requirements) and 47 designs for plays in the repertory of the Hôtel de Bourgogne. Most scholars believe that the designs are by the compiler, Laurent Mahelot, although some historians have suggested that he was merely the theatre's machinist and that the designs are by Georges Buffequin, the major scenic designer of the period.

Mahelot's compilation demonstrates clearly that in 1635, scenic practices were still essentially Medieval. Since the unity of place was not yet usual, most plays required a number of locales, each of which was represented by a mansion. All mansions were present simultaneously, arranged along the sides and across the back of the stage so as to leave the center free for the actors. The back scene usually represented a single place, while typically there were two mansions on each side. Many of the mansions were of such a general nature—a house, a wood, a palace, a grotto, a cave, a tomb, a prison, a tent, a seacoast—that they reappeared in a number of different settings. When a play required more mansions than could be accommodated on stage at once, units were converted by removing painted canvas coverings or by opening curtains to reveal an interior. A few visual characteristics relate the settings to Italian practices: some of the painted backcloths are done in perspective; the balanced pairs of mansions resemble Serlio's arrangement of angled wings; in some settings, decorative details are repeated so as to give greater unity to the whole. In spite of these elements, the effect is more Medieval than Italianate.

A few machines are mentioned by Mahelot. Boats with passengers

SETTING at the Hôtel de Bourgogone (c. 1635) for duRyer's *Lisander and Caliste*. From *Le Memoire de Mahelot.* . . . [Courtesy Bibliothèque Nationale, Paris]

move from one side of the stage to the other; gods and other supernatural characters appear above the stage; clouds, fire, smoke, and sound effects are specified. Such properties as human heads and sponges filled with blood are noted. Furniture is restricted to an occasional throne or stool.

Le Mémoire also gives some information about costumes, since it lists all items supplied by the company. It reveals that actors supplied their own garments except for monks, devils, ghosts, coachmen, and valets, or when a number of identical costumes were required. By the 1630's, considerable splendor in dress was evident. The inventory made of Charles LeNoir's wardrobe in 1637 appraised it at the modern equivalent of $8000; one individual costume was valued at $400.

The second part of the *Mémoire* lists 71 titles of works in the repertory of the Hôtel de Bourgogne in 1646–47, but unfortunately includes neither notices nor designs. It may be assumed that scenic practices gradually moved away from simultaneous settings composed of Medieval mansions to unified settings as the unity of place was increasingly adopted after the *Le Cid* controversy. Certainly, by 1680 settings were appreciably simpler than in 1635, a point which will be pursued later.

The Italian Ideal in Staging, 1625–1700

Although Italianate scenery had been introduced at court before 1625, it was not exploited until after 1640. Perhaps to provide a model, Cardinal Richelieu had the architect LeMercier construct the first theatre in France with a permanent proscenium arch and a stage designed for flat wings. Called the Palais Cardinal, this theatre had a stage 59 feet wide by 46 feet deep, and an auditorium 59 feet wide by 65 feet deep. Two undivided galleries surrounded the hall, while most of the ground floor was taken up by an amphitheatre which rose in broad steps from a small pit. Since the theatre was intended only for invited guests, the auditorium did not follow the arrangement used in the public theatres.

The Palais Cardinal was opened in January 1641 with *Mirame,* with scenery and special effects designed by Georges Buffequin. Since *Mirame* required only one setting, the potentialities of the theatre were not fully displayed until later in 1641 when the *Ballet de la Prosperité des Armes du France,* with nine settings, was produced. When Richelieu died in 1642, the theatre came under the control of the crown and thereafter was called the Palais Royal.

Richelieu's position as Chief Minister was assumed by Cardinal Mazarin, an Italian with a taste for opera, which he sought to introduce into France. His first production in 1645 set in motion a series of events which

INTERIOR of the theatre built by Cardinal Richelieu in 1641 (later the Palais Royal). [From a contemporary print]

were to bring Giacomo Torelli to Paris. A visiting *commedia dell'arte* troupe was so fearful of the opera that it begged the Queen to import a designer and choreographer from Italy to increase the appeal of their spectacle. Consequently, she wrote to the Duke of Parma, who dispatched the aid she requested.

By 1645, Torelli was probably the most famous scene designer in Italy because of his productions at the Teatro Novissimo in Venice. Torelli accepted the royal summons without realizing that he was to work with the *commedia dell'arte* players. Upon learning the truth, he at first refused, but eventually agreed upon the condition that he be allowed to do other productions as well. For his first opera in Paris, he chose *La Finta Pazzi*, the work that had made him famous in Venice. Staged at the Petit Bourbon in December, 1645, before the court, it was a complete success. Most historians date the triumph of the Italian ideal in France from this production.

To house this opera, Torelli had also converted the Petit Bourbon into an Italianate theatre. In it he erected a platform six feet high to make a stage about 49 feet wide by 48 feet deep, somewhat larger than the one he had used in Venice. He also installed his chariot-and-pole system of scene shifting, probably the chief improvement over Richelieu's theatre.

In 1646, Torelli remodeled the Palais Royal to accommodate the chariot-and-pole method of shifting, and in 1647 *Orphée* was staged there at a tremendous cost, which Mazarin paid out of state funds. The presence of so many Italians, the hostility which the French nobles felt against Mazarin, and the use of state money to finance operas aroused considerable resentment. Mazarin, seeking works more suited to French taste, com-

SETTING by Torelli for Act II of Corneille's *Andromède*
(1650). [Contemporary engraving by Chauveau]

missioned Corneille to write *Andromède,* called a "machine play," since it differed considerably from the Italian operas. Although the story progressed through spoken episodes, each act provided an excuse to introduce elaborate machinery during a pantomimic episode accompanied by music. Most of the scenery and machines had already appeared in *Orphée.* Staged at the Petit Bourbon in 1650, *Andromède* was sufficiently successful that it began a vogue for machine plays, which the Marais sought to meet. With such productions as *The Golden Fleece, The Loves of Jupiter and Semele, The Loves of Venus and Adonis,* and *The Marriage of Bacchus and Ariadne,* the Marais ran into virtual bankruptcy because of the sums required for these spectacles.

In the late 1640's, ballet began to recapture the popularity it had enjoyed at court before 1620. It was especially prominent between 1651 and 1669, when Louis XIV appeared in many ballets. These productions, called *ballets d'entrées,* did not require the technical proficiency of modern ballet. Rather, they were allegorical stories, explained by a spoken libretto and pantomimed by performers in movements based upon ballroom dances of the time. One of the more characteristic works, *The Ballet of the Night* (1653), was divided into 43 "entries," featuring such groups as hunters, bandits, shepherds, gypsies, astrologers, the Four Elements, Venus, Aurora, and finally the Sun, danced by Louis XIV.

The majority of the ballets had librettos by Isaac Bensérade (1613–91). In 1654 Mazarin commissioned Bensérade to write an opera with ballets between the acts. For this production, *The Marriage of Peleus and Thetis,* Torelli designed seven sets and a number of spectacular special

237

Le décor du premier acte de l'*Andromède* de Corneille (d'après la gravure de Chauveau).

SETTING by Torelli for Act I of Corneille's *Andromède* (1650). [From Bapst's *Essai sur l'Historie du Théâtre* (1893)]

effects. Louis XIV appeared in six roles. Although ballet remained popular, opera was largely abandoned after this production until the 1670's.

Preparations for the wedding of Louis XIV precipitated several changes. In 1659, Mazarin sent to Italy for Gaspare Vigarani (1586–1663), famous at this time as a scenic designer and builder of theatres. The Petit Bourbon was torn down, and in its place a new wing was erected on the Louvre by LeVau. In it, Vigarani set up the largest theatre in Europe, the Salle des Machines. Although only 52 feet wide, the new theatre was 226 feet long; of this length, only 94 feet were occupied by the auditorium, leaving 132 feet of depth for a stage which had a proscenium arch only 32 feet wide. This enormous depth is symptomatic of the trend toward settings of ever-increasing size. Completed in 1660, the Salle des Machines was inaugurated in 1662 with the opera *Hercules in Love,* a transparent compliment to the King. Interlarded with ballets, the opera also featured Vigarani's scenery and machines, on one of which, 60 feet deep by 45 feet wide, the entire royal family and their attendants were flown. This machine was used again in *Psyche* (1671) to display 300 deities surrounded by clouds. Because of its size and poor acoustics, the Salle des Machines was seldom used after the 1660's.

When Mazarin imported Vigarani, he had not intended to exclude Torelli, but the latter's enemies rallied around Vigarani, and after Mazarin died in 1661 Torelli was ordered to leave France. He returned to his native Fano, where he later built a theatre. There he staged his last production in 1677, the year before he died. Although Torelli left Paris under a cloud, to

CARLO VIGARANI'S SETTING for Lully's *Atys*, 1676. [Courtesy Nationalmuseum, Stockholm]

him must go the primary credit for establishing the Italian ideal in France.

When Vigarani died in 1663, his post as court designer was given to his son, Carlo (1623–1713), who retained it until 1680. Carlo Vigarani's principal work was done at the court of Versailles and at the opera in Paris. The palace at Versailles was begun in 1627 by Louis XIII, but the court was not moved there until 1682. Nevertheless, between 1663 and 1674, Louis XIV staged several festivals there, for which temporary theatres were set up at various spots in the palace grounds. One of the most spectacular of the celebrations was that of 1664, called "The Pleasures of the Enchanted Island," which extended over three days, and included processions, tournaments, ballets, and plays.

Throughout the 1660's, "comedy ballets," in which scenes in dialogue alternate with ballet entries, were a favorite at court. Many of these were written by Molière and Jean-Baptiste Lully (1632–87), destined to become the founder of French opera. Lully was born in Italy, but came to France when only 12 years old. Appointed a court musician in 1653, he was superintendent of all court music by 1661. In this capacity, he worked closely with Molière and others on court entertainment. His experience with ballets, machine plays, and other forms, familiarized him with French musical taste. In 1672 he obtained from Louis XIV a monopoly on musical performances in Paris, and in 1673, after Molière's death, he wrested control of the Palais Royal from Molière's widow to use as the home of his Royal Academy of Music and Dance (commonly called the Opéra). Although the terms of Lully's monopoly were vague, he interpreted them to

A SCENE from the first day of *Pleasures of the Enchanted Island* given by Louis XIV at Versailles in 1664. In this picture Molière and Madeleine Béjart are in the arbor at the center. [From a contemporary engraving by Silvestre]

cover any performance which required more than six instruments, two trained singers, or elaborate spectacle. The latter provision is indicative of the period's association of spectacle with opera, for as the neo-classical ideal triumphed, the staging of drama had become increasingly simple. Lully's monopoly put an end to the "machine plays" at the Marais, further weakening that company, which had steadily declined since 1647.

Between 1672 and 1687, Lully created a series of works considered to mark the origin of French opera. His principal collaborator was Phillippe Quinault (1635–88), author of 14 librettos, of which the most famous are *Atys* (1676) and *Armide* (1686). Vigarani designed the scenery until 1680, when he returned to Italy.

Vigarani was succeeded by Jean Berain *père* (1637–1711). Educated entirely in France, Berain is credited with establishing the visual style associated with the reign of Louis XIV. Employed at court in 1671 to design embroidery, tapestry, woodcarving, and furniture, he succeeded Henri Gissey as "Designer of the Cabinet of the King" in 1674. Since Gissey had customarily designed costumes for the opera, Berain also assumed this job. After 1680, Berain was principal designer for the court and the opera until his death, when he was succeeded by his son, Jean Berain *fils* (1678–1726), who held the posts until 1721. To the Berains goes the credit for establishing a distinctively French style of design emphasizing heavy lines, reverse curves, and encrusted ornamentation. In his stage designs, Berain usually restricted himself to one set for each act, but employed many machines and special effects. This combination of static scenery and dynamic machinery was to remain typical of French operatic design through the 18th century.

BERAIN'S SETTING for *The Triumph of Love,* a ballet by Bensérade and Lully (1681) at the Palais Royal. [Courtesy Bibliothèque Nationale, Paris]

After 1682, when the seat of government was moved from Paris to Versailles, the influence of the court on the public stage declined. After 1690, Louis became increasingly puritanical and the stage was tolerated rather than encouraged. Henceforth, the future of the French theatre lay almost entirely with the public troupes. Nevertheless, the taste of the court in the 17th century was largely responsible for establishing the Italian ideal, which was to form the basis for future developments.

French Drama, 1660–1700

Following its decline during the years of the Fronde difficulties, French drama began to recover in the late 1650's. Tragedy returned to favor with *Timocrate* (1656) by Thomas Corneille (1625–1709), younger

241

brother of Pierre Corneille. Author of more than 40 plays, the best of which are *Ariane* (1672), *Le Festin de Pierre* (1673), and *Le Comte d'Essex* (1678), Thomas Corneille was one of the most successful dramatists of his time, although his reputation has suffered by comparison with his brother. Pierre Corneille returned to writing in 1659 with *Oedipe* and continued until 1674.

Although many of Pierre Corneille's late works are of unquestioned merit, they are overshadowed by Jean Racine's (1639–99) plays, with which French tragedy reached its peak. Racine received an excellent education which instilled in him a lasting admiration of the Greek dramatists, whose example he sought to follow. His first tragedy, *La Thébaïde*, was produced in 1664 by Molière, who, in spite of the financial failure of the play, also produced Racine's second work, *Alexander the Great,* in 1665. Dissatisfied with the production, Racine permitted the Hôtel de Bourgogne to present the same play two weeks later, an unprecedented breach of contract. Furthermore, Racine allegedly induced Mlle. DuParc, Molière's principal tragic actress, to join the Hôtel de Bourgogne troupe. This double treachery led to a permanent rupture between the two men.

Racine's reputation, established by *Andromaque* in 1667, grew steadily during the next ten years with *Britannicus* (1669), *Bérénice* (1670), *Bajazet* (1672), *Mithridate* (1673), *Iphigénie* (1674), and *Phèdre* (1677). After *Phèdre,* Racine gave up playwriting, perhaps because his enemies had contrived to make a success of Jacques Pradon's (1632–98) *Phèdre,* produced at the same time as Racine's play, and his own a relative failure. At about this time, Racine was appointed historiographer to Louis XIV and abandoned his literary life. Some years later, he wrote *Esther* (1689) and *Athalie* (1691) for Mme. de Maintenon's school at St. Cyr. Neither play was performed professionally during his lifetime. In addition to his tragedies, Racine wrote one comedy, *Les Plaideurs* (1668), based in part on Aristophanes' *The Wasps.*

Racine's reputation is based upon the tragedies written between 1667 and 1677, of which *Phèdre* is the acknowledged masterpiece. Racine's greatness stems in part from his ability to develop compelling dramatic actions out of the internal conflicts of his protagonists. In contrast with Corneille's use of simple characters and complex plots, Racine constructed simple plots and complex characters. Because Racine's protagonists vacillate between two courses of action, torn between their sense of duty and their uncontrollable desires, dramatic interest is centered on the inner struggle rather than on the external events, which are important only as they contribute to the inner crisis. The plays begin some time after the protagonist has become aware of his dilemma. In a state of high emotion, he usually lays his soul bare to a *confidant* during the opening scene. Although no information is withheld, neither the audience nor the characters can foresee the outcome. The protagonist's psychological struggle makes up the dramatic action. Therefore, Racine was able to express his tragic vision adequately within the confines of the neo-classical ideal.

Upon Racine's retirement, tragedy began a long decline, which was not immediately apparent, since at the time other writers seemed worthy successors. The most important of these were Campistron, Longpierre, and LaFosse. Jean Galbert de Campistron (1656–1723) wrote seven tragedies between 1683 and 1691 which led critics to consider him the leading tragedian of his time. Of his plays, the most popular were *Andronic* (1685), which reverses the situation in *Phèdre* by having a man fall in love with his stepmother, and *Tiridate* (1691), a play about incestuous love. Campistron concentrated upon the victims of tragedy, and consequently his effects are essentially pathetic. After 1691, he retired to enter the King's service.

Hilaire Bernard de Roqueleyne Longpierre (1659–1731) also concentrated upon pathetic situations, although, like Racine, he placed major emphasis upon internal psychological conflicts. His major work is *Medée* (1694), notable in part because the fourth act is entirely a monologue. Antoine de LaFosse (1653–1708) did not begin writing until 1696 and composed only four tragedies. Nevertheless, many critics believed that, had he begun earlier, he would have surpassed Racine. Today he is remembered primarily for *Manlius Capitolanus* (1698), which remained in the repertory of the Comédie Française until 1849. In spite of these new writers, the tragic impulse was nearly over by 1700.

Like tragedy, comedy reached its peak in the 1660's and 1670's. As Racine represents the summit of tragic writing, so Molière does in comedy. Building upon the comedy of intrigue which Corneille and Scarron had popularized, Molière added interest with characterization. Through his work, comedy was raised to a level equalling that of tragedy.

Molière (Jean-Baptiste Poquelin, 1622–73), the son of a prosperous upholsterer and furniture maker, was given an excellent education and was destined for a court position until he joined with nine other young people to form the Théâtre Illustre in 1643. Having failed in Paris, the troupe set off in 1646 on a tour of the provinces which lasted until 1658. At this time, about 12 or 15 other companies were touring in France, and Molière's company soon joined with that of Charles Dufresne (c. 1611–c. 1684). By 1651, Molière was head of the troupe. Molière now turned to writing plays, his first important work being *L'Étourdi*, performed at Lyons in 1655. The turning point in the troupe's fortunes came in 1658, when it was invited to play at court by the King's brother, who had seen it perform in the provinces. The troupe was sufficiently well received to be granted the title Troupe de Monsieur and the use of the Petit Bourbon for public performances.

The company was not very successful with the public until it performed Molière's *Les Précieuses Ridicules* (1659), a satire on contemporary affectations. After this, its fortunes were assured. When the Petit Bourbon was torn down, Molière was allowed to use the Palais Royal, built by Richelieu and remodeled by Torelli. Here the company played from 1660 until 1673, enjoying a position of preeminence in comedy similar to that accorded the Bourgogne in tragedy. The Marais was now relegated to the third rank.

The reputation of the Palais Royal troupe derived primarily from Molière's plays, the core of its repertory. Now remembered principally for his comedies of character, Molière wrote other kinds of plays as well. Many of his works tended toward farce in the manner of the *commedia dell'arte*, by which he was much influenced. Some of the most popular of these were *Sganarelle, or The Imaginary Cuckold* (1660), *The Doctor in Spite of Himself* (1666), and *The Tricks of Scapin* (1671). Other works were written especially for court festivities, although most were later performed for the general public. Of these, a large number were "comedy ballets," such as *The Bores* (1661), *The Forced Marriage* (1664), *The Princess of Elide* (1664), and *Monsieur de Pourceaugnac* (1669). Others, such as *Amphitryon* (1668) and *Psyché* (1671) were "machine plays" with much spectacle. For most of the court plays, Molière collaborated with Lully, who provided the music. Occasionally Molière attempted serious drama, as in *Don Garcie de Navarre* (1661), but with little success.

Molière's great achievements are his comedies of character and manners, such as *The School for Husbands* (1661), *The School for Wives* (1662), *Tartuffe* (1664, 1667, 1669), *The Misanthrope* (1666), *The Miser* (1668), *The Learned Ladies* (1672), and *The Imaginary Invalid* (1673). His observations on contemporary manners and types in these

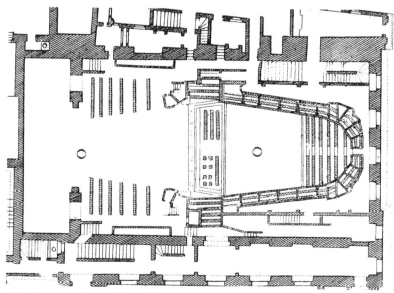

PLAN of the Palais Royal. [From Blondel, *Architecture Française* (1754)]

works embroiled him in much controversy. The first important battle was precipitated by *The School for Wives,* which questioned the right of guardians to dispose of their wards. Although enormously popular, the play was attacked on both artistic and moral grounds. Molière answered in two plays: *The Critique of The School for Wives* (1663) and *The Rehearsal at Versailles* (1663). Louis XIV's grant of an annual pension to Molière did much to silence the criticism. By far the bitterest controversy centered around *Tartuffe,* an attack upon hypocrisy interpreted by many as a condemnation of religion. After the play was forbidden, Molière rewrote it twice, once in 1667 and again in 1669, before it was deemed acceptable. When the final version was produced in 1669 it had an initial run of 44 performances, a record for the time. Louis XIV's attitude toward the quarrel is probably indicated in his granting Molière's company the title *Troupe de Roi* and an annual subsidy in 1665.

These quarrels clearly indicate that Molière had made comedy a vital reflection of contemporary life and manners. There is little bitterness in Molière's plays, for though he ridiculed customs and character types, he did not believe that men could be changed; thus, he shows those things which deform human nature without implying that it can be perfected. Consequently, his characters remain much the same at the end of the plays as at the beginning. This probably explains why his resolutions, usually brought about by some external force, are open to criticism. When, as in *The Misanthrope,* no external power intervenes, the action remains unresolved.

In his long plays, Molière usually conforms to the neo-classical ideal of five acts and the unities. Some of the plays are written in verse, others in prose. While his language is varied, it is rarely witty for its own sake; aptness to character and situation is the secret of his dialogue. Many of the plays are set in drawing rooms, a clear departure from previous comedy, which had usually been placed out-of-doors in the manner of Roman comedy. With Molière, the settings are a reflection of the manners and characters depicted, and his example did much to popularize the interior setting for comedy. Molière wrote for his own company and knew who would play each character. Furthermore, he directed his own plays and often played the leading role himself. Hence, details were probably added during rehearsals which do not appear explicitly in the scripts.

Acting Companies, 1660–1700

When Molière died in 1673, Paris had five professional troupes: Molière's, Lully's opera company, a *commedia dell'arte* troupe, and the companies of the Hôtel de Bourgogne and the Marais. All received some financial assistance from the government. By 1700, only two were left.

At Molière's death, many doubted his company's ability to continue. To allay anxieties, the troupe resumed performances after one week. Soon, however, a number of actors seceded, and Lully was able to evict the troupe from the Palais Royal. Another theatre in the rue Guénégaud was found, but the Marais troupe wished to buy it. Louis XIV now intervened, ordering the closing of the Marais and the amalgamation of the two companies. The combined groups opened at the rue Guénégaud in July 1673.

This situation continued until 1679, when Mlle. Champmeslé, the Bourgogne's principal tragic actress, left to join the troupe at the Guénégaud. This crisis was also resolved by a crown order joining the troupes to form the Comédie Française, the world's first national theatre. The new company gave its first performance on August 25, 1680 at the theatre in the rue Guénégaud. The Comédie Française was given a monopoly on the performance of spoken drama in French, the rights of the Confrèrie de la Passion having at last been abrogated in 1675.

Almost immediately, however, an exception to this monopoly was made for the *comedia dell'arte* troupe, since it had for some time been performing works in French. Although *commedia* companies had at first played only intermittently, after 1660 a troupe headed by Tiberio Fiorillo

THEATRE in the Rue Guénégaud. Note the chandeliers over the stage, and the spectators on stage and in the boxes. [From a contemporary engraving by Mariette]

THE *Commedia dell'arte* troupe of the Hôtel de Bourgogne, 1689. [From *Almanach de l'An* 1689]

(1608–94), made Paris its permanent home. Other famous actors in this company were Domenico Biancolelli (*c.* 1637–88), a favorite of Louis XIV and the popularizer of Arlequin in France; Marc'Antonio Romagnesi (*c.* 1633–1706), who at first played the lover and later the Dottore; and Angelo Constantini, who made many innovations in the character of Mezzetin. In 1680, the troupe was given the Hôtel de Bourgogne.

Periodically, the *commedia* troupe was in trouble because of the audacity of its plays, but it overcame all difficulties until 1697, when it was expelled from Paris following an alleged attack upon Mme. de Maintenon, Louis XIV's second wife, in *The False Prude*. There were to be no more Italian troupes in Paris until 1716. After 1697, the Parisian theatre was reduced to the Comédie Française and the Opèra.

The Organization of the French Acting Companies

All of the French acting troupes of the 17th century were organized on the sharing plan, all regular members participating in the management and dividing the profits. The number of members varied with the company's prosperity. Before 1650, there were usually 8 to 12; when Molière returned to Paris in 1658, his troupe included 10 members, but was increased to 12 (8 men and 4 women) in 1659. When the Comédie Française was formed in 1680, 21¼ shares were divided among 27 members (17 full shares, 7 one-half shares, and 3 one-quarter shares). Thus, an actor's share varied according to his importance in the company.

Since the number of shares in the Comédie Française was fixed by the First Gentlemen of the Chamber (the court officials who superintended the troupe), not all actors were members, or *sociétaires*. No new member could be admitted until an actor resigned, retired, or died. To become a *sociétaire,* an actor bound himself to the company for 20 years and made himself liable to a heavy fine if he quit. When a vacancy occurred, the *sociétaires* elected a new member, usually from among the *pensionnaires,* actors who worked for the troupe on salary. If a performer desired a position with the Comédie Française, he was required to play a series of roles in the regular public performances; if the troupe wished to retain him, they placed him on salary until a vacancy in membership occurred. Not all *pensionnaires* became *sociétaires.* The *sociétaires* had a voice in all matters of policy, including the acceptance of new plays. The actor with the longest service acted as head, or *doyen,* of the troupe. The Comédie Française also continued the pension system which had evolved among the earlier troupes. Under it, an actor could retire after 20 years of service with an annual pension of 1000 francs. The troupe was provided an annual subsidy of 12,000 francs by the government.

With the formation of the Comédie Française, the actor achieved considerable security. His assured position as a *sociétaire,* however, encouraged complacency and arrogance. His opportunities for employment had also become more restricted, since Paris now had only one troupe.

Of the actors who achieved fame in the years between 1660 and 1700, several were associated with Molière. Madeleine Béjart (1618–72) was already an established provincial actress when Molière met her. She is credited with inducing him to become an actor and was intimately involved in his work until her death. In the early years, she played tragic heroines, but later turned to the saucy maids of Molière's comedies. Geneviève (*c.* 1622–75), Joseph (*c.* 1620–59), who played young lovers, and Louis Béjart (1625–78), who played comic valets, were also members of the troupe. Armande Béjart (1642–1700), who became Molière's wife in 1662, made her debut in 1663 and thereafter played the heroines in his plays. A versatile actress, she did much to hold the company together after her husband's death. In 1677, she married Isaac François Guérin d'Étriché (*c.* 1636–1728), who acted until he was past eighty and had become *doyen* of the Comédie Française.

Perhaps even more than Molière's wife, LaGrange (Charles Varlet, *c.* 1639–92) was responsible for the continuation of the company. Employed in 1659 to replace Joseph Béjart as the young lover, he also kept the company's records until 1685. His *Registre,* which records receipts, performances and all deliberations, is the principal source of information about Molière's troupe and the early years of the Comédie Française. LaGrange also wrote the only contemporary biography of Molière, published in 1682 with the first edition of Molière's works.

Of tragic performers, the most important were Mlle. DuParc, Mlle. Desoeillets, Mlle. Champmeslé, and Michel Baron. Mlle. DuParc (1633–68) joined Molière's troupe in the provinces and remained with him until 1666, when Racine is said to have lured her to the Bourgogne, where she was the leading tragic actress until her death. Mlle. Desoeillets (1621–70) served a long apprenticeship in the provinces before coming to Paris around 1660. Playing first at the Marais, she moved to the Bourgogne in 1662; there she was the leading performer until Mlle. DuParc joined the company in 1666, and again after Mlle. DuParc died. Short and not very pretty, she nevertheless gave moving performances which won her a devoted following. Mlle. Champmeslé (1642–98) came to the Marais in 1669, also after a career in the provinces. Within six months she was considered the finest tragic actress in Paris and had moved to the Bourgogne. She retained her position of supremacy until her death, creating such great tragic roles as Phèdre. Supposedly her desertion of the Bourgogne motivated the formation of the Comèdie Française. She passed on her declamatory style to two of her pupils, Mlle. Desmares and Mlle. Duclos, the leading tragic actresses of the early 18th century.

The void left at the Bourgogne by the death of Montfleury in 1667 and the retirement of Floridor in 1671 was not filled until Michel Baron (1653–1729) deserted Molière's troupe in 1673. Baron had been a child actor even before Molière took him into his home in 1666 and trained him further. His adult career began in 1670 as Domitien in Corneille's *Tite et Bérénice.* By the time of Molière's death, Baron was noted as a fine serious actor of the natural school; soon after he joined the Bourgogne in 1673, he was recognized as the leading tragic actor of the day and continued to be so regarded until he retired in 1691. His return to the stage in 1720 will be considered later. To many, Baron was the epitome of great acting and he is still thought by many to have been the finest serious actor of the 17th century.

Although an actor tended always to play the same type of role, he was not as yet employed to play a specified range of characters, as he was to be in the 18th century. The casting of a new play was done by the author, and actors were forbidden to refuse a role. Old plays were cast by the company in consultation. Rehearsals, perfunctory by modern standards, were held in the late morning. Although authors allegedly staged their own plays, they probably relied heavily upon the advice of a leading actor. Once a play had been performed, the actors were considered ready to present it at any time

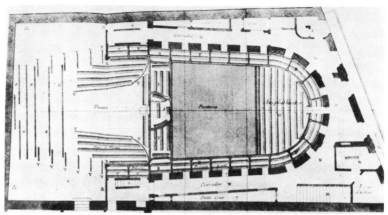

PLAN of the theatre used by the Comédie Française from
1689 until 1770. Note the benches on stage for spectators.
[From Mantzius' *History of Theatrical Art* (1905)]

thereafter. A company in this period usually had about 70 plays in its active
repertory, which were rotated in a daily change of bill.

Until the 1650's, an author was paid a fixed sum for each play. Later,
he was assigned shares for the initial run, after which he received no further
payments. As long as the play remained unpublished, it was considered the
exclusive property of the company that had bought it; after publication,
any company could produce it without paying a fee.

The expenses of a company were subtracted before the sharing actors
were paid. The troupe, however, did not supply costumes. Although most
characters wore contemporary garments, classical, Near-Eastern, and Indian
figures were usually played in elaborate and costly costumes quite unlike
those worn in daily life. The typical dress of classical heroes, the *habit à la
romaine,* an adaptation of Roman armor, tunic and boots, surmounted by a
full-bottomed wig and plumed headdress, cost about 2000 livres, a sum
roughly equivalent to one-third of the actor's annual income. This financial
burden was somewhat relieved by the royal practice of paying actors 400
livres for each costume they provided in plays mounted especially for court.
In spite of his expenses, the actor of the late 17th century was well paid by
the standards of the time. Between 1660 and 1673, a full share in Molière's
troupe brought an annual income varying from 2000 to 5500 livres; in
1700, the average earnings of a full share at the Comédie Française was
about 4900 livres.

Until 1680, the troupes played only three or four days each week, the
preferred days being Tuesday, Friday, and Sunday. After 1680, the troupes
began to play daily; in the 1682–83 season, the Comédie Française gave 352
performances. The usual starting time was now 4 or 5 P.M. Attendance was
not high, the average at the Comédie Française between 1680 and 1700
being about 450 persons, in theatres designed to hold 1500–2000 persons.

Spectators still stood in the pit and moved about freely. Others sat on the stage, a practice which some scholars date from the first production of *Le Cid*. By the late 17th century, benches were installed on either side of the stage, reducing the playing area to about 15 feet in width. All entrances and exits had to be made from upstage and little illusion of place was possible. This confined acting area and the presence of spectators on three sides undoubtedly affected the acting style.

Theatre Architecture and Scenic Practices, 1660–1700

The public theatres of Paris remained relatively unchanged from the 1640's until after Molière's death. In 1673, the Marais was abandoned, and the Palais Royal was refurbished for the Opéra. Little is known of the theatre in the rue Guénégaud, occupied by the Marais-Molière troupe from 1673 to 1680 and by the Comédie Française from 1680 until 1689. Built in 1670 by the Marquis de Sourdéac, it housed Lully's operatic productions until he gained control of the Palais Royal.

The Comédie Française was ordered to leave the rue Guénégaud in 1687, when the Sorbonne decided to build a new college nearby. Not until 1689 was it able to acquire a new home, the Étoile tennis court in the rue Neuve-des-Fosses in the St. Germain-des-Prés quarter of Paris. Remodeled by the architect Francois d'Orbay at a cost of 200,000 livres, it put the company in debt for many years. It was to be the home of the Comédie Française until 1770.

D'Orbay ignored the exterior walls of the tennis court and constructed inside them a horseshoe-shaped auditorium. On the ground floor, a standing pit was backed by an amphitheatre raised about six feet above it. Along the walls, two levels of 19 boxes were surmounted by an undivided gallery. The total capacity of the auditorium was about 2000.

The stage was about 41 feet deep by 54 feet wide, but the available acting area was considerably restricted by five rows of benches on either side of the stage. A few benches were also placed in the orchestra pit, which was not used by the musicians because of objections raised by the Opéra. When musicians were needed, they were placed in a box at the rear of the auditorium. The stage was equipped for flat wings and shutters, but since scene shifts were seldom required, the machinery was minimal.

This stage reflects the changes which had occurred in scenic practices since the 1630s. *Le Mémoire de Mahelot, Laurent, et d'Autres Décorateurs*, the last part of which was compiled between 1678 and 1686, contains notices of 53 plays performed at the Hôtel de Bourgogne between 1678 and

SCENE from Brécourt's *The Village Wedding* (1666). Note the spectators on the stage. [From the first edition of the play]

1680, and 69 notices of plays staged at the rue Guénégaud between 1680 and 1686. Most of these notices were written by Michel Laurent.

The principal change indicated by Laurent's notices of 1678–86, in comparison with those by Mahelot in 1634–35, is the movement toward simplicity. By Laurent's time, most settings represented a single place composed of flat wings. Shutters may have been pierced by doors, since entrances from the sides were almost impossible because of onstage spectators.

The typical background for tragedies was the *palais à volonté,* a neutral setting suited to the action but without particularized details. Consequently, it could serve as a background for all scenes in the same town without any changes, for it was so anonymous that it might represent a street, a square, a vestibule, or a palace. A variation was composed of tents near a battlefield, often with a sea or city in the background. For comedy, the *chambre à quatre portes* was typical. It differed in no important way from the *palais à volonté,* except that it depicted domestic architecture, usually an interior, whereas the *palais à volonté* was more formal. The unity of place was never completely adopted, however, for in some plays the settings changed with each act. In others, a shutter or curtain was opened to reveal another place behind the one previously shown. Thus, by the end of the 17th century, the typical setting at the Comédie Française supplied a suitable, though neutral, background which placed little emphasis upon illusion and concentrated attention upon the actor.

The Close of the 17th Century

By 1700, then, Paris had two troupes with monopolistic privileges dividing between them the whole range of drama. The Opéra depended much upon Italianate scenery and machines for the effectiveness of its musical dramas and ballets. The Comédie Française relied little on spectacle, although it too had adopted the Italian mode in scenery and the neoclassical ideal in drama.

With this stability came a change in attitude. Rather than searching for new horizons, dramatists looked to the past for standards. The prevailing mood can be seen in the "Battle of the Ancients and Moderns" which raged in the French Academy and elsewhere after 1688 over the relative merits of classical and 17th century French writers. In general, the battle, which continued into the 18th century, was decided in favor of the French authors. In practice, this meant that Corneille and Racine became the standard for tragedy and Molière for comedy, and that dramatists sought to copy their style and techniques. Attempts to maintain past glory inevitably led to stagnation and decline. Although for another century French drama continued to set the standard for all Europe, its period of greatest vitality was over.

9

THE ENGLISH
THEATRE, 1642–1790

*F*rom 1642 until 1660, theatrical performances were forbidden in England, but upon the restoration of the monarchy they were rapidly revived. Combining old conventions with recent continental developments, a modified neoclassicism emerged. In the 18th century, as governmental regulation increased, new dramatic types appeared and emphasis on spectacle grew. Restoration practices underwent many significant changes. By 1790, the English theatre was on the threshold of the Romantic era.

The Theatre Under the Commonwealth

Because theatrical performances between 1642 and 1660 were illegal, few records relating to them have survived, although playing certainly continued. At first, the actors complied with the law. The King's Men sold its wardrobe and its Globe Theatre was torn down. Actors soon began to perform surreptitiously, however, and by 1647 performances were being given at The Fortune, Cockpit, and Salisbury Court theatres. Although Parliament ordered officials to halt the violations, suppression was sporadic and ineffectual. When the law prohibiting performances expired in 1648, open playing was immediately resumed. In 1649, Parliament passed a new law ordering that all actors be apprehended as rogues. The interiors of the Fortune, Cockpit, and Salisbury Court were dismantled. The actors continued to perform, nevertheless, using the Red Bull, which had escaped demolition or, when that appeared too dangerous, private houses, tennis courts, or inns. Often officials were bribed to ignore violations. The usual form of entertainment was the "droll," a short farcical play condensed from a longer work.

Apparently, the actors believed that the theatre would be legalized. Around 1650, William Beeston (c. 1606–82) acquired the Salisbury Court, rebuilt it, and began to train a company of boys. The Cockpit passed into the hands of John Rhodes, a bookseller, who also organized a young company. Perhaps most significantly, William Davenant, who in the 1630's had succeeded Jonson as the principal writer of court masques, began to stage operatic productions openly. The initial offering, *The First Day's Entertainment at Rutland House,* was presented in May 1656.

A DRAWING, probably showing a composite of the stages used during the Commonwealth for "drolls." Note that characters from several plays are shown. Note also the use of chandeliers and footlights. [From Kirkman's *The Wits,* a collection of drolls, published in 1672]

The production of *The Siege of Rhodes,* also in 1656, is a far more important event, however, for it marks the first clear use in England of Italianate scenery for a public performance. Designed by John Webb (1611–72), pupil and son-in-law of Inigo Jones, the settings were mounted on a stage measuring only 22 feet in width, 18 feet in depth and 11 feet in height. Behind the proscenium, a series of fixed wings, painted to represent rocky cliffs, terminated in movable shutters which, in combination with set pieces, depicted the various places required by the action.

These first entertainments were given in Rutland House, Davenant's residence, but in 1658–59 Davenant presented at least three others at the Cockpit, in which a proscenium arch was erected. Although some opposition was expressed, by this time the restoration of the monarchy was imminent and no action was taken. On the other hand, Davenant was not violating any law, for his pieces were musical entertainments, which had not been forbidden.

The Reestablishment of the Theatre

As soon as it became evident that the monarchy would be restored, preparations for reopening theatres began. In March 1660, Davenant leased Lisle's Tennis Court and went to France to urge his claims with Charles II. Sir Henry Herbert resumed the position of Master of Revels, which he had held under Charles I, and licensed three companies: one under John Rhodes at the Cockpit, another under Michael Mohun at the Red Bull, and a third under William Beeston at the Salisbury Court. Meanwhile, Charles II, unaware of Herbert's actions, had awarded a monopoly on theatrical production in London to Davenant and Thomas Killigrew (1612–83), who had grown up at the English court and had been with the royal family throughout its exile. Not until late 1660 were Davenant and Killigrew able to suppress the troupes licensed by Herbert. At first they ran a single company, but soon formed two. Killigrew, as head of the King's Company, took the older, more experienced actors, while Davenant's Duke's Company was left with the younger performers.

This monopoly was challenged almost immediately by George Jolly (*fl.* 1648–73), who during the Commonwealth years had headed a touring company in Germany. It was there in 1655 that he had performed for the future Charles II and had received some commitment from him. Consequently, in late 1660, Jolly was granted a license to perform in London. In 1662, he went on tour, Davenant and Killigrew having rented his license. During his absence, the two managers convinced the King that they had bought Jolly's license and in 1664 secured a new patent issued in their

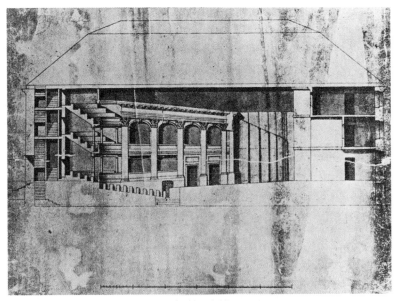

SECTIONAL PLAN of a theatre, now believed for Wren's Drury Lane, 1674. [Reproduced by kind permission of the Warden and Fellows of All Souls College, Oxford]

names. Following this treachery, Jolly returned to London and resumed performances until 1667, when the King finally silenced him. Perhaps to avoid further trouble, Jolly was employed by Davenant and Killigrew to head their training school for actors. After 1673, no more is heard of him.

Davenant and Killigrew also had difficulties with Sir Henry Herbert, who sued them for usurping many privileges formerly held by the Master of Revels. Eventually Herbert was deprived of the right to license theatres and companies in London, although he continued to authorize companies outside of London and to license all new plays. Thus, Davenant and Killigrew established almost complete control over the theatrical performances in London. The patents granted to them were to remain in effect until 1843, seriously hampering future growth.

Acting Companies, 1660–1700

Although Killigrew began with the advantage of experienced actors, his company did not prosper as did Davenant's. Killigrew devoted little attention to the theatre, delegating authority to three of his actors. Perhaps as a result, the company was wracked by constant dissension. Davenant, on the other hand, supervised his theatre closely until his death in 1668, after

257

which the actors Betterton and Harris assumed the artistic direction under the management of the Davenant family. By 1682 Killigrew's company was in such serious financial difficulties that the two troupes were merged.

The United Company continued until 1695, when several actors seceded to form another troupe after a series of events had placed them in an untenable position. In 1688, Charles Davenant had sold the controlling interest in the theatre to his brother Alexander; in 1693, when Alexander fled England to escape his creditors, it was revealed that his money had come from Christopher Rich and Sir Thomas Skipworth. Rich, a lawyer without any theatrical experience, assumed control of the company and proved himself so unpleasant, withholding salaries and favoring those actors who catered to his whims, that the major performers, under Betterton's leadership, secured a license from William III to form a second troupe. This separation was to last from 1695 until 1707.

In addition to the London companies, a number of troupes were licensed to perform in the provinces, while the Dublin theatre was controlled by its own Master of Revels. In 1637, John Ogilby (1600–76) had been given a license to open a theatre in Dublin and was named Master of Revels for Ireland. Ogilby's patent, dormant after 1641, was renewed in 1661, and in 1662 he opened the Smock Alley Theatre, the first built in Great Britain after the Restoration. Upon Ogilby's death, the patent passed to Joseph Ashbury, who for the next 45 years maintained the finest company outside of London.

English Drama, 1660–1700

One of the problems facing managers in 1660 was the acquisition of a suitable repertory. At first they depended on pre-Commonwealth plays which the Master of Revels divided between the companies. Of these, the works of Beaumont and Fletcher were the most popular; Jonson's, though much admired, were seldom produced, and many of Shakespeare's were revised to bring them more nearly into line with neo-classical principles. Many of the older works proved too outmoded and were dropped as soon as new ones could be obtained.

The plays written between 1660 and 1680 were much indebted to French and Spanish authors. The emphasis upon love versus honor in these foreign works led to English "heroic" tragedy, popularized through the plays of Roger Boyle, Earl of Orrery (1621–79), notably *The Tragedy of Mustapha* (1665), *The Black Prince* (1667), and *Tryphon* (1668). Other popular writers of this genre were Elkanah Settle (1648–1724), author of *Cambyses, King of Persia* (1671) and *The Empress of Morocco* (1673); Nathaniel Lee (1653–92) with *The Rival Queens* (1677); and John Dryden (1631–1700) with *The Indian Queen* (1664), *The Indian Emperor* (1665), *The Conquest of Granada,* parts 1 and 2 (1669–70), and *Aureng-Zebe* (1675). In these works, an idealistic hero and a beautiful heroine are faced with a conflict between love and honor; often the background is martial, and frequently a happy ending is contrived. Filled with ranting speeches in rhymed couplets, the plays now seem hopelessly stilted. The genre was dealt a heavy blow in 1671 by *The Rehearsal,* written by George Villiers, second Duke of Buckingham (1628–87), which burlesqued the typical themes and plot devices of heroic tragedy. Buckingham's play outlived its target, remaining in the repertory until the late 18th century.

As heroic drama declined, it was replaced by neo-classical blank verse tragedy. Treating relatively simple plots and observing the unities, the form was first seen in Dryden's *All for Love* (1677), adapted from Shakespeare's *Antony and Cleopatra,* and it remained the dominant mode through the rest of the century. By far the best serious dramatist of the age was Thomas Otway (1652–85), whose *The Orphan* (1680) and *Venice Preserv'd* (1682) were favorite vehicles until the late 19th century. English neoclassicism was always more liberal than continental varieties. Unity of action was interpreted to permit a number of related subplots, and the unity of place was considered observed if the characters could move between all of the locales within the 24-hour time limit.

Building upon Davenant's Commonwealth "entertainments," opera flourished during the Restoration. It differed from heroic tragedy only in the addition of music, song, and spectacle, while its principal departure from Italian opera lay in the substitution of spoken passages for recitative. Not only were Shakespeare's *Macbeth* and *The Tempest* adapted to the operatic mode, but such original works as Thomas Shadwell's (1642–92) *Psyche* (1674–75) and Dryden's *Albion and Albianus* (1685) and *King Arthur* (1692) achieved great popularity. This English strain of opera was to decline rapidly after the vogue for Italian opera began in 1705.

The Restoration is noted especially for its diverse comic drama: comedies of humours, comedies of intrigue, farces, and comedies of manners. Because of Jonson's reputation, "humours" were much exploited during the Restoration. Of the major authors, Thomas Shadwell was the most successful writer of humorous comedy with *The Sullen Lovers* (1668), *The Humourists* (1670), *The Squire of Alsatia* (1688), and *Bury Fair* (1689). Each of these plays introduces a series of eccentric characters in a story of contemporary life, told with frank and outspoken dialogue.

Perhaps because of the influence of Corneille and the Spanish dramatists, the comedy of intrigue was also popular in these years. The best examplar of this genre was Mrs. Aphra Behn (1640–89) with such plays as *The Rover,* parts 1 and 2 (1677–80). Farce reached its height in the works of Edward Ravenscroft (*fl.* 1671–97), whose *London Cuckolds* (1681) and *The Anatomist* (1697) were played throughout the 18th century.

Above all, however, the Restoration is noted for its sprightly comedy of manners. Dryden, the most versatile dramatist of the age, contributed to its formation with such works as *Sir Martin Mar-All* (1667), *The Mock Astrologer* (1668), and *Marriage à la Mode* (1672), each of which includes a pair of carefree, witty lovers. The fully-developed comedy of manners, however, is usually traced to the plays of Sir George Etherege (*c.* 1634–91), who, after a somewhat erratic beginning in *Love in a Tub* (1664), set the pattern for later writers with *She Would if She Could* (1668) and *The Man of Mode* (1676). Here for the first time are found the characters drawn from the upper classes and their preoccupation with seduction, arranged marriages, the latest fashions, and witty repartee.

Of the later writers in this vein, two, Wycherley and Congreve, were of special importance. William Wycherley (1640–1715) began writing for the stage in 1671 with *Love in a Wood,* and continued with *The Gentleman Dancing Master* (1672), *The Country Wife* (1675), and *The Plain Dealer* (1676). Although these plays are well constructed and present subtly depicted characters, their moral tone has offended many critics. *The Country Wife,* in which the hero circulates the rumor that he is sexually impotent in order to facilitate his seductions, is often cited as evidence of the moral laxity of Restoration comedy. The comedy of manners reached its peak in the plays of William Congreve (1670–1729), whose *Love for Love* (1695) and *The Way of the World* (1700) are still considered masterpieces, because of their brilliant scenes, sparkling dialogue, and clear-cut characterizations.

The subject matter and tone of the comedies of manners has led to much debate over their moral viewpoint. In them, the wise are rewarded and the foolish are duped; virtue consists of unsentimental self-knowledge. The self-deceived are ridiculed and gulled, often by protagonists who use their own superior insights to justify their treatment of the fools. Discussions about the acceptability of these standards of behavior have often obscured the remarkable accomplishments of the Restoration dramatists.

By 1700, a change in English drama was already becoming evident. The Puritan tide which had been stemmed under Charles II rose again after William and Mary were crowned in 1689. A number of attacks were launched on the theatre, but none was effective until Jeremy Collier's *A Short View of the Immorality and Profaneness of the English Stage* (1698) appeared. Collier succeeded where others had failed because he began with the accepted neo-classical doctrine that the purpose of drama is to teach and to please and showed the disparity between the ideal and the reality.

Most dramatists found it impossible to answer Collier effectively, since they too had accepted moral teaching as the basic aim of literature. A few playwrights made public recantations, Congreve gave up writing, and English drama turned in new directions.

English Drama of the 18th Century

The transitional drama is best exemplified in the work of Colley Cibber (1671–1757) and George Farquhar. In Cibber's *Love's Last Shift* (1696), *The Careless Husband* (1704), *The Double Gallant* (1707), and *The Lady's Stake* 1707), profligate characters pursue their fashionable follies until the fifth act, when they undergo rapid and sentimentalized conversions. George Farquhar (1678–1707) preserved much of Congreve's wit, but set his plays in the country and resolved them in a manner which removed all moral objections. His best plays are *The Constant Couple* (1699), which introduced Sir Harry Wildair, one of the most popular characters of the 18th century, *The Recruiting Officer* (1706), and *The Beaux' Stratagem* (1707), the latter two still perennial favorites.

The new direction in comedy was first fully established in *The Conscious Lovers* (1722) by Sir Richard Steele (1672–1729). Based on Terence's *Andria*, Steele's play transfers the action to 18th century London. In it, the penniless heroine Indiana, after withstanding many trials, is discovered to be the daughter of a rich merchant, thus making a happy resolution possible. The few humorous scenes fall to the servants. With Steele's play, the purpose of comedy was altered; it now sought to produce "a pleasure too exquisite for laughter," to arouse noble sentiments through the depiction of trials bravely borne by sympathetic characters who are rescued from their sufferings and handsomely rewarded.

Today the drama of the 18th century is usually called "sentimental," for the characters appear unnaturally good and their problems too easily overcome. These plays were accepted in the 18th century, nevertheless, as truthful representations of human nature. The disparity in attitude is explained by our changed view of human psychology. The 18th century conceived of man as naturally good, a state which he could retain by following his instincts, but from which bad examples might lead him. It was thought possible to reclaim men from vice by appealing to those virtuous human feelings which had been covered up. For this reason, the rapid reformation of characters seemed believable to 18th century audiences. Pathetic situations were useful devices in plays because they demonstrated the goodness of the characters who withstood trials, and they provided the spectator an occasion for displaying his own virtue, since such emotional responses as weeping were thought to be the signs of a properly sensitive and moral nature.

Although Steele was to have no important successors in comedy until after 1750, the new vein was exploited effectively in tragedy much earlier. In the early 18th century, Nicholas Rowe (1674–1718) had written a number of pathetic tragedies, such as *The Ambitious Step-Mother* (1701), *Tamerlane* (1701), *The Fair Penitent* (1703), and *The Tragedy of Jane Shore* (1714), which were to hold the stage until the 19th century. Other important serious playwrights included Ambrose Philips (1675–1749), whose *The Distrest Mother* (1712), based upon Racine's *Andromaque,* remained a popular vehicle for actresses for over a century; Joseph Addison (1672–1719), whose *Cato* (1713) was considered a masterpiece; and James Thomson (1700–48), whose *Sophonisba* (1729) was one of the most admired plays of its time. These tragedies, however, were all based upon historical or mythological subjects and drew their characters from the ruling classes. A significant new direction was taken in 1731 when George Lillo (1693–1739) wrote *The London Merchant,* in which the hero-apprentice, George Barnwell, is led astray by a prostitute and ends on the gallows in spite of his abject repentance. Lillo chose his subject from everyday life because he believed that the lessons of traditional tragedy, with its characters drawn from the nobility, were not sufficiently applicable to the ordinary man. Although Lillo had many imitators, none achieved his success. His nearest rival was to be Edward Moore (1712–57), whose *The Gamester* (1753), depicting the downward career of a gambler, was a favorite play of the late 18th century.

As domestic tragedy declined in popularity after 1750, sentimental comedy flourished, perhaps because audiences preferred to see characters rescued from misfortune rather than punished for mistakes. Of the later writers, the most important were Hugh Kelly (1739–77), whose *False Delicacy* (1768) treats the disentanglement of three pairs of unsuited lovers; Richard Cumberland (1732–1811), whose *The West Indian* (1771) tells the story of a young rake who, after being reformed by marriage, is rewarded by the discovery that his wife is an heiress; and Thomas Holcroft (1745–1809), whose *The Road to Ruin* (1792) shows a gambler so touched by his father's shame that he is restored to virtue. The sentimental drama, with its emphasis upon moral teaching through poetic justice, was to develop in the 19th century into melodrama.

Robust comedy did not altogether die out. Between 1720 and 1760, however, "laughing" comedy was restricted primarily to farce, usually one-act plays performed as afterpieces. Samuel Foote (1720–77) did much to keep the comic spirit alive through such works as *The Knights* (1749), *The Orators* (1762), *The Minor* (1760), and *The Maid of Bath* (1771), which also contain much personal satire.

After 1760 a few writers began to oppose sentimentalism. George

Colman the Elder (1732–94) approached the spirit of Restoration comedy in *The Jealous Wife* (1761) and other plays. The most important later comic writers, however, were Oliver Goldsmith (1730–74) and Richard Brinsley Sheridan. Goldsmith's *The Good Natur'd Man* (1768), an attack upon the style of Kelly, Cumberland and others, is stilted and structurally weak, but *She Stoops to Conquer* (1773) is a comic masterpiece. Its skillful manipulation of several plot strands to create an amusing and rapid action was an effective argument in favor of "laughing" comedy.

Sheridan (1751–1816) is noted primarily for *The Rivals* (1775) and *The School for Scandal* (1777), which recall Congreve's comedies of manners with their sparkling wit and vivid pictures of the fashionable world. Both Sheridan and Goldsmith were sufficiently influenced by their time, however, to punish deviations from morality and uphold the traditional values. They did much to recapture the past brilliance of English drama, and, with the exception of Shakespeare, have held the stage more consistently than any other dramatists. Unfortunately they had no followers, and after 1780 English drama moved steadily toward melodrama.

As neoclassicism declined during the 18th century, there arose a number of minor dramatic types: pantomime, ballad opera, comic opera, and burlesque. Pantomime combined elements from *commedia dell'arte* and farce with topical satire and stories drawn from classical mythology. *Commedia dell'arte* troupes had appeared occasionally in England since the 16th century, and *commedia* types had been incorporated into the dances and entr'acte entertainments of English performers since the late 17th century. But it was not until 1702 that John Weaver arranged the dances into a connected story. It remained for John Rich (1692–1761), son of Christopher Rich and manager of Lincolns Inn Fields and Covent Garden theatres, to establish the accepted pattern of English pantomime, first clearly seen in *Harlequin Sorcerer* (1717). In Rich's works, serious scenes based on classical mythology alternated with comic episodes featuring *commedia* characters. The comic scenes were mute, but the serious plot used dialogue and song. Music accompanied much of the action. The dominant feature was spectacle, motivated by Harlequin's acquisition of a magic wand which could transform places or characters.

Unlike most pantomimes, Rich's were long-lived. In 45 years he created only about 20, 13 of which were first performed between 1717 and 1732. Nine became mainstays in his repertory; they were refurbished at regular intervals and were alternated from season to season. Under the name Lun, Rich was also the most famous and accomplished pantomimist of the 18th century.

By 1723, pantomime was the most popular form of theatrical entertainment. Although they served only as afterpieces, many pantomimes were more popular than the plays they accompanied. Prices were always raised when new pantomimes were offered, and several had initial runs of 40 to 50 performances. Rich trained a number of other pantomime players. The most famous was Harry Woodward (1717–77), who deserted Rich in 1738 and for the next 20 years mounted pantomimes at Drury Lane in competition with his former master. After 1760, the central role of Harlequin declined in favor of the more sentimental clown.

Rich is also associated with the rise of ballad opera, since it was he who produced the first one, *The Beggar's Opera* (1728) by John Gay (1685–1732), after it had been refused by Drury Lane. Ballad opera emerged in part out of the vogue for Italian opera, which began around 1705 and accelerated in 1710 with the arrival of George Frederick Handel (1685–1759) in England. In 1719, the Royal Academy of Music was founded as the home of opera. Although always in financial difficulties after 1730, the opera continued to enjoy great prestige with the aristocracy through the rest of the century. In the ballad opera, dialogue alternates with lyrics sung to popular tunes. Gay's work was more than popularized opera, however, for its story of London low-life satirized the political conditions of his time and set the tone for much of the minor drama during the next ten years. None of the other ballad operas, however, achieved the stature of the first one.

After the passage of the Licensing Act in 1737, ballad opera declined rapidly. In its place arose a new musical drama, the comic opera, with sentimental plots and original music. The most famous writer of the new type was Isaac Bickerstaffe (1735–1812), with such works as *The Maid of the Mill* (1765) and *Lionel and Clarissa* (1768). Other works in this vein

SCENE from *The Beggar's Opera*. Note the spectators on stage. [An engraving by William Blake after the painting by William Hogarth]

include Sheridan's *The Duenna* (1775), John O'Keeffe's (1747–1833) *The Poor Soldier* (1783), and George Colman the Younger's (1762–1836) *Inkle and Yarico* (1787).

The satirical burlesque, which differed from ballad opera principally in the absence of music, appeared in the 1730's. The finest writer of this form was Henry Fielding (1707–54), who began his dramatic career with adaptations from Molière and then turned to topical satire in his burlesque of contemporary tragedy, *Tom Thumb, or the Tragedy of Tragedies* (1730). His later plays, such as *Pasquin* (1736), *Tumble-Down Dick* (1736), and *The Historical Register of 1736* (1737), burlesqued the major figures and events of the day. Other famous burlesques include Henry Carey's *The Tragedy of Chrononhotonthologos* (1734) and *The Dragon of Wantley* (1737). Like ballad opera, burlesque waned after the passage of the Licensing Act in 1737. By far the best of the later works was Sheridan's *The Critic* (1781), a satire on tragedy, critics, authors, and the vogue of spectacle. It replaced Buckingham's *The Rehearsal* and was regularly performed until the end of the 19th century.

The 18th century theatre was by no means restricted to production of contemporary plays. The pattern which was followed throughout the 18th century had been set during the Restoration, when a company's repertory of 35–40 plays was divided about equally between pre-Commonwealth plays and new plays or successes from recent seasons. By the early 18th century, the repertory had increased to 40–75 plays, and by the last half of the century to 75–80 works. After 1750, about one-third of the repertory

SCENE from Sheridan's *School for Scandal* at Drury Lane in 1777. [From a contemporary engraving]

was drawn from Shakespearean and other pre-Commonwealth plays, another third was made up of Restoration or early 18th century works, and the remaining third was composed of recent successes or new plays. Consequently, playgoers were offered more plays from the past than from recent years, and new plays constituted the smallest portion of the repertory. Between 1737 and 1777 only about three new full-length plays were given each season. Consequently, though the repertory offered much variety, the dramatist had little incentive to write.

Not only were the opportunities for production few, but the financial rewards were uncertain. For a time after the Restoration, a few playwrights were attached to companies at a fixed salary or as a shareholder. Dryden, for example, held a share in the King's Company from 1668 until 1678, in return for providing three plays each year. As the supply of plays began to exceed the demand, however, other financial arrangements were found more economical. After 1680, dramatists were paid by the "benefit" system, under which they received the proceeds (less house expenses) of the third night of the initial run. After 1690, they might also be given a benefit on the sixth night, if the play ran so long, and in the 18th century on every third night of the original run. Few plays ran beyond the third night, however, and some did not run that long, in which case the writer received nothing for his work. In any case, he lost all control over his plays after their initial runs. Although a few plays brought considerable rewards to their authors, this was exceptional.

The greatest demand for new plays came during the ten years preceding the passage of the Licensing Act in 1737, for during this time a number of minor theatres were open, some of which specialized in new plays. This act, which brought severe censorship and the closure of many theatres, reduced the playwright's opportunities for the rest of the century.

Governmental Regulation of the Theatre

The Licensing Act of 1737 was an attempt to solve problems which had existed since the late 17th century. When William III granted Betterton's troupe a license in 1695, despite the crown monopoly held by Christopher Rich, he set a precedent which was later to cast considerable doubt on the validity of the patents.

The two companies continued in opposition until 1707, when they were reunited by crown action. Rich immediately returned to his oppressive policies, and, having ignored orders to meet his actors' demands, was silenced in 1709. Rich still held both of the original patents, however, and bided his time, now moving to the Lincolns Inn Fields theatre, upon which he had taken a lease.

The Drury Lane was reopened in 1710 under a license, and with the exception of the years between 1715 and 1719, when a patent was granted to Sir Richard Steele, it was to operate under a renewable license thereafter. Upon the death of Queen Anne in 1714, the ban against Rich was raised, and his son opened the Lincolns Inn Fields theatre under the original patents.

By 1720, the validity of patents was being questioned because Charles II's grants had never been confirmed by Parliament, and because the crown itself had made so many exceptions to them. This doubt led several men to defy the patents. The Haymarket Theatre, built by John Potter, was opened in 1720, and by the 1730's four unlicensed theatres were operating in London. The confusion was compounded in 1733 when the courts dismissed the legal actions brought by the two licensed theatres against actors who had seceded from the Drury Lane to act elsewhere. Since this decision seemed to deny the validity of the patents, clarification was needed.

The immediate motivation for the Licensing Act, however, was Prime Minister Walpole's sensitivity to the political satires being offered at unlicensed theatres. Following a particularly scurrilous attack, a bill was rushed through Parliament. Since it was not thoughtfully devised, it created as many problems as it solved. The main provisions of the Licensing Act of 1737 were simple: (1) it prohibited the acting for "gain, hire, or reward" of any play not previously licensed by the Lord Chamberlain, and (2) it restricted authorized theatres to the City of Westminster (the official seat of government). The Drury Lane and Covent Garden thus were confirmed as the only legitimate theatres in England, for no provisions were made for troupes in any other city.

At first the law was obeyed, but in 1740, Henry Giffard, who had managed the best of the unlicensed troupes between 1731 and 1737, reopened the Goodmans Fields Theatre. Ostensibly charging admission only for concerts, to which plays were added free, Giffard sought to evade the Licensing Act by interpreting literally the prohibition against unauthorized acting for "gain, hire, or reward." The attention drawn to this theatre by David Garrick's debut in 1741 soon brought its closure. Others used similar ruses; Samuel Foote offered his "free" entertainments to those who paid for a "Dish of Chocolate" or to attend an "Auction of Pictures." Such ventures were tolerated for a time but most were eventually forbidden. It was the closure of the New Wells Theatre that prompted William Hallam to send a troup to America in 1752, the real beginning of the American theatre.

Other public entertainments did not require licensing until 1752, when abuses led to the passage of a new bill. Under it, all places of entertainment within a 20-mile radius of London were required to secure licenses from local magistrates. Although regular drama was expressly forbidden, the permissible kinds of entertainment were left indefinite.

No law as yet provided for theatrical entertainments outside of the area adjacent to London. Nevertheless, the provincial theatre had continued to operate, and a number of regular circuits had grown up. By the 1760's, the larger towns were objecting to being denied legitimate theatres. As a result, Parliament authorized theatres in specific towns: Bath and Norwich in 1768, York and Hull in 1769, Liverpool in 1771, Chester in 1777. By the end of the century, almost every major town had a "theatre royal," or crown-authorized theatre. With this legitimization, the provincial theatre flourished until the late 19th century.

In London, no exception to the monopoly held by Drury Lane and Covent Garden was made until 1766, when, in recompense for having been crippled by a prank instigated by the Prince of Wales, Samuel Foote was granted a license to present plays at the Haymarket between May 15 and September 15, a period during which the patent houses presumably would be closed. Although Foote's license was granted only for his lifetime, he sold it to George Colman in 1777 and it was renewed until 1843. Thus, the Haymarket became a third legitimate theatre.

Still another bill was passed in 1788 which permitted magistrates outside the 20-mile radius of London to license theatres for legitimate drama. As a result, the theatre was once again legitimized throughout the

INTERIOR of the Haymarket as it appeared in the late 18th century. On stage is a scene from a pantomime. [From Wilkinson, *Londina Illustrata* (1825)]

British Isles. After the act of 1788, the possibilities of confusion were almost as great as before 1737, for there were now four distinct licensing authorities: (1) the Lord Chamberlain, who licensed all plays and theatres in the city of Westminster; (2) local magistrates within 20 miles of London, who licensed places of minor entertainment; (3) local magistrates outside the 20-mile radius, who licensed legitimate theatres in their districts; and (4) Parliament, who authorized "theatres royal" in specific towns. The confusion was not to be exploited until the 19th century, when changing conditions led managers to search for ways to evade the legal restrictions.

Financial Policies

By 1700 theatre managers had evolved most of the financial policies which were to serve for the next 200 years. Since the first owners of the patents had insufficient capital to finance theatre buildings and to purchase the necessary scenery and costumes, they sold shares. These were of two kinds: shares in buildings and shares in acting companies. From the Restoration on, theatres were to be erected on leased land with money obtained by the sale of shares. The shareholders were then paid a fixed sum for each day that the company performed.

For a time after 1660, the old system under which actors shared in the company's profits was revived, but as the theatre declined in prosperity, actors came to prefer a fixed salary. By 1690 the sharing arrangement had been abandoned. It was revived by Betterton's troupe from 1695 to 1707, after which the London companies gave it up altogether, although it continued in the provincial theatres until the 19th century.

As the actor's control declined, that of outside investors increased. Davenant and Killigrew established the pattern by mortgaging their patents, scenery, and costumes. When the mortgages were not redeemed, partial ownership of the companies passed to persons who had no interest in the theatre except as a commercial venture. Thus, Christopher Rich, ostensibly to protect the investors, assumed control of the United Companies in 1693, even though he had no theatrical experience of any kind. He was merely the first of many such persons to gain control over London theatres.

Although there might be many investors, the financial risk fell on the men who leased and ran the theatres. Few managements survived long, and consequently few are significant. Rich was evicted from Drury Lane in 1709, but his son, John, managed Lincolns Inn Fields from 1714 to 1732 and Covent Garden from 1732 to 1761. After 1767, when Rich's heirs sold their interest, Covent Garden was weakened by dissensions among the owners. In 1771, control passed to Thomas Harris, who retained it into the 19th century.

Between 1710 and 1733 the Drury Lane was very successful because of the policies of the "triumvirate" of actors, Colley Cibber, Robert Wilks, and Thomas Doggett (replaced after 1713 by Barton Booth), who shared the managerial duties. After 1733, however, Drury Lane was in grave financial difficulty until 1747, when stability was restored under David Garrick and John Lacy. With Garrick assuming responsibility for staging and Lacy for finances, this management was to be the most admired of the 18th century. After Garrick's retirement in 1776, control passed to a group under the leadership of Richard Brinsley Sheridan. Most of the duties, however, fell to Thomas King, an actor. He was given so little authority that the theatre had declined considerably by 1788, when John Philip Kemble replaced King.

The Haymarket Theatre saw many short-lived managements until 1766, when it became the third licensed house. From 1766 until 1777 it was managed by Samuel Foote, and after 1777 by George Colman. Both men supervised their companies closely.

The success of theatre management, then, was somewhat erratic. Most of the failures can be attributed to managers who either knew little of the theatre and were unwilling to delegate authority to experienced persons, or to businessmen who sought merely to exploit the theatre. On the whole, the theatre was increasingly prosperous.

Despite occasional retrenchments, the trend between 1660 and 1790 was toward larger companies and more carefully mounted productions, which demanded greater financial resources. Whereas the typical acting company of the Restoration had included 35–40 members, that of 1776 had about 70. In addition to actors, each company employed treasurers, ticket takers, "numberers" (to count spectators as a check on the ticket takers), prompters, dancers, musicians, bill distributors, scene painters, candle snuffers, stagehands, wardrobe keepers, dressers, laundresses, and other maintenance personnel. In 1776, the major troupes employed about 200 persons.

Expenditures and profits were calculated on each playing day. By the 18th century "benefits" were an important part of theatrical life; each manager needed to know his daily expenses because these were subtracted from the beneficiary's receipts. In the early 18th century, the daily expenses were about 40 pounds; by 1735 they had risen to 50 pounds; and by the late 18th century to 85 pounds.

Since the manager depended primarily upon ticket sales for income, he had only two paths open to him as his expenses increased: to raise the price of tickets, or to enlarge seating capacity. Although at times he did both, he was cautious about increasing prices. Consequently, the scale of entrance fees did not change markedly. During the Restoration the basic charges were: boxes, 4 shillings; pit, 2 shillings 6 pence; middle gallery, 1s 6d; upper gallery, 1s. In the late 18th century, the comparable prices were 5s, 3s, 2s, and 1s. The usual prices were raised for premieres, or when expenditures for costumes or scenery were thought to justify an advance. On special occasions, such as a benefit for a particularly popular actor, the pit was converted into boxes and additional seating erected on the stage. Such alterations also brought a considerable increase in prices, although little of the additional income went to the manager.

After 1690 spectators were allowed to enter at the end of the third act at "half price," except when a new pantomime or other attraction was to be given as an afterpiece. If prices had been raised because of the afterpiece, the spectator who left at the end of the main piece was refunded the additional charge. Besides tickets, the managers realized some income from the sale of food, chocolate, playbooks, and playbills.

Steadily increasing expenses, however, forced most managers to enlarge their theatres to accommodate additional spectators. Most of the changes in theatre auditoriums were motivated by this need, whereas those in the stage resulted from changing fashions in spectacle.

Theatre Architecture

Although the Salisbury Court, Cockpit, and Red Bull Theatres were used for a short time following the Restoration, none was thought sufficiently suited to Italianate scenery. Consequently, Killigrew used Gibbons' Tennis Court from 1660 until 1663, when his Theatre Royal in Bridges Street was opened. Little is known of it, for it burned in 1672. Another structure, usually called the Drury Lane Theatre, was erected on the same site. Opened in 1674 and used until 1791, it measured 58 feet by 140 feet.

In 1661, Davenant converted Lisle's Tennis Court into the Lincolns Inn Fields Theatre. Measuring only about 30 by 75 feet, it became increasingly inadequate for the operatic spectacles that Davenant favored. Consequently, in 1671 it was replaced by the Dorset Gardens Theatre, a structure 57 by 140 feet, designed by Christopher Wren. The Dorset Gardens was seldom used after the union of the troupes in 1682 and was torn down in 1709. When Betterton's company was licensed in 1695, it reopened the Lincolns Inn Fields Theatre.

STAGE of Dorset Gardens (the proscenium doors are partially indicated at the extreme sides). The scene is from Settle's *Empress of Morocco*. [From Wilkinson's *Londina Illustrata* (1825)]

Thus, between 1660 and 1700 there were three theatres of importance—Drury Lane, Lincolns Inn Fields, and Dorset Gardens. Although they varied in size and details, they established the pattern for English playhouses until the 19th century.

The auditorium was divided into pit, boxes, and gallery. Unlike the French, the English pit was raked to improve sightlines and equipped with backless benches for all spectators. There were two or three galleries. The first was partitioned into boxes, while the uppermost remained open. The middle gallery, when present, might be divided between boxes and an open area. The early theatres were small; at the Drury Lane, for example, the distance from the stage to the back of the auditorium was only about 36 feet. The seating capacity was limited also; in the 17th century, Drury Lane held only about 650 persons and Lincolns Inn Fields even fewer.

Although the auditorium was similar to that of continental theatres, the stage differed. It included both a proscenium arch and an open platform in front of the proscenium. The Drury Lane of 1674 had a stage about 34 feet deep, divided into two equal parts by the proscenium. Two or three doors, surmounted by balconies, opened onto the apron at either side. These doors were the usual entrances for all characters, since most of the action took place on the apron. As in Elizabethan times, an exit through one door and reentry through another was sufficient to indicate a change of place. The apron thrust the action into the auditorium, rather than confining it behind the picture frame.

The floor of the stage was raked upward from the front of the apron to the back wall. Behind the proscenium, grooves were installed to accommodate wings and shutters, while trapdoors and flying machinery provided for special effects. These basic characteristics, with minor changes, were to continue through the 18th century.

Between 1700 and 1790 only a few theatres were important: Drury Lane, Lincolns Inn Fields, The Kings Theatre, the Haymarket, and Covent Garden. The Drury Lane was altered several times during the 18th century; after the major renovations of 1762 and 1775, it seated about 1800 as compared to 650 in 1700. When Lincolns Inn Fields was abandoned in 1705, Christopher Rich razed it and erected a new theatre on the site. This building, which seated about 1400, was used from 1714 until 1732, when it was replaced with Covent Garden. The Kings Theatre (until 1714 called the Haymarket or Queens Theatre), built in 1705, was devoted entirely to opera from 1707 until 1789, when it was gutted by fire. The Haymarket, built in 1720, was used by unlicensed companies until 1766, after which it took its place as a major theatre. The Covent Garden, built in 1732 to replace Lincolns Inn Fields, remained in use until 1808. Originally it seated about 1300–1400, but by the 1780's had been enlarged to hold 2180, and in 1793 to hold about 3000. The last renovation was made in part because the Drury Lane was being rebuilt to hold 3600. Thus, the size of the auditoriums increased through the 18th century, although marked changes did not occur until after 1760. In spite of the increase in size, the basic pattern remained constant. All were divided into pit, boxes, and gallery, and until the 1790's none had more than three levels.

As the auditorium grew, so did the stage. Around 1700, the stage back of the proscenium at Drury Lane was increased to about 30 feet, and by 1750 some theatres had stages as deep as 50 feet. At the same time, the apron dwindled. Around 1700, Rich removed one set of proscenium doors and shortened the apron, thus setting the pattern for the 18th century, during which there was only one door on either side. The apron, now reduced to about 12 feet, remained the principal playing area, however, until at least 1765, after which it was used less extensively.

The facilities for production were also increased during the 18th century by the acquisition or construction of smaller structures adjoining the main buildings. In spite of all additions and alterations, most of the theatres were considered inadequate by 1790, and they were soon to be replaced by larger, more elaborate buildings.

INTERIOR of Drury Lane c. 1790, just before it was rebuilt. [From Wilkinson, *Londina Illustrata* (1825)]

Scenic Practices

After 1661 the conventions of the English stage differed little from those of Italy and France. Wings, borders, and shutters were the standard units, although roll drops were sometimes used in the place of shutters after 1690. Sets were shifted by means of grooves installed on the stage floor and overhead. Upon a whistled signal from the prompter, stagehands made the necessary changes. Since the front curtain was raised after the Prologue and not lowered until the end of the performance, all changes were made in full view of the audience. Even entr'acte entertainments were given in front of a full stage setting until about 1750, after which an "act drop" was used as a background. Heavy properties or furniture could be set up and removed behind the shutters. Occasionally they were brought on by servants in full view of the audience.

Between 1660 and 1790 each theatre accumulated a stock of scenery which was used over and over again. When a new theatre was built, settings were commissioned even before the repertory was fixed. This practice was made possible by the neo-classical attitude that specific time and place are irrelevant in drama, and that attempts to particularize only diminish universality. Thus, settings were so anonymous that they could be used in many different plays. One author, writing about 1750, lists the necessary scenes as: (1) temples, (2) tombs, (3) city walls and gates, (4) palace exteriors, (5) palace interiors, (6) streets, (7) chambers, (8) prisons, (9) gardens, and (10) rural prospects. He adds that other settings are needed only occasionally. Settings designed for the specific needs of a particular play were occasionally used in minor genres emphasizing spectacle, as in pantomime, which was often built around magical transformations. Even this scenery, however, was reused in other plays.

The development of spectacle was retarded by the presence of spectators on the stage. Although well-established before 1642, this practice was not revived until about 1690, and was not usual until about 1700. It continued until 1762, when Garrick effectively banished the audience from the stage. Between 1700 and 1762, rows of benches extended upstage from the proscenium, and at benefits additional amphitheatrical seating often was erected across the back of the stage. On the other hand, the audience was usually forbidden to sit on the stage during productions which depended upon spectacle.

Since most plays were performed in stock scenery, ticket prices were raised when new sets were used. The additional revenue which this provided may be one reason why spectacle increased. Rich's successful exploitation of spectacle in pantomimes led him to experiment with it in regular drama. In the 1730's he added a procession and coronation scene to *Henry VIII*, in 1750 a funeral procession to *Romeo and Juliet*, and in 1761 the

A DESIGN by James Thornhill for *Arsinoe* at the Drury Lane Theatre, 1706. [Victoria and Albert Museum. Crown Copyright]

coronation of George III to several of Shakespeare's history plays. Spectacle was ordinarily reserved for the minor genres, however, until about 1765, when Garrick returned from the continent with new ideas of staging. Through the remainder of the century, scenery was to become more specific and new settings more common. Of the 37 new plays presented at Drury Lane between 1765 and 1776, 19 were given entirely new scenery.

The increasing interest in spectacle was accompanied by a change in the status of the scene painter. From 1660 until about 1735, no theatre had a scene painter on its regular staff; settings were commissioned as needed from easel painters. By the late 18th century, two or more scene painters were attached to each major theatre. This probably explains why so little is known of scene designers before 1760. During the Restoration, John Webb worked with Davenant, and Samuel Towers, Robert Robinson, and Robert Streeter painted settings for Killigrew. It seems probable that the principles of transferring a complex design to flat wings were not yet well understood in England, since some painters took so long and were paid so well. For example, Isaac Fuller sued Killigrew in 1669, claiming that he had not been paid for a single setting which he testified had required six weeks to paint; the court awarded him 335 pounds for his work at a time when a leading actor was paid about 2½ pounds per week. In 1674–75, another painter was paid 800 pounds to do settings for one play. By the early 18th century, however, payments were considerably less, perhaps because the painters now had greater facility. Since, before 1760, scenery was commissioned only sporadically, the average yearly expenditure for settings was small. Covent Garden spent only 253 pounds in the season of 1746–47, and only about one-tenth of a company's budget was ever spent on settings until after 1760.

From occasional references we know the names of many scene painters of the 18th century. Some of the more important are John DeVoto, who worked between 1719 and 1744; George Lambert (1710–65), a landscape painter who did settings for Rich at Lincolns Inn Fields and Covent Garden (some of his scenery remained in use until 1808); Francis Hayman and Thomas Lediard, who painted settings for Drury Lane in the 1730's.

In 1749, Rich began to import designers from the continent. The most significant of these was Jean-Nicholas Servandoni (1695–1766), famous for his work at the Paris Opera and elsewhere in Europe. Rich seems to have had Servandoni paint settings for which he had no immediate use, for one was introduced at Covent Garden as late as 1773 as never having been used before. Other important artists who worked at Covent Garden include Giovanni Battista Cipriani, a Florentine painter who came to London in 1755; Nicholas Thomas Dall, a Dane who settled in England around 1760, considered one of the finest painters of his age; and John Inigo Richards (?–

1810), a distinguished painter noted especially for his picturesque land-scapes.

The most important designer of the late 18th century, however, was Philippe Jacques DeLoutherbourg (1740–1812), a French artist who had studied with Boucher and Boquet of the Paris Opera. Engaged by Garrick in 1771 to oversee all elements of spectacle, he continued in this position until 1781, when he resigned because Sheridan proposed to cut his salary of 500 pounds. DeLoutherbourg continued to design settings occasionally until 1785. Between 1771 and 1785, he prepared more than 30 productions, of which a few are of special importance: *A Christmas Tale* (1773), with its subtle lighting effects; *The Wonders of Derbyshire* (1779), which depicted actual places in England and established the vogue for "local color"; and *Omai, or a Trip Around the World* (1785), a travelogue based on Captain Cook's voyage. In other productions, DeLoutherbourg recreated such recent events as the Portsmouth Naval review (1773) and a fashionable outdoor festival (1774). From 1781 to 1786, he maintained a miniature theatre, the Eidophusikon. On a stage six by eight feet, he created remarkable illusions of specific places and weather conditions through painting, lighting, sound effects, and music.

DeLoutherbourg's contributions were many. He introduced reproductions of real places on the stage. To increase illusion, he broke up the stage picture with ground rows and set pieces to gain a greater sense of depth and

A SKETCH by DeLoutherbourg for a battle scene in *Richard III*. [From *The Magazine of Art* (1895)]

277

reality, and to avoid the symmetrical composition imposed by parallel wings and shutters. He used miniature figures at the rear of the stage to depict battles, marching armies, and sailing vessels; and sound effects, such as waves, rain, hail, and distant guns, to increase the illusion. He revamped the lighting system, installing overhead battens, using silk screens and gauze curtains to gain subtle variations in color and to simulate various weather conditions and times of day. Perhaps most important of all, DeLoutherbourg achieved a unity of design by overseeing all of the visual elements of his productions. Before DeLoutherbourg, the various settings for the same play were often done by different painters. Furthermore, a play might be given one new set, with others taken from stock. Thus, although a manager probably had a vague agreement with his painters about the kind of scenes to be provided, there seems to have been little attempt to coordinate efforts. DeLoutherbourg's practices established a standard which was not to be fully achieved by his successors until well into the 19th century.

The work of DeLoutherbourg and others reflects the growing interest in both local color and history. The rediscovery of Herculaneum in the mid-18th century aroused public curiosity about past civilizations, and soon an interest in picturesque places and customs began to replace the neo-classical preoccupation with generalized, universalized times and places. Settings became more specific, and composition began to move away from the symmetrically-balanced settings typical of the preceding period. These new trends were not fully developed, however, until the 19th century.

Lighting

Little is known of lighting practices during the Restoration. Performances were given in the afternoon, and windows probably provided some illumination. Chandeliers hung above the apron and behind the proscenium. Pepys, in his *Diary,* often complains of headaches produced by looking into the candles. Footlights were certainly in use by 1673, for they are depicted in an illustration printed in that year. Since most of the action occurred on the apron, both auditorium and stage were illuminated throughout performances.

By 1744, lights were apparently being mounted on vertical "ladders" behind each wing and dimmed by "scene blinds," for an inventory made at Covent Garden in that year lists 12 pairs of "scene ladders," 24 "scene blinds," and 192 tin candlesticks. Footlights were mounted on pivots which allowed them to be lowered below the stage level for dimming. Lamps were

THE SO-CALLED FITZGIGGO RIOTS at Covent Garden in 1763. The on-stage characters are dressed for Arne's *Ataxerxes*. Note the men's Near Eastern dress as compared to the fashionable clothing of the women. Note also the chandeliers over the stage. [From Paston's *Social Caricature in the Eighteenth Century* (1905)]

used in some positions, since reflectors made candles wilt. It is difficult to say when these arrangements began; possibly they date from the Restoration.

Although Garrick is credited with reforming stage lighting in 1765, the nature of his reforms is unclear. He seems to have removed all visible light sources from the stage and to have increased brightness, perhaps with lamps and reflectors. During the 1770's, DeLoutherbourg made other changes. Using silk screens to reflect light, and perhaps transparent silk filters, he gained considerable control over color for the first time. This increased concern for lighting is reflected in the costs: in 1745, theatres were spending about 340 pounds a year on lighting, while during the 1770's expenses rose to 1,970 pounds.

In 1785 the Argand, or "patent," lamp was introduced. Using a cylindrical wick and glass chimney to control the relative proportions of oxygen and oil, it produced a much brighter and steadier light than earlier instruments. After this time, oil largely superseded candles for stage lighting. Since the chimneys could be colored, experimentation with color effects also increased.

Improvements in lighting and emphasis upon illusion encouraged managers to place more of the action behind the proscenium arch. This trend was not fully completed during the 18th century, however, and the auditorium continued to be lighted as a part of the total picture.

A SCENE from Whitehead's *The Roman Father* at Drury Lane in 1750. At center is Garrick. Note the *habit à la romaine* worn by the men, and the few exotic touches at the shoulder and waist on the women's dresses. [Courtesy Folger Shakespeare Library]

Costume Practices, 1660–1790

For the most part, the principles governing costume between 1660 and 1790 differed little from those of pre-Commonwealth times or from those of 17th century France. Since time and place were considered unimportant, most characters wore contemporary garments. Furthermore, since neo-classicism tended to idealize nature, most actors dressed their characters as sumptuously as possible. As in the earlier period, however, some deviations from contemporary dress were usual. Classical heroes wore the *habit à la romaine,* while Near-Eastern characters were identified by turbans, baggy trousers, and long fur-trimmed gowns. On the other hand, actresses playing classical or Near-Eastern roles merely added feathered headdresses to otherwise contemporary dress. Until about 1750, actresses often wore black velvet in tragedy, but after that time appeared increasingly in the latest fashions.

Conventionalized costumes continued for a few characters, notably Falstaff (played in ruff and Cavalier boots), Richard III (in Elizabethan pumpkin hose), and Henry VIII (after the manner of Holbein's portrait). Other conventions included costuming Hamlet in black, adding ermine trim to Lear's otherwise contemporary dress, and placing Macbeth in the uniform of a British officer.

Concern for greater realism and appropriateness began in the 1740's. In 1741, Charles Macklin clothed Shylock in a black gabardine gown, long trousers, and red hat, which he considered realistic Jewish dress. After 1750, Garrick occasionally attempted to costume pre-Commonwealth plays in Elizabethan garments, although he continued to perform all those written after 1660 in 18th century dress. Garrick's costumes were neither historically accurate nor consistent, but his concern indicates the awakening interest in history and the desire to reflect it in costuming. At first, there were no guides to historical costume, but in 1757 there appeared in London *Recueil des Habillements,* a collection of designs taken from paintings by Holbein, Van Dyke, Hollar, and others, "to which are added the habits of the principal characters on the English stage." In 1775, Joseph Strutt was to provide more accurate information in *The Dress and Habits of the Peoples of England.* As with scenery, however, costuming was not significantly altered by these trends until the 19th century.

Between 1660 and 1790, the principal sources for costumes were the company's wardrobe and the actor's own garments. Each company maintained a "common stock" of costumes, which were preserved and added to regularly. Throughout the 18th century, companies always spent more on costumes than on scenery. In time, wardrobes became extremely large, since nothing was thrown away and costumes were frequently refurbished. In staging a coronation scene in 1761, Garrick is said to have used garments which had been in stock since 1727. In the late 1760's, the Covent Garden wardrobe had grown so large that it had to be moved to a separate house adjoining the theatre.

At a glance, these practices suggest that a company provided adequate costumes for its repertory, but this is not completely true. In the second half of the 18th century, a company bought only an average of twelve new women's and twelve new men's outfits each year. Since an acting company included about 70 actors and a repertory of 75–80 plays, this rate of acquisition would probably have left most actors rather shabbily dressed if all depended upon the company's wardrobe.

It is probably for this reason that actors with sufficient means supplied most of their own costumes; some demanded a special allowance for this purpose. The actors' desire to dress as sumptuously as possible led to intense rivalries. As a result, costumes usually reflected the actor's purse rather than the character's position, and a Queen played by a poorer actress might appear shabby alongside an attendant played by a performer of greater means.

The company wardrobe was available to all actors. Wardrobe keepers checked out costumes to players, who were free to select whatever they wished to wear. In the late 18th century, this practice was curtailed somewhat as the choice of garments was more frequently assigned to the wardrobe keepers. In addition to looking after the costumes, the wardrobe keepers made and altered garments, purchased new supplies and took an inventory annually. Laundresses to keep the clothes clean and "dressers" to assist the actors during performances were also employed.

Acting Companies, 1660–1790

A major innovation of the Restoration was the appearance of women in the acting companies. By 1661 both Davenant and Killigrew had a full complement of actresses, and after this time men appeared only in such female roles as witches and comic old women, a practice which persisted through the 18th century.

Between 1660 and 1790 actors usually entered a company on a probationary status and learned by watching others. In the 1660's and 1670's, Davenant and Killigrew maintained a training company, and in the 1740's Macklin ran an acting school, as did Thomas Sheridan somewhat later, but none of these operations was a marked success. At Drury Lane between 1710 and 1730, the young actors had to attend three sessions a week to learn singing and dancing, and the established actors were sometimes paid to teach the beginners. Garrick instructed his young actors, and Rich trained several pantomime players. Such attempts were sporadic, however, and most performers learned through trial and error.

The beginner, or "utility" actor, played an enormous number of small roles each season and eventually discovered the types for which he was best suited. After a few years, he advanced into a "line of business" (a limited range of character types) in which he usually remained for the rest of his career. It is impossible to determine when lines of business were first recognized, for they may extend back to pre-Commonwealth times. By the late 18th century four clearly distinguishable ranks existed: (1) players of leading roles, (2) players of secondary roles, (3) players of third-line parts (often called "walking ladies" or "walking gentlemen"), and (4) general utility performers. The first rank was usually restricted to players of heroes and heroines of tragedy and light comedy, although an unusually popular performer in another line might command a salary of the highest rank. The lesser ranks included specialists in such lines as low comedy roles, "singing chambermaids," fathers, eccentric types, witches, and hags.

The extent to which an actor specialized depended both upon his versatility and the size of the company in which he performed. A small, provincial company required its actors to play a wider range of parts than the large London troupes. Most actors had a serious and a comic line, although they were seldom equally good in both. Lines of business were not related to an actor's age. Garrick played Hamlet until he was 59, and actresses often performed Juliet throughout their lives. Lines of business led to the "possession of parts," since once an actor was cast in a role he continued to play it as long as he remained in the company. Under the repertory system, each actor was assigned a large number of roles which he was supposedly able to perform on 24-hours' notice. Actors jealously guarded their parts and the redistribution of roles when a new actor was brought into a company often created a crisis. This problem increased in the late 18th century, when troupes began to employ more than one performer in a single line of business. The number of parts which a leading actor "possessed" varied. Mrs. Oldfield played about 26, Barton Booth about 35, and Garrick 96. Most actors were employed by the season, although some were given contracts for longer periods. On the other hand, Macklin performed under short-term engagements after 1743, inaugurating the "starring" arrangements which were to dominate the 19th century theatre. Other London performers starred with provincial troupes during the summer months.

The actor's income varied considerably. Salaries, although quoted by the week, were paid only when the theatre was open, and any closure brought a proportionate loss to the actors. Except for leading performers, little is known about actors' earnings prior to 1750. In the 1690's, Mrs. Barry received about 70 pounds a year; by the 1740's, a top-ranking actor earned about 180 pounds; in the 1760's, the four ranks of actors were paid 287 pounds, 148 pounds, 70 pounds, and 42 pounds.

During the 18th century, the actor's salary was augmented by a yearly "benefit." Benefit performances for groups of actors began in the 1660's and were first accorded to individual performers in the late 1680's. After 1695, Betterton began offering benefits as an inducement to actors to remain with his company; after 1700 the custom was gradually extended until every employee of the playhouse shared in a benefit performance. At first the benefits were scattered through the season, but after 1712 they were normally concentrated in the period between Easter and summer. Major performers had separate benefits, while lesser actors and non-performing personnel shared benefits. Typically the beneficiary received all the excess beyond house expenses.

A well-attended benefit might bring a performer more income in a single evening than he made throughout the rest of the year, especially since spectators often voluntarily paid higher admission fees and presented gifts of money or jewelry to popular performers. On the other hand, the receipts sometimes did not meet the house expenses and the actor lost money. The lure of a profitable benefit, however, probably permitted managers to pay actors considerably less than might otherwise have been demanded.

Usually an experienced actor (or "acting manager") was appointed to stage the plays when the theatre manager was not qualified for this task. Betterton was acting manager of the companies in which he worked for most of the years between 1668 and 1709; at Drury Lane between 1710 and 1732, the triumvirate of actor-managers divided the rehearsal duties; John Rich staged pantomimes and spectacles, but employed such actors as James Quin, Lacy Ryan, and James Lacy to rehearse the regular drama; Charles Macklin was acting manager at Drury Lane from 1734 to 1743, and Garrick was in charge of the repertory and staging at that theatre from 1747 until 1776.

The first three rehearsals of a new play fell to the dramatist, who presumably helped the actors with interpretation. The acting manager had complete responsibility for all revivals. Rehearsals were few by modern standards; they were held from about 10 A.M. until 1 P.M. and seldom extended beyond two weeks. Garrick was sometimes more meticulous and occasionally prolonged rehearsals to eight weeks. Little time was spent on blocking or movement patterns. Actors learned by experience how to move about the stage and when to give the dominant positions to the major performers. Most scenes were played on the apron or near the front of the stage, and lines were addressed to the audience as much as to the other characters. Since furniture was seldom used, actors stood throughout and gave little thought to creating realistic stage pictures. During rehearsals, the players made no attempt to give full portrayals. Consequently, innovations were not revealed until the first performance, when they surprised fellow actors as much as the audience. The typically brief rehearsals usually meant that on opening night actors were still uncertain of their lines and depended much on improvisation. Furthermore, their relatively secure positions seem to have made many actors neglectful. As a result, managers sought to impose discipline through an elaborate system of fines for such faults as tardiness at rehearsals and failure to learn lines.

The orderly operation of a company depended much upon the prompter, whose duties included securing licenses for the plays, copying out the actors' "sides," holding rehearsals when requested to do so, drafting the playbills, enforcing the company's rules, and assessing fines. During performances he gave cues for scene shifts and music, dispatched call boys for actors, and prompted as necessary. Some of these men, notably John Downes, William Chetwood, and Richard Cross, have left invaluable records of the theatres in which they served.

Acting was a mixture of tradition and innovation. Roles were passed down from one generation to the next, and with them went the traditional interpretation. When one actor succeeded another, he was expected to learn the business used in that company, since the repertory could not be restaged to suit him. Because so much of playing became traditional, new conceptions of characters, or even new line readings, often produced sensations. Thus, Charles Macklin revolutionized the role of Shylock in 1741 by departing from the traditional low-comedy interpretation. On the other hand, Garrick built his reputation through the unique qualities he was able to achieve without altering the basic tradition of his roles.

CLOSET SCENE from *Hamlet,* supposedly showing Betterton at the left as Hamlet. [From Rowe's edition of Shakespeare's works (1709)]

The style of acting varied from formal to realistic. Until about 1750, the dominant approach was oratorical, as epitomized in the playing of Betterton, Booth, and Quin. Macklin and Garrick urged the adoption of a style based upon direct observation of life, although they too probably idealized reality. The two styles came into direct conflict in the 1740's when Quin and Garrick were the leading performers of London. The triumph of Garrick served to establish the more realistic approach as a standard for the remainder of the century. Garrick's victory parallels the changes evident in the other theatre arts, since it marks a movement away from the idealized generality of neoclassicism, which Quin favored, to a more specific and individualized characterization. The neo-classical and oratorical style persisted, however, even among Garrick's troupe, and two rather distinct styles were often seen in the same play.

So many outstanding performers appeared on the English stage between 1660 and 1790 that only a few can be noted here. Of the pre-Commonwealth actors who returned at the Restoration, the most important were Michael Mohun (c. 1620–84) and Charles Hart (?–1683), leading members of Killigrew's company. Of the younger group, the most famous were Edward Kynaston (c. 1640–1706), at first the player of women's roles and then of heroic parts; James Nokes (?–1696), actor of foolish old husbands, clumsy fops, and ridiculous old women; Cave Underhill (c. 1634–1710), noted for his low comedy playing; Henry Harris (?–c. 1682), friend and rival of Betterton; William Mountfort (1664–92), portrayer of the heroes of Restoration comedy; and John Lacy (?–1681), outstanding in ridiculous characters. By far the most important actor of the Restoration was Thomas Betterton (c. 1635–1710). On the stage from 1660 until 1709, he excelled in heroic and tragic parts and was universally considered the greatest actor of his day. Betterton performed a wide range of roles, both comic and serious, although he was probably best in such parts as Hamlet, Othello, Hotspur, and Brutus. He remained completely in character throughout a performance and commanded universal attention with his restrained but powerful action and speech. His somewhat formal and elocutionary style established the model for others. Of the actresses, three were outstanding: Nell Gwynn, Mrs. Barry, and Mrs. Bracegirdle. Nell Gwynn's (1650–87) acting career was brief, 1665–69, but sufficient to establish her fame as a comedian, especially in roles requiring male attire, dancer, and speaker of witty prologues and epilogues. Elizabeth Barry (1658–1713) played leading tragic roles opposite Betterton. Anne Bracegirdle (c. 1663–1748), trained by Betterton, excelled in comedies of manners from 1680 until 1707, when she retired at the height of her career.

Between 1710 and 1735 the outstanding actors were Colley Cibber, Robert Wilks, Thomas Doggett, Barton Booth, and Anne Oldfield. Cibber (1671–1757) entered the United Company in 1690. Remaining with Rich when the more experienced actors seceded in 1695, he was soon playing leading roles and writing popular plays. From 1710 until 1733, he was one of the managers and leading performers of Drury Lane. In 1740, he published his autobiography, a principal source of information about the English theatre between 1690 and 1735. As an actor, Cibber was best in the roles of fops. Robert Wilks (c. 1665–1732), who began his acting career in Ireland in 1691, was well established at the Drury Lane by 1698, where he played leading roles and served as acting manager. From 1710 until his death he was one of the managers of Drury Lane. Although successful in tragedy, he was especially admired as the dashing young hero of comedy. Thomas Doggett (c. 1670–1721) was considered the finest low comedian of his day. He began his career in Dublin and several provincial companies before coming to London in 1691. He went with Betterton to Lincolns Inn Fields in 1695. Taken into the management of Drury Lane in 1710, he resigned in 1713 and seldom acted afterward. Barton Booth (1681–1733) began his career in Dublin about 1698 and came to London in 1700. He played secondary roles until 1713, when he made a great sensation in Addison's *Cato*. By royal order, he was admitted to the management of Drury Lane. From 1713 to 1727, when ill health forced him to retire, he was considered the finest tragic actor of London and Betterton's true successor. Anne Oldfield (1683–1730) went on the stage in 1700 and achieved her first success about 1704. After the retirement of Mrs. Barry and Mrs. Bracegirdle she was considered the finest actress of her time. She played both comic and serious roles, but was especially admired in high comedy. She was buried in Westminster Abbey, the first actress to be so honored.

By 1733 these actors were either dead or retired. During the next ten years there was a dearth of outstanding performers. The leading actor was James Quin (1693–1766), who began his career in Dublin in 1712, came to Drury Lane in 1714, and in 1718 joined John Rich, for whom he worked as acting manager. He returned to Drury Lane in 1734 and retired in 1751. Although his declamatory style in tragedy led to his being compared unfavorably with Garrick, he was universally admired in such comic roles as Falstaff. Despite Garrick's reputation, Quin was at the height of his popularity when he retired.

Although Garrick is often credited with inaugurating the more natural style of acting, he was anticipated by Charles Macklin (1699–1797). Born in Ireland, Macklin began acting about 1719 and continued until 1789. He first came to London about 1725, but his style was considered too prosaic and he returned to the provinces until 1730. He served as acting manager at Drury Lane from 1734 until 1743, when he and other actors, including Garrick, seceded. Refused a license, they capitulated, but the manager would not employ Macklin again. For a time he ran an acting school, and thereafter played short engagements in London and elsewhere. Macklin's reputation was based primarily upon a few roles, especially Shylock and the protagonists of his own comedies, such as *Love à la Mode* (1759) and *The Man of the World* (1781). Although he was more devoted to naturalistic acting than was Garrick, Macklin's limited range as an actor and his quarrelsome nature restricted his success. He specialized in bluff, hearty old men, and eccentric characters.

From the 1740's until 1776, David Garrick (1717–79) dominated the English stage. After making his London debut at Goodman's Fields Theatre in 1741, he alternated between Drury Lane and Covent Garden until 1747, when he became joint manager of Drury Lane, a position which he held until his retirement in 1776. Garrick influenced the theatre through

MACKLIN AS SHYLOCK in the trial scene of *The Merchant of Venice*. [From a contemporary engraving]

his managerial policies as much as through his acting, for in addition to being a careful and devoted director, he was responsible for several significant innovations. As an actor, he had an extremely wide range, playing almost every kind of character, although he was considered best as Lear, Macbeth, and Hamlet. He had a mobile face, piercing eyes, and expressive body, all of which he used to great effect in the pantomimic byplay for which he was famous. His agreeable and well-controlled voice was somewhat lacking in fullness. Through intense concentration upon the immediate situation, Garrick made whatever he did seem compellingly real. Above all, he seemed to grasp the complexities of each role, and he gave them more fully-rounded portrayals than did any of his contemporaries.

Garrick's fame has overshadowed the many other fine performers of the late 18th century. Among the actresses who worked with him were Peg Woffington (*c.* 1714–60), noted especially for her portrayal of spirited heroines of comedy and for "breeches" parts (that is, those played in male attire); Kitty Clive (1711–85), who began her career in 1728 and remained a favorite with audiences in farce and spirited comedy; and Frances Abington (1737–1815), noted for high comedy roles. Susanna Cibber (1714–66), daughter-in-law of Colley Cibber, began her career as a singer

GARRICK AND MRS. PRITCHARD in *Macbeth*. Note the use of 18th century costumes. [From the *English Illustrated Magazine* (1776)]

but turned to acting in 1736. Appearing almost entirely in tragedy, she modified her declamatory style somewhat after joining Garrick in 1753. Mrs. Hannah Pritchard (1711–68) was universally considered the finest tragic actress of her time. So thoroughly did she make Lady Macbeth her own that Garrick never appeared in the play after she died.

Garrick's greatest rival was Spranger Barry (1719–77), who began his career in Ireland in 1743 and came to London in 1746. From 1750 to 1758 he played at Covent Garden in competition with Garrick. Although Garrick outshone him in most roles, Barry was considered superior as the romantic lover. From 1766 until his death, he often appeared at Drury Lane.

Other performers of note include: George Ann Bellamy (c. 1727–88), remembered principally as Garrick's Juliet: Mary Ann Yates (1728–87), who replaced Mrs. Cibber in tragedy; Edward Shuter (1728–76), famous for his comic old men and for his entr'acte entertainments; Richard Yates (1706–96), a low comedian and Harlequin; Thomas King (1730–1805), a player of comic old men and acting manager under Sheridan at Drury Lane; John Henderson (1747–85), considered Garrick's successor, but whose early death prevented him from establishing a lasting reputation; and Elizabeth Farren (1759–1829), an outstanding actress of fine ladies, who left the stage to marry the Earl of Derby in 1797. By 1790 the leadership in acting was passing to the Kemble family, who were to dominate the next generation.

Audiences and Performances

During the Restoration, the theatrical season ran from October to June; in the 18th century, it opened in mid-September and continued until the end of May. In the fall, the theatres played two or three times a week until mid-October, when they began to perform daily except Sundays. Although performances were forbidden on Wednesdays and Fridays of Lent, sacred oratorios were permitted on those days after 1740. All theatres were closed during Passion Week. The number of performances in a regular season averaged from 170 to 200. During the Restoration, the apprentices gave occasional programs during the summer months, but summer playing was not usual until the 1740's, and, since these performances were illegal, they were often interrupted. After 1766, when the Haymarket was licensed to perform from May 15 to September 15, London always had a summer season.

Performances were advertised in various ways: posters set up around the city; handbills distributed at coffee houses, private homes, and elsewhere; advertisements in newspapers, after these began to appear in the early 18th century; and announcements made from the stage each evening. The performance time was gradually moved from midafternoon to early evening. During the Restoration, the beginning time was 3 or 3:30 P.M.; by 1700, it had been moved to 4 or 5; between 1700 and 1710, the time varied from 5 to 5:30 to 6; after 1710, the usual hour was 6 P.M., although the minor houses often played at other hours. The doors of the theatre were usually opened long before performances began and, since seats were not reserved, many persons came early or sent servants to hold seats. By the 1730's, tickets for boxes could be bought in advance and eventually those seats were numbered. Each part of the house—boxes, pit, and galleries—had its own entrance, ticket sellers, and ticket takers. Since most seats were unnumbered, squabbles over places often occurred.

The evening's bill was complex. In the Restoration, it consisted of a full-length play, with singing and dancing between the acts. Around 1700, Christopher Rich added acrobats, trained animals, and other circus-like performers in an attempt to compete more effectively with Betterton's troupe; this kind of entertainment was never completely absent from the theatre thereafter. Around 1715, the afterpiece was introduced and soon became standard. Thus, after 1720, a typical evening's bill was arranged in this way: approximately one-half hour of music preceded the performance; then came the Prologue, followed by a full-length play; the intervals between acts were filled with miscellaneous variety entertainment; following the main play, an afterpiece (a pantomime, farce, or comic opera) was performed; and the evening concluded with a song and dance. Performances lasted three hours or longer.

The relationship between audience and performers was close. Actors often took their grievances to the spectators, who demanded explanations from alleged offenders. Riots, precipitated by changes in casting or entrance charges, and violations of well-established customs, were frequent.

The theatre gained steadily in popularity as commercial prosperity enlarged the potential play-going public. Consequently, by 1790 the theatre buildings had grown too small. Also by this time, new values had undermined neoclassicism. England was ready for new developments in both its theatre and drama.

ITALY
AND FRANCE
IN THE
18TH CENTURY

*I*n the 18th century, Italy continued its leadership in scenic design but contributed little of significance in play writing. France, on the other hand, retained its lead in drama. As the theatre of other countries gained strength and new tastes developed, the influence of both Italy and France waned. By 1790, their supremacy was no longer assured.

The Evolution of Italian Scenic Design

By the late 17th century, Italian scenic practices had been adopted in most of Western Europe. Settings composed of flat wings, shutters, and borders were erected on proscenium-arched stages, permitting rapid scene shifts and spectacular effects. The accepted visual conventions were those popularized by Torelli and Vigarani. The typical setting showed a perspective alley composed of large buildings leading to a distant prospect. The important theatrical centers of Italy were Venice, Parma, Bologna, Milan, Turin, Rome, and Naples.

By the 1650's, the Austrian court in Vienna was also attracting influential Italian scenic designers. Here between 1652 and 1707, Giovanni Burnacini (1600–65) and Ludovico Ottavio Burnacini (1636–1707) staged some of the most lavish entertainments in Europe. Of their more than 115 productions, the most elaborate was probably *The Golden Apple* (1668), which required 23 settings and 35 machines; in the final scene, three groups of dancers performed simultaneously; one in the sky, one on the sea, and one on land.

SETTING by Lodovico Burnacini for Minato's *La Monarchia Latina Trionfante* (1678) in Vienna. [From *Die Theater Wiens* (1899)]

Although settings in general increased in size and splendor during the late 17th century, they remained within the visual conventions which had been established before 1650. Significant changes, most of which are associated with the Bibiena family, were not made until after 1700. Of the many Bibienas, the most important were Ferdinando (1657–1743), Francesco (1659–1739), Giuseppe (1696–1757), Antonio (1700–74), and Carlo (1728–87). The family's reputation was first established through Ferdinando's work at Bologna and Parma. By 1708 he was sufficiently famous to be summoned to Barcelona, where he staged the festivities for the marriage of the future Emperor Charles VI. In 1711, Charles VI appointed him court architect at Vienna to succeed Burnacini. Thereafter the Bibienas were in demand wherever an interest in opera developed. During the 18th century they were employed in such major cities as Paris, Lisbon, London, Stockholm, Berlin, Dresden, and St. Petersburg.

The contributions of the Bibiena family were numerous. Around 1703, while working at Bologna, Ferdinando introduced angle perspective, perhaps his most significant innovation. Rather than a single vanishing point at the rear of the setting, Bibiena used two or more vanishing points at the sides. Whereas previous designers emphasized a central vista, Bibiena placed buildings, walls, statues, or courtyards at the center of the picture and relegated vistas to the sides.

SETTINGS by Ferdinando Bibiena for Pariati's *Angelica Vincitrice di Alcina* (1716) in Vienna. [From *Die Theater Wiens* (1899)]

Bibiena also altered the scale of settings. Before his time, the stage had been treated as an extension of the auditorium, and the scenery had been proportioned accordingly. Thus, in Torelli's settings the tops of the buildings are always visible. Furthermore, the auditorium's rectangular arrangement was continued in the central perspective alley created by the scenery. Bibiena, on the other hand, divorced both the angle and the scale of his settings from those of the auditorium. Consequently, since a scene could now be depicted from any eye point, the former symmetrical arrangement was no longer necessary. Furthermore, the wings near the front of the stage were painted as though they were merely the lower portion of a building too large to be contained in the narrow confines of the stage. Vanishing points were placed extremely low so as to increase the effect of apparent size. As a result, Bibiena's settings seem so vast that they often create a mood of fantasy and unreality.

The Bibienas continued the trend toward excessive ornamentation which had begun in the late 17th century. Columns are twisted and entwined with garlands, S-curved supports are added to beams and pediments, encrustations abound everywhere. Although unadorned classical forms were still used, the typical setting followed the style usually called "Baroque."

STAGE SETTING by Guiseppe Bibiena. [From a contemporary engraving]

In spite of its apparent size, a setting using angle perspective often required less space than one with a central alley, for the effect of vastness was created by side vistas not fully shown. Many of the settings divide the stage into a foreground, intended for the actors, and a background representing distant objects. A drop, cut to form arches or a series of columns, often delimits the acting area at the rear and provides a frame through which distant prospects are seen. The chariot-and-pole system of scene shifting also aided composition, for an obelisk, tree, or other seemingly free-standing object could be mounted at any point on the stage. Nevertheless, it is extremely difficult to recreate the floor plans of 18th century settings, since engravings give few clues about the division into wings, shutters, and borders.

Although Ferdinando Bibiena popularized the *scena per angolo,* it was also developed quite independently by Filippo Juvarra (1676–1736), who adopted angle perspective in Naples around 1706. After working in Rome, he moved to Turin, where he became the leading architect of northwestern

Italy. Juvarra's architectural training probably accounts for the principal differences between his stage settings and those of the Bibienas. He appears to have worked from a floorplan, often indicated at the bottom of his designs. Consequently, his settings appear less fantastic than those by Bibiena. They are essentially curvilinear and lead the eye back to the foreground rather than off to the sides, as often happens in the Bibienas' work. Juvarra also experimented with "unit settings," in which the background elements were altered behind a fixed foreground. Some of his settings appear to be made entirely from draperies; others include such exotic elements as tropical foliage and near-Eastern architectural forms.

A DESIGN by Filippo Juvarra. [Victoria and Albert Museum. Crown Copyright]

In addition to the Bibienas, several other families of scenic designers were active. Members of the Mauro family worked in the principal theatrical centers of Italy and Germany from the 17th century until 1820. Beginning with Gaspare Mauro (*fl.* 1657–1719), the family designed settings in Venice, Turin, Parma, Monaco, Milan, Dresden, Vienna, and elsewhere. The Quaglio family, beginning with Guilio (1601–58) and ending with Eugen (1857–1942), continued as designers through six generations. Although of Italian origin, they worked principally in Austria and Germany. From 1778 until 1917 they maintained headquarters at Monaco, where the museum preserves many of their designs. The Galliari family, of which the most famous members were Bernardino (1707–94) and Fabrizio (1709–90), were active from the early 18th century until 1823. Although they worked in many cities, they were associated primarily with Turin and Milan.

VIEW OF THE INTERIOR of the Royal Theatre, Turin, about 1750. Drawing by P. D. Olivero. Note the servants with food and drink in the auditorium, the *habit à la romaine* worn by the actors, the elaborate court dress of the woman (requiring train bearers), and the elaborate stage settings. [Courtesy Museo Civico, Turin]

DESIGN by Guiseppino Galliari of classical ruins (about 1780). [Courtesy Museo Civico, Turin]

The visual style established between 1700 and 1750 underwent many changes in the late 18th century as new interests emerged. With the development of comic opera, domestic and rustic scenes became common. In Italy, comic opera evolved from the *intermezzi* performed with serious operas. The first to achieve widespread fame was Pergolesi's *La Serva Padrona* (1733). Variations on comic opera (such as the English ballad opera, the German *singspiele,* and the French *opéra comique*) appeared throughout Europe. By the late 18th century, the larger opera houses were maintaining two separate troupes, one for comic and one for serious opera.

The increased interest in history also affected scene design. The rediscovery of Pompeii in 1748 and its systematic excavation after 1763 captured the imagination of Europe. Scenic designers began to show classical structures in various stages of ruin with shrubs or vines growing from cracks. Interest in history also led to works based upon the national past or on folk literature. Usually set in the Middle Ages, they brought Gothic architecture into the theatre, which had previously used classical forms almost exclusively. The interest in particular times and places also motivated the introduction of picturesque landscapes and "local color." The late 18th century also saw a reaction against florid operatic and scenic forms. Christoph Willibald Gluck (1714–87) sought to recapture the simplicity of the early Florentine opera, and the change in operatic style was paralleled by a return to pure classical architecture.

Perhaps the most important innovation was the introduction of "mood" into design. Before the late 18th century, settings were painted for clarity of detail. Now designers began to emphasize the atmospheric values of light and shadow. The key figure in this trend was Gian Battista Piranesi (1720–78). Although he designed many stage settings, Piranesi's influence was exerted primarily through his more than 1000 engravings of Roman ruins and contemporary prisons published between 1745 and 1778. His drawings of ruins contributed much to the interest in "ruined" antiquity,

ENGRAVING of a prison by Piranesi. [From Piranesi's *Carceri d'Invenzioni* (1761)]

and his prisons, with their marked contrasts in light and shadow, accelerated interest in atmospheric qualities. Scene designers began to depict picturesque places as seen by moonlight or interiors illuminated by a few shafts of light. Color played only a minor role in this trend, for the palette was limited. Settings were painted in sepia or pastel shades of green, yellow, and lavender. Mood, therefore, was achieved primarily through the juxtaposition of masses of light and shadow.

In spite of the trend toward greater visual variety, the types of places represented in late 18th century operas can be reduced to about ten. Because each locale was idealized, settings could be reused for a number of different works. The basic compositional techniques remained unchanged, for the *scena per angolo* continued to dominate. The major innovations after 1750 were restricted to new motifs and an increased concern for mood, both of which were to contribute to the development of Romanticism.

ITALY AND FRANCE IN THE 18TH CENTURY

Italian Drama of the 18th Century

If Italy's designers dominated the theatre of Europe, the same cannot be said for its dramatists, for few of them achieved fame. Because of the prestige of opera, most Italian playwrights were content to compose librettos, and the most prized honor was the post of poet to the Imperial Court at Vienna. Here the two most famous Italian writers of the early 18th century worked. Apostolo Zeno (1668–1750), author of more than 60 operas, was considered the leading author of the years 1700 to 1725. He was soon overshadowed by his successor, Metastasio (Pietro Trapassi, 1698–1782), honored as the greatest poet of his age. Metastasio attempted to write librettos that could be performed effectively without music. Thus, his plays resemble neo-classical tragedies, with the exception that they are in three acts and end happily. Since the characters are either good or evil and virtue is always triumphant, they are essentially melodramas. Although Metastasio wrote only about 30 librettos, the most famous of which are *Adriano* (1731), *Issipile* (1732), and *The Clemency of Titus* (1734), they were set to music more than 1000 times before 1840. The shallowness of these works from a modern view makes it difficult to understand the 18th century's admiration, bordering on worship, of Metastasio.

Except for opera, serious drama was not popular in 18th century Italy. Before 1750, the only tragedy of note is *Merope* (1713) by Francesco Scipione di Maffei (1675–1765). It tells the story of Merope, who, on the verge of slaying her unknown son, discovers the truth and is able to effect revenge upon the real cause of her misery. It was out of such unpromising beginnings that Italy's most famous tragedian appeared around 1775. Vittorio Alfieri (1749–1803) sought to present the most powerful emotions in the simplest possible dramatic form. Everything not essential is pared away. As a result, his plays resemble those of Racine more than they do other 18th century tragedies. Of his works, which include *Oreste* (1776), *Antigone* (1783), and *Myrra* (1789), the acknowledged masterpiece is *Saul* (1782). In it, attention is concentrated upon Saul, the remnant of a great man, now vacillating between madness and sanity, petty tyranny and greatness. The action is simple, for it grows out of Saul's inner torment. Other works by Alfieri are somewhat flawed by his strong political convictions, which sometimes led him to place too great emphasis upon doctrinal messages. It was Alfieri's political ideas which influenced most of his successors, none of whom rose to his level.

Comedy fared little better than tragedy. Until 1750, the comic impulse was largely channeled into the *commedia dell'arte*. Unfortunately, after

1700 this formerly vital form had grown repetitious. Minor masks, music, and spectacle had been added to increase its variety but, as sentimentalism grew, *commedia* came to seem crude and unfeeling. It was in this atmosphere that Carlo Goldoni (1707–93), Italy's greatest comic dramatist, appeared. He began his career in 1734 by writing scenarios for *commedia* troupes in and around Venice, the last stronghold of the *commedia dell'arte*. From the first he objected to many of the form's conventions; in 1738, he began his reforms by writing out the principal role in his *Man of the World*. This was sufficiently well received that by 1743 he was writing out all of the parts, and by 1749 was beginning to alter the traditional character types.

GOLDONI's *The Mistress of the Inn* (1753). [From an edition of Goldoni's plays published in 1789]

In 1750, Goldoni's *The Comic Theatre* attacked the antiquated methods of the *commedia,* called for abandoning masks (because they prevented subtle facial expression), adopting better stage speech, and substituting subjects based on life for the traditional situations of *commedia.* Since he had already abolished most of the improvisation, his program advocated altering all the form's essential characteristics. By 1761, when he left Venice, Goldoni had done much to banish fantasy, vulgarity, and nonrealistic conventions from the *commedia,* substituting instead realism, humor, and sentiment. The stock characters had been humanized and softened. Pantalone, for example, was no longer the ridiculous, miserly, and lecherous old man, but an honest merchant, good father, and solid citizen. In this manner, Goldoni obliterated the distinctions between the *commedia* and regular comedy. In 1762, Goldoni settled in Paris, where he wrote for the Comédie Italienne until his retirement in 1773.

Goldoni was one of the most prolific writers of the century. Of his 150 comedies, 10 tragedies, and 83 musical dramas, many are mere trifles, but others are among the finest works of the age. He was enormously inventive, and found many ingenious ways of unifying plots. Sometimes he used a place, as in *The Coffee House,* at others an object, as in *The Fan,* or a character type, as in *The Women's Gossip,* to weld together a number of actions. Although Goldoni depicted almost every profession and class, he favored the middle and lower classes, and often characterized the nobility as decadent and useless. Above all he idealized his female characters, as his most famous play *The Mistress of the Inn* (1753) illustrates well. The sentimental strain is found throughout Goldoni's work, but there is always sufficient wit and humor to avoid the cloying sentimentality which afflicts many plays of the era. Nevertheless, Goldoni's work, despite its charm and vivacity, is lacking in depth.

Carlo Gozzi (1720–1806) strongly objected to Goldoni's alterations of the *commedia,* his sentimentalism, and his treatment of the upper classes. Gozzi's counterattack took the form of *fiabe,* dramatic and satiric fairy tales written for the *commedia* masks. Gozzi emphasized those elements which Goldoni sought to suppress: fantasy, enchantment, and improvisation. Thus, he chose his subjects from fairy tales or legends (which provided many opportunities for spectacular effects), and used them to satirize the sentimental trends of current literature. As a result of this topicality, a modern reader can only guess at their effectiveness, especially since all leave some portions to be improvised. Although his *The Love for Three Oranges* (1761), *King Stag* (1762), *Turandot* (1762), and *The Magic Bird* (1765) were extremely popular in the 18th century, Gozzi's fame was not lasting. He brought a new life to the *commedia* for a few years, but after 1770 its strength rapidly declined. Thereafter, Italian comedy was to follow the major European trends.

French Drama of the 18th Century

Although today French drama of the 18th century ranks low in critical estimation, during its own time it was considered the finest in the world. Most of the tragic writers sought to follow in Racine's footsteps, but, since they substituted involved plots and complex character relationships for his emphasis upon internal conflicts, their work failed to achieve greatness. The major trends can be seen in the work of LaGrange-Chancel, Crébillon, and Voltaire.

Joseph de LaGrange-Chancel (1677–1758) wrote 14 plays after 1694. The most popular, *Ino and Mélicerte* (1713), tells the story of Ino, now a slave in the household of her former husband, the King, who believes her to be dead. The present queen is plotting to kill Ino's son, Mélicerte, who is unaware of his own identity. A number of other complex relationships are clarified in a series of recognition scenes, which thwart the evil queen and restore Ino to happiness. The trend toward melodrama, evident in this plot, was accelerated by Prosper Jolyot Crébillon (1674–1762), whose extremely complex dramas were designed to arouse horror in the spectator. Crébillon often selected stories filled with atrocities, as in *Atreus and Thyestes* (1707), in which Thyestes is served a drink concocted from the blood of his sons. Crébillion's preference for complex plots is well illustrated by *Électre* (1708), in which Aegisthus is provided with a son and daughter so as to motivate complications based on the love of Aegisthus' children for Electra and Orestes. Crébillon's best play is *Rhadamisthe and Zénobie* (1711), in which the unrecognized heroine is loved by Rhadamisthe (her cruel husband, who is present in disguise although he is presumed dead), her father-in-law, and her brother-in-law, Arsames. After the death of Rhadamisthe and numerous recognition scenes, Zénobie finds happiness in marriage to the virtuous Arsames. This play, considered one of the finest of the 18th century, held the stage until 1830.

Voltaire (Francois-Marie Arouet, 1694–1778) dominated tragedy in the 18th century, as he did all French literature and thought. Beginning with *Oedipe* (1718), he wrote 53 plays, of which more than half are tragedies. Although superior in many respects, they continue the trend toward complex plots, involved character relationships, and sudden reversals based upon recognitions.

Voltaire's best work, *Zaïre* (1732), tells the story of the slave, Zaïre, who is loved by her master, the Sultan Osman. Her discovery that she is the daughter of Lusignan, the Christian former king of the area and a fellow-slave, is kept from the Sultan, who grows insanely jealous of her meetings with Nerestan, Zaïre's recently-discovered brother, and kills them both. Voltaire's philosophical interests are reflected in many of his plays. *Alzire* (1736), for example, argues that a religion should be valued only to the extent that it produces humanitarian results. The trend toward sentimentalism is reflected in Voltaire's frequent use of the *voix du sang* (an instinctive attraction to blood relatives) as a dramatic device to foreshadow recognition scenes.

As a result of his residence in England from 1726 to 1729, Voltaire sought to liberalize the neo-classical ideal in France. His reforms, however, were restricted to permitting ghosts and a limited amount of violence on stage, widening the permissible subject matter, and increasing spectacle. Voltaire's attempts to use spectacle more effectively were frustrated by the presence of spectators on the stage, and it was largely due to his influence that the practice was abolished in 1759. This innovation, coming at just the time when public interest in history and local color was growing, encouraged the exploitation of spectacle in the regular drama. Voltaire's *Tancrède* (1760) turned attention to the Middle Ages and began a vogue for plays about the French national past, which was to be explored in such later popular works as Pierre Laurent de Belloy's *The Siege of Calais* (1765) and *Gaston and Bayard* (1771).

In his desire to liberalize the French stage, Voltaire called attention to Shakespeare's works, previously neglected in France. Although they were sometimes read in their original form, Shakespeare's plays were considered much too "irregular" for the stage. Even the drastic adaptations of Jean-Francois Ducis (1733–1816), several of which were produced after 1769, were too exotic for French taste. This response illustrates how solidly entrenched neoclassicism continued to be, in spite of the reforms introduced by Voltaire and others.

Comedy, perhaps because of its less privileged position, underwent more changes than tragedy. The influence of Molière, dominant until about 1720, is seen in the comedies of Dancourt, Regnard, and LeSage. Florent-Carton Dancourt (1661–1725) made his debut at the Comédie Française in 1685 and eventually became the leader of the troupe. Of his more than 50 comedies, two are of special importance, *The Fashionable Gentleman* (1687) and *The Fashionable Middle-Class Women* (1692). The first introduces a type prominent in later plays, the *chevalier d'industrie* or gigolo, while the second satirizes the attempts of merchants' wives to become ladies of fashion. Dancourt's other plays treat a wide variety of character types and social customs. Jean-Francois Regnard (1655–1709) wrote for the *commedia* troupe from 1688 to 1694, when he turned to the Comédie Française. His finest works are *The Gambler* (1696), a comedy of character, and *The Universal Heir* (1708), a farce. Alain-René LeSage (1668–1747), after adapting plays by Lope de Vega, Rojas Zorilla, and Calderón, launched a remorseless attack upon contemporary tax collectors in *Turcaret* (1709). Often called the first great French comedy of manners, it depicts a world of clever rascals who prey upon each other. The controversy aroused by the play left LeSage estranged from the Comédie Française. As a result, he confined himself thereafter to novels and comic operas, produced by the illegitimate theatres at the Parisian fairs.

The trend toward sentimentalism, which began around 1720, is most evident in the works of Destouches, Marivaux, and LaChaussée. The reputation of Philippe Néricault Destouches (1680–1754) is based primarily upon two plays, *The Married Philosopher* (1727) and *The Con-*

SCENE from Regnard's *The Universal Heir* at the Comédie Française, 1708. [From the original edition of the play]

ceited Count (1732), which resemble Steele's *The Conscious Lovers.* In *The Conceited Count,* a penniless but arrogant nobleman reforms following an emotional appeal by his father, who later comments: "My son is proud, but his heart is excellent; that makes up for all."

Pierre Carlet de Chamberlain de Marivaux (1688–1763) came to prominence in 1720 with *Arlequin Refined by Love.* This play was presented by the Italian troupe, which had returned to France in 1716. The majority of his 35 plays were produced by the Italians, whose acting style was much better suited to Marivaux's subtle presentation of emotions than was that of the French troupe. Most of Marivaux's plays are concerned with awakening love. Unlike earlier comedies, in which lovers are kept apart by some external force, the obstacles in Marivaux's plays arise from the inner feelings of the characters. In *The Game of Love and Chance* (1730), for example, two friends arrange a marriage between their children on the condition that the boy and girl are willing; the young couple, who do not know each other, are skeptical, and each hits upon the scheme of changing places with a servant so as to observe the other; each then falls irresistibly in love with a supposed servant. Here, as in most of Marivaux's plays, interest is focused on subtle changes in feeling rather than upon external intrigues. Consequently, Marivaux is sometimes compared with Racine.

305

Marivaux is also noted for his distinctive prose style, often labeled *mari-vaudage*. With his emphasis on feeling, Marivaux contributed significantly to the development of sentimentalism, but his charm and wit raise him far above his contemporaries. Because of his interest in psychological conflicts, his critical stature has grown steadily since the late 19th century. In France today, his comedies are second in popularity only to those of Molière.

With *False Antipathy* (1733) and *The Fashionable Prejudice* (1735), Pierre Claude Nivelle de LaChaussée (1692–1754) established the *comédie larmoyante*, or tearful comedy, as one of the most popular dramatic types. In LaChaussée's works, a protagonist is faced with a formidable set of obstacles, designed to arouse sympathy and compassion, from which he is rescued by the revelation of previously unknown facts. Thus, they resemble contemporary tragedy in the use of plots based upon concealed informa-tion. Until 1750, *comédie larmoyante* was to be the dominant comic mode in France. Voltaire also contributed to the development of sentimental comedy with such works as *The Prodigal Son* (1736) and *Nanine* (1749), with their mingling of comic and domestic scenes.

In spite of the popularity of sentimental drama, most critics doubted its value because it deviated from the neo-classical doctrine that comedy should ridicule the foibles of middle and lower class characters. It gained its first critical support in the 1750's when Denis Diderot (1713–84) raised his influential voice in its favor. At this time Diderot's *Encyclopédie*, published in 28 volumes between 1748 and 1772, was the rallying point for advanced thinkers of the time (the *encyclopédistes* or *philosophes*). Diderot argued that neoclassicism was too narrow in its restriction of the acceptable dramatic types to comedy and tragedy, and that additional "intermediate" genres—the *drame*, or domestic tragedy, and a comedy concerned with virtue—should be added. He also suggested many innovations in staging, for he believed that drama would move an audience profoundly only if it created a complete illusion of reality. Consequently, he advocated subject matter chosen from everyday life, presented on a stage which duplicated real rooms. He urged the use of prose dialogue, detailed pantomime, and the "fourth wall" convention in acting (that is, behavior which takes no cognizance of the audience). Diderot's ideas, much in advance of their time, were not fully exploited until the late 19th century. To illustrate his theories, Diderot wrote *The Illegitimate Son* (1757) and *The Father of a Family* (1758), neither of which was very successful but which paved the way for the *drame*.

Diderot had a number of followers who sought inspiration in English drama. Bernard-Joseph Suarin (1706–81) adapted Moore's *The Gamester* as *Beverlei* (1768), and Louis-Sebastien Mercier (1740–1814) adapted *The London Merchant* as *Jenneval* (1769), as well as writing such original works as *The Judge* and *The Indigent Man*. The best of the *drames* was *A Philosopher Without Knowing It* (1765) by Michel-Jean Sédaine (1719–

97). Its subject, the story of a young man who survives an unwonted duel to become the friend of his former enemy, is a typical one, but the play rises above other *drames* because of its superior characterization and less obvious didacticism. Since the Comédie Française did not encourage it, the *drame* had little chance to develop, except in the minor theatres, where it was to mingle with pantomime and music and emerge in the 19th century as melodrama.

The late 18th century produced only one major dramatist, Beaumarchais (Pierre-Augustin Caron, 1732–99). Now remembered chiefly for his comedies, Beaumarchais also wrote a number of *drames*, such as *Eugénie* (1767) and *The Two Friends* (1770). His assured fame rests on *The Barber of Seville* (1775) and *The Marriage of Figaro* (1783). The former, a comedy of intrigue in which an elderly guardian's plans to marry his young ward are thwarted, introduces Figaro, the culmination of all the comic servants of French drama. Although *The Marriage of Figaro* uses the same characters as the earlier play, its tone is quite different, for intrigue is now subordinated to commentary upon society and class relationships. It is a far more complex play than *The Barber of Seville*. In these two works, Beaumarchais recaptured the spirit of "laughing" comedy, much as Goldsmith and Sheridan had done in England.

Act V of Beaumarchais' *The Marriage of Figaro* (1785). [From the original edition of the play]

The typical plays, however, continued to be sentimental and often capitalized as well on the growing interest in history and local color. These trends are epitomized in Charles Collé's (1709–83) *The Hunting Party of Henri IV* (1774), in which the disguised King mingles with the common people.

By 1790, then, French drama had taken a few tentative steps away from neoclassicism. Although the typical subject matter and treatment often differed considerably from those of 1700, no startling innovations had been made before the Revolution inaugurated a new era in France.

Parisian Acting Troupes

In 1700 there were only two legitimate troupes in Paris, the Opéra and the Comédie Française, each with monopolistic privileges. These companies were to remain the major ones throughout the century, although they were to encounter considerable competition. The first challenge came from the illegitimate theatres at the fairs, especially those of St. Germain, which ran from February 3 until Easter, and St. Laurent, which ran from the end of June until near the end of October. Together they were open about six months each year. The fairs had featured entertainers, such as acrobats, dancers, and exhibitors of trained animals and freaks, since the 16th century. In the late 17th century, crude dramatic skits and *commedia dell'arte* plays had been introduced, and when the Italian company was expelled from France in 1697, the fair troupes seized the opportunity to enlarge their activities. After 1698, the Opéra and the Comédie Française strove continuously to suppress these troupes, which used various ruses to evade the monopolies. Because of their desire to offer entertainments not prohibited by the monopolies, the fair troupes experimented with dramatic forms; the popularity of these "irregular" dramas did much to undermine the neo-classical ideal.

The first significant minor form to emerge was comic opera. Forbidden to use dialogue, the troupes began to condense the necessary information into couplets, which were printed on placards held by small boys, dressed as cupids and suspended above the stage; the couplets, set to popular tunes, were sung by confederates planted in the auditorium. By 1714, the Opéra was in such financial difficulties that, in return for a sizable fee, it authorized one of the fair troupes to use music, dance, and spectacle. After this time, the entertainments were called *opéras comiques*. Between 1713 and 1730, LeSage exploited this form so successfully that he is often called the founder of French comic opera. In his works, spoken dialogue was mingled with verses set to popular tunes. Featuring *commedia* characters, these short pieces parodied tragedies, operas, and current fashions. The fair companies' bills, which always included sideshow variety acts, contrasted sharply with the staid performances of the Comédie Française and the fashionable repertory of the Opéra.

SCENE from a Fair theatre play, *The Quarrel of the Theatres*. The French troupe is represented by the figure taking away the wing on the right and the Italian troupe by the figure taking away the one on the left. [From a volume of Fair plays published in 1722]

The theatre was further diversified in 1716, when the Duc D'Orleans, Regent for the young Louis XV, invited a *commedia dell'arte* troupe to Paris. Installed in the Hôtel de Bourgogne, the Italians were led by Luigi Riccoboni (c. 1676–1753), who in 1713 had attempted unsuccessfully to establish a national theatre in Verona. Riccoboni had recognized the decline of *commedia* and was attempting to vary his troupe's offerings. Thus, when his company's initial popularity in Paris declined, he performed Maffei's *Merope* and Italian translations of French tragedies and tragicomedies. In 1718 he added a few works in French, and in 1719 began to present parodies in the manner of the fair troupes. By 1721, Riccoboni had added four French actors to his company and had induced such authors as Marivaux to provide him with plays. In 1723, the troupe became a second state theatre with the official title, Comédiens Ordinaires du Roi (usually called the Comédie Italienne). At the same time it was awarded an annual subsidy and placed under a set of governing rules similar to

309

those of the Comédie Française. Its repertory was confined to *commedia dell'arte,* comedies, and parodies.

The fair companies, which had been suppressed since 1718, although they continued to perform surreptitiously, resumed open playing in 1723, after Louis XV attended a performance. This apparent sanction won them many years of unmolested prosperity. From 1723 on, then, Paris had three legitimate troupes and a number of semilegitimate fair companies.

In the 1740's, *opéra comique* began to drop its farcical and satirical subject matter in favor of more sentimental stories. Charles-Simon Favart (1710–92) was especially successful with the new type. His *Acajou* (1744) was so popular that the Opéra suspended the fair troupe's privileges,

Types et personnages de la Comédie Italienne.

ACTORS of the Comédie Italienne in the 18th century. [From Bapst's *Essai sur l'Histoire du Théâtre* (1893)]

bought with a yearly fee, and attempted to take over *opéra-comique.* This led to so violent a controversy that the crown issued an injunction, destined to last from 1745 until 1751, against comic opera. In these years, English pantomime was introduced successfully at the fairs and remained a staple of the minor theatres for the rest of the century.

Two significant innovations were made in *opéra-comique* after its revival in 1751. First, ordinary characters began to replace the *commedia* figures. As a part of this shift, local color also came into the minor theatres

CHARLES SIMON FAVART. [From *Die Theater Weins* (1893)]

long before it was a staple at the major houses. Second, after the great success of Pergolesi's *La Serva Padrona* in 1752, original music replaced the popular tunes. Possibly because of the increased popularity brought by these innovations, *opéra comique* was lost to the fair troupes in 1762. In that year the reorganized Comédie Italienne was awarded a monopoly on comic opera, and Goldoni was imported to write for the troupe. *Opéra comique* and Goldoni's comedies proved so popular that French plays were dropped altogether from the repertory of the Comédie Italienne between 1769 and 1780.

When the fair troupes were deprived of *opéra comique,* they returned to the original form of comic opera in which songs were set to popular tunes. Now called *comédies-en-vaudevilles,* plays of this type were to retain their appeal until well into the 19th century. Pantomime also increased in popularity as it became more melodramatic. In pantomimes showing innocent characters rescued from villains, music was used to underscore emotional scenes and spectacle. By 1780, the introduction of dialogue had created such anachronistic types as *pantomimes dialoguées et parlées.* After the Comédie Italienne dropped its French comedies in 1769, the minor troupes also began to perform *drames* and comedies, perhaps because

311

THE FAIR OF ST. OVID, one of the lesser fairs. Shown on the right is Nicolet's booth. [From Pougin, *Dictionnaire du Théâtre* (1885)]

French playwrights now had no other outlet if their works were refused by the Comédie Française.

After 1760 the fair troupes began to relocate on the Boulevard du Temple, a fashionable recreational spot. Since they still played at the fairs, they were now able to perform throughout the year. Of the troupes which moved to the Boulevard, four were important: those of Audinot and Nicolet, the Théâtre des Associés, and the Variétés Amusantes. Because of these troupes, secondary Parisian groups are still referred to as "boulevard theatres." The minor troupes were dealt a serious blow in 1784, when the Opéra was granted authority over them. Those agreeing to pay a substantial yearly fee were permitted to continue, but those defying the grant were expropriated or suppressed.

After the retirement of Goldoni in 1773, the Comédie Italienne began to decline in popularity. In 1780 it was once more reorganized, and both its Italian plays and performers were dropped, thus severing the troupe's last connections with Italy. French comedies and *drames* were returned to the repertory. The spoken drama did not prosper, however, and in 1790 the repertory was reduced to *opéra comique*. In 1791, the National Assembly abolished all monopolies, thus freeing the theatres from the former restraints. Although other restrictions would soon be imposed, the act of 1791 marks the end of an era.

Throughout the 18th century, the Comédie Française maintained its monopoly on "regular" comedy and tragedy. Consequently, most of the major playwrights wrote for it, since only the lesser or "irregular" forms were permitted at the Comédie Italienne and the fairs. These restrictions often meant that a play refused by one company had to be rewritten to

An entr'acte at Nicolet's theatre on the Boulevard du Crime. [From Pougin's *Dictionnaire du Théâtre* (1885)]

meet the genre restrictions placed on another troupe. The limited demand for new works led to the acceptance of plays years before they were produced. It is probably for this reason that in the late 18th century the Comédie Française was required to produce one new play or revival each month.

Of all the troupes, the Opéra enjoyed the greatest prestige. Probably for this reason, it was allowed to exploit other companies. After 1714 it collected considerable revenue by permitting other theatres to use music, dance, or elaborate spectacle. After 1762, the Comédie Italienne paid the Opéra from 20,000 to 54,000 francs yearly for the right to present musical plays, and after 1784 the boulevard theatres were subsidiaries of the Opéra.

The Comédie Française and the Comédie Italienne were sharing companies. When the Comédie Italienne became a state troupe in 1723 it was placed under the supervision of the Gentlemen of the Chamber, who also oversaw the Comédie Française, under regulations similar to those governing the older company. Ostensibly, all decisions were made at weekly meetings of the actors, who administered their own affairs. After 1759, even the *pensionnaires* were included in deliberations. On the other hand, the Gentlemen of the Chamber had to ratify all decisions, including the choice of plays and actors, changes in financial procedures, and alterations in the theatre buildings. They sometimes ordered the admission of actors as *sociétaires* (even if this forced others to retire), redistributed shares, and interfered in other ways.

The Opéra was organized along entirely different lines. Although the

313

crown provided a subsidy and laid down the rules under which it func-
tioned, the management was farmed out to an entrepreneur. Because of its
large expenses, the Opéra was always in financial difficulties, and by 1749
had accumulated a debt of more than one million francs. In that year, it
was ceded to the City of Paris. Having failed to achieve a sound fiscal
policy, the city also farmed out the management after 1757. By 1780 the
situation was so chaotic that the crown resumed its control and placed a
court official in charge. This arrangement continued until the Revolution.
In spite of its abysmal financial and managerial record, the Opéra was the
favored troupe with aristocratic audiences throughout the century. It
presented the most spectacular productions in Paris, and after 1775 was
considered the finest opera company in Europe. The fair theatres were run
entirely as private ventures. Each was operated by a manager, who assumed
both risks and profits.

The troupes increased in size during the century. In 1713, the Opéra
had 121 performers (singers, dancers, and musicians), but by 1778 it had
grown to 228. By the 1770's, the Comédie Française included about 50
actors and the Comédie Italienne about 70. Although growth brought
increased expenses, it was probably less responsible for the troupes' constant financial difficulties than were their strange fiscal policies. Both the
Comédie Française and the Comédie Italienne received subsidies (ranging
from 12,000 to 15,000 francs), required each new *sociétaire* to invest from
8,000 to 15,000 francs in the company, and collected large sums in annual
rentals for private boxes. Most of this money, however, was divided among
the *sociétaires* rather than going into a common fund, with the result that
the troupes were never able to meet unexpected expenses. Consequently,
the Comédie Française owed 487,000 francs in 1757 and the Comédie
Italienne 400,000 in 1762, even though *sociétaires* were sometimes receiving as much as 30,000 francs a year, as compared to a *pensionnaire's* salary
of less than 2000 francs. Thus, while the troupes in theory were sharing
companies, they appear to have shared income more than expenses. Occasionally the crown made special grants or ordered economies to reduce
indebtedness, but no effort was made to reform fiscal policies.

The dramatic troupes played daily. At first the season extended from
November 2 until Easter, but after 1766 it ran from November 15 until
May 15. In 1700, the curtain time was 5 P.M.; it later changed to 5:15 or
5:30. Each theatre was required to list its bill two weeks in advance.
Normally a different play was offered each day, except when a popular new
piece was produced. At the Opéra, performances were given only three days
a week. Its season was divided into two parts: October to Lent, and Easter
to mid-May. In 1700, performances began at 4, but after 1714 at 5:15. The
Opéra ran each production as long as it drew an audience and sometimes
performed no more than four or five works in a season.

The evening's bill was simpler than in a London theatre. The Comédie Française normally presented a long play and an afterpiece. After 1757, ballets were given as entr'actes. The Comédie Italienne often gave programs made up of several short pieces. Its bills were organized so as to reserve certain days of the week for each of the genres in its repertory. In the 1740's it added a dance troupe; after 1750, pantomimes and displays of fireworks were typical offerings. The Opéra normally presented a major work with incidental ballets. The ballet increased in importance after the 1770's, when Jean-Georges Noverre (1727–1810) became the ballet master. Noverre began his career in 1743 in *opéra-comique* and later worked in several major European cities. In 1760 he published his revolutionary work, *Letters on the Dance and Ballet,* which was largely responsible for transforming the *ballet d'entrées* into works resembling modern ballets. At the fair theatres, variety was the key, for there the carnival atmosphere predominated. Thus, the Parisian theatre included as wide a range of entertainment as did the English, although the restrictions on the companies led to more specialization by each troupe.

In the 18th century, the payment of authors was also regulated by the government. After a dramatic troupe's daily expenses and a poor tax (ranging from $\frac{1}{6}$ to $\frac{5}{18}$) had been deducted from receipts, the author was paid $\frac{1}{9}$ (after 1781, $\frac{1}{7}$) of the revenue for a long play and $\frac{1}{18}$ (after 1760, $\frac{1}{12}$) for a short play. This arrangement continued until the receipts fell below a prescribed amount, after which the dramatist received no further payment. Since the Opera sought long runs, its scheme of payments differed. For long works, the librettist and composer each were paid 100 francs for the first ten performances and 50 francs for the next twenty; for short pieces, 60 francs for the first ten and 30 francs for the next twenty.

Although this scheme guaranteed the playwright an income for his work, the actors found ways of decreasing it. The most significant was the exclusion of income from annual box rentals from the calculations. Beaumarchais' objections to this practice led him in 1777 to found the Bureau Dramatique (the origin of the present Society of Authors) to represent dramatists. Largely because of this organization's efforts, the National Assembly in 1791 passed the world's first copyright law. It secured to authors and their heirs complete control over dramatic works until five years after the author's death. The playwright was now able to collect fees for each performance of his works.

Actors and Acting

The 18th century also brought the first successful attempt to establish an orderly system for training actors. Until the 1780's, most French actors received their training while playing utility roles in a provincial troupe. A

315

few beginners were accepted into the Parisian companies after being coached by leading actors, who were paid 500 francs for each acceptable pupil. These methods were eventually judged insufficient, and in 1786 the Royal Dramatic School, forerunner of the present Conservatoire, was founded as an adjunct to the Comédie Française.

Admission to a Parisian troupe was difficult. An applicant had first to be approved by a committee of actors; he then played at least three roles in public performances; if successful, he was accepted as a *pensionnaire* until a vacancy occurred among the *sociétaires*. By the late 18th century, a *pensionnaire* either had to be admitted as a *sociétaire* or released by the end of his second year with the troupe. This rule led to reassignments of shares or forced retirements in order to keep desirable performers.

A young actor often began as understudy, or *double,* to a major performer. As in England, most casting was governed by "lines of business." The major lines in tragedy were kings, tyrants, lovers, princesses, mothers, and female lovers, while the major lines in comedy were old men, lovers, valets, peasants, old women, coquettes, and soubrettes. In addition, there were a number of secondary lines, while the bottom rank was made up of general utility players. Certain tragic and comic lines were usually filled by the same actors. For example, the *jeune premier* played the lover in both comedy and tragedy, while the actress who played princesses in tragedy assumed the roles of coquettes in comedy. As a rule, an actor remained in the same line of business throughout his career.

The 18th century produced many distinguished performers, most of whom were members of the Comédie Française. Between 1700 and 1720, a period noted for its formal and oratorical style, the major actors were Mlle. Desmares, Mlle. Duclos, and Beaubour. Charlotte Desmares (1682–1753) succeeded Mlle. Champmeslé, her aunt, as leading actress of the Comédie Française in 1698 and retained that position until she retired in 1721. Her principal rival was Mlle. Duclos (Marie-Anne de Chateauneuf, 1668–1748), Mlle. Champmeslé's understudy and pupil. After the vogue in acting style changed around 1720, she lost most of her following; by the time she retired in 1736, she was judged very old-fashioned. Pierre-Trochon de Beaubour (1662–1725) replaced Baron at the Comédie Française in 1691. His good looks and excellent declamation assured him the position of leading actor until he retired in 1717.

Around 1720, the performance style became more realistic, partially because of Michel Baron's return to the stage from 1720 to 1729. It was also established by Adrienne Lecouvreur (1692–1730), who made her debut in 1717 and became the leading actress of the company after the retirement of Mlle. Desmares in 1721. She died suddenly in 1730 and was refused Christian burial, being interred in some unknown spot in the same year that Mrs. Oldfield was buried in Westminster Abbey. The leading actor of this period was Quinault-Dufresne (1693–1767), admitted to the Comédie

ACTORS of the Comédie Française in the 18th century. Note the *habit à la romaine* worn by the actor in the foreground. [From an engraving based upon a painting by Watteau]

Française in 1712 as understudy to Beaubour, whose roles he inherited in 1717 and retained until his retirement in 1741.

In the succeeding period, the leading performers were Mlle. LaGaussin, Grandval, and Mlle. Dangeville. Mlle. LaGaussin (Jeanne-Catherine Gaussens, 1711–67, daughter of Baron's valet), was accepted into the Comédie Française in 1731 and was its leading actress until overshadowed by Mlles. Dumesnil and Clairon. Her ability to express tenderness and grief made her especially effective in "tearful comedy." Charles-Francois de Grandval (1710–84) began in 1729 as understudy to Quinault-Dufresne, whose roles he inherited in 1741. He remained the company's leading actor until 1768. Marie-Anne-Botot Dangeville (1714–96) was admitted to the Comédie Française in 1730 and was its principal comedienne until her retirement in 1763. Garrick thought her the finest actress on the French stage.

Perhaps the most famous players of the 18th century were Mlle. Dumesnil, Mlle. Clairon, and LeKain. Mlle. Dumesnil (Marie-Françoise Marchand, 1713–1803) began her acting career in the provinces around 1733. Accepted as an understudy at the Comédie Française in 1737, she became a *sociétaire* in 1738 and was soon the leading performer of such strong tragic roles as Clytemnestra and Medea. In his *Paradox of Acting*, Diderot depicts her as dependent upon inspiration. She retired in 1776. Mlle. Clairon (Claire-Josèphe-Hippolyte Léris de la Tude, 1723–1803) began her career in 1736 at the Comédie Italienne and, after performing in

317

the provinces and at the Opéra, was admitted to the Comédie Française in 1743 as understudy to Dumesnil. Diderot idealizes her as an artist conscious of every detail in performance. Voltaire and Garrick also considered her superior to Dumesnil. At first declamatory in style, Clairon was persuaded by the critic Marmontel in 1753 to assume a more conversational tone. This change made her question the old traditions of costuming and in 1755 she began to adopt more realistic and historically accurate stage dress. She retired in 1766 at the height of her career. Mlle. Clairon's reforms were supported by Henri-Louis LeKain (1729–78), who was admitted to the Comédie Française in 1751 largely because of Voltaire's influence. He worked hard to overcome his vocal and physical shortcomings, but was not awarded a full share in the company until 1758. His talents were not fully recognized until after Gradval's retirement in 1768. Thereafter, LeKain was considered the greatest tragic actor of his age.

LeKain's principal successors were Larive and Molé. Larive (Jean Mauduit, 1747–1827) was appointed understudy to LeKain in 1775 and succeeded to many of his roles in 1778. In spite of his handsomeness and fine voice, he never achieved LeKain's reputation. He retired in 1788. Francois-Rene Molé (1734–1802), after several years in the provinces, was admitted to the Comédie Française in 1760. Thereafter he was the leading player of young comic heroes and inherited as well several of LeKain's serious roles. He left the troupe in 1791.

The principal tragic actresses of the late 18th century were Mme. Vestris and Mlle. Raucourt. Mme. Vestris (Françoise-Marie-Rosette Gourgaud, 1743–1804), after studying with LeKain, was admitted to the company after the retirement of Clairon and Dumesnil. Mlle. Raucourt (1756–1815) made her debut in 1775 as understudy to Mme. Vestris. Dismissed in 1776 following a scandal, she was readmitted in 1779. She was excellent in stern tragic roles but lacking in tenderness.

The finest comic actor of the late 18th century was Préville (Pierre-Louis Dubus, 1721–99), who played in the provinces before joining the Comédie Française in 1753. Préville revolutionized the playing of low comedy roles, which had previously been treated as fat and alcoholic bunglers. Préville, who was handsome, slender, and graceful, used these qualities in his carefully differentiated characterizations. He retired in 1786.

Although most of the famous actors were associated with the Comédie Française, a few achieved fame at the Comédie Italienne. Luigi Riccoboni, leader of the original troupe, was excellent as the "first lover." Giovanna Benozzi, the second *amoureuse*, was the inspiration for many of Marivaux's heroines. Perhaps the most famous performer of the Comédie Italienne was Marie-Justine Favart (1727–72), wife of Charles-Simon Favart. After playing at the fairs, she joined the Comédie Italienne in 1749 and continued there until 1771. A performer of great versatility, she was also a leader in costume reforms. The restriction to minor forms and the frequent reorganization of the company prevented the development of lasting traditions and outstanding actors at the Comédie Italienne.

With the coming of the Revolution, the French actor at last achieved full civil and religious rights. The National Assembly forbade discrimination against players, and though this act did not make performers socially acceptable universally, it removed the legal grounds which had encouraged prejudice in the past.

Theatre Architecture

The major theatres of Paris remained virtually unchanged until after 1750, when interest in theatre architecture increased. Articles appeared in Diderot's *Encyclopédie*; Dumont's *Parallèle des plus belles salles de spectacle d'Italie et de France* (1763) compared the outmoded French theatres with their newer Italian counterparts. Perhaps as a result, the structures which replaced the old ones followed the Italian trends toward the ovoid auditorium and an enlarged stage.

The first major change in the Parisian theatres came in 1763 when the Palais Royal burned. From 1763 until 1769, the Opéra performed in the Théâtre des Tuileries, converted from the stage (an area 52 by 132 feet) of

CEREMONY at which the bust of Voltaire was crowned in 1778. At this time the Comédie Française was performing in the Théâtre des Tuileries. [From Pougin, *Dictionnaire du Théâtre* (1885)]

319

the Salle des Machines. With its three tiers of boxes, it recreated many of the features of the Palais Royal. The Opéra's new theatre opened in 1769 and burned in 1781. The troupe then moved to the new Porte-Saint-Martin Theatre, where it remained until 1794.

The Comédie Française continued to use its converted tennis court until 1770. Alterations were minor. Several large boxes were divided into smaller ones that could be rented by the year; about 180 seats were installed at the front of the pit when spectators were banished from the stage in 1759, while the amphitheatre was reduced to maintain the space allotted to standing spectators. In 1770, the troupe moved to the Théâtre des Tuileries, recently vacated by the Opéra, until its new theatre, on the site of the present-day Odéon, was opened in 1782. The new building provided seats for all spectators and abolished the standing pit for the first time. The auditorium was ovoid in shape and the stage much better equipped than that of the older theatre.

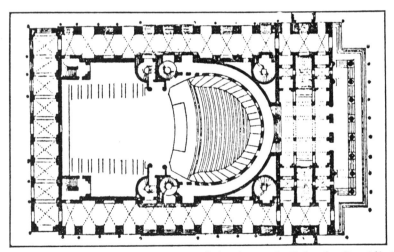

PLAN of the theatre built by the Comédie Française in 1782. It was later to become the home of the Odéon. [From Donnet and Kaufmann, *Architectonographie des theatres* (1836–57)]

The Comédie Italienne played in the Hôtel de Bourgogne from 1716 until 1783, when this theatre, built in 1548, was abandoned. Changes in the Bourgogne during the 18th century paralleled those made at the Comédie Française. A number of large boxes were subdivided in 1760, and in 1765 benches were installed at the front of the pit to accommodate the spectators who were banished from the stage at that time. Perhaps out of a desire to compete with the Comédie Française, the Comédie Italienne moved into a new building in 1783. It, too, incorporated the latest Italian features, but it retained a "standing pit" for 650 spectators. In 1788, the attempt to furnish this area with benches was met with such opposition that it was abandoned.

THE STAGE AND AUDITORIUM of the Hôtel de Bourgogne in
1769. [Courtesy Bibliothèque Nationale, Paris]

INTERIOR of the theatre built by Victor Louis in the 1780s.
Later the home of the Comédie Française, it was being used
by the Variétés Amusantes when this picture was drawn
about 1790. [From *L'Ancienne France* (1887)]

Not until the beginning of the 19th century was the seated pit fully accepted in Paris.

The Boulevard theatres also began to construct elaborate theatres in the late 18th century. The Varietés Amusantes, designed by Victor Louis and opened in 1785, was one of the finest theatres in Paris, and after 1799 was to become the home of the Comédie Française.

By the time of the Revolution, the major theatres of Paris had been modernized. Although seating capacity had been enlarged, the major changes appear to have been motivated by the desire to improve sightlines and to provide better facilities for spectacle.

Scenic Practices

Although as early as the 1730's Voltaire urged more appropriate spectacle, little was done to implement his suggestions until spectators were banished from the stage in 1759. Thus, until about 1760 the *palais à volonté* and the *chambre à quatre portes* continued as the typical settings.

The removal of spectators was probably hastened by the desire to provide more elaborate settings. An important turning point in the attitude toward spectacle can be seen in the production of Voltaire's *The Orphan of China* (1755), which was given new and allegedly accurate Oriental costumes and settings. The Comédie Italienne also began to introduce local color during the 1750's, and both theatres increased their use of spectacle after 1760. Voltaire's *Trancrède* (1760) directed attention to the Middle Ages, and soon other plays were being set in such locales as Norway, Russia, Spain, America, and the Near East, and in many different periods. Diderot's call for greater fidelity to everyday life was met in such plays as Voltaire's *L'Écossaise* (1760), set in the common room of an inn, and Beaumarchais' *Eugènie* (1767), which sought to reproduce a domestic background. In spite of these innovations, however, the majority of plays continued to be presented in stock scenery.

Considerable emphasis was placed on spectacle at the Opéra throughout the century. After the retirement of Jean Bérain in 1721, the most important designer was Jean-Nicolas Servandoni (1695–1766), a Florentine who worked for the Opéra from about 1728 to 1746. His principal contributions to French design were the *scena per angolo* and monumentality in the manner of the Bibienas. Servandoni is also noted for his "mute spectacles," mounted in the Salle des Machines between 1738 and 1742 and again from 1754 to 1758. In these, he recreated faithfully a number of well-known places. The naturalism of these actorless spectacles probably did much to motivate the other theatres of Paris to improve their settings.

A STAGE SETTING by Servandoni. [From Bapst's *Essai sur l'Histoire du Théâtre* (1893)]

BOUCHER'S SETTING for *Armide* at the Opéra in the 1740s.
[From an engraving by Saint-Aubin]

Servandoni's successors at the Opéra changed so rapidly that none was able to establish a dominant style. Among the later designers the most important were Boucher, Boquet, and Algieri. Francois Boucher (1703–70), who worked for a number of theatres after 1740, was noted for his idyllic landscapes. Louis-René Boquet (1717–1814) was famous for his ballet costumes as well as his scenery, in which Chinese decorative motifs

323

were prominent. Pietro Algieri, who designed settings from about 1748 to 1761, turned attention away from the fantasies of Boucher and Boquet to more formal architectural settings. Many of the best-known French painters, such as Gillot, Saint-Aubin, Wailly, and Moreau *le jeune,* also designed settings. Nevertheless, scenic design in France seldom met the standards set by the Italian designers of the period. The frequent changes in management and the constant financial difficulties at the Opéra, the continued adherence to the neo-classical ideal, and the reticence of the actors to authorize large expenditures for scenery at the Comédie Française did much to keep scenic practices in old paths. Although new directions had been suggested before the Revolution, they had not yet been fully exploited.

Costume Practices

Costume practices in France differed little from those of England. Most characters were dressed in contemporary garments and as sumptuously as the performers could afford. Ordinary fashionable garments were used in both comedy and tragedy until 1727, when Adrienne Lecouvreur adopted the much more elaborate court dress for tragedy. Her practice soon became standard for all tragic heroines. The actors also adopted court dress for tragedy except in classical roles, for which the *habit à la romaine* was retained, although it, too, grew more elaborate and conventionalized, as the plumed helmet was replaced by a three-cornered hat and the skirt of the tunic was hooped. The use of traditional costumes for a few roles continued through the 18th century. Molière's ridiculous characters, such as Harpagon, Sganarelle, Scapin, and Gros-Réné, were most subject to this treatment, all being costumed in the style of the mid-17th century.

As in England, costumes came from two sources: the company's wardrobe and the actor's privately-owned garments. Each company owned an extensive wardrobe, but since it was reused constantly, the costumes were often threadbare. As a result, it was used primarily by the lesser performers. By 1730 the major actors were engaging in bitter competitions to outdo each other in the lavishness of their stage dress. When Adrienne Lecouvreur died, her wardrobe was sold for 40,000 francs, and Mlle. Raucourt was given a wardrobe valued at 20,000 francs when she made her debut in 1772.

The ideal of lavishness began to be challenged in the 1750's. The first significant change came in 1753, when Mme. Favart wore an authentic peasant dress as the heroine of *The Loves of Bastien and Bastienne.* In 1761, she supposedly sent to Constantinople for an authentic dress to wear

LeKain and Dumesnil in Voltaire's *Sémiramis*. Note Mlle. Dumesnil's elaborate 18th century court dress and LeKain's formalized costume. [From an English print of 1772]

Mlle. Clairon's costume for *The Orphan of China* (1755). Although it marked a change to more accurate costuming, it fell considerably short of authenticity. [From a contemporary print]

325

MME. FAVART in her Turkish costume for *The Three Sultans* in 1761. [From *Costumes et Annales des Grands Théâtres de Paris* (1786–89)]

in *The Three Sultans*. The new trend came to the Comédie Française also in the 1750's, under the leadership of Mlle. Clairon and LeKain. For his *The Orphan of China* (1755), Voltaire asked the artist Joseph Vernet to design clothing which, though based on Chinese dress, would not provoke laughter. The results were more nearly Turkish than Chinese in appearance. The innovation was favorably received, nevertheless, and thereafter Clairon and LeKain sought to dress each role appropriately. In 1756, LeKain outraged audiences by appearing in *Sémiramis* with bare arms, disarrayed hair, and bloody hands. Voltaire disapproved of so much realism, calling it "too English." Voltaire's *Tancrède* (1760) introduced Medieval costumes, and thereafter other periods and locales were occasionally represented in costumes. Beaumarchais described in detail the dress for each of his characters, even when the plays were contemporary.

None of these reforms had far-reaching effects. Many of the actors refused to accept the changes and others were inconsistent in their use of them. By 1790, the reforms had amounted to little more than the abandonment of hooped petticoats for classical figures and of plumed headdresses for all characters, and the adoption of 16th century garments for all historical periods other than classical or contemporary. Since, with rare exceptions, each actor chose his own costumes, inconsistencies abounded. The state of costuming is well illustrated in Levacher de Charnois' *Costumes et Annales des Grand Théâtres de Paris* (1786–89), in which pictures of actors in their costumes are followed by historically accurate drawings of the same garments.

Nevertheless, the seeds of change had been planted. The conflict between the old outlook, in which art was expected to idealize, and the new, in which art was expected to copy life, had begun. As yet, neo-classicism still reigned, but its foundations had been undermined. With the coming of the Revolution, many of the institutions which had encouraged the retention of the older practices were swept away. Although the way was now made easier for new ideas, their triumph would not be complete for many years.

THE THEATRE
IN NORTHERN
AND EASTERN
EUROPE DURING
THE 18TH CENTURY

Although by 1700 the professional theatre was firmly established in England, France, Italy, and Spain, it had scarcely begun in Northern and Eastern Europe. The 18th century witnessed an upsurge in dramatic activity, however, and by 1800 the theatre was established almost everywhere. Although it remained weak in many of the new territories, in Germany the theatre had become one of the most vigorous in the world.

The School Drama in Northern Europe

The slowness of Northern Europe to develop a professional theatre can probably be attributed to the unsettled religious and political conditions during the 16th and 17th centuries. Before this time, its theatre had developed along much the same lines as in France and England. During the Middle Ages some of the most elaborate productions in all of Europe were staged in Germany, and, as elsewhere, these civic theatrical activities were followed by a school drama.

The school drama, usually called the "Christian Terence" because it mingled Christian teaching with Latin comic devices, received its first strong impetus in Germany when the plays of the 10th century nun, Hrosvitha, were published in 1501. Modeled on Terence's comedies, Hrosvitha's six plays, previously unknown, had led by 1530 to the regular production of Latin plays in schools and universities.

The story of the prodigal son was a favorite with the early school dramatists. Noteworthy examples include Gnapheus' *Acolastus* (1529) and Macropedius' *Petiscus* (1536), *Asotus* (1537), and *Rebeles* (1539). Of the late 16th century plays, those by Cornelius Schonaeus were the most influential, especially after 1592, when they were published under the general title, *Christian Terence, or Sacred Comedies*. Most of the plays in the "Christian Terence" tradition were composed by schoolmasters in Protestant territories. Essentially tragicomedies, they were at first written in Latin but were eventually translated into German, Dutch, and other vernacular languages.

In the Catholic areas of southern Germany, Austria, and Eastern Europe, the school drama developed under the influence of the Jesuits. The Society of Jesus, founded in 1534 and given Papal sanction in 1540, gained strength rapidly, and by the early 17th century had opened nearly 300 schools in Europe, many of them in southern Germany and Eastern Europe. Their productions of didactic plays began about 1550 and continued until 1772. The plays were usually presented in Latin, although by the end of the 17th century they were occasionally given in the vernacular. Intended only for invited audiences, productions were restricted to one or two a year. In many Teutonic areas, the Jesuit plays maintained a higher standard of playwriting and production than did the professional troupes.

That the school drama did not stimulate a strong secular drama, as in other countries, can probably be explained by the total disruption of normal activities between 1618 and 1648 by the Thirty Years War. Beginning as a struggle between Protestants and Catholics, the war was trans-

SCENE from a Jesuit drama, *Pietas Victrix*, of the 17th century. [From *Die Theater Wiens* (1899)]

formed into a battle against Austria's territorial ambitions. At the end of the conflict, the population and resources of Germany were seriously depleted, and the territory divided into some 360 separate political units. Consequently, it was to be many years before there would be centers capable of supporting a vigorous public theatre.

The Early Secular Theatre in Germany

Although Hans Sachs (1494–1576) had laid the foundations for a German secular theatre, he had no significant successors. Rather, the professional theatre in Germany owes its origin to English troupes, which began to tour on the Continent around 1586. Among the early companies, the most important were those of Robert Browne, between 1590 and 1605, John Spencer, from 1605 to 1623, and John Green, from 1606 to 1628. Of the later groups, the best was that headed by George Jolly between 1648 and 1660.

In the beginning, most of the English troupes were attached to courts, although all traveled at least part of each year. As opera gained in prestige after 1650, the dramatic companies became increasingly dependent upon the uneducated public. To attract a German-speaking audience, the English actors had to adapt their plays, originally drawn from the London public theatres. Plots were simplified and comedy, pantomime, and music

330

were increased. The clown, usually called Stockfisch, John Posset, or Pickelherring, became the most important figure in every play. The English actors gradually inserted German phrases, speeches, or scenes, and by 1626 had begun to add German actors to the troupes. By 1650 a few companies were composed entirely of Germans, and by 1680 English actors had virtually disappeared.

The first important German troupe was that managed by Carl Andreas Paulsen from 1650 to 1687 and thereafter by Johannes Velten (1640–95). Unlike most actors of the period, Velten was well-educated. Having read the plays of such men as Corneille and Molière, he sought to raise the level of the German theatre by adapting these works for his troupe. Not even Velten, however, could accomplish much under the existing theatrical conditions. Since there were no cities of any size, troupes were forced to travel constantly in search of new audiences. They competed vigorously for the right to perform at fairs held annually in the major towns, since it was here that the largest crowds assembled. Wherever they played, they were required to contribute up to one-fourth of their receipts to local charities. Since there were no permanent theatres, the actors set up their stages in riding schools, inns, fencing grounds, rooms above markets, and tennis courts. They had to change their bills daily and replenish their repertories often in order to attract the small potential audience. Velten's troupe usually had about 87 plays in its repertory.

A program was made up of a long play and an afterpiece, both of which might include such incidental entertainment as songs, dances, and acrobatic feats. The main offering, called the *Hauptaktion* (chief play) or

An 18TH CENTURY itinerant troupe. [From *Die Theater Wiens* (1899)]

331

Haupt-und-Staatsaktion (chief and state play), might be either serious or comic. The afterpiece, or *Nachspiel,* was usually a farce. It is not known who wrote these plays. Most of the long works were hodgepodges of serious and comic scenes, of bombast and violence, villainous machinations and fortunate escapes. No matter how serious the play, the clown was usually the central figure.

By 1700, all of the earlier clowns had coalesced in the character Hanswurst. Given his distinctive traits by Joseph Anton Stranitzky (1676–1726), Hanswurst was compounded of many elements: Harlequin, familiar to German audiences because of the tours of *commedia dell'arte* troupes; the Medieval fool; and the various clowns introduced by English actors. Stranitzky's Hanswurst was a jolly, beer-drinking peasant with a Bavarian accent. His costume consisted of a Tyrolean hat, red jacket, long trousers, white neck ruff, and a pointed beard. Although Hanswurst's attributes and dress varied somewhat in different parts of Germany, the outlines established by Stranitzky were usually retained.

Originally a member of Velten's troupe, Stranitzky settled in 1708 in Vienna, where he virtually created the public theatre. Until his death he was the mainstay of the Karntnertor, Vienna's first permanent public theatre, built by the town council in 1710. Here Stranitzky established such

STRANITZKY AS HANSWURST. [From *Die Theater Wiens* (1899)]

Biel Orth hab ich durchreist Zu Wien will ich verbleiben
Ich bitt mein Herr laßt mich in eüre Bande schreib

a vigorous tradition of improvisation that regular drama made little headway until after 1750.

In the early 18th century, then, several factors contributed to the theatre's low state: a repertory designed to attract an unsophisticated audience; the uneducated actors, who were little better than sideshow performers; and conditions which made it impossible to rehearse and mount plays with care. Under the circumstances, it is not surprising that the aristocracy held the professional theatre in contempt. Not until after 1725 were effective measures taken to change this image.

The Court Theatres of Germany

Between 1650 and 1775, the ruling classes of Germany sought their theatrical entertainment outside the public theatres. As the vogue for opera spread, the dramatic troupes which had been retained by the courts in the early 17th century were abandoned. Although the first operatic performance in Germanic territories was given in 1618 at Salzburg, few others followed until after the war ended in 1648. The decisive peace-making role of France established its influence throughout Germany, where practically every ruler sought to create a miniature French court. Opera, ballet, and spectacle became a regular part of court life. Affluent rulers imported Italian or French designers, musicians, and singers, while the less prosperous relied upon native Germans to copy the foreign models.

INTERIOR of the theatre built by Burnacini at the Imperial Court at Vienna in 1665. [From a contemporary engraving]

The pattern was set at Vienna in 1652, when Burnacini was imported from Venice to stage court entertainments. An elaborate court theatre was built in 1665, and the most famous composers and librettists of the age were brought from Italy. As a result, Vienna was to be the most important center of operatic production from about 1660 until 1740. Other German rulers soon followed the Austrian example. At Munich, an opera house was built in 1654, and in the 1660's Francesco Santurini was brought from Venice to design scenery for it. Opera theatres were erected in Dresden sometime between 1664 and 1667 and in Gotha about 1683. By the end of the 17th century, opera and Italianate scenery were to be seen at practically every court in Germany. Although rulers occasionally witnessed dramatic performances, they confined their financial support almost entirely to opera or to foreign troupes.

Considering its prestige, it is not surprising that opera also became the favored form with the prosperous middle class. Before the end of the 17th century, some of the more populous commercial centers had been able to establish public opera houses. Hamburg had a company from 1678 to 1738 and Leipzig from 1693 to 1720, although both performed only sporadically. Thus, with both the aristocracy and the bourgeoisie, opera was the favored form and drama only gradually won their support.

The Reforms of Gottsched and Neuber

The first steps toward a more significant drama were taken by Johann Christoph Gottsched (1700–66). Educated at the University of Königsberg, Gottsched was to become the intellectual leader of Germany. Among his many interests, the development of German as a medium for literary expression ranked high. Latin was still the language of the universities (the first lecture in the vernacular had not been given until 1687), while French was spoken by the aristocracy. Consequently, there were few German plays other than the crude works offered by the professional actors. Gottsched was not the first well-educated German dramatist, however, for in the 17th century Andreas Gryphius (1616–64), influenced by Corneille, created skillfully constructed plays, such as *Papinianus* (1659), and Daniel Caspar von Lohenstein (1635–83) had written a series of bloodthirsty melodramas. Neither of these men, however, had an outlet for his work and consequently exerted no lasting influence.

The theatre attracted Gottsched because he saw in it a means of reaching the illiterate masses. Therefore, he sought a liaison with a professional company. His opportunity came in 1727, when he met Carolina Neuber (1697–1760). The daughter of a lawyer and government official,

Frau Neuber had run away from home in 1717 with Johann Neuber, whom she married in 1718 after joining an acting troupe. They later entered the Haack-Hofmann company, the direct descendent of Velten's company, and succeeded to its management in 1727. At the same time they also acquired the title, "Royal Polish and Electoral Saxon Court Comedians," which brought with it the right to play during the annual fair at Leipzig, then the intellectual capital of Germany and Gottsched's home.

In 1727, the Neubers and Gottsched agreed to work together toward the reform of the theatre. This liaison, which was to last until 1739, is significant as the first alliance between a leading literary figure and a professional acting company. Unfortunately, it was easier to formulate high ideals than to achieve them. First, a completely new repertory had to be obtained, for Gottsched wished to eliminate *Haupt-und-Staatsaktion* plays, improvisation, burlesque afterpieces, and Hanswurst. Gottsched and his circle set out to supply the new works, principally by translating or imitating French neo-classical plays, which to them represented the ideal form of drama. The most famous of the new works was Gottsched's *The Dying Cato* (1731), reprinted ten times before 1756; plays by Destouches, LaChaussée, Voltaire, and others also came to be performed regularly.

As her contribution, Frau Neuber sought to raise the level of theatrical performances. She insisted upon careful rehearsals and the abandonment of improvisation; she assigned each actor additional duties, such as painting scenery, making handbills, or sewing costumes; she policed the performers' personal lives in an attempt to overcome moral prejudices against actors. She was doomed to disappointment, however, for it was impossible to attract a new kind of spectator rapidly enough to replace those alienated by the new drama. In order to survive, she was forced to compromise, much to the impatience of Gottsched. In 1735, more than half of her afterpieces still included Hanswurst and, although in 1737 she banished him from the stage in a short play of her own composition, by 1738 he had crept back into many of her productions under another name. Furthermore, the company still had to tour, for Gottsched's followers were too few to support a year-round theatre in Leipzig, and elsewhere enthusiasm for the reforms was lacking. Her problems are illustrated by an eight-month season in Hamburg, second only to Leipzig as a cultural center. Here in 1735, her 203 performances included 75 full-length and 93 one-act plays. Considering the problems of maintaining such a large repertory, it is not surprising that her performances did not always achieve the polish which she so optimistically promised.

Although Frau Neuber attracted some powerful supporters, notably the ruler of Schleswig-Holstein, she did not succeed as she had hoped, and after 1735 began to rebuke audiences publicly for their lack of taste. She alienated many of her supporters in Hamburg and Leipzig, and in 1739 broke with Gottsched. Thereafter, her career declined. In 1740 she went to

St. Petersburg, but the death of the Empress Anna six months after her arrival led to the closure of her theatre. Returning to Leipzig in 1741, she found Schönemann, one of her former actors, established in her theatre. There followed a pitched battle, in the course of which Neuber satirized Gottsched and his ideas. Although her attack signalled the end of Gottsched's leadership, it did not aid her. She remained in Leipzig for a few years, then moved on to Vienna and elsewhere until her death in 1760.

Although Gottsched and Neuber were not always successful, neither were they failures. By the 1740's regular drama was being performed by all troupes, and Neuber's production techniques were being adopted by others. Thus, although Gottsched and Neuber were often ridiculed by later dramatists and actors, they made the future gains possible.

Acting Troupes, 1740–70

Between 1740 and 1770, Neuber's principles were perpetuated and extended by a number of troupes. The earliest of these was formed in 1740 by Johann Friedrich Schönemann (1704–82), who had entered the Neuber troupe in 1730. Originally a clown, he played comic valets in Neuber's company. When he formed his own group, he borrowed both her methods and her repertory. His actors were young and many were well-educated; their vitality and refinement won much support in Leipzig. Three of the performers—Sophie Schröder, Konrad Ackermann, and Konrad Ekhof—were to become famous. Sophie Schröder (1714–92), a well-educated woman in need of employment after leaving her husband, was persuaded by Ekhof to take up acting. Although she had no theatrical experience, she immediately became the leading actress of the Schönemann company. Her career is inextricably tied to that of Konrad Ackermann (1710–71), who did not begin acting until he was almost 30. His family background and fine education probably contributed to that stately presence for which he was noted. If Frau Schröder and Ackermann prospered immediately, the same cannot be said for Konrad Ekhof (1720–78). Short and homely, he had to work hard to win acceptance. Frau Schröder and Ackermann left Schönemann after one season, but Ekhof remained with him for 17 years. By 1752, he was the company's leading man. He had also become the first important theorist of the German stage, and now sought to establish a school to train actors. Although he was able to institute his plan, classes were soon abandoned because of the indifference and mockery of fellow actors.

After Schönemann's troupe was given the title "Court Comedians to the Duke of Schwerin" in 1751, it divided its time between Schwerin and

Hamburg. This comparative stability, however, encouraged Schönemann to pursue his mania for horsetrading, with the result that the company declined. In 1757, after Ekhof had resigned in protest, the company collapsed and Schönemann retired. Ekhof was induced to return, but having little interest in management, he requested Heinrich Koch to take charge. New friction caused Ekhof to join Ackermann's troupe in 1764.

Heinrich Koch (1703–75) entered Neuber's company in 1728 and remained with her until she left Leipzig in 1749. Obtaining her former license, he toured in that area until he joined the Schönemann troupe in 1758. Between 1758 and 1763, Koch succeeded in playing most of each year in one city, Hamburg, a feat not yet accomplished by any troupe. In 1766, following the Seven Years War, he returned to Leipzig, where he built that city's first permanent theatre. In spite of the city's importance as the cultural center of Germany, all previous theatres were temporary. Koch played at the court theatre in Weimar from 1768 to 1771 and in Berlin from 1771 until his death in 1775. He was probably the first German manager to achieve Neuber's ideals. Paying careful attention both to staging and to public taste, he was eventually able to abandon touring and establish a company in one location.

The third major company was that of Konrad Ackermann. With Sophie Schröder, whom he married in 1749, he worked in a number of companies, touring as far afield as Russia, before establishing a more stable organization in 1753. In 1755, he built a permanent theatre in Königsberg, the first in Germany intended for use by a dramatic company. Unfortunately, in 1756 the Seven Years War (1756–63) forced Ackermann to flee to the West, where he played in Switzerland, Alsace, and elsewhere before coming to Hamburg in 1764. In this year, Ekhof joined the company. With the Ackermanns, Ekhof, Sophie Hensel (1738–89), and young Friedrich Schröder, the troupe was probably the finest in Germany. In 1765 Ackermann built Hamburg's first permanent theatre. Rivalries in the company led to friction. It was probably for this reason that Ackermann agreed to give up his company and rent his theatre to the Hamburg National Theatre.

The Hamburg National Theatre grew out of ideas set forth by Johann Friedrich Löwen, Schönemann's son-in-law, in a pamphlet on the state of the German theatre. He blamed its low repute on uncultivated managers and actors, the profit motive, the lack of stage support, the necessity of touring, and the shortage of German dramatists. To remedy the situation, he proposed the establishment of a permanent, subsidized, nonprofit theatre, run by a salaried manager; he advocated an academy for training actors, high salaries and a pension system to attract the best performers, and prizes to encourage dramatists. Löwen persuaded twelve businessmen to back his venture, of which he was to be the artistic director and Abel Seyler (1730–1801), a businessman and friend of Sophie Hensel, the business manager. The actors, with a few exceptions, were drawn from Ackermann's company. Lessing, by this time considered Germany's finest playwright, was induced to become resident critic and advisor to the company and to edit a theatrical journal designed to create interest in the repertory and educate the public.

The Hamburg National Theatre was opened with high hopes in April 1767. Löwen soon lost authority over the actors, however, and only Ekhof could maintain some discipline. Furthermore, in spite of the stated goal of presenting a higher standard of drama, the theatre was forced to add variety acts to keep up attendance. The venture came to an inglorious end in 1769.

The only lasting achievement of the Hamburg National Theatre was Lessing's *Hamburg Dramaturgy*, one of the major contributions to German criticism. Although it accomplished little, the Hamburg National Theatre remains a landmark as the first German attempt to establish a theatre on noncommercial lines. While it was not truly a "national" theatre, it popularized the notion that Germany needed such theatres and paved the way for those which were soon to appear.

German Drama, 1740–87

By the 1740's, Gottsched and his circle had laid the foundations for a new repertory but had provided no plays of lasting value. As their influence declined after 1740, a new group of dramatists arose. Of these, Schlegel, Gellert, and Lessing were most important. Johann Elias Schlegel (1719–49) wrote a number of tragedies and comedies, but the best of his works was *Hermann* (1741), a tragedy based on German history. C. F. Gellert (1715–69), in such plays as *Betschwester* (1745) and *Das Loos in der Lotterie* (1747), developed the sentimental strain of comedy and domestic tragedy.

Both of these writers are overshadowed, however, by Gotthold Ephraim Lessing (1729–81), Germany's first significant playwright. He began his career with *The Young Scholar* (1748), performed by Carolina Neuber, but his reputation was not fully established until 1755 when *Miss Sara Sampson* swept Germany and won a complete triumph for domestic drama. In addition to Gellert's works, such English plays as Lillo's *The London Merchant* and Moore's *The Gamester* had paved the way for Lessing's domestic tragedy. Set in 18th century England, *Miss Sara Sampson* reshapes and softens the Medea legend by placing the major emphasis upon the young girl who becomes the victim of Medea's wrath. Tears flow abundantly from the softhearted characters. First performed by Ackermann's troupe, *Miss Sara Sampson* was soon the most popular play in Germany and the most widely imitated. Lessing gave further impetus to domestic drama by translating Diderot's works into German. This "middle-class" drama won the theatre a wide following among the bourgeoisie for the first time. Lessing had turned only gradually to English drama as a suitable model for German writers. Thus, it was not until about 1760 that he broke completely with Gottsched's emphasis upon French drama. Thereafter, he sought both in his plays and criticism, especially the *Hamburg Dramaturgy,* to replace the narrow neoclassicism of French drama with the more liberal practices of English writers.

SCENE from Act V of Lessing's *Minna von Barnhelm.* [Engraving from an 18th century edition of the play]

Lessing's second influential play, *Minna von Barnhelm* (1767), is often called Germany's first national comedy. Treating events immediately following the Seven Years War, the play presents lovers drawn from opposing sides who symbolize current problems and divisions within Germany. The union of the lovers at the end of the play, therefore, has a significance beyond the literal meaning. In spite of its topical subject, it is one of the most durable of 18th century comedies. Although the play is sentimental, the resourcefulness and humor of Minna lend it freshness. Like *Miss Sara Sampson, Minna von Barnhelm* was phenomenally popular and gave rise to numerous imitations.

Lessing's third influential drama, *Emilia Galotti* (1772), adapts the classical story of Appius and Virginia to an 18th century background. By avoiding the sentimentality of *Miss Sara Sampson,* it approaches more nearly the spirit of tragedy. Lessing's depiction of the despotic ruler of a small state led many to interpret his work as a criticism of contemporary political and social conditions.

Lessing's last important work, *Nathan the Wise* (1779), a dramatic poem not intended for the stage, is considered by many the greatest philosophical drama of the 18th century. In it, he depicts characters representing Judaism, Islam, and Christianity to demonstrate that universal love is the only fruitful doctrine. Probably because it was not written for performance, its structure is much freer than that of Lessing's other plays. It is also the first major German work in blank verse, previous plays having used either the Alexandrine or prose. After Goethe adopted Lessing's innovation, blank verse became the standard for tragedy. *Nathan the Wise* was soon performed and has continued to be one of the most frequently produced German works.

Thus, Lessing, through his plays and criticism, established a new standard by leading drama away from Gottsched's narrow path and by demonstrating that a native playwright could attract a wide following. It would be a mistake, however, to assume that the repertory had been transformed by the time Lessing died in 1781. The majority of plays continued to be adaptations or close imitations of foreign works. Nevertheless, the hold of French drama had been broken, and the English drama had replaced it as a model.

In spite of Lessing's reforms, he had remained within the mainstream of 18th century rationalism, which viewed the universe as ruled by a benevolent god, man as essentially good, and the human mind as capable of solving all important problems. His own plays, while freer in structure than the French dramas of the period, represent a "revised classicism" rather than any markedly new approach. His criticism, however, had served to undermine the hold of neoclassicism. Before he died, a new and more radical group of dramatists had appeared. Between 1770 and 1800, Germany was to see many experiments with dramatic form.

The revolt against the past was centered in the "Storm and Stress," or *Sturm und Drang,* school of writers. Traditionally dated from 1767 to 1787, the Storm and Stress movement reached its peak in the 1770's. Major writers and works include Goethe's *Goetz von Berlichingen* (1733), Jacob M. R. Lenz's (1751–92) *The Tutor* (1774) and *The Soldiers* (1776), Heinrich Leopold Wagner's (1747–79) *The Child Murderess* (1776), Johann Anton Leisewitz's (1752–1806) *Julius von Tarent* (1776), Friedrich Maximilian Klinger's (1752–1831) *Storm and Stress* (1776), and Friedrich Schiller's *The Robbers* (1782), *Fiesko* (1782), and *Intrigue and Love* (1783).

Scene from Klinger's *Die Zwillinge*. [From the original edition of the play]

The Storm and Stress plays have often been described as completely formless rebellions against neoclassicism, primarily because *Goetz von Berlichingen,* with its 54 scenes and tangle of plots, and *Storm and Stress,* with its rhapsodic emotionalism, have been taken as typical of the school. In actuality, most of the plays are written in five acts; as many observe the unities of time and place as violate them. Storm and Stress was a frankly experimental movement of young men in revolt against 18th century rationalism. Since they agreed upon no alternative philosophy, the plays show wide variations both in thought and expression. *The Robbers* displays a liberal, Rousseauistic outlook, while *The Soldiers* upholds the need for class distinctions; *Julius von Tarent* is written in a strict neo-classical form, while *Goetz von Berlichingen* uses a loose, episodic structure; the naturalistic subject matter of *The Child Murderess* contrasts sharply with the lyrical emotionalism of *Storm and Stress;* and the diction ranges from the formal verse of *Julius von Tarent,* through the staccato, expressionistic utterances of *Storm and Stress,* and the conversational prose of *The Tutor.* The very diversity of the plays was bewildering, for the young authors seemed to be

341

challenging all artistic and social values. The subject matter was often shocking. *The Soldiers* proposes a state-sponsored system of prostitution, while in *The Child Murderess* a rape occurs just offstage and a child is killed on stage. The plays made many new demands on staging. *Goetz* moves from one place to another as rapidly as a film scenario, and other plays require detailed settings which are clearly described in stage directions.

The few Storm and Stress plays which were produced achieved little success. The major exceptions were *Goetz von Berlichingen,* which began a vogue for plays based on German history, and Schiller's works. Nevertheless, they were widely read and discussed and helped to break down old barriers and pave the way for more popular writers in the new style. They probably aided also in gaining acceptance for Shakespeare's plays, then being introduced on the German stage, for they seemed to many critics similar in structure and outlook. Out of these beginnings, a more mature drama was to come between 1785 and 1805.

The Establishment of National Theatres, 1770–1800

While the drama was breaking new ground in the 1770's, the theatre was consolidating its former gains. A number of journals appeared which kept the scattered troupes in touch with each other and helped to create common ideals of theatrical production. The number of troupes also increased. From the six in Neuber's time, they had grown to about 14 in 1776. Most important, state-supported theatres were founded.

The first state theatre was established at Gotha in 1775 from the remnants of the Hamburg National Theatre troupe. When the Hamburg theatre closed in 1769, Abel Seyler had formed a new company, including Sophie Hensel and Ekhof, which, after touring for a time, had settled in Weimar between 1772 until 1774. When the Weimar theatre burned, Seyler moved to Gotha. There in 1775 a scheme for the formation of a state theatre was proposed and carried out. Although Seyler left, Ekhof and the better actors remained.

The Gotha Court Theatre was a nonprofit organization, in which each member was a state employee with pension rights. Ekhof, who was responsible for staging the plays, was at this time the most respected actor in Germany. He brought to Gotha a number of talented young men who received fine training and later became the leading actors of Germany after Ekhof's death. Ekhof was very conservative in his tastes, however, and did nothing to forward the new drama. In 1779, upon Ekhof's death, the theatre was closed.

Before the Gotha venture ended, a far more important state theatre had begun in Vienna. Although it had always been the most powerful Germanic city, Vienna had lagged behind others in the development of a public theatre. While the court had spent lavishly on opera, it had almost completely ignored German drama, considered so inferior that the Empress Maria Theresa (1717–80) never saw a German play until 1771. Court entertainments were usually provided by French actors, who performed in the Burgtheater, a converted tennis court.

The general public had been served by the Karntnertor theatre since 1710, but because of the traditions established by Stranitzky and his successors, such as Joseph von Kurz (1715–84), improvised drama had been the usual fare until about 1750. Written drama began to gain a foothold after Koch appeared in Vienna in 1748, but it was not until the 1760's, when Professor Joseph von Sonnenfels waged a compaign in its favor, that regular drama was widely accepted. Thus, a new era in the Austrian theatre was inaugurated in 1776, when the Emperor Joseph II founded the Teutsches Nationaltheater (more commonly called the Burgtheater after the theatre in which it performed). Its organization and procedures were modeled after the Comédie Française. Although the Burgtheater encountered many difficulties in its early years, it gradually moved to the forefront of the German theatres because generous state support permitted it to assemble a fine company. By 1825, it was considered the finest of all German troupes.

A third state theatre was founded at Mannheim in 1779, when the ruler, Karl Theodor, succeeded to the Electorate of Bavaria and moved his court to Munich. As a gift to his subjects in Mannheim, he created the Hof-und-Nationaltheater. Under the supervision of Baron H. von Dalberg, the company was an amalgamation of Seyler's troupe and the recently disbanded Gotha company. At first, Seyler had primary responsibility for production, but after 1781 Dalberg took charge and made the theater one of the finest in Germany, especially between 1784 and 1795.

After 1780 state theatres were established throughout Germany. Among the most important were those at Cologne, Mainz, Salzburg, Weimar, and Passau. Destined to become the most important was that formed at Berlin in 1786. As in other states, the drama was given little encouragement in Prussia during the early 18th century. Frederick the Great (reigned 1740–86), who was devoted to French culture, had engaged a French troupe for his private theatre and had supported lavish opera productions. Although both Schönemann and Koch played in Berlin, they received no recognition from the court. Thus, a new era was marked when Frederick William II established the Court Theatre in 1786. The new troupe used the theatre formerly occupied by the French company and received an annual subsidy.

Thus, in the years between 1775 and 1800 far-reaching changes occurred in the German theatre. In contrast with the period between 1725 and 1740, when troupes were virtually ignored by the aristocracy, rulers now vied with each other in establishing theatres, much as they had formerly competed in operatic staging. The theatre was now viewed as a cultural institution to be made available to all the people, and as an instrument of German unity. The continued division of Germany into many states, however, perpetuated a decentralized theatre.

The establishment of state theatres was paralleled in the same period by the building of permanent theatres in towns other than the seats of national governments. Before 1800 there were permanent theatres in Linz, Innsbruck, Brunn, Frankfort-on-Main, Augsburg, Nürnberg, Altona, Breslau, Riga, and elsewhere. By the 1790's there were more than 70 Germanic companies, over half of them permanently located. Touring was now restricted to minor troupes.

F. L. Schröder

The most influential troupe in the years between 1770 and 1800 was that of Friedrich Ludwig Schröder (1744–1816). The son of Sophie Schröder, he was on the stage from the time he was three years old. Separated from the Ackermanns at the time of the Seven Years War, he learned to fend for himself by joining with itinerant performers, who taught him acrobatics and dancing. Later, he rejoined his parents and came into contact with Ekhof, who first made him realize what great acting might be. When the Hamburg National Theatre was formed in 1767, Schröder left the company and performed for a time with Kurz, from whom he learned improvisational playing. Schröder returned to Ackermann's Hamburg troupe in 1769 and became artistic director of the company when his step-father died in 1771.

The challenge of management seems to have transformed Schröder. Previously a careless performer who could scarcely be induced to rehearse, he now became a firm disciplinarian who insisted upon perfection in every detail. Consequently, his was the first company in Germany to become a truly integrated ensemble. Furthermore, he produced a distinguished repertory. Not only did he perform Lessing's works, but was the first manager to champion Shakespeare and the Storm and Stress writers. In 1774 he gave the premiere of *Goetz von Berlichingen,* a play which most managers considered unproducible. Beginning in 1776 with *Hamlet,* Schröder had performed eleven of Shakespeare's plays by 1780, although in severely adapted versions.

SCHRÖDER in the role of Falstaff. [From *Literatur und
Theaterzeitung* (1780)]

In addition to his managerial duties, Schröder performed about 39 new roles each year, and between 1771 and 1780 translated, adapted or wrote 28 plays. Although he remained a versatile actor, he gradually moved away from light comedy to tragic roles. He won an enthusiastic following, and the "Hamburg style" became the standard for all Germany. By 1780, he was universally recognized as Germany's greatest actor.

Despite his success, Schröder remained merely the employee of his mother, who retained complete financial control over the company. In 1780 she still paid him the same salary as in 1771. For this and other reasons, Schröder resigned his post in 1780 and for the next six years played at leading theatres throughout Germany.

Meantime, the Hamburg company had disintegrated. In 1786 Schröder returned and assumed complete control of the company. For the next 12 years, he made it the most respected troupe in Germany. In spite of universal acclaim, his greatest contribution had been made before 1780, for now Schröder seemed content merely to repeat his earlier successes. He retired in 1798, while at the height of his career.

Schröder is still considered by many the greatest actor Germany has ever known. In his lifetime he played more than 700 parts. He was instrumental in establishing the "natural" school of acting which was to dominate for many years.

Evolution of Staging in the 18th Century

The trend toward greater security is reflected in every aspect of the theatre. As audiences increased in size, the companies could reduce the number of plays in the repertory. This change, in turn, permitted more careful preparation. Nevertheless, not until the last part of the century was ensemble playing achieved, largely because of Schröder's influence. He began the practice of reading each play to the assembled cast and guiding them in their characterization. He demanded strict order and punctuality at all rehearsals and performances. The superior quality of his productions led other companies to adopt his procedures.

The acting style moved increasingly toward realism. In Neuber's time, good acting was considered to be quite unlike everyday behavior. Ekhof and Schröder, however, turned to life as the standard, and Schröder especially sought to make his characters convincingly natural on the human level. As a result, even the great tragic figures came to be portrayed as ordinary creatures.

So long as there were no permanent theatres, spectacle was not extensively developed. Furthermore, the necessity of touring forced companies to rely upon a few settings which might be adapted for almost any play. Before 1725, three sets were considered sufficient: a wood for all exterior scenes; a hall for palaces; and a cottage room for domestic interiors. After 1750, the typical stock settings were somewhat more numerous: a Prachtsaal (or *palais à volonté*), a street, a village, several middle-class rooms, a prison, and several hills and shrubs. Changes of place were difficult to handle before permanent theatres were built. Consequently, up to the 1770's many companies hung a curtain about half way back on the stage so that shallow and full stage scenes could be alternated while changes were made behind the curtain.

The 1770's brought significant innovations in spectacle. Permanent theatres introduced the chariot-and-pole system of scene shifting just when changing standards created a demand for more appropriate, varied, and detailed settings. The success of *Minna von Barnhelm* (1767) and the subsequent vogue for plays with war backgrounds brought the first attempts to create authentic settings and costumes. Managers often sought the cooperation of the local army garrison; Schröder is said to have borrowed 80 soldiers for one of his productions in 1771.

Concern for historical accuracy was stimulated by *Goetz von Berlichingen* and the series of chivalric plays (or *Ritterstücke*) which it stimulated. Schröder's production of *Goetz* in 1774 was the first to use scenery and costumes intended to evoke a historical milieu. Although innacurate in detail, they were sufficiently popular to make historical spectacle standard for plays in the Ritterstücke tradition. Dalberg extended the principle in the 1780's, when he staged Shakespeare's *Julius Caesar* at Mannheim with unprecedented attention to antiquarian detail and picturesque splendor.

By the 1790's dramatists were writing plays which demanded the use of practical bridges, walls, and other complex set pieces. Doors and windows began to be set up between wings, thus marking the first steps toward the box set. As elsewhere, however, the trends toward greater realism and accuracy of detail were not to be fully exploited until the 19th century.

Costumes followed the same general trends. Before 1725, extreme simplicity was the rule. Each actor was expected to own a pair of black breeches, while the manager supplied him a coat and waistcoat. This basic costume, used in all roles, was adapted by the addition of simple accessories: a king carried a scepter and wore a feathered headdress; a classical hero draped a scarf diagonally across his chest and wore a helmet. Actresses wore the most fashionable garments they could afford. Lace was often made from cut paper.

As the influence of French drama increased, the costuming conventions of the Parisian troupes were adopted. Most tragic heroes and heroines were played in French court dress, while classical heroes wore the *habit à la romaine* and Near Eastern characters adopted baggy trousers and turbans. Performers began to accumulate their own wardrobes and managers increased the common stock.

Beginning with Gottsched, intermittent attempts were made to introduce a measure of historical accuracy. Gottsched recommended the use of Roman togas in classical plays and, after their break, Frau Neuber revenged herself on him by following his prescriptions. Audiences were not yet ready for this innovation and found Gottsched's *The Dying Cato* farcical. In 1766, Koch created a considerable stir when he opened his new theatre in Leipzig with Schlegel's *Hermann* done in period dress. It was not until the 1770's, however, that historical costumes became common. For his production of *Goetz* in 1774, Schroder dressed the knights in armor, monks and bishops in appropriate ecclesiastical garments, and the courtiers, citizens, and gypsies in allegedly accurate clothing. This feature of the production, considered a major innovation, elicited the greatest number of comments from critics. The succeeding Ritterstücke plays came to accept historical costuming as a basic convention. All of these plays, however, used garments of single period—the 16th century. In 1776, Roman dress was adapted for some classical plays at Gotha, and in the 1780's Dalberg introduced it at Mannheim.

In the 1770's, authors of domestic plays began to prescribe the costumes to be worn by their characters, often enumerating the colors and details at length. Thus, before 1800 managers were becoming aware of the need for individualized costumes, although the old traditions still dominated.

Other theatrical customs also changed. Through much of the 18th century, performances were not permitted on Saturdays, Sundays, holidays, or during Lent and Advent. Gradually the strictures were relaxed, but it was not until about 1800 that daily playing throughout the year was permitted. As in other countries, the starting time was moved to a later hour. Frau Neuber's performances began at 4 or 4:30 P.M.; by the 1770's the usual hour was 5, and by 1800, 5:30.

Iffland and Kotzebue

As the theatre achieved full acceptance between 1775 and 1800, drama similarly attained maturity between 1785 and 1805. The theatre now attracted audiences from every class largely because of the work of Iffland and Kotzebue, while real distinction was achieved by Goethe and Schiller.

August Wilhelm Iffland (1759–1814) began his acting career in the Gotha company under Ekhof and joined the newly-established Mannheim state theatre in 1779. During the following decade, the Mannheim theatre was one of the most vital in Germany. Schröder played there in 1780 and introduced Shakespeare into the repertory; Schiller's first three plays were first produced there, and for a time Schiller was resident dramatist; Dalberg led the way in theatrical innovations.

At Mannheim, Iffland soon came to the fore both as actor and dramatist. From 1784, when his *Crime from Ambition* established his fame as a writer, until 1796, when he left the troupe, Iffland was the greatest influence on the Mannheim stage. Thirty-seven of his plays were first performed by the company and his renown throughout Germany served to elevate this theatre in public esteem. As Iffland's plays became well-known, he was sought for starring engagements and became a major force throughout Germany. In 1796, he was appointed head of the Berlin state theatre, which he welded into one of the finest ensembles of his time. After Schröder's retirement in 1798, Iffland was considered Germany's leading actor.

As a performer, Iffland depended primarily upon his expressive body and face, for his voice was weak. Since his major strength lay in the portrayal of sentiment, he is often said to form the bridge between neoclassic and romantic styles.

IFFLAND AND MADAME BETH-
MANN in a scene from *Die
Hausfreunde*. [A contempo-
rary engraving]

Iffland's own plays provided him with his best acting vehicles. Offering idealized portraits of ordinary men and women, their touching situations tended to romanticize the simple life. His *The Foresters,* in which unsophisticated country people are contrasted with scheming city dwellers, was performed until the 20th century. Although Iffland now seems a precursor of romanticism, he opposed the new movement and sought to keep the romantic drama out of the repertory at Berlin. Nevertheless, the popularity of his sentimental portraits of humanity paved the way for the Romantic school.

August Friedrich von Kotzebue (1761–1819) was even more popular as a playwright than Iffland. From 1787, when he won his first success with *Misanthropy and Repentance,* until his death, he was the most popular playwright in the world. Between 1787 and 1867, one fourth of all the Burgtheater's performances were of Kotzebue's plays; at other theatres the proportion was often higher. Thirty-six of the plays were translated into English, and several remained starring vehicles throughout the 19th century. His more than 200 plays range through domestic drama, historical spectacle, verse plays, and farces.

Kotzebue's success can probably be explained by his ability to adapt new trends to public tastes. Thus, while he used many of the themes and

Scene from Kotzebue's *Misanthropy and Repentance.* [From the edition of the play published in 1790]

devices introduced by Storm and Stress dramatists, he was successful where they had failed. He knew how to titillate audiences without shocking them and how far he could depart from accepted conventions without confusing the unsophisticated spectator. He combined sensational subjects, striking spectacle, and humanitarian sentiments so successfully that he helped to create the vogue for melodrama that was to dominate the 19th century stage. Largely because of Kotzebue's plays, German drama was considered by 1800 the most vital and popular in the world.

Goethe, Schiller, and Weimar Classicism

If Iffland and Kotzebue raised German drama to the peak of its popularity with the theatre-going public, Goethe and Schiller were to be remembered as Germany's greatest playwrights. In their joint work at

Weimar, they also created a distinctive style of production which spread the fame of that small town throughout Germany.

Johann Wolfgang von Goethe (1749–1832) is usually considered the greatest literary figure Germany has known. A "universal genius." Goethe's interests ranged through almost every field, and in most he made significant contributions. He began his literary career at a very early age, but it was his play *Goetz von Berlichingen* (1773) and his novel *Werther* (1774) which made him the most famous young writer of his time and the center of the Storm and Stress school. Throughout Europe, Goethe's Werther came to epitomize the longings of the new generation.

In 1775, at the request of the young ruler, Duke Karl August, Goethe settled in Weimar, which he made one of the cultural centers of Germany. Arriving shortly after Seyler and Ekhof had departed, Goethe became the leader of the amateur group which provided the town's only theatrical entertainment. After the enthusiasm of the amateurs waned, the theatre, which had been built in 1780, was leased in 1783 to a professional troupe under the direction of Joseph Bellomo. Given a small subsidy and a limited supply of scenery and costumes, Bellomo's troupe remained in Weimar until 1790.

Goethe's visit to Italy from 1786 to 1788 marks a turning point in his outlook. His new appreciation of the classical past made him reject his former Storm and Stress period and write for a time in the classical mode. His *Iphigenia in Tauris* (1787) is often considered one of his greatest achievements. Within the framework of the ancient myth, it depicts man's ethical evolution from a narrow concern for self to an awareness of the broader claims of humanity.

In 1790, Karl August dismissed Bellomo's troupe and established a state theatre like those which had been appearing elsewhere. Since the population of the Weimar duchy was only 6000, the Duke could not afford a first-rate company. Failing to attract a suitable director, he appointed Goethe to the post. The Weimar Court Theatre opened in 1791 with a mediocre company under the artistic direction of Franz Fischer, an actor. Goethe took little interest in the theatre until 1796, when a visit from Iffland gave him a vision of what the troupe might become if given sufficient guidance. This interest was deepened by Schiller, who stimulated Goethe to take over the active direction of the company.

Friedrich Schiller's (1759–1805) career had developed along quite different lines than Goethe's. The son of an army officer, Schiller had been forced by the Duke of Württemberg to enter military school. When, following the success of his first play, *The Robbers* (1782), Schiller was forbidden to write, he fled to Mannheim; there he was appointed resident dramatist to the state theatre.

Like Goethe, Schiller underwent a significant change during the 1780's. While working on *Don Carlos,* he began to reassess his values in the light of his study of history. He wrote no plays between 1787 and 1798, devoting himself instead to historical studies. His *The Revolt of the Netherlands* and *A History of the Thirty Years War* won him fame as a historian and an appointment as professor of history at the University of Jena, only five miles from Weimar. As a result of this proximity, Goethe and Schiller became the closest of friends and exerted a strong mutual influence. In 1798, Schiller left Jena and settled in Weimar, where he assisted Goethe. Between 1798 and 1805 Schiller wrote his mature works and Goethe made the Weimar theatre one of the most famous in Germany.

Although in many ways Goethe and Schiller were almost opposite in temperament, they were united by a common artistic view. Now often grouped with the Romantic school, they considered themselves quite distinct from it. To them, the Romantics seemed content either to reproduce the life they saw around them or to escape into fantasy, while the theatre under the influence of Schröder and Iffland seemed bent on reducing all experience to the level of domestic drama. Goethe, under the impact of his visit to Italy, and Schiller, after his study of history and philosophy, sought to counter the major artistic trends of their day. Although both wrote some plays in the classical style, it was not the formal characteristics of ancient drama which attracted them so much as its spirit. For them, the formal conventions of Greek tragedy served merely as devices to "distance" the spectator from the play's events so that they might perceive the ideal patterns behind everyday reality. Thus, Goethe and Schiller argued that drama should transform ordinary experience rather than create an illusion of real life. Consequently, they adopted verse, conventionalized structural patterns, and a stylized production style in order to lead spectators beyond their normal perceptions into the realm of ideal truth. Out of these views came "Weimar Classicism."

Schiller's late plays are complex works in which philosophical, historical, and personal problems are interwoven to produce many layers of meaning. For most, Schiller chose subjects which represent turning points in history. *Wallenstein's Camp* (1798), *The Piccolomini* (1799), and *Wallenstein's Death* (1799) form a trilogy on the Thirty Years War, on a vaster scale than any work since the time of Shakespeare. *Mary Stuart* (1800), *The Maid of Orleans* (1801), and *William Tell* (1804) treat decisive events in English, French, and Swiss history.

Goethe turned his attention to transforming the second-rate Weimar troupe into a true ensemble. The actors' geographical origins and lack of education were evident in every performance, because of the wide range of accents and stage behavior. Since they had so many roles to learn, most had come to depend upon improvisation. To remedy this situation, Goethe laid down a set of rules which, without a knowledge of the actors' problems, might seem elementary. They cover linguistic matters, proper enunciation,

SCENE from Schiller's *Wilhelm Tell* (1804) at Weimar.
[From a contemporary engraving]

ways of overcoming regional dialects, control of tempo and tone, principles
of movement and grouping, posture and stance, and social behavior. All
aim at achieving grace, dignity, and ease.

Since he did not trust either the taste or previous training of his actors,
Goethe became an absolute dictator. He began each new production with a
series of reading rehearsals during which he corrected errors in line readings, pronunciation, and interpretation. He also gave considerable attention to the proper speaking of verse. To aid blocking, he divided the stage
into squares, to which he related the actors' movements. He often consulted
painters about pictorial composition, and he was so concerned with rhythm
and cadence that on occasion he allegedly beat time with a baton. Rather
than seeking to create the illusion of reality, Goethe attempted to achieve a
harmonious and graceful picture which, in combination with intelligent
line readings, would attune the spectator to an ideal beauty. By requiring
absolute adherence to his directions, Goethe achieved the most perfect
ensemble yet seen anywhere. He was one of the first directors in the
modern sense. Critics, however, could not agree whether Goethe's productions were theatrically effective. His numerous admirers praised them
extravagantly; others suggested that uniformity was so complete that the
actors could exchange roles without noticeable effect.

Goethe treated the audience as autocratically as he did the actors. He
forbade them to express approval except by applause or disapproval except
by silence. From his box in the theatre, he reprimanded them if they

responded incorrectly and ordered their arrest if they misbehaved. He assumed the role of schoolmaster to all Weimar.

The remodeled Weimar theatre was opened in 1798 with Schiller's *Wallenstein's Camp*. The combined fame of Goethe and Schiller attracted many visitors and soon "Weimar Classicism" was famous throughout Germany. The repertory was not confined to works by Goethe and Schiller. The state subsidy covered only about one-third of the company's expenses, and Goethe had to arrange the repertory to insure adequate income. Consequently, of the three weekly performances, one was usually devoted to musical plays or opera, one to popular drama (especially the works of Kotzebue and Iffland), and the third to plays that Goethe admired. The actors complained, probably with good cause, that Goethe spent two-thirds of the rehearsal time on plays of the last type. Goethe often experimented with unusual production devices or plays. He used half masks in Terence's *The Brothers,* revived some *commedia dell'arte* scripts, and presented plays by Shakespeare, Calderón, and other authors not normally found in the repertories of the period.

After Schiller died in 1805, Goethe gradually lost interest in the theatre. In 1807 the troupe was invited to Leipzig, where it was much admired for its ensemble. The actors were now in demand and, joining other troupes, they disseminated the Weimar style widely during the first half of the 19th century. Goethe gradually lost control of the Weimar troupe to Caroline Jagemann (1777–1848), an actress and the Duke's mistress. He resigned his post in 1817, but remained advisor to the theatre until his death. After Goethe's resignation, the Weimar theatre slowly sank back into obscurity.

Of Goethe's later works, the most famous is *Faust,* the first part of which was published in 1808 and the second in 1831. Not intended for the stage, this dramatic poem seeks to depict man's search for fulfillment. Its episodic structure and philosophical viewpoint are similar in all important respects to the work of the Romantic playwrights. Thus, while Goethe stands as the culmination of German Classicism, he also contributed much to the Romanticism which came to the fore after 1798.

Theatre and Drama in Other Countries of Northern Europe

By 1800 Germany had assumed a position of leadership in the European theatre, while other countries of Northern Europe continued to play a subordinate role. The theatres of Belgium and Holland could boast a continuous history since the Middle Ages, when spectacular religious dramas had been staged in Belgium and Chambers of Rhetoric had flourished in Holland. As the religious drama declined, the French-speaking areas of Belgium came under the influence of the public theatre in France. The Academy of Music, the first opera house in Belgium, was established in Brussels in 1687. In 1700, the Théâtre de la Monnaie was opened, and, though altered many times, continues as the principal theatre of Brussels. In 1705, the first permanent dramatic troupe was assembled. Since that time the Belgian theatre has, with a few interruptions, enjoyed a continuous history.

The Flemish and Dutch areas of the Low Countries were subject to both French and German influences. By the beginning of the 17th century, the Chambers of Rhetoric were in decline. In Amsterdam the only two remaining societies were united in 1617 under the more fashionable name of The Academy. By 1638, the city had built the Schouwburg Theatre to accommodate The Academy along with other cultural activities.

INTERIOR of the Schouwburg, Amsterdam, in 1638.
[From a contemporary engraving]

Designed by Jacob von Campen, who had studied in Italy, the Schouwburg represents a compromise between the Rhetoric and Italian stages. The platform, raised about seven feet, had no proscenium or front curtain. Along the sides and back, pilasters were spaced several feet apart to accommodate flats, each of which might represent a different locale or part of a single place. At times, the pilasters across the back were used to form an open colonnade. The stage picture, therefore, varied from multiple settings similar to those at the Hotel de Bourgogne to modified perspective settings in the Italian manner. Some of the flats were double-sided to allow for quick changes. When needed, the central portion of the rear facade could be enclosed to form an inner stage. The main stage was divided into two

355

parts by a curtain which could be closed to permit changes or opened to indicate a shift in locale. At times, mansion-like structures were set up on the stage. There was also a permanent upper stage in the form of a balcony extending across the back and part way down the sides. Similar to the *théâtre supérieure* of the Théâtre du Marais in Paris, the upper stage might be treated as part of a unified setting or used to represent one or more separate locales. The ovoid auditorium consisted of a standing pit, 46 feet wide by 23 feet deep, surrounded by a row of ten raised boxes, surmounted by an open gallery. This building was replaced in 1664 by another with a stage of the Italian type. A professional company was installed at this time; thereafter, the theatre in Holland reflected the major French or German developments.

Further north, the professional theatre was slower in appearing. Until the 18th century, Norway and Denmark (unified as a single country until 1814) were dependent upon French, English, or German troupes. After 1700 the court maintained a French troupe, while the general populace was restricted to traveling companies of the type common in Germany at that time.

The turning point came in 1720, when Frederick IV dismissed his French company. One of the actors, René Magnon de Montaigu, had been away from France for 35 years and wished to remain in Denmark. He joined with Étienne Capion, another Frenchman and former actor, to petition the King for permission to open a public theatre. Upon receiving a favorable response, they built a small theatre (seating about 400) and opened it in 1722. When Capion went bankrupt in 1723, he ceded his share to Montaigu, who in turn failed in 1727. Montaigu was then permitted to use the court theatre and was provided a small subsidy until 1730. The theatre was then closed under pressure from puritan forces.

In spite of these difficulties, Danish theatre and drama dates from these early years, during which Denmark's first playwright, Ludwig Holberg (1684–1754), appeared. Well educated, Holberg had traveled throughout Europe. In 1718 he became a professor at the University of Copenhagen and in 1719–20 published a satirical story, *Peder Paars,* usually considered the beginning of Danish literature. The work was revolutionary, for Latin was still the language of learned men and French that of polite society. Holberg was requested by Capion and Montaigu to provide them with plays. By 1723 he had written 15 full-length plays, and eventually wrote 18 others. Of these, *Jeppe of the Hill* (1722) and *Erasmus Montanus* (printed 1731) are probably the best known. Although using many of the conventions of Roman comedy, many of Holberg's plays resemble robust Medieval farces with appended moral conclusions. For example, *Jeppe of the Hill* tells the story of a henpecked peasant, who is kidnapped while drunk, led to believe that he is a great lord, and then returned to his village during another fit of drunkenness. This comic story concludes with the argument that class barriers must be maintained since, as Jeppe has shown, the lower classes would become tyrannical if given power. A fusion of native elements and borrowings from Plautus and Molière, Holberg's works became the backbone of the Danish repertory.

A PERFORMANCE of Holberg's *Jeppe of the Hill* at the theatre in Copenhagen in the mid-1720s. A 20th century reconstruction. [Courtesy Theatermuseum, Copenhagen]

When the theatre was reopened in 1746, Holberg provided a few more plays, but the bulk of his work had been done before 1730. The fortunes of the new theatre were as uncertain as those of the old until 1772, when the Royal Danish Theatre, still in existence, was created. It predates all of the German state theatres.

The bulk of the late 18th century repertory was foreign, for Holberg had few successors. Johann Herman Wessel (1742–85), a prolific translator, also gained considerable fame by writing parodies of foreign works. Johannes Ewald (1743–81), Denmark's first important serious playwright as well as one of its greatest lyric poets, provided *Rolf Krage* (1770), the first significant Danish tragedy, and *The Fishermen* (1780), the first serious Danish play to treat ordinary people sympathetically. Ewald also called attention to the rich heritage of North European folklore and legend and laid the foundations for the succeeding Romantic movement.

The theatre of Sweden has a long if somewhat undistinguished history. Although plays were written in the vernacular from about 1550, the religious wars served to divert attention from the arts. A public theatre was maintained from about 1690, although the court gave its principal support to ballet and opera.

Not until the reign of Gustav III (1746–92) did the theatre flourish. After he came to the throne in 1771, Gustav promoted literature and the arts along French lines. He established a Swedish Academy, wrote plays, and encouraged native writers and performers. Despite his efforts, the results were essentially lifeless imitations of the French originals.

A VIEW of the stage at the Drottningholm Theatre, showing a *palais à volonté* setting of the 18th century in place. [Courtesy Theatermuseum, Drottningholm]

Gustav's reign is now remembered primarily because of the theatre at Drottningholm, a royal residence near Stockholm. Erected between 1764 and 1766, this building was closed in 1792 and left untouched until 1921. As a result, 30 stage settings, the stage machinery, and the auditorium of an 18th century court theatre have been preserved intact. It is now one of the major theatrical museums of the world. The theatre at the royal residence at Gripsholm has also survived.

The Theatre in Russia to 1800

The 18th century also saw the establishment of theatre and drama in Russia. As in other parts of Europe, folk and ritual drama can be found in Russia from the earliest times, and wandering entertainers can be traced back as far as the 10th century A.D. If an extensive liturgical drama existed, however, few traces have survived. Drama was introduced into the Jesuit schools of the Ukraine in the 17th century, and until the 18th students sometimes toured as far east as Siberia during the summer, performing in private homes.

The first clear record of the theatre in Moscow is found in 1672. After Tsar Alexey (reigned 1646–76) failed to secure a theatrical troupe from the West, Johann Gottfried Gregory, a Lutheran minister and school-teacher in the resident German colony, agreed to produce plays for the theatre which Alexey had built in his palace. Although Gregory's productions were Haupt-und-Saatsaktion plays complete with Pickelherring, Alexey was so enthusiastic that he forced the aristocracy to attend. He also established a subsidized theatre school to train additional performers. Upon Alexey's death in 1676, both the theatre and the school were abandoned.

When Peter the Great (reigned 1682–1725) decided to use the theatre in his campaign for Westernization, he had to begin over again. In 1702, he imported Johann Kunst's company from Danzig and installed them in a theatre on what is now Red Square. Since few of his people understood German, Peter selected several Russians to be trained by the foreign actors. This theatre, already disrupted by the movement of the capital to St. Petersburg in 1712, was abandoned upon Peter's death.

Between 1725 and 1750 theatrical activities were largely confined to the court. For the coronation of the Empress Anna (reigned 1730–40), the Polish King sent a *commedia dell'arte* troupe. Their success led to the importation of Francesco Araia, a Neopolitan composer, in 1735, and of Jean-Baptiste Landet, a French dancing master and the founder of Russian ballet, in 1738. Carolina Neuber's troupe was invited to St. Petersburg in 1740, but the death of the Empress Anna cut short Neuber's engagement.

Under the Empress Elizabeth (reigned 1741–62), the Italians and French fought for supremacy in the court theatre. Eventually a French company was employed to perform plays twice a week, while the Italians continued their spectacular operatic productions. By 1750, the Russian court was abreast of the latest Western trends. There was as yet, however, neither a public theatre nor a native Russian repertory.

Around 1750 a number of developments began a new era in the Russian theatre. First, a talented Russian dramatist Alexander Sumarokov (1717–77), began to write plays. Using the French neo-classical form, Sumarokov took his stories from Russian sources. His tragedies and satirical comedies mark the beginning of the Russian classical school. In 1749, the success of the cadets at the Academy of the Nobility with Sumarokov's first play, *Khorev* (1747), induced them to present other works by Sumarokov.

Another major train of events was set in motion around 1750 when Fyodor Volkov (1729–63), a merchant's son who had seen theatrical performances in St. Petersburg, decided to present plays in Yaroslavl. Assembling a troupe from his family and friends, Volkov fitted up a barn as a theatre. Enthusiasm was so great that he had moved into more adequate quarters before being summoned to play for the Empress in 1752. Impressed by their work, the Empress sent some of the actors to the Academy of the Nobility for further education and permitted them to give performances for the general public. Thus, Volkov is usually considered the founder of the Russian professional theatre.

In 1756, the Empress established a state theatre to perform comedies and tragedies in Russian. Sumarokov was appointed director, although the ultimate authority resided in a court official. The troupe was made up largely of Volkov's actors. The relatively slight value placed on this Russian company, however, is indicated by its subsidy of 5000 rubles as compared with the 20,000 given the French actors and the 30,000 to the Italian opera troupe. The Russian plays, treated condescendingly by the court, were attended primarily by the middle class.

Under Catherine II (reigned 1762–96) the theatre spread throughout Russia. Playwrights increased, although few won lasting fame. Leadership passed from Sumarokov to his son-in-law, Yakov Kniazhnin (1742–91), who after 1769 wrote seven tragedies and a number of comedies in the neo-classical style. By far the best of 18th century Russian dramatists was Denis Fonvizin (1745–92). Beginning in 1761, he achieved his first significant success in 1766 with *The Brigadier General*, a satire on the newly-rich and the general Russian tendency to praise everything from Western Europe and to dislike everything Russian. His lasting reputation rests principally upon *The Minor* (1781), a satirical picture of the brutish, uneducated rural gentry.

The majority of the plays in the repertory, however, were translations. As the plays of Diderot, Destouches, Mercier, Lillo, Lessing, and Beaumarchais were translated in the 1760's, domestic tragedy and sentimental drama began to dominate the repertory. Musical plays in the manner of ballad opera or *opéra comique* also gained an enormous following. The most popular of these works was A. Ablesimov's (1742–83) *The Miller, the Witchdoctor, the Cheater and the Matchmaker* (1779), which held the stage through the 19th century.

Under Catherine, the state continued its firm control over the theatre. All plays were subject to strict censorship, and the court and state-subsidized theatres operated under regulations established by the crown. Although opera continued to be the favored form with the aristocracy, the dramatic troupes achieved increased security. In 1766 a pension system was inaugurated, and after 1789 the companies were allowed four annual benefit performances, the proceeds of which were divided among all the actors. In 1779 an acting school was established, and in the 1790's a second state theatre was opened in St. Petersburg. In general, acting companies followed "lines of business" similar to those current in France. A state document of 1766 lists the lines as follows: first, second, and third comic

INTERIOR of the Bolshoi Theatre, St. Petersburg, during the
reign of Catherine II. [From Aseyev, *Russkoe teatralno*]

and tragic lovers, noble fathers, comic fathers, first and second domestics,
moralizers, clerks, confidants, first and second tragic and comic female
lovers, first and second chambermaids, old women, and confidantes.

After the death of Volkov in 1763, the most famous actor was Ivan
Dmitrevsky (1734–1821), who began his career in Volkov's Yaroslavl
troupe. In 1765 and 1767 he went abroad, where he is said to have studied
the acting of Clairon, LeKain, and Garrick. He acted only rarely after 1787,
but beginning in 1784 was an influential teacher. In 1791 he was appointed
supervisor of all performances in the state dramatic troupes. A carefully
controlled performer who planned every effect, Dmitrevsky was best in the
classical repertory. Yakov Shusherin (1753–1813), on the other hand, was
famous for his portrayal of sentimental roles. Between 1786 and 1810 he
was the most popular actor on the St. Petersburg stage.

By the end of the 18th century, itinerant companies were touring to all
of the principal cities of Russia. Many privately owned theatres also had
appeared; some gave public performances, while others were maintained by
nobles for private entertainments. Few of the public companies were
successful. In Moscow, for example, the public theatre was open only
sporadically. After one venture, lasting from 1759 to 1761, failed, there was
no professional troupe there until 1786, when M. E. Medox's company
struggled along until 1796. Moscow was not to have a state troupe until the
19th century.

By far the majority of the privately owned theatres were maintained
by the great landowners. Under Catherine II, the aristocracy began to
patronize the arts as a sign of their enlightenment, and many nobles

361

established small courts. Here, theatrical troupes, composed of serfs owned by the nobles, were maintained. In 1797, there were 15 serf theatres in Moscow alone, many of which rivaled in quality the court and state theatres of St. Petersburg. Prince Yusopov, owner of 21,000 serfs, established separate ballet, opera, and dramatic companies and a training school. Count Peter Sheremetyev built three separate theatres, one of which had three tiers of boxes. His principal troupe had 230 members, and he retained an agent in Paris to keep him abreast of all the latest developments in Western Europe. His productions, famous for their lavishness, were attended by the royal family, important nobles and foreign dignitaries. Sometimes landowners sold entire companies or rented them out for public performances. The most important serf companies operated between 1790 and 1810, but others continued until the abolition of serfdom in 1861.

By 1800, then, the Russian theatre and drama had gained a firm foothold. Few important dramatists had appeared, and the theatre was largely imitative of French and Italian practices, but the basis for future developments was clearly present. As the Russian experience indicates, by 1800 the professional theatre had spread throughout Europe. Although in some areas it was still weak, the 19th century was to bring its full flowering.

FRANCE, ITALY, AND SPAIN IN THE 19TH CENTURY

*A*lthough the French Revolution removed many strictures which had discouraged new developments in the theatre, other controls were soon imposed. After the fall of Napoleon, however, the gradual relaxation of regulations led to an increasingly varied theatre in Paris. Drama underwent many significant changes as the dominant style shifted from neoclassicism to Romanticism and Realism. The new movements brought progressively greater concern for authentic and detailed spectacle, and this complexity, in turn, increased the need to plan and coordinate all parts of a production. By the 1880's, the foundations of the "modern" theatre had been laid.

363

The Parisian Theatre, 1789–1815

During the period of political uncertainty which followed the fall of the Bastille in 1789, the minor theatres grew ever bolder in their encroachments on the privileges of the major troupes, who protested in vain. After the monopolies were abolished in 1791, numerous new companies were formed. It is difficult to chronicle their development, for many soon expired, and others adopted new names with bewildering frequency in the desire to reflect changing political currents and to remain in favor with the ruling factions. Estimates of the number of troupes between 1791 and 1800 range from 50 to 100.

Most of the theatres catered to mob tastes by offering a wide range of popular entertainments combined with appeals to patriotic sentiment. The first burst of freedom, during which censorship was lifted, had given way by 1793 to repressive measures and severe punishments for any alleged opposition to the Revolution. Consequently, little drama of merit appeared. By far the most popular playwright of the Revolution was Marie-Joseph Chénier (1764–1811), whose *Charles IX* (1789) and *Henri VIII* (1791) set the political tone for others. In spite of their revolutionary sentiments, however, Chénier's plays remained clearly within the neo-classical tradition.

During the 1790's, the former crown theatres lost much of their prestige. In 1791, the Comédie Française, already weakened by internal strife, split into two troupes. The actors sympathetic to the Revolution, including Talma, Mme. Vestris, and Mlle. Desgarcins, joined those of the Variétés Amusantes to form the Théâtre de la République in 1792. After 1793, when the actors at the Comédie Française were imprisoned, this company was considered the finest in Paris. The Comédie Italienne, now the Théâtre Favart, was dangerously weakened by its fierce competition with the Théâtre Feydeau. The Opéra survived only because it was taken over by the city of Paris.

By 1799 France was weary of the intrigues and fanaticism which had characterized the government since 1793. Consequently, it welcomed the emergence of Napoleon, who, beginning in 1799 as one of a triumvirate, was crowned Emperor in 1804 and remained in complete control until 1814. As early as 1799, Napoleon made clear his opposition to partisan drama by suppressing several plays favorable to his own cause. As a result, the theatre began to turn away from political subjects.

The changed atmosphere also brought renewed stability to the major troupes. In 1799, the two branches of the Comédie Française were reunited; in 1800 their theatre was declared state property and its use ceded to the troupe; in 1801, its pensions and subsidies, interrupted in 1791, were reinstated. In 1801, the Théâtre Feydeau and the Théâtre Favart were united in the state-subsidized Théâtre National de l'Opéra-Comique. In 1802, the Opéra was brought under state control once more and in 1803 was granted a subsidy.

The favors shown the major troupes were paralleled by repressions of minor theatres, for which Napoleon had little respect. In 1806, he decreed that works in the repertories of the state troupes could not be performed by any other theatres, that all plays must be passed by a censor, and that no new theatres might be established without special permission. In 1807, he took more drastic measures. First, he authorized four state-supported theatres: the Comédie Française (for regular comedy and tragedy) ; the Théâtre de l'Impératrice, later the Odéon (for lesser drama) ; the Opéra (for grand opera and serious ballet) ; and the Opéra-Comique (for light opera and comic ballet). These troupes were to continue into the 20th century. Second, he ordered the closure of all minor theatres except four: the Théâtre de la Gaîté and the Ambigu-Comique (both to perform melodramas and pantomimes) ; and the Théâtre des Variétés and the Vaudeville (both to perform short plays, parodies, and comédies-en-vaudevilles). Other theatres, such as the Porte Saint-Martin and the Cirque Olympique, were eventually allowed to reopen, but they too were restricted to minor genres. Until 1831, the number of theatres in Paris was strictly controlled, and each was restricted to works of specified types. Thus, theatrical conditions between 1807 and 1831 differed little from those of the 1780's. As before the Revolution, the principal innovations were to come from the Boulevard theatres.

French Drama, 1800–50

Just as Napoleon sought to pattern his empire after Rome, so too he favored a classical drama. It is often said that, in return for supporting the theatre, he demanded a new tragic dramatist each year. Unfortunately, he was doomed to disappointment, for, although many writers attempted to fulfill his dream, none found lasting favor with the public. Probably the best serious playwright of the time was Népomucène Lemercier (1771–1840), author of *Pinto* (1800) and *Christophe Colombe* (1809), but his work lacked force and vitality.

Ironically, it was the despised Boulevard theatres that produced the only truly popular plays, and these were melodramas rather than the tragedies for which Napoleon longed. Although melodramatic works, most often in the form of tragicomedy or pastoral, can be traced back to classical Greece, the term "melodrama" did not come into widespread use until about 1800. All of the characteristic elements of melodrama had long been present in the Boulevard theatres, but it was René Guilbert de Pixérécourt (1773–1844) in his *Victor, or the Child of the Forest* (1798), who gave them their typical form. The popularity of Pixérécourt's works and those of Kotzebue combined to establish melodrama as the dominant dramatic type of the 19th century.

The basic characteristics of melodrama can be summarized briefly: a virtuous hero or heroine is relentlessly persecuted by a villain and is rescued from his machinations only after a series of thrilling escapades; an episodic story unfolds rapidly after a short expository scene; each act ends with a strong climax; all important events occur on stage and often involve elaborate spectacle, such as battles, floods, earthquakes, or scenes of local color, such as festivals, dances, or picturesque working conditions; the typical plot devices include disguise, abduction, concealed identity, and strange coincidence; strict poetic justice is meted out, for, although he may triumph until the final scene, the villain is always defeated; comic relief is provided by a servant or companion to one of the principal characters; song, dance, and music provide additional entertainment or underscore the emotional values of scenes. Melodrama, with its simple, powerful stories, unequivocal moral tone, and elements drawn from popular entertainment, could be understood and enjoyed by the least sophisticated of theatregoers. Probably for this reason, melodrama was largely responsible for bringing into the 19th century theatre a large popular audience comparable to that enjoyed by motion pictures and television in the 20th century.

Although Pixérécourt, with his more than 120 works, was the most successful of the melodramatic playwrights, he had many competitors. Of these, the most influential was Victor Ducange (1783–1833), whose *Thirty Years, or the Life of a Gambler* (1827) was performed throughout the world.

Melodrama paved the way for French romantic drama by popularizing departures from neo-classical precepts and by creating a large potential audience for it. Furthermore, melodrama's plot devices were taken over by romantic drama to such an extent that many of the plays can be distinguished from melodrama only because of a few differences: romantic drama employs the five-act form (as opposed to melodrama's three acts); avoids the happy ending; and is more dependent upon diction. In broad outline, nevertheless, the characteristic French romantic drama was merely elevated melodrama.

The Romantic movement was slow in getting underway in France, perhaps because of political events. Its first important impetus came with the publication of Mme. de Staël's *Of Germany*. Born Germaine Necker, Mme. de Staël (1766–1817) was the daughter of Louis XVI's minister of finance and the wife of the Swedish ambassador to France. A bitter enemy of Napoleon, she spent the years of his reign in Germany, where she became familiar with romanticism. *Of Germany,* which described the new literary movement, was published in France in 1810 but was suppressed until Napoleon's downfall in 1814. The notoriety of Mme. de Staël's feud with Napoleon led to the book's wide dissemination and gave currency to its ideas. The debate over the relative merits of neoclassicism and romanticism now began in earnest.

Stendhal (Henri Beyle, 1783–1842) contributed to the controversy with his *Racine and Shakespeare* (1823, 1825), in which he urged Shakespeare's plays as more suitable models than those of Racine. The major statement of the Romantic doctrine came in Victor Hugo's preface to *Cromwell* (1827). Hugo (1802–85) set forth few ideas not already current; he called for the abandonment of the unities of time and place, denounced the strict separation of genres, and advocated greater emphasis upon the specific historical milieu of an action. Perhaps most important, he insisted that art should go beyond the neoclassicist's "idealized nature" to one which included both the sublime and the grotesque. Since for Hugo the sublime was related to man's spiritual qualities and the grotesque to his animal nature, he argued that a truthful depiction of humanity requires that both be represented in every literary work.

The culmination of the debate came in 1830 with the production of Hugo's *Hernani* at the Comédie Française. A pitched battle between the Romantics and traditionalists, during which the actors were scarcely heard, raged for 45 nights. The bitterness of the contest is probably explained by the feeling on both sides that the future course of literature depended upon the outcome. Several events had accelerated the trend toward romanticism after 1827: Charles Kemble's troupe of English actors had performed Shakespeare's plays to admiring Parisian audiences in 1827; Macready had appeared in English romantic plays in 1828; Sir Walter Scott's novels were attracting an ever-wider reading public; and Shakespeare's plays were being read and produced in France. By 1829, romantic dramas were making their way into the repertory of the Comédie Française: Alexandre Dumas *père's Henri III and His Court,* Casimir Delavigne's *Mariano Falieri,* and Alfred de Vigny's adaptation of *Othello* as *The Moor of Venice* had all been produced in 1829. Now the conservative audience sought to halt the trend.

In *Hernani,* Hugo deliberately violated many of the rules which the advocates of neoclassicism sought to retain. First, he made innovations in the Alexandrine, which had been the accepted verse form for tragedy since the 17th century. Second, he used many words which had long been ruled out as beneath the dignity of tragedy. Third, he broke the unities of time and place. Fourth, he showed deaths and violence on stage. Fifth, he shifted the mood of his scenes frequently and mixed humor with seriousness.

THE BATTLE over *Hernani* (1830). Onstage is the final scene. [From Grand-Carteret's *XIXe Siècle* (1892)]

Although *Hernani* is merely a melodrama with an unhappy ending, it won the day; hence, the romantic movement in France is usually dated from its production. Hugo's popularity increased with such plays as *Marion Delorme* (1831), *The King Amuses Himself* (1832), and *Ruy Blas* (1838).

Other important romantic dramatists include Dumas *père*, Vigny, and Musset. The plays of Alexandre Dumas *père* (1803–70) are of two types: historical spectacles, such as *Henri III and His Court, Christine* (1829), and his dramatization of *The Three Musketeers;* and domestic dramas, such as *Antony* (1831). Although Dumas had a surer sense of dramatic situation than did Hugo, he lacked Hugo's poetic gift, and, when he attempted to express profound emotion or significant thought, often lapsed into puerility.

Alfred de Vigny (1797–1863) began his dramatic career by adapting the works of Shakespeare and went on to write historical spectacles, such as *The Marshal of Ancre.* He is now remembered primarily for his *Chatterton* (1835), the story of a poet-martyr, outcast from society because of his special insight, which epitomizes the romantic idealization of the misunderstood genius.

Of all the romantic works, the plays of Alfred de Musset (1810–57) have fared best, although originally they were virtually ignored. After the failure of his first play, *A Venetian Night* (1830), Musset ceased writing for production. Consequently, his later works shift time and place freely and depend little upon spectacle. Like Racine and Marivaux, Musset is pri-

A SKETCH by Hugo for his play *Le Roi s'amuse*.
[From Loliée, *La Comédie Française* (1907)]

marily concerned with the inner feelings of his characters, especially their inability to resist love's compelling force. Musset's characters are essentially selfish, however, and seek desperately to protect their egos. Sometimes the results are happy, as in *A Door Should Either be Shut or Open,* and sometimes tragic, as in *No Trifling with Love.* Musset seldom strayed from his preoccupation with love, but his *Lorenzaccio,* the story of a Hamlet-like character who seeks to right the Florentine state, is one of the finest historical dramas of the 19th century. Musset's plays, most of which were written between 1830 and 1840, were not produced until about 1860. Since that time, they have never been absent from the repertory.

Despite the battle over *Hernani,* romantic drama did not find a congenial home at the Comédie Française, and the dramatists had to turn to the Odéon and the Boulevard theatres. Their lot was eased after 1831, when the genre restrictions on theatres were abolished. After this time, the Boulevard theatres, now seeking to broaden their repertories, welcomed the new drama enthusiastically. There, romantic drama mingled with melodrama and absorbed still more melodramatic qualities, while melodrama tended to become more refined.

By the 1840's the enthusiasm for romantic drama had waned. The failure of Hugo's *Les Burgraves* in 1843 is usually considered to mark the end of the romantic era. Romanticism was succeeded by the "theatre of common sense," which attempted to find a middle ground between neo-classicism and romanticism. The leader of the new group was François Ponsard (1814–67), who came to prominence in 1843 with *Lucrèce*. As with most compromises, the "theatre of common sense" soon lost its appeal, and by the 1850's was giving way to the new realistic school.

The Development of Realism

Dissatisfaction with romanticism stemmed from political and social problems as well as from aesthetic taste. Romanticism had emphasized the disparity between man's spiritual longings and his physical limitations and had implied that human perfection lies in striving after those higher goals perceived through the imagination. This concentration upon spiritual perfection tended to distract attention from the very real political and social problems of the early 19th century.

The French Revolution had aroused high hopes for a society based on equality and the "brotherhood of man." These dreams were shattered, however, first by the Reign of Terror and then by Napoleon's political ambitions. After Napoleon's downfall, monarchies were reestablished throughout Europe, and restrictive measures were taken to insure against future rebellions. Consequently, the masses were deprived of many rights, while attempts at improving social and political conditions were discouraged. Repressive legislation came at just the time when the Industrial Revolution was drawing workers to urban centers and creating vast new social problems. Thus, at the time when planning was most needed, the governments were least inclined to undertake it. The desirability of reforms was acknowledged only after a series of revolutions, beginning in 1830 and culminating in 1848, made it impossible to ignore the problems. By 1850, the Romantics, even though they had championed freedom, seemed too idealistic to cope with the realities of economic and social problems. The desire for a more pragmatic approach paved the way for Realism.

Realism owed much to the "positivism" of Auguste Comte (1798–1857), author of *Positive Philosophy* (1830–42) and *Positive Polity* (1851–54). Comte classified the sciences according to their relative simplicity, placing sociology at the apex as the most complex and important of the sciences. Since to him the ultimate aim of all knowledge was the betterment of human life, Comte argued that all the sciences must contribute to sociology, which, after the rigorous application of the scientific method, would supply the necessary knowledge for predicting human behavior and controlling society. Comte's arguments fell on willing ears, not only among scientists and philosophers, but also among artists, who sought to make art "scientific." Out of these attempts, realism emerged.

The realistic mode in art had been attempted sporadically since the time of the Greeks. Beginning in the Renaissance, pictorial illusion had dominated the theatre. Melodrama and romanticism had accelerated the demands for authenticity of spectacle and psychological motivations. All of the approaches before 1850, however, emphasized "beautiful" nature, norms, picturesque local color, or pleasing contrasts. Although Hugo argued for the inclusion of the grotesque in art, his own works avoided the sordid. Now, artists and critics began to advocate a close and objective observation of life, no matter how squalid or elevated.

As a conscious movement, realism appeared first about 1853. By 1863 the theoretical foundations had been fully expressed in such periodicals as *La Révue de Paris, L'Artiste, Le Figaro, Réalisme* (first published in 1856), and *Le Present.* The main tenets of the new movement were that art must depict truthfully the real, physical world; truth can be attained only through direct observation; only contemporary life and manners can be observed directly; the observer must strive to be as impersonal as a scientist.

The pioneer dramatists of the realistic school were Dumas *fils* and Augier. Although quite unlike them in many respects, Eugène Scribe (1791–1861) had supplied the pattern upon which they were to build. Between 1811 and 1861, Scribe contributed over 300 pieces to Parisian theatres, twenty-three of them to the Comédie Française. He ranged through *comédies-en-vaudevilles,* opera libretti, comedies, and serious drama. Perhaps the best of his works were *Marriage for Money, A Glass of Water,* and *Adrienne Lecouvreur.* Today, Scribe is remembered primarily as the popularizer of the "well-made play" formula. Often used as a term of derision, the well-made play merely perfected dramatic devices which had been current since the time of Aeschylus: careful exposition and preparation, the cause-to-effect arrangement of incidents, the building of scenes to a climax, the use of withheld information, startling reversals, and suspense. Because they sacrificed depth of characterization and thought to intrigue, Scribe's plays now seem shallow. To theatregoers of the 19th century, however, they appeared more substantial, probably because they manipulate so skillfully the attitudes and prejudices of the day. Although Scribe was not associated with the realistic movement, his "well-made" play formula, emphasizing logical development from cause to effect, supplied Dumas *fils* and Augier a suitable form for their ideas.

Alexandre Dumas *fils* (1824–95) came to public attention with his novel, *The Lady of the Camellias,* played throughout the world in Dumas' dramatization as *Camille.* Although today *Camille* (performed 1852) seems merely an idealized treatment of the "prostitute with a heart of gold," it was forbidden production for three years because of its realism. Set in Paris in the 1840's, the play used prose dialogue and depicted a protagonist based upon a well-known courtesan of the time. Although Hugo's *Marion Delorme* had also treated a courtesan, its story was historical and its dialogue poetic. Consequently, it had not aroused the objections which greeted Dumas' work.

DUMAS FILS' *Madame Aubray's Ideas* (1867), Act IV. [From *Monde Illustré* (1867)]

By 1855, Dumas had undergone a change of attitude and in *The Demi-Monde* he treated unsympathetically the same kind of characters that are presented sentimentally in *Camille*. He now set out to show that "women with a past" must be prevented from marrying into good families. From this time, Dumas wrote "thesis plays" about current social problems, utilizing Scribe's well-made play formula to create suspenseful and entertaining stories. His works are marred by didacticism, for in each a message is clearly stated by an articulate *raisonneur,* or author's mouthpiece. In spite of this lack of objectivity, Dumas considered himself a realist and his duty the betterment of society. In the preface to *A Prodigal Father* (1868), he wrote: ". . . if I can exercise some influence over society . . . if I can find some means to force people to discuss the problem, and the law-maker to revise the law, I shall have done more than my duty as a writer, I shall have done my duty as a man."

Émile Augier (1820–89) was a more versatile writer than Dumas *fils*. He began his career in 1844 as an adherent of the "theatre of common sense" but, after seven verse plays, adopted the realistic style. One of his first prose works, *Olympe's Marriage* (1855), was intended as a direct reply to Dumas' *Camille,* for it shows the results of a courtesan marrying into an aristocratic family. It is Augier's most didactic play. His more characteristic works are comedies of manners, such as *M. Poirier's Son-in-Law* (1854) in which Augier depicts the struggle for supremacy between the nobility and the well-to-do merchant class. Other plays treat the power of money, the influence of the church on politics, and other problems.

AUGIER's *Olympe's Marriage* (1855). The large picture shows a scene from the second act, while the inset depicts the final scene. [From a contemporary lithograph]

After the initial shock, both Dumas *fils* and Augier came to be accepted as sane and healthy men seeking to bring good sense to the theatre. Because they both provided suspenseful plots in the Scribean tradition, they were not thought to differ in any essential way from less serious playwrights, such as Sardou and Labiche.

Victorien Sardou (1831–1908), Scribe's true heir, was one of the world's most popular playwrights between 1860 and 1900. Like Scribe, he used the well-made play formula and adapted it to almost every dramatic type. His early successes included comedies, such as *A Scrap of Paper* (1860) and *Our Intimates* (1861), and satires on contemporary life, such as *The Family Benoiton* (1865). He later wrote a number of plays for

Sarah Bernhardt, including *Fedora* (1882) and *Tosca* (1887). His *Patrie!* (1869) and *Theodora* (1884) were among the most lavish historical spectacles of the 19th century and elicited praise even from the Naturalists for their faithful depiction of particular milieus. To George Bernard Shaw, Sardou's shallow plots seemed to epitomize the decadence of the late 19th century theatre, which he labelled "Sardoodledom."

SCENE from Sardou's *Patrie* at the Théâtre de Porte Saint-Martin, 1869. Settings by Cambon. [From a contemporary engraving]

Eugène Labiche (1815–88) was one of the finest writers of farce in the 19th century. Uninterested in theories, Labiche wrote for the popular audience and only reluctantly agreed to the publication of his plays. Most of his works, of which *The Italian Straw Hat* (1851) is representative, appear delightfully irresponsible, but others, such as *M. Perrichon's Journey* (1860) and *Dust in the eyes* (1861), make penetrating observations on human nature.

By the 1880's French drama had assimilated the Scribean formula into the realistic mode. Even the most popular playwrights now tried to reflect real life through the visual elements of their plays. Realism was no longer offensive: even Dumas *fils* and Augier, the most serious dramatists, wrote primarily about persons like those in the audience and always upheld conventional morality. It was now clear that no revolution would come from their work. It remained, then, for Antoine and the Naturalists, to be considered in a later chapter, to make the break with the popular tradition and inaugurate the "modern" theatre in France.

Theatrical Conditions in the 19th Century

The number of theatres in Paris grew steadily through the 19th century. Although the government retained firm control over licensing, the eight companies authorized by Napoleon in 1807 had grown to 28 by 1855. Between 1864, when the licensing restrictions were removed, and 1900 the number increased to about 50. Of these, the four state-supported troupes commanded the greatest prestige. After genre restrictions were removed in 1831, the Odéon and Opéra-Comique often rivaled the Comédie Française and Opéra in the quality of works presented and in the mounting of their productions. Throughout the century, the Boulevard theatres were the most experimental, often championing new playwrights or methods of production long before they were accepted by the state troupes. Of the secondary theatres, the most influential were the Vaudeville, Gymnase, Porte Saint-Martin, Gaîté, and Ambigu-Comique.

With the exception of the Comédie Française, all of the Parisian troupes were run by managers who employed actors on a salary basis. The Comédie Française, on the other hand, continued to be a sharing company, operating under rules much like those in effect before 1791. The new regulations, established in 1812 by the "Decree of Moscow," sought to correct some of the earlier problems. A reserve fund was established to insure pensions and deficits, and the number of shares was reduced to 20. Each *sociétaire* was now guaranteed a minimum annual wage and, in addition, was paid a small fee for each day he performed. Profits were still divided among the shareholders. By the late 19th century, the troupe had about 50 members, of which less than half were *sociétaires*. The government subsidy was also gradually increased from 100,000 to 240,000 francs. Ostensibly the actors were responsible for making all decisions of policy and for running the company, but the supervisor, who replaced the Gentlemen of the Chamber, sometimes assumed considerable authority.

The other state theatres were assigned to managers, who had full control over the companies and repertories, although their work was subject to close governmental scrutiny. The Opéra continued to be the most favored troupe. Its subsidy often amounted to 600,000 francs, and between 1811 and 1831 all private theatres were required to pay it up to $\frac{1}{20}$ of their receipts.

All of the Parisian theatres retained the repertory system until the end of the 19th century, although the long run seriously altered the old patterns. In the early years of the century, only unusually popular plays were performed for a number of consecutive evenings. Typically the bill was changed every day. By the end of the century, however, most theatres were running each play as long as it drew audiences. Thus, although a number of plays were performed each season, they were now usually presented consecutively rather than in rotation. The old pattern might be used to fill in while a new play was being prepared, but only the Comédie Française maintained the original system. Runs of 100 nights were still unusual, however, and 20 performances were considered sufficient to repay the investment.

The change in programming had several results. The number of plays in each company's repertory was considerably reduced, for an entire season could usually be filled up with less than ten works. Since most of the long-running plays were new, the classics tended to be dropped from the repertory except at the Comédie Française and a few other theatres. The new conditions also led to greater specialization, as theatres built reputations for presenting a particular kind of play. Restricting the repertory to a few works, all of the same basic type, led to the employment of more specialized actors. Furthermore, since long-running plays sometimes did not make use of all members of a company, by 1900 it was becoming more economical to employ actors for each play rather than by the season. Touring companies, common by the end of the 19th century, were also undermining the provincial troupes and were rapidly making Paris the only theatrical center in France. These trends would not be completed until the 20th century.

Most theatres presented one long and one short play each evening, but some of the minor theatres offered entire programs of short pieces. Others performed the equivalent of 12 acts on one bill. After 1850, the short play was usually performed first, as a "curtain raiser" rather than after the long play as had been the previous practice. This change seems to have been adopted to offset the effects of "fashionable lateness" among spectators. Matinee performances, also introduced in the 19th century, had become standard by 1900.

Every theatre had a paid claque to insure correct and adequate response. Some actors even specified in their contracts the amount of applause they were to receive at their first entrance in each play. As a result of this paid approval, other spectators tended to restrict overt response to disapproval.

The government controlled advertising. Bills, all of a uniform size, were posted together at a specified place. Each theatre was assigned a specific color to distinguish its bills. Throughout the century, the government collected eleven percent of all tickets receipts as a "poor tax." Ticket agencies had appeared by 1900 and were accused of buying up all seats for popular plays so that they might resell them at advanced prices.

Spectators at Parisian theatres had to present their tickets to three persons: the theatre's official ticket taker, the government employee who made a record of the poor tax, and the representative of the Society of Dramatic Authors who calculated royalties. The Society of Dramatic Authors, which had succeeded the Bureau Dramatique in 1829, was a "closed shop" that boycotted any theatre refusing to accept its authority over contracts. The standard contract specified the maximum permissible delay between the acceptance and production of a play, required that each play be performed at least three times, and allowed a cessation of rehearsals for ten days so that the author might revise his work. Dramatists received from 10 to 15 percent of each performance's receipts. The society also established a pension fund for playwrights who had been members for more than 20 years, and who had had more than a minimum number of plays produced. Before 1900, the dramatist's copyright had also been extended to his lifetime plus 50 years. French playwrights were the first in the world to collect a royalty for each performance of their works and to achieve the financial security of a pension fund.

Acting and Directing

During the 19th century, acting and directing moved toward more illusionistic detail. For example, melodrama and romantic plays emphasized powerful emotions and provided opportunities to portray situations, especially violence and death, previously banished from view. Rachel's playing of Adrienne Lecouvreur's death throes aroused both admiration and horror because of its lifelikeness. In addition to this emotional realism, interest grew in creating the illusion of everyday life. As plays based on contemporary situations proliferated after 1850, ever-increasing attention was given to the minutiae of daily existence. Each step toward greater lifelikeness was deplored by critics who believed that art should idealize rather than copy life, and even those who approved of the trend usually denounced any attempt to represent sordidness on the stage. Consequently, until Antoine's time, stage realism seldom went beyond picturesque local color, historical accuracy in visual detail, or typical middle-class milieus.

Melodrama initiated a concern for "directing," for much of its effect depended upon the precise manipulation of coincidence and spectacle. Plots often revolved around overheard conversations, fortunate entrances, and spectacular feats of physical courage, and the resolutions often saw the villain foiled by an earthquake, a volcanic eruption, or some other fortuitous cataclysm. The effectiveness of many melodramas, therefore, depended upon the precise coordination of many elements. It was for this reason that Pixérécourt insisted upon absolute control over the staging of his works. He later declared that his preeminence as a dramatist was due to his care in production. Pixérécourt was probably the first French director in the modern sense; Hugo, Dumas *père*, Sardou, and several other dramatists continued Pixérécourt's practices and were among the century's outstanding directors as well as writers. Most of them were concerned primarily with picturesque local color, historical accuracy, or precision of action, however, rather than with creating the illusion of daily life.

Through most of the century actors tended to form a semicircle at the front of the stage for all scenes and to retire upstage when they had no lines. This pattern was only gradually broken. By 1835, critics were noting that a few actors had begun to sit on the arms of chairs, to lean on tables, and even to remain seated while speaking. Both Sardou and Dumas *fils* credit Adolphe Montigny (1805–80), director of the Gymnase theatre, with making the first significant break with the past. Beginning around 1853, Montigny placed a table downstage center in order to prevent the semicircular formation. Next, he put chairs around the table, seated the actors, and made them speak to each other rather than to the audience, as had been typical in the past. Finally, he furnished his settings like real rooms and placed properties, such as cigar boxes, handkerchiefs, or letters, about the stage to motivate movement from one place to another. In this way, he gradually arrived at an illusion of real life. According to Sardou, Montigny's success encouraged others to adopt his innovations.

Many practices prevented the achievement of complete illusion or perfect ensemble. Supernumeraries were almost always recruited off the streets, and they rarely rehearsed with the company before performing. Most theatres employed someone to secure and rehearse the supernumeraries and to provide leadership on stage during performances. Often the group differed each night. Furthermore, the emphasis during the 19th century upon starring actors worked against ensemble effects. After 1850, it became increasingly common for managers to build productions around stars, while the rest of the company merely filled in. Even the Comédie Française did not escape entirely from this trend, and the actors there were especially loath to give up any of their authority to a director.

Actors continued to be employed according to lines of business until about 1875, when the trend toward long runs had begun to undermine the repertory system which had encouraged the traditional classifications. Type casting continued, nevertheless, and lines of business were not completely abandoned until the 20th century. Most French actors still received their training while in service, but the Conservatoire, attached to the Comédie Française, assumed increasing importance in theatrical life, especially as the repertory system began to decline.

By the late 19th century, the theatre was in a state of transition. Most companies now employed a director and two or three assistants to oversee the various aspects of staging and performance. In spite of the greatly increased attention to all aspects of production, however, a unifying approach was still lacking. Since all parts of a production were assigned to different individuals who worked independently of each other, the overall effect was disjointed. The theatre awaited someone to weld these individually conceived elements into an artistic whole.

Actors

The leading actors between 1790 and 1825 were Talma, Mlle. Duchenois, Mlle. Mars, Fleury, and Mlle. George. François-Joseph Talma (1763–1826), often called the greatest of all French actors, spent much of his youth in England, but returned to France in 1785 and was one of the first students at the École Royale Dramatique when it opened in 1786. Entering the Comédie Française in 1787, he was a constant source of friction because of his dissatisfaction with the troupe's acting style, costuming practices, and politics. He attained his first success in 1789 in *Charles IX,* a work which contributed to the separation of the company in 1791. After the troupe was reunited in 1799, Talma remained its acknowledged leader until his death. He was a favorite of Napoleon, who often summoned him to play before the rulers of Europe. Talma was devoted to authenticity in costume and to detailed study of every role. To this care, he joined intense feeling and vigor. It is sometimes said that he was by temperament a Romantic but by circumstance doomed to perform in neo-classical plays.

Mlle. Duchenois (Catherine Rafuin, *c.* 1777–1835) was Talma's usual companion in tragedy. In 1802 her debut as Phèdre was so successful that the play was repeated for eight nights. Although she was notoriously ugly, her "profound tenderness and melodious sorrow" won her a devoted following. She seldom played after Talma's death and retired altogether in 1830.

While Talma and Mlle. Duchenois dominated tragic acting, Mlle. Mars and Fleury were the most famous performers of comedy. Mlle. Mars (Anne Boutet, 1779–1847), on the stage from childhood, joined the Comédie Française in 1799 and after 1805 was the idol of Paris. All critics spoke of her in glowing terms. Although noted for her shrewishness offstage, as an actress she seemed the ideal woman. When the Comédie Française began to go into debt in the 1830's, she resigned as a *sociétaire* so that she might demand an exorbitant salary as a *pensionnaire,* thus setting a precedent that was to plague the troupe through much of the century. She continued to play young heroines until her retirement at the age of 62.

Abraham-Joseph Fleury (1750–1822) joined the Comédie Française in 1778 and taught at the Conservatoire from its founding in 1786. His elegant manner in comedy made him a fit companion for Mlle. Mars. He retired in 1818.

Mlle. George (Marguerite Weymer, 1787–1835), daughter of a provincial manager, made her debut at the Comédie Française in 1802 at the age of 15. Her rivalry with Mlle. Duchenois was intensified when Napoleon took her as his mistress, and the Empress Josephine retaliated by taking Mlle. Duchenois under her protection. In 1808, Mlle. George left Paris to play in St. Petersburg, Stockholm, and elsewhere before returning in 1813. After Napoleon's downfall, she fled France once more until 1822. After this time her career was bound up with that of Jean-Charles Harel, manager of the Porte Saint-Martin and Odéon theatres. Harel was very sympathetic to the Romantics and produced many of their plays. In these, Mlle. George played the heroines and did much to popularize the new drama.

Melodrama and romantic plays brought many Boulevard actors to the fore. Of these, the most popular were Mme. Dorval, Bocage, and Deburau. Mme. Dorval (Marie Delaunay, 1798–1849), after studying at the Conservatoire, played for a time in the provinces before joining the Porte Saint-Martin troupe in 1818. Here she played in melodrama until the theatre was permitted to perform other genres. An intuitive actress, she was best at portraying vehement emotion and seductive charm. She declined a position at the Comédie Française because that company refused to include several of her vehicles in its repertory.

Bocage (Pierre-François Touze, 1797–1863), a weaver in his youth, was admitted to a provincial company largely because of his handsomeness. After being refused an engagement at the Comédie Française in 1821, he turned to the Boulevard theatres, where he was soon regarded as the greatest stage lover of his day. After 1845 he also served as manager of the Odéon.

Jean-Gaspard Deburau (1796–1846) was born into a family of touring acrobats. In 1811, he settled in Paris, where he was associated principally with the Théâtre des Funambules. His fame came after 1825 as he developed the character, Pierrot, a pale, lovesick, ever-hopeful seeker after happiness. In this role, he became one of the most popular performers in Paris.

The most renowned romantic actor of France, Frédérick Lemaître (1800–76), entered the Conservatoire at the age of 15, and performed at the circus in pantomime and melodrama while still undergoing this rigorous classical training. In 1823, he achieved renown by turning the villain of a melodrama into a comic caricature. Thereafter he took considerable liberties with his roles until he was employed by Harel at the Odéon and Porte Saint-Martin, where he became a dedicated performer. Lemaître was the most versatile actor of his day, for he refused to be bound by the usual lines of business. He delighted in astonishing audiences by novel interpretations and passionate outbursts. The peak of his popularity was reached between 1830 and 1850, but he went on acting until his death, long after his popularity had waned.

Of similar temperament but performing an entirely different kind of repertory, Rachel (Elisa Félix, 1820–58) epitomized the tempestuous actress. The daughter of a peddler, she was befriended while a child street singer and sent to a dramatic school. Withdrawn by her father who wished to exploit her talent, she made her professional debut in 1837 at the Gymnase. In 1838, she was engaged at the Comédie Française, where she soon became its greatest attraction. She refused to become a *sociétaire,* however, and insisted upon an enormous salary (as much as 10,000 francs for each appearance). Her performances revived the popularity of the classical repertory, which had declined markedly after romanticism came to the fore. While she filled the Comédie Française on the nights when she played, she impoverished the company by taking most of the receipts. Largely because of this experience, the Comédie has since that time refused to give any performer star billing, all actors being listed according to seniority.

Rachel's repertory was restricted to about 12 roles, only one of which, Scribe's Adrienne Lecouvreur, was from a contemporary play. She was unsuited to comedy and could not portray tenderness, womanly softness, gaiety, or heartiness; her strength lay in scorn, triumph, rage, malignity, and lust. Within her range, however, she had no peers. By 1841 she was in demand for foreign tours and began to play throughout Europe; in 1855 she appeared in America. Tuberculosis brought a decline in her powers, and in her last years she conserved her strength for the great moments and rushed through other scenes. Nevertheless, her intensity and power established a standard remembered through the rest of the century.

In the last half of the century, the Comédie Française attracted a number of excellent actors. Among the best were Gôt, Coquelin, Worms, and Mounet-Sully. Edmond Gôt (1822–1901), at the Comédie Française from 1844, was noted for his excellent performances in classical and contemporary comedy. Constant-Benoît Coquelin (1841–1909) performed at the Comédie Française from 1860 to 1886, after which he toured throughout the world before settling in Paris as manager of the Porte Saint-Martin theatre. Here he created the role of Cyrano de Bergerac, written especially for him. At his best in Molière's comic roles or in flamboyant romantic parts, Coquelin was noted for his mastery of acting techniques, about which he often wrote in such works as *The Art of the Actor* (1889).

Gustave-Hippolyte Worms (1836–1910), who made his debut at the Comédie Française in 1858, played young lovers in both comedy and tragedy. After a successful engagement in Russia, he returned to the company in 1877. Much admired for his "natural" acting, he was also a teacher at the Conservatoire.

Mounet-Sully (Jean-Sully Mounet, 1841–1916) entered the Comédie Française in 1872 and was soon considered the best tragic actor of his day. With his striking physique, beautiful voice, and fiery temperament, he brought considerable originality to all the great tragic roles in both the classical and romantic repertory.

BERNHARDT AND MOUNET-SULLY in Racine's *Phèdre*. [From a contemporary lithograph]

The most famous actress of the late 19th century was Sarah Bernhardt (1845–1923). After performing at the Comédie Française from 1862 to 1880, she resigned because of her impatience with the troupe's traditions. The rest of her career was devoted to starring tours throughout the world and to the management of a series of Parisian theatres. Noted for her slim figure, dark eyes, "golden" voice, and her portrayals of seductiveness, pain, tearful rage, and death, she achieved her greatest success as Camille, Tosca, Adrienne Lecouvreur, Phaedra, Dona Sol in *Hernani,* and the title role in Rostand's *L'Aiglon.* Her mastery of the techniques of acting and her magnetic personality combined to create an image of the "grand actress."

As this brief summary indicates, the great 19th century actors achieved international reputations, and after 1850 worldwide tours were frequent.

Although these tours probably did much to establish high standards, they are also symptomatic of the craze for starring performers. Motion pictures were to continue and exploit this taste even further.

Theatre Architecture

It would be impossible to discuss all of the theatre buildings of Paris between 1790 and 1900. Not only did the ever-increasing number of troupes lead to the construction of new buildings, but a large percentage of the theatres were rebuilt either because of fires or Napoleon III's (reigned 1852–70) replanning of Paris, which destroyed many structures to make way for a network of "grand boulevards."

One of the few theatre buildings to survive was that occupied by the Comédie Française. Built in 1785 by Victor Louis, already famous as the architect of the Bordeaux theatre, it was intended for the Opéra. After a complex chain of intrigues led to its rejection by that company, it was acquired by the Variétés Amusantes, which later amalgamated with one branch of the Comédie Française as the Théâtre de la République. In 1799, when the troupe was reunited, the theatre passed into the possession of the Comédie Française. The building was partially destroyed by fire in 1900, but was rebuilt according to the original plans. Thus, with the exception of some interior remodeling, the present Comédie Française follows the design of 1785. Having been built for the Opéra, this theatre was more elaborate than those intended for drama, and, perhaps for this reason, it has continued to meet the needs of the company.

Although not housed in such historic buildings, two other stage troupes still occupy sites important in the 18th century. After the Revolution, the Odéon acquired the theatre which had been built for the Comédie Française in 1782. Burned and rebuilt twice by 1818, it is the present home of the state-subsidized Théâtre de France. The Opéra-Comique, after occupying a number of buildings, settled in its present home on the site of the theatre built for the Comédie Italienne in 1783.

The Opéra occupied a series of buildings before moving to its present site in 1874. This structure in many ways marks the culmination of trends which had begun during the Italian Renaissance. Since it is both indicative of the 19th century ideal and the end of a tradition, it merits detailed attention.

Designed by Charles Garnier, begun in 1862, and completed in 1874, the Opéra cost about 40 million francs. Enormous foyers and stairways lead to the auditorium with its four levels of galleries. The seating capacity is about 2100 persons. A proscenium arch 55 feet wide frames a

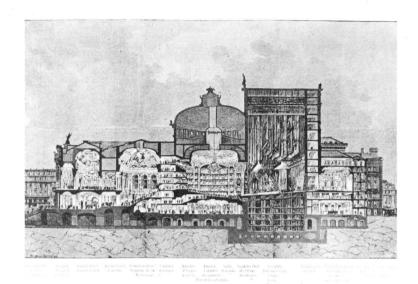

SECTIONAL PLAN of the Paris Opera opened in
1874. [From *Monde Illustré* (February 6, 1875)]

stage 175 feet wide by 85 feet deep. The depth can be increased to about
150 feet by including the dance salon immediately behind the stage. The
floor from the front of the stage to the back of the dance studio is raked
upward two inches in every 40 inches. Above the stage there is 119 feet of
space, and below it 50 feet. The stage floor is divided from front to back
into ten sections, or *plans,* each of which is subdivided into (1) several slots
about 1½ inches wide, (2) narrow traps about 18 inches wide, and (3)
larger traps about 40 inches wide. Any part of a subdivision or entire plan
can be opened the width of the proscenium arch. This flexibility permits
the operation of almost any effect from beneath the stage. Scenery is shifted
by chariots, each about 10 feet long and with four upright poles upon
which flats can be mounted. In addition, scenery may be flown or moved
through the stage traps. When it was built, this was the most elaborate
theatre in the world.

A number of minor changes occurred in theatre architecture during
the 19th century. Although the Parisian theatres were by no means uniform in design, they tended to follow the same basic pattern. By 1900 an
area forward of the stage, called the "orchestra," was fitted out with
comfortable arm chairs. This kind of seat was introduced at the Opéra-
Comique in 1840 and gradually adopted by other theatres. The rest of the
ground floor was occupied by the pit, which continued to use the less
comfortable benches. Throughout the century, women were forbidden in
most theatres to sit in the orchestra or pit. The ground floor was surrounded by a row of boxes, or *baignoires,* above which rose two or three

additional galleries. In the first, two or three rows of chairs were backed by boxes, while the second gallery was devoted entirely to boxes and the third entirely to benches. The more fashionable theatres had a number of lavish *loges à salon,* fitted up like sitting rooms complete with bell cords, so that the occupants could ring for service during the performances. The seating capacity of the theatres averaged from 1200 to 2000. Not until near the end of the century was there much concern for safety. The aisles were narrow and often filled with folding chairs; there were no fire exits and ventilation was minimal. After 400 persons perished in the fire which destroyed the Opéra-Comique in 1887, attention was at last turned to greater safety.

The proscenium arch was usually very high in order to provide adequate sightlines for spectators in the galleries, which not only rose to the ceiling but extended along the sides of the auditorium to the proscenium. The proscenium arch was also usually very thick, for in most theatres a box was set into it on the level of each gallery. This thickness created a wide apron which was much used by the actors, especially before realism was fully established. The prompter was housed in a box at the front of the apron. The floor of the stage raked up toward the rear. The chariot-and-pole system remained the usual method of scene shifting, although it was supplemented by flying and the movement of set pieces by hand. During the 19th century, space above and below the stage was greatly enlarged to permit more effective handling of the increasingly detailed settings.

Scenic Practices

Although local color and historically accurate motifs had been introduced before the Revolution, they were not exploited fully until the 19th century. During the 1790's many theatrical entertainments sought to recreate actual places and real events, but a consistent emphasis upon spectacle is first evident in the Boulevard theatres between 1800 and 1830. Here it served at least two major functions: as a plot device in dramatic action and as a novelty designed to attract audiences. Both promoted the increased use of detailed settings and special effects.

Early 19th century melodramas often depended upon natural disasters to forward the plot. For example, Pixérécourt's *Daughter of the Exile* shows a flood uprooting trees, inundating the stage, and carrying the heroine away on a plank. Similarly, his *Death's Head* uses a volcanic eruption to engulf the stage and foil the villain. The Cirque Olympique recreated famous battles, using a troupe of more than 100 persons and 30 horses, in which a troupe of cavalry not uncommonly arrived at the crucial moment. Thus, many of the Boulevard plays depended heavily upon spectacle to keep plots moving or to resolve them.

Emphasis was also placed on the novelty of the spectacle. Playwrights sought to include new places or examples of local color never before represented on the stage. Consequently, a variety of historical periods, exotic locales, and fantastic settings appeared.

Spectacle was so highly developed by 1828 that the new Ambigu-Comique opened with a play in which the "Muse of the Mise-en-Scéne" demanded admission to Mount Parnassus. As evidence of her worth, she displayed all the scenic marvels of the theatre and so impressed the other Muses that she was granted admission to their ranks. Nevertheless, spectacle did little to enrich characterization, for usually it merely provided variety in an otherwise routine story.

During this period two designers, Daguerre and Ciceri, laid the foundations for many later developments. Daguerre is especially important for his work with the panorama and diorama, which brought illusion ever closer to reality. The panorama, invented and patented by Robert Barker in 1787, was first seen in Edinburgh in 1788 and in London in 1792. Robert Fulton (1765–1815), an associate of Barker and later the inventor of the steamboat, secured a French patent on the panorama in 1799. He then sold it to an American, James Thayer, who opened two panoramas in Paris in 1800.

Panoramas were displayed in circular buildings in which the audience, occupying a central platform, was completely surrounded by a continuous painting. To the spectator, the total effect was that of being set down at a spot from which he had a view in every direction.

Louis-Jacques Daguerre (1787–1851) began his career as an assistant to Pierre Prévost (1764–1823), one of the first painters of panoramas, but his interest in optics, which was to culminate in the invention of the Daguerreotype, led him to experiment with variations on the panorama. Thus, in 1822 he began to display his Diorama. Here the spectator was not surrounded by the painting, but rather sat on a platform which revolved every 15 minutes to show him one of two different paintings, each about 71 feet wide by 45 feet high, on proscenium-like stages. Daguerre's improvement lay in his ability to create the illusion of constant change. While Daguerre's partially transparent scenery remained stationary, he varied its appearance by manipulating the direction, intensity, and color of the natural light which entered through overhead openings. By controlling light, he was able to depict the gradual change from fair weather to storm, from day to night, and through many other conditions. Daguerre was not long content with his accomplishment, and soon perfected the *diorama à double effet*. Here some details were painted on the front and some on the rear of a transparent cloth. Through changes of light, Daguerre could make details visible or invisible. One of his most famous dioramas, "Midnight Mass at St. Étienne-du-Mont," showed the church empty by day, its gradual filling with people for the midnight mass, and its return to emptiness.

The panorama was displayed throughout the world in the early 19th century and was soon adapted to theatrical needs. It was always more useful in the theatre than the diorama because it did not depend upon the manipulation of stage lighting. On the other hand, the panorama had to be altered considerably for stage purposes, since it could no longer surround the audience; thus, it assumed the shape which Daguerre adopted for his dioramas. Perhaps for this reason, after the 1820's the terms panorama and diorama were often used interchangeably.

A STAGE DESIGN by Daguerre (1822). Note how the distant view of the Alps is framed by the foreground structures. [From a contemporary lithograph]

Moving panoramas were introduced into the theatre in the early 19th century. For these, a continuous scene was painted on a cloth of enormous length, suspended from an overhead track, and attached at either end to an upright roller, or "spool." When the spool was turned, the cloth moved across the stage. In this way, characters, ships, horses and carriages, while remaining in full view, apparently moved from one place to another without any abrupt change in the setting, as would have been necessary had wings and drops been used. Before the end of the 19th century, the moving panorama was coupled with "treadmills" for such scenes as the chariot race

TREADMILLS and a moving panorama used to create the effect of a horserace. [From *L'Illustration* (14 March 1891)]

in *Ben Hur,* for which the stadium was painted on a panorama and moved past the galloping horses, which were kept on stage by the treadmills.

The panorama and diorama also permitted designers to dispense with sky borders, which by the early 19th century were considered unsatisfactory, since they destroyed illusion by making breaks in the sky. Panoramas permitted a new arrangement. Flats representing architectural units or natural objects were erected at the front of the stage to form an arch, through which was seen a distant view painted on a panorama curving across the back and down the sides of the stage. Not only did this eliminate sky borders, but an entire scene, with the exception of the downstage masking pieces, could be painted on a continuous surface. This practice eventually led to the development of the neutral cyclorama to surround the acting area.

The panorama and diorama, then, contributed in many ways to illusionism. In Paris, their theatrical uses were first fully exploited at the Panorama-Dramatique, where between 1821 and 1823, panoramic spectacles with only two characters made up the entire repertory.

While Daguerre contributed to scenic design primarily through his experiments with optical illusion, Pierre-Luc-Charles Ciceri (1782–1868) was the most influential designer of the period, probably because of his ability to depict the favorite visual themes of the time: quaint local color, nostalgic ruins, and picturesque historical milieus. From about 1810, Ciceri was the Opéra's principal designer, but he also worked for the Opéra-Comique, Comédie Française, Porte Saint-Martin, Panorama-Dramatique, and other theatres. After 1822, he was in such demand that he opened the first scenic studio in Paris. Here he eventually employed specialists (one for architectural details, another for landscapes, and so on), a practice which was to prolong the use of different designers for a single production. From Ciceri's time, the independent scenic studio began to replace those maintained by individual theatres. After 1850, Ciceri was supplanted by his students, who dominated stage design for the rest of the century. Among these the most important were Charles-Antoine Cambon (1802–75), Charles Séchan (1803–74), Edouard Desplechin (1802–70), and Philippe Chaperon (1823–1907).

Décor d'Oedipe roi, par Chaperon. (Gravure extraite de la *Revue des Arts décoratifs*, année 1881–1882.)

SETTING by Chaperon for *Oedipus Rex*. [From *Revue des Arts Décoratifs* (1881–82)]

Interest in spectacle accelerated after 1820. The new Opéra, opened in 1822, incorporated all of the latest developments, including gas lighting and a water system for realistic fountains and waterfalls. After 1825, when Baron Taylor was appointed its supervisor, even the Comédie Française began to follow the new trends. Taylor, previously director of the Panorama-Dramatique, employed Ciceri in 1826 to provide historically accurate settings for a number of plays.

After 1828, interest in spectacle led to the publication of *livrets scéniques,* or promptbooks, describing in detail scenery and special effects used in the Parisian theatres, with suggestions for simplifying spectacle in less well-equipped theatres. After 1830 concern for historical accuracy increased, for the romantic playwrights were scornful of the inconsistencies often seen in production of melodramas. Hugo consulted the Commission on Historical Monuments and other sources before making the sketches which he provided for his plays. Dumas *père* often publicly castigated producers who failed to provide sufficiently accurate spectacle for his works.

By 1840, dramatic critics were giving detailed accounts of scenery, costumes, and lighting seen in the theatre and often criticized even the fairy-tale pantomimes for alleged inaccuracies. The classical repertory, for which the *palais à volonté* had continued in use, largely escaped the trend toward historical accuracy until 1842, when the revival of *Le Cid,* with its six new settings, established a new pattern.

The movement toward historical realism reached its peak in the late 19th century with Sardou's spectacles, which were so detailed that even the Naturalists praised them. *Hatred* (1874), set in Medieval Siena, used armor costing 120,000 francs, costumes costing 192,000 francs, and settings costing 60,000 francs, unprecedented expenditures for a stage play.

Although local color and historical accuracy were the most popular forms of scenic illusionism, realism of daily life also made headway. Under its impact, the box set, complete with ceiling, gradually came into use for interior scenes. It is impossible to say when the box set was first used, but it probably developed out of tentative beginnings in the late 18th century. By the 1820's, it was no longer unusual. Only gradually, however, was it furnished with complete realism, for until 1850 most of the properties and furniture were mere painted cut-outs. In 1846, *Pierre Fevrier* created a sensation with its real furnishings and its decorated floor cloth, simulating black and white marble squares, the first seen in Paris. After 1850, realistic details increased markedly. By 1876, *My Friend Fritz* at the Comédie Fran-çaise featured a farmyard in which real water flowed from a pump and real cherries were picked from the trees; in another scene, real food and drink were consumed onstage.

By the end of the 19th century, methods of obtaining scenery were relatively standardized. The director, after consultation with the play-wright, gave a summary of requirements to the scenic designers, who then made cardboard models of the sets. When these were approved, scale drawings were made to guide the theatre's carpenters, who built the settings. After completion, the scenery was sent to one of Paris' five or six scenic studios for painting. Each theatre hired a relatively small number of stagehands, for since French plays almost never changed place within acts, shifting was usually confined to intermissions when haste was not of major concern.

In 1900 the same settings were still being used for many different plays. Thus, while a company might have many more settings than in the 18th century, it did not consider it necessary to have specially designed scenery for each play. Furthermore, since the various settings for a single production were often designed by different artists, unity was still lacking.

BACKSTAGE at a theatre in the late 19th century. Note the division of the floor; note also the poles supporting the flats. [From Pougin, *Dictionnaire du Théâtre* (1884)]

Costume Practices

As with scenery, costuming between 1790 and 1900 paid increasing attention to realistic detail. In the early years, Talma did much to popularize historical accuracy in tragic costuming. As early as 1787 he startled audiences by appearing in a toga with bare arms and legs, the first attempt to achieve authenticity in classical dress. Although a consistent approach was long in developing, progress was steady. Comedy, slower to accept the new trends, continued to be performed in contemporary dress until after 1815. Gradually 17th century garments were adopted for Molière's plays, although Mlle. Mars refused to accept the changes and continued to wear the latest fashions. Talma's influence was reenforced by that of Baron Taylor when he became superintendent of the Comédie Française in 1825. After 1830, the Romantics further accelerated the trend toward historical accuracy, and by 1840 critics were universally scornful of anachronisms.

Nevertheless, the changes were only gradually reflected in the hiring of personnel. After 1850, theatres began to employ special designers for

Costumes for Dumas' *Don Juan de Marana*
(1836). [From *Revue du Théâtre* (1836)]

historical plays and increased their staffs of tailors and seamstresses to
construct and maintain garments. Special supply houses were founded to
meet the demand for armor and other articles too difficult to be made by
the theatres. Professional wig makers supplied wigs and several hairdressers
were hired to assist the actors. By the late 19th century, Racinet's *Le
Costume Historique* (completed 1888) had become the standard guide
both for the design and storage of costumes.

Costume practices were not completely revolutionized, however, for
many actors continued to supply their own wardrobes and the actresses
were often outfitted by the *grand couturiers*. Even when a manager employed a costume designer, the leading actors felt free to supply their own
dress and were often praised by critics for their novel touches. Although
consistency was most nearly achieved in historical spectacles, even here it
was seldom complete. As with scenery, the same costumes were used for
many different plays.

Lighting

Lighting continued 18th century practices until 1822, when the Opéra
introduced gas. The flexibility and greater intensity of gas light soon led
other theatres to adopt it, although the Comédie Française did not install it
until 1843. Even then, the Comédie retained its oil footlights because
the actresses considered gas light too harsh. Allowing greater control over
intensity and direction, gas encouraged more realistic lighting effects. Since
spotlights had not yet been invented, however, stage lighting still consisted
primarily of general illumination.

The movement toward more specific illumination dates from the 1840's, when experiments with the carbon arc and limelight began in France. In 1846 a carbon arc was used at the Opéra to create the effect of a rising sun, and in 1860 a carbon arc was equipped with a hood and lens to create the first effective spotlight. Originally used as "follow" spots or for special effects, these spotlights were only gradually exploited in the modern manner; their full potentialities were not realized until the 20th century.

Electricity began to replace gas shortly after the incandescent lamp was invented in 1879. The Opéra introduced some of the new lamps in 1880 and lighted its stage entirely with electricity after 1886. The Comédie Française changed to electricity in 1887, the same year in which a fire, attributed to gas, took 400 lives at the Opéra-Comique and hastened the adoption of electricity by all theatres. Since incandescent lamps were still weak in intensity, they had to be supplemented by the more powerful carbon arcs and limelights. By 1900, the equipment for "modern" lighting was becoming available, but its use still awaited development.

The 19th century, then, brought increased attention to every aspect of theatrical production. Still missing, however, was a theory of theatrical production capable of welding the diverse elements into a unified whole. In the 1880's, this need began to be articulated and met. The results will be discussed when we turn to the modern theatre.

Theatre and Drama in Italy in the 19th Century

Between 1800 and 1861, Italy was preoccupied with political developments. During the Napoleonic Wars, it was overrun by France, who merged many of the smaller states and reduced the power of the church over temporal affairs. During this period, the national consciousness was awakened for the first time. The fall of Napoleon in 1815 brought the return of conditions much like those that had existed before 1800. The reinstatement of foreigners as rulers over many of the states served to keep alive the desire for independence and Italian unity; following a series of rebellions in 1848, Italy finally became a nation in 1861. Drama tended to reflect these events.

Until 1815 tragedy followed the example of Alfieri and comedy that of Goldoni, but immediately after the fall of Napoleon, romanticism was introduced into Italy with the publication of Mme. de Staël's *Of Germany*. Since it was soon associated with liberalism and nationalism, romanticism served to bring literary and political interests together.

Only a few important dramatists emerged. Ugo Foscolo (1778–1827), with his *I Sepolcro* (1807) and *Ajace* (1809), is usually considered a precursor of romanticism. Partially because he was forced to flee Italy in 1815, Foscolo's works were popular throughout this period. The first important romantic dramatist, Alessandro Manzoni (1785–1873), combined religious themes and liberal political sentiments in such plays as *The Count of Carmagnola* (1820) and *Adelchi* (1822). By far the most famous writer of the period, however, was Giambattista Niccolini (1782–1861), a Florentine professor who wrote in the style of Alfieri before turning to romanticism. His plays, by pointing clear parallels between present and past events, consistently urged liberation from foreign rule and church influence. Although they now seem dull, his *Giovanni da Procida* (1830) and *Arnaldo da Brescia* (1843) inspired Italians with their sense of national destiny.

After the union of Italy in 1861, political sentiments no longer provided dramatists with themes capable of transcending regional interests. Because each area clung to its own customs and dialect, most playwrights wrote with a particular region in mind. Since 1861 Italian writers have only rarely captured the national consciousness, and even fewer have achieved international fame.

Scene design in Italy followed the same general trends as in France. Among the more important designers were Lorenzo Sacchetti (1759–1829), who worked in Venice, Vienna, and Prague; Alessandro Sanquirico (1777–1849) of the Teatro alla Scala in Milan; and Antonio de Pian (1784–1851), who worked in Venice and Vienna. Although Italy continued a leader in opera, its influence lessened. The outstanding Italian composers spent much of their lives in France and elsewhere, and the worldwide demand for Italian performers and scenic artists declined. In Germany, where Italian opera troupes had been common since the 17th century, the last foreign company was dismissed in 1832. Elsewhere, native performers gradually replaced Italians. Stars continued to be welcomed everywhere, but other Italian personnel were less popular.

Opera continued to dominate the theatrical life of Italy, and the few dramatic companies were forced to tour. This inconvenience, however, brought many actors wide fame. Three performers, Ristori, Salvini, and Rossi, achieved international acclaim.

Adelaide Ristori (1822–1906) was on the stage from the age of 12. At 14, she was playing leading roles in the company of Giuseppe Moncalvo (1781–1859). In 1838 she joined the Royal Theatre at Turin, where she received formal training in classical poetic drama. By 1850 she was famous throughout Italy for her studious and regal performances and in 1853 took her company to Paris. From that time until 1885, when she retired, she toured throughout Europe; she made four visits to America and in 1874 went around the world. Although she made no striking innovations, she raised the received tradition to new heights.

Tomasso Salvini (1829–1915) began his career at the age of 14 in the troupe of Gustavo Modena (1803–61) at Padua. By 1848 he was in Ri-

SETTING by Sanquirico for Meyerbeer's *Il Crociato in Egitto*
at the Teatro alla Scala, 1826. [From Sanquirico's *Raccolta
di varie Decorazioni sceniche* (1828)]

stori's company in Rome, where he won his first fame as Alfieri's Orestes.
Around 1860 he began a series of international tours. Salvini excelled as
Macbeth, Lear, Alfieri's heroes and, above all, as Othello. An actor of great
passion and energy, he is said to have terrified his leading ladies because of
his complete absorption in his roles. Throughout the world, Salvini's name
became synonymous with fiery tragic acting. He retired in 1890.

Ernesto Rossi (1829–96) entered the theatre in 1846, replacing Salvini in Modena's company. He later performed with Ristori, and in 1857
took his own troupe to Vienna. After that time, he toured all over the
world in plays by Alfieri and Shakespeare. A polished performer, he was
considered by many too studied, an opinion which probably explains his
failure to rival the fame of Ristori and Salvini.

Italy's contribution to theatre and drama in the 19th century, then,
was minor. For the most part, it followed old traditions or adopted new
trends after they were established elsewhere.

The Theatre in Spain, 1700–1875

After the death of Calderón in 1681, the Spanish theatre rapidly
declined. Until well into the 18th century, writers sought unsuccessfully to
recapture the glory of the Golden Age, and theatres drew their repertories
primarily from the past. During the 18th century, many attempts were

made to turn attention to the neo-classical ideal. Under Philip V (reigned 1700–46), Louis XIV's grandson, a Spanish Academy was formed, and Ignacio de Luzán (1702–54) sought through his critical treatises to familiarize his countrymen with neo-classical principles. Despite these efforts, no playwright adopted the new mode until after 1750.

Under Carlos III (reigned 1759–88) *autos sacramentales* were abandoned in 1765 and the public theatres were forbidden to perform religious plays. By the end of his reign, the popularity of 17th century plays was at last being challenged by neo-classical dramas. Most of the new works were translations, but native tragedy was accepted after the appearance of Vincente García de la Huerta's *La Raquel* (1778) and Lopez de Ayala's *Destruction of Numancia* (1778), while neo-classical comedy was established by Tomás de Iriarte's *The Pampered Youth* (1788) and *The Ill-Bred Miss* (1791).

By far the most important dramatist of the 18th century was Leandro Fernández de Moratín (1760–1828). The son of a writer, he spent some time in Paris in the 1780's before writing his own plays between 1786 and 1805. Moratin's acknowledged masterpiece is *The Consent of Young Maidens* (1805), which tells of the rivalry between an uncle and nephew for the hand of a young girl. Unlike most plays on this theme, Moratin's concentrates upon character rather than intrigue; all of the complications stem from the inability of the young people to be frank with their elders. Because of its truthful observation and sincerity, *The Consent of Young Maidens* is considered the best Spanish play between 1680 and modern times.

If Moratín was the finest playwright of his age, Ramón de la Cruz (1731–94) was the most popular. Originally a writer of comedies, in 1764 he turned to the *zarzuela,* which he transformed by banishing the mythological figures and replacing them with contemporary character types. In this form, the *zarzuela* has continued to be one of the most popular Spanish dramatic genres. Cruz also achieved renown for his *sainetes,* or one-act farces performed between the acts of longer works.

Theatrical conditions changed little during the 18th century. In Madrid, the Corral de la Cruz and the Corral del Príncipe continued to be the only public theatres performing Spanish drama. In the 1740's the original structures were replaced (the Teatro de la Cruz in 1743 and the Teatro del Príncipe in 1745), but the only important change was the addition of a proscenium arch. Moratín states that the scenic practices and other customs continued to be those of the Golden Age.

A third theatre, the Caños del Peral, was built by an Italian troupe in 1708. After 1715, it was used entirely for opera, then in great favor with the court and aristocracy. Farinelli (Carlo Broschi, 1705–82), the greatest opera singer of his age, came to Spain in 1737 and staged lavish operas at the Buen Retiro palace between 1747 and 1759.

SCENE from Moratín's *The Consent of Young Maidens.* [From the original edition of the play]

During the last part of the 18th century many attempts were made to reform the public theatres, but almost nothing was accomplished until Isodoro Maiquez (1768–1820) came to the fore. The son of an actor, Maiquez made his debut at the Teatro del Príncipe in 1791. Around 1800 he went to Paris, where he is said to have studied with Talma, whose ideals he attempted to realize in the Spanish theatre upon his return. Maiquez became head of the Príncipe troupe and was able to turn acting away from the old declamatory style to a more natural delivery.

Significant progress was thwarted, however, by political events. Napoleon's brother, crowned king of Spain in 1808, was replaced in 1815 by one of the most repressive regimes in Europe. Consequently, many of Spain's writers lived abroad until conditions eased after the death of Ferdinand VII in 1833. Most spent the years of exile in Paris, where they witnessed the romantic revolution.

The Spanish counterpart of the battle over *Hernani* came in 1835 with the production of Angel de Saavedra's (1791–1865) *Don Alvaro, o la Fuerza del Sino*. Although its success established romanticism in Spain, the vogue was short-lived and declined rapidly after 1840. Among the more important romantic dramatists were Martínez de la Rosa (1787–1862) with *Venice Conspiracy* (1834), Antonio García Gutiérrez (1812–84) with *El Trovador* (1836), José Zorrilla (1817–92) with *Don Juan Tenorio* (1844),

Antonio Gil y Zárate (1796–1861) with *Carlos II* (1837), and Mariano José de Larra (1809–37) with *Macías* (1834).

The period from 1840 to 1875 brought the transition from romanticism to a tentative realism. Among the important writers of this period were Ventura de la Vega (1807–65), whose *Man of the World* (1845) followed Moratín's style; Manuel Tamayo y Baus (1829–98), whose *Love's Madness* (1855) develops the story of Queen Juana's jealousy and whose *Lo Positivo* (1862) treats domestic and social problems; Adelardo López de Ayala (1828–70), whose *El tanto por ciento* (1861) and *Consuelo* (1878) are reminiscent of Augier's plays. By 1875, the foundations had been laid for the more complete realism which would be developed by "modern" Spanish playwrights.

INTERIOR of a Spanish Theatre about 1845.
[From a contemporary print]

After 1833, the theatre also underwent a number of significant changes. As the popularity of drama grew in the 1830's, a number of minor houses were opened in Madrid and elsewhere. By 1849 theatrical conditions were so chaotic that a state council was created to establish guidelines for the regulation of public theatres. This council was to accomplish the first significant reforms since the 17th century.

The Teatro del Príncipe was renamed the Teatro Espagñol and made the Spanish national theatre, a position which it still holds. Its building was remodeled, gas lighting was installed, and its production methods modernized. (The Teatro de la Cruz was abandoned in 1856.) The use of theatres to support charities was now discontinued so that the revenue might be used to raise the level of performance. All theatres were classified into three ranks, and each was restricted to particular dramatic genres.

Although the latter provision was never fully enforced, it encouraged the growth of minor dramatic types. In 1870, of Madrid's 32 theatres, only eight were devoted to regular drama. Furthermore, the major theatres found it difficult to compete with the minor houses, which soon established the custom of offering an evening's bill composed of four distinct entertainments. This flexibility in the length of programs and the hours of attendance greatly increased the popularity of the minor houses. This custom has continued to plague theatres wishing to present full-length plays and has seriously affected playwriting.

During the 19th century, then, the theatre of Spain burgeoned, growing from a few companies in 1800 to more than 50 by 1875. From an antiquated institution, it had been brought more nearly into line with current practices in other European countries. Nevertheless, it retained much of its insularity, participating in major international movements only at a distance.

THE THEATRE IN GERMANY AND RUSSIA DURING THE 19TH CENTURY

*I*n the years between 1798 and 1805, Germany developed the theoretical foundations of romanticism which were to influence all of Europe. Nevertheless, it produced few significant playwrights. Following the conquest of Germany by Napoleon, drama tended to become either pessimistic or nationalistic in outlook; by 1860, its vitality was gone. After the fall of Napoleon, the theatres were placed under bureaucratic restraints which discouraged change. A few men sought to awaken the theatre, and by the 1880's Wagner and Saxe-Meiningen had startled producers into a new awareness of the theatre's possibilities. In Russia, government censorship and control seriously hampered the theatre's development. Greater freedom in the 1880's began to stimulate changes. By 1890, both Germany and Russia were on the threshold of a new era in the theatre.

The Development of Romanticism in Germany

The 18th century had witnessed the gradual decline of the neo-classical ideal as domestic tragedy, sentimental comedy, and comic opera gained in popularity. Critics had cast doubt on the unities of time and place, the strict separation of genres, and the concept of decorum. The preoccupation with norms and universal characteristics gave way to an interest in local color and history, and the former emphasis upon man as a rational creature was undermined by a growing faith in feeling and instinct as guides to moral behavior. Writers began to idealize the distant past when man allegedly had lived in a "natural" state, free from the shackles of despotic rulers. Thus, although the rejection of strictures took many forms, all contributed to shaping a new view of human nature, political theory, and literary forms. Most of the trends in drama came together around 1800 in Romanticism.

As a conscious movement, romanticism in Germany dates from 1798, when a group of writers in Berlin adopted the term as descriptive of their work. The basic conception was first set forth in *Das Athenaeum,* a literary journal published between 1798 and 1800. The German Romantics were not in revolt against a stagnating theatre as were their French counterparts, for they appeared at the very time when Goethe and Schiller were perfecting German drama. Rather, they saw themselves as clarifying and developing conceptions derived from "Sturm und Drang," Goethe, and Schiller. They also borrowed liberally from the philosophy of Immanuel Kant (1724–1804) and other German Idealists in formulating the theoretical position for a "Romantic" art.

The philosophical foundations of romanticism are complex, but its fundamental tenets can be summarized briefly.

First the German Romantics argued that behind all earthly phenomena lies a higher truth, for all that exists was created by an absolute being (variously called God, Spirit, Idea, Ego). Consequently, all creation participates in eternal truth and all things are parts of the whole and of each other. Truth, then, is defined in terms of the infinity of existence, rather than in observable norms, as the neoclassicist had held.

Second, since all creation has a common origin, a thorough and careful observation of any part may give insights into the whole. The less spoiled a thing is—that is, the less it deviates from its natural state—the more likely it is to embody some fundamental truth. Hence, the Romantic writer preferred as his subjects nature and unspoiled "natural" men, living in primitive times or rebelling against the restraints of society.

Third, human existence is compounded of dualities: the body and the soul, the physical and the spiritual, the temporal and the eternal, the finite and the infinite. Because of his dual nature, man is divided against himself, for he must live in the physical world although his spirit strives to transcend this limitation. Art is of enormous significance, for it allows man to "become whole again," since in the aesthetic experience he is freed momentarily from the divisive forces of everyday existence. Art makes "the supersensuous sensuous" by giving higher truth concrete form so that it can be apprehended; through these glimpses of truth, man becomes more fully aware of his own potentialities and of all being. Fourth, to see the unity behind the apparent diversity of existence requires an exceptional imagination, found only in the artist-genius and philosopher. Thus, art is a superior form of knowledge and the genius a superior individual.

Romantic theory implies that happiness and truth are to be sought in a noncorporeal spiritual realm, thus making them impossible to achieve in earthly life. Furthermore, since spirit, as a part of the absolute, is eternal and infinite, the human mind with its physical limitations can never encompass truth in its totality. Thus, the romantic playwright was faced with an impossible task, for not only was the highest truth always beyond his grasp, but the profound intuitions granted him as a genius could never be embodied adequately through the limited physical means available to him. Consequently, the demands of the stage were often viewed as too restricting, and many dramatists made no attempt to write for production.

Given these conceptions, it is not surprising that the Romantics rejected the unities of time and place, the strict separation of genres, the rationalistic outlook, and narrow didacticism. To them, Shakespeare's plays seemed most nearly to approach the desired goal; consequently, they were adopted as models. For many dramatists, however, Shakespeare merely meant freedom from restraint, and they justified their own disorganized and episodic works by his example. It was the subjectivity and lack of discipline in romantic plays which alienated Goethe and Schiller, who in other respects had much in common with the romantic authors. Even though Goethe labeled the movement "sickly," his *Faust*, with its enormous scope, its picture of eternal human striving, and its attempt to encompass the infinite variety of existence, epitomizes much of romantic thought and sums up the German literary experience between 1770 and 1830.

Of the group who called themselves Romantics, only two, Schlegel and Tieck, were deeply concerned with drama. August Wilhelm Schlegel (1767–1845), through his lectures and essays, formulated and disseminated romantic theory in Germany and elsewhere. Mme. de Staël's *Of Germany* drew heavily on his work and carried his ideas into France and Italy, while

Coleridge adapted Schlegel's conceptions in England. Because of Schlegel's influence, the distinctions between classicism and romanticism gained currency almost everywhere. Schlegel considered Shakespeare the greatest of all dramatists and translated 17 of the plays, which became as much a mainstay of the German as of the English repertory in the 19th century. In his criticism, Schlegel paid little attention to dramatic form, preferring instead to discuss tragic and comic "moods" as states of perception out of which differing approaches come. Thus, mood, emotion, and character were for him the main ingredients of drama, while plot was treated as a contrivance used by lesser playwrights to keep a story moving. These ideas were to exert considerable influence on 19th century playwriting.

Long before he met the other Romantics, Ludwig Tieck (1773–1853) had developed a profound interest in Elizabethan drama and had written a number of "fantastic comedies" in the manner of Gozzi's *fiabe,* satirizing 18th century rationalism and theatrical practices. Tieck's comedies are surprisingly modern in tone, for they frequently break the dramatic illusion and call attention to the theatrical devices being used. After he embraced romanticism, Tieck wrote a number of tragedies, of which *Kaiser Octavianus* (1804) is typical. The basic subject is the development of Christianity and the union of all men in a universal church. Extremely episodic, it is held together primarily by the allegorical figure of Romance. The prologue became famous for its evocation of twilight as a time of mystery and enchantment when imagination replaces the world of sensual reality. To Tieck's contemporaries, this passage seemed to describe so well the outlook of the Romantics that they began to call them the "twilight men."

The early Romantics were held together by close personal ties, but as their ideas spread and as they separated, the movement became increasingly diverse. Consequently, literary historians now divide the German Romantics into groups, such as the Heidelberg Romantics and the Berlin Romantics. Few of the romantic plays were produced, and even fewer found favor with the German public. Romantic ideas and techniques were made acceptable to the ordinary theatregoer primarily through the work of such playwrights as Kotzebue. They were also popularized through "fate tragedy," the vogue for which was established by Zacharias Werner's (1768–1823) *The 24th of February* (1809), which tells of a series of widely separated tragic events, all stemming from a curse and all occurring on the 24th of February. This play also spread the influence of Schiller, who previously had been derided by the Romantics because of his attempt to unite literature and the theatre, a task which they thought impossible because of the limitations that production placed upon the playwright's genius. The phenomenal success of Werner, who had taken his inspiration from Schiller's *The Bride of Messina,* wrought a change of attitude and led to many imitations of Schiller's plays.

SCENE from Werner's *The Twenty-Fourth of February*, Act V. [From *Le Monde Dramatique*]

Heinrich von Kleist (1777–1811) the finest German dramatist of the early 19th century, had no direct connection with the Romantics, and critics disagree as to whether he should be considered one of them. Receiving no encouragement, he committed suicide in 1811 without having seen any of his plays produced. Goethe, to whom Kleist submitted some of his work, was repelled by it. Kleist remained completely unknown until Tieck published his works in 1821. By 1900 his reputation far exceeded that of any of the Romantics, and his plays still figure prominently in the German repertory.

Kleist's best-known dramas are *Penthesilea* (1806–08), *The Prince of Homburg* (1811), and *The Broken Jug* (1811). *Penthesilea,* set in the time of the Trojan War, depicts completely self-centered characters who are destroyed by uncontrollable desires. It is essentially a psychological study of lust and the irrational element in love. *The Prince of Homburg,* Kleist's acknowledged masterpiece, tells of a young army officer who is sentenced to die even though his disobedience has led to a military victory. After a scene in which he begs for his life and admits that his action was motivated by ambition, he is pardoned. *The Broken Jug,* a long one-act play about a Falstaffian judge who seeks to hide his involvement in a case being tried before him, is one of a few comedies of the romantic era that remain playable. Kleist probably failed to achieve recognition in his own time because, unlike the other Romantics, he emphasized man's sensual, rather than spiritual, nature. By the time he died, forces destined to make his works more acceptable were already emerging.

Post-Romantic German Drama

A change in the German consciousness came after 1805–06, when Napoleon overran Germany and Austria. An increasingly nationalistic outlook was eventually to make possible a united Germany. After the defeat of Napoleon in 1815, repressive political regimes were installed in all the German states, now reduced to about 38 in number. Since censorship discouraged innovations, the repertory came to be a mixture of the classics, including the works of Lessing, Goethe, Schiller, and Shakespeare, and innocuous new dramas. In addition to Kotzebue, such writers as Eduard von Bauernfeld (1802–90), Ernst Raupach (1784–1852), Roderich Benedix (1811–73), Friedrich Halm (1806–71), Charlotte Birch-Pfeiffer (1800–68), and Salomon Hermann Mosenthal (1821–77) met the popular demand.

Under these conditions, few significant writers appeared. Many of these were associated with the movement called "Young Germany" which began to emerge in the 1820's out of the disillusionment with romanticism and idealist philosophy. Although Young Germany, with its concern for the problems of everyday existence, marks a transition from romanticism to realism, it did little more than cast doubt upon old values. Among the leaders of Young Germany were Karl Gutzkow (1811–78), whose most famous work is *Uriel Acosta* (1846), and Heinrich Laube (1806–84), best known for *Prinz Friedrich* (1845). Today Grabbe and Büchner seem the most important members of this school, although they were virtually unknown in their own time.

In his play *Comedy, Satire, Irony and Deeper Meaning* (1822), Christian Dietrich Grabbe (1801–36) depicts society as governed by selfish interests, outworn clichés, and static conventions. The play's chaotic structure reflects Grabbe's view of the world. *Don Juan and Faust* (1829) symbolizes in its two principal characters the separation between the masses and the intellectuals, between the sensual and the spiritual, which Grabbe thought characteristic of his age. Most of Grabbe's works are unsuited for production; his *Napoleon, or the One Hundred Days* (1831), for example, calls for the European continent as a stage and an army as actors.

Georg Büchner (1813–37) wrote only three plays, *Danton's Death* (1835), *Leonce and Lena* (1836), a slight satire, and the uncompleted *Woyzeck* (1836). *Danton's Death*, an episodic drama about the Reign of Terror, tells the story of an idealist who, seeing his highest aims wrecked by pettiness, comes to suspect that his ideals were merely a disguise for his sensual appetites. His superior sensitivity, which causes him to question the meaning of existence, will permit no resolution of his doubts, and he ends in despair and death. *Woyzeck,* one of the first plays to treat a lower-class protagonist sympathetically, shows the gradual degradation of a man trapped by his heredity and environment. The play foreshadows Naturalism in its subject matter, and Expressionism in its structural devices and dialogue. Because his outlook and techniques were considerably in advance of his time, Büchner seemed very modern when his plays were rediscovered in the late 19th century. Since 1900, Büchner has assumed considerable importance in dramatic literature.

The German playwright most honored in his own lifetime was Friedrich Hebbel (1813–63). Largely self-educated, Hebbel began his playwriting career in 1839 with *Judith.* Among his most important works are *Genoveva* (1840–41), *Maria Magdalena* (1844), *Herod and Miriamne* (1847–48), and the trilogy *The Niebelungen* (1855–62). Like many of his contemporaries, Hebbel underwent a serious crisis in belief after first accepting the romantic outlook. Unlike Büchner, who never passed beyond pessimism, Hebbel found consolation in his own version of Hegel's philosophical position. Thus, he came to view society as a reflection of Absolute Spirit, which lies behind human existence and works out its own perfection through humanity. In Hebbel's view, the most significant human problems arise because values tend to harden into conventional patterns rather than remaining flexible to meet changing situations. Consequently, advances in morality are accomplished only after a violent conflict has destroyed worthwhile human beings seeking a better way of life; death serves to destroy faith in the old patterns, however, and to make way for new ones. Since the new values will rigidify in their turn, the process must be repeated. Thus, Hebbel viewed history as a series of conflicts and his plays reflect this preoccupation with moral evolution.

In Hebbel's works, the main characters are representative of the old and the new orders. Since the old has the power of established authority behind it, the new, which can rely only upon faith, is usually destroyed. This destruction, however, foreshadows the triumph of the position which has seemingly been defeated. Through such a view, Hebbel reconciled his sense of the world's current imperfections with the possibility of improvement. His most famous play, *Maria Magdalena,* is now usually studied as a forerunner of Realism, because its characters are drawn from ordinary life, its dialogue is in prose, and its story ends in the suicide of the heroine, a victim of society's narrow-mindedness. Thus, the play can be viewed as a realistic depiction of 19th century German life. Nevertheless, like Hebbel's other plays, it too embodies the conflict between old and new values, and the heroine's death serves to make way for the new by raising serious doubts about the old.

Although Hebbel overshadowed his contemporaries, a few rose above the general level. Of these, the most important were Gustav Freytag (1816–95), who, with such plays as *The Journalists* (1852), helped to naturalize the "well-made play" in Germany, and Otto Ludwig (1813–65), many of whose works, especially *The Forester* (1850), were forerunners of Realism. After the death of Hebbel in 1863, German drama entered a period of decline. The general level is probably best exemplified in the work of Ernst von Wildenbruch (1845–1909), an ardent admirer of the Hohenzollern rulers and of the German national past. His work gained especial popularity following the unification of Germany in 1871. Wildenbruch had a considerable gift for writing crowd scenes and for depicting picturesque lower-class life, but much of his work, such as *Heinrich und Heinrichs Geschlecht* (1896), is claptrap.

During the 19th century, Austria also began to produce dramatists of note. Its first important serious playwright, Franz Grillparzer (1791–1872), who began his career in 1817 with *The Ancestress,* wrote regularly for the stage until 1838, when the censor forbade one of his plays. Thereafter he withheld his plays from the stage; consequently, many were not produced until after his death. Among his more important works are a trilogy on the Golden Fleece (1822), *The Fate and Fall of King Ottokars* (1824), and *The Jewess of Toledo* (1837). Grillparzer's serious works reflect the influence of Schiller and "fate tragedy," even though he was in conscious rebellion against Schiller's tendency to show man achieving greatness in defeat. Sharing the disillusionment of his contemporaries, Grillparzer concentrates upon characters whose awareness of higher ideals comes to nothing.

Austrian genius seemed most at home, however, in the folk and

SCENE from Grillparzer's *Traum ein Leben* at the Burgtheater in 1834. [From Weddigen, *Geschichte der Theater Deutschlands* (1904)]

peasant play, which had been popular since Stranitzky introduced Hans-wurst. The tradition was continued by Raimund, Nestroy, and Anzen-gruber. Ferdinand Raimund (1790–1836), a comic actor and the manager of Vienna's Leopoldstädter Theater (founded in 1781), wrote a series of plays in which peasant life is interwoven with supernatural and fairy-tale elements. Regional dialects, folklore, allegory, and farce are the major ingredients of such plays as *The Barometer-Maker and the Magical Island* (1823) and *The Alpenking and the Misanthrope* (1828).

Johann Nepomuk Nestroy (1801–62) began his career as an opera singer but later turned to comic acting. From 1854 to 1861, he was manager of the Karl Theater in Vienna. In addition to fairy-tale plays, Nestroy wrote dialect farces and parodies which were extremely popular throughout Austria and Germany. One of his plays was to serve Thornton Wilder as a basis for *The Matchmaker*.

Ludwig Anzengruber (1839–89) continued the tradition of the peas-ant play but turned it to the more serious purpose of presenting a faithful picture of rural life. *The Priest of Kirchfield* (1870) reflects the contro-versy over the recently-promulgated doctrine of papal infallibility, while his *The Double Suicide* (1875) is reminiscent of *Romeo and Juliet*. Anzengruber was not always serious, however, and his *The Cross Signers* (1872) is a variation on *Lysistrata*. Because of his realism, Anzengruber was little appreciated until the end of his life, when the rise of Naturalism

NESTROY (at the left) in *Lumpazivagabundus*. The exag-geration of costumes for comic effect is typical of the early 19th century. [From *Schriften der Gesellschaft für Theater-geschichte* (1908)]

called attention to his depiction of characters rooted in particular environments. His fame aroused new interest in peasant drama, as a result of which a theatre was founded in Bavaria in 1891 especially to produce and tour folk plays.

After 1850, foreign plays, especially those of Scribe, Sardou, Augier, and Dumas *fils,* made up an increasingly large part of the German and Austrian repertory. Mingled with the classics, they helped to compensate for the lack of good native plays. The period of stagnation was ultimately broken around 1890 with the emergence of the "modern" school.

Theatrical Conditions in the 19th Century

The vitality of the German theatre between 1805 and 1815 was seriously affected by the French occupation, during which many state troupes lost their subsidies. While the downfall of Napoleon brought the reinstatement of financial aid, it also brought political control. Court officials with no theatrical experience were installed as superintendents of the state theatres, on the grounds that they would mediate between the public good and the sometimes-prejudiced views of theatrical workers. The result was the undermining of the stage managers' authority and the imposition of a bureaucratic structure on each company. Initiative was soon destroyed and routine efficiency replaced innovation. The experience of the Berlin troupe is typical. Under Iffland, the company had become the finest in Germany, but after his death the company settled into comfortable mediocrity under the regime of Count Karl von Bruhl, a court official.

If few companies were truly outstanding, the theatre in general prospered. Actors were relatively secure because they were now civil servants with pension rights. Company deficits were made up by the state, which also supplied buildings with good facilities. By 1842, Germany had 65 permanent theatres employing about 5000 actors, singers, and musicians. By the time Germany became a nation in 1871, both state and municipal governments took it for granted that they should support the theatre. Because of the German attitude toward the theatre, each sizable city had a troupe of reasonably good quality. On the other hand, decentralization made it difficult for any theatre to become dominant. Censorship also contributed to mediocrity by discouraging outspoken plays. The repertory was made up primarily of "safe" works drawn from the classics and innocuous new plays. As a result of all these factors, the German theatre of the 19th century tended to be competent but rarely inspired.

Theatrical production followed the same general trends evident elsewhere, as the century brought increased care in every aspect of performance. Historical accuracy in setting and costumes grew steadily. Iffland's production of Schiller's *The Maid of Orleans* in 1801 created a sensation with its accurate costumes and elaborate spectacle on a scale previously reserved for opera. The coronation procession required more than 200 performers. Since Iffland's successor, Count von Bruhl, was even more insistent upon correctness, the Berlin theatre played a major role in popularizing historical accuracy. Nevertheless, during the first half of the 19th century five periods of costumes were considered sufficient for all plays: Classical, Medieval, 16th century, 17th century, and mid-18th century. More detailed treatment did not come until after 1850, when additional information became available in Jakob Weiss' authoritative histories of costume, published between 1856 and 1872. Further research was stimulated after 1874, when the Meiningen players aroused new interest in fidelity to history.

Accuracy in scenery was stimulated by the work of Karl Friedrich Schinkel (1781–1841), who designed the setting for *The Maid of Orleans* in 1801. Trained in Italy and Germany, Schinkel was the best-known theatre architect and scene designer of his day. He also opened the Diorama in Berlin in 1827, patterned on Daguerre's innovations. In operation until 1850, the Diorama exerted considerable influence on stage scenery by encouraging the use of moving and still panoramas and dioramas.

By 1825, the Vienna Burgtheater was gaining ascendancy over the Berlin troupe. Thereafter, its practices set a standard for many other

CORONATION SCENE from Schiller's *Maid of Orleans* as staged by Iffland at Berlin in 1801. The setting is by Karl Friedrich Schinkel. [From Weddingen's *Geschichte der Theater Deutschlands* (1904)]

theatres. It first demonstrated its superiority under the management of Josef Schreyvogel (1768–1832) between the years of 1814 and 1832. Under Heinrich Laube, the playwright, between 1849 and 1866, and Franz Dingelstedt (1814–81), between 1871 and 1880, it became noted for its lavish and accurate pictorial settings.

By the second half of the 19th century, a number of companies were famous for care in staging. Before going to the Burgtheater, Dingelstedt had won acclaim for his Shakespearean productions at Munich between 1851 and 1857, and at Weimar between 1857 and 1867. Dingelstedt appears to have been the first producer anywhere to present Shakespeare's history plays as a cycle. He rearranged the scenes, added music and dance, staged the crowd scenes with care, and used lavish pictorial settings. Similarly, Friedrich Haase (1827–1911), while director of the theatre at Coburg-Gotha between 1866 and 1868, won fame for his historically accurate production of *Hamlet*. He later extended his reputation with other productions of this type while manager of the Leipzig Municipal Theatre between 1870 and 1876. Laube, Dingelstedt, Haase, and Saxe-Meiningen (who was to crown the efforts of his predecessors) drew much of their inspiration from the work of Charles Kean, which they had seen in London.

Thus, during the second half of the 19th century historical accuracy was accepted as an ideal almost everywhere. Nevertheless, the same settings were still reused for different plays of the same historical period. Consequently, although the number of settings was greater than in the 18th century, stock scenery was still the rule.

SCENE from Dingelstedt's production of *Romeo and Juliet* at the Burgtheater, Vienna. [Courtesy National Library, Vienna]

411

INTERIOR of the Burgtheater in the late 19th
century. [From *Die Theater Wiens* (1893)]

FRIEDERICH HAASE'S PRODUCTION of *The Merchant of Venice*
in Leipzig, 1872. [From the *Leipziger Illustrierte Zeitung*
(1872)]

412

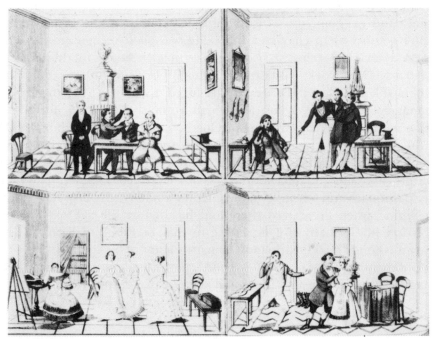

Nestroy's *House of Temperaments,* produced at the Theater an der Wien in 1837. Note the use of four rooms simultaneously. [From a contemporary lithograph]

While most settings continued to be composed of wings and drops, the box set was used with increasing frequency for interiors. Apparently the box set began to evolve in the late 18th century when a door or window was set up between two wings. Gradually other units were added, until the acting area was completely enclosed. By the 1830's Nestroy, in his *The House of Temperaments,* could demand a setting which showed two rooms on the stage level and two above. Nevertheless, the box set did not become usual for interior scenes until after 1875.

The kind of ensemble attained by Schröder and Goethe declined in the 19th century. It was most consistently achieved at the Burgtheater, which was noted for its integrated productions and careful rehearsals. Elsewhere, ensemble playing emerged only sporadically, since emphasis was usually placed on starring performers. Traveling stars, popularized in the 18th century by Schröder and Iffland, grew in number during the 19th century, especially after the opening of the first railroad in 1835. Managers thought it necessary to engage a series of stars, for while the theatre was the favorite form of entertainment, the German public was not attracted by the standard repertory unless performed by noted actors. Since the visitors seldom rehearsed extensively with the local companies and often insisted that other roles be curtailed so as not to detract from their own, ensemble effect was difficult to attain.

In the years after Iffland's death, the major performers were Devrient and Esslair. Ludwig Devrient (1784–1832) made his debut in 1804 in a minor touring company. Unsuccessful at playing persons of his own age, he achieved success in character roles. He was soon recognized as one of the finest actors in Germany, becoming especially noted for his portrayals of Richard III, Shylock, Falstaff, and Franz Moor (in Schiller's *The Robbers*). Upon Iffland's death, Devrient was hired by the Berlin theatre as stage manager for comedy, a position which he held from 1815 until 1828. The stage manager for tragedy, one of Goethe's former actors, thought Devrient quite unsuited for tragedy. As a result, Devrient was largely restricted to comic roles during the years of his greatest vitality. In 1828 he went to the Burgtheater; for the next four years, he electrified Viennese playgoers with his passionate and versatile acting. Unfortunately, his powers were already declining when he arrived there and he died at the age of 48. Devrient's position in Germany is comparable to that of Edmund Kean in England; each was considered the foremost romantic actor of his country.

Ferdinand Esslair (1772–1840) performed in traveling companies until 1820, when he was appointed stage manager and leading actor of the

LUDWIG DEVRIENT as King Lear. [From Weddingen, *Geschichte der Theater Deutschlands* (1900)]

Munich court theatre. An extremely handsome and graceful man, Esslair was best in the roles of romantic heroes, especially Schiller's protagonists. He was much in demand as a visiting performer and played throughout Germany.

Among the later stars, the most famous were Karl Seydelmann (1795–1843), Wilhelm Kunst (1799–1859), Bogumil Davison (1818–72), Emil Devrient (1803–72), a nephew of Ludwig Devrient, and Friedrich Haase. Until about 1850, the Weimar style dominated tragic acting, but under the influence of such men as Seydelmann and Davison, a more natural delivery gained ascendancy. Often two conflicting styles were evident in the same production.

Innovators and Reformers

Not everyone was content with the prevailing conditions. Among the early innovators seeking higher artistic standards, the most important were Tieck and Immermann. Ludwig Tieck's interest extended far beyond the playwriting which had first introduced him to the theatre. By 1820 he was considered Germany's leading authority on the theatre because of his critical essays, his performances as a platform-reader, and his translations of Shakespeare's plays. Nevertheless, Tieck's ideas about theatrical production were considered impractical. In 1824 he was appointed advisor to the Dresden troupe, but had no authority and his advice was seldom taken. It was not until 1841, when he was 64 years old, that Tieck was given a chance to implement his ideas.

The difficulties which Tieck encountered are explained by the dominance of Weimar Classicism in German theatres of the period. Since Tieck advocated psychologically realistic acting on a platform stage, he called for an approach almost opposite to that popularized by Goethe. Many of Tieck's ideas stemmed from his intensive study of Shakespeare. In his novel, *Der junge Tischlermeister* (1837), Tieck describes a performance of *Twelfth Night* on an Elizabethan public stage. Later, with the architect Gottfried Semper, he sought to reconstruct the Fortune Theatre, the first attempt of this kind. Tieck was also the first modern critic to advocate a return to the open stage, for he believed that true illusion results from convincing acting and is destroyed by pictorial realism. He also believed that every element of a production should be supervised by a single and autocratic director.

Tieck's chance to try out his ideas came in 1841, when William IV of Prussia decided to devote his court theatre at Potsdam to experimental productions. He summoned Tieck to stage Sophocles' *Antigone,* an innovation in itself, since professional productions of Greek tragedies were practically unknown at this time. Tieck was given complete authority over the production. He extended the apron over the orchestra pit in a semicircle and constructed a Greek *skene*, which served as the only background for the action. After its success at Potsdam, the production was moved to the state theatre in Berlin and was soon adapted by companies at Dresden, Leipzig, Mannheim, Munich, and Karlsruhe.

Tieck's most influential production was *A Midsummer Night's Dream,* presented in 1843. For it, he adapted Elizabethan conventions to the proscenium theatre. Letting the forward part of the stage form a large open space, he constructed a unit to the rear, with curving stairs leading to an acting area eight feet above the stage. The two stairs framed an inner stage on the lower level. The sides of the stage were masked by tapestries hung at right angles to the proscenium. This production was repeated 40 times during the first season at the Berlin theatre, and was imitated by numerous troupes throughout Germany. Because of illness, Tieck was never able to complete another production. *Henry V,* which he planned to do without any set changes, had to be abandoned.

Tieck's work was made possible only because William IV ordered all theatrical personnel to follow Tieck's orders. The bypassing of the perma-

TIECK'S PRODUCTION of *A Midsummer Night's Dream* at Berlin in 1843. [From a contemporary lithograph]

nent managers created considerable friction; after Tieck's retirement, the old methods were resumed. Nevertheless, Tieck's ideas were to be revived and pursued more consistently at the end of the century.

Karl Immermann (1796–1840) combined the ideas of Goethe and Tieck, for while he advocated the declamatory acting style, he accepted many of Tieck's theories about spectacle. Immermann believed that the salvation of the theatre lay in drama of high quality rather than in the technical excellence then being emphasized by most managers. At the Stadttheater in Dusseldorf between 1837 and 1840, he tried to implement his ideas through a repertory composed largely of works by Shakespeare, Calderón, Goethe, Schiller, Lessing, and other major writers. For some Shakespearean productions, he erected a facade setting on his proscenium stage; for other productions, he employed some of the finest painters of his time to design settings and costumes. Since the public proved indifferent to his ambitious—and unsubsidized—productions, Immermann failed.

IMMERMAN'S STAGE for Shakespearean plays. [A contemporary print]

It was not until about 1875 that widespread critical and public support for innovations was achieved, largely through the work of Wagner and Saxe-Meiningen. Richard Wagner (1813–83) was brought up in a theatrical household, his stepfather and four of his brothers and sisters being employed in the theatre. Wagner was destined to play a major role in his country's growing desire for a German opera free from foreign influence. Although his first opera, *Die Feen,* was written in 1831, he did not achieve critical success until 1842 with *Rienzi,* which also brought him an appointment as conductor at the Dresden opera house. Banished for his part in the revolution of 1848, he spent twelve years in exile. During this time, he formulated those theories which were to influence the course of the modern theatre.

Wagner rejected the contemporary trend toward realism, arguing that the dramatist should be a myth-maker rather than a recorder of domestic affairs. To him, true drama was concerned with the ideal world, which is left behind as soon as spoken dialogue is admitted. He suggested that drama should be "dipped in the magic fountain of music" to combine the greatness of Shakespeare and Beethoven. He also argued that music, through melody and tempo, permits greater control over performance than is possible in spoken drama, in which interpretation is subject to the performers' personal whims. Thus, for Wagner the effectiveness of music-drama depends upon performance as well as upon composition, and he argued that the author-composer should supervise every aspect of production in order to synthesize all parts into a *Gesamtkunstwerk,* or "master artwork." From these ideas were to stem much of modern theory about the need for a strong director and a unified production.

In addition to his theories, Wagner's practice also exerted considerable influence, especially on theatre architecture. To house his idealized music-drama, Wagner set out to create a new kind of opera house. The structure which he eventually built is said to have been suggested as early as 1841 by Schinkel. The first concrete plans were made in 1864 by Gottfried Semper (1803–79), who had worked with Tieck on his reconstruction of the Fortune theatre, and were later reworked by several persons, including the architects Wilhelm Neumann and Otto Brückwald and the machinist Karl Brandt. Originally planned for Munich, the opera house was built in Bayreuth.

Begun in 1872 and opened in 1876, the new opera house was soon famous throughout the world and inspired many reforms in architectural design. Since Wagner wished to create a "classless" theatre, he abandoned the box, pit, and gallery arrangement. The main part of the auditorium had thirty stepped rows of seats; there were no side boxes or center aisle, each row leading directly to a side exit. At the rear of the auditorium was a single large box surmounted by a small gallery. The total seating capacity was 1745. To insure good sightlines, the auditorium was shaped like a fan, measuring about 50 feet across at the proscenium and 115 feet at the rear of the auditorium. Since all seats were said to be equally good, a uniform price was charged. The orchestra pit was hidden from view, much of it extending underneath the apron of the stage. This feature helped to create a "mystic chasm" between the real world of the auditorium and the "ideal" world of the stage, an effect reenforced by darkening the auditorium during performances and by framing the stage with a double proscenium arch.

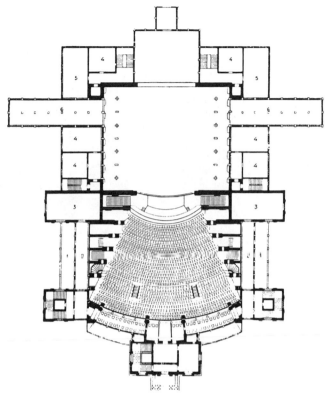

PLAN of Wagner's theatre at Bayreuth. [From
Sach's *Modern Opera Houses and Theatres*
(1896–98)]

The arrangement of the auditorium was the theatre's greatest innovation; the stage was essentially conservative in design. The floor was raked
upward toward the back, and the chariot-and-pole system of scene shifting
was retained. The principal innovation was a system of steam vents to
create realistic effects of fog and mist, and a "steam curtain" to mask scene
changes. The proscenium opening, about 40 feet wide, gave onto a stage 80
feet deep by 93 feet wide. About 100 feet of overhead space and 32 feet of
below-stage space were provided. The building also included ample workshops, storage, dressing rooms, and rehearsal space.

Although Wagner's theories later inspired several nonillusionistic
approaches, his own productions aimed at complete illusion. He forbade
the musicians to tune their instruments in the orchestra pit and allowed no
applause during performances or curtain calls at the end. He sought precise
historical accuracy in scenery and costumes and employed such devices as
moving panoramas. For a production of *Siegfried,* for example, he used a
dragon with realistic scales and movable eyes and mouth. To Wagner, the

419

THE AUDITORIUM AND STAGE at Bayreuth. The setting for
Parsifal designed by Max Brückner. [From *Le Théâtre*
(1899)]

ideal was to be reached through total illusion. Thus, Wagner's theatrical practice was grounded solidly in the 19th century tradition. Nevertheless, his conceptions of the master artwork, the director, the unified production, and theatre architecture were to inspire many pioneers of the "modern" theatre.

While Wagner's opera house was being constructed, another potent force, the Meiningen Players, came to the fore. Although plays had been performed in the Duchy of Meiningen since the late 18th century, a court theatre was not opened until 1831, and the productions remained commonplace until Georg II (1826–1914) succeeded to the throne in 1866. Georg II, Duke of Saxe-Meiningen, had received extensive art training, had been at the Prussian court in Berlin at the time when Tieck worked there, and had seen Charles Kean's Shakespearean productions in London and the superior ensembles of the Burgtheater and the Comédie Française. His intense interest in the theatre was well developed before the Prussian invasion of Meiningen forced his father to abdicate in his favor.

Upon succeeding to the throne in 1866, Georg II immediately began to change the repertory of the court theatre and to take a personal interest in its affairs. In managing the troupe, the Duke at first depended heavily upon Friedrich von Bodenstedt (1819–92), and after 1871 on Ludwig Chronegk (1837–91). Trained as a singing comedian, Chronegk had been employed at Meiningen in 1866 as a comic actor. His appointment as director came as a surprise to the company, for there seemed little in his background to justify it. Nevertheless, the fame of the troupe probably owes as much to Chronegk as to Saxe-Meiningen. Not only was he an indefatigable worker, but it was he who conceived and arranged the tours which made the company famous. A third major influence was Ellen Franz (1839–1923), an actress who in 1873 became the Duke's third wife. After this time she assumed responsibility for proposing the repertory, adapting the texts, and supervising stage speech. Thus, it is difficult to assign credit for the company's accomplishments, although it is now typical to allot sole responsibility to the Duke.

From 1866 until 1874 the company played entirely in Meiningen. When it did appear in Berlin in 1874, it took the astonished spectators completely by surprise. After its initial success, the company began a long series of tours. Between 1874 and 1890, it played in 38 cities in nine countries, including Russia, Sweden, Austria, Denmark, Belgium, Holland, and England, giving about 2600 performances of 41 plays. By 1890, when it gave up touring, the Meiningen commanded the greatest respect of any company in the world.

The accomplishments of the Meiningen Players were due to its methods rather than to its aims. The Duke, like most producers of his day, sought to create the illusion of reality with accurate spectacle and lifelike acting. His repertory, composed primarily of works by Shakespeare, Schiller, Grillparzer, and other 19th century Romantic playwrights, was not unlike that of other producers except in its inclusion of more plays of high merit. Although he presented Ibsen's *Ghosts* for a few performances, the other contemporary plays in his repertory were poetic, romantic works.

The Meiningen also resembled other groups of the time in emphasizing pictorial illusion, in which it excelled all previous standards because of its greater accuracy. The Duke divided each century into thirds and further distinguished among national differences within each time period. As a result, his productions attained unprecedented authenticity. Accuracy was further insured by the Duke's refusal to permit actors to tamper with their costumes. In most theatres of the time, the stars either supplied their own garments or altered as they saw fit those provided by the theatre. Actresses often wore crinoline petticoats under dresses of all periods. Furthermore, the Duke insisted upon authentic materials in place of the usual cheap substitutes. He used heavy upholstery fabrics, imported materials from France and Italy, some of which were made to his specifications, and introduced genuine chain mail, armor, swords, axes, halberds, and other instruments. In Roman plays, the actors wore togas of enormous length. Authentic period furniture was used. The success of the Meiningen Players led to the establishment of theatrical supply houses which manufactured furniture, properties, costume materials, and armor for stage use.

Saxe-Meiningen designed all of the costumes, scenery and properties used by his troupe. The settings were usually painted by Max Brückner, a well-known landscape artist of Coburg, who also designed Wagner's settings. Strong colors were used in scenery for the first time, reversing the former practice of having actors play against pastel scenery. This innovation probably accounts for the adverse comments on the "garishness" of the Meiningen settings. The Duke was opposed to sky borders and used foliage, beams, banners or other devices as overhead masking. He avoided symmetrical balance, for he thought this unnatural, and was careful to keep each detail in correct proportion and to blend painted and three-dimensional elements convincingly. He was also one of the first artists consistent in considering the stage floor as part of the design, breaking it up with fallen trees, rocks, hillocks, steps, and platforms.

SCENE from the Meiningen Players' production of Schiller's *Maid of Orleans*. Compare this picture with the earlier one by Schinkel. Saxe-Meiningen has used only the central door of the cathedral and has achieved a sense of a large crowd with a confined space. [From *Leipziger Illustrierte Zeitung*]

While its use of scenery and costumes was probably superior to that of other troupes, the company's principal source of power was the total effect, especially the ensemble acting. The Duke maintained as complete authority over his actors as over the scenic investiture. Because he could not afford major performers, his company was composed either of beginners or of older actors who had not attained outstanding success. Although guest actors sometimes performed with the troupe, they had to conform to the company's rules against stars. Perhaps to discourage any tendency toward the "star complex," Saxe-Meiningen required all actors not cast in leading roles to appear as supernumeraries. This, in turn, made possible the effective crowd scenes for which the company was noted. Saxe-Meiningen used no supernumeraries who were not permanent members of the troupe. While this limited the number of persons available for crowd scenes, the effect of large masses was achieved by settings which forced the actors into the wings, suggesting great numbers offstage, and by diagonal and contrasting movements to create effects of confusion and agitation. In rehearsing crowd scenes, the Duke divided his actors into small groups, each under the charge of an experienced performer who aided in training those under him. Each member of a mob was given individualizing characteristics and specific lines; then all were carefully coordinated. The results, contrasting sharply with the usual mob scenes, were considered revolutionary.

Fortunately, the Duke could depend upon long rehearsal periods. Since Meiningen had a population of only 8000, the theatre was open only twice a week for six months of the year. This schedule and the Duke's authority made it possible to rehearse in a way quite different from that in use elsewhere. Each work was rehearsed from the first with full settings, furniture, and properties. Costumes were not always available from the beginning, but were always used for some time prior to the premiere. Actors were required to "act" from the first day rather than merely "walking through" the part as was typical in other theatres. Rehearsals, held in the evening after the Duke's state duties were completed, often lasted five or six hours and continued until the play was judged ready for performance, even if this required several months. Because he did not work against a deadline, the Duke conceived many details as he went along, and rehearsals were frequently delayed while the furniture was rearranged or new plans made.

The impact of the Meiningen Players came from the complete illusion attained in every aspect of the production. Thus, the company stands as the culmination of trends which had begun in the Renaissance. More important, it stands at the beginning of the new movement toward unified production, in which each element is carefully selected because of its contribution to the total effect; the actor had given way to the director as the dominant artist in the theatre. Saxe-Meiningen's example influenced such men as Antoine and Stanislavsky, who were to figure significantly in the formation of the modern theatre. By the time the Meiningen Players discontinued touring in 1890, the theatre was already entering the new era which they had helped to inaugurate.

Russian Drama in the 19th Century

The Russian theatre, like that of other countries, expanded steadily during the 19th century. Strict governmental censorship, especially after 1825, did much to retard both theatre and drama and to discourage authors who otherwise might have contributed more significantly to world drama.

During the Napoleonic era, Vladislav Ozerov (1770–1816) was the most popular playwright, probably because his works appealed to patriotic sentiment at a time when Russia was endangered by France. Written in the neo-classical style, his plays, notably *Dmitri Donskoi* (1807), were extravagantly praised but soon forgotten.

By far the best dramatist of the early 19th century was Alexander Griboyedov (1795–1829), remembered primarily for *Woe from Wit* (1822–25), one of the masterpieces of Russian drama. As in Molière's *The Misanthrope,* the disillusioned hero of *Woe from Wit* seeks to make others aware of the shortcomings of a materialistic and hypocritical society. To demonstrate his point, Griboyedov brings together a gallery of character types representative of Moscow life. This emphasis upon characterization probably explains the comedy's lasting appeal. It is sometimes said to be the only significant Russian play in the neo-classical style. Like many important works, it was forbidden production at first. The complete version was not seen until 1869; since then, it has never been absent from the Russian repertory.

By the time Griboyedov's play was written, romanticism was emerging. Alexander Pushkin (1799–1837) is usually given major credit for establishing the new ideal in literature. His one play, *Boris Gudonov* (1825), with its variety, magnitude, poetic strength, and historical subject, marks the first victory over neoclassicism in drama. Sometimes called the first Russian play on a political theme, it deals with the relationship of a ruler to his subjects. Censorship kept the play out of print until 1831 and from production until 1870. Mussorgsky's operatic version, presented in 1873, has largely supplanted the original text in the theatre. Mikhail Lermontov (1814–41), one of Russia's finest romantic poets, also wrote a few plays after 1830, when his *The Spaniards* appeared. He is now remembered primarily for *Masquerade* (1835), in which corrupt society is blamed for a man's murder of his wife. Censorship kept this play from the stage until the 1860's.

Given the severity of the censor, it is not surprising that most Russian plays were either innocuous or flattering to the ruler. Consequently, romanticism flourished primarily in the patriotic spectacles encouraged by Nicholas I. One of the most successful writers of such plays was Nestor Kukolnik (1809–68), whose *The Almighty's Hand the Fatherland Has Saved* (1834) depicts the election of Michael Romanov, Nicholas I's ancestor, to the throne. Nikolai Polevoy (1796–1846) exploited the same vein, although he achieved his greatest success with melodramas, which had become popular in Russia following the production in 1829 of Victor Ducange's *Thirty Years.* Polevoy's greatest contribution was the introduction of Shakespeare to the Russian stage through his translation of *Hamlet* in 1837. Thereafter, the works of Shakespeare became increasingly prominent.

As elsewhere, the repertory in Russia was dominated by melodrama and musical plays. A large number were translations, especially of French works, but native writers cultivated the taste. The *comédie-en-vaudevilles,* a one-act comedy with couplets sung to familiar tunes, was especially popular. It reached its high point in the work of Alexander Pisarev (1803–28), but many other writers followed his example through the remainder of the century.

A more realistic drama began to appear in the 1830's with the work of Nikolai Gogol (1809–52). As a playwright Gogol is now remembered primarily for *The Inspector General* (1836), the story of a young man mistaken for an official from St. Petersburg. Satirizing the corruption and boorishness of provincial officials, the play was original for its time, since it included neither a love story nor sympathetic characters. Its claim to realism lies almost entirely in its grotesque characterization and its preoccupation with pettiness, hypocrisy, and corruption. Its production, allegedly after the personal approval of the Czar, encouraged other authors to turn to more realistic portraiture.

Psychological realism was first exploited by Ivan Turgenev (1818–83), considered Russia's major author after 1852, when his collection of short stories, *A Sportsman's Sketches,* appeared. After 1863, Turgenev lived abroad, where he became the best-known of all Russian authors. Most of his plays were written between 1843 and 1852, but their influence on other dramas came much later; his finest work, *A Month in the Country* (1850) was not produced until 1872. Turgenev's major concern in *A Month in the Country* is the inner life of the characters. While he renders the daily routine of a country estate faithfully, he does so only as a means of showing the permanent psychological changes wrought in several characters by the presence of a young tutor. Turgenev's contribution to realism comes from his use of quiet domestic detail to reveal inner turmoil. Upon his work, Chekhov was to build.

Before Turgenev's plays appeared on the stage, realism had already been popularized through the work of Alexander Ostrovsky (1823–86), Russia's first professional playwright and the first Russian writer to devote himself exclusively to drama. Ostrovsky wrote his first play in 1847; from 1853 until his death, he completed at least one new drama each year. Working primarily from observation, Ostrovsky is often credited with creating a peculiarly Russian drama free from Western influence. Although he wrote in a variety of forms and used a wide range of subjects, his major works draw on the life he knew best, that of the middle class. He sought to eliminate Gogol's penchant for caricature and avoided stage tricks and irrelevant spectacle, concentrating instead upon characters and their relationships to each other and to a particular milieu. Ostrovsky is best known for *Enough Stupidity in Every Wise Man* (sometimes called *The Diary of a Scoundrel*), *The Forest,* and *The Thunderstorm. Enough Stupidity in*

Every Wise Man is the comic chronicle of a man's rise through his manipulation of other people's vanities. *The Thunderstorm*, which shows the tragic outcome of parental tyranny, is noteworthy for its use of the storm as a symbol of turmoil in human affairs. In this and other ways, Ostrovsky anticipates Chekhov.

SCENE from Ostrovsky's *A Good Post*, produced at the Maly Theatre, Moscow in 1864. [From *Teatr*]

Ostrovsky was instrumental in founding the Russian Society of Dramatic Authors and Composers in 1866. Until this time, the dramatist usually received no pay for his work beyond a set fee from the state troupes; provincial companies did not pay. After 1866, playwrights gradually won full copyright protection.

Of Ostrovsky's contemporaries, the most important were Pisemsky, Sukhovo-Kobylin, and Saltikov-Shchedrin. A. F. Pisemsky (1820–81) wrote many kinds of plays but is now remembered primarily for one of the most naturalistic works of the 19th century, *A Bitter Fate* (1859), which antedates by many years the Naturalistic movement in France. The story is simple: a peasant learns that his wife has been seduced by a wealthy landowner; he kills the child born to her and turns himself over to the authorities. A masterfully written work, it more nearly realizes the aims of the French Naturalists than any of their own dramas. Alexander Sukhovo-Kobylin (1817–1903) is noted primarily for a trilogy of plays treating the Russian legal and bureaucratic systems, with which he was personally entangled. *Krechinsky's Wedding* (1854) is relatively lighthearted, but *The Case* (1861) and *Tarelkin's Death* (not produced until 1917) seem intended to arouse shudders rather than laughter. The work of Mikhail Saltikov-Shchedrin (1826–89) is related to that of Sukhovo-Kobylin, for he too gives a satirical picture of corruption in his *The Death of Pazukhin* (1857, banned until 1900).

Near the end of the 19th century, Leo Tolstoy (1828–1910), already famous as a novelist, turned to playwriting. Of his dramas, the most important is *The Power of Darkness* (1886, first performed in Russia in 1895), a story of greed and murder among Russian peasants. Like *A Bitter Fate,* it is one of the most effective of naturalistic plays. *The Fruits of Enlightenment* (1889, produced 1892) satirizes the preoccupation of the nobility with trifles and superstitions, while *The Living Corpse* (or *Redemption,* 1900) is a problem play about the conflict between marriage laws and the Christian demand for self-sacrifice.

Although the major Russian plays of the late 19th century fall into the realistic school, they were by no means the standard fare of the public theatres, which continued to favor melodrama, farce, musical drama, and romantic spectacles. Of the writers opposed to the realistic trend, probably the most important was Alexey K. Tolstoy (1817–75), whose plays idealized the Russian past and emphasized the clash of strong personalities against picturesque historical backgrounds. His trilogy, *The Death of Ivan the Terrible, Tsar Fyodor Ivanovich,* and *Tsar Boris* (written between 1865 and 1870) are among the finest of their genre.

Thus, during the 19th century Russia produced a number of outstanding playwrights, many of whom are still scarcely known in the West. It is difficult to avoid speculating about the heights which might have been reached had censorship been less strenuous and theatrical conditions more favorable.

Russian Theatrical Conditions in the 19th Century

During the 19th century the Russian theatre expanded constantly, but always under close government supervision. Prince Alexander Shakhovskoy (1777–1846), Director of Repertory in the Imperial Theatres from 1801 to 1826, initiated several important changes. In 1805 a state theatre was opened in Moscow, for which the crown purchased a company of 74 serf actors from A. E. Stolypin and others from Prince Volkonsky. In 1809 a training school was added; gradually, the Moscow troupes grew in theatrical importance, although the St. Petersburg companies continued to receive favored treatment and higher subsidies. Shakhovskoy, after visiting Paris and other Western theatrical centers, also attempted to raise the level of production, and worked out regulations for governing the troupes which were to remain in effect from 1825 until 1917.

Until 1882 the Imperial theatres had a monopoly on theatrical production in St. Petersburg and Moscow. Through most of the century St. Petersburg had three theatres: the Bolshoi, used mainly for ballet and opera; the Maly (replaced by the Alexandrinsky in 1832), used primarily for drama; and the Mikhailovsky, devoted primarily to foreign works. Moscow had two theatres, one for opera and ballet and the other for drama. Both companies were originally housed in temporary buildings. In 1824, the Maly, home of spoken drama, was opened; it still remains in use. In 1825 the Bolshoi was inaugurated for opera and ballet; after it burned in 1853, it was replaced in 1856 with the present building. Because of their prestige, the state troupes set the standard for all Russia, which for the most part depended upon touring companies of poor quality.

INTERIOR of the Moscow Bolshoi Theatre c. 1850. [From Barkhin, *Architektura Teatra* (1947)]

Following the revolt of 1825, Nicholas I instituted a strenuous censorship which brought every aspect of the Russian theatre under close supervision. Although conditions eased after his death in 1855, it was not until Alexander III came to the throne in 1881 that significant changes occurred. In 1882, the monopolies were abolished. In actuality, they had been violated for many years by performances disguised as private entertainments. The Nobility Assembly, the Painters Club, the Merchants Club, and others had regularly scheduled "dramatic evenings," and "family reunions" often featured theatrical entertainment. By 1875 about 25 theatrical groups were performing regularly in Moscow and St. Petersburg.

After the monopolies were rescinded, the public theatre expanded rapidly, although the state troupes continued to command the greatest prestige. The quality of the provincial theatres also improved. Prior to the

1880's, even the best companies had to tour and, even then, felt it necessary to import stars to increase their appeal. As soon as a provincial actor established a reputation, he was hired by the Imperial troupes. Costumes and scenery were meager, and amateurs were often employed as stage-hands. By the 1870's permanent theatre buildings had been built in eight provincial cities, but not until about 1890 were companies able to settle down permanently. The first provincial troupe to establish a reputation for excellence was that of N. N. Solovtsov (1857–1902), which performed in Kiev and Odessa between 1892 and 1902. Aside from a few large towns, however, Russia continued to be served by touring groups. In 1897 the provincial theatres held the first All-Russian Convention of Theatrical Workers to discuss common problems.

A number of outstanding actors appeared in the 19th century. In the early years, the St. Petersburg performers were dominant. Yekaterina Semyonova (1786–1849), trained by Dmitrevsky, played leading roles in both comedy and tragedy, although she excelled in the latter. She was unsuited to domestic drama. Because of her popularity, she was paid considerably more than other performers and given a special allowance for costumes. When Mlle. George arrived from Paris in 1808, a battle for supremacy was waged until the French actress left in 1811. Aleksey Yakovlev (1773–1817), also trained by Dmitrevsky, made his debut in 1799. An impulsive actor who depended primarily upon inspiration, Yakovlev was especially popular in Ozerov's tragedies, then at the height of their vogue. During the second quarter of the 19th century, the St. Petersburg stage was dominated by Vassily Karatygin (1802–53). Tall, handsome, and vocally gifted, he played roles of almost every type. He was a master technician who paid careful attention to costume, makeup, and every detail of his performances.

After 1825, the lead in drama gradually passed to Moscow, largely because of its superior actors. Among the early performers, the most important were Mochalov and Shchepkin. Paul Mochalov (1800–48) was on the stage from the age of 17. An uneven, emotional actor, he swept audiences away when he was at his best. He was especially admired in melodrama and in such roles as Richard III and Hamlet. According to Stanislavsky, Mikhail Shchepkin (1788–1863) was the first great Russian actor. Born a serf, Shchepkin's early career was spent in a serf troupe. He began to travel with a professional company in 1808 and obtained his freedom in 1821. By 1823 he was a member of the Moscow troupe with which he remained the rest of his life. After 1832 he taught at the dramatic school and toured frequently throughout Russia. Shchepkin was a painstaking technician who strove for naturalness in acting. Because of his influence, ensemble effects were achieved at the Maly long before they were usual elsewhere in Russia. He initiated the practice of reading the play to the company before the roles were cast and guided other actors in their characterizations. He excelled in Gogol's comedy, and his natural style is said to have encouraged playwrights to draw more realistic characters.

Shchepkin's major successor was Prov Sadovsky (1818–72), whose success in Ostrovsky's plays led to the Maly's designation as "the House of Ostrovsky." Discovered in the provinces by Shchepkin, in 1839 Sadovsky came to the Maly, where he played minor roles until Ostrovsky's plays offered him parts suited to his style of performance. While Shchepkin had excelled at external detail, Sadovsky's ability to project both internal and external realism created more fully-rounded characterizations than any previously seen.

Other important actors of the Maly included Shumsky, Fedotova, Yermelova, Lensky, and Yuzhin. Sergei Shumsky (1821–78) was a follower of Shchepkin and continued his tradition of careful attention to detail and technical excellence. Glikeria Fedotova (1846–1925), on the stage from the age of 16, was at her best in Ostrovsky's character roles. Maria Yermelova (1853–1928), after beginning her career in ballet, changed to drama in 1870 and achieved her first important success in 1876 in Lope de Vega's *The Sheep Well*. She continued on the stage into the Soviet period and was the first actress to become a "People's Artist." Alexander Lensky (1847–1908) went on the stage in 1865 and in 1876 settled in Moscow, where he became a noted stage lover and excellent teacher. After 1898 he served as a director and teacher at the Novy Theater. Alexander Yuzhin (1857–1927) was an outstanding interpreter of heroic roles and a staunch defender of realistic detail. In 1909 he became director of the Maly.

The St. Petersburg troupes were more inclined to cultivate popular taste and to ignore ensemble effects. Perhaps for this reason, they produced fewer outstanding actors than did the Maly. Among the most important performers were Martynov, Davidov, and Savina. Alexander Martynov (1816–60), a pupil of Karatygin, was noted principally for comic acting, in which he developed a realism similar to that practiced by Shchepkin. Vladimir Davidov (1849–1925) played in the provinces from 1867 until 1880, when he came to St. Petersburg. He remained on the stage until 1922. Noted primarily for comic playing, he combined realistic detail with broad theatricality. Maria Savina (1854–1915), on the stage as a child, played at the Alexandrinsky Theatre after 1874. She was noted for her truthful playing and avoidance of clichés. At her best as society women, she appeared in works by Gogol, Turgenev, Ostrovsky, and Tolstoy.

Through most of the 19th century, actors in the state troupes were hired according to lines of business adopted from French usage. State-approved rules governed rehearsals, the behavior of actors, and every aspect of their lives. In 1839, they were placed under civil service and divided into three ranks according to length of service. Until the 1860's, actors were trained either in service or at the state dramatic schools, which combined the course of study for actors, dancers, and singers. After the private

Russian Musical Society opened a conservatory in St. Petersburg in 1862 and another in Moscow in 1866, the state schools reevaluated their approach. Training for opera and ballet were separated from acting, and graduates were no longer automatically eligible for employment in the Imperial theatres. In 1882, lines of business were abandoned as the basis of employment in the state troupes. Although type casting continued, greater flexibility became possible.

Opera, which had been primarily an aristocratic entertainment, began to win a wider following in the 1830's, when Mikhail Glinka (1804–57) initiated the Russian school of composers. Nevertheless, foreign influence remained dominant throughout the century. Ballet, also under foreign influence, reached a peak of excellence before the end of the 19th century. Between 1801 and 1829, Charles Didelot, a Frenchman, introduced Noverre's reforms into Russia. He emphasized vertical movement, replaced the soft shoe with one permitting difficult turns, introduced leotards, and shortened skirts. Foreign stars, such as Marie Taglioni (1804–84), the most celebrated ballerina of her day, were imported beginning in the 1830's and gave further emphasis to technical excellence. It was not until the late 19th century, however, that Russian ballet was given its distinctive form by Marius Petipa (1822–1910). Born in France, Petipa came to Russia in 1847 and was appointed ballet master of the Imperial Schools in 1862. After 1870 he was the virtual dictator of ballet in Russia. He choreographed 74 long works and 30 "entertainments," in which considerable emphasis was placed on sets and costumes as well as upon story-telling dance. By the time he retired in 1903, Russian ballet had assumed the characteristics for which it is still noted.

Until after 1850 most theatres relied upon a few stock settings. Although the box set was introduced in the 1830's, it found little favor until much later. In 1853, one of Ostrovsky's plays is said to have startled audiences with its simple and accurate spectacle. The heroine appeared in a cotton dress and with natural hair rather than the usual fashionable garments and coiffure. Thereafter, realism of detail grew steadily, especially at the Maly, upon which Ostrovsky exerted considerable influence. In the final year of his life, Ostrovsky was made head of the theatre, the first time that a professional had been appointed to such a post, but he died before he could implement the reforms that he envisioned.

It was not until the 1880's that theatres began consistently to pay attention to accurate settings. Until then, most theatres used conventionalized settings, devoid of national or period flavor. Such settings had been popularized by Andreas Roller (1805–91), a German designer who dominated Russian scenic practices, since his pupils or disciples held the major posts in the state theatres. Nevertheless, archeologically correct settings began to appear sporadically after the 1860's. In 1865, the Alexandrinsky Theatre employed an archeologist to assist with historically accurate set-

SETTING by A. Roller for a ballet. From Syrkina's *Russkoe teatralne dekoratsione iskusstvo*]

SETTING from M. A. Shishkov for Griboyedov's *Woe from Wit*. [By Syrkina]

tings and costumes for Tolstoy's *The Death of Ivan the Terrible,* and after 1870 such major Russian painters as Bocharov and Shishkov began to turn attention to accuracy of detail. In 1880, Shishkov organized a special class in theatrical design at the Art Academy, and by the 1890's a number of prominent painters were working for the private theatres. Nevertheless, Ostrovsky's response to the Meiningen Players in 1885 tells much about Russian attitudes of the time: he labeled them a talented group of amateurs who placed far too much emphasis upon spectacle except in the admirable crowd scenes. On the other hand, Stanislavsky was deeply impressed by the Meiningen troupe's attention to pictorial values, which contrasted so sharply with the typical Russian approach. Stanislavsky states that in Russia around 1890 three sets of period costumes were considered sufficient for all plays, and that, since these were used repeatedly, they were usually old and dirty. He adds that actresses still insisted upon wearing stylish and inappropriate clothing and that the secondary characters could always be identified by their drabness.

True ensemble effects of the type exemplified by Saxe-Meiningen's company were not to be achieved in Russia until after 1898, when the Moscow Art Theatre was founded. Prior to this time, however, a few Russian companies had pointed the way. Especially important was the troupe founded in 1882 by O. A. Korsh (1852–1921) in Moscow. Korsh maintained a high standard of production, introduced many significant plays from Western Europe, established matinee performances in Russia, and trained a number of actors later to be famous. The company continued until 1932, many years after Korsh's death. In Korsh's theatre, the early productions achieved a consistent style and all roles were cast and prepared with care. By the 1890's, however, this meticulousness had begun to fade. Nevertheless, by 1898 the conditions and possibilities of a new theatre had been established. It remained for Stanislavski and Nemirovich-Danchenko to consolidate the gains and to inaugurate a new era in the Russian theatre.

THE ENGLISH
THEATRE IN
THE 19TH CENTURY

*A*lthough the English theatre expanded rapidly after 1790, until 1843 the provisions of the Licensing Act denied most companies the right to present regular drama. Furthermore, the financial depression which followed the Napoleonic Wars made theatrical ventures risky. After 1843, the English theatre gradually recovered both financially and artistically to become one of the most respected in the world. During the last half of the 19th century, pictorial realism reached its apex and actor-managers began to establish unified production as a goal. By 1900, however, illusionism was under attack and the English theatre, like that of other countries, was undergoing changes which would soon transform it.

The Licensing Act, 1790–1843

The population of London doubled in the years between 1790 and 1843, when it exceeded two million. A large proportion of the increase came in the working classes, who now began to attend the theatre in large numbers. The expanding demand for entertainment had several important effects. First, the patent theatres were enlarged. The seating capacity of Covent Garden was increased in 1792–93 to about 3000, and in 1794 Drury Lane was rebuilt to accommodate more than 3600. Second, minor theatres were opened. The first were licensed in the 1780's by magistrates outside the City of Westminster (the official seat of government) under the provisions of the law of 1752. After 1804, when the Earl of Dartmouth became Lord Chamberlain, an important change occurred. He interpreted the Licensing Act as authorizing minor theatres within the City of Westminster, so long as they did not infringe upon the rights of the patent houses. Consequently, beginning in 1807 he issued a number of permits for new theatres. By 1843, there were 21 companies in the London area as compared to six in 1800. Furthermore, the Lord Chamberlain authorized longer seasons for the Haymarket, originally restricted to five months during the summer. By 1812, it was open seven months, and by 1840 ten months.

Third, the repertory was affected. While only the patent houses (Covent Garden, Drury Lane, and the Haymarket) were authorized to perform regular drama, any theatre was permitted to give the lesser forms and incidental entertainment. In an attempt to retain audiences in the face of the new competition, the patent theatres increased their offerings of minor drama. Furthermore, in seeking to cater to all tastes, the evening's bill was extended until it lasted five or six hours. Sometimes as many as three plays were performed on the same evening; a bill composed of two full-length plays, an afterpiece, and numerous variety acts was not unusual between 1820 and 1843. Many persons felt that the patent theatres had abdicated their responsibility for producing regular drama by adopting a repertory not unlike that seen in the minor houses. Consequently, around 1810 and again in the 1830's, attempts were made to establish a "third theatre" which would be devoted entirely to the standard repertory. Although nothing came of these efforts, they focused attention upon the need for reform. As the repertory of the major theatres changed, especially after 1810, a number of the former spectators deserted the drama for opera, which was performed at the King's Theatre where even the frequenters of the pit were required to wear formal evening dress. The popular audience

435

which remained for drama seemed to care little for poetic plays, and by 1843 it was widely believed that Shakespeare meant ruin at the box office.

Although the patent houses were free to perform the minor genres, other theatres could not play regular drama. Consequently, they sought loopholes in the Licensing Act which would allow them to compete more effectively with the major theatres. Two dramatic types, the burletta and the melodrama, came to their rescue. By 1800 burletta, imported into England in the mid-18th century as a type of comic opera, had become such an ambiguous label that the Lord Chamberlain accepted as a burletta any work that had no more than three acts, each of which included at least five

ASTLEY'S AMPHITHEATRE, showing the use of the ring and the stage. [From Wilkinson, *Londina Illustrata* (1825)]

songs. This ambiguity was first exploited by Robert Elliston, manager of the Surrey Theatre. One of the finest actors of his day, Elliston was not content to perform in the usual fare of the minor theatres. In 1809 he transformed Farquhar's *The Beaux' Stratagem* into a burletta and followed it with *Macbeth* presented as a "ballet of action." Thereafter, almost any work might be altered to meet the licensing requirements.

Melodrama, which all minor theatres were allowed to perform, offered a similar loophole. Characteristically it was written in three acts and was accompanied by a musical score. Thus, regular plays could be made into melodramas by dividing them into three parts and adding musical accompaniment. This stratagem became so perfunctory that *Othello* is said to have been performed as a melodrama with the mere addition of a chord struck on the piano every five minutes.

Although minor theatres were occasionally penalized for such evasions, the distinctions between patent and minor theatres became increasingly blurred. The resulting dissatisfaction made reform inevitable. In 1843, the Theatre Regulation Act abolished the privileges of the patent houses. Thereafter any licensed theatre could perform works of any type, so long as the plays were licensed in advance by the Lord Chamberlain. This bill remained in effect until 1968.

English Drama, 1790–1850

Theatrical conditions between 1790 and 1843 contributed to the romantic notion that fine drama can never be adequately embodied in theatrical production, and that genius is never appreciated by the mass audience. Thus, while most of the major English poets of the early 19th century wrote plays, few of these works were intended for production, and few had any success when presented. Most of the poetic plays written between 1790 and 1850 were neo-Elizabethan in subject matter and approach, for they treated historical themes and sought to recapture Shakespeare's glory.

One of the most admired playwrights of the early 19th century was Joanna Baillie (1762–1851), who between 1798 and 1812 published three volumes of *Plays of the Passions*, each drama treating one dominant emotion. While the verse is of high quality, the plays are unsatisfactory because character and story are subordinated to a single motivation. Only *DeMontfort* (acted 1800) achieved any success in the theatre, although Miss Baillie's works were extravagantly praised by other writers.

Most of the romantic poets attempted drama. Samuel Taylor Coleridge (1772–1834), the major theorist of romanticism in England, wrote *Remorse* (1813), William Wordsworth (1770–1850) *The Borderers* (1795–96), and John Keats (1795–1821) *Otho the Great* (1819). Percy Bysshe Shelley (1792–1822) was probably the best dramatist of the time, but his plays *The Cenci* and *Prometheus Unbound* were not acted until the 20th century. *The Cenci* (1819), which tells of Beatrice Cenci's revenge upon her father for his inhuman behavior, comes closer to Jacobean drama than any play of its period. George Gordon, Lord Byron (1788–1824) was the most successful of the romantic poets in the theatre. Not only did he write more plays, but more were suited to the stage. As a member of the governing committee of Drury Lane, Byron probably had more knowledge and interest in production than did his contemporaries. Nevertheless, only

437

Marino Faliero (1821) was acted during his lifetime, although all of his plays were eventually performed. *Sardanapalus* (1821) offered such producers as Charles Kean irresistible opportunities for historical spectacle, while *Werner* (acted 1830), the story of a man destroyed by an obsession for revenge, became one of Macready's vehicles.

Although Sir Walter Scott (1771–1832) had an abiding interest in the theatre and wrote several plays, his influence came primarily through his novels, most of which were adapted by others for performance. With their emphasis upon local color and history, they helped to establish the vogue for the historical romance. Robert Browning (1812–89), author of many "dramatic" poems, seemed naturally fitted for writing dramas. At Macready's urging, he accepted the challenge, but *Strafford* (1837), *A Blot on the 'Scutcheon* (1843), and *Colombe's Birthday* (1853) gained no marked success, since they concentrate upon the eccentric and fail to achieve universality. For many years Thomas Noon Talfourd's (1795–1854) *Ion* (1836), based upon the classical myth, was hailed as the long-awaited masterpiece. Macready performed it regularly until about 1850, but its reputation faded rapidly thereafter.

At the time, the dramatist who seemed most clearly destined for greatness was James Sheridan Knowles (1784–1862), who first gained renown with *Virginius* (1820), soon a standard play in theatres throughout England and America. Knowles consolidated his fame with *William Tell* (1825), *The Wife* (1833), and *The Hunchback* (1832). His success stemmed from a skillful blending of melodramatic stories with a pseudo-Shakespearean form. For a time, he gained a considerable critical and popular following.

If serious playwriting did not fare well, melodrama did. Although many melodramatic elements can be found in the sentimental comedy and domestic tragedy of the 18th century, they were not fully developed until the end of the century, when the impact of Kotzebue's work turned attention to the new form. Thirty-six of Kotzebue's plays were translated into English, and *The Stranger* and *Pizarro* remained in the repertory throughout the 19th century. Melodrama also received considerable impetus from native playwrights, especially Matthew Gregory Lewis (1775–1818), usually called "Monk" Lewis because of his famous novel, *Ambrosio, or the Monk* (1795). Dramatized many times, this novel and *The Castle Spectre* (1797) began a vogue for "Gothic" melodramas. Set in the Middle Ages, these plays often transpired in ruined abbeys, and featured outcasts, ghosts, long-lost relatives, and long-concealed crimes. In 1802, Thomas Holcroft (1745–1809) gave the trend toward melodrama additional strength with *A Tale of Mystery,* an adaptation of Pixérécourt's *Coelina.* Soon melodramas were attracting large audiences; they were to be the mainstay of the minor theatres.

Until the 1820's the majority of melodramas were rather exotic, either because they were set in some remote time or place, or because they featured the supernatural or highly unusual. Pierce Egan's *Life in London* (1821), dramatized by Egan and others as *Tom and Jerry, or Life in London,* began a trend toward melodramas of contemporary life. Egan's work featured a number of well-known places in London and told a story based on everyday events.

The trend begun by Egan was developed by Jerrold, Fitzball, and Buckstone. Douglas William Jerrold (1803–57) began his playwriting career in 1821 and gained his greatest success with a series of "nautical" melodramas, of which *Black-Eyed Susan* (1829) was to become one of most popular plays of the century. Although remembered primarily for his melodramas, Jerrold wrote many kinds of plays, including blank-verse tragedy. After 1841, he gave up dramatic writing to work for the magazine *Punch.* Edward Fitzball (1792–1873) had dramatized a number of Scott's novels before turning to original compositions; soon his nautical melodramas were almost as famous as those of Jerrold. He is now remembered, however, because he initiated the vogue for melodramas based on actual crimes. His *Jonathan Bradford, or the Murder at the Roadside Inn* (1833) had an initial run of 161 nights, a record not broken until 1860. One of the most prolific playwrights of the century, Fitzball continued to turn out plays until his death. John Baldwin Buckstone (1802–79), a popular actor and manager, wrote or adapted more than 200 plays between the 1820's and the 1870's. His early work, especially *Luke the Labourer* (1826), helped to popularize the "domestic" melodrama. Many of Buckstone's later plays were farces, pantomimes, or dramatizations of recent novels.

Although the older exotic melodrama continued, the domestic plays began to dominate after 1830. A number of other types also appeared. Astley's and the Royal Circus featured melodramas which incorporated daring feats of horsemanship, and Sadler's Wells had a water tank installed in 1804 so that it might perform "aquatic" plays featuring sea battles and rescues from drowning.

Until around 1840, melodrama made its greatest appeal to the unsophisticated theatregoer. With the work of such men as Bulwer-Lytton and Marston, however, appeared a "gentlemanly" melodrama which was to attract the more discriminating audience with works both theatrically effective and critically acceptable. Although much of Knowles' work falls into this category, it was Edward George Bulwer-Lytton (1803–73) who established the type. Already noted for his novels, Bulwer-Lytton was persuaded by Macready to turn to playwriting. Three of his works, *The Lady of Lyons* (1838), *Richelieu* (1839), and *Money* (1840), all of which owe much to Macready's suggestions, held the stage throughout the 19th century. John Westland Marston (1819–90) also helped to establish the type with *The Patrician's Daughter* (1842) and *Anne Blake* (1852), both of which treat contemporary subjects in poetic dialogue but in a melodramatic form. With "gentlemanly" melodrama, the theatre began to regain its former prestige with the upper classes.

Theatrical Conditions, 1790–1843

Between 1790 and 1817, the theatre maintained its stability largely because of the work of John Philip Kemble (1757–1823). When Kemble became acting manager of Drury Lane in 1788, it had fallen considerably from the height to which Garrick had lifted it. Richard Brinsley Sheridan, the manager, had devoted himself increasingly to politics but had failed to delegate sufficient authority to Thomas King, who ran the theatre in his absence. Although Kemble reestablished the reputation of the Drury Lane, he tired of coping with the crises induced by Sheridan's frequent financial difficulties. In 1802 he moved to Covent Garden, where he remained until his retirement in 1817. Under his management, the Covent Garden became the leading theatre of the English-speaking world.

By the time Kemble retired, Europe was in a period of financial crisis which was to last until 1840. Scarcely a theatrical management escaped bankruptcy between 1817 and 1843. The rapid decrease in income can be seen at the Drury Lane, where receipts diminished from 80,000 pounds in

THE INTERIOR of Covent Garden Theatre around 1800. The setting on stage is for an oratorio. [From *The Microcosm of London* (1902)]

1812–13 to 43,000 pounds in 1817–18. Nevertheless, the owners of the buildings were slow to lower their rental charges. At the Drury Lane between 1819 and 1827, Robert Elliston paid 10,000 pounds annually for his lease, and it was only in 1832, after Elliston and several of his successors had failed, that the rent was lowered to 6000 pounds. Pressure on the managers was reduced somewhat by a decline in other expenses. At Covent Garden, nightly expenses fell from 300 pounds in 1809 to 154 pounds in 1836. Between 1833 and 1835 the major theatres were in such straits that Alfred Bunn (1798–1860) was able to lease both Drury Lane and Covent Garden and run them with a single company. Of the patent houses, only the Haymarket, a small theatre free from major competition during the summer months, remained relatively prosperous.

Some of the difficulties during these years are explained by the greater financial outlay required by the increasingly elaborate spectacle. It is sometimes suggested that the enormous auditoriums made subtlety in acting impossible and shifted emphasis to visual effects. Covent Garden was destroyed by fire in 1808 and Drury Lane in 1809. In the new Covent Garden (1809) the distance from the stage to the back of the upper gallery was 104 feet, and at the new Drury Lane (1812) only slightly less. Such size, coupled with the growing interest in melodrama, local color, and history, undoubtedly encouraged greater emphasis upon the visual elements.

Increased concern for spectacle was evident as early as the 1790's, when Kemble began to mount Shakespearean revivals with the same care pre-

THE INTERIOR of Drury Lane as it appeared before it burned in 1809. Note the five levels of galleries. [From *The Microcosm of London* (1902)]

viously lavished upon minor drama by Garrick and DeLoutherbourg. The major designer of the Kemble era was William Capon (1757–1827), who came to the fore when the Drury Lane was reconstructed in 1794. This theatre now had a stage 85 feet wide and 92 feet deep, with a proscenium opening 43 feet wide by 38 feet high. One of Capon's sets in 1799 showed the nave, choir, and side aisles of a 14th century cathedral; it measured 56 feet in width, 52 feet in depth, and 27 feet in height. Capon continued as principal designer at Drury Lane until it burned in 1809, after which he worked at Covent Garden. Some of his scenery was in use as late as 1840. Unlike DeLoutherbourg, Capon designed primarily for regular drama and was one of the first important advocates of historical accuracy in scenery. Nevertheless, consistency had not yet been attained, for often several different designers, each working independently, provided settings for one play, and frequently one act was newly mounted while the others were performed in stock scenery.

ONE of Capon's Gothic settings. [From *The Magazine of Art* (1895)]

Kemble's attitude toward scenery and costumes marks a transition from the generality favored by the neoclassicists to the individuality advocated by the romantics. Thus, although he often clothed the major characters in pseudo-historical garments, the minor personages usually wore traditional costumes taken from the company's wardrobe. Similarly, while Mrs. Siddons discarded fashionable dress in tragedy, she substituted for it conventionalized "draperies" of no particular era. Kemble always put theatrical effectiveness above archeological accuracy. Thus, he set *Corio-*

lanus in late rather than in early Rome because he thought audiences unprepared to accept the architecture of the earlier period, and the costumes for *King Lear* were given merely a "Saxon tendency." Consequently, while he acknowledged the desirability of historical and individualizing detail, Kemble applied it sporadically and inconsistently.

During Kemble's lifetime, complex practical scenic pieces also increased markedly in number. For example, Sheridan's *Pizarro* (1799) required a gorge spanned by a bridge which could be cut loose so that the hero might escape. Such devices became common as melodrama grew in popularity. In 1811, under the influence of equestrian drama, Kemble even employed a troupe of mounted cavalry. He also made increased use of processions, coronations, and other mass effects. By the time he retired in 1817, it was accepted that all drama should be "illustrated" as completely as possible.

Robert Elliston, manager of Drury Lane from 1819 to 1826, continued the emphasis upon spectacle. His *King Lear* (1820) featured trees that actually bent in the wind and storm noises so realistic that Lear could not be heard. Elliston installed a water system to achieve greater illusion, and one of his principal designers, Clarkson Stanfield (1793–1867), introduced the moving diorama (panoramas had been used in London theatres since about 1800).

The major step toward antiquarianism came in 1823, when James Robinson Planché (1796–1880) persuaded Charles Kemble (1775–1854), manager of Covent Garden from 1817 to 1832, to use historically accurate costumes for every role in Shakespeare's *King John*. Although the actors feared that they would be laughed at, the audience allegedly welcomed the innovation. In 1824, both historically accurate costumes and scenery were used for Kemble's production of *Henry IV, Part I*. In spite of the success of these productions, Kemble did not repeat the experiment until 1827, and it was not until Macready accepted it in 1837 that authenticity was consistently exploited. Thus, while Planché's work in 1823 must be considered a landmark, it did not bring an immediate revolution in theatrical practice.

Planché continued to be a leader in the movement toward antiquarianism. Finding it difficult to obtain information for his costume designs, he undertook extensive research which resulted in his *History of British Costume* (1834), long the standard English work in this field. He continued his study of heraldry and was frequently consulted by producers. Thus, Planché not only provided impetus to authentic staging, but also supplied the information which made it possible.

By the 1830's it was assumed that each theatre would prepare a number of handsomely mounted productions each season. The increased financial outlay meant, however, that longer runs were required to justify the investment. Consequently, from this time the trend toward long runs accelerated, although it was not to be widely exploited until after 1850.

COSTUME for Philip Falcon-bridge as designed by Planché for Charles Kemble's production of *King John* in 1823. [From the edition of the play published in 1824]

Between 1790 and 1843 a number of important actors emerged. Until 1815, the stage was dominated by the Kemble family. Almost all of the twelve children of Roger Kemble (1721–1802), a provincial actor-manager, appeared on the stage, but lasting fame was achieved only by John Philip and Sarah Kemble Siddons (1755–1831). As an adult, John Philip Kemble was on the stage from 1776. Coming to London in 1783, he only gradually gained favor, but from 1790 until his retirement was considered the leading actor of the English-speaking world. Mrs. Siddons was on the stage from childhood; attaining no success at Drury Lane in 1775, she returned to the provinces until 1782. From her reappearance in London until her retirement in 1812, she was recognized as the greatest tragic actress of her day.

Kemble and Mrs. Siddons established a style usually called "classical" because of its emphasis upon stateliness, dignity, and grace. In Kemble, this style often gave the impression of coldness and restricted his excellence to such roles as Cato, Coriolanus, Cardinal Wolsey, Brutus, Rolla, and the Stranger. His characterizations were always worked out studiously and sustained with care. As a result, he was often accused of self-consciousness. Mrs. Siddons, while attaining a comparable dignity, rose far above her brother because of her greater emotional intensity. She was especially noted

A PRINT showing the Kemble family in *Henry VIII*. At the front is Mrs. Siddons as Queen Katherine; seated at the left is John Philip Kemble as Cardinal Wolsey; in the background is Charles Kemble as Henry VIII.

A LITHOGRAPH showing Charles Kemble's production of *Henry VIII* in 1830.

for her playing of Lady Macbeth, Queen Katharine, Volumnia, and Mrs. Haller.

Other members of the Kemble family included Stephen (1758–1822), who acted primarily in the provinces but became famous in London for his Falstaff; Eliza Kemble Whitlock (1761–1836), who, after performing in the provinces, migrated to America in 1794 to become one of the most noted actresses in the new country; Charles, who excelled as the young heroes of John Philip Kemble's productions and later managed the Covent Garden theatre. Much of Charles Kemble's later fame was associated with his daughter, Frances Anne Kemble (1809–93), a popular leading lady from her debut in 1829 until her retirement in 1834. Charles Kemble retired in 1836 and later served as Examiner of Plays for the Lord Chamberlain.

The Kemble school of acting was continued by Charles Mayne Young (1777–1856), who succeeded to many of John Philip Kemble's roles until his retirement in 1832; J. M. Vandenhoff (1790–1861); and J. W. Wallack (1791–1864), who became a leading figure in the American theatre. Eliza O'Neill (1791–1827) was considered by many to be Mrs. Siddons' true successor.

The classical approach was challenged after 1814 by the romantic school. Although Edmund Kean was the greatest exponent of the new style, he was preceded in it by George Frederick Cooke (1756–1812). On the stage from 1776, Cooke did not appear in London until his powers were already declining in 1800. Addicted to drink, Cooke was unreliable and disappeared for long periods. When in full possession of his powers, no one could so captivate an audience. At his best in villainous roles such as Richard III and Iago, he cared little for grace or nobility but was unequaled at portraying hypocrisy and evil. He favored realistic acting and even wrote out poetic dialogue as prose so as to avoid emphasizing rhythm or rhyme. His last years, 1810 to 1812, were spent in America; as the first major English actor to undertake a starring tour of the United States, he established a precedent which was to have important consequences.

If Cooke prepared the way for romantic acting, Edmund Kean (1787–1833) perfected the style. On the stage as the child prodigy Master Carey, Kean began his adult career at 14 in a provincial company. He did not appear in London until he was 27, but from his debut there in 1814 he was considered a major star and, after Kemble's retirement, the foremost actor of his day. Like Cooke he excelled in somewhat villainous roles, such as Richard III, Shylock, Sir Giles Overreach, and Barabas; he seldom appeared in comedy. Although it is sometimes said that Kean depended upon inspiration, this is a misconception. He worked out every movement and intonation with care. Once set, a role was much the same at every performance, although Kean sometimes revised a characterization, and his intentions were often subverted by his alcoholism. In later years, he was inclined to save his strength for the great moments and to slight the remainder of a role. Unlike Kemble, Kean did not value grace and dignity; he was willing to cringe or crawl on the floor if he thought it necessary to convey the proper effect. Thus, he tended to emphasize realism of emotion, whereas Kemble had sought to convey an ideal nobility. Kean's style pleased the new audiences, but his erratic behavior had lowered his popularity considerably before his death in 1833.

Largely because of Kean's example, starring engagements became the norm for major performers after 1815. In London, Kean was never a regular member of an acting company. Instead, he frequently demanded 50

EDMUND KEAN in the role of Richard III. [A contemporary engraving]

pounds or more for each time he performed. (Kemble had never received more than 36 pounds a week, and Mrs. Siddons never rose above 30 pounds a week.) His demonstration that a star could command a high salary with a limited repertory established a precedent followed by many of his successors.

Although no comic actors achieved the lasting fame enjoyed by Kemble and Kean, many won popular acclaim in the years between 1790 and 1843. In addition to his importance as a manager, Robert Elliston was universally admired as the young hero of comedy and later in such character roles as Falstaff. Charles Mathews (1776–1835) was noted especially

447

for his "At Homes," in which he portrayed a succession of character types based upon observation. Beginning around 1808, this superior kind of mimicry made him a leading attraction throughout England and took him to America for tours in 1822 and 1834. Above all, however, it was the era of the low comedian. For the first time, such performers as Joseph Munden (1758–1832), John Liston (1776–1846), and Robert Keeley (1793–1869) commanded salaries equaling or exceeding those of major serious actors. Other outstanding stars included Tyrone Power (1795–1841), noted for his comic Irish portrayals, and T. P. Cooke (1786–1864), famous as the hero of nautical melodramas.

Audiences were also attracted by the eccentric and unusual, and the early 19th century brought a craze for child actors, of which the most famous was William Henry West Betty (1791–1874), often called the Young Roscius. When Master Betty came to London in 1804 after winning fame in the provinces, his following became so great that Kemble and Mrs. Siddons gave up playing for a time. On one occasion, Parliament was adjourned so that its members might see him perform. Betty's fame soon passed, and after 1811 he sank into obscurity.

Except during starring engagements, actors were still employed by the season at a weekly salary and a yearly benefit. Although "lines of Business" continued to be the norm, specialization increased. After 1809, Kemble employed the equivalent of three troupes, one for serious drama, one for comedy, and one for music and dance. Thereafter, the trend in large companies was to hire actors who were outstanding in a limited range; diversity was achieved because each troupe included many specialized performers.

Rehearsals were still perfunctory. Although Kemble aimed at ensemble effects, he did little beyond holding line rehearsals, probably because by this time conventional groupings and movement served in most instances. It was customary for actors to space themselves an arm's length apart so as not to inhibit gestures. Because the footlights had a large cluster ("the rose"), an actor moved to this bright spot each time he had an important speech. After delivering his lines, he then moved three steps to the left or right to make way for the next speaker. This continuous shifting of places was typical of acting until after 1850.

Macready and Mme. Vestris

In the 1830's two managers, Macready and Mme. Vestris, began to bring order out of the chaos which had reigned since about 1815 and to lay the foundations for the recovery of the theatre.

William Charles Macready (1793–1873) had no intention of going on the stage until a financial crisis in his father's theatre at Birmingham forced him to leave school in 1810. By 1816 he was playing in London, where he was soon considered a serious rival to Kean, although it was not until Kean's death that he was acclaimed England's foremost actor. As a performer, Macready combined much of Kemble's dignity and studiousness with Kean's fire. Unlike Kemble, however, he sought to give an illusion of everyday life, and included many domestic and familiar details in his stage business. He was famous for his lengthy pauses, during which he seemed to reflect and compose his responses.

Macready's profound dissatisfaction with theatrical conditions eventually led him into management as the only effective means of reforming them. From 1837 to 1839 he managed Covent Garden and from 1841 to 1843 Drury Lane, each with more artistic than financial success. In spite of difficulties, however, Macready introduced many innovations which were to form the basis of later practices.

Macready was one of the early directors in the modern sense. He did not allow actors to choose their own stage positions, but sought instead to impose blocking upon them. He was often derided and defied, but he did not give up. Furthermore, Macready insisted upon acting during rehearsals rather than "saving himself" for performances, the usual practice of the day. While he did not convert all of his company, his superior success as a performer and director won many converts.

Macready paid attention to every detail of his productions. Although

MACREADY'S PRODUCTION of *Othello*, 1837, at Covent Garden. [From Scharf's *Recollections* (1839)]

449

he presented stock plays which were repeated many times each season, he introduced and lavished attention upon a few new productions each year. He was the first director who consistently sought historical accuracy in both costumes and scenery. His usual designer was Charles Marshall (1806–80), one of the finest landscape artists of the day, but he also employed many other noted designers. For *Henry V*, Clarkson Stanfield designed a moving diorama to illustrate the sea voyage from Southampton to Harfleur, and Col. Hamilton Smith (1776–1859), a noted antiquarian, was often consulted on costumes.

Macready sought to improve the repertory. He placed considerable emphasis upon Shakespeare's plays and claimed much credit for restoring the original texts, although he was not always scrupulous in this matter. He

THE INTERIOR of Drury Lane Theatre, 1841. On stage is the wrestling scene in Macready's production of *As You Like It*. The setting is by Charles Marshall. [From *London Interiors* (1841)]

persuaded some of the foremost literary figures of his time to write for the stage and from these efforts came "gentlemanly melodrama." Macready also considered it a point of integrity to perform no work more than four times a week, regardless of its popularity. (From this policy stemmed many of his financial difficulties.)

Macready maintained a company of high quality. Helen Faucit (1817–98), an actress of the Kemble school who made her London debut in 1836, was generally considered the finest actress of the day. Mrs. Mary Warner (1804–54) was recognized as the leading performer of such mature roles as

450

Lady Macbeth. Samuel Phelps, soon to attain fame as a manager, was second only to Macready as an actor.

Continually disappointed in his efforts to achieve a stable theatre of high quality, Macready gave up management in 1843 and thereafter was a touring star. His last appearance in America in 1849 was marred by the Astor Place riot, stemming from his rivalry with Edwin Forrest. Macready retired in 1851.

Whereas Macready's influence came through his productions of regular drama, Mme. Vestris' most significant work was with the minor forms. Born Lucia Elizabetta Bartolozzi (1797–1856), in 1813 she married Armand Vestris (1788–1825), a famous dancer of the time. In 1815 she went on the stage, playing in both London and Paris. She achieved her first outstanding success in a "breeches role" in *Giovanni in London* (1821), a burlesque of Mozart's *Don Giovanni*. She remained one of the most popular performers of light comedy and burlesque until her retirement in 1854.

Mme. Vestris' importance, however, stems from her work as a manager, notably at the Olympic Theatre from 1831 to 1838. Here she had the assistance of J. R. Planché, who wrote many of the plays in her repertory, which was restricted to burlesques, extravaganzas, and similar minor types. At this time, the burlesque was a broad caricature of a popular drama, myth, or current event. In its original form, the extravaganza was a whimsical treatment of a myth or fairy tale placing special emphasis upon dance and spectacle. Both burlesque and extravaganza usually made considerable use of music. Because of their common characteristics, they were eventually intermingled and the type designations lost their specificity. Burlesque seems to have appealed to the 19th century taste for broad humor, while extravaganza was a precursor of musical comedy. Both were extremely popular, especially between 1830 and 1870. Planché, one of the most prolific writers of these forms, turned out about 175. With their whimsy and wordplay, Planché's works were to be a major influence on the operettas of Gilbert and Sullivan.

As a manager, Mme. Vestris is important for several reasons. First, she paid close attention to every element of production and coordinated them into an integrated whole. Second, she gave special consideration to spectacle and is usually credited with introducing the box set into England. The origin of the box set is obscure, but it probably came into being gradually. In 1808, Monk Lewis' *Venoni* required two rooms simultaneously, a demand repeated in George Colman's *The Actor of All Work* in 1817. Fitzball's *Jonathan Bradford* (1833) utilized four rooms simultaneously, two above and two below. While it is unclear how these scenic requirements were met, they suggest some version of the box set. Nevertheless, Mme. Vestris was probably the first producer to use this type of setting consistently; she may also have been the first to enclose the acting area

THE OLYMPIC THEATRE as it appeared in
the 1820's. [From Wilkinson, *Londina
Illustrata* (1825)]

completely. There is much dispute over the date when the box set was
introduced at the Olympic, but 1832 seems most likely. By 1834 it had been
seen at Drury Lane and by 1837 was in use at Covent Garden. Nevertheless,
the box set remained something of a novelty and was not widely adopted
until after 1870.

Not only did Mme. Vestris use box sets, she equipped them like rooms
in real life. Rugs were laid on the floor, knobs were attached to doors, and
bookcases, books, and bric-a-brac were included to give the appearance of
reality. This care extended to costumes. With Planché's encouragement,
Mme. Vestris substituted garments like those worn in real life for the
exaggerated costumes usually seen in burlesque. Thus, she was the first
producer to treat minor drama with the respect formerly reserved for the
classics.

Mme. Vestris was also instrumental in simplifying the evening's bill.
She curtailed her offerings so that the program ended no later than 11 P.M.,
a drastic measure since programs at this time usually lasted until one or two
A.M. The popularity of the innovation began the trend which eventually
led to the one-play bill.

In 1838 Mme. Vestris gave up the Olympic Theatre and married
Charles Mathews the younger (1803–78), a performer of light comedy
roles in her company. Together they managed the Covent Garden from
1839 to 1842 and the Lyceum from 1847 to 1856. At both they continued
the policies begun at the Olympic. At the Lyceum, they were assisted by

William Roxby Beverley (*c.* 1814–89), one of the finest designers of the day. Their insistence upon the highest quality in every detail led them into financial difficulties, and both managerial ventures ended in bankruptcy. Nevertheless, their reforms were to inspire others and to produce important results in the 1860's.

Theatrical Conditions, 1843–60

When the Theatre Regulation Act was passed in 1843, the London stage seemed at a low ebb, despite the work of Macready and Mme. Vestris. Many persons assumed that the new law would bring rapid change and many new theatres. In actuality, the period between 1843 and 1860 was to be one of reassessment and gradual recovery. Unlike the years between 1810 and 1843, when many new buildings were erected, no new theatre was built in London until after 1860. Yet in retrospect, out of the years 1843–60 grew an unprecedented prosperity and prestige.

After 1843, Drury Lane and Covent Garden rapidly lost their positions of dominance. Covent Garden soon became the home of opera, while Drury Lane turned increasingly to spectacle and musical drama; both have continued these specialties to the present day. Of the patent theatres, only the Haymarket retained its prestige, and between 1843 and 1850 was London's foremost home for regular drama. Between 1837 and 1853, the Haymarket was managed by Benjamin Webster (1797–1882), a former member of Mme. Vestris' troupe. In 1844, Webster also acquired the Adelphi, which specialized in melodramas, notably those of J. B. Buckstone. In 1853, Webster ceded the management of the Haymarket to Buckstone, who retained it until 1876. Under Buckstone, the Haymarket maintained its reputation for comedy; it lost its privileged position in serious drama except when visiting stars performed there. Webster rebuilt the Adelphi in 1858 and remained at its head until 1874.

Webster and Buckstone were continuers of a tradition rather than innovators. Major new developments were to come from Sadler's Wells and the Princess' Theatre. In 1844, Sadler's Wells was a remote house noted for its bloodthirsty melodramas. Since about 1730 it had been offering theatrical entertainments, and it was the principal target of the bill of 1752, which required the licensing of all places of entertainment. In the early 19th century it had gained renown for its aquatic dramas and later as the summer home of Joseph Grimaldi (1778–1837), the most famous clown of pantomime.

It is unclear why Samuel Phelps (1804–78), an actor since 1826 and Macready's principal support since 1837, chose this out-of-the-way, run-

THE RECONSTRUCTED Haymarket Theatre, opened July 1821. [From Wilkinson, *Londina Illustrata* (1825)]

down theatre for his experiment in management, but it is probably explained by the low rental. Contrary to expectations, not only was Phelps financially successful but he made Sadler's Wells the principal home of poetic drama between 1844 and 1862. Phelps' significance lies in his demonstration—at a time when it was almost universally believed that only popular entertainment could attract a large audience—that fine drama could be successful. The source of Phelps' popularity was unmistakable, for his repertory was composed almost entirely of poetic drama. Except for six of the minor works, Phelps produced all of Shakespeare's plays in versions more complete than any since Shakespeare's time. Unlike his successors, who rearranged the plays to avoid scene shifts and made drastic cuts to allow scope for spectacle, Phelps made only minor cuts and transpositions.

Although he mounted his productions with care, Phelps' lack of funds precluded sumptuous costumes and settings, and, while he sought historical accuracy, he never sacrificed dramatic values. Perhaps his most famous production, *A Midsummer Night's Dream* with settings by Fenton, used a moving diorama to shift the scene from one part of the forest to another; much of the action took place behind a scrim which created a misty atmosphere.

Phelps suffered most from the lack of first-rate actors. For the first two seasons, Mrs. Warner played leading roles. She was followed by Isabella

Glyn and several lesser actresses. Because of their inexperience the actors were coached extensively by Phelps, who also played leading roles ranging from Lear to Bottom. As a performer, Phelps was universally praised for his judgment, taste, absence of tricks, and faultless elocution (which Macready and Charles Kean were slighting in their attempts to achieve greater realism). His faults were monotonous pace and slow delivery. Despite its actors, Sadler's Wells had the most devoted audience of any theatre in London.

It is sometimes charged that as a manager Phelps merely continued Macready's work. While this is partially true, Phelps succeeded where Macready failed, and it was he who reestablished that faith in poetic drama which Macready's financial troubles had undermined. After he gave up Sadler's Wells in 1862, Phelps toured widely. For a time in the 1860's he restored Drury Lane to its former glory with a series of Shakespearean productions. He continued on the stage until 1877, by which time his style was considered old-fashioned.

If Phelps revived poetic drama, Charles Kean (1811–68) perfected pictorial realism and brought the fashionable audience back to the theatre. Son of Edmund Kean, he went on the stage in 1827 but, lacking his father's powers, he gained little recognition until 1838. In 1842, he married Ellen Tree (1806–80), his leading lady thereafter. His first experience as a director came in 1841, when he staged *Romeo and Juliet* for Webster. During his third tour of America between 1845 and 1847, he produced *King John* and *Richard III* in New York, following Macready's prompt-books closely. The most detailed productions yet seen in America, their success probably encouraged Kean to go into management. In 1850, he leased the Princess' Theatre in London.

The Princess' was the last theatre opened in London before the passage of the Theatre Regulation Act. During the 1840's it was noteworthy primarily because it presented the American actors Edwin Forrest, Charlotte Cushman, Anna Cora Mowatt, and E. L. Davenport. Its period of glory, however, was to come with Kean's management between 1850 and 1859.

Kean's work is significant for several reasons. First, it brought fashionable audiences back to the theatre. Probably much of the credit should go to Queen Victoria, who in 1848 revived the office of Master of Revels and appointed Kean to it. Queen Victoria requested many theatrical performances for Windsor Castle and also began to attend the Princess' Theatre. The combination of her prestige and the respectable tone of Kean's management soon made his theatre a fashionable resort.

Second, Kean rearranged the evening's bill. Because fashionable playgoers tended to dine late, Kean opened his performances with a short curtain-raiser to offset the effect of late arrivals. Furthermore, he eliminated all

CHARLES KEAN'S PRODUCTION of *Richard II*. An interpolated scene showing the entry of Bolingbroke into London. [From the *Illustrated Times* (March 28, 1857)]

incidental entertainment. Thereafter, variety acts were increasingly relegated to the music halls, and theatres began to specialize in a limited range of theatrical entertainment.

Third, Kean hastened the trend toward "gentlemanly melodrama" begun by Macready. Although now remembered primarily for his Shakespearean productions, Kean presented only 17 of Shakespeare's plays, and his greatest success as an actor came in such melodramas as Boucicault's *The Corsican Brothers* and *Louis XI,* both adapted from French works which blend Romantic drama and melodrama. Such plays were to enjoy enormous popularity through the remainder of the century.

Fourth, Kean helped to establish the long run as a policy. Before 1850 a few melodramas had attained long runs, but Kean was the first producer to cultivate extended engagements for standard plays. The policy was first fully exploited in 1855, when *Henry VIII* was given 100 successive performances. Considering the enormous investments, it was probably inevitable that long runs would be adopted to recover the outlay. From this time, theatres tended to replace the repertory of plays rotated nightly with a series of plays, each performed as long as the demand continued.

Fifth, and probably most important, Kean developed antiquarianism further than any English producer. His first significant attempt to insure accuracy in every detail came in 1852 with *King John.* Beginning with *Macbeth* in 1853, he provided the audience with a printed list of the authorities he had consulted in his search for authenticity. Kean considered his election in 1857 to the Society of Antiquaries one of his greatest honors. Despite his

456

care for details, however, Kean could never induce Ellen Tree to abandon the hooped petticoats she wore under garments of every period.

Often called the "illustrator" of Shakespeare's texts, Kean replaced descriptive passages with spectacle. As designers, Kean had the services of such gifted men as Thomas Grieve (1799–1882), William Telbin (1813–73), and Frederick Lloyds. About 400 watercolor sketches of Kean's productions have survived, providing one of the most complete pictures of a 19th century producer's work.

Last, Kean helped to establish the director as the primary artist in the theatre. He employed no stars and gained his effects primarily through care for details and the coordination of the whole. Despite his fame, Kean was financially unsuccessful, for he always spent more than he made. Any deficit, however, can be attributed to his high standards rather than to lack of patronage, for his theatre was always well attended. After his retirement from management, Kean toured throughout the world in starring engagements.

English Drama, 1850–90

In the second half of the 19th century, English drama continued at a low ebb, although a number of writers achieved contemporary fame. Between 1844 and 1878, Tom Taylor (1817–80) wrote more than 70 plays ranging through almost every type. His greatest success was achieved with comedy and domestic drama. Among his most famous works were *Masks and Faces* (1852), based on the life of Peg Woffington; *Still Waters Run Deep* (1855), which created a stir because of its discussion of sex; *Our American Cousin* (1858), made famous by E. A. Sothern's playing of Lord Dundreary; and *The Ticket-of-Leave Man* (1863), a story of low-life featuring the detective Hawkshaw.

Between 1857 and 1882 Henry James Byron (1834–84) wrote nearly 150 plays ranging from sentimental comedy to burlesque and extravaganza. *Our Boys* (1875) achieved a run of 1362 performances, a record which stood for many years. Byron's plays epitomize the general level of dramatic entertainment in the late 19th century, which seldom penetrated beneath the surface of ideas or stock characters.

A more important dramatist was Dion Boucicault (1822–90), for he adapted French romantic drama to English tastes. Beginning his career in 1841 with *London Assurance*, Boucicault wrote his major works after residing in France from 1844 to 1848. Between 1853 and 1860 he lived in America and later divided his time between the United States and England. The basic ingredients of his plays, sentimentality, wit, sensationalism, and local color, were established between 1852 and 1860 and seldom varied thereafter except in details. His major works, such as *The Corsican Brothers* (1852), *The Sidewalks of New York* (1857), *The Octoroon* (1859), *The Colleen Bawn* (1860), *Arrah-na-Pogue* (1864), and *The Shaughraun* (1874), end with sensational and spectacular scenes requiring the full resources of the theatre. Fires, explosions, snowstorms, avalanches, and other disasters abound. His eagerness to exploit new inventions made him a major influence on theatrical production as well as playwriting.

While Boucicault tended to perfect and extend old devices, Thomas William Robertson (1829–71) is significant for pointing the way toward future developments. Son of a provincial actor, he began his career as a performer and served for a time as Mme. Vestris' stage manager. He began writing in 1851 and achieved his first success in 1864 with *David Garrick*. All of his major works, *Society* (1864), *Ours* (1866), *Caste* (1867), *Play* (1868), and *School* (1869), were performed by the Bancrofts. With their stories of contemporary life and emphasis upon realistic settings, properties, and stage business, his dramas mark a break with the past and foreshadow the realistic mode. Because he had no immediate successors, the vein opened by Robertson was not exploited until the 1890's, largely because the vogue for Sardou's plays swept all before it after 1870.

Between 1850 and 1900, burlesque, extravaganza and musical drama continued to attract the largest audiences. After 1870, the Christmas pantomime assumed the characteristics which it still retains. Most of the innovations came first at Drury Lane, where between 1869 and 1879 the Vokes family of dancers and pantomimists replaced the traditional short pieces with full-length fairy-tale pantomimes. In the 1880's, Augustus Harris (1851–96), manager of the Drury Lane, began to import music hall performers to play the "principal boy" (a breeches role) and the "dame" (played by a man) and to perform specialty acts. After this time, comedy gained the ascendancy, and the element of fantasy was relegated to a skimpy plot which served as excuse for the comic routines, dances, and spectacle.

Meanwhile the extravaganza was transformed by Gilbert and Sullivan. William Schwenk Gilbert (1836–1911), encouraged by Robertson to take up dramatic writing, achieved his first success with *Pygmalion and Galatea* (1871) and wrote a number of other plays before beginning his collaboration with Arthur Sullivan (1842–1900) in 1875. Their first work, *Trial by Jury*, also brought an alliance with Rupert D'Oyly Carte (1844–1901), who produced the operettas and in 1881 built the Savoy Theatre to house them. After writing *H.M.S. Pinafore* (1877), *The Pirates of Penzance* (1879), *The Mikado* (1885), and *The Gondoliers* (1889), Gilbert and Sullivan quarreled and, although they wrote two other works, their successful collaboration was at an end. The operettas have held the stage continuously. With their light-hearted melodies, whimsical humor, and good-

PUSS IN BOOTS, a pantomime at Drury
Lane, 1887. [From *The Graphic* (Jan. 7,
1888)]

natured satire, they turned the extravaganza in the direction of Aristophanic comedy.

The success of Gilbert and Sullivan prompted other developments in
musical comedy, especially through the work of George Edwardes (1852–
1915). Business manager of the Savoy Theatre for a time, in 1885 Edwardes
became manager of the Gaiety Theatre. Here, beginning with *In Town*
(1892) and *The Shop Girl* (1894), Edwardes established a type of musical
comedy in which a sketchy plot provided an excuse for songs, elaborate
production numbers performed by beautiful chorus girls, and specialty acts.
In this form, musical comedy was to flourish without significant change
until the first World War.

The music hall also prospered in the late 19th century, as regular
drama was separated from the incidental entertainment which had accompanied it since 1700. The music hall emerged slowly from the "music
rooms" attached to taverns. Around 1850, Charles Morton (1819–1904)
began the new trend when he erected a special building for entertainment.
Other tavern owners followed his example, but it was many years before
the link with taverns was broken. Gradually, however, the separation came
and the entertainment was made acceptable to middle-class audiences.
Sketches and short plays were added to the bills, and famous actors and
concert artists were induced to appear in the music hall theatres that were
erected throughout England. Edward Moss (1852–1912) and Oswald Stoll

(1866–1942) created famous circuits and attempted to substitute the term "variety" for "music hall." With the advent of the motion picture, variety declined rapidly. In the last quarter of the 19th century, however, the music halls offered serious competition to the legitimate drama.

Theatrical Conditions, 1860–80

By 1860 the major work of both Phelps and Kean was over, and the theatre was well on its way to recovery. For the first time since 1843, new theatres were built. The 21 theatres of 1860 had increased to 30 by 1870. The population of London also grew from 3,316,932 in 1864 to 4,766,661 in 1881. The new prosperity was accompanied by a number of changes, most evident in the work of Fechter, Boucicault, and the Bancrofts.

Charles Fechter (1824–79), son of a German father and French mother, made his acting debut in 1844 at the Comédie Française, where he often supported Rachel. Soon dissatisfied, he resigned his position and played for a time in Berlin and London before returning to Paris in 1848. He was soon recognized as the foremost stage lover of his day, and for a time was joint manager of the Odéon. Resigning after a disagreement, he decided to go to London.

Fechter opened at the Princess' Theater in 1860 and in 1861 created a sensation with his production of *Hamlet*. Unfamiliar with the English tradition, Fechter's interpretation of Hamlet was markedly different from any previously seen. Playing in the familiar style of gentlemanly melodrama and in settings furnished like ordinary rooms, he made the play seem contemporary. From 1863 to 1867, Fechter managed the Lyceum Theatre, where he featured translations of French plays and won a reputation as one of the finest actors of his time. In 1870 he went to America, but failed to gain a wide following because his powers were fading. In 1876 he retired.

Fechter's influence was considerable. First, he extended the vogue for gentlemanly melodrama begun by Macready and Kean. Second, he popularized a more realistic acting style, for he played the classics in precisely the same manner as contemporary drama. Thereafter, poetic drama grew in favor largely because it was merged with the 19th century taste for spectacular melodrama. Third, Fechter revived interest in the box set, which he used for most interiors. He gave up the practice of entering between the wings, which actors traditionally had done even when the wings represented solid walls. While Fechter did not bring about a revolution in theatrical practice, he encouraged renewed concern for illusionism.

After Dion Boucicault returned to England in 1860, he introduced several innovations. He seems to have originated the "out-of-town tryout" when *Arrah-na-Pogue* was played in the provinces before opening in London in 1865. Accepting the long-run policy, Boucicault recognized its implications and was the first to employ actors for the run of the play rather than on a seasonal contract.

Boucicault was also the first English playwright to achieve financial security. During the early 19th century the previous practice of paying authors with benefit performances was often replaced by the payment of set sums (100 pounds for a five-act play and proportionately less for shorter works) on the third, sixth, and twentieth nights of the original run. Few playwrights between 1810 and 1860, however, received more than 400 pounds. Jerrold testified that for *Black-Eyed Susan*, one of the most popular works of the 19th century, he had received a total of 70 pounds. By 1830 dissatisfaction had led to the formation of the Dramatic Authors' Society. Largely because of its agitation, Parliament in 1833 passed England's first copyright law. While the act protected all plays written after 1823, it did not cover dramatizations of novels, and the force of the bill was further reduced by a court decision which invested the acting rights to printed plays in their publishers. Thereafter, dramatists sought to keep their works out of print. Thus, the new bill gave authors some protection but did not greatly improve their lot.

Boucicault's innovation did not stem from any new legal sanction. Rather, because of the popularity of his plays, he demanded and received a percentage of the receipts from every performance. Consequently, *The Shaughraun* is said to have earned him $500,000. In 1865, the Bancrofts began to pay Robertson a set fee for each performance of his works; thereafter, the royalty system gradually gained in favor. The playwright's position was further improved by the International Copyright Agreement of 1886 and the U.S. Copyright Act of 1870, which together secured the dramatist's control over his works throughout most of the world.

Probably the most significant management between 1860 and 1880 was that of the Bancrofts at the Prince of Wales' Theatre, for here many earlier trends came together. Although it is difficult to discover a practice which they initiated, the Bancrofts combined a number of innovations to create a theatre quite unlike any other of the period.

Mrs. Bancroft, born Marie Wilton (1839–1921), was on the stage as a child, appearing with both Macready and Charles Kean. Her success as an adult actress began in burlesque drama in 1856. At the age of 26 she decided to manage her own company. The only theatre she could afford to rent was the out-of-the-way Queen's Theatre, so run down that it was known as the "dust hole." Nevertheless, after indemnifying him against loss, she induced H. J. Byron, the popular dramatist, to join her as co-manager and to supply the theatre with plays. Now called the Prince of Wales', the theatre opened in 1865. In securing Byron's services, Miss Wilton obviously intended to present a repertory composed primarily of burlesques and light comedy. Thus, it was only at Byron's urging that she produced Robertson's *Society,* a play previously refused by several other managers. Its run of 150 nights began an association which soon made Byron superfluous, and in 1867 he withdrew from the management. In the same year, Miss Wilton married Squire Bancroft (1841–1926), her leading man. Bancroft had made his debut in 1861 and had played in the provinces until he joined Miss Wilton's company in 1865. From 1867 until 1879 the Bancrofts were joint managers of the Prince of Wales' Theatre, and from 1880 until 1885, when they retired, of the Haymarket.

It is difficult to distinguish the Bancrofts' contributions from those of Robertson, for not only was he their major playwright, but he also directed the plays during the formative years. On the other hand, Robertson had little success with any other troupe. Consequently, it would appear that their joint success stemmed from their compatibility.

THE BANCROFTS' PRODUCTION of Robertson's *Ours* at the Prince of Wales's Theatre, 1866. [From *The Illustrated London News* (1866)]

The distinctive Robertson-Bancroft style first appeared with *Caste* (1867). While several earlier producers had emphasized realistic visual detail, they had used spectacle primarily as embellishment. In Robertson's plays, on the other hand, character and stage business are inseparable, for the attitudes and emotions of his personages are revealed more often through the minutiae of everyday domestic tasks than through dialogue. Without spectacle Robertson's plays scarcely exist, and the printed versions require lengthy and detailed stage directions to be comprehensible. They mark the advent of a new kind of realism in England.

Robertson worked with the actors of the Bancroft troupe on every detail. He sought to substitute understatement for bravura acting and to emphasize ensemble effects. The company had no stars and even the Bancrofts often played small roles. Most of the actors were young and greeted the innovations with enthusiasm. Lines of business, still dominant in other troupes, were not observed. Rehearsals, long by the standards of the period, were treated as seriously as performances.

The Bancrofts' contributions came primarily in contemporary drama. Only two of their productions were of "classics" and these were unsuccessful, for the company's acting style was not suited to period plays. Nevertheless, the prestige of the Bancroft company was comparable to that enjoyed earlier by Charles Kean, and contemporary drama was raised considerably in critical esteem.

The Bancrofts embraced the long run. In their 20 years of management they produced only 31 plays, and about one-half of all performances were of Robertson's works. After they began to present a series of plays for extended runs, they employed many of their actors on a "run of the play" contract. They abandoned the benefit system, still prevalent in most theatres, and raised salaries markedly. When other managers were paying actors five to ten pounds weekly, the Bancrofts were offering 60 to 100 pounds.

The Bancrofts also helped to establish several other important innovations. Their production of *Caste* in 1867 was the first in England to tour with a full company and all scenery and properties. By 1880 there were many "road" theatres in England and provincial companies were beginning to decline. The Bancrofts also helped to establish the single-play bill by dropping the curtain raiser. Although many theatres retained the more complex program, audiences no longer demanded lengthy productions. The Bancrofts aided in establishing matinee performances. Used occasionally since the 1850's, matinees became usual with the Bancrofts with their production of Sardou's *Diplomacy* in 1878. Matinees were adopted for Gilbert and Sullivan's operettas in the 1880's and were accepted almost everywhere by 1900.

Many of the Bancrofts' contributions involved spectacle and theatre architecture. Their productions won full acceptance for the box set. After 1875 as much care was devoted to accuracy in modern plays as in Shakespearean productions. The Bancrofts also firmly anchored acting behind the proscenium arch. The retreat from the apron had begun with Garrick, but, despite several attempts to abandon the proscenium doors, they were not removed at Drury Lane until 1822 and at Covent Garden in 1823. In 1831 the Olympic became the first minor house to dispense with them. The apron persisted, however, and actors continued to use it. After 1867, the "fourth wall" was always respected at the Prince of Wales' Theatre. When the Bancrofts moved to the Haymarket in 1880, they extended the gilded proscenium arch across the bottom of the stage to emphasize the picture frame. By 1900 the use of the apron had been curtailed almost everywhere.

The Bancrofts were also instrumental in establishing the orchestra as the favored seating area. In 1800, the pit still consisted only of backless benches. The King's Theatre, which was used for opera, converted some of its benches into comfortable seats with backs in 1828, and in 1843 the Haymarket added a few of these "stalls." Gradually other theatres accepted the change, although the stalls were restricted to a few rows at the front while the pit continued to occupy the remainder of the ground floor. In 1863, the Haymarket replaced its stalls with upholstered chairs, and the last pit benches were removed when the Bancrofts took over the Haymarket in 1880. Other theatres gradually followed this example. With the introduction of stall seating came the numbering and reservation of places. The practice of reserving seats reenforced the long run, since popular plays encouraged the booking of seats in advance and advance sales encouraged the extension of runs.

These changes are representative of many others in auditorium design. From the Restoration, the pit had been surrounded by boxes only slightly raised above it. Around 1820, however, the Adelphi Theatre established a new trend when the boxes were raised to permit the extension of the pit to the outside walls. Other changes came after 1860. Probably most important was the movement away from large houses. The Criterion, opened in 1874, held only 660, and the Prince of Wales' seated only 814. Few theatres built after 1875 held more than 1500. This reduction in size meant fewer galleries, while the growing prestige of stall seating motivated the replacement of boxes with open balconies, usually called the Dress Circle, Upper Circle, and Gallery. Furthermore, the balconies were foreshortened on the sides so that they no longer extended to the proscenium wall. As a result, the proscenium arch could be lowered. The cantilevering of balconies, which began around 1900, permitted the removal of supporting posts. All of these changes did much to improve sightlines and comfort. Many of the innovations stem from the work of C. J. Phipps (1835–97), designer of about 40 theatres in England.

Theatrical Practice, 1880–1900

Between 1880 and 1900 the English theatre was dominated by the actor-manager, Henry Irving (1838–1905). Born John Henry Brodribb, Irving played in the provinces from 1856 to 1866. After he came to London, he performed with several leading actors before going to the Lyceum Theatre in 1871 as leading man and stage manager. At that time, the Lyceum was under the management of H. L. Bateman (1812–75), an

American who had taken the theatre to star his daughters, Kate (1843–1917), Virginia (1853–1940), and Isabel (1854–1934). Kate and her sister Ellen (1844–1936) had achieved notoriety in America as child prodigies in such roles as Richard III, Macbeth, and Shylock. Ellen had retired at the age of 16, but Kate had won considerable fame as an adult performer before the family came to London. After Bateman died in 1875, his wife continued as manager until 1878, when the Lyceum passed to Irving. Under Irving's management from 1878 to 1898, the Lyceum became the foremost theatre of London. Irving also played throughout England and made eight tours of America. He retired in 1902.

As an actor, Irving gained his first outstanding success in 1871 as Mathias in *The Bells,* a thrilling melodrama about a man who confesses under hypnosis to the murder of a Jewish pedlar. This role remained one of Irving's most popular throughout his career. He continued to build his reputation in such melodramas as W. G. Wills' (1828–91) *Charles I* (1872) and *Eugene Aram* (1873). In 1874, his *Hamlet* ran for 200 nights, a new record for a Shakespearean play. By the time he became a manager, he was considered the finest serious actor in London. In 1878 he had already been on the stage for more than 20 years and his success had been won only through long and diligent work. Irving had few natural attributes upon which to build; throughout his career critics voiced grave reservations about his playing. He mispronounced many words, walked, as one critic put it, like a man trying to get over a plowed field hastily, and at times interpreted roles in a bizarre fashion. On the other hand, he was a master of byplay which clarified every reaction and thought. His roles were boldly conceived and carefully portrayed. Like Charles Kean, Irving was at his best in melodrama. Although he is now remembered chiefly as a Shakespearean actor, Shylock was the only Shakespearean role in which he consistently appeared with success. Irving promoted no new playwrights and never appeared in the new realistic drama.

Irving's fame is bound up with that of his leading lady, Ellen Terry (1847–1928), who came from a large family of actors, two others of whom were well known. Kate (1844–1924), on stage with Ellen as a child in Charles Kean's company, went on to perform Ophelia to Fechter's Hamlet before retiring in 1867. She was to be the grandmother of John Gielgud. Fred Terry (1863–1933), outstanding in romantic roles for the Lyceum company, managed his own troupe from 1900 to 1930. As an adult, Ellen Terry had played in the provinces, for the Bancrofts, and at the Court Theatre before joining Irving in 1878. She remained Irving's leading lady until he retired in 1902. She then managed the Imperial Theatre for a time, allowing her son, Gordon Craig, to try out many of his ideas. After her marriage in 1907 she performed only occasionally, although she did not retire fully until 1925. At her best in such roles as Beatrice in *Much Ado About Nothing,* Olivia in *Twelfth Night,* and Portia in *The Merchant of*

SCENE from Irving's production of Tennyson's *Becket* in 1893. The design is by Hawes Craven. [From the souvenir program]

Venice, Miss Terry had an excellent sense of timing and great command of stage movement and speech. To all of her roles she brought freshness and vitality.

Despite the personal fame of Irving and Ellen Terry, the reputation of the Lyceum rested upon the total effect of its productions. Building upon the tradition of Macready and Charles Kean and stimulated by the London appearance of the Meiningen Players in 1881, Irving's work climaxed the trend toward pictorial realism. Although never the stickler for accuracy that Kean had been, Irving sometimes employed archeologists to aid him. For example, Sir Lawrence Alma-Tadema (1836–1912) designed the costumes and scenery for *Cymbeline* (1896) and *Coriolanus* (1901). At other times he commissioned designs from such famous painters as Edward Burne-Jones (1833–98). In addition, he employed the finest scenic artists of the day, Hawes Craven and Joseph Harker. Craven (1837–1910) had worked in London since 1857 for such producers as Fechter and the Bancrofts, and to him probably should go much of the credit usually given to Irving. Craven was later to open a scenic studio which supplied many theatres with settings. Joseph Harker (1855–1927) began his career as an assistant to Craven and later took major responsibility for many of Irving's productions. After leaving Irving he became Herbert Beerbohm Tree's principal designer. Continuing to work into the 1920's, Harker was one of the major links between Victorian and modern scenic practices. Although Irving employed the finest artists available, he had no consistent policy. Sometimes one person designed the scenery and costumes for a production, but more frequently the tasks were divided among a number of artists.

Many of the innovations at the Lyceum resulted from changes in the method of shifting scenery. In 1881, grooves were abandoned. By adopting "free plantation," Irving could place scenery wherever he desired and achieve complete flexibility. Irving's solution was the culmination of many earlier trends. Since the beginning of the century, heavy set pieces had increased in number. Many had been shifted by means of large elevator traps located upstage. While a "short scene" occupied the forward part of the stage, a "set scene" was arranged behind a drop and revealed when needed. In this way, heavy pieces could be shifted without the necessity of closing the front curtain. Other complex changes were often made while the "act drop" was serving as a background for the entr'acte entertainment. Irving was the first producer who used the front curtain to mask major changes of scenery, although he too continued the alternation of short and long scenes to avoid breaks in the action.

During the 19th century the arrangement of the stage floor also grew increasingly complex as the requirements of spectacle changed. After 1850 the stage was usually constructed in the following manner. The supporting joists, which ran parallel to the footlights, were arranged in groups of three or four set about 1½ to 2 inches apart. The spaces between the joists could be covered with narrow strips of wood or left open to form "cuts," through which pieces of scenery, such as ground rows, might be raised or lowered. Occasionally, a vertical moving panorama ran from overhead through a cut to aid the illusion of climbing or falling. The groups of joists were spaced about four feet apart. On them were laid the floorboards, all of which could be removed to form "bridges," through which large set pieces could be raised or special effects manipulated.

Bridges also accommodated the many traps required by 19th century plays. The "vampire" trap, named for Planché's *The Vampire* (1820), consisted of two spring-leaves which parted under pressure and immediately reclosed. It could be set into the floor or a flat to permit an actor to sink seemingly into the earth or walk through a solid wall. The "Corsican" trap (so-called because of its use in *The Corsican Brothers*) or "ghost glide" was more complex. For it, a bridge was removed the full width of the stage. Over it was placed a surface constructed like the covering of a roll-top desk. Beneath the bridge was an inclined track upon which a wheeled platform ran. As the platform moved up the track, the actor standing on it was forced up through a "bristle" trap (an opening covered with bristles colored to match the floor). The roll-top covering over the bridge was geared to move with the platform so that no opening in the floor was ever seen by the audience. Thus, figures appeared to rise from the earth while gliding through space.

As the desire for complete illusion grew, so did the use of three-dimensional scenic elements. Charles Kean still depended primarily upon two-dimensional painted pieces; it was not until the 1870's that steps,

AN ENGLISH STAGE of the late 19th century. Note the treatment of the stage floor and the overhead grooves for the sliding flats. [From *The Magazine of Art* (1889)]

platforms, and similar three-dimensional units were common. Edward Godwin (1833–86), father of Gordon Craig, seems to have begun the trend with his settings for the Bancrofts' *The Merchant of Venice* in 1875. Godwin later built a Greek stage inside a circus, anticipating Max Reinhardt's experiments by many years. It was probably Irving's desire to make more effective use of three-dimensional pieces that motivated his removal of the grooves, which were suited only to flat wings. Since he then had to depend primarily upon manual shifting, Irving employed about 135 persons to "arrange and conduct the scenes" and rehearsed them as thoroughly as he did his actors. Irving's innovation was soon to outmode the raked floor, on which it was difficult to handle scenery not mounted parallel to the footlights.

Irving also paid careful attention to costumes, but his chief improvement over his predecessors lay in the care given to minor characters. Even Kean had dressed the supernumeraries in armor made of zinc and tinsel and had substituted glazed cotton for satin. Irving allegedly applied the

[IRVING'S PRODUCTION of *Romeo and Juliet*. The setting is by William Telbin. Note the extensive use of three-dimensional scenery. From *The Illustrated London News* (1882)]

same standard to all costumes and consequently achieved a more unified effect.

Irving was probably the first English producer to make an art of stage lighting. Lighting underwent many changes during the 19th century. The first major innovation came with the introduction of gas. Although William Murdoch had experimented with gas at the end of the 18th century, it was not sufficiently developed for purposes of illumination for several years. It was adopted for exterior lighting at Covent Garden in 1815 and may have been installed in the auditorium of the Lyceum in the same year. It was first used for stage lighting in 1817 at both Covent Garden and Drury Lane.

Gas did not win immediate acceptance, however, for it presented many problems. Since there were as yet no gas mains, each theatre had to install and maintain its own plant, an expensive undertaking. Furthermore, gas gave off unpleasant fumes and oppressive heat; the danger of fire was always great. It was not until the 1840's, when a dependable supply became available, that gas was widely adopted.

Gas eventually triumphed because of its advantages over candles and oil. For the first time, the stage could be lighted as brightly as desired. Since the burners did not have to be trimmed, as did the wicks of candles and lamps, they could be distributed more advantageously. As a result, border

469

lights were used more extensively. Furthermore, complete control over intensity was now possible. At first each gas pipe was controlled separately, but in the 1840's the "gas table," comparable to the modern control board, made it possible for an operator to control all lights from one position. After 1850 many of the objections to gas were eliminated by the "fishtail" burner, which increased efficiency and reduced fumes by controlling the relationship of the fuel to oxygen. In the 1880's, an incandescent mantle made gas even safer, but by this time electricity had begun to replace it.

Two lighting instruments, the limelight and carbon arc, were of special importance during the 19th century. The limelight ("calcium" or Drummond light) was invented by Thomas Drummond in 1816. It consisted of two cylinders of compressed gas, one of hydrogen and one of oxygen, which were directed against a column of lime so as to heat it to incandescence. Placed inside a hood and fitted with a lens, the limelight was the prototype of the spotlight. Macready was the first to recognize its potentialities for the stage, but after using it for a time in 1837 he gave it up as too expensive. Nevertheless, by the 1850's it had been adopted widely and played a prominent role in the productions of Samuel Phelps and Charles Kean. Its mellow and brilliant rays were first used for creating such atmospheric effects as sunlight or moonlight; only gradually was its potentiality for lighting the acting area developed. Eventually it came to be used primarily as a "follow" spot to emphasize starring performers. The major disadvantage of the limelight was its need for constant supervision: since the lime had to be kept in proper alignment with the gases and flame, it required a separate operator for each instrument.

The carbon arc was first demonstrated in 1808 by Sir Humphrey Davy. The lack of a satisfactory source of power left its theatrical uses unexplored until the 1840's. By 1860, it had been placed in a housing and equipped with a lens to create a spotlight. It was not widely used, however, until after 1880, when electricity began to replace gas. To create a carbon arc, each electrical pole was attached to a stick of carbon; when the carbons were brought into close juxtaposition, the current leaped between them, creating an incandescence. Giving off a rather harsh light, the carbon arc also tended to be noisy and to flicker. Many of the drawbacks were eliminated with the invention in 1876 of the Jablochkoff Candle, which kept the carbon in proper alignment without the aid of an operator. The carbon arc served the same purposes as the limelight.

In 1879, Edison's invention of the incandescent lamp made it possible to light the entire stage electrically. The change to electricity was rapid, largely because several disastrous theatre fires made managers anxious to dispense with gas. As the first illuminant which did not require an open flame, electricity was widely adopted, even though it was not yet equal to gas in versatility. In 1881, the Savoy Theatre became the first in England to be lighted throughout by electricity. By 1900, almost all theatres had made the change. Because early incandescent lamps could be made only in very low wattages, the carbon arc and limelight continued as important supplements. Beginning in 1905, significant improvements in the filaments of lamps made higher wattages possible. As the potential intensity of lamps was increased thereafter, the carbon arc and limelight declined, but remained important until after the first World War.

While such technical advances created new potentialities for stage lighting, few producers knew how to use them for artistic effect. After the introduction of gas, brightness was overemphasized for several years. Under this garish light the two-dimensionality of the painted scenery was readily apparent, a significant factor in motivating greater use of three-dimensional detail. While many producers experimented with more subtle effects, it was Irving who first fully exploited stage lighting. He continued to use gas to the end of his career, employing electricity only for special effects.

Irving's improvements were gained through care for details. He broke up the footlights and borders into short sections, each of which was equipped with different colors and controls. He experimented with transparent lacquered glass to achieve varied hues, and with several means of distributing light more effectively. Critics almost always commented on his lighting, although many termed it arbitrary and distracting because each moment had obviously been contrived for beauty and effectiveness. Irving also introduced black masking pieces at the front of the stage to prevent "light spill" and was the first English producer who consistently darkened the auditorium during performances. It required 30 "gas men" to mount and operate the lights at the Lyceum.

Irving's care with each element of production was crowned by even greater care in their coordination into an integrated whole. It was in this regard that Irving's work was superior. Irving's position in England is comparable to that of Saxe-Meiningen in Germany, for while his emphasis upon pictorial realism summarized the 19th century tradition, his work as a director made way for the future.

Irving's greatest success came between 1878 and 1888, when the relative failure of *Macbeth* marked the beginning of his decline. Nevertheless, it was not until 1892 that his most lavish production, *Henry VIII,* was staged. In 1896 his health began to fail, and in 1898 he gave up management, although he continued to perform until 1902.

In 1895 Irving became the first actor in English history to be knighted, an indication that actors had at last achieved social acceptance, as well as a measure of Irving's preeminence. In 1897 Squire Bancroft was knighted, and by 1914 such performers as John Hare, Johnston Forbes-Robertson, and Herbert Beerbohm Tree had been similarly honored. Comparable awards were not given to women until 1925, when Ellen Terry was named Dame Commander of the British Empire.

The Continuing Tradition, 1900–1914

Although the "modern" theatre began to emerge in the 1890's, pictorial realism continued as the principal goal until the first World War. Furthermore, most of the major figures of the London stage between 1900 and 1914 had been trained in the Bancroft-Irving tradition, and they made few innovations. Of the actor-managers, the most important were John Hare, the Kendals, Forbes-Robertson, Martin-Harvey, Wyndham, and Tree.

John Hare (1844–1921) had won a considerable following before he left the Bancrofts in 1875 to manage the Court Theatre. In partnership with the Kendals, he managed St. James' Theatre from 1879 to 1888, when he moved to the Garrick. He retired in 1911. Hare was considered one of London's most versatile actors and most careful managers.

Madge Kendal (1848–1935), Robertson's sister, and her husband William Hunter Kendal (1843–1917) played for the Bancrofts and Hare before entering management in 1879. They retired in 1908. Mrs. Kendal was noted for her technical skill and subtle playing in the Bancroft tradition. Both were considered models of personal and professional behavior.

Johnston Forbes-Robertson (1853–1937) differed from most of the major actors of his day in being an excellent speaker of verse, an art which he had learned from Samuel Phelps. On the stage from 1874 until 1913, Forbes-Robertson acted with Phelps, the Bancrofts, and Irving. He also served as leading man to Helena Modjeska (1844–1909), the Polish actress who appeared with great success in England and America between 1877 and 1905, and to Mary Anderson (1859–1940), an American actress who won fame in England between 1883 and 1889 for her Shakespearean performances. Occasionally Forbes-Robertson undertook management, but his reputation rested primarily upon his acting. Some critics consider him the finest Hamlet of all time.

John Martin-Harvey (1863–1944) made his debut in 1881 and from 1882 played for Irving, whom he succeeded as manager of the Lyceum Theatre. In his first independent production, an adaptation of Dickens' *A Tale of Two Cities*, he won such popularity that he was condemned to play the role of Sidney Carton through most of his remaining career. He gained renown in 1912 for his performance in Reinhardt's London production of *Oedipus Rex*. Until about 1910, Martin-Harvey continued Irving's practices, but gradually accepted modern trends and after the First World War abandoned pictorial realism altogether. More than any other producer, he successfully bridged the Victorian and the modern stage.

Charles Wyndham (1837–1919) became an actor in 1862 but did not achieve success until he opened the Criterion Theatre in 1874. He made this theatre and those which he later acquired—Wyndham's (1899) and the New Theatre (1903)—famous for light drama. His productions were considered impeccable. Wyndham is also credited with replacing the short handbill with the modern theatre program.

TREE'S PRODUCTION of *Henry VIII* (1910). The setting is by Joseph Harker. [From *The Daily Mirror* (1910)]

The most famous actor-manager between 1900 and 1914 was Herbert Beerbohm Tree (1853–1917). On the stage from 1878, he assumed the management of the Haymarket in 1887. From the profits made on melodramas and light contemporary plays he built Her Majesty's Theatre in 1897. Although he had little previous experience with Shakespearean drama, Tree's new theatre was to be the principal home of Shakespeare between 1900 and 1914. Tree employed two of Irving's former designers, Harker and Walter Hann, and often consulted such archeologists as Alma-Tadema. His *A Midsummer Night's Dream* (1900) featured live rabbits and a carpet of grass with flowers that could be plucked. Although the scene changes added 45 minutes to the playing time, the literal realism of this production attracted more than 220,000 spectators. Through Tree's work, Shakespeare probably gained his widest public following. Beginning

473

in 1905, Tree annually staged a festival of Shakespeare's plays, many performed by other companies.

Although not a very good actor, Tree often starred in his own productions. On the other hand, he employed the best performers available, and he worked on every production with unbounded enthusiasm. As the repertory system declined, Tree became concerned about the lack of effective training for young actors. Consequently, in 1904 he established an acting school which was to become the Royal Academy of Dramatic Art.

With the outbreak of the First World War in 1914, Tree gave up his Shakespearean productions. Before the war ended, he was dead. With him died the 19th century tradition, for after the war the actor-manager system was largely abandoned and pictorial realism was considered old-fashioned.

By 1917, the forces which created the modern English theatre had already been at work for more than 25 years. The new tradition, although in many ways quite unlike the old, owed much to those practices it was to supplant.

15

THE AMERICAN
THEATRE TO 1915

*I*n America the theatre began to emerge about 1750. Interrupted by the
Revolution, it grew steadily after 1785. By 1800, it was firmly established
along the Atlantic Coast, and after 1815 followed the path of westward expansion. In the early years, the American theatre emulated practices current
in England, from whence came many of its performers and most of its
repertory. Native actors and dramatists only gradually gained recognition.
After 1870, the resident stock company was superseded by traveling troupes,
and New York became the center of production. After 1895, as businessmen
gained control, financial gain became the principal motive in theatrical
production. By 1915, revolts against this condition had begun to stimulate
changes that would at last make American drama a potent international
force.

The Colonial Theatre

At first, life in the American colonies was too harsh to permit theatrical activities. The earliest record of a performance is not found until 1665, when three men in Virginia were hauled into court for performing a playlet, *The Bear and the Cub*. No other instances are noted until the end of the century, when students presented plays at Harvard College and at William and Mary. In New York sometime between 1699 and 1702, Richard Hunter obtained permission to give theatrical entertainments, but it is not certain that he did so. In 1703 Anthony Aston, the first professional actor to arrive in America, gave a few performances in Charleston and New York to earn money for his return passage to England. In 1714, the first extant American play, *Androboros* (or "Maneater"), written by Robert Hunter, Governor of New York, was published. A rather crude satire, it ridiculed Hunter's political opponents.

Between 1715 and 1735, theatrical activities increased. In 1716, William Levingston of Williamsburg, Virginia, built the first theatre in America, and here Charles and Mary Stagg arranged entertainments, the precise nature of which are uncertain, until about 1732. In Philadelphia, strolling players performed in 1723 and 1724; in Lancaster, performances were given irregularly between 1730 and 1742; and in New York, amateur players staged plays and fitted out a theatre between 1730 and 1733. In Charleston, South Carolina, amateurs gave a season of three plays in 1735 and built a theatre for performances in 1736 and 1737. This flurry of activity came to an end in the late 1730's, however, probably because of the religious fervor which accompanied the appearances of George Whitefield and John Wesley in the colonies.

A significant new beginning was made in 1749, when a company under the leadership of Walter Murray and Thomas Kean made its initial appearance in Philadelphia. Almost nothing is known about the origin or qualifications of the actors. Probably most were amateurs. This troupe played in Philadelphia until 1750, and then moved on to New York and various towns in Virginia and Maryland. Little is heard of it after 1752. Regardless of its artistic stature, the Murray-Kean company was the first to present seasons of some length in several towns. It established a precedent which was to be followed by its more important successor, the Hallam troupe.

Before turning to the Hallams, however, it is necessary to glance briefly at Jamaica, where theatrical performances had been given sporadically since about 1680. The arrival in 1745 of John Moody, an English strolling player, marked a significant change. After playing with an amateur group, he returned to England in 1749 to recruit professional actors. In 1751, he sent a company, headed by David Douglass (?–1786), to Jamaica. It was probably Moody who alerted English actors to opportunities in the colonies at a time when the Licensing Act had seriously curtailed the theatre in England. His news came at an especially crucial moment in the career of the Hallams.

William Hallam, one of a large family of actors, had opened the New Wells Theatre in Goodman's Fields, London, in 1740. At first he presented only minor entertainments, but in 1744 turned to more ambitious works in spite of the Licensing Act. Although he prospered for several years, in 1751 his theatre was closed. It was at this time that Hallam conceived the idea of sending a troupe to America. The new company was headed by his brother, Lewis Hallam (1714–56), an actor of secondary roles, with Mrs. Lewis Hallam as the leading actress. Consisting of 12 adults and Hallam's three children, the troupe was organized on the sharing plan, which was then still typical of English provincial troupes. Upon arriving in America, they fitted out a theatre at Williamsburg and opened in September, 1752. From this date can be traced the effective beginning of the professional theatre in America.

In addition to Williamsburg, the Hallams played in New York, Philadelphia, and Charleston before sailing to Jamaica in 1755. When they arrived, David Douglass was preparing to leave for England to recruit new actors, and the amalgamation of the troupes solved difficulties for both companies. Lewis Hallam died in 1756, and in 1758 Mrs. Hallam married Douglass, who remained head of the troupe until the Revolution. From 1758 to 1764, Douglass' company played in the mainland colonies. During these years, Mrs. Douglass continued as the leading actress, while Lewis Hallam, Jr. (c. 1740–1808) was now the leading man. Between 1759 and 1761, Douglass performed in New York, Philadelphia, Annapolis, Williamsburg, and elsewhere, and in 1761–62, his presentations of "moral dialogues" in Rhode Island were the first professional performances in New England.

After another interval in Jamaica, Douglass returned to the mainland from 1766 to 1775. By now, he had developed considerable optimism about the future and began to build substantial permanent playhouses. The first, the Southwark Theatre in Philadelphia, was opened in 1766. In 1767, he built the John Street Theatre in New York, and thereafter erected theatres in major towns between New York and Charleston. During these years, Douglass also performed the first American play to be given a professional production, Thomas Godfrey's (1736–63) *The Prince of Parthia*. A neoclassical tragedy with echoes of many Shakespearean works, it was given in Philadelphia in 1767. At the outbreak of the Revolution in 1774, the Continental Congress called for the cessation of theatrical entertainment.

In 1775, Douglass sailed for Jamaica. Although many members of his company were to return after the war, Douglass' theatrical career soon ended.

The colonial theatre between 1752 and 1774 differed little from the English provincial theatre of the day. The Hallam-Douglass company had to tour, for as yet there was no center capable of supporting a permanent theatre. The expense and inconvenience of travel made it necessary to keep the troupe small and the scenic investiture simple. The performers were at best third-rate; they doubled in roles and appeared in entr'acte entertainments as well. Thus, while the artistic level was not high, the company established the foundations upon which later and more substantial companies would build.

During the Revolution, there were no professional performances, although British soldiers presented plays in Boston, New York, and Philadelphia, and American troops performed on a less ambitious scale. American playwrights were more active than performers. Mercy Otis Warren (1728–1814) satirized British sympathizers in *The Adulateur* (1773) and *The Group* (1775), Hugh Henry Brackenridge (1748–1816) wrote a blank-verse play, *The Battle of Bunker Hill* (1776), and to John (or Joseph) Leacock is attributed the five-act prose work, *The Fall of British Tyranny* (1776). The most effective play of the period is Robert Munford's (c. 1730–84) *The Patriots* (c. 1776–77), a satire on "super patriots" who label all opponents enemy agents. Although the literary output of the period is slight, it is still significant as the first flurry of dramatic writing in America.

The Reestablishment of the Theatre, 1782–1815

Professional performances were resumed soon after hostilities ended. In 1782, Thomas Wall, a former member of Douglass' troupe, appeared in Baltimore, and in the next year he joined forces with Dennis Ryan. As "The American Company," their troupe played between New York and Charleston during the next few years. In 1784 Lewis Hallam brought a company to the new country, and in 1785 John Henry (1738–94), another of Douglass' players, came with his. In 1785, Hallam and Henry joined forces to create "The Old American Company," destined to be the new country's major troupe until 1794 and the foundation of New York's theatre.

Between 1794 and 1815, however, Philadelphia was the dominant theatrical center. It began with little promise, for the prohibition against acting was not repealed until 1789. In 1791 Thomas Wignell (1753–1803),

INTERIOR of the Chestnut Street Theatre, Philadelphia. [From *The New York Magazine* (1794)]

Hallam and Henry's principal low comedian, and Alexander Reinagle, a musician, set out to establish a company there. Desiring to create a theatre of high quality, they erected the Chestnut Street Theatre, the finest in America. Allegedly modeled upon the Theatre Royal at Bath, it seated about 1200 and had a stage 71 feet deep by 36 feet wide. While it was being built, Wignell sailed for England, where he engaged the best company yet seen in America. Among his recruits were Eliza Kemble Whitlock (1761–1836), sister of John Philip Kemble and Mrs. Siddons; Mrs. Oldmixon (?–1835–36), a favorite singer at Covent Garden; and James Fennell (1766–1816), an actor of enviable reputation both in Edinburgh and London.

The troupe was further strengthened in 1796 with the addition of Mrs. Merry, Warren, and Cooper. Anne Brunton Merry (1768–1808) had been the leading actress at Covent Garden before retiring upon her marriage in 1792. Financial reverses soon made it necessary for her to return to the stage; the lack of a suitable engagement in England brought her to America, where she remained at the head of her profession until her death at the age of 40. After her first husband died, she married successively Wignell and Warren. William Warren (1767–1832), an actor of old men's roles, was connected with the Chestnut Street Theatre from 1796 until 1829, and from 1806 until 1827 shared in its management. Thomas Abthorpe Cooper (1776–1849), one of England's most promising young actors, came to America in 1796 because he was unable to find a suitable engagement at home. Within a few years he was considered America's leading actor. Essentially a tragic performer, he popularized the Kemble style in America. In 1797, Wignell added John Bernard (1756–1828) to his troupe. A performer of heroes in high comedy, Bernard had played at Covent Garden and elsewhere before coming to America. In Philadelphia, Boston, New York, and Albany, Bernard did much to raise the level of performance before returning to England in 1819. With this superior company and under sound management, the Chestnut Street Theatre forged to the front. Its high standards were maintained by Wignell and Reinagle's successors, Warren and William Wood (1779–1861), joint managers of the company from 1810 to 1826.

The secondary position of the New York theatre between 1794 and 1815 is explained in part by dissensions within the company. In 1792, John Hodgkinson (c. 1765–1805), a versatile and ambitious provincial actor, joined the troupe, and by 1794 had replaced Henry in the management. By this time, Hallam's popularity was declining, and his jealousy of Hodgkinson seems to have interfered with the orderly operation of the theatre. Perhaps for this reason, William Dunlap (1766–1839), the leading playwright of the period, was induced to join the management. Shortly afterward, Hallam gave up his share, as did Hodgkinson in 1798, although both continued to act with the company and to create dissension. Thus, by the time Dunlap became sole manager in 1798, the troupe was in serious difficulty despite attempts to strengthen it with new talent. In 1793, Mrs. Charlotte Melmoth (1749–1823), an actress who had won considerable fame at Covent Garden and Drury Lane, had arrived to play principal tragic roles, and in 1795, Joseph Jefferson I (1774–1832), a popular comic actor who was to found an important theatrical family, joined the company. In spite of these and other additions, factions within the troupe made it difficult to maintain discipline and to achieve high artistic standards.

The New York theatre had also been weakened financially by Hodgkinson's insistence upon taking the company to New England and by competition from the Chestnut Street troupe, which still made occasional visits to New York. Furthermore, by 1798 the John Street Theatre was inadequate and a new home had to be built. In 1798 the Park Theatre, destined to be New York's leading theatre until the 1840's, was opened. As sole manager, Dunlap struggled along until 1805, when bankruptcy overtook him. In 1807, Thomas A. Cooper became manager, and the Park entered a period of prosperity. In 1808–09, Cooper sold a share in the company to Stephen Price (1783–1840), a lawyer and businessman who proved to be a skillful manager. After Price demonstrated his abilities, Cooper spent an increasing amount of time on starring tours, and by 1815 had given up management altogether.

It was Cooper and Price who did most to popularize tours by starring actors, a practice destined to undermine resident troupes. Although actors had played short engagements with companies since about 1800, it was the importation of George Frederick Cooke in 1810 which created a demand for stars of the first magnitude. Cooper and Price served as Cooke's agents in America and engaged Dunlap to travel with him to Boston, Philadelphia, and Baltimore. This tour was so profitable that others were inevitable, although the War of 1812 prevented immediate successors.

The 1790's also introduced the professional theatre in Boston. Although Joseph Harper had given performances in 1792, the prohibition against acting was not rescinded until 1793. The Federal Street Theatre was erected in the same year and Charles Stewart Powell assembled an inferior company in England. Managements changed often and conditions remained unsettled until 1802, when Snelling Powell (1774–1843) assumed control. The company was especially strong between 1806 and 1811, when John Bernard shared in the management and attracted a number of outstanding players. After 1802, the Federal Street Theatre had no competitors until 1827.

Charleston emerged as the fourth important theatrical center of the 1790's. While the Ryan-Wall troupe had played in Charleston as early as 1785, no continuing company settled there until 1795, when John Joseph Sollee assumed control of the City Theatre. Much of the vitality of the Charleston theatre came from the influx of French refugees, both at the time of the French Revolution and following the slave uprising in Santo Domingo in 1793. In the 1790's many plays were performed in French, and many outstanding actors were of French origin. Perhaps the most important French artist was Alexandre Placide (c. 1750–1812), a dancer, acrobat, and pantomimist from the Parisian fair and boulevard theatres, who appeared with all of the major troupes in America before becoming manager of the Charleston theatre from 1798 until 1812.

By the 1790's, then, the theatre was firmly established along the Atlantic seaboard. Four main circuits were established: the Charleston troupe controlled all of the towns northward to Richmond; the Philadelphia troupe controlled Baltimore, Annapolis, and later Washington; the New York company toured for a time in the adjacent area, but after 1800 tended to remain fixed; and the Boston troupe dominated New England. While there were other lesser ones, these were the principal companies until 1815. After 1790, the major troupes abandoned the sharing arrangement in favor of salaries and a yearly benefit, although lesser groups continued the older tradition through much of the 19th century. Performances were still given only three times a week, and the length of seasons in each town was variable, since most troupes toured and yellow fever and the discomfort of winter cold and summer heat often required the suspension of playing.

For the most part the repertory was English. Nevertheless, American playwrights, notably Tyler, Dunlap, and Payne, laid the foundations for a native drama. Royall Tyler (1757–1826) is remembered now for *The Contrast* (1787), the first American comedy to be professionally produced. Owing much to Sheridan's plays, it is saved from mere imitativeness by the Yankee servant, Jonathan, whose frank and naive responses to New York social life illuminate the manners of the period.

SCENE from *The Contrast* (1787). [From the first edition of the play (1790)]

Tyler's success may have inspired William Dunlap to turn to playwriting. Dunlap had spent the years between 1784 and 1787 in England and had seen most of the important performers and plays of the time. After the success of his *The Father* (1789), he went on to write some 60 plays, at least 13 of which were adapted from works by Kotzebue. His most famous original drama, *André* (1798), is based on an actual incident involving a British spy during the Revolutionary War. The majority of Dunlap's plays were written before 1812, after which he devoted his time primarily to painting. Dunlap is also important for having written *A History of the American Theatre* (1832) and the first history of American art, published in 1834.

John Howard Payne (1791–1852) came to public attention when only 14 years old as the publisher of *The Thespian Mirror,* a critical journal. In the following year, his first play, *Julia* (1806), was acted at the Park Theatre, and in 1809 he made his acting debut, billed as a child prodigy. With Stephen Price as his manager, he enjoyed a considerable vogue for a short time, but by 1811 his popularity had waned. In 1813, he went to England, where he spent the next 20 years as dramatist and critic. Payne wrote or adapted between 50 and 60 plays. Of these, the best known were *Brutus* (played by Edmund Kean in 1818), *Charles II* (performed by

Charles Kemble in 1824), and *Clari* (1823), famous for the song, "Home, Sweet Home." Payne was America's first internationally successful dramatist. After 1832, he ceased writing for the stage.

The Expanding American Theatre, 1815–50

As in England, the theatre in America between 1815 and 1850 was one of paradoxes, for while it constantly expanded, it was often in danger of ruin because of the general financial depression. The growth of the theatre is most clearly manifested in its extension into new territories as settlers moved westward. Although there had been a few theatrical performances west of the Alleghenies before 1815, these had been given primarily by amateurs. Only in New Orleans, where a French theatre was opened in 1791, was there extensive dramatic activity.

The first major step toward a professional theatre in the "west" came in 1815 when Samuel Drake (1769–1854) took a company overland from Albany to Pittsburg and down the Ohio River to Kentucky. Here Drake established a circuit, including Lexington, Louisville, and Frankfort, although he ventured at times into Ohio, Indiana, Tennessee, and Missouri. His scenery was designed to meet all situations. An adjustable cut-drop served as a proscenium which could be erected in any large room; a roll drop served as a front curtain; three sets of wings (one for exteriors, one for fancy interiors, and a third for plain interiors) and six roll drops (garden, street, wood, palace, parlor, and kitchen) served all scenic demands. Plays were altered so that they could be performed by his company of 10 actors, who also doubled in backstage capacities. Drake's work is typical of all the pioneers who came after him, for like the Hallams he improvised to meet whatever situation he encountered and remained in each town as long as attendance permitted. Typically, troupes began by touring over a large area and, as the population increased, gradually confined themselves to an ever smaller territory until touring could be given up altogether.

Drake soon had a number of competitors. The most important between 1820 and 1840 was James H. Caldwell (1793–1863), an English light comedian who came to America in 1816. Appearing first in Charleston and Richmond, he moved to New Orleans in 1820. Between 1825 and 1835, Caldwell dominated the theatre in the Mississippi Valley, for he controlled theatres in Natchez, St. Louis, Nashville, and elsewhere. Thus, Caldwell could offer attractive contracts to touring stars as they came to include the West in their tours around 1830. After suffering serious financial losses during the depression of 1837, he gave up his theatrical interests in 1843.

Caldwell was succeeded by Ludlow and Smith. Noah Ludlow (1795–1886) came west with Drake, and in 1817 set off to tour through Tennessee, Alabama, and elsewhere, giving the first theatrical performances ever seen in many areas. He alternated between management and acting engagements until 1835, when he formed a partnership with Solomon Smith (1801–69). Beginning his acting career in 1823, Smith had played for a number of managers in the West before joining Ludlow. Between 1835 and 1853 they dominated the St. Louis theatre, controlled the Mobile theatre until 1840, and from 1843 to 1853 succeeded to Caldwell's position of preeminence in New Orleans. Thus, during the 1840's they were the most powerful managers in the West. Ludlow and Smith are also important for having written accounts of their experiences, major sources of information about the "frontier" theatre.

Most of the theatres in the West were situated on rivers easily reached by boat. Few were located north of the Ohio River. Chicago did not see a professional production until 1833 and had no permanent theatre until 1847. Small itinerant companies were to be seen almost anywhere, however, for just as the new territory provided a buffer against financial crisis and overpopulation in the East, so too it offered a chance to actors who had been unsuccessful in the major theatrical centers. Most itinerant companies set up temporary theatres in each town they visited. In the 1830's, however, a new answer, the showboat, was conceived. While actors had long traveled by water, no one seems to have thought of fitting out a boat as a theatre until 1831, when William Chapman (1764–1839), an English actor who had come to America in 1827, converted a flatboat, and gave performances on it while sailing from Pittsburg to New Orleans. Unfortunately, flatboats had to be abandoned when they reached the end of the down-river trip, and it was not until 1836 that a steamboat, which could return up-river, was converted into a theatre. Showboats were eminently practical, for they allowed traveling companies to take well-equipped theatres wherever there was a navigable river. Interrupted by the Civil War, showboating resumed immediately afterward. The most lavish "floating palaces" were in service between 1875 and 1900, when A. B. French, E. A. Price, and E. E. Eisenbarth dominated the river. Showboats continued in regular use until about 1925, after which they became quaint relics.

While the frontier was being settled, the Eastern cities continued to grow. The population of New York increased from 60,600 in 1800 to 312,710 in 1840, and Philadelphia grew from 41,000 in 1800 to 93,665 in 1840. The demand for theatrical entertainment resulting from this growth was met in several ways. Existing theatres were enlarged. The Chestnut Street Theatre, which originally seated 1200, was remodeled in 1805 to hold 2000, and the Park Theatre in New York was enlarged in 1807 to accommodate 2372. After both theatres burned in 1820, they were rebuilt for audiences of between 2000 and 2500. In New York, the Bowery

SPALDING & RODGERS CIRCUS CO
ON BOARD FLOATING PALACE,
WILL Exhibit in Terre Haute on Saturday, April 23d, at 2 and 7 o'clock, P. M.
PRICE OF ADMISSION.
Dress Circle, all armed Chairs..........................50 cer
Family Boxes, Cushioned Seats........................25 "
Gallery...25 "
Gallery for Colored persons............................50 "
The Company will perform at the following places:
   Monday 18, Mt. Carmel at 2 & 7 p. m.
   Tuesday 19, Vincennes at 2 & 7 p. m.
   Wednesday 20, Russelville at 2 & 7 p. m.
   Thursday 21, Hudsonville at 2 & 7 p. m.
   Friday 22d at Darwin at 2 & 7 p. m.
April 9, '63 33 3t.

A SHOWBOAT CIRCUS, 1853. [Reprinted from Hulbert, *The Ohio River* (1906)]

Theatre, built in 1826, seated 3000. The number of weekly performances was also increased. In 1820, the Park Theatre began to play six times a week, a move which was adopted in 1823 by the Chestnut Street Theatre. Others soon accepted the new trend.

Additional companies were established. By 1825 there were about 20 permanent troupes in America, and by 1850 about 35. In addition, there were countless temporary, itinerant groups. In the major cities of the East, expansion followed a typical pattern. Usually a second theatre began as an amphitheatre or circus, which also gave occasional theatrical entertainments, and then progressed to a full season of plays. In New York in 1812, a circus was converted into the Olympic Theatre (later called the Anthony Street and then Pavilion Theatre). By the 1830's, New York had four theatres playing regularly and the number increased steadily thereafter. In spite of competition, the Park Theatre retained its preeminence. By 1815, the managment had passed to Stephen Price and Edmund Simpson (1784–1848), an English actor who came to New York in 1809. After 1840 Simpson was sole manager until 1848, the year in which the Park Theatre burned, thus ending its dominance of New York theatrical life. One of the most ambitious of the Park's competitors was the Bowery Theatre, the largest in the country when it opened in 1826. It soon turned to melodramas so gory that it came to be called the "slaughter house."

A similar pattern can be seen in Philadelphia. In 1812, a former circus began to offer occasional dramatic entertainments and later became the Walnut Street Theatre. When the Arch Street Theatre opened in 1828, a

A PERFORMANCE at the Park Theatre, New York, in 1822.
On stage is Charles Mathews the Elder. [Courtesy New
York Historical Society]

three-way struggle for supremacy left all of the companies weakened.
William Wood, who had left the Chestnut Street Theatre in 1826, headed
the Arch Street Theatre, but both he and Warren, who had continued to
manage the Chestnut Street, were bankrupt before the season of 1828–29
ended. Both then retired. Nevertheless, after 1828, Philadelphia usually
had at least three theatres in operation. The Chestnut Street's preeminence
passed to the Arch Street during the 1830's, and after 1850 the Walnut
Street came to the fore. The Chestnut Street was closed in 1855.

In Boston, the Federal Street Theatre encountered its first competition
in 1827 when the Tremont Street Theatre was opened. The two companies
were amalgamated in 1829, but new competition appeared in 1832 with the
opening of the National Theatre. Thereafter, Boston always had more than
one troupe. The most important company was to be that of the Boston
Museum. Opened in 1841 as a collection of sideshow exhibits, the Museum
included a music salon in which short entertainments were given. By 1843,
regular plays were being offered, and in 1846, following the enormous

486

popularity of *The Drunkard* (1844), a melodrama written by the company's stage manager, William H. Smith (1806–72), a regular theatre was erected. This was to house one of America's leading companies until 1893.

The rapid expansion of the theatre during a period of financial crisis brought many bankruptcies and frequent changes of management. The battle for audiences was reflected in many ways, but perhaps most importantly in the increased use of visiting stars after Edmund Kean's visit to America in 1820–21. Then considered the finest actor of the English-speaking world, Kean set an example which made it easy to persuade other major actors to cross the Atlantic. After 1820, Price spent much of his time in London recruiting performers for American tours. Stars came with ever-increasing frequency: Charles Mathews in 1822 and 1833–35; Macready in 1826–27, 1843–45, and 1849; Charles Kean in 1830, 1839, and 1845–47; Charles and Fanny Kemble in 1832–34; Mme. Vestris and Charles Mathews the Younger in 1838. At first, tours were restricted to the Atlantic Coast, but as transportation improved, stars ventured to New Orleans and up the Mississippi River.

In the beginning, visits from major actors served to elevate the quality of local companies, but after 1830 lesser actors began to tour as starring engagements came to be a mark of distinction. Few good actors were content to remain within the confines of a local troupe. The quality of performances also began to suffer after 1830, for the stars usually arrived too late for adequate rehearsals, performed only in vehicles adapted to their talents, and relegated local leading actors to secondary roles. Often stars demanded enormous salaries and one or more benefits, leaving the managers with little profit from their visits. Managers were soon trapped by the system, for audiences ceased to attend the theatre unless some novelty were offered. While these evils were not immediately evident, the resident stock company was eventually undermined by them.

The struggle for survival was also reflected in the repertory. Entr'acte entertainments increased in number and variety, novelties (such as child actors, animals, and specialty performers) abounded, and melodrama and minor forms composed an ever-larger part of the repertory. While this pattern did not differ markedly from that current in England, it was complicated by the American ambivalence toward foreign plays and performers. As Americans developed a national consciousness after the war of 1812, the mass audience tended to be suspicious of anything foreign, while the better educated and more sophisticated groups looked to Europe for their standards and gave only condescending attention to native talent. Consequently, after 1815 American dramatists and performers gained recognition only gradually and were usually accepted by the mass audience before winning critical approval.

The majority of actors, both major and minor, were English-born and

487

English-trained. The dominant performer up to 1825 was Cooper, but his "classical" style was less admired as Kean's approach triumphed. Of the new school, perhaps the most important was Junius Brutus Booth (1796–1852). On the stage from 1813, Booth came to America in 1821 and remained for the rest of his life. Although he managed theatres for brief intervals, he was essentially a touring star, one of the first to appear in the Mississippi Valley and the first major actor to play in California. It is sometimes said that Booth did more than any other performer to create a taste for tragic acting. His erratic behavior made him undependable, however, and lessened his potential influence in the major theatrical centers. Other English actors who contributed significantly to the American stage in this period were Mary Ann Duff and the Wallacks. When Mary Ann Duff (1794–1857) came to America in 1810, she had had little experience or training, and did not emerge as a leading player until 1818. Edmund Kean, Forrest and Cooper all acclaimed her the greatest tragic actress of her day, and Kean declared her superior to any actress on the English stage. Henry J. Wallack (1790–1870) and James Wallack (1791–1864), actors in the Kemble tradition, divided their time between England and America after 1818, serving with distinction both as actors and managers.

Although there had been many native-born actors before his time, Edwin Forrest (1806–72) was the first American performer to win lasting fame. On the stage from the age of 14, Forrest gained much of his early experience in frontier theatres. He made his New York debut in 1826 and by 1828 was the major attraction at the Bowery Theatre. Thereafter, he was considered America's leading actor. Following the Astor Place Riot of 1849 and his sensational divorce, his popularity diminished somewhat and he appeared infrequently after 1852. He retired in 1872.

Forrest established an "American" style of acting (sometimes called the "physical" or "heroic" style). A man of powerful physique and great vocal strength, he disliked the repressed acting of the Kemble and Macready schools. His athletic and uninhibited performances made him the idol of unsophisticated theatregoers, but he won only grudging admiration from others. Forrest was always more vigorous than most of his contemporaries, many of whom sought to emulate him.

The first native-born actress to win international fame was Charlotte Cushman (1816–76). Originally an opera singer, she turned to drama when her voice failed. After serving as a utility actress at the Park Theatre from 1837 to 1840, she played leading roles in Philadelphia and New York. Appearing with Macready in 1843, she was much affected by his methods, which she adopted so successfully that she was often called the "female Macready." In 1845, she went to London, where she won immediate and lasting fame, soon being considered the finest tragic actress of the English-speaking world. After 1852 she appeared only sporadically and confined herself to a restricted repertory, notably Lady Macbeth, Queen Katherine in *Henry VIII*, and Meg Merrilees in *Guy Mannering*. In some ways, Cushman's acting style was not unlike Forrest's, for it depended upon energy and constant motion, but her intelligent line readings and emotional control won her a much wider following among sophisticated audiences. James E. Murdoch (1811–93) also gained wide recognition both in America and England. On the stage from 1829 until the late 1850's, Murdoch exerted considerable influence on others through his textbooks on elocution.

CHARLOTTE CUSHMAN as Meg Merrilies in *Guy Mannering*. [From a contemporary engraving]

Perhaps the greatest boon to the native-born actor came from plays with American themes and native types, for foreign-born actors found it difficult to play in many of these works. Between 1815 and 1850, a number of American dramatists achieved limited fame. James Nelson Barker (1784–1858) wrote ten plays, of which five survive. The first to be acted was *Tears and Smiles* (1807), a comedy of manners, not unlike *The Contrast*, on Philadelphia society. His *The Indian Princess* (1808), a romantic drama about Pocahontas, was the first play about Indians to reach the stage. His best play, *Superstition* (1824), treats witchcraft in New England. Mordecai Manuel Noah (1785–1851) contributed a number of patriotic plays, such as *She Would Be a Soldier* (1819), *The Siege of*

Tripoli (1820), and *Marion, or the Hero of Lake George* (1821). Simply written, Noah's plays depend much upon spectacle and action. Richard Penn Smith (1799–1854) wrote 20 plays, 15 of which were performed, ranging from farce to romantic tragedy. While most of his comic works were adapted from French sources, several of his serious plays, notably *William Penn* (1829) and *The Eighth of January* (1829), treated American themes. Samuel Woodworth (1785–1842) wrote a number of domestic dramas, such as *The Deed of Gift* (1822) and *The Widow's Son* (1825), but is remembered now primarily for *The Forest Rose* (1825), which introduced the popular Yankee character Jonathan Ploughboy.

Several native dramatists were encouraged by Edwin Forrest, who after 1828 offered prizes for plays by American authors. The most important of the dramatists who wrote for Forrest were Bird and Stone. Robert Montgomery Bird (1806–54) began his playwriting career in 1827 with *The City Looking Glass,* one of the first American plays of low-life. He subsequently supplied Forrest with some of this most lasting vehicles, *The Gladiator* (1831), *Oralloosa* (1832), and *The Broker of Bogota* (1834). John Augustus Stone (1801 34) is remembered primarily for *Metamora* (1829), a play in which Forrest performed throughout his career. Other dramatists who provided Forrest with plays include Robert T. Conrad (1824–71) with *Jack Cade* (1835), and George H. Miles (1824–71) with *DeSoto* (1852).

American plays of the early 19th century popularized two important native types: the Indian and the Yankee. The Indian was presented sympathetically, following the romantic tradition of the "noble savage," and provided strong roles for serious performers. The Indian had been introduced in American drama as early as 1766 in Robert Rogers' *Ponteach,* but Barker's *The Indian Princess* sketched the outline which was to be followed by others. The vogue for Indian dramas was given its major impetus by George Washington Parke Custis' (1781–1857) *The Indian Prophecy* (1827) and *Pocahontas* (1830). Between 1825 and 1860, more than 50 Indian plays were performed in America. The type was dealt a serious blow by John Brougham's burlesque, *Po-ca-hon-tas* (1855), but not until after 1870 was the "noble savage" tradition abandoned.

The Yankee character was the province of the comic actor or "specialty" performer. Although the Yankee had appeared in many plays after his introduction in *The Contrast* (1787), the idea of making him the central character seems to have stemmed from Charles Mathews' *A Trip to America* (1824), a work satirizing various American types. With his "At Homes," Mathews also did much to popularize the "specialty" performer in America. After 1825, the Yankee became a favorite character and a number of "specialists" appeared. The Yankee was the symbol of the American common man, simple and naive on the surface, but upholding democratic principles and despising pretense and sham. The first important actor of Yankee roles was James H. Hackett (1800–71), who conceived the character Solomon Swap in *Jonathan in England* (1828), the first important Yankee play. Hackett gave up Yankee roles in 1836, but continued his distinguished career as manager and actor, being especially noted for his portrayal of Falstaff. Hackett was succeeded by George Handel Hill (1809–49), by 1832 considered the best of the Yankee specialists. In addition to monologues and skits, Hill performed full-length plays, such as J. S. Jones' *The Green Mountain Boy* (1833) and *The People's Lawyer* (1839). With Hill, the Yankee became more sympathetic and sentimental. Dan Marble (1810–49) achieved fame after 1836 in the role of Sam Patch, a more generalized American type, while Joshua Silsbee (1813–55) was the acknowledged master of Yankee roles after the deaths of Hill and Marble. Silsbee turned the type once more toward broad and eccentric humor. Of the later specialists, John E. Owens (1823–86) was the most famous. The height of the Yankee vogue came between 1830 and 1850 and was instrumental in establishing a native American comedy.

The Negro, another important native type, also fell to specialists. The Negro may be found in American drama from the beginning as a faithful servant or comic caricature, but a new treatment began about 1828 when Thomas D. Rice (1808–60) introduced his "Jim Crow" song and dance. Soon a major star, Rice spawned a host of imitators, most notably Barney

GEORGE HANDEL HILL in *The Yankee Pedlar*. [From an aquatint published in London, 1838]

491

Williams, Jack Diamond, Barney Burns, and Bob Farrell. Rice's success also helped to create the Minstrel Show. In an effort to enlarge his repertory, Rice began to offer "Ethiopian Operas" around 1833. Building upon these, Dan Emmett (1815–1904) put together a full-length entertainment, "Virginia Minstrels," in 1843. The Minstrel Show form was established in 1846 by E. P. Christy (1815–62).

The Minstrel Show was divided into two parts. In the first, the performers were arranged in a semicircle, the tambourine player at one end and the "pair of bones" player at the other. These "end" men came to be called Tambo and Bones. The "middle" man, or Interlocutor, served as Master of Ceremonies and exchanged jokes with the end men between musical numbers. The second part, or "olio," consisted of specialty acts and songs. The Minstrel Show reached the peak of its popularity between 1850 and 1870. After 1870, companies began to increase in size, some including more than 100 performers. The popularity of the form declined, nevertheless, and by 1896 only ten companies remained. By 1919 there were only three, and soon the Minstrel Show was a mere curiosity.

T. D. RICE dancing "Jim Crow" at the Bowery Theatre, New York, in 1833. [From a contemporary lithograph]

Another native type, the city boy, came into prominence in the 1840's, perhaps to give the increasing urban population its own folk hero. City low-life had appeared on the stage occasionally since Pierce Egan's *Tom and Jerry, or Life in London* was adapted in the 1820's as *Life in Philadelphia, Life in New York,* and so on. The city boy was not popular, however, until Benjamin Baker's *A Glance at New York* (1848) introduced the volunteer fireman and good-natured roughneck, Mose the Bowery Boy. The phenomenal success of this play led to many sequels in which Mose visits various countries and becomes embroiled in new situations. Frank S. Chanfrau (1824–84) spent much of his career acting this role. The Bowery Boy faded in popularity after the 1860's, but was assimilated into other plays about city life.

By the 1840's, American writers and actors were no longer novelties. Perhaps for this reason, Anna Cora Mowatt (1819–70) won immediate and widespread acceptance with *Fashion* (1845), a comedy of manners about New York social life. Of a well-to-do family, Mrs. Mowatt turned to writing around 1840 when her husband lost both his fortune and his health. Since playwriting paid little, Mrs. Mowatt went on the stage in 1845. With no

FRANK CHANFRAU as Mose the Fireboy. [From a contemporary print]

previous experience, she was a star from the first. In such roles as Juliet and Rosalind, she won fame both in America and England before retiring in 1854.

Between 1815 and 1850 spectacle began to be given greater emphasis. For the most part, plays continued to be staged in stock settings, but occasionally an effort was made to provide more specific and elaborate backgrounds. Interest in historical accuracy is first found in John J. Holland's Gothic settings for Joanna Baillie's *De Mountfort,* presented at the Park Theatre in 1809. Archeological detail did not make a deep impression, however, until 1845–46, when Charles Kean staged *Richard III* and

493

King John at the Park Theatre. Thereafter, accuracy was gradually accepted as an ideal.

Panoramas and dioramas were introduced in an attempt to gain greater realism. Nontheatrical panoramas had been seen in New York since the 1790's, and in the 1820's Daguerre's dioramas were regularly shown. Perhaps as a result, Dunlap was commissioned by the Bowery Theatre in 1827 to write *A Trip to Niagara,* in which a journey by steamboat up the Hudson River was staged. Mme. Vestris allegedly attracted attention to more detailed settings and properties during her tour in 1838, and it is possible that she introduced the box set in America at this time.

Lighting practices followed closely those current in England. In 1816, the Chestnut Street Theatre was the first in the world to light the stage with gas, and by the 1840's the new medium was in use by most major companies. In 1850 the approach to spectacle in American theatres was still haphazard, and it would be many years before a more consistent ideal would be adopted.

Continued Growth, 1850–70

The years between 1850 and 1870 brought still further expansion of the American theatre. As the westward movement accelerated, especially after the discovery of gold in California in 1848, the theatre kept pace. In California, the first professional performances in English were given in 1849, when Sacramento's Eagle Theatre began to offer three programs each week to the miners. In San Francisco, the first theatre was opened in 1850 and by the following year the number had grown to three. From this time, San Francisco was to be the major theatrical center of the far west. In 1853, Catherine Sinclair (1817–91), Edwin Forrest's divorced wife, opened the Metropolitan Theatre, where she assembled the first outstanding company of the West. Here most of the visiting stars appeared until 1869, when the California Theatre, under John McCullough and Lawrence Barrett, began to offer serious competition.

The rush of stars to the new territory began in 1852, when Junius Brutus Booth toured the mining camps. In spite of tedious journeys overland or by sea, many major stars of the time followed. Most came from the East, but one native performer, Lottie Crabtree (1847–1924), was to gain national fame. On the stage from the age of eight, she was a major star and had embarked on her first eastern tour by the age of 17. In vehicles written especially for her, she usually played several characters to demonstrate her versatility. In several of the plays she portrayed a ragged waif who regenerates drunken miners. All allowed her to display her talents for singing, dancing, and playing the banjo.

New mining strikes led to still further expansion of the western theatre. The Comstock Lode, discovered in 1859, had by the mid-1860's spawned five legitimate theatres and six variety houses in Nevada City, Nevada. Similarly, mining towns attracted actors to Idaho, Montana, and Colorado. In the late 1850's touring groups began to appear in Oregon, where a theatre was established at Willamette in 1861. Washington saw its first professional troupe in 1862, but no permanent theatre was established there until 1879.

A FRONTIER THEATRE in Cheyenne, Wyoming.
[From *Frank Leslie's Illustrated Newspaper* (October 13, 1877)]

In Utah, the Mormons began to produce plays as early as 1850, and in 1862 they erected the Salt Lake Theatre, the first major structure built in Salt Lake City. Performances were at first given by amateurs, but in 1863 professional actors began to be added and a permanent company was maintained after 1865. The theatre in all the western areas was considerably strengthened with the opening of the first transcontinental railroad in 1869.

Between 1850 and 1870 the number of permanent companies increased throughout America. The 35 of 1850 had grown to about 50 in 1860, and remained constant until after 1870. Numerous itinerant groups also played in less populous areas. The dependence upon visiting stars continued, although a number of managers sought to counteract its adverse effects. Among these the most important were William Mitchell, William E. Burton, and J. W. Wallack. At the Olympic Theatre in New York between 1839 and 1850, William Mitchell (1798–1856) maintained an outstanding theatre without using starring performers. He specialized in light entertainment, however, and it remained for William E. Burton (1804–60) to extend Mitchell's policy to standard drama. Born in London, Burton had been a low comedian in the English theatre from 1821 to 1834, when he came to America. A popular actor and successful manager in Philadelphia until 1848, he opened Burton's Chambers Street Theatre in New York, where between 1848 and 1856 he maintained the most respected company in America. Because the Chambers Street Theatre seated only 800, in 1856 Burton moved to the Metropolitan Theatre, one of the largest in the world. Success did not follow him, and he soon had to import stars. He gave up management in 1858 and retired in 1859. With his excellent company and broad-ranging repertory, Burton demonstrated at the Chambers Street Theatre that success did not require stars. He also gained much prestige with his productions of Shakespeare's plays in historically accurate settings and costumes.

NEW YORK CITY.—OLD LANDMARKS—INTERIOR OF BURTON'S THEATRE, CHAMBERS STREET.

INTERIOR of Burton's Chambers Street Theatre. [From a contemporary print]

Before Burton retired, his preeminence had already been seriously challenged by James W. Wallack, who in 1853 had taken over the Lyceum Theatre and renamed it Wallack's Lyceum. From 1855 until the 1880's, Wallack's was the leading theatre of America. He was succeeded as manager by his son, Lester Wallack (1820–88), a fine romantic leading actor, who continued his policies until 1887. Also prominent in the troupe was James W. Wallack, Jr. (1818–73), a performer of tragic roles. Maintaining a high standard of production, Wallack presented a repertory made up primarily of standard works. Another outstanding company was assembled by Laura Keene (c. 1820–73), an English actress who had worked for Mme. Vestris. Following her American debut in 1852, she played for Wallack before going on tour. Between 1855 and 1863, she ran her own theatre in New York, serving as manager and leading actress in a series of lavishly mounted productions in the style of Mme. Vestris. After 1863 she toured, and she was playing at Ford's Theatre in Washington on the night of President Lincoln's assassination.

Not all of the major troupes were located in New York. The Boston Museum, one of the finest in the country, owed much of its prestige to William Warren, Jr. (1812–88), who performed there from 1847 until 1883. Because of his wide range, Warren is considered by many critics the finest comic actor of his age. Philadelphia's Arch Street Theatre, under the direction of Mrs. John Drew (1820-97), became famous throughout America for its fine company and the training it gave young actors. Born Louisa Lane, Mrs. Drew was on stage as a child, came to America in 1827, and married John Drew (1827–62), an actor of Irish roles, in 1850. Although she retained the management of the Arch Street from 1860 until 1892, the theatre's reputation was made during the 1860's. After 1870, Mrs. Drew toured widely, especially in the role of Mrs. Malaprop. In Chicago, John H. McVicker (1822–96), after working for Ludlow and Smith and inheriting Dan Marble's Yankee roles, formed his own company in 1857. Until his death, his Chicago theatres were among the finest outside of New York. In St. Louis, Ludlow and Smith were succeeded by Ben DeBar, who dominated the theatre there from 1853 until the 1880's.

While the resident stock company continued to be the standard theatrical organization between 1850 and 1870, it was gradually undermined by several innovations. One of the most damaging was the introduction of the long run. Before 1850, successful new plays had usually been given from 7 to 15 times and then placed in the repertory to alternate with other plays. In 1852–53, *Uncle Tom's Cabin* was played for 300 consecutive performances. Although atypical, this run is symptomatic of the new trend toward extended engagements even in well-established stock companies. At the Boston Museum, for example, the average run in the 1860's was 14–40 performances, in the 1870's, 20–50, and in the 1880's, 50–100.

The increase in the length of runs brought a decrease in the size of the repertory. In 1851–52, the Boston Museum gave 140 plays (68 full-length and 72 afterpieces), but by 1875 the number had declined to 75 and by 1893 to 15. At Wallack's Theatre in 1855–56, 60 plays were performed, but in 1875 only 15–25, and in 1885 only 5–10. While some of the decrease can be attributed to the gradual abandonment of the afterpiece around 1870, it is indicative as well of a new approach to repertory playing under which a series of plays were given for long runs, while the older scheme of alternating plays was used merely in the intervals between successful productions.

With the extended run came greater emphasis upon new plays. Although between 1850 and 1870 Shakespearean and other standard works continued to make up a sizable portion of the repertory, the majority of long-running plays were new works. Adaptations of recent novels, melodramas, extravaganzas, and burlesques were prominent. Probably the most popular play of the period was *Uncle Tom's Cabin*, based on Harriet Beecher Stowe's novel. Although it was adapted many times, the most popular version was George L. Aiken's, first played in Troy, New York, in 1852 as two separate plays and then combined into a single six-act work. It was written for the Howard family (George C. Howard as St. Clare, Mrs. Howard as Topsy, and their daughter, Cordelia, as Little Eva), who played it until 1887. Although the craze for *Uncle Tom's Cabin* died down before 1860, it revived in the 1870's, when about 50 travelling companies were performing it. There were still 12 companies in 1927. Melodrama gained new vitality as well through the work of Dion Boucicault, who came to America in 1853 and spent much of his time here until his death in 1890.

Between 1850 and 1870, burlesque was one of the most popular dramatic types. Parodying well-known plays, performers, or topical events, and featuring songs and dances, it appealed to the taste for broad comedy. Probably the most successful writer of burlesques was John Brougham (1810–80), an Irishman who had worked for Mme. Vestris before coming to America in 1842. A popular comic actor, Brougham tried his hand unsuccessfully at management several times, adapted many popular novels for the stage, and wrote numerous original works. Of all his plays, the most famous was *Po-ca-hon-tas, or The Gentle Savage* (1855), a parody of the "noble savage" tradition, popular since the 1820's. Many others also wrote and performed in burlesques. George L. Fox (1825–77), one of the most talented comic actors of the 19th century, was famous for his travesties of *Macbeth, Richard III,* and *Hamlet.* He also revived pantomime with his *Humpty Dumpty* (1868), in which he played Clown more than 1200 times. Mrs. John Wood (1831–1915) was probably the best burlesque actress of the day, winning special acclaim in *The Sleeping Beauty* and *The Fair One with the Golden Locks.*

Of the serious dramatists of this period, the best was George Henry Boker (1823–90). Son of wealthy parents, he began to write plays about 1848. His first work, *Calaynos* was produced in London in 1849 and in Philadelphia in 1851. His *Francesca da Rimini* (1855) is considered by many the finest poetic tragedy of the 19th century. Boker worked hard to secure more adequate legal protection for dramatists. Although probably not due to his efforts, a copyright act was passed in 1856. Unfortunately, it failed to give effective protection because it merely provided for the

498

UNCLE TOM'S CABIN as produced by William Brady in 1901. The scene shows Eliza crossing the frozen river. [Courtesy Harvard Theatre Collection]

499

registration of works in local courts. The transfer of registration to the Library of Congress in 1870 did much to correct the weaknesses, but full protection of the American playwright was not to come until the acceptance of the International Copyright Agreement in 1891 and the passage of a revised American Copyright Act in 1909.

The Triumph of the Touring Company, 1870–95

The years between 1870 and 1895 brought enormous changes as the resident company was undermined by touring groups, as New York became the only major center of production, and as the long run superseded the repertory system. By 1870, the resident stock company was at the peak of its development in America. The 50 permanent companies of 1870, however, had dwindled to 20 in 1878, to eight in 1880, to four in 1887, and had virtually disappeared by 1900.

While the causes of this change are numerous, probably the most important was the rise of the "combination" company (that is, one that travels with star and full company). Sending out a complete production was merely a logical extension of touring by stars. By the 1840's, many major actors were already taking along a small group of lesser players, for they could not be sure that local companies could supply adequate support in secondary roles.

There is much disagreement about the origin of the combination company. Boucicault claims to have initiated it around 1860 when he sent out a troupe with *Colleen Bawn,* but a book published in 1859 speaks of combination companies as already established. Joseph Jefferson III also declared that he was a pioneer in the movement. In actuality, the practice probably began tentatively during the 1850's only to be interrupted by the Civil War. It mushroomed in the 1870's, as the rapid expansion of the railway system made it increasingly feasible to transport full productions. In 1872, Lawrence Barrett took his company, but no scenery, on tour; in 1876, *Rose Michel* was sent out with full company, scenery, and properties. By the season of 1876–77 there were nearly 100 combination companies on the road, and by 1886 there were 282.

During the early years of the combination system, local managers maintained companies to perform during the intervals between traveling productions. Often the local company toured small towns in the vicinity while the visitors occupied its theatre. As local support was withdrawn from the resident troupes, managers dismissed their actors and became mere landlords. The new system did not end the emphasis upon stars, but now they traveled with full productions. Henry Irving toured America eight

SCENE from Boucicault's *The Colleen Bawn*. [From the 1864 edition of the play]

times between 1883 and 1902; Salvini five times between 1872 and 1889; Coquelin three times between 1889 and 1900; and Sarah Bernhardt nine times between 1880 and 1918. While foreign stars usually played in a small repertory, American troupes most frequently performed a single play.

These changes did not occur overnight, and several of the major companies held out against the new system for many years. Nevertheless, Wallack's closed in 1888, the Arch Street Theatre in 1892, and the Boston Museum in 1893. Most of the significant contributions of the years between 1870 and 1895, nevertheless, came from those managers who maintained permanent troupes. Of these, the most important were Edwin Booth, Augustin Daly, and Steele Mackaye.

As a young man, Edwin Booth (1833–93) accompanied his father, Junius Brutus Booth, on his tours and made his own acting debut in 1849 in Boston. From 1852 to 1856 he played with various companies and toured in California, Australia, and the southern United States before appearing at Burton's Theatre in New York. From 1856 until his death, he was one of the country's major stars. In 1863, he leased the Winter Garden Theatre in New York and gave a number of Shakespearean productions which surpassed in quality any yet seen in America. His *Hamlet* ran for 100 nights, a record not broken until the 20th century. When his brother killed Lincoln, Booth retired from the stage for a time. In 1868, his new Booth's Theatre introduced several innovations. The stage floor was flat and had no grooves. Several elevators were used to raise set pieces from the 50 feet of working space below the stage, and flying machinery raised other pieces into the 76 feet of overhead space. Thus, Booth introduced "free plantation" of scenery many years before it was adopted by Irving in England. Booth's Theatre also had no apron, and box settings were used extensively to increase the

501

illusion of reality. Booth produced on such a lavish scale that by 1874 he was bankrupt. From then until his retirement in 1891, he played starring engagements in America and abroad.

Booth believed that the theatre should confine itself to the best drama and that the actor's function is to reveal the beauty and wisdom contained in great plays. He studied his roles tirelessly and executed them with infinite care. He was noted for his elegant and graceful movements, the use of vocal tone to reveal mood and meaning, the combination of emotional intensity with clarity of interpretation, the consistency of his characteriza-

BACKSTAGE at Booth's Theatre, 1870. Note the use of the trap and stage braces. [From *Appleton's Journal* (May 28, 1870)]

tions, and his freedom from mannerisms. Not having great physical strength, he depended much upon his flexible and expressive voice. At his best in tragic roles, notably Hamlet, Iago, Othello, and Richelieu (in Bulwer-Lytton's play), Booth is considered by many historians the greatest actor America has produced.

Augustin Daly (1836–99) was a critic before winning fame with *Leah the Forsaken* (1862), adapted from Mosenthal's *Deborah*. His first original work, *Under the Gaslight* (1867), also saw his debut as a producer. In 1869 he leased the Fifth Avenue Theatre and formed his own company. From this time until his death he was one of the most influential figures in the American theatre. His most important work was done after 1879, when he opened Daly's Theatre, his company's third home. After playing in London in 1884, 1886, and 1888, he opened his own theatre there in 1893.

Daly's significance derives from several sources. He contributed much to the development of realism. Many of his own plays emphasized realistic special effects (the hero tied to the tracks in the path of an approaching train; the heroine locked in the stateroom of a burning steamboat) and new subject matter. His *Horizon* (1871) was the first work to present the Indian as villain and to emphasize the difference between Eastern and Western standards of conduct. More important, Daly helped to establish

INTERIOR of Daly's Theatre, 1879. [From a contemporary print]

the director as the major force in the theatre. He retained absolute control over every element of his productions. In many ways, he was comparable to Saxe-Meiningen in Germany, and Irving and the Bancrofts in England. Daly assumed the right to coach his actors in interpretation, stage business, and blocking. He abandoned the traditional practice of casting according to lines of business. Because of his working methods, Daly usually attracted young performers, many of whom he raised to stardom. Consequently, he was one of the earliest "star makers." Daly's first star was Agnes Ethel (1852–1903), who with almost no previous experience played the leading role in *Frou-Frou* (1870), Daly's first important production. She retired from the stage in 1874. Next came Fanny Davenport (1850–98), daughter of E. L. Davenport (1815–77), one of the most versatile actors of the 19th century. After an apprenticeship in Mrs. Drew's company, she came to Daly in 1869, emerged as a leading actress in 1875, and then left Daly to star in her own productions. Daly's most famous discovery was Clara Morris (1846–1925), who came to the fore when Agnes Ethel left the company. Catapulted to fame in 1872 by her performance in *Article 47,* she too soon left the company. At her best in roles of pathetic suffering, she was so realistic in her emotional outbursts that she was called the "Queen of Spasms." Her style palled after 1890, and ill health forced her to give up the stage soon afterward.

ACT I of Daly's production of *The Merchant of Venice.* [Courtesy Theatre Collection, Harvard University]

Daly's mainstays after 1879 were "the big four": Ada Rehan (1860–1916) and John Drew II (1853–1927), players of leading roles; James Lewis (1840–96) and Mrs. G. H. Gilbert (1822–1904), chief comic actors. Between 1879 and 1892 they helped Daly create the finest ensemble in America. Both Drew and Miss Rehan had been trained by Mrs. Drew and continued to perform together until 1892, when Drew left Daly's company. For Daly, Miss Rehan played more than 200 roles, of which her best was Katherine in *Taming of the Shrew.* Her personal magnetism and beautiful voice made her one of the most popular actresses of her day. Unable to adapt to other working conditions after Daly's death, she retired in 1905.

Steele Mackaye (1842–94), actor, playwright, director, inventor, designer, and teacher, was more versatile than Daly but probably less influential because few of his enterprises were sustained long enough to demonstrate their worth. As an actor and teacher, he is remembered primarily for introducing the Delsarte method in America. After studying with François Delsarte (1811–71) in France, Mackaye came to believe that Delsarte's system could reform the stage. Delsarte placed primary emphasis upon gesture and sought to establish a "science of movement," in which external signs would be closely related to various bodily organs, faculties, and states of mind. He aimed at making acting more natural by analyzing human behavior meticulously and reproducing it "scientifically." In Mackaye's application, the Delsarte system seems to have worked well, but others came to use it mechanically and transformed it into a set of prescribed gestures and postures. Because of these absurdities, the Delsarte system fell into disfavor in the 20th century, after having been the most accepted approach to the teaching of elocution and acting in the late 19th century.

Mackaye's influence was also exerted through acting schools. As stock companies declined after 1870, the old scheme of in-service training for the actor was no longer practical. As a result of his study with Delsarte and at the Comédie Française's Conservatoire, Mackaye believed that systematic instruction was needed. Thus, in 1872–73 he created a short-lived acting school, the first in America, at his St. James' Theatre in New York. His greatest contribution, however, came in 1884, when at his Lyceum Theatre he began another training program which was to become the American Academy of Dramatic Art. Two of Mackaye's students founded other schools: Samuel S. Curry created the Curry School of Expression, and Charles W. Emerson the Emerson School of Oratory. As the most important of the early acting schools, these three spread Mackaye's ideas.

Mackaye also wrote or adapted 19 plays, three of which were especially successful: *Hazel Kirke* (1878–80), *Won at Last* (1877), and *Paul Kauvar* (1887). After achieving an initial run of 486 performances in New York, *Hazel Kirke* was taken on the road by 14 different companies in 1884. It is also significant in the development of realism, for although essentially melodramatic, it contained no villain and all the characters were drawn with sympathy and fidelity. *Paul Kauvar* was noteworthy for its crowd scenes staged in the manner of the Meiningen company.

Mackaye was one of the most fertile inventors of the late 19th century. His Madison Square Theatre, opened in 1879, had two elevator stages, each 22 feet wide by 31 feet deep, which permitted complete scene changes in 40 seconds. His Lyceum Theatre in 1885 was one of the first to use electric lighting and to emphasize safety devices. In a play on the westward movement written and staged for "Buffalo Bill" Cody at Madison Square Garden, Mackaye created a realistic cyclone and stampede. Many of Mackaye's grandest schemes were never realized. For the Chicago Exposition of 1893, he designed a "Spectatorium" with 25 stages on which to portray Columbus' voyage to the New World and the subsequent story of America's development. A financial panic prevented its completion, but the surviving plans show that his conception was feasible. Few American producers have been so inventive, and few have been dogged by so many misfortunes.

Other important managers included Daniel Frohman and A. M. Palmer. Daniel Frohman (1851–1941), who succeeded Mackaye at the Lyceum Theatre, maintained one of the finest companies in New York until 1902. Many of Charles Frohman's stars established their reputations in the Lyceum company. Daniel Frohman succeeded to the management of the extensive Frohman enterprises upon his brother's death in 1915. A. M. Palmer (1838–1905) also maintained outstanding companies at the Union Square Theatre from 1872 to 1896, at the Madison Square Theatre from

SECTIONAL PLAN of the Madison Square Theatre, opened in 1879. Note the two stages, one above the other, mounted on elevators. The orchestra is placed above the proscenium opening. [From *The Scientific American* (April 5, 1884)]

1884 to 1891, and at Wallack's from 1891 to 1896. Palmer's success stemmed primarily from his executive ability, for he left the production work to others. Although his selection of plays was not daring and he hired actors only after they had proven their abilities elsewhere, he recognized and rewarded proven merit and maintained high standards.

As the emphasis shifted to new works, playwriting emerged as a profession. Bronson Howard (1842–1908), America's first professional dramatist, began his playwriting career in 1864, but did not attract wide attention until his *Saratoga* (1870) ran for 101 nights. Of his 18 plays, *The Banker's Daughter* (1878), *Young Mrs. Winthrop* (1882), and *Shenandoah* (1888) are the best known. *Shenandoah*, a play set against the background of the Civil War, launched Charles Frohman on his producing career.

Howard was also one of the first dramatists to receive regular royalty payments. In 1891, he founded the Society of American Dramatists and Composers, the forerunner of the present-day Dramatists' Guild.

Much of the drama of this period illustrates the trend toward greater realism. While fidelity of spectacle had been increasing throughout the century, realism of character and situation were slower in arriving. A step toward more daring subject matter was taken with the production of *Camille*. Considered by many too bold, the play was first presented by Laura Keene as a dream from which the heroine awakens. Matilda Heron (1830–77), on the other hand, translated the play faithfully in 1857 and played it without idealizing the characters. It ran for 100 nights, and Miss Heron was hailed for her naturalistic acting.

Realism was more often confined to local color. Building upon the popularity of Bret Harte and Mark Twain, such works as Bartley Campbell's (1843–88) *My Partner* (1879) exploited frontier life. Local color was also emphasized in Augustus Thomas' (1857–1934) plays, *Alabama* (1891), *In Mizzoura* (1893), and *Arizona* (1897). Thomas' best works, however, turned in other directions. *The Witching Hour* (1907) deals with hypnosis and telepathy, while *The Copperhead* (1918) tells the story of a northern patriot who pretends to be a southern sympathizer in order to aid his country during the Civil War.

Local color of a quite different sort appears in the plays of Edward Harrigan (1845–1911), a comic writer who extended the "Bowery Boy" tradition. His early fame was gained in variety houses in partnership with Tony Hart (Anthony Cannon, 1857–91). Harrigan began writing sketches and went on to full-length plays about life among various immigrant groups in New York. Combining knockabout farce and realism, most of the plays end with some outrageous denouement, such as the explosion of a fireworks factory followed by bodies falling through the ceiling. Harrigan performed in his own works and mounted them with absolute fidelity of background and dress. After 1895, Harrigan performed only rarely. Little appreciated by contemporary critics, he is now recognized as a faithful observer of his milieu.

Realism was developed most extensively in the plays of Gillette and Herne. William Gillette (1855–1937), on the stage after 1875, wrote his first play, *The Professor*, in 1881. Of his 20 works, the most important are *Held by the Enemy* (1886), the first major play on a Civil War theme, *Secret Service* (1895), and *Sherlock Holmes* (1899). Gillette's most realistic drama, *Secret Service*, also has a Civil War background. Built around minutiae, the play's stage directions take up more space in printing than does the dialogue. One act requires an authentic telegraph office, complete with a working telegraph key. Although Gillette's plays are essentially melodramas, they create the illusion of real life through the accumulation of external details. Gillette was also one of the finest actors of his day. By

507

concentrating upon the moment-by-moment development of the action, he sought to create the "illusion of the first time" regardless of how often he had performed a role.

James A. Herne (1839–1901) began his career in 1859 as an actor. During the 1870's while serving as a stage manager in San Francisco, he adapted several plays, some in collaboration with David Belasco. He first attracted favorable critical attention with *Drifting Apart* (1888), a work about the evil effects of drink on a Massachusetts fishing village. Encouraged by William Dean Howells and other realists, Herne thereafter consciously sought fidelity in writing, staging, and acting. His most important play, *Margaret Fleming* (1890), is usually considered the most realistic American drama of the 19th century. It tells the story of a woman who, upon learning of her husband's infidelity, takes his illegitimate child to rear with her own. While it includes much realistic visual detail, its major emphasis is upon psychological conflicts. Its subject matter made it unacceptable to commercial managers, and Herne had to present it in halls and out-of-the-way theatres. After suffering heavy financial losses, he recovered his fortunes with *Shore Acres* (1892), a play about a quiet, lovable, New England character. Although in the realistic mode, it did not offend moral sensibilities and was soon a popular favorite. While not a great playwright, Herne did more than any other American dramatist to establish the realistic mode.

Despite the trend toward realism, the majority of theatres continued to emphasize more popular fare. After 1870, minor dramatic forms were combined with variety acts to create new conceptions of burlesque and vaudeville. Burlesque began to change in 1866 when a troupe of ballet dancers, stranded in New York, were incorporated into *The Black Crook*. The resulting combination of spectacular scenery, lightly-clad girls, music, dance, and song was so popular that it ran for 16 months and spawned many imitations. This vogue was given further impetus in 1869 by the appearance of Lydia Thompson and her "British Blondes" in burlesques which emphasized feminine charms more than parody, the previous domain of burlesque. Soon burlesque had assumed its modern form: a collection of variety acts mingled with musical numbers featuring beautiful women. With its sexual emphasis, it came to appeal primarily to male audiences. Burlesque reached the height of its popularity just prior to the First World War, but it was not until around 1929 that the "striptease" became a feature which placed burlesque on the fringes of legality.

Modern vaudeville grew out of the same movement. In the 1880's, Tony Pastor (1837–1908) reshaped the burlesque to make it suitable for the family audience. From about 1890 until about 1930, vaudeville was one of the most popular of theatrical entertainments. Essentially a collection of variety acts, it also featured sketches and short plays in which leading actors performed.

By 1895 the actor's position in the theatre had changed radically. Benefits had been abandoned in the 1870's in favor of straight salary payments. With the triumph of the traveling company, actors now had to go to New York to seek employment. Furthermore, they were hired for the run of a play rather than by the season, and since there was as yet no union to protect their rights, they received no salary during rehearsal periods and were often stranded when productions closed on the road. From the position of dominance which he had held for some 200 years, the actor was now subordinate to both the director and the producer.

Joseph Jefferson III as Rip van Winkle. [From *Leslie's Weekly* (May 1, 1902)]

Most of the major actors of the period have already been mentioned, but a few others deserve attention. Joseph Jefferson III (1829–1905), one of the most beloved actors of the 19th century, was on the stage from the age of four. He early established a reputation for comic playing, but *Rip van Winkle* was to be the mainstay of his repertory after 1865. Noted for ease, expressive action, and inventive byplay, he mingled pathos and humor in a unique combination. John McCullough (1832–85) came to America from Ireland at the age of 15. From 1861 to 1866 he played secondary roles in Forrest's company. Of similar disposition and build, McCullough adopted Forrest's approach. After playing in San Francisco from 1866 until

509

1875, he came under Mackaye's influence and altered his acting style. By the time he died, he was considered second only to Booth as a tragic actor. Lawrence Barrett (1838–91) had few attributes to recommend him for the stage. Accepted by Burton in 1857, he worked his way up slowly. Virtually illiterate when he began, Barrett perfected his knowledge until he came to be known as the "scholar" of the American theatre. In the 1880's, he became Booth's partner and costar. Noted for his clarity of conception, he was somewhat faulty in execution because of his self-consciousness and artificial elocution. Richard Mansfield (1854–1907) went on the stage in 1880 and achieved his first success in 1883 as Baron Chevrial, a doddering lecher in *A Parisian Romance*. After 1886, he maintained his own company and each year added a new role to his repertory, alternating long runs of new works with his repertory of past hits. Best in melodramatic and eccentric parts, his lack of subtlety limited his success in major tragic roles. With his lavishly mounted productions, Mansfield was often compared with Irving as actor and manager.

The Triumph of Commercialism, 1895–1915

By 1895, the traveling road show had become the usual source of theatrical entertainment in America. While a few resident troupes remained, the long-run hit had become the goal, and New York was virtually the only theatrical center. These conditions brought many new problems. Perhaps the most obvious difficulties were those connected with booking. The manager of a local theatre now had to go to New York to arrange a season of attractions. If he wished to schedule a 40-week season, he often had to deal with 40 different producers, each of whom was negotiating with many other local managers. Thus, booking was difficult and haphazard and since producers often defaulted on their agreements, local theatres were frequently faced with sudden cancellations. To remedy these ills, new approaches evolved. Theatres in a restricted area joined together to arrange bookings, and agents began to serve as middlemen between managers and producers.

In this confusion, a small group of men saw the possibility of gaining control of the American theatre. In 1896 Sam Nixon and Fred Zimmerman of Philadelphia, Charles Frohman, Al Hayman, Marc Klaw, and Abraham Erlanger of New York formed the "Theatrical Syndicate." Of these men, only Frohman was directly involved in theatrical production, the others being booking agents or theatre owners. The new organization began by offering a full season of stellar attractions, on the condition that local managers book exclusively through the Syndicate. This offer was welcomed by many managers, for it permitted them to deal with a single agent and to obtain outstanding productions. Managers who refused to deal with the Syndicate were systematically eliminated through simple, if ruthless, maneuvers. The Syndicate did not seek to gain direct control over all theatres in the country; rather, it concentrated on key routes between large cities, for unless productions could play along the way, touring was financially impossible. Where it could not gain control over key theatres, the Syndicate built rival houses and booked the finest productions at reduced prices until the competing theatres were bankrupt. New York producers who refused to cooperate were denied bookings and many actors were "blackballed," since the Syndicate would not send on tour any production in which they appeared. By 1900, the Syndicate was in effective control of the American theatre. Now in a position to influence the choice of plays, it refused to accept works not likely to appeal to a mass audience, and favored productions which featured stars with large personal followings. Thus between 1900 and 1915, the American theatre became largely a commercial venture.

Of the Syndicate members, Charles Frohman (1854–1915) was by far the most important, since he was the only one directly involved in theatrical production. Working his way up from program seller to business manager and agent, Frohman had entered management in 1889. In 1893, he opened the Empire Theatre in New York, where he maintained a fine stock company for many years. In 1896, he extended his interests to London and later controlled five theatres there. At the height of his power he employed some 10,000 persons. As an entrepreneur, Frohman was guided by two convictions: public taste is infallible, and stars are necessary to attract audiences. Thus, he sought to provide the mass public with works which would please, and launched many new stars.

Several of Frohman's stars were already well-established performers when he engaged them. These included John Drew II, William Faversham (1868–1940), a popular matinee idol, Viola Allen (1869–1948), noted primarily for her Shakespearean performances, and Otis Skinner (1858–1942), outstanding in romantic dramas and sentimental comedies. Other Frohman stars were Henry Miller, Margaret Anglin, Maude Adams, Ethel Barrymore, E. H. Sothern, and Julia Marlowe. Henry Miller (1860–1925) had played in several companies before becoming the leading actor in Frohman's Empire stock company. In 1897 he went on the road, but in 1906 formed his own company and in 1918 opened his own theatre in New York. Closely associated with Miller through much of his career was Margaret Anglin (1876–1958), leading actress of the Empire troupe. After 1910, her interests turned increasingly to standard drama and she made an enviable reputation for her Greek and Shakespearean productions. Maude Adams (1872–1953) was on stage from childhood, but her fame rests upon her work in Frohman's productions. Now remembered primarily for her appearances in J. M. Barrie's plays, she was Frohman's greatest money-maker for many years, perhaps because she accepted only roles showing optimism and wholesomeness. Retiring from the stage in 1918, she returned for occasional engagements after 1931. Ethel Barrymore (1879–1959) had served a brief apprenticeship with her uncle, John Drew II, and with Henry Irving before becoming a star overnight in *Captain Jinks of the Horse Marines* in 1901. By the 1920's she was considered America's leading actress, even though she had appeared in no significant plays and depended primarily upon her own forceful personality. From the 1930's, she worked almost exclusively in films. After 1904 the careers of E. H. Sothern (1859–1933) and Julia Marlowe (1870–1950) were bound up together. Previously Sothern had toured with McCullough and had been a leading actor in the Lyceum company, while Miss Marlowe, on the stage from childhood, had gained considerable fame for roles in standard works. From 1904 to 1924, they were the principal purveyors of Shakespeare to American audiences. Although inferior to many of their predecessors, they kept the classical tradition alive at a time when most of their contemporaries were appearing in new plays.

Despite the Syndicate's strength, it did not go unopposed. James A. Herne, Mr. and Mrs. Harrison J. Fiske, James O'Neill, David Belasco, and others held out, although with the exception of the Fiskes all eventually came to terms with the Syndicate. Minnie Maddern (1865–1932) was on the stage from the age of three and had achieved considerable fame by 1889, when she married Harrison Grey Fiske (1861–1942), a dramatist and editor of the most influential theatrical newspaper of the day, *The New York Dramatic Mirror*. After she returned to the stage in 1893, Mrs. Fiske championed the new realistic drama and was the first American to give Ibsen an extensive hearing through her productions of *A Doll's House, Hedda Gabler, Rosmersholm, Pillars of Society,* and *Ghosts*. When the Syndicate closed its theatres to her, she and her husband leased the Manhattan Theatre, where from 1901 to 1907 they produced many outstanding plays in which they sought to subordinate stars to ensemble effect. As a performer, Mrs. Fiske relied upon direct observation of life and a close study of psychology. She moved away from lines of business and encouraged actors to play as wide a range of roles as possible. She probably did more than any other American performer of her day to pave the way for the modern theatre.

James O'Neill (1847–1920), now remembered as the father of Eugene O'Neill, was one of America's most popular actors from the 1880's until the first World War. Despite great promise, he became identified with the leading role in *The Count of Monte Cristo*, which he first played in 1883, and rarely appeared in other works.

The most significant opposition to the Syndicate came from David Belasco (*c.* 1854–1931), a producer and dramatist who shared many of Frohman's ideals. Born in San Francisco, he was on the stage as a child and

Mrs. Fiske in a scene from Edward Sheldon's *Salvation Nell* (1908). [From *The
Theatre* (1909)]

wrote his first play at the age of 12. By the time he left California in 1882,
he had written or adapted over 100 works and had staged some 300. In New
York he served as manager of the Madison Square Theatre after Mackaye
left it, and later was Mackaye's stage manager at the Lyceum. Between 1887
and 1890 he collaborated with Henry C. DeMille (1850–93) on four very
successful plays for the Lyceum, and during the 1890's continued to build
his reputation as a dramatist with such hits as *The Girl I Left Behind Me*
(1893), *The Heart of Maryland* (1895), and *Zaza* (1899). Although he
had produced plays occasionally during the 1890's, it was not until 1902
that he acquired his own theatre. In 1907 he opened the Stuyvesant
Theatre (renamed the Belasco in 1910), where every modern improvement was installed. Here he continued his work until 1928. Belasco never
maintained a stock company and always worked on the single-play principle.

As a producer, Belasco is now remembered for three reasons: his power
as a star maker, his realism in staging, and his opposition to the Syndicate.

513

Like Frohman, Belasco depended much on stars, many of whom he coached carefully and for whose capabilities he tailored plays. Among his stars were Mrs. Leslie Carter (1862–1937), featured in many of Belasco's works from 1895 to 1905; Blanche Bates (1873–1941), noted especially for her appearances in Belasco's *Madame Butterfly* (1900) and *The Girl of the Golden West* (1905), and later in many of Frohman's productions; Frances Starr (1886–   ), a versatile actress who starred in such works as Belasco's *The Rose of the Rancho* (1906) and Eugene Walter's *The Easiest Way* (1909); and David Warfield (1866–1951), a burlesque performer until Belasco transformed him into a leading dramatic actor in such plays as *The Auctioneer* (1902), *The Return of Peter Grimm* (1911), and *The Merchant of Venice* (presented in 1922).

BELASCO'S PRODUCTION of *The Governor's Lady* showing the replica of a Childs' Restaurant which he erected on stage. [From *The Theatre* (1912)]

Above all, Belasco is now remembered for his staging. Like Daly and Mackaye, Belasco insisted upon controlling every aspect of his productions. With him, naturalistic detail reached the peak of its development in America. For *The Governor's Lady* (1912), a Childs Restaurant was reproduced on stage and the Childs concern stocked it daily with food which was consumed during the performance. For *The Easiest Way,* Belasco bought the contents of a boarding-house room, including the wallpaper, and had it transferred to his stage. His crowd scenes were famous for their authenticity and power. In collaboration with Louis Hartman, he experimented extensively with stage lighting. In *Madame Butterfly,* the passage of night was shown realistically through a 12-minute sequence which moved through sunset to night to dawn. Belasco replaced footlights with spotlights mounted in the auditorium and developed new color media. In his search for perfection, however, Belasco remained firmly within the 19th century tradition, for he sought merely to bring the maximum of illusion to a repertory in the Boucicault tradition.

Belasco first came into conflict with the Syndicate when he sought to take *The Auctioneer* on the road in 1902. Further difficulties led to a court battle in 1906. By 1909 Belasco's productions were in such demand that the Syndicate was forced to accept Belasco's terms, even though he refused to book exclusively through it. Its concessions to Belasco marked the first important break in the Syndicate's power.

The willingness of the Syndicate to make concessions had been hastened by the rise of the Shuberts. Three brothers, Sam (1876–1905), Lee (1875–1954), and Jacob J. (1880–1963), after beginning in Syracuse, New York, leased a theatre in New York City in 1900. When the Syndicate closed its theatres to their productions in 1905, they began to establish a rival chain. By this time, the high-handed methods of the Syndicate had created much dissatisfaction, and the Shuberts were welcomed by many local managers as allies. By 1908 several theatres had defected to the Shuberts, and the revolt accelerated after 1910 when the National Theatre Owners Association was formed. The struggle between the Shuberts and the Syndicate reached its peak in 1913, after which the Syndicate's grip was broken. Further weakened by the death of Charles Frohman in 1915, the Syndicate ceased to be an effective force after 1916. Unfortunately, the Shuberts became as dictatorial and monopolistic as the Syndicate had been. As producers, they were noted for lavish musicals with little substance. Although they largely gave up producing plays after 1945, they continued to control "the road" until 1956, when the government ordered them to sell many of their theatres. Their theatrical holdings are still sufficiently extensive to exert considerable influence on the theatre in America.

Under the conditions which governed the American theatre between 1895 and 1915, it is not surprising that significant playwriting did not flourish. Probably the most successful dramatist was Clyde Fitch (1865–1909). After being commissioned by Richard Mansfield to create *Beau Brummel* (1890), he wrote about 60 plays, of which the most important were *Barbara Frietchie* (1899), *Captain Jinks of the Horse Marines* (1901), *The Girl with the Green Eyes* (1902), *The Truth* (1907), and *The City* (1909). During the season of 1900–01, ten of Fitch's works were being played in New York or on the road. A careful observer, Fitch reflected the life of his times. Noted for his quiet, intense scenes, Fitch probably failed to achieve true depth because of the haste with which he wrote. As the first American playwright to publish his works regularly, he established a pattern continued until the present.

William Vaughan Moody (1869–1910) seemed the dramatist with greatest promise. Moody was a professor at the University of Chicago and a poet of stature when he began writing closet dramas about 1900. His first produced work, *The Great Divide* (1906), performed by Henry Miller and Margaret Anglin, was considered a landmark because it combined considerable literary merit with an exciting action which dramatized the "great divide" between the effete and self-conscious East and the rough and open-hearted West. Moody's only other play to reach the stage, *The Faith Healer* (1909), was not well received, perhaps because of its protagonist, who believes in his ability to heal through faith. Moody's early death blighted the hopes of those who saw in his work the promise of a truly significant American drama.

By 1915, the theatre was beginning to decline in popularity. While increased ticket prices were partially responsible, effective competition, most notably from spectator sports and motion pictures, was also appearing. Soon after Thomas A. Edison demonstrated the "kinetoscope" in 1894, "penny arcades" began to show short motion pictures. Only one person at a time could be served, however, until George Eastman's flexible film and Thomas Armat's projector made it possible to show movies to an assembled audience.

In 1905, the first motion-picture theatre was opened in McKeesport, Pennsylvania, and by 1909 there were 8000. The early theatres seated only about 100 and offered only short films. In 1914, the Strand Theatre in New York, with its 3300 seats, began the trend toward larger houses. But it was not until D. W. Griffith's *The Birth of a Nation* (1915), the first full-length picture, surpassed Belasco's realism and melodramatic power that films became a serious competitor for the theatre. With their superior ability to capture spectacle and their markedly lower admission costs, motion pictures began to draw away that audience which had sought illusionism and thrills in the theatre. Unfortunately, the commercialization of the theatre had alienated a large part of the more discriminating spectators, leaving no effective buffer against disaster.

The competition from films did not bring an overnight revolution. In 1915, there were still about 1500 legitimate theatres outside of New York and the number of theatrical productions on Broadway continued to increase until the season of 1927–28. The invention of sound motion pictures in 1927 and the depression of 1929 dealt serious blows, however, and by 1930 only 500 theatres remained outside of New York. Thereafter, the number steadily declined.

Although these new directions were not apparent in 1915, it was already clear to many that the old production methods were outmoded and that commercialization had gradually reduced the repertory to works calculated to appeal to the mass audience. Reassessment, new methods, and changing ideals were to create the modern American theatre.

THE THEATRE
OF THE ORIENT

*T*hus far only the theatre of Europe and America has been considered. While it was developing, however, another quite different tradition was taking shape in Asia. Equally as diverse as the theatre of the West, it deserves a much fuller discussion than is possible here, for almost every country of the Orient has a long and distinctive theatrical past. Since the practices of India, China, and Japan have been most influential, the following account will concentrate upon them, especially those which were to attract Western producers seeking alternatives to illusionism. Practically unknown in the West until the late 19th century, the Oriental theatre is now recognized as an important influence upon the modern Western theatre.

The Theatre in India

The theatre in India is one of the most ancient in the world. Precisely when it began, however, is uncertain, for the early Indians paid little heed to chronology. According to Hindu legend, Brahma taught the art of drama to the sage Bharata, who recorded the lessons in *Natyasastra* (The Science of Dramaturgy) somewhere between 200 B.C. and 200 A.D. Since Bharata's treatise codifies traditions of dance, drama, makeup, costume, and acting, these skills must have been well established by this time.

Taking its material primarily from the two epics, *Mahabharata* and *Ramayana* (both probably written between 500 B.C. and 320 A.D.), a Sanskrit drama of high order appeared around 320 A.D. Rather than concentrating upon character development or philosophical issues, it was organized around *rasas*, fundamental moods, to which all other dramatic elements were subordinated. Thus Sanskrit plays are not categorized as comedy, tragedy, or melodrama, but according to one of the nine *rasas:* erotic, comic, pathetic, furious, heroic, terrible, odious, marvelous, or peaceful. While a single work may employ many moods, incompatible ones are avoided, and since the final aim is to induce composure and harmony, all plays end happily. Death and violence are banished from the stage, and right and wrong are clearly differentiated. Joy and sorrow may be mingled, but all must be resolved into happiness in an ending which shows good triumphant over evil.

The plays are complex, nevertheless, because of their many elements. The heroic and the domestic, the exalted and the commonplace exist side by side. The mixture is exemplified in the typical practice of making the hero's confidant a bald, dwarfish, gluttonous clown, who provides considerable comic relief from a basically serious story. The diversity may also be seen in the dialogue, a mixture of verse (used for heightened expression in scenes of intense emotion) and prose (used for more ordinary scenes) and of Sanskrit (the learned language, spoken by gods, kings, Brahmins, ministers, generals, and sages) and Prakrit (the everyday dialect, used for women, children, servants, soldiers, peasants, and persons of low birth). Considerable variety is also achieved by intertwining several subsidiary plots, ranging from the farcical to the serious, around the main story.

Plays vary in length from one to ten acts. According to the accepted rules, the events of a single act must be confined to a 24-hour period, while no more than one year may elapse between successive acts. In technique, the Sanskrit drama resembles the epic poem, for it employs narrative to set scenes and to describe events occurring between acts, while the action shifts freely among various locales, including both heaven and earth. Bharata describes ten kinds of plays, including monologues, farces, operatic works, and social plays. The most important is the heroic drama, based upon mythology or history, in which an exemplary hero defends a righteous cause. Usually there is also a love story in which the lovers are kept apart by some evil force until the end of the play.

About 25 Sanskrit plays have survived. Of these the most important are *The Little Clay Cart,* attributed to King Shudraka (probably of the 4th century A.D.), and *Shakuntala,* by Kalidasa (late 4th–early 5th century, A.D.). *The Little Clay Cart,* a social play according to the traditional Hindu classifications, tells of the love of a Brahmin for a courtesan. The plot is entirely invented. Written in ten acts, it has a number of subplots, most of which come together in the resolution. The true prince, previously aided by the courtesan, recaptures his throne and unites the Brahmin and courtesan, who have narrowly escaped death at the hands of the evil prince.

Shakuntala, a heroic drama in seven acts, is generally considered the finest of all Sanskrit dramas. It tells of King Dushyanta's meeting with Shakuntala (the foster daughter of a hermit), their love and separation (prolonged by a curse pronounced by a rejected suitor), and their eventual reunion. Renowned in part for its beautiful descriptive passages evoking the forest, stream, and other natural phenomena, it moves freely between heaven and earth, forest and court, from the serious and romantic to the comic. The lyrical and the fantastic mingle with the everyday as the play moves through a wide range of human experience.

Other Sanskrit dramatists include King Harsha (7th century A.D.), with *The Pearl Necklace, The Lost Princess,* and *Nagananda;* Bhavabhuti (late 7th century), with *The Story of the Great Hero, The Later Story of Rama,* and *The Stolen Marriage;* and Vishakhadatta (9th century A.D.), with *The Signet Ring of Rahshasa.* None captured the strength of the earlier works, however, and after the Mohammedan invasions of the 12th and 13th centuries, Sanskrit drama ceased to be a potent force.

Since Hindu drama was concerned ultimately with the internal and spiritual rather than the external and material, it turned away from realistic production techniques. Its spiritual inspiration was always recognized in the elaborate ritualistic ceremonies performed before the play to propitiate the gods and prepare performers and spectators for the drama. Given only on special occasions, such as a religious festival, a marriage, coronation, victory, or state visit, the performances lasted four or five hours. The audience was usually restricted to the court and aristocracy.

There were no permanent playhouses in ancient India. Bharata's treatise specifies that those set up for performances are to be 32 yards long by 16 yards wide and divided into two equal parts (auditorium and stage). Four pillars (white, red, yellow, and blue) are to be used to indicate where members of the various castes are to sit. The total seating capacity was only about 400. A curtain divided the stage area into two equal parts, the front half to be used for the dramatic action and the rear half as dressing rooms and off-stage space. The stage may have had two levels, the lower for the majority of the action and the upper for the less frequent scenes set in heaven, in a tower or other high place.

No scenery was used. At the beginning of the play, a prologue established the time, place, and situation. In each scene, descriptive passages and pantomime evoked place as needed. The actors used stylized movement and gestures to suggest such actions as climbing a hill, picking flowers, crossing a stream, riding a horse, or driving a chariot. A walk around the stage indicated a long journey. Because scenery was not used, place could shift rapidly as one scene flowed into the next.

Primary emphasis was placed upon the actor, said to have four basic resources at his disposal: movement and gesture; speech and song; costume and makeup; and psychological insight. Movement and gesture, although based upon natural behavior, were limited to rigidly prescribed signs as described by Bharata and other Hindu writers. Classified according to the parts of the body and inner feelings, gestures were codified into thirteen movements of the head, six of the nose, six of the cheek, seven of the eyebrows, nine of the neck, five of the chest, thirty-six of the eyes, thirty-two of the feet, and twenty-four of the single hand. All were to be combined (according to character type, mood, and situation) to create a sign language as complex as speech.

A similar classification was made of verbal speech and music, in both of which an elaborate scheme of intonation, pitch, and tempo were mingled according to the emotion, character, and situation. Each play was accompanied throughout by music played on the drum and stringed instruments. The drum was considered most essential, for it followed the dialogue closely and enhanced rhythmic effects. Singing was also used extensively. Through entrance or exits songs, the musicians provided information about the situation or characters, while other songs indicated changes in mood or bridged gaps in the action.

Costume and makeup for each character were also strictly prescribed. The makeup indicated the character's caste, social position, place of birth, and historical period. Color was used symbolically: the Sun and Brahma were golden, Gods orange, high caste characters red, low caste characters blue, and so on. Ornaments such as earrings, bracelets, belts, necklaces, and headgear differentiated characters within categories. Properties were used symbolically. The presence of an elephant was indicated by the use of a goad, a horse by a bit, and a chariot by a whip.

Characters were divided into clearly differentiated categories. For example, there were four basic types of hero: the sublime, the impetuous, the gallant, and the quiet. Emotions were classified as nine: love, laughter, pathos, anger, energy, fear, disgust, wonder, and quietude. The actor, then, sought to weld conventionalized gestures and movements, speech and intonation, costume and makeup, emotion and character type into a performance capable of arousing the appropriate *rasa*.

While the Sanskrit theatre ceased to be active after the 13th century, Hindu dance had a more fortunate history. Dance is undoubtedly even more ancient than drama and was obviously well developed by the time Bharata wrote his *Natyasastra,* for in it he codified 108 dance poses. Hindu dance probably reached its peak during the 4th and 5th centuries A.D., although treatises analyzing its subtleties continued to be written until the 15th century. With the coming of the Mohammedan invaders, the dance retreated southward to the state of Madras, where it was preserved by temple dancers. When Indian nationalism began to reassert itself in the 1890's, this traditional dance form, now called the *Bharatanatyam,* came into prominence once more and has since been highly prized. Although originally probably performed by more than one dancer, it is now a woman's solo dance noted for its grace.

Classical dance has also survived in three other forms: the Kathak, characterized by intricate footwork and precise rhythms; the Manipuri, noted for its swaying and gliding movements; and the Kathakali, a dance drama. In all there are elements of pure dance and of mime, but only the Kathakali tells a connected dramatic story.

Kathakali is now about 300 years old and is restricted to South India. Its subject matter is taken primarily from the Hindu epics. Perhaps because it is pantomimic, Kathakali has exaggerated many of the features found in Sanskrit drama and has brought violence and death onto the stage. Its stories center around the passions and furies of gods and demons, or the loves and hates of superhuman characters; the forces of good and evil clash in desperate struggles, but good always wins. The actors rely entirely upon dance, mime, costume, and makeup, although musicians also help to tell the story through song and instrumental accompaniment. The gestural language includes more than 500 separate signs. Characters fall into about seven basic types, each with its own costume and symbolic makeup, which takes hours to apply. Because it is so energetic, Kathakali uses boys to perform female roles. The Kathakali dancer must begin his training as a child and is not considered mature until he has performed a role for about twenty years. Kathakali is presented in a temple courtyard or other open space, upon a stage about 16 feet square covered with a flower-decked canopy and lighted by torches. Performances last all night. Kathakali is such a complex form that few attempts have been made to bring it to Western audiences, but in recent years it has attracted increased attention, especially since a troupe appeared in Paris, London, and Montreal in 1967.

Alongside the classical forms, popular dramatic types have existed

KATHAKALI DANCERS OF INDIA. [From
Gargi, *The Theatre in India.* Courtesy
Theatre Arts Books]

from earliest times, although their history is less well known. Bharata lists
18 kinds of "lower" drama. Of the popular entertainments, puppet plays
are among the oldest; the shadow play, in which silhouettes of puppets are
projected on cloth, can also be traced far back into history. Both were to
spread eastward and westward to become popular entertainments in Europe and Asia.

Folk drama probably has its roots in the plays performed for the
common people during the early Christian era, but its history can be traced
no further back than the 15th or 16th centuries. Each area of India has its
own characteristic folk plays. In some locales, they assume operatic form
and feature legendary heroes or themes of love and chivalry; in others, they
are light farces, dance dramas, or devotional plays. Regardless of type,
almost all have common characteristics. A narrator usually sets the scene,
calls out each character as needed, and describes events not shown on stage.
All are performed on an open stage surrounded on three sides by the
audience. No scenery is used. The acting is stylized, but uses conventions

fully understood by the audiences of the area. Music accompanies the entire performance. Most plays continue all night in the light of flickering torches.

The puppet and folk plays kept Indian traditions alive during the centuries of Muslim and English occupation. When they arrived in the 18th century, the British introduced Western drama, and in the 19th century Indian plays written in the Western style began to appear. Of the modern playwrights, Rabindrinath Tagore (1861–1941) has been most successful in blending Indian and Western traditions in such plays as *Chitra* (1894), *King of the Dark Chamber*, (1914), and *The Cycle of Spring* (1917).

Although the revival of the Indian national consciousness has re-directed attention to Sanskrit drama and other classical forms, the great diversity of local languages and customs has not yet permitted the development of a characteristic modern style. The Indian theatre is now extremely diverse, ranging through productions of the Sanskrit play and folk drama to modern realistic works. The influence of India, nevertheless, continues to derive primarily from its classical forms.

The Chinese Theatre

In China, ritual dance can be traced back to the Shang Dynasty (1766–1122 B.C.), but it did not emerge as a form of entertainment until the Han Dynasty (200 B.C.–200 A.D.). Even then, it was not dramatic. Important steps toward drama appear to have been taken during the T'ang Dynasty (618–906 A.D.), for the Emperor Ming Huang (712–54) established a school for training singers and dancers, the Academy of the Pear Orchard. Most scholars now agree that the theatrical performances of this period were probably composed of dance dramas which bore little resemblance to the later and more characteristic form of Chinese drama. Song, dance, and dialogue were first fused into a connected story sometime during the Sung Dynasty (960–1279) and first flourished during the Yuan Dynasty (1280–1368), perhaps because the Mongol Yuan emperors excluded intellectuals from government posts, leaving them no outlet for their energies other than literature.

Yuan drama (which actually began during the Sung Dynasty and did not reach its fulfillment until the Ming Dynasty, 1368–1644) was the first to be written in China according to the rules which were later to become set conventions. The stages in its development are obscure, for no accurate contemporary records exist. In general, however, in Yuan times two principal schools of drama—the Southern and the Northern—can be distinguished because of differences in prosody, music, and composition. The Southern school adhered to strict rules of prosody, used a musical scale of five tones, and employed rather esoteric dialogue filled with scholarly allusions. The musical accompaniment was primarily that of the flute, while the overall feeling of the plays was one of softness and gentleness. The Northern school, on the other hand, took considerable liberties with the rules of prosody, used a seven-tone scale, and wrote dialogue based upon everyday speech. Stringed instruments provided the principal accompaniment, and the overall effect was lively and vigorous.

These two schools were equally important until the 16th century, when the Southern school began to dominate, although by this time it had absorbed many characteristics of the Northern school. The dramas of the new type often extended to thirty or more acts, each relatively complete and separately titled. Thus, acts could be eliminated or played in various combinations. In the first act of the long plays a secondary character explains the story, which does not begin to unfold until the second act. In succeeding acts, many plot strands are introduced and all are happily resolved in the final act. This new style of drama was to dominate until the 19th century, although it underwent many stylistic changes. Under the Ming Dynasty, Soochow became the cultural center of China and the major home of drama. Perhaps because the patronage of the court gradually led to dilettantism, the drama had begun to deteriorate before the rebellion of 1853 put an end to Soochow's dominance and to the old dramatic style.

The theatre in Peking now came to prominence. Throughout the period of Soochow's preeminence, other local styles had persisted in many regions of China. Around 1790, troupes from Anhui settled in Peking and gradually absorbed characteristics from other areas. After the destruction of the Soochow theatre, these troupes assumed the lead and during the reign of Emperor Huang Hsu (1875–1908), established the Peking opera, as the new style is usually called, as the major classical form. Although other styles have continued, the Peking mode remains dominant.

The Peking opera shows a considerable decline in literary quality from the earlier period. Its plays are classified under two headings: civil plays, dealing with social and domestic themes, and military plays, involving the adventures of warriors or brigands, although the two are often mingled. Many of the plays are derived from two novels, *Romance of the Three Kingdoms* and *The Water's Edge*, both probably dating from the Yuan or Ming Dynasties. *Romance of the Three Kingdoms* recounts the daring exploits of three military leaders during the years of upheaval between 220 and 265 A.D., while *The Water's Edge* tells of the adventures of several "Robin Hood" figures of the 11th century who were forced into hiding by the failure of a reform program. Other plays are based upon history, legend, mythology, folklore, popular novels, and romances. An entire Peking play is often no longer than one or two acts of the older form, from which scenes are often borrowed. A program is usually made up of a succession of short pieces performed without intermission. All plays end happily. The text of a work is seldom strictly followed, for all great actors make changes at certain points and each troupe has its own versions of standard works. The dramatic action is often obscure because the beginnings and endings are neglected, interest being focused upon the high points of the story. A play, however, is merely an outline for a performance, and the audience goes to see a production rather than to hear a literary text.

Despite many changes in Chinese drama through the centuries, most of its basic conventions have remained relatively fixed. Many of these are related to the playhouse, its arrangement and equipment. The earliest stages were probably the porches of temples—simple platforms with an ornate roof—and the influence of the temple stage continues to the present time. The stage of the Chinese theatre is an open platform, often almost square, covered by a roof supported by lacquered columns. Raised a few feet above the ground and surrounded by a wooden railing about two feet high, the stage is equipped only with a carpet, two doors in the rear wall (the one on stage right is used for all entrances and that on stage left for all exists), between which hangs a large embroidered curtain. The only permanent properties are a wooden table and two chairs.

This simplicity allows for rapid changes of place, which are indicated through speech, action, or properties. In addition to statements about place, actors may pantomime knocking at gates, entering rooms, or climbing stairs. A circle around the stage indicates a lengthy journey. The table and chairs may be used to symbolize a law court, banqueting hall, or other interior scene, for each of which furniture is arranged according to a prescribed formula. The significance of the table and chairs is further extended through their combination with other simple properties: an incense tripod on the table indicates a palace; paper and an official seal indicate an office; an embroidered divided curtain hung from a bamboo pole signifies a general's tent, an Emperor's chamber, a drawing room, or a bride's bedroom, depending upon the other properties with which it is combined. The table and chairs may also be used less representationally. Two chairs back to back may stand for a wall; chairs at the end of a table may form a bridge; a chair may represent a tree or the door of a prison; a table may stand for a hill, cloud, or other high place.

Other properties serve to clarify setting and action. A blue cloth upon which a wall is painted may represent a fort, city gate, or mountain pass; a whip indicates that an actor is riding a horse; two yellow flags upon which wheels are painted signify a chariot or wagon; four pieces of cloth carried by an actor running across the stage represent the wind; a banner with a fish design indicates water; a stylized paddle is used to mime rowing. A rolled water banner on a tray becomes a fish, while a corpse is represented

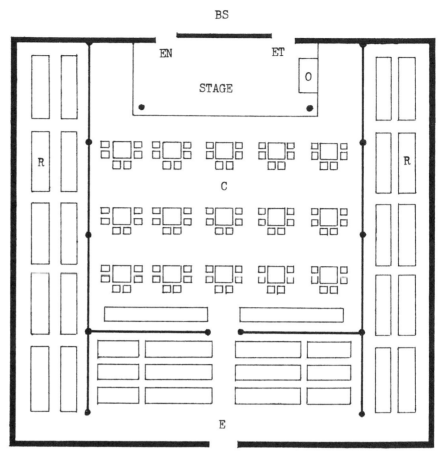

BS-Backstage
EN-Entrance to stage
ET-Exit from Stage

O-Orchestra
E-Main Entrance to Auditorium
R-Raised Side Seats

C-Tables & Stools for Audience

GROUND PLAN of a Chinese theatre. [Drawing by Douglas Hubbell]

by a paddle wrapped in a garment. Weapons, although modeled after real ones, are made of bamboo, wood, or rattan and are decorated. Thus, the audience's imagination is stimulated, but much is left to fill in. Perhaps the departure from realism is best illustrated by the presence on stage throughout the performance of assistants who help the actors with their costumes and bring on, remove, or rearrange properties as needed. No attempt is made to disguise their presence; in contrast with the gaudily-attired actors, they wear ordinary street clothes, often of an extremely informal type.

Traditionally, the musicians also remain in full view throughout the performance and are dressed in the same style as the stage assistants. They come and go freely and are never considered part of the stage picture. (In contemporary Communist China, the musicians are often seated in an orchestra pit and kept offstage.) Music is an integral part of every performance. It provides an atmospheric background, accompanies the many sung passages, controls the timing of movements, and welds the performance into a rhythmical whole. Since Chinese musical notation is very imprecise, theatre musicians learn their parts by rote. Most music used in the Peking opera has been worked out collaboratively between actors and musicians; most is borrowed from already existing sources and recombined according to the requirements of a particular play. Although they may be classified as string, wind, and percussion, the instruments of the Chinese orchestra have no counterparts in the West. The leader of the orchestra plays a drum which establishes the time and accentuates the rhythm. Gongs, cymbals, brass cups, flutes, stringed instruments, and more exotic items complete the orchestra. Songs are accompanied only by flute and strings, but entrances and exits are signaled by deafening percussion passages. Much of the on-stage action is performed to a musical background.

It is the actor, however, who is at the heart of the Chinese theatre. On a bare stage furnished only with a few properties and served by drably clothed stage attendants and musicians, the lavishly and colorfully dressed actors speak, sing, and move according to rigid conventions. Acting roles are divided into four main types: male, female, painted face, and comic. The male roles (*sheng*) include scholars, statesmen, patriots, and similar types. They range from young to old and from the dandy to the warrior. They are subdivided according to whether they involve fighting and acrobatics or are restricted to singing and dancing. Actors playing these roles wear simple makeup and, except for young heroes, beards. The female roles (*tan*) are subdivided into six types: the good and virtuous wife or lover; coquettish types; warrior maidens; young unmarried girls; women of evil character; and old women. Originally all *tan* roles were played by women, but from the reign of Ch'ien Lung (1735–96) until the 20th century actresses were forbidden. Perhaps as a result, the *tan* roles were always considered secondary until Mei Lan-fang (1894–1961), the most famous of Chinese actors, raised them to prominence. After 1911, actresses returned to the stage and now have largely supplanted the male *tan* actors. The painted face (*ching*) roles are so called because of the brilliant and elaborate patterns painted on the actors' faces. The *ching* roles include warriors, bandits, courtiers, officials, gods, and supernatural beings, but the basic attribute of all is their swagger and exaggerated strength. They are also subdivided according to whether they are good or evil, whether fighting and gymnastics are required, and so on. The clown (*ch'ou*) speaks in an everyday dialect, is free to improvise, tells many jokes, and is the most realistic of the characters. He may be a servant, businessman, jailer, watch-man, soldier, shrewish mother-in-law, or matchmaker. He combines the skills of the mimic and the acrobat.

Upon entering the stage, each important character describes his basic nature and appearance in a half-spoken, half-chanted passage. This is often followed by other lines in which he explains the story and tells his name, family background, and other information. Such speeches clarify situation and character, and consequently permit the dramatist to concentrate upon particular moments by summarizing much of the surrounding action. The

MEI LAN-FANG in a duel scene from *The Rainbow Pass*. [From *Theatre Arts* (1935)]

actor's delivery of lines is also rigidly controlled by conventions. Each role has its prescribed timbre and pitch, and to maintain a rhythm syllables are often drawn out without regard for conversational usage. Even spoken passages are governed by strict rhythms and tempos. Chanted and sung passages are freely inserted into spoken monologues or dialogues. Thus, the script is rendered in an extremely stylized manner.

All stage movement is related to dance, being rhythmical, mimetic, and symbolic. Furthermore, every word is accompanied by movement intended to enhance or explain its meaning. Stage gesture has been fully codified. There are seven basic hand movements, many special arm move-ments, more than twenty different pointing gestures, more than twelve special leg movements, and a whole repertory of sleeve and beard movements. Methods of walking or running vary with each role. The prescribed gestures and movements are combined according to character, mood, situation, or other conditions.

Costumes, most of which are heavily patterned and gaudy in color, are also extremely important in the Chinese theatre. Each of the more than 300 standard items is designed to describe its wearer's character type, age, and social status through color, design, ornament, and accessories. Color is always used symbolically: red for loyalty and high position, yellow for royalty, dark crimson for barbarians or military advisors, and so on. The designs also have symbolic significance: the dragon is the emblem of the emperor; the tiger stands for power and masculine strength; the plum blossom indicates long life and feminine charm. Headgear is almost as varied as the garments; the approximately 100 variations are all used symbolically. Most costumes are made of rich materials regardless of the wearer's rank, but occasionally linen or cotton is used for very poor characters or clowns.

The visual appearance is completed by makeup. Bearded *sheng* actors and old women wear very little makeup. For the other female roles, the face is painted white and the eyes surrounded by a deep red shading into pink. A similar makeup, although with less marked contrasts, is used for the unbearded *sheng* roles. The clown's distinguishing feature is the white patch around the eyes; the various types of clowns are differentiated by distinctive black markings. By far the most complex makeup is that of the *ching* roles, the entire face being painted in bold patterns symbolic of the particular character.

Such a complex and formalized system of performance requires long and rigorous training. The would-be actor enters a school between the ages of seven and twelve, where he undergoes a period of strict discipline for six years. At first his training is generalized, but as the student shows his suitability for a particular type of role his training is specialized. If an actor is to achieve fame, he must remain within the prescribed conventions of his role but somehow endow it with his own personality.

The peculiar flavor of the Chinese theatre also owes much to the audience. Most of the early public theatres were temporary; the permanent structures were to take much of their inspiration from the teahouse, where around the 17th century actors began to perform for customers seated at tables. The later permanent theatres retained this arrangement, the ground floor being fitted out with tables and stools at which spectators were served tea while watching the play. The permanent theatres also added a raised platform around the sides and back of the auditorium, where poorer spectators sat on benches. A balcony, divided into sections much like the boxes of a Western theatre, was also added. In some periods the balcony was occupied by the wealthy class, but in others it was reserved entirely for women. After 1911, the traditional arrangement of the auditorium began to change and now most urban theatres are furnished with Western style chair seating. Audience behavior has changed little, however, for the spectators carry on conversations, eat and drink, and come and go freely. Audiences are usually familiar with the plays; each member has his favorite passages to which he attends carefully, only to ignore others. Like the playwright, the spectator is more concerned with significant moments than with overall effect.

The Chinese theatre has been known in the West longer than that of any other oriental country. As trade with China increased in the 18th and 19th centuries, familiarity with its art followed. A vogue for Chinese decorative motifs swept Europe in the 18th century, and Voltaire's *The Orphan of China* (1755) became the first Western play to draw upon a Chinese source. Nevertheless, it was not until the 20th century that Chinese theatrical conventions began to impinge upon the Western consciousness. Even then, they were felt most through such Western adaptations as *The Yellow Jacket* (1913) by J. H. Benrimo, *The Circle of Chalk* (1923) by A. H. Klabund, and *Lady Precious Stream* (1938) by S. I. Hsiung. To most Westerners, the Chinese theatre remains an exotic and little understood phenomenon, although appreciation of its conventions has grown in recent years because of the appearance of a Peking opera company in Europe and the wide distribution of a filmed performance.

Western-style drama has made some impact upon China during the 20th century. Melodramas, especially, have figured prominently in the many political struggles that have haunted China during the past 100 years. Nevertheless, the Peking opera remains the most characteristic Chinese dramatic form.

The Theatre of Japan

As in other countries, the theatre in Japan can be traced from ritual dances. Increasing in importance after the 7th century A.D., they were to give rise to three distinct forms—Noh, the doll theatre, and Kabuki. Of these, the first to appear was Noh. Originally there were two types of Noh. One, the *dengaku-no* or *ennen-no,* performed by monks as entertainments following important Buddhist ceremonies, was probably derived from the folk dances of the rural communities. The second, the *saragaku-no,* was raised to such preeminence by Kanami Kiyotsugu (1333–84) and his son Zeami Motokiyo (1363–1444) that by the 15th century it had become the only type regularly performed. Although there were many later Noh dramatists, Kanami and Zeami remain the most important. Of the approximately 240 works still in the active repertory, more than 100 were written by Zeami, who also formulated the principles of Noh acting and laid the foundations of production practices.

Originally Noh plays appealed to a wide range of spectators, and "subscription performances" were often given on temple grounds to raise money for shrines. Its conventions were also flexible until about 1615. The changes in Noh and other Japanese forms cannot be fully understood without reference to political conditions. From 1338 until 1590 Japan was wracked with civil wars. In the settlement which followed, the Emperor appointed Tokugawa Ieyasu *shogun.* The *shoguns,* who became the secular rulers of Japan, rigidly upheld the feudal system, under which each rank and trade was carefully regulated. After 1641, they systematically isolated Japan from the rest of the world. Perhaps as a result of the narrow sphere within which they were free to act, the Japanese cultivated elaborate ceremonies and rituals in daily life, a preoccupation which is reflected in all their arts.

In the early 17th century, when the *shoguns* took them under their protection, the Noh actors were accorded *samurai* status, which placed them among the privileged classes, and were granted a stipend raised through a system of national requisitions. Five schools, or branches, of Noh were recognized and the headship of each was made hereditary. These schools still exist. By 1650, Noh traditions had become fixed.

After 1650 "subscription Noh" was revived, now on a purely commercial basis, and continued at intervals thereafter. Nevertheless Noh remained primarily an aristocratic form. With the fall of the *shoguns* in 1868, Noh lost its privileged position and survived mainly because of the efforts of societies formed by admirers of Noh and by occasional favors from the ruling family. Since the Second World War, its status as a national treasure had been increasingly recognized, and its survival now seems assured.

Noh has a limited appeal, however, for it is essentially a relic of the past. The language, that of the upper classes of the 14th century, is unintelligible to most spectators. Written partly in prose and partly in verse, most of the lines are either sung melodically or intoned. The few spoken passages—usually less than one-third of the total—are recited in a highly stylized manner. Ordinary speech is used only when a player comes on stage between the parts of a two-act piece to summarize what happened during the first act. Most Noh plays are shorter than the average Western one-act play and seem undramatic by Western standards. The Noh is essentially a musical dance-drama for which the script serves as a framework for choreographically ordered movement. It is not concerned with action but with a situation expressed in lyrical form. All Noh plays culminate in a dance, and the dialogue and song which precede it serve primarily to outline the circumstances which motivate it. A chorus sings the actor's lines while he is dancing and narrates many of the events through the rest of the play.

Noh dramas are usually classified into five types: *shin,* which praise the virtues of some god; *nan,* or battle plays; *jo,* or plays about women; *kyo,* usually plays about demented persons, although almost any play which does not fall into the other categories may be included; and *ki,* or plays about such supernatural creatures as demons and goblins. These categories control programming, typically one play from each type being given in the order listed above. Since the Second World War, however, it has become common to present only three plays. Despite the five categories used by the Japanese, most of the Noh plays can be divided into two types: those set entirely in the real world, and those which feature apparitions (by far the greatest number). In the latter, the past is usually revealed in retrospect. For example, in Zeami's *Atsumori* a priest, formerly a warrior, is seeking to atone for having killed Atsumori; a reaper whom he meets reveals himself as the ghost of Atsumori, and they refight their battle in the culminating dance of the play.

The individual Noh dramas are separated by *Kyogen,* or short farcical interludes composed entirely of humorous dialogue. *Kyogen* have no musical accompaniment, and the maskless actors never appear in Noh plays. Although their effectiveness is derived from humorous exchanges and pantomime, they are performed according to a strictly controlled formal pattern. Most *Kyogen* have only two characters, although occasionally more appear.

The casts of the Noh plays are also small, often no more than two, although as many as six may be used. The principal character, or *shite,* and the secondary character, or *waki,* may each have a companion. Child actors, or *kokata,* play young princes, emperors, and other youthful roles, and sometimes an additional supporting actor appears. All of the performers are men. They wear masks made of painted wood, many handed down for generations. Masks fall into five basic types—aged, male, female, deities, and monsters—although each may have many variations. In addition, special masks are sometimes used.

Costumes, rich in color and design, are based upon the official dress of several centuries past but have been adapted to give an air of grandeur and to increase the performer's stature. Most are of silk decorated with elaborate embroidery, but they are never as gaudy as those used in the Chinese theatre. The garments may be placed in four categories: the outer garments; garments worn indoors or without an overdress; lower garments, such as divided skirts; and headdresses. Each category has many variations, but garments may be reused in several different types of roles. On his feet, the actor wears *tabi.* Costumes are often changed or adjusted on stage.

Properties are few and conventionalized. The fan is by far the most important, for it can be used to suggest the blowing of the wind, the ripple

SCENE from a Noh play. [From Haar, *Japanese Theatre in Highlight.* Courtesy Charles E. Tuttle Co., Tokyo]

of water, a rising moon, falling rain, and many subtle emotional responses. The meaning of the fan is determined by the actor's movement and the music. Occasionally the actor may use a sword or spear. Stage properties are also simple. A wooden stand may represent a palace, mountain, bed-chamber, or other place; a bamboo frame represents a boat. There is no machinery or scenery.

The Noh stage has been standardized since about 1615. Its two principal areas, the stage proper (*butai*) and the bridge (*hashigakari*), are both roofed like the shrines from which they are descended. The stage roof is supported by four columns, each with its own name and significance. At the upstage right pillar, *shitebashira* (principal character's pillar), the *shite* pauses when he enters to announce his name and where he comes from. While reciting this speech, he faces the pillar at the downstage right corner, the *metsukebashira*. The pillar at the downstage left corner is called *wakibashira* (or sometimes *daijinbashira,* "prime minister's pillar"), be-cause of its association with the secondary character. The upstage left pillar, *fuebashira* (flute pillar), indicates the flute player's position on stage.

The stage is divided into three principal areas, although none is marked off architecturally except by the pillars. The largest area, the main-stage, is enclosed within the four pillars and is about 19 feet square. Back of

THE NOH THEATRE, showing stage and auditorium. From
Zoe Kincaid's *Kabuki*. [Courtesy Macmillan and Company]

the upstage pillars is the rear stage (*atoza*), occupied by an orchestra
composed of two or three drummers and a flute player. To stage left of the
main stage is the *waki-za*, occupied by the chorus of eight to ten members.

There are two entrances to the stage. The principal one, the bridge
(*hashigakari*), is a railed gangway about six feet wide and from 33 to 52
feet long leading from the dressing room. In front of this bridge are planted
three small pine trees symbolizing heaven, earth, and man. The bridge is
used for all important entries. The other entrance, the "hurry door,"
upstage left and only about three feet high, is used by subordinate characters, the chorus, musicians, and stage assistants. The rear wall of the stage
and bridge are made of wood. On the wall back of the orchestra is painted a
pine tree and bamboo, perhaps as reminders of the natural scenery which
formed the background of the earliest performances. The audience views
the stage from two sides, being seated in front of the main stage, along its
stage right side and in front of the bridge.

The Noh performance is one of the most carefully controlled in the
world. Every movement of hands and feet and every intonation follows a
set rule. The orchestra supplies a musical setting and controls the timing.
Every episode is drawn out to great length so as to extract the full flavor of
the ritualistic action.

534

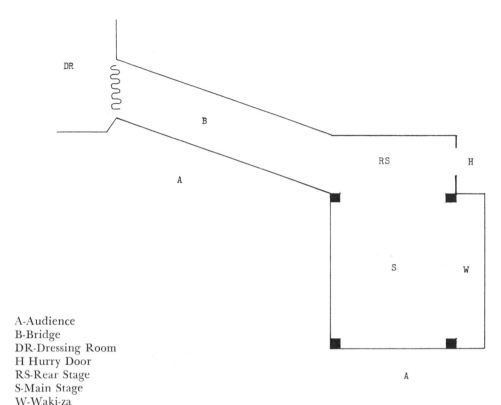

A-Audience
B-Bridge
DR-Dressing Room
H Hurry Door
RS-Rear Stage
S-Main Stage
W-Waki-za

GROUND PLAN of a Noh stage. [Drawing by Douglas Hubbell]

Puppets were also perfected in Japan through the *ningyo shibai,* or doll theatre. Although puppet entertainers can be traced back to the Heian era (781–1185 A.D.), it was not until the Keicho era (1596–1614) that the present doll theatre began. After undergoing many changes, it was given its definitive form by Takemoto Gidayu (1650–1714), who established a doll theatre in Osaka in 1685, while its most characteristic dramatic works were written by Chikamatsu Monzaemon (1653–1724), one of Japan's most famous dramatists, who worked with Takemoto.

The dolls underwent many changes, becoming ever more complex. Originally the puppeteers used a head only, but later hands and feet were added, and by 1678 rather complete figures were in use. In 1730, a mechanism was introduced which allowed the dolls to move their eyes; in 1733 jointed and movable fingers were added; later, the puppets were fitted with movable eyebrows. As the figures grew in complexity, the number of operators increased. Originally one handler, hidden from view, was sufficient, but by 1734 each doll was operated by three men, all entirely visible to the audience. One person manipulated the head and right arm, a second the left arm, and a third the feet. In 1736, the dolls were doubled in size to their present height of three or four feet.

The doll stage also grew in complexity. The use of movable stage settings after 1715 soon led to the invention of stage machinery which has since been adopted throughout the world. In 1727, elevator traps were introduced to raise scenery through the floor, and after 1757 they were used to create different stage floor levels. Perhaps most important, in 1758 the revolving stage—a circular platform used for changing settings—was invented.

The doll theatre reached the height of its popularity during the 18th century, when its conventions were fixed. After 1780 it was overshadowed by Kabuki and now survives only in one company, the Bunraku, located in Osaka, although it often plays in Tokyo, where provisions have been made for it in the new National Theatre.

The long and narrow stage of the doll theatre is divided into three levels from front to rear, each indicated by low partitions between which the doll handlers sit. All locales are represented scenically and changed as required by the story. Numerous properties are used.

A SCENE from the doll theatre in Japan, showing the handlers and their dolls. [From Haar, *Japanese Theatre in Highlight*. Courtesy Charles E. Tuttle Co., Tokyo]

A doll performance begins with the appearance of an announcer clad in black and wearing a hood (this costume is worn by all the stage assistants except the principal doll handlers, the musicians, and the narrator), who proclaims the title of the play and the names of the *samisen* player and the narrator. An orchestra is seated on stage left, while the *samisen* player and the narrator are placed downstage left. The *samisen,* a three-stringed instrument related to the lute, has a skin-covered base and is simultaneously plucked and struck. Extremely varied in sound, it can follow the rise and fall of the voice, give special emphasis, and provide punctuations to the narration and action. Its accompaniment is considered essential in the doll theatre. The narrator tells the story (the handlers do not speak) and expresses the feelings of each doll. He smiles, weeps, starts with fear and astonishment.

The doll handlers and the dolls occupy center stage. The dolls vary somewhat in size and complexity according to their importance in the play. The female dolls ordinarily do not have feet, because of their long skirts, and minor characters do not have movable mouths, eyes, and eyebrows. The handlers seek to become one with their dolls and to absorb themselves in the drama. They undergo long and arduous training before appearing on stage, first learning to operate the feet (usually about 10 years is spent mastering this operation), then progressing to the left hand (requiring another ten years), and then to the head and right arm. Their artistry has exerted considerable influence upon the Kabuki.

Of the three major Japanese theatrical forms, Kabuki is the most popular and vital, for it has been most sensitive to changing conditions. It is also the least "pure" of the forms, for it has borrowed freely from Noh, the doll theatre, and other sources.

Kabuki is usually traced back to about 1600, when O Kuni, a ceremonial dancer, began to give public performances of variations on Buddhist dances. Her success led to further elaboration and to many imitators. The early troupes were composed of women, whose easy virtue led the *shogun* in 1629 to prohibit the appearance of women on stage. Women's Kabuki was succeeded by Young Men's Kabuki, which was suppressed in 1652, for the boys proved to be as seductive as the women. Next, came Men's Kabuki, destined to be the permanent form, although the men were required to shave their foreheads and to eschew any emphasis upon physical charms.

Kabuki developed rapidly, and between 1675 and 1750 evolved most of its characteristic techniques. New methods of acting were introduced, fully-developed plays replaced the former improvised entertainments, and artistry replaced personal appeal. Many practices and much of the repertory were borrowed from the doll theatre, which Kabuki surpassed in popularity at the end of the 18th century. Many purists consider that true Kabuki ended in 1868, for under the impact of Western ideas it underwent several changes. Since the second World War ticket prices have made Kabuki something of a luxury, while the patronage of tourists has brought alleged debasements of the traditional practices. Nevertheless, Kabuki remains the most popular of Japanese theatrical forms, and its future now seems assured since the Japanese National Theatre, opened in 1966, has provided it a home.

Kabuki drama has undergone many changes. Originally, improvised sketches were inserted into dance performances, and it was not until the second half of the 17th century that works of a more ambitious nature began to appear. The first two-act play was given in 1664 and no important writer emerged until the 1670's, when Chikamatsu Monzaemon began to write for the Kabuki troupes. In 27 years he provided between 25 and 50 plays, although none now exists in its original form, and none ranks with the works he wrote for the doll theatre after 1704. Many of his approximately 100 doll plays were later taken into the Kabuki repertory.

Next to Chikamatsu, the most important Kabuki dramatist is Takedo Izumo (1691–1756), who worked with Chikamatsu and succeeded him as principal writer for the Osaka doll theatre. His masterpiece is *Chushingura* (1748), originally a doll play but now the most popular of all Kabuki dramas. Eleven acts long, it requires a full day in performance. Based upon an actual event, it tells of 47 faithful retainers who avenge the wrongs done to their master.

As drama increased in importance, the staff of each troupe came to include a playwright and a number of assistants apprenticed to him. When a new work was needed, the dramatist outlined a plot and his assistants then worked together on it, a practice which continued until 1868. Only one dramatist after Izumo is of special importance. Kawatake Mokuami (1816–93) bridged the old and the new system (under which writers worked alone) to become famous for his domestic plays, especially those about thieves and other low-life characters. Kawatake's dramas have remained so popular that it is rare to see a Kabuki program today that does not contain a selection from his approximately 50 plays.

Kabuki drama is not considered to be literature, however, for, like most Eastern dramatic forms, it serves merely as a basis for performance. Kabuki plays are usually divided into three categories: *jidaimono,* or plays with historical backgrounds; *sewamono,* or plays with domestic or low-life backgrounds; and *shosagoto,* or dance plays. Within these divisions there is much variety, for Kabuki writers never thought in terms of precisely defined forms and no clear line was drawn between comic and serious works as in Noh. Nevertheless, Kabuki has few purely comic plays, and most of these are dance pieces in one act. Other works are sometimes called comedies because they end happily. Most Kabuki plays are essentially melodramas, although they vary considerably in mood. Most are made up of loosely connected episodes joined together to create works of many acts and of considerable length. More interested in a series of climaxes than in a complete story, the playwrights often wrote strong scenes but failed to clarify their connection with others in the same play. This practice of composing relatively discrete episodes probably explains the modern prac-

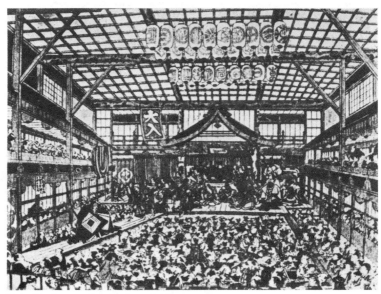

THE INTERIOR of a Kabuki theatre in the late 18th century. Note the large *hanamichi* on the left and the smaller one at right. Note also the vestigial temple roof. [From *Theatre Arts*]

tice of performing programs made up of parts of plays (often even parts of acts) rather than of complete works.

Kabuki programs have traditionally been lengthy. In the 18th century, performances began in the early morning and ran until about six P.M. In 1868, the maximum length of performances was set at eight hours a day. (Night performances were not given until 1878, when gas lighting was introduced.) Since the Second World War, it has been usual to give two programs a day, one lasting from about 11 A.M. until 4 P.M., and the second from about 4:30 P.M. until 9:30 P.M.

Many critics consider dance to be the basis of Kabuki, although dance must be understood to include rhythmical movement, studied posture, and conventionalized gesture. Originally only the female roles were danced, but by the late 18th century dance was such an essential part of all performances that a professional choreographer was added to each company. Since then dance has grown more complex and new forms have been specially created for Kabuki. The choreographers founded schools and granted licenses to students when they reached a certain level of proficiency. Many of the present schools date back to the 18th century.

Dance in Kabuki is always expected to reflect the verbal text. It seeks to distill the essence of real emotions and deeds into stylized gesture, movement, and posture. Thus, weeping becomes a rhythmical movement of the head accompanied by precise hand gestures. Kabuki dance is accompanied by narrative and descriptive music which helps to establish its

SCENE from a Kabuki play at the Kabuki-za, Tokyo. [From *Décor de Théâtre dans le Monde depuis 1935*]

character but always remains subordinate. The music for each play is traditional. Because Kabuki has borrowed from several sources, the placement of the musicians on stage varies: sometimes they sit upstage, sometimes they are at stage left, sometimes at stage right. Onstage musicians wear the ceremonial dress of the *samurai* (divided skirt, kimono, stiff horizontal shoulder pieces). When not performing, they sit upright and motionless. In addition to the onstage musicians, others provide special musical effects from behind a screen on stage right. Although the orchestra includes flutes, drums, bells, gongs, cymbals, and strings, the most essential instrument is the *samisen*. Singing and narration to its accompaniment is one of the most characteristic features of Kabuki.

Song and narration are important in Kabuki, especially in dance plays or those taken from the doll theatre. Since actors never sing, in these works a narrator sets the scene, comments on the action, and speaks part or all of the dialogue as in the doll theatre. In those plays in which most of the lines are spoken by actors, the narrator or chorus still sings or recites some passages. Even the actor's spoken lines follow conventionalized intonational patterns.

Kabuki acting is a combination of speaking and dancing. Because it follows established rules, it requires long and diligent study. The actor begins his training at the age of six or seven, first studying dance and then proceeding to diction, intonation, and the wearing of costumes. Since there are many children's roles, the student is usually on stage from the beginning of his career and learns his profession at first hand. Most of the leading performers come from a few families for whom acting is a hereditary profession. Each family has an elaborate system of stage names, some of which are so honored that they are awarded only to those considered undisputed masters of their art. An actor is almost never judged mature until after he has reached middle age.

The roles in Kabuki are divided into a few basic types: *tateyaku,* loyal, good, and courageous men; *katakiyaku,* villainous men; *wakashu kata,* young men, who if mild in disposition are called *nimaime; doke kata,* comic roles, including comic villains; *koyaku,* children's roles; and *onnagata,* women's roles of various kinds, all played by men.

Kabuki actors do not wear masks, but most use boldly patterned makeup to exaggerate the muscular conformation of the face. Upon a white base red and black patterns are normally painted, although demons and evil characters may use blue or brown. The *onnagata* usually adds roughing at the corner of the eye but otherwise leaves the face completely white. Married women blacken their teeth and obliterate their eyebrows. For some of the more athletic male roles, the arms and legs are made up in a conventional pattern. The makeup of each role is symbolic of the character.

Every role also has its traditional costume. Most are based upon historical garments which have been altered for dramatic purposes. Dress from different periods is often seen in a single play, for historical accuracy is of no importance in Kabuki. Pattern and color are usually subdued. Some costumes weigh as much as 50 pounds and stage attendants must assist the actors in keeping them properly arranged on stage.

In visual style Kabuki lies somewhere between the conventionalism of the Noh stage and the illusionism of the Western theatre. This combination can be seen most clearly in the properties, stage, and scenery. Properties range from the symbolic to the relatively realistic. The fan is used much as in Noh and can indicate riding a horse, shooting a bow and arrow, the rising moon, or an opening door. A scarf serves a multitude of similar purposes. On the other hand, many properties are representational, although none is intended to be convincingly real. The Kabuki horse probably best exemplifies the degree of illusionism; a wooden framework shaped like a horse, covered with velvet and ridden by an actor, is supported by two actors, whose legs clearly show. Many other properties—armor, swords, human heads, tigers, elephants, monkeys, household goods—are treated in much the same fashion.

The stage also marks a compromise between convention and illusionism. Originally the Kabuki performers used the Noh stage, but by the 1660's they had already widened the bridge and added a curtain to conceal the stage. Some scenic pieces began to appear in the late 17th century, and gradually the doll theatre's innovations were adopted. Elevator traps to handle scenic units were installed in 1736 and were being used to raise and lower actors by 1744. In 1793 the revolving stage was adopted and after 1827 was built in two sections, one revolving inside the other, which could be worked independently. A forestage had become a permanent feature of the Kabuki theatre by 1736 and was the principal acting area after 1745.

THE KABUKI HORSE. Note the legs and feet of the human actors supporting the frame. [From Zoe Kincaid's *Kabuki*. Courtesy Macmillan and Company]

Some time between 1724 and 1736 one of the Kabuki's most distinctive features, the *hanamichi,* was introduced. A raised gangway which connects the stage with a small room at the rear of the auditorium, the *hanamichi* is used for all major entrances and exits, as well as for many important scenes. The *hanamichi* was so popular that a second had been introduced by the 1770's. By 1830, the Kabuki stage had achieved its characteristic form. The Noh roof had been abandoned, and the stage now occupied the full width of the auditorium and was equipped with revolving stage and elevator traps. The area between the two *hanamichi* was divided into numerous square enclosures, or floor boxes, in which spectators sat on mats. Another row of these boxes ran along each side of the auditorium.

After 1868, several changes were made as a result of Western influence. The proscenium arch was introduced in 1908 and became standard after 1923, as did Western-style seating. The second *hanamichi* was eliminated, although it is still sometimes installed temporarily when required for a particular play. Except for the introduction of flying machinery, electric lighting, and the proscenium arch, however, the stage has remained relatively unchanged. The proscenium arch of the present Kabuki-za in Tokyo is 90 feet wide but only about 20 feet high, and the auditorium is only 60 feet deep. Thus the spatial relationship between stage and audience differs considerably from that of the typical Western theatre.

Unlike Noh, Kabuki uses a great deal of scenery, although it decorates the stage rather than conceals it. Every locale in a Kabuki play is suggested scenically. The scenery is changed in full view of the audience by means of the revolving stage, elevator traps, grooves, or by visible stage attendants. Perhaps because Kabuki emphasizes lateral composition, no more than two sets are erected on the revolving stage at once; sets are never pie-shaped and almost all scenery is placed parallel to the front of the stage. Painting is usually flat and is not intended to appear three-dimensional. Typically the stage is enclosed at the rear by flats upon which are painted a distant view, but illusionism is avoided by letting the cracks between individual flats show and by using a black curtain to cut off the top of the scene.

Sometimes relatively realistic Japanese buildings are erected on stage, but the entry gates to houses are often removed by stage assistants when no longer needed, and other theatrical conventions constantly remind the audience of the contrivance. Many scenic pieces are used symbolically. White mats represent snow, blue mats water, gray mats the ground; different kinds of trees indicate changes of locales. This mingling of the familiar with the conventional makes Kabuki more accessible to the Westerner than any of the traditional Oriental forms.

Japan has also developed a Western-style drama. The earliest type, the *shimpa,* was not very successful and died out after 1905. In 1909, the Free Theatre Society began to stage works by such authors as Gorki, Maeterlinck, Shaw, Chekhov, and Ibsen. Western influence was not widely felt, however, until motion pictures became popular. A realistic form, the *shingeki,* has developed in recent years but few plays have achieved outstanding popularity. It is ironical that, while the West has been seeking to alter its dramatic forms by adapting the conventions of Oriental drama, Japan has been trying to make its theatre more realistic in the Western sense.

Other Oriental Countries

Every Oriental country has its own dramatic traditions. Those of Korea have been shaped most by China and Japan, yet remain quite distinctive. The theatre of Southeastern Asia, on the other hand, owes most to Indian traditions and to the Hindu epics. Most Asian countries have developed dance drama to a high level, and some have produced historical and religious plays as well.

Perhaps the most distinctive form in Southeastern Asia is the shadow play, especially as developed in Java and Bali. Probably originating as early as the 7th century A.D., it took its subject matter from the *Mahabharata* or

Ramayana. In the Javanese shadow play, or *wayang kulit,* flat leather puppets act out the plots, while a puppet-master chants the story, manipulates the puppets with wooden sticks, directs the music, and produces special sound effects. A performance lasts throughout the night (approximately nine–ten hours) and is divided into phases related to the passing hours. Typically, the *wayang kulit* is organized as follows: first, a problem or situation is established; then an intrigue begins, usually in the stronghold of the hero's enemies; next, the hero, accompanied by clown-servants, appears (this happens at midnight); the action reaches its climax in a battle fought between the hero and several powerful giants (this phase of the story usually begins about 3 A.M. and lasts until dawn); the action is resolved with the triumph of the hero over the forces of evil. The plays are accompanied throughout by music (played by an orchestra made up primarily of percussion instruments), which varies according to the phase of the story and the hour of the night. Although the plays may be viewed purely as entertainment (the audience ranges from young children to old men), they also embody moral lessons and have mystical overtones as well.

There are many variations upon the shadow play, and each has its own

A SHADOW PLAY. In the background is the screen, orchestra, and puppet master, while the audience is seated in the foreground. [From *Theatre Arts* (1936)]

special name according to the kind of puppets used and the source of the subject matter. The shadow play also gave rise in the 11th century to performances by living actors, the *wayang topeng,* in which dancers panto-mime an action while a narrator recites the story. This form, still practiced in Java, takes its inspiration entirely from the puppet theatre. The Java-nese shadow play extends conventionalization perhaps as far as it has yet been taken, for it reduces humanity to stylized shapes manipulated by a master who speaks for all.

The Western world was largely ignorant of the Eastern theatre until the 19th century. The Sanskrit plays were the first to be translated and read, but Oriental theatrical conventions were unappreciated until Eastern companies began to appear in the West. A Chinese troupe played in Paris in 1895, a Japanese group appeared in London in 1900, and individual performers toured with some frequency thereafter. Nevertheless, it was not until such Western producers as Meyerhold, Vakhtangov, Brecht, and Artaud began to advocate and use them that Eastern conventions began to affect Western practices. At first viewed as perverse or exotic, the innova-tions have been increasingly accepted since the Second World War, largely because of the influence of Brecht and Artaud. Although it is doubtful that most Westerners still truly understand the Oriental theatre, they have been stimulated by it to seek new theatrical means. Thus, the Eastern and the Western traditions have at last made significant contact.

THE MODERN
THEATRE, 1875–1915

During the last quarter of the 19th century, a few dramatists and producers began to seek means for restoring the theatre to the esteem it had held in ancient Greece. Not all of the reformers shared common ideals, for some sought to make the theatre an instrument for social change, while others saw in it a path into the mystery of the universe or into the subconscious mind, and still others sought in it a "communion" not unlike that of ritual. Yet all shared a faith in the theatre's capacity to generate significant insights and humanizing ideals. Out of these strivings came the "modern" theatre, usually dated from Ibsen's prose dramas of the 1870's. By the time of the First World War, the new forces were beginning to triumph, although the ordinary playgoer still found many of them difficult to comprehend. The ferment of the years between 1875 and 1915 can best be seen by dividing it into two aspects, the realist and the idealist, although the two often merged.

Ibsen

As faith in science grew during the 19th century, attention turned increasingly to the direct and objective observation of life as the primary source of truth. This change was accompanied by a rejection of those idealistic philosophies which locate ultimate reality in forces which cannot be comprehended through the senses. In art, Romanticism gradually gave way to Realism, and during the 1850's such dramatists as Dumas *fils* and Augier began to concentrate upon contemporary social problems, while producers gave increasing attention to lifelike settings. By 1875, however, the innovations of the 1850's had already become accepted conventions. If important changes were to come, new influences were needed. Although the sources of change were numerous, the most important were the plays of Ibsen and the French Naturalists.

Henrik Ibsen (1828–1906), after publishing his first play in 1850, was appointed resident dramatist and stage manager at the newly-created Norwegian National Theatre in Bergen in 1851. By 1857 he had assisted in staging 145 plays, and had written seven of his own. From 1857 until 1862, he worked at the Norwegian Theatre in Christiana. After 1863, he lived abroad except for brief intervals.

Between 1850 and 1899, Ibsen wrote 25 plays. Most of the early works are Romantic verse-dramas about the Scandinavian past. These include *Lady Inger of Ostraat* (1855), *The Vikings at Helgeland* (1858), and *The Pretenders* (1863). The most important early works, however, are *Brand* (1866) and *Peer Gynt* (1867). *Brand,* a dramatic poem, depicts an uncompromising idealist who sacrifices everything, including his family, to his vision. This work established Ibsen's reputation, while the financial security which it brought made it possible for him to work as he pleased. *Peer Gynt* supplies a strong contrast to *Brand,* for its protagonist is a man who avoids issues by skirting around them. A skillful blending of fantasy and reality, *Peer Gynt* was interpreted by many as a satire on the Norwegian character.

Following *Peer Gynt,* Ibsen made a sharp break with his past. He now declared his intention of abandoning verse because it was unsuited to creating the illusion of reality. Since his first work in the new vein, *The Emperor and Galilean* (1873), is set in Roman times and deals with the conflict between Christianity and Paganism, it was not until *Pillars of Society* (1877) that the future direction of his work became apparent. With *A Doll's House* (1879), *Ghosts* (1881), and *An Enemy of the People* (1882), Ibsen established his reputation as a radical thinker and controversial dramatist. Above all, it was *A Doll's House* and *Ghosts* which shocked conservative readers and served as a rallying point for supporters of a drama of ideas. In *A Doll's House,* Nora, upon realizing that she has always been treated as a doll, chooses to leave her husband in order to become a person in her own right. In *Ghosts,* Mrs. Alving, conforming to traditional morality, has remained with a depraved husband only to have her only son go mad, presumably from inherited syphilis. Thus, both plays questioned the inviolability of marriage, while the allusion to venereal disease in *Ghosts* made it such a storm center throughout the world that it was forbidden production in many places.

Ibsen soon turned in new directions. In *The Wild Duck* (1884), *Rosmersholm* (1886), *The Master Builder* (1892), *John Gabriel Borkman* (1896), and *When We Dead Awaken* (1899) he made increasing use of symbolism and of subjects more concerned with personal relationships than with social problems. In actuality, the basic theme of Ibsen's plays remained relatively constant: the struggle for integrity, the conflict between duty to oneself and duty to others. Mrs. Alving of *Ghosts* discovers too late that she has destroyed her life by overvaluing duty to others, whereas in many of the late plays the protagonists, while pursuing some private vision, destroy the happiness of others and finally their own. In his many variations on this theme, Ibsen brought together trends which had been developing throughout the 19th century. Thus, his drama marks both a culmination of the old and a point of departure for the new.

Much of Ibsen's work contributed to the development of realism. In the prose dramas, he refined upon Scribe's "well-made play" formula and made it more fitting to the realistic style. Ibsen discarded asides, soliloquies, and other non-realistic devices, and was careful to motivate all exposition. Most often a character who has just arrived elicits information in a manner which appears completely natural by asking questions about happenings during his absence. All scenes are causally related and lead logically to the denouement. Dialogue, settings, costumes, and business are selected for their ability to reveal character and milieu, and are clearly described in stage directions. Each role is conceived as a personality whose behavior is attributable to hereditary or environmental causes. Internal psychological motivations are given even greater emphasis than external visual detail. In these ways, Ibsen provided a model for writers of the realistic school.

Ibsen's late plays were to influence non-realistic drama as extensively as the earlier prose plays did realistic works. In them, ordinary objects (such as the duck in *The Wild Duck*) are imbued with significance beyond their literal meaning and enlarge the implications of the dramatic action. Furthermore, many of the plays border on fantasy. In *Rosmersholm,* a white horse appears at crucial moments, and in *When We Dead Awaken* the mountain heights exert an irresistible pull. This sense of mysterious forces at work in human destiny was to be a major theme of idealist drama.

Whether realistic or idealistic, almost all dramatists after Ibsen were influenced by his conviction that drama should be a source of insights, a creator of discussion, a conveyor of ideas, something more than mere entertainment. He gave playwrights a new vision of their role.

Zola and the French Naturalists

While Ibsen was writing his prose works, the French Naturalists were also demanding a new drama. The principal spokesman of the movement was Émile Zola (1840–1902), an admirer of Comte and an advocate of the scientific method as the key to all truth and progress. Believing that literature must either become scientific or perish, Zola argued that drama should restrict itself to illustrating the "inevitable laws of heredity and environment" or to recording "case studies." He wished the dramatist, in his search for truth, to observe, record, and "experiment" with the same detachment as the scientist. Zola compared the writer with the doctor, who seeks the causes of a disease so that it may be cured; he does not gloss over infection, but brings it out into the open where it can be examined. Similarly, the dramatist should seek out social ills and reveal them so that they may be corrected.

Zola's first major statement of the Naturalist doctrine came in his Preface to *Thérèse Raquin* in 1873 and was expanded in *Naturalism in the Theatre* (1881) and *The Experimental Novel* (1881). He attracted a number of followers, many of whom were even more radical in their demands for theatrical reform. Jean Jullien (1854–1919), for example, argued that a play should be a "slice of life" transferred to the stage without regard for dramatic effect. Thus, many of the Naturalists sought to obliterate distinctions between art and life in their zeal to approximate scientific truth.

Naturalism, like many movements before it, was handicapped by a dearth of plays embodying its principles. Although Edmond and Jules Goncourt, famous for their Naturalistic novels, wrote plays occasionally, their *Henriette Maréchal* (1865) and similar works had failed to interest the public. In the 1880's, a Naturalistic dramatist of power at last appeared: Henri Becque (1837–1899), whose *The Vultures* (1882) effectively embodied the Naturalistic outlook, although the author resisted all attempts to associate his play with Zola's ideas. *The Vultures* shows the fleecing of a family of women by their supposed friends following the death of the father; there are no sympathetic characters, the ending is pessimistic and cynical, and there are no obvious climaxes, merely a slow progression toward the inevitable outcome. *La Parisienne* (1885) depicts a wife who considers her infidelity an asset to her husband's advancement in business. In these plays, Becque raised Naturalism to its highest point.

By 1887, Naturalism had found its way into the state theatres and the public was beginning to respond favorably to it. An example of changing taste can be seen in the reception of Alphonse Daudet's *L'Arlésienne,* a failure in 1872 but a success in 1885. Becque's *The Vultures* was performed by the Comédie Française, a bastion of conservatism. Nevertheless, those works which had been produced did not raise any serious questions about traditional values, for censorship was strict. Thus, while several Naturalistic plays had been presented and staging sometimes reproduced the minutiae of life, the complacency of the public and of theatrical workers had not been disturbed. Something more was needed if significant change was to come. This new element was to be added by the "independent theatre movement," begun by Antoine in 1887.

Antoine and the Théâtre Libre

André Antoine (1858–1943) seemed a most unpromising source of revolution in 1887, for he was merely a clerk in a gas company, and his theatrical experience was limited to supernumerary acting with Parisian professional companies and occasional appearances with an amateur group. When Antoine sought to produce a program of new plays, including a dramatization of Zola's *Jacques Damour,* his amateur circle refused to cooperate, and Antoine set off on his own. In search of a name for his company, he adopted "Théâtre Libre." The success of his first program won him the endorsement of Zola and other influential figures. His second program was attended by the major theatrical critics, who wrote lengthy reviews. Before the end of 1887, Antoine was famous. He gave up his clerk's job and until 1914 devoted himself to theatrical production.

Organized on a subscription basis, the Théâtre Libre was open only to members and therefore was exempt from censorship. As a result, many of the best plays available to Antoine were those that had been refused licenses, and most were naturalistic. Much of the notoriety of the Théâtre Libre stemmed from its *comédies rosses* (plays in which the usual principles of morality are reversed), many of which repelled even Antoine's select audience. These rather extreme works gave Naturalism its reputation for depravity but paved the way for greater freedom in the regular theatres.

Although Antoine preferred to present French plays, he found the supply of worthwhile scripts limited. Consequently, in 1888 he began to produce one foreign work each year. After Tolstoy's *The Power of Darkness,* he went on to Ibsen's *Ghosts* and *The Wild Duck.* In this way, controversial foreign as well as domestic plays were given their first Parisian performances.

In addition to serving as a showcase for new dramas, the Théâtre Libre also became the proving ground for new production techniques. Although Antoine had used a realistic approach from the beginning, he intensified his search for authenticity after witnessing the Meiningen Players and Irving's company in 1888. He now sought to reproduce environment in every detail. In *The Butchers* (1888), for example, he hung real carcasses of beef on the stage. The "fourth wall" was observed consistently; in

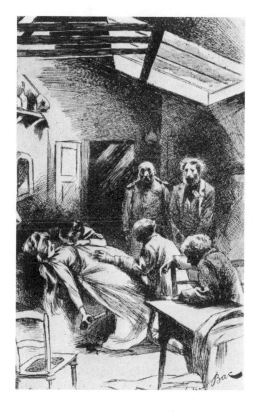

FINAL SCENE from Antoine's production of Ibsen's *The Wild Duck* at the Théâtre Libre. [From a contemporary lithograph]

designing settings, he arranged rooms as in real life and only later decided which wall should be removed. Often furniture was placed along the curtain line, and actors were directed to behave as though there were no audience. Through his belief in the importance of environment, Antoine helped to establish the principle that each play requires its own setting quite distinct from that of any other work. After witnessing the Meiningen company, Antoine also gave special attention to ensemble acting. Although most of his performers were amateurs, he coached them carefully and autocratically. He discouraged conventionalized movement and declamatory speech, seeking natural behavior instead.

Antoine's success worked against him, for as soon as a playwright or actor established his worth, he was employed by a major company. Furthermore, Antoine's high standards of production kept him constantly in debt. Even at the height of its popularity, the Théâtre Libre gave no production for more than three performances. By 1893, the company began to weaken and in 1895 the venture came to an end. Antoine had given 62 programs composed of 184 plays. In addition to playing in Paris, he had toured in Belgium, Holland, Germany, Italy, and England. His fame was worldwide, and the example he had set was to be followed in several other countries.

SCENE from Ménessier's *La Terre* at the Théâtre Antoine, 1902. [Directed by Antoine. From *Le Théâtre* (1902)]

Antoine did not stay away from the theatre long. In 1897 he opened his Théâtre Antoine, run as a fully professional theatre, and in 1906 he was appointed director of the state-subsidized Odéon, which he completely modernized. Although he practiced it less assiduously, realism still dominated his work. Probably his most famous productions of this era were of French classical dramas, in which he attempted to recreate the theatrical conventions of the 17th century. Costumed actors served as on-stage audience, chandeliers were hung over the stage, and candle footlights were conspicuous. Through this approach, he helped to establish a realism based upon past theatrical conventions rather than upon architecture and dress, as had been the usual case. By the time he resigned in 1914, he had presented a total of 364 works. No one else had influenced the French theatre of the period as profoundly as Antoine.

After 1890, most of the major new French dramatists were realists. Of these, the most important were Porto-Riche, Curel, Hervieu, and Brieux. Georges Porto-Riche (1849–1930) was noted for subtle characterizations which emphasized internal conflicts. Probably his best play is *A Loving Wife* (1891) in which a husband tries to rid himself of his wife by arousing her interest in another man, only to discover that he cannot give her up. François de Curel (1854–1928) had his first play produced by Antoine in 1892. He made few concessions to popular taste, and his disregard for ordinary principles of dramatic construction often obscured his intentions. His concern for internal psychological conflicts, however, did much to forward realistic subject matter. Among his best works are *The Fossils* (1892), depicting a decaying aristocracy, and *The Lion's Feast* (1898), in which the protagonist attempts to improve the lives of workingmen. Paul Hervieu (1857–1915), like Dumas *fils*, bases his plays upon theses which determine plot and character. Most involve family situations. Perhaps the best of his dramas is *The Pincers* (1895), the story of a woman who, having been refused a divorce by her husband, turns down a similar request from him years later in order to protect the son fathered by her lover of long ago. Eugène Brieux (1858–1932) was said by Shaw to be the most important dramatist in Europe after the death of Ibsen. Given his first production by Antoine in 1892, Brieux went on to write *The Red Robe* (1900), showing the difficulty of obtaining justice from judges concerned primarily with promotion, *Damaged Goods* (1902), concerning syphilis and its transmission to a child, and *Maternity* (1903), in which a blistering attack is launched on a society which does not permit legal birth control. As Brieux's plays reveal, subjects which had been unacceptable to the general public when Ibsen began his work were to be seen in commercial theatres by 1900.

The Freie Bühne and German Realism

The pattern which emerged in France was repeated in Germany. The first step toward theatrical reform came in 1883, when the Deutsches Theater was opened in Berlin by Adolf L'Arronge (1838–1908) and Ludwig Barnay (1842–1924), with a company headed by Josef Kainz (1858–1910), who had worked in the Meiningen troupe, and Agnes Sorma (1865–1927), later to be Germany's leading actress. Here a repertory of old and new plays were produced in the manner of the Meiningen Players. While it raised the level of production in Berlin, the Deutsches Theater ignored new playwrights other than those in the Schiller tradition.

Meanwhile, a group calling itself "Youngest Germany" had begun to advocate a new art based upon an objective observation of reality, while another calling itself *Durch* (or "Through") went even further than Zola in its demands for a Naturalistic drama. Both groups found inspiration in Ibsen's plays, sixteen of which had been translated into German by 1890.

As in France, however, the new movement lacked focus until an "independent" theatre was formed. Taking its inspiration from the Théâtre Libre, the Freie Bühne was organized in Berlin in 1889. Unlike Antoine's company, however, the German group was a democratic organization with officers and a governing council. Otto Brahm (1856–1912), a dramatic critic, was elected president and became its guiding spirit. In order to secure the services of professional actors, the Freie Bühne gave its performances on Sunday afternoons; its actors and most of its personnel were regularly employed by established theatres. Each production usually involved different actors, over whom Brahm had little control. Thus, the Freie Bühne exerted little influence on theatrical production. Its major contribution was made by giving a hearing to plays forbidden by the censor. The opening production of *Ghosts* was followed with plays by Hauptmann, the Goncourts, Zola, Becque, Tolstoy, Anzengruber, and Strindberg. After the season of 1890–91, regular performances were discontinued, although occasional programs were arranged when a play was forbidden a license. The Freie Bühne came to an end altogether in 1894, when Brahm was named director of the Deutsches Theater.

The only important German dramatist introduced by the Freie Bühne was Gerhart Hauptmann (1862–1946). The furor which greeted his *Before Sunrise* (1889), the story of a Silesian family which sinks into viciousness after the discovery of coal on their land, established Hauptmann as a major new playwright. During the next 50 years he wrote about 30 plays. Of the early works, the best is *The Weavers* (1892), remarkable for its group-protagonist of workers engaged in an abortive revolt. Like Ibsen, Hauptmann went on to write plays in a more symbolic vein, notably *The Assumption of Hannele* (1893) and *The Sunken Bell* (1896). After 1912, his plays became increasingly non-realistic. Before his death, Hauptmann had lost much of his prestige because of his passive attitude under Hitler's regime. All of Hauptmann's work shows great compassion for human suffering, but his protagonists, who are victims of circumstances beyond their control, are more pitiable than heroic.

The Freie Bühne stimulated the formation of several other stage societies in Germany. Although none achieved the fame of the original group, they helped to pave the way for a new drama. Perhaps of equal importance, a "people's" theatre was organized by socialist groups interested in raising the cultural standards of the working classes. Using the Freie Bühne as a model, the Freie Volksbühne was organized in Berlin in 1890 to produce plays at Sunday matinees, for which season tickets were distributed by lot at a nominal price. Beginning with 600 members, the organization included 12,000 by 1908. In 1892, the Neue Freie Volksbühne, founded by the former director of the original group, began a similar program. By 1905, it was offering its subscribers a choice among productions at several major theatres. Before the First World War the two groups had amalgamated, and their membership of 50,000 was soon to open one of the most modern theatres in Germany with its own permanent company. The workers' theatre movement flourished throughout Germany and Austria. To it must go considerable credit for creating the broad-based theatregoing public which continues in Germany even today.

Before 1900, the new realistic drama was being accepted almost everywhere. At the Burgtheater in Vienna a wide selection of recent works was presented between 1890 and 1898, when Max Burckhardt was director of the theatre. His successor, Paul Schlenther, a friend and admirer of Hauptmann, continued his policies. A somewhat similar pattern was followed elsewhere, for as public interest in the new plays grew the repertory expanded to include them.

In addition to Hauptmann, other important new dramatists included Sudermann, Halbe, Hirschfeld, and Fulda. Hermann Sudermann (1857–1928) was even more instrumental than Hauptmann in making Naturalism acceptable to the public, for he tended to retain the well-made play techniques and to conform more nearly to accepted morality while writing about "advanced" subjects. His most popular play, *Magda* (1893), concerning a singer whose bohemian life brings her into conflict with her father, became a favorite vehicle of actresses. Sudermann continued to write until well into the 20th century, although his reputation declined after about 1905. Max Halbe's (1865–1944) work is typified by *Youth* (1893), the story of a young girl killed by her half-witted brother while he is seeking to destroy her lover. George Hirschfeld (1873–1943), a strong exponent of Naturalism, is most famous for *The Mothers* (1896), the story of a working-class girl who leaves a composer when she realizes that she cannot fit into his life. Ludwig Fulda (1862–1939) won fame for *Comrades* (1894), a satire on the "new" woman, and *The Lost Paradise* (1890), a Naturalistic play about class conflicts.

In Austria, Schönherr, Bahr, and Schnitzler were probably the best dramatists. Karl Schönherr (1867–1943), writing in the vein of Anzengruber, painted realistic pictures of Tyrolean peasant life in such works as *Earth* (1908) and *The She-Devil* (1914). Hermann Bahr (1863–1934) demonstrated his firm grasp of all the new movements, which were reflected successively in his more than 80 works. His most popular play is *The Concert* (1909), a comedy about a wife's attempt to cope with her pianist-husband's amorous adventures. By far the most important was Arthur Schnitzler (1862–1931), a recorder of the melancholic worldweariness which characterized the turn of the century, and of the shallow sexual attitudes which accompanied it. The most famous of his works is *Anatol* (1893), a series of short plays, each of which records a different love intrigue. Even in the midst of happiness, Anatol knows that his momentary pleasure will dissolve into jealousy and boredom. A similar, though more shocking work to audiences, is *Reigen* (1900, variously translated as *Hands Around, La Ronde,* and *Round Dance*), with its ten characters who engage in a series of love affairs. Schnitzler, a friend of Freud, was much concerned with the centrality of sexual behavior, but was also convinced that love cannot be built upon pure ego satisfaction. While he seldom strayed from this theme, Schnitzler occasionally wrote on other subjects, as in *Professor Bernhardi* (1912), a play about anti-semitism.

The Independent Theatre and Realism in England

After the death of Robertson in 1871, the English theatre was given over largely to works in the tradition of Boucicault and Sardou or to lavish productions of the classics. A new direction was not evident until the 1890's, when Jones and Pinero appeared. These writers hold a place in English drama comparable to that of Dumas *fils* and Augier in French, for both were sufficiently new to be slightly scandalizing, yet both were sufficiently conventional to be acceptable to the censor and the theatregoing public.

Henry Arthur Jones (1851–1929) began his playwriting career with a successful melodrama, *The Silver King* (1882), and did not turn to more serious drama until after 1890 with *The Dancing Girl* (1891), *The Liars* (1897), and *Mrs. Dane's Defence* (1900). His most unusual play, *Michael and His Lost Angel* (1896), treated a love affair between a minister and one of his parishioners. Although Jones had high ideals for drama, he was not an original thinker. He aroused suspense and titillation without giving any significant new insights.

Arthur Wing Pinero (1855–1934) began his career in 1874 as an actor and turned to writing in 1877. His first major success came with a farce, *The Magistrate* (1885), a form in which he excelled. Although Pinero never professed interest in a "drama of ideas," it was his *The Second Mrs. Tanqueray* (1893), the story of a "woman with a past," which brought the first change in public attitudes, for when it proved a popular hit, producers began to look more favorably upon "Ibsenesque" drama. Although Pinero continued to write for another 30 years, turning out such successful plays as *The Notorious Mrs. Ebbsmith* (1895), *Iris* (1901), and *Mid-Channel* (1909), his popularity declined steadily after 1910.

While Jones and Pinero paved the way for public acceptance, the development of a more significant drama owes most to Ibsen. By 1880, William Archer had begun to translate Ibsen's plays and by 1890 all were available in English. In 1889, Janet Achurch (1864–1916) presented *A*

SCENE from Act I of the original production of Pinero's
The Second Mrs. Tanqueray, with Mrs. Patrick Campbell
and George Alexander. [From *The Graphic* (1893)]

Doll's House, the first unadapted version of a play by Ibsen seen in
England. Miss Achurch was to be one of the new drama's most ardent
champions, appearing in many plays by Ibsen, Shaw, and others. Her
production of *A Doll's House* reminded critics of how far behind the
Continent English drama had fallen and supplied one of the motivations
for founding the Independent Theatre.

Modeled on the Théâtre Libre and the Freie Bühne, the Independent Theatre was headed by J. T. Grein (1862–1935), a Dutch-born critic
who had lived in London for many years. Like its predecessors, the Independent Theatre was organized on a subscription basis to avoid censorship,
and like the Freie Bühne it gave its productions on Sundays in order to
gain the cooperation of theatre managers and actors. The opening play in
1891, *Ghosts,* prompted more than 500 articles, most of them vituperative.
The second program, Zola's *Thérèse Raquin,* created almost as great a
storm. This publicity began to make the general public aware of the new
drama for the first time.

Between 1891 and 1897, the Independent Theatre presented 26 plays,
mostly translations. It did little in the way of mounting the plays. Thus,
like the Freie Bühne, it served primarily as a rejuvenator of drama rather
than as an influence upon production. Grein had hoped to produce new

English plays, for he was convinced that the low state of English drama was attributable to the conservatism of producers. He soon found, however, that no significant plays were available. His disappointment prompted Shaw to complete *Widower's Houses,* the production of which in 1892 launched Shaw's career as a dramatist.

George Bernard Shaw (1856–1950), previously a novelist and critic, wrote regularly for the theatre from 1892 until his death. Unlike most of the new writers, who tended to be gloomy and intensely serious as a reaction against the shallowness of their predecessors, Shaw wrote primarily in the comic form. This choice may be explained in part by Shaw's interest in persuasion, which was best served by having characters arrive at perceptions which remove the barriers to a happy resolution. Shaw also delighted in using paradoxes to make both characters and audiences reassess their values. Thus, *Arms and the Man* (1894) punctures romantic notions about love and war, while *Major Barbara* (1905) upholds a munitions manufacturer as a greater humanitarian than an officer in the Salvation Army. Many of Shaw's plays, notably *The Doctor's Dilemma* (1906) and *Getting Married* (1908), are essentially extended discussions of specific problems. Other works, such as *Man and Superman* (1901) and *Back to Methuselah* (1919–21), show Shaw's interest in "creative evolution" and the "life force," which he believed were striving to create a "superman" by working through superior individuals. In still other plays, as in *Caesar and Cleopatra* (1899) and *Saint Joan* (1923), Shaw sought to correct popular views of historical figures and events. Perhaps his least characteristic work is *Heartbreak House* (1914–19), a parable about Europe at the time of the First World War. Shaw labeled it a play in the Chekhovian manner, perhaps to indicate its difference from his other works.

Although Shaw is related to the realistic movement through his concern for ideas and social problems, he differed markedly from most of the writers of this school. While recognizing the importance of heredity and environment, Shaw always implies that man has freedom of choice. Furthermore, although his characters often speak in dialect, they are always articulate and seldom follow closely the patterns of everyday speech. Shaw was not objective, for he chose his characters and invented his stories to illustrate a point of view. His comic method eventually won a wide audience for the drama of ideas.

Shaw was not immediately successful, however, for at first his unconventional ideas and paradoxical situations only puzzled or irritated audiences. His reputation was built slowly through the efforts of organizations which succeeded the Independent Theatre. The first of these was the Incorporated Stage Society, founded in 1899 to present modern plays. At first its programs were given on Sunday afternoons but, as its membership grew from the original 300 to 1500 by 1914, it added Monday matinees as well. By the time the group disbanded in 1939 it had presented about 200 works, many of which would otherwise not have been seen. It served as an experimental theatre which kept the English theatrical world abreast of the latest movements both at home and abroad.

The most significant producing group in this period was that at the Court Theatre, where between 1904 and 1907 Harley Granville-Barker (1877–1946) and John Vedrenne (1863–1930) gave the new drama its first full hearing in a public theatre. Barker had begun his career as an actor in 1891, had worked with several organizations, including the Incorporated Stage Society, and had established himself as a dramatist before being invited to assist Vedrenne with a production of *Two Gentlemen of Verona*.

GRANVILLE BARKER'S PRODUCTION of Shaw's *Caesar and Cleopatra* at the Court Theatre. At right as Caesar is Forbes-Robertson, for whom Shaw wrote the role. [From *Play Pictorial* (1907)]

This beginning soon developed into a permanent arrangement, under which one play was offered each evening for several weeks while another little-known or seldom-performed work was given at matinees. If the matinees engendered enough enthusiasm, the play was moved to evening performances. Even successes, however, were not played consecutively for more than a few weeks. Between 1904 and 1907, the Court presented 32 plays by 17 different authors, including Euripides, Hauptmann, Ibsen, Galsworthy, and Yeats. The mainstay of the theatre, however, was Shaw, eleven of whose plays were presented. It was these productions which established Shaw's popularity with the general public.

The Court made other important contributions. It was noted for ensemble acting by a company which included some of the best actors of the period: Lillah McCarthy (1875–1960), Edith Wynne Matthison (1872–1955), Louis Calvert (1859–1923), Lewis Casson (1875–   ), and Godfrey Tearle (1884–1953). There were no stars. Since Barker believed that it is the director's primary task to give a thoughtful interpretation of the playwright's script, he sought to find in each work the style suited to it. Nevertheless, the dominant style of the Court productions was a subtle realism which avoided bravura. Simplicity and suggestion were the keynotes of both the acting and scenery. In 1907, Barker and Vedrenne moved to the Savoy Theatre, but closed after one season because of lack of attendance and trouble with the censor. When Charles Frohman established a repertory company at the Duke of York's Theatre in 1910, he employed Barker to head it. After presenting 17 plays in 17 weeks and incurring a sizable deficit, Barker resigned.

In spite of these failures, the Barker-Vedrenne experiments engendered several imitators, especially in the provinces, where repertory companies began to be opened once more. The first important company was established by Miss A. E. F. Horniman (1860–1937) in 1907 in Manchester. Until it was discontinued in 1921 this was to be one of the best theatres in England, offering a wide variety of English and Continental plays. Its encouragement of local writers gave rise to the "Lancashire School," of which Stanley Houghton (1881–1913), author of *Hindle Wakes* (1912), and Harold Brighouse (1883–1958), author of *Hobson's Choice* (1916), were the most important. Other vigorous repertory companies were founded at Liverpool in 1911 and at Birmingham in 1913. The Birmingham Repertory Company, under the direction of Barry Jackson (1879–1961), was to be especially influential after the first World War.

In addition to Shaw, a number of other dramatists in the realistic vein appeared after 1900. John Galsworthy (1867–1933), already one of England's most successful novelists, turned to playwriting in 1906 with *The Silver Box,* in which the justice meted out to a poor and a rich man for the same crime is contrasted. His later plays, *Strife* (1909), *Justice* (1910), and *Loyalties* (1922), were in the same vein. All are objective treatments of social problems which demonstrate Galsworthy's considerable gift for creating dramatic dialogue and clear-cut conflicts. Harley Granville-Barker won fame as a dramatist with such plays as *The Marrying of Ann Leete* (1902), *The Voysey Inheritance* (1905), *Waste* (1907), and *Madras House* (1910). Similar to Shaw in his interests, Barker lacked Shaw's sense of the comic, and his discussions now seem cold and deficient in intensity. St. John Hankin (1869–1909) was the most gloomy dramatist of the period. In such works as *The Return of the Prodigal* (1905) and *The Last of the DeMullins* (1908), he attacked abuses but offered no alternatives to the conditions depicted.

The Moscow Art Theatre and Realism in Russia

Russia also had to await the "independent theatre" movement before needed reforms were to come. Although such Russian dramatists as Turgenev, Ostrovsky, and Pisemsky had already inaugurated a realistic school of writing, theatrical production still preserved conventions inherited from the 18th century. The visit of the Meiningen Players in 1885 and 1890 had revealed to many Russian producers how far behind they were. Little progress was made, however, until the formation of the Moscow Art Theatre by Constantin Stanislavsky (1863–1938) and Vladimir Nemirovich-Danchenko (1858–1943) in 1898.

The Moscow Art Theatre differed from the other independent theatres in being a fully professional organization from the beginning and in emphasizing theatrical production rather than neglected plays. Its first program, Alexei Tolstoy's *Tsar Fyodor Ivanovich,* created a sensation because of its painstaking recreation of the Russia of 1600, its ensemble acting, and its absence of stars. Public interest waned, however, until the production of Chekhov's *The Sea Gull* established the originality of both the author and the company.

Anton Chekhov (1860–1904) began his dramatic career with vaudeville sketches and short plays in the comic-pathetic vein and then went on to long plays. When *The Sea Gull* (1896) was performed at the Alexandrinsky Theatre in St. Petersburg, it was a failure because the actors did not understand their roles and had not learned their lines. As a result, Chekhov was determined to give up playwriting. After reluctantly permitting the Moscow Art Theatre to perform *The Sea Gull,* he was inspired by its success to write three other plays: *Uncle Vanya* (1899), *The Three Sisters* (1901), and *The Cherry Orchard* (1904). Upon these four plays Chekhov's reputation rests.

Each of Chekhov's four major plays is set in rural Russia and depicts the monotonous and frustrating life of the landowning class. All of the characters aspire to a better life, but none knows how, or has the initiative, to achieve his goals. The plays are built upon infinite detail, the connection among which is not always obvious. Yet gradually a unifying mood, clearly delineated characters, and a complete and simple action emerge. The absence of startling climaxes, strong suspense, and clear purpose has caused many readers to misunderstand the plays, which require detailed study and attention to nuance if the pattern behind the surface is to become clear.

The methods of the Moscow Art Theatre were well adapted to the

Act I of Chekhov's *The Sea Gull* at the Moscow Art Theatre, 1898. Setting by V. A. Simov. [From *Moscow Art Theatre, 1898–1917* (Moscow, 1955)]

demands of Chekhov's plays. Stanislavsky always undertook a long study of each play before rehearsals began. He insisted upon careful attention to detail from each actor, and he sought to recreate the milieu only after visiting the site of the play's action, or after extensive research.

Despite its success with *The Sea Gull,* the Moscow Art Theatre ended its first season in debt and was saved only by the generosity of patrons. With the new support, it was able in 1902 to build its own theatre, with workshops and such up-to-date equipment as a revolving stage. It increased its acting company from 39 to 100 members. Thereafter, it staged from three to five new plays each year, while keeping successful works in the repertory. The influence of the Moscow Art Theatre was soon felt throughout Russia, and by 1906 it was sufficiently well-known abroad that it undertook a foreign tour.

Stanislavsky is now remembered above all for his attempts to perfect a method of acting. He became fully aware of the need in 1906 and made the first outline of his ideas in 1909, but he did not set down his system in writing until he published *My Life in Art* (1924) and *An Actor Prepares* (1936). The entire plan was not available outside of Russia until the appearance of *Building a Character* (1949) and *Creating a Role* (1961). Because of this piecemeal publication, the ambiguities in the theory, and the many changes made by Stanislavsky as he refined upon the method, many conflicting interpretations of "the Stanislavsky system" have arisen.

Although no summary is entirely acceptable to all of Stanislavsky's admirers and critics, the method appears to be based upon the following principles. (1) The actor's body and voice should be thoroughly trained so that they respond efficiently to all demands. (2) The actor should be schooled in stage techniques, since he must be able to project his characterization to an audience without any sense of contrivance. (3) The actor should be a skilled observer of reality, out of which he builds his role. (4) The actor should seek an inner justification for everything he does on stage. In doing so, he depends in part upon "the magic 'if' " (that is, the actor says, "If I were this person faced with this situation, I would . . .") and "emotion memory" (a process by which the actor relates the unfamiliar dramatic situation to some analogous emotional situation in his own life). (5) If the actor is not merely to play himself, he must undertake a thorough analysis of the script and work within the "given circumstances" found there. He must define his character's motivations in each scene, in the play as a whole, and his relationship to each of the other roles. The character's primary "objective" becomes the "spine" of the role, around which everything else revolves. (6) On stage, the actor must focus his attention upon the action as it unfolds moment by moment. Such concentration will lead to the "illusion of the first time" and will guide the actor in subordinating his ego to the artistic demands of the production. (7) An actor must continue to work to perfect himself as an instrument.

Various aspects of this method have been emphasized by different interpreters. Taken as a whole, it is an attempt to analyze each phase of the actor's work and to make it as efficient as possible. Stanislavsky was never fully satisfied with his system and cautioned others against adopting it without making changes required by different artistic needs and cultural backgrounds.

Although the Moscow Art Theatre had no stars, a number of outstanding actors came to the fore. In addition to Stanislavsky, these included Moskvin, Kachalov, and Knipper. Ivan Moskvin (1874–1946), a small man, was best suited to self-effacing characters such as Epikhodov in *The Cherry Orchard*. His was the art of understatement in which a few subtle touches brought out the emotional values of a scene. Vassily Kachalov (1875–1948), a tall, handsome man with a beautiful voice, was at his best in the roles of romantic heroes, rebels, or intellectuals. Olga Knipper (1870–1959), Chekhov's wife, played a wide variety of roles, but was best known as Madame Ranevskaya of *The Cherry Orchard*.

In addition to Chekhov, the Moscow Art Theatre also encouraged Maxim Gorky (1868–1936), already famous as a writer of realistic stories. *The Lower Depths* (1902), set in a flophouse and featuring a collection of characters defeated by life, became one of the troupe's greatest successes. With his concern for the outcasts of society, Gorky won a reputation as spokesman for the proletariat that would give him enormous influence with the Soviets.

The Revival of Idealism in France

The realistic and naturalistic trends did not go unchallenged. Although the years between 1850 and 1900 were resolutely anti-idealistic, the sweeping claims made for science brought several reactions. The most significant protest came from the Symbolists, who officially launched their attack through a "manifesto" issued in 1886. Taking its inspiration from the works of Edgar Allan Poe, the English Romantic poets, Ibsen's symbolic plays, Dostoevsky's novels, and Wagner's theories, Symbolism attracted representatives from all the arts. To these men, subjectivity, spirituality, and mysterious internal and external forces represented a higher form of truth than that to be derived from the mere observance of outward appearance. This deeper significance, they argued, cannot be represented directly but can only be evoked through symbols, legends, myths, and moods.

As with Naturalism, Symbolism made no marked impression in the theatre until an "independent" group, modeled on the Théâtre Libre, appeared. In 1890, Paul Fort (1872–1962), a 17-year-old poet, founded the Théâtre d'Art, where by 1892 he had presented works by 46 authors, ranging from adaptations of the *Iliad* and the *Bible* to modern plays. Most of the programs were given for only a single performance, and the actors, most of whom were amateurs, were not always adequate. Unlike Antoine, Fort received only hostile critical notices and threats of violence from anonymous letter-writers. Thus, the idealist theatre was given little encouragement, perhaps because it was incomprehensible to a public accustomed to illusionism.

When Fort abandoned his theatre in 1892, it was absorbed into the Théâtre de l'Oeuvre, headed by Aurélien-Marie Lugné-Poë (1869–1940). An actor and stage manager at the Théâtre Libre, Lugné-Poë was converted to the idealist outlook after seeing and appearing in some of the productions at the Théâtre d'Art and after becoming acquainted with such painters as Vuillard and Bonnard. The Théâtre de l'Oeuvre opened in 1893. Until 1897, Lugné-Poë used the same style for all of his productions. Guided by the motto "the word creates the decor," he reduced scenery to simple compositions of lines and color painted on backdrops. Using settings by Toulouse-Lautrec, Maurice Denis, Odilon Redon, Vuillard, Bonnard, and Roussel, Lugné-Poë sought to create a unity of style rather than an illusion of place.

The opening production, *Pelléas and Mélisande*, was typical. No properties or furniture were used; the stage was lighted from overhead and most of the action passed in semidarkness; a gauze curtain gave the impression that mist enveloped the stage; backdrops, painted in grayed tones, emphasized the air of mystery; costumes were vaguely Medieval, although the intention was to create draperies of no particular period. The actors spoke in a staccato chant like priests and, according to some critics, behaved like sleepwalkers; their gestures were stylized. Given this radically new approach, it is not surprising that the spectators were mystified.

Lugné-Poë's repertory was made up primarily of French plays mingled with some works by Ibsen, Hauptmann, Sanskrit dramatists, and others. Of the French dramas, those by Maeterlinck were the best. Maurice Maeterlinck (1862–1949), after coming to Paris from Belgium, turned to playwriting in 1889 and by 1896 had written *The Intruder* (1890), *The Blind* (1890), and *The Death of Tintagiles* (1894). Of his early work, the best known is *Pelléas and Mélisande* (1892), in which a young woman, after marrying a prince who has found her in a forest, falls in love with his brother and dies of grief. The interest does not reside in the triangular relationship, however, but in the mood of mystery which envelops it and which is evoked through a multitude of symbols, such as a wedding ring dropped into a fountain, doves that fly away from a tower, subterranean pools and grottoes, enveloping shadows, and blood stains that cannot be washed away. In the early 1890's, Maeterlinck argued that the most dramatic moments are those silent ones during which the mystery of existence, ordinarily obscured by bustling activity, makes itself felt. After 1896, Maeterlinck revised his view and modified his style to include more straightforward action. The most famous of his later plays is *The Blue Bird* (1908), an allegory about the search for happiness.

One other non-realistic play of the 1890's has assumed increasing importance in recent years. *Ubu Roi*, written by Alfred Jarry (1873–1907) at the age of 15, was presented by Lugné-Poë in 1896. Now often cited as the first "absurdist" drama, *Ubu Roi* parodies traditional tragedy, inverts middle-class values and pushes them to an extreme of grossness.

The first major phase of the anti-realistic movement came to an end in 1897 when Lugné-Poë broke with the Symbolists after concluding that most of their plays were immature and that his commitment to a single style of production was too limiting. His decision was influenced by Ibsen, who convinced Lugné-Poë that extreme stylization was not suited to his plays. The Théâtre de l'Oeuvre closed in 1899, but Lugné-Poë was to revive it before the First World War began and to continue his work until 1929. Nevertheless, it is his Symbolist productions of the 1890's which constitute his most significant contribution to the theatre. Through tours with his company and articles written about his work, Lugné-Poë influenced almost every departure from realism between 1893 and 1915.

JARRY's *Ubu Roi* at the Théâtre Antoine, 1908. Gémier directed the play and appeared as Père Ubu. [From *Figaro* (February 16, 1908)]

Appia and Craig

While Lugné-Poë was producing plays in the 1890's, two other men, working independently of each other, Appia and Craig, were beginning to lay the theoretical foundations of modern nonillusionistic theatrical practice. Adolphe Appia (1862–1928), born in Switzerland, first came into contact with the theatre through his musical studies. Deeply impressed by Wagner's music-dramas and theoretical writings, Appia recognized that the usual mounting of the operas did not properly embody Wagner's theories. After years of thought, he published *The Staging of Wagner's Musical Dramas* (1895) and *Music and Stage Setting* (1899). Here and in *The Work of Living Art* (1921) he set forth ideas about theatrical production which eventually were to be accepted almost universally.

Beginning with the assumption that artistic unity is the fundamental goal of theatrical production, Appia sought to analyze the failures to achieve it. He concluded that stage presentation involves three conflicting visual elements: the moving three-dimensional actor; the perpendicular scenery; and the horizontal floor. In painted two-dimensional settings he found one of the major causes of disunity and recommended that they be replaced with three-dimensional units (steps, ramps, platforms) which enhance the actor's movement, and which blend the horizontal floor with the upright scenery. Above all, however, Appia emphasized the role of light in fusing all of the visual elements into a unified whole. Since to him light was the visual counterpart of music, which changes from moment to moment in response to shifting moods, emotions, and action, Appia wished to orchestrate and manipulate light as carefully as a musical score. Attempts to implement this theory, which require control over the distribution, brightness, and color of light, have led to much of modern stage-lighting practice. Appia also argued that artistic unity requires that one person control all of the elements of production. Thus, his ideas strengthen the role of the director.

DESIGN for Wagner's *Parsifal* by Appia, 1896.

Appia had few opportunities to try out his ideas in actual productions. His most extensive work was done in collaboration with Émile Jaques-Dalcroze (1865–1950), the advocate of "eurythmics" as a system of rhythmical discipline. After 1913, Appia worked with Jaques-Dalcroze at his school in Hellerau for a time, and in the early 1920's designed a few settings for Wagnerian operas at La Scala in Milan. For the most part, however, Appia's influence came through his books.

Gordon Craig (1872–1966), son of Ellen Terry and Edward Godwin, began his career as an actor in Irving's company. His first important experience as a designer was gained in his mother's company at the

Imperial Theatre in London in 1903. An exhibit of his work in 1902 and the publication of his book, *The Art of the Theatre* (1905), created such controversy that within a few years he was well known throughout Europe. In 1905, he designed a play for Brahm in Berlin, in 1906 one for Eleanora Duse in Florence, and in 1911 one for the Moscow Art Theatre. Everywhere controversy followed him. He continued to set forth his provocative and original ideas in *On the Art of the Theatre* (1911), *Towards a New Theatre* (1913), *The Theatre Advancing* (1921), and *The Mask,* a periodical issued between 1909 and 1929. In 1908 he settled in Florence, where he ran a school for a time. Although Appia had set forth many of the same ideas, it was Craig who publicized them. To many conservative producers, Craig seemed as dangerous "a crank" as Ibsen had in the 1880's.

GORDON CRAIG'S SETTING for *Hamlet* at the Moscow Art Theatre, 1911. [From *Moscow Art Theatre, 1898–1917* (Moscow. 1955)]

While Appia and Craig agreed upon many important points, they differed on others. With Appia, the actor and text were always of prime importance, whereas with Craig they were treated as material to be moulded by the master artist, the director. Craig thought the actor too anxious for praise and the playwright too prone to moralizing; occasionally he suggested that the theatre would benefit by the elimination of both. Craig's primary influence was upon the visual elements of production. He was opposed to realism and urged the elimination of all nonessential details. His own designs use simple forms to capture the feeling of a work without representing any actual place. Often vast in scale, they have been denounced by many critics as impractical. Their value, however, did not reside in their practicality but in the vision they convey and in their radical departures from the accepted practices of the period. Together, Appia and Craig laid the theoretical foundation upon which almost all modern theatrical practice has been built.

Strindberg and Freud

During the first decade of the 20th century, another major influence on modern drama, the non-realistic plays of the Swedish dramatist, August Strindberg (1849–1912), appeared. Strindberg established his reputation as a realistic dramatist with *The Father* (1887) and *Miss Julie* (1888), both of which demonstrate his preoccupation with conflict between men and women. *Miss Julie* won high praise for its emphasis upon heredity and environment, its unusual setting (which showed one corner of a kitchen), and its use of pantomimes to replace intermissions.

Powerful as these plays are, they were not so influential as those which Strindberg wrote after a bout with insanity between 1896 and 1899. Partially because of his recent experiences and partially under Maeterlinck's influence, Strindberg now began to write "dream plays," of which he said: "The author has tried to imitate the disconnected but seemingly logical form of the dream. Anything may happen; everything is possible and probable. Time and space do not exist. On an insignificant background of reality, imagination designs and embroiders novel patterns, free fancies, absurdities and improvisations. The characters split, double, multiply, vanish, solidify, blur, clarify. But one consciousness reigns above them all—that of the dreamer; and before it there are no secrets, no incongruities, no scruples, no laws." In such plays as *To Damascus* (a trilogy, 1898–1904), *The Dream Play* (1902), and *The Ghost Sonata* (1907), Strindberg reshaped reality according to his own subjective vision. Time and place shift frequently and without regard for logical sequence, the real and the imaginary blend, and the seemingly commonplace is invested with a sense of doom. Through all, there runs Strindberg's despair of achieving happiness and his deep compassion for human suffering. As the first dramatist to construct plays according to the logic of dreams, Strindberg was hailed by some as a genius and denounced by others as a madman.

From 1907 to 1910, he was associated with August Falck (1882–1938), an actor and producer, at the Intimate Theatre in Stockholm. Seating only 161, this theatre was intended as a home for Strindberg's plays, some of which were written especially for it and called "chamber plays" in recognition of the theatre's limitations. By the time Strindberg died in 1912, he was one of the most famous writers in the world. Although his plays have never been widely popular in the theatre, they have never ceased to be a source of controversy and inspiration.

Strindberg's reputation increased as the psychoanalytic theories of Sigmund Freud (1856–1939) gained currency. Freud's explanation of human behavior, with its emphasis upon the unconscious mind, dreams as a key to understanding suppressed desires, and the human propensity for telescoping experience, gave strong authority for Strindberg's dramaturgy. Furthermore, just as Comte, Zola, and others had placed primary emphasis upon social environment as a determinant of human behavior, Freud turned attention toward equally powerful psychological causes. His interest in sexual drives as the key to human behavior also did much to break down taboos against sex as a suitable subject for drama.

Freud's pervasive influence on modern drama is also explained in part by his having provided a quasi-scientific basis for behavior which in idealist drama had been attributed to "the mystery of fate," "intuition," or other equally vague and subjective concepts. By locating the source within the human mind, Freud made it possible for realistic dramatists to accept behavior previously considered irrational because it had no verifiable basis. Freud's conception of reality, which intermingles the rational and irrational, the objective and subjective, the real and the fantastic, was to break down many of the barriers between realistic and non-realistic drama.

Idealist Drama in Germany

Although a number of German dramatists, most notably Hauptmann and Sudermann, alternated between realistic and non-realistic styles, Hofmannsthal and Wedekind rejected realism more forcefully. Hugo von Hofmannsthal (1874–1929) was related to the French Symbolists in his general outlook. A poet of considerable power, his early work, dating from 1891, was too subjective to have wide appeal, but he later found a richer vein in well-known materials. *Elektra* (1903), *Oedipus and the Sphinx* (1905), *Everyman* (1912), and *The Great Theatre of the World* (1922) were among his most successful plays. Many of his works breathe an air of decadence, and in all a sense of fate seems to lead the characters down mysterious paths. Many of Hofmannsthal's dramas are now kept alive only in Richard Strauss' operatic settings, but his *Everyman* still figures prominently in the annual Salzburg Festival.

Franz Wedekind (1864–1918) is more nearly related to Strindberg than to the French Symbolists. After working as a journalist, publicist, and actor, Wedekind toured Germany in a repertory of his own plays, which were never widely appreciated during his lifetime. Wedekind's first important play was *Spring's Awakening* (1891), the story of two adolescents' struggle with sexual awareness. One commits suicide, and the other is saved from a similar fate by the mysterious "Man with the Mask." Like Wedekind's other plays, *Spring's Awakening* is a mixture of naturalism and symbolism, of brutal frankness and lyricism. His interest in sexual themes was continued in *Earth* (1895) and *Pandora's Box* (1904), in both of which the protagonist, Lulu, confuses lust with love. Wedekind's other plays also show his preoccupation with the relationship between sex and love. In some of the final works, such as *Samson* (1914) and *Herakles* (1917), the sexual fantasies border on lunacy. Although the uneven quality of Wedekind's dramas makes it difficult to assess his accomplishment, his reputation was to grow steadily and to exert considerable influence on later writers.

After 1900, German producers experimented increasingly with non-realistic staging. Some of the most important innovations were made at the Munich Art Theatre, founded in 1907 by Georg Fuchs (1868–1949), a critic and theorist, and Fritz Erler (1868–1940), a designer, in a theatre designed by Max Littman (1862–1931). In two books, *The Theatre of the Future* (1905) and *Revolution in the Theatre* (1909), Fuchs expressed the need for a theatre to meet the needs of modern man and declared pictorial illusionism outmoded. Under the slogan "retheatricalize the theatre," he sought to unite all the arts in a new kind of expression.

For the project, Littmann designed a theatre with an auditorium and sunken orchestra pit similar to those at Bayreuth. The stage, however, differed markedly. The acting area could be extended into the auditorium

CROSS-SECTION of the Munich Art Theatre. Note the stepped seating, hidden orchestra pit, proscenium doors, and bridge over the stage. [From *Theatre Arts* (1918)]

by covering over the orchestra pit, while an adjustable inner proscenium, containing a door at stage level and a balcony above, made it possible to adjust the size of the stage opening. The stage floor was broken into sections, each of which was mounted on an elevator, permitting the floor to be arranged into levels. The stage was surrounded by four cycloramas, each of a different color, which could be changed electrically.

For settings, Fuchs and Erler depended primarily upon levels, a few set pieces, and lighting. Nonillusionistic, painted curtains were employed occasionally, and scenic pieces were sometimes added to the inner proscenium. The performers were kept near the front of the stage, often on a ledge so narrow that critics characterized the acting as being in bas-relief. Nevertheless, Fuchs sought to emphasize the three-dimensionality of the actor by placing him against a simplified background which suggested the play's mood without reference to historical period or ordinary reality. Fuchs also sought to fuse the various elements through rhythm, which he called "primal." Ultimately, he hoped to reestablish that sense of communion between audience and performer which he thought had characterized the ancient theatre but which had been lost with pictorial illusionism.

Max Reinhardt (1873–1943) was to synthesize all of the trends which had developed since the 1880's. On stage as an actor from the age of 19, he was brought to the Deutsches Theater by Otto Brahm in 1894. While acting with Brahm's troupe, Reinhardt experimented with staging at a cabaret and developed a strong appreciation for its intimate atmosphere. His first experience as a producer was gained between 1902 and 1905 at the Kleines Theater, where he presented nearly 50 plays drawn from many countries and styles. His major work began in 1905, when he succeeded Brahm as director of the Deutsches Theater. In 1906, he opened the Kammerspiele, a small theatre, in conjunction with the larger house. The flexibility in programming and style of production which this arrangement permitted was to influence almost all of the state theatres in Europe and eventually the educational theatre of America.

Reinhardt's influence came in large part through his diversity. Unlike major producers who preceded him, almost all of whom had used the same style for every play they presented, Reinhardt believed that each play required a different style. His eclecticism, therefore, reconciled many conflicting movements, for with him each style had its uses. With Reinhardt, each new production became a problem to be solved, not through the employment of proven formulas but through clues found within the work itself. Furthermore, his conception of theatrical style included the physical arrangement of the theatre and the spatial relationship of the audience to the performers. In his view, some plays required intimate surroundings, others large spaces; some needed a proscenium, others an open platform. For example, he staged *Oedipus Rex* in a circus, because this arrangement seemed most appropriate to the spirit of Greek tragedy.

REINHARDT'S PRODUCTION of the pantomime *Sumurun,* with settings by Ernst Stern, at the Kammerspiele, Berlin, 1910. [From *The Theatre* (1912)]

He was to extend such experiments with styles of production and theatre architecture after the First World War.

Reinhardt believed that the director must control every element of production. For each play he prepared a *Regiebuch* in which he recorded each detail of movement, setting, properties, sound, lighting, and costume. Some critics charge that Reinhardt's actors were mere puppets which he manipulated, while others maintain that Reinhardt was so sensitive that he knew exactly how to help each performer. In any case, Reinhardt worked closely with his actors to achieve performances world-famous for their stylistic excellence. Among his actors, the best known were Alexander Moissi (1880–1935), noted especially for his Shakespearean and Greek roles; Max Pallenberg (1859–1934), a versatile comic actor; Albert Bassermann (1867–1952), famous for his performances in Ibsen's plays and later as an actor in American films; Werner Krauss (1884–1959), and Emil Jannings (1887–1950).

Reinhardt also worked closely with his scene designers, notably Ernst Stern (1876–1954), Alfred Roller (1864–1935), Oscar Strnad (1879–1935), and Emil Orlik (1870–1932). Often his productions centered around a motif, a ruling idea, or the staging conventions of a past period; they ranged through every style from naturalism to extreme stylization. Reinhardt has been accused of debasing the ideas of others, but he did more than anyone to make the new movements acceptable to the general public.

The Non-Realistic Theatre in England

In England, few playwrights departed markedly from the realistic mode. Oscar Wilde (1856–1900), a member of the "Art-for-Art's Sake" movement which paralleled French Symbolism, rejected the idea that drama should be utilitarian or that the popular audience is a suitable judge of merit. He suggested that life should seek to become a work of art rather than art imitating life. Nevertheless, of Wilde's plays, only *Salomé* (1893), resembles French Symbolist drama, although his phenomenally popular comedy, *The Importance of Being Earnest* (1895), illustrates his general outlook through its parody of the stock devices of comedy and its epigrams which puncture the conventional sentiments of his time. On the surface, *Lady Windermere's Fan* (1892), *A Woman of No Importance* (1893), and *An Ideal Husband* (1895) appear to be much like Pinero's social dramas, but a closer examination will show that Wilde deliberately lets the machinery of his plots show until the plays become near-parodies.

J. M. Barrie (1860–1937), after beginning as a journalist and novelist, turned to drama in 1892 and wrote regularly for the stage until 1936. Through all of his work shines an optimistic, whimsical view of life in which humor is infused with sentiment. His most successful play is *Peter Pan* (1904), a sentimental fantasy which romanticizes childhood and the child's view of reality. Other popular works include *The Admirable Crichton* (1902), *What Every Woman Knows* (1908), and *Dear Brutus* (1917).

While few English plays departed from the realistic mode, several innovations in staging were to lead away from illusionism. Many of these stemmed from interest in staging Shakespeare's works. An early step toward more simplified staging was taken by Frank Benson (1858–1939). After acting with Irving, Benson founded his own troupe in 1883 and continued to tour the provinces in a Shakespearean repertory until 1933. Benson produced almost all of the plays seen at the annual festival at Stratford-on-Avon (instituted in 1879) between 1886 and 1913, and after 1900 gave a few performances in London each year. Benson began by producing plays in the style of Irving, but by 1900 he had reduced the scenic background to a few stock settings and was placing primary emphasis upon the actors. Although his solution was at best a compromise, Benson helped to make simplified staging acceptable to the public.

A more drastic reform was sought by William Poel (1852–1934). After his debut as an actor in 1876, Poel worked for Benson and others before founding the Elizabethan Stage Society in 1894. Thereafter, he concentrated upon the plays of Shakespeare and his contemporaries. He dressed his actors in Elizabethan garments and sought to recreate the stage of the Elizabethan public theatre. Above all, Poel desired continuity of action, a lively pace, and an intimate relationship between performers and audience. Although his productions did not generate much enthusiasm, they demonstrated the advantages of unbroken playing and of concentrating attention upon text and performers.

POEL'S PRODUCTION of *Measure for Measure* in 1893. Shown here is Act II, scene 2. Note the costumed spectators on either side of the stage. [Courtesy Victoria and Albert Museum. Crown Copyright]

Poel's approach represents another form of antiquarianism, one which sought to substitute the theatrical conditions of a past era for historical accuracy in the older sense. It is typical of similar approaches then being tried in several countries. At the Royal Court Theatre in Munich beginning in 1889, Perfall and Savitts had attempted to approximate the Elizabethan plan with a structure erected on a picture frame stage; Antoine adopted a similar approach to 17th century French plays at the Odéon, and Reinhardt was to utilize staging conventions from many periods.

Between 1912 and 1914, Granville-Barker synthesized several earlier trends in his Shakespearean productions at the Savoy Theatre. Barker, who had worked for Poel before going to the Court Theatre, amalgamated Poel's continuous staging with the visual simplicity advocated by Craig and others. Barker remodeled the Savoy Theatre by adding an apron and doors forward of the proscenium. Back of the proscenium the stage was divided into a main acting area and a modified inner stage, raised a few steps, and equipped with curtains. This division of the stage into three parts allowed a continuous flow of action and eliminated the extensive cutting and re-

GRANVILLE BARKER'S PRODUCTION of *Twelfth Night* at the Savoy Theatre, 1912. Settings by Norman Wilkinson. [From *The Daily Mirror* (1912)]

arrangement of the scripts usual in illusionistic staging. Barker employed such artists as Norman Wilkinson (1882–1934) and Albert Rutherston (1884–1953) to design scenery and costumes. Settings were composed primarily of painted, draped curtains, while the costumes were of no certain period. Such bright colors as magenta, scarlet, and lemon replaced the somber tones usual in Shakespearean productions. The forest of *A Midsummer Night's Dream* (presented in 1914) contained no three-dimensional trees, consisting rather of a painted drapery, while Titania's bower was made of gauze suspended from a crown of flowers. The gilded fairies wore bronze tights and moved like marionettes in order to set them off from the mortals. Although many conservative critics were deeply offended by Barker's productions, his approach was to triumph after the war.

The Irish Renaissance

Although Dublin had been one of the major English theatrical centers since the 17th century, no attempts had been made to create an indigenous drama until Irish national sentiment began to emerge in the 19th century. The first significant step was taken in 1898, when the Irish Literary Society was established in Dublin. Between 1899 and 1902, this group produced seven short plays and demonstrated the possibility of creating an Irish theatre. The leaders of the Society were William Butler Yeats (1865–1939), Lady Augusta Gregory (1863–1935), George Moore (1853–1933), and Edward Martyn (1859–1923). After a disagreement brought an end to their theatrical productions, another organization headed by W. G. Fay (1872–1947) and Frank Fay (1870–1931) took the title "The Irish National Dramatic Company," and shortly afterward amalgamated with the remnants of the Irish Literary Society. An appearance in London won the support of Miss A. E. F. Horniman, who acquired the Abbey Theatre for them and provided a subsidy until 1910.

At first the group gave only three performances a month, but after they obtained a permanent home they began to present a different play each week. It was not until 1908 that they could afford to pay royalties or actors' salaries. Nevertheless, their finest achievements came before 1910, when the best actors began to leave.

Of its playwrights two—Yeats and Synge—were important. Yeats' playwriting career extended from 1892 until 1938. Much of his work resembled that of the French Symbolists, many of whom he had known in Paris. Of his early plays, the best is probably *Cathleen ni Houlihan* (1902), in which the spirit of Ireland, incredibly old but forever lovely, is embodied in the figure of an old woman who is transformed into a young girl. About 1920, Yeats came under the influence of the Oriental theatre and thereafter increasingly emphasized masks, dance, music, and chant. *At the Hawk's Well* (1920) and *Purgatory* (1938), in which pantomime is accompanied by descriptive choral passages, are representative of his late style.

John Millington Synge (1871–1909) was the best dramatist of the Irish Renaissance. Combining poetic imagination with true dramatic instinct, his plays were more viable than those of Yeats. Of his short plays, *Riders to the Sea* (1904), in which Maurya sees the last of her seven sons killed by the sea, is universally considered a masterpiece. His best long play is *The Playboy of the Western World* (1907), an ironical comedy about a man who is treated as a hero because he has allegedly killed his father. Its implied criticism of the Irish character created riots wherever it was presented and, although the publicity did much to spread the fame of the Abbey Theatre, it contributed to many misconceptions about Synge's purpose.

Lesser dramatists encouraged by the Abbey Theatre include Lady Gregory, noted especially for her one-act comedies such as *Spreading the News* (1904) and *The Workhouse Ward* (1908); Lord Dunsany (1878–1957), whose *The Glittering Gate* (1909) and *If* (1921) helped to win acceptance for non-realistic drama; St. John Ervine (1883–   ), whose *Jane Clegg* (1913) and *John Fergusson* (1915) present powerful character studies in the realistic vein; and Lennox Robinson (1886–1958), whose *The Whiteheaded Boy* (1916) and *The Far-off Hills* (1928) developed native Irish themes. Robinson was long one of the leaders of the Abbey Theatre, notably in the years following the First World War.

The Abbey Theatre gained international fame for its ensemble acting. In addition to the Fays, associated with the troupe until 1908, the company included Dudley Digges (1879–1947), destined to become one of the mainstays of the Theatre Guild in New York after 1919; Arthur Sinclair (1883–1951), who performed with the troupe until 1916; Sinclair's wife, Maire O'Neill (1887–1952), and her sister, Sara Allgood (1883–1950), later a well-known film actress in America. Although the Abbey was to recapture some of its former glory with the plays of Sean O'Casey during the 1920's, its major contribution had been made by 1915.

Russian Idealism

In Russia, the revolts against realism were centered at first around *The World of Art,* a periodical begun in 1898 by Sergei Diaghilev (1872–1929). In addition to keeping Russians abreast of events in the artistic centers of Europe, the magazine sought to encourage Russian artists and composers. Diaghilev's major contribution, however, was to stem from ballet. After Petipa retired, Prince Sergei Volkonsky, Director of the Imperial Theatres, and Mikhail Fokine (1880–1942), choreographer at the Mariinsky Theatre, introduced several innovations. Fokine disliked the long narrative works which Petipa had favored, and sought more limited subjects which offered greater opportunity for novel choreographic design. Using music by such composers as Igor Stravinsky, he emphasized complex rhythms and harmony of mood.

Meanwhile Diaghilev had been arranging exchanges of art with other countries, and in 1909 he took opera and ballet companies, including Fokine's, to Paris for a six-week season. Their ecstatic reception led to the formation of Diaghilev's Ballets Russes, which then toured throughout Europe. Everywhere they were praised both for their dancing and for their scenic design. When the war began, many members of the company remained in the West.

The scenic style of the Ballets Russes did not depend upon any new technical devices, for it relied upon painted wings and drops. Nevertheless, it departed markedly from illusionism, for its line, color, and decorative motifs were considerably stylized to reflect moods and themes rather than specific periods or places. Costumes also emphasized exaggerated line, color, and mass. Thus, although the artists retained familiar forms and decorative motifs, they created a quality of exoticism and fantasy through stylization. Their influence upon European scenic design is incalculable. The Ballets

Russes designers included Leon Bakst (1866–1924), Alexandre Benois (1876–1960), Alexander Golovin (1863–1930), Mstislav Dobuzhinsky (1878–1958), and Natalie Gontcharova (1881–   ). Bakst and Benois later settled in Paris, where they continued to work.

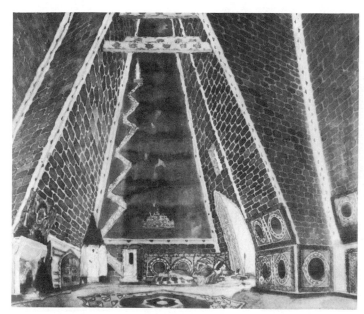

A SETTING by Bakst for *Tamar* at the Ballets Russes, 1912. [From the souvenir program]

Around 1905, Symbolism penetrated Russian literary circles and was to be the dominant non-realistic force until the Revolution. At this time, Stanislavsky became interested in Maeterlinck and in 1904–05 presented a bill of his short plays. This experience helped to convince Stanislavsky that his company needed to enlarge its approach, and in 1905 he established a studio to experiment with non-realistic styles. To supervise the works, Stanislavsky employed Vsevelod Meyerhold (1874–1942), a former member of the Moscow Art Theatre who had left in 1902 to form his own troupe. At the new studio, Meyerhold produced two plays, but his subordination of the actors to a directorial concept displeased Stanislavsky so much that he discontinued the experiment.

The Moscow Art Theatre went on to produce other non-realistic works, including Maeterlinck's *The Blue Bird* in 1908 and *Hamlet* in 1911, the latter with scenery by Gordon Craig. It also encouraged Leonid Andreyev (1871–1919), Russia's foremost non-realistic dramatist. After beginning in the realistic mode, Andreyev was converted to Symbolism in 1907, the year in which he wrote his most famous play, *The Life of Man,* an allegory which seeks to summarize the human experience. Stanislavsky staged it against black curtains, using rope to outline windows, doors, and walls, and with considerable stylization in acting. Andreyev later turned to writing in a more concrete style, although *He Who Gets Slapped* (1915), a drama with a circus background, demonstrates his continuing penchant for allegory.

ANDREYEV's *The Life of Man* at the Moscow Art Theatre, 1907. Setting by V. E. Egerov. [From *The Moscow Art Theatre, 1898–1917* (Moscow 1955)]

In 1911, the Moscow Art Theatre established the First Studio, under the direction of Leopold Sullerzhitsky (1872–1916), primarily to give training in the Stanislavsky system, but also to encourage non-realistic approaches. Here a number of future leaders, notably Richard Boleslavsky, Mikhail Chekhov, and Eugene Vakhtangov, received their training. But, if Stanislavsky experimented with non-realistic approaches, any marked departure from realism was ultimately unacceptable to him since all tended to "dematerialize" the actor.

The most important early experiments with non-realistic staging were undertaken in the company maintained by Vera Kommissarzhevskaya (1864–1910). On the stage from 1891, she attracted an enormous following and opened her own theatre in St. Petersburg in 1904. Interested in new approaches, she employed Meyerhold when he left Stanislavsky. In his first production, Ibsen's *Hedda Gabler,* Meyerhold assigned each character a color and a limited number of sculpturesque gestures; he used costumes devoid of realistic detail and a greenish-blue setting with white furniture. He ignored Ibsen's stage directions. For Wedekind's *Spring's Awakening,* he placed everything to be used in the production on stage at once and spotlighted each area as needed. When audiences did not respond favorably to these and other experiments, perhaps because Meyerhold did not exploit the considerable talents of Kommissarzhevskaya, Meyerhold was asked to leave. Immediately afterward he was employed by the Director of Imperial Theatres.

When he staged Molière's *Don Juan* at the Alexandrinsky Theatre in 1910, Meyerhold removed the front curtain and footlights, extended the forestage into the auditorium, kept the house lights on throughout the performance, used costumed stagehands to change properties and scenery, and set the actors' dancing movements to Lully's music. After the enormous success of this production, he went on to stage several operas at the Mariinsky Theatre. Between 1910 and 1914, Meyerhold also established studios where he experimented with circus and *commedia dell'arte* techniques. In one studio the performers mingled with the audience and converted the entire auditorium into an acting area. Actors worked out their own scripts and experimented with geometrically patterned movement, improvisation, and rhythm. Meyerhold also became interested in Oriental theatre and began to turn the scenic background into a mere apparatus for acting—a collection of steps and levels. He was to continue and extend his work after the Revolution. In these early years, Meyerhold clearly believed that the director is the major creative force in the theatre and that a script is merely material to be moulded and reworked as the director wishes. His was probably the most persistent exploration of the possibilities and limitations of the theatre as a medium of expression.

At Kommissarzhevskaya's theatre, Meyerhold was succeeded by Nikolai Evreinov (1879–1953). Although equally opposed to realism, Evreinov

MEYERHOLD'S PRODUCTION of Przybszewski's *The Eternal Story* at Kommissarzhevskaya's Theatre, 1906. Setting by Denissov. [From Volkov, *Meyerhold* (Moscow, 1929)]

sought to enlarge the actor's place in the theatre by emphasizing flamboyance, theatricality, and the grotesque. Evreinov is probably most famous for his "monodramas," the basic principle of which was first set forth in his "Apology for Theatricality" in 1908. He suggested that man's inborn theatrical instinct leads him into "role playing" and makes him seek to transform reality into something better. Consequently, he argued, the theatre should not imitate life, but life should seek to become like theatre at its best. In his "monodramas" he aimed to help the audience achieve its desires by making it the alter-ego of the protagonist. Through identification, the audience supposedly participated directly in the experience and was led to perceptions of the higher reality. In staging, Evreinov sought to treat everything as seen through the mind of the protagonist. Lighting, sound, and scenery reflected the character's changing moods and emotions. The most famous of the monodramas was *The Theatre of the Soul* (1912). Although never very popular, Evreinov's monodramas contributed to Expressionism and to motion picture techniques.

Theodore Kommissarzhevsky (1874–1954) worked with his sister, Evreinov, and others before opening his own theatre in 1910. Probably the most balanced Russian producer, he sought to remain faithful to each playwright's intention, an attempt which led to an eclecticism not unlike Reinhardt's. In the 1920's he emigrated to England, where he contributed significantly to the staging of Shakespeare's plays at Stratford-on-Avon, and later to America, where he staged many operas and plays.

Alexander Tairov (1885–1950) worked for a number of producers before opening his own theatre, the Kamerny (or Chamber) Theatre in Moscow in 1914. Tairov argued that there is no relationship between art and life and that the theatre must be viewed as analogous to the sacred dances of an ancient temple. Like Meyerhold, he viewed the text as an excuse for creativity, although he objected to Meyerhold's suppression of the actor, who, according to Tairov, is the basic creative force in the theatre. Because he was concerned with rhythmical movement, Tairov's settings were composed primarily of steps and levels. Productions were approached as if they were musical compositions; speech was a compromise between declamation and song, and movement always tended toward dance. The effect was nearer to ritual than to the usual dramatic performance. By the time of the Revolution, Tairov had staged 14 plays drawn from a wide variety of countries and dramatic types. Most productions featured his wife, Alice Koonen, his ideal interpreter. Tairov was to continue his work after the Revolution.

By 1917, Russian experimenters had introduced techniques far removed from those employed by Stanislavsky in 1898. Some methods were as determinedly non-realistic as have ever been devised. One of the least advanced countries of Europe at the end of the 19th century, Russia had witnessed some of the most daring theatrical experiments, although, with

TAIROV'S PRODUCTION of Wilde's *Salome,* 1917. Costumes and setting by A. Exter. [From Moussinac, *New Movement in the Theatre*]

the exceptions of the Ballets Russes and the Moscow Art Theatre, the work was little known outside its borders.

The Revival of Idealism in France

After the closing of the Théâtre de l'Oeuvre in 1899, Paris settled once more into its somewhat complacent conviction that it was the artistic capital of Europe. Antoine's productions became the standard, and non-realistic experiments were few and sporadic. Thus, the appearance of the Ballets Russes in 1909 came almost as a revelation. A new wave of experimentation was given further impetus by the publication in 1910 of *L'Art Théâtral Moderne* by Jacques Rouché (1862–1957). After describing the work of Fuchs, Erler, and Reinhardt in Germany, of Meyerhold, Stanislavsky, and Kommissarzhevskaya in Russia, and the theories of Appia and Craig, Rouché went on to call for similar experiments in France. Not only was his book widely read and discussed, Rouché himself set out to implement his appeal at the Théâtre des Arts between 1910 and 1913. Rouché did not aim at extreme stylization, but sought a simplicity in which color and line characterize a milieu and mood without calling attention to themselves. He found his ideal designer in Maxime Dethomas (1867–1929). Rouché was the first French producer to be truly eclectic. From 1914 to 1945 he was director of the Opéra, where he renovated the repertory and brought to it a new generation of scene designers.

Rouché's work had important consequences. Lugné-Poë revived the Théâtre de l'Oeuvre, where he presented a series of plays with designs by

COPEAU'S ADAPTATION of *The Brothers Karamazov* at Rouché's Théâtre des Arts, 1911. Setting by Dethomas. [From *L'Illustration Théâtrale* (April 11, 1911)]

Jean Variot, who reenforced Rouché's influence. More important, Rouché inspired Jacques Copeau (1879–1949) to open his own theatre. A dramatic critic, Copeau gained his first practical experience at the Théâtre des Arts when his adaptation of *The Brothers Karamazov* was produced there in 1911. Copeau was convinced that Rouché's suggested reforms put too much emphasis upon visual elements, and that no significant progress could come except from the drama itself.

HAMLET at the Théâtre de l'Oeuvre, 1913. Directed by Lugné-Poë and Gémier. Settings by Jean Variot. [From *Le Théâtre* (1913)]

In 1913, Copeau published his manifesto for a new theatre. In it, he adopted a position almost opposite to that of Meyerhold and Tairov, for he argued that the director's primary task is the faithful translation of the dramatist's script into a "poetry of the theatre." Furthermore, he stated that the actor, as the "living presence" of the author, is the only essential element of theatrical production, and that a rejuvenation of the drama could best be served by a return to the bare platform stage.

Copeau assembled a company of ten actors, including Louis Jouvet, Charles Dullin, Suzanne Bing, Romain Bouquet, and Valentine Tessier, all of whom were to be significant in the postwar theatre, and retired to the country to perfect his first productions. Meanwhile, with the assistance of Francis Jourdain, Copeau converted a small hall into the Théâtre du Vieux Colombier, seating only 400. The proscenium arch was removed to create an open platform raised a few steps above the auditorium. At the rear of the stage an alcove surmounted by a balcony completed the acting facilities, which were not unlike those of the Elizabethan public theatre. This basic structure could be altered by the addition of curtains and set pieces, but it always remained essentially the same. Copeau presented 15 plays, including works by Shakespeare, Molière, Heywood, Claudel, and others, in 1913–14, before the war forced him to stop. The actors scattered, but in 1917 Copeau was asked by the French government to revive the troupe and take it to New York as cultural propaganda. Between 1917 and 1919 he presented plays for American audiences before returning to Paris to reopen his theatre there. It is impossible to overrate the importance of the Théâtre du Vieux Colombier, for with its formation the leadership of the French theatre passed from Antoine to Copeau, who was to dominate the postwar theatre in France.

The Theatre in Italy and Spain, 1875–1915

Between 1875 and 1915, both Italy and Spain were more emulative than innovative. Italy's major creative energies continued to be poured into opera. In drama, realism arrived first in the works of Paolo Ferrari (1822–89), a writer in the vein of Dumas *fils*, and then through the "Verist" school. Since Italy was still divided by differences in dialect and customs, the Verists are usually separated into groups centered in Milan, Turin, and Naples. Of the Milanese school, Marco Praga (1862–1929), with such dark, hopeless plays as *The Virgins* (1889), was the most famous. At Turin, Giuseppe Giacosa (1847–1906) was the dominant figure with his Ibsenesque plays *The Rights of the Soul* (1894) and *Like Falling Leaves* (1900). Of the Neapolitan school, Roberto Bracco (1862–1943), with his dramas about victimized women, as in *Maternity* (1903) and *Nellina*

(1908), was the best. In Sicily, Giovanni Verga (1840–1922) won fame with his Zolaesque plays of brutal violence, *Cavalleria Rusticana* (1884) and *The She-Wolf* (1896). Neoromanticism found its major exponent in Gabriele D'Annunzio (1863–1938), who, under the influence of Maeterlinck, wrote such plays as *The Dead City* (1898), *La Giocanda* (1898), and *Francesca da Rimini* (1902).

The strong Italian acting tradition was continued by such outstanding players as Ermete Zacconi (1857–1948), Giovanni Grasso (1875–1930), and Ruggero Ruggeri (1871–1954). By far the most renowned, however, was Eleanora Duse (1859–1924). On the stage from the age of four, she became Rossi's leading lady in 1879. After touring South America in 1885, she formed her own company and played throughout the world. She retired in 1909, but returned to the stage in 1921 and died in Pittsburg while on tour. Duse played an extremely wide range of roles, many of them favorites of Bernhardt, with whose flamboyance her quiet style contrasted sharply. Noted for subtlety, she used simple means to convey complex conceptions. She scorned makeup and prided herself on her ability to make the physical adjustments required by each role. To many discerning critics, she was the greatest of modern actresses.

In Spain, the realistic drama found its first important exponent in José Echegaray (1848–1927), notably in *The Son of Don Juan* (1892), patterned on Ibsen's *Ghosts*, and *The Great Galeoto* (1881), a play about the

ELEANORE DUSE in Ibsen's *Rosemersholm* at the Norwegian National Theatre in Oslo, 1906. [From *Bühne und Welt* (1906)]

power of gossip to ruin lives. After the war of 1898 had stripped Spain of her last shreds of glory, a new movement, "the Generation of '98," sought to modernize literature by seeking inspiration outside Spain. The most famous of the new writers was Jacinto Benavente (1866–1954), a versatile dramatist who composed nearly 300 works ranging through every style and form. Of his realistic plays, the best is probably *The Passion Flower* (1913), the story of a man's love for his step-daughter, while of the non-realistic works *The Bonds of Interest* (1907), a philosophical work using *commedia dell'arte* conventions, is the best known.

For the most part, however, Spanish drama tended to remain sentimental and melodramatic underneath a facade of realistic detail. Serafín Álvarez Quintero (1871–1944) and Joaquín Álvarez Quintero (1873–1938) wrote more than 150 plays of this type, such as *The Merry Heart* (1906) and *Malvoloca* (1912). In much the same vein, Gregorio Martínez Sicrra (1881–1947) wrote *Cradle Song* (1911) and *The Kingdom of God* (1916).

The modern movement in Spain was helped considerably by the Teatro Intim, founded in imitation of the "independent theatres" of Europe by Adria Gual (1872–1932) in 1898 at Barcelona. Here a cross section of drama from Aeschylus to the present was offered for more than 30 years. With his experiments in production styles, Gual brought many of the new trends to Spain.

The major Spanish actors of this period were María Guerrero (1868–1928) and her husband, Fernando Diaz de Mendoza (1862–1930). From 1896 until 1909 they managed the Teatro Espagñol, and from 1909 until 1924 the Teatro de la Princesa (later renamed the Teatro María Guerrero). The Mendoza-Guerrero company toured South America 22 times and elsewhere with less frequency.

Major Technical Innovations, 1875–1915

Between 1875 and 1915 several important technical innovations were introduced, the majority in Germany. Many were motivated by the need to shift the heavy three-dimensional settings which were replacing the wings and drops designed for movement by the chariot-and-pole system. One of the most important of the new devices was the revolving stage, the first of which was installed at the Residenz Theater in Munich in 1896 by Karl Lautenschläger, who had encountered the device in Japan. Its ability to accommodate several settings and to change them merely by revolving the turntable, led to its wide adoption after 1900. Another solution, the rolling platform stage, was introduced by Fritz Brandt at the Royal Opera House in Berlin around 1900. With it, settings could be mounted on a large platform offstage and then moved on stage by means of rollers set in tracks. The elevator stage also was widely adopted. At the Munich Art Theatre, the Burgtheater, and elsewhere, the stage was divided into segments, each of which could be adjusted to create a variety of levels for the action or to raise heavy objects from beneath the stage. A still more complex arrangement was installed in the Dresden state theatres between 1904 and 1914 by combining sliding platforms with elevators. These complex mechanical devices were supplemented with flying, manual shifting, and with small wagons mounted on casters. The wider adoption of the new stage machinery in Germany than elsewhere is probably due to two factors: the expense, absorbed in Germany by the state, and the decline of realism before the devices were widely adopted elsewhere, for the growing emphasis upon simplified settings made complex machinery less desirable.

Many German theatres of this period also installed plaster domes (or *kuppelhorizants*) which curved around and over the stage to give the effect of infinite space and eliminated the need for overhead and side masking pieces. To fulfill the same function, other theatres used a cloth cyclorama hung from a batten which curved around the stage.

Many experiments with stagelighting were conducted. Light bridges and other new mounting positions were tried. Footlights began to be replaced with spotlights mounted in the auditorium. After 1907, improvements in the filaments of incandescent lamps made it possible to increase wattage. By 1913, 1000-watt lamps were available in Europe, and color media and spotlights were beginning to be common. One of the most ambitious lighting systems was devised by Mariano Fortuny (1871–1949), in collaboration with the General Electric Company of Berlin. Fortuny directed strong lights against colored silk panels, which reflected the light onto a *kuppelhorizant* and then onto the stage. With elaborate machinery for changing the panels and controlling the light, the system gave the most subtle variations of any then known, but its complexity and cost prevented its widespread adoption. Nevertheless, it is indicative of the growing interest in lighting as an important element of design.

Auditoriums also underwent considerable change, largely under the influence of Wagner's theatre at Bayreuth. Boxes tended to disappear, the number of balconies decreased (often there was none), center aisles were eliminated, and sightlines were improved. As the interest in breaking down the barriers between performers and audience grew, the apron stage returned to favor and in some instances the proscenium arch was eliminated. Thus, the Italianate theatre, dominant since the 17th century, was seriously challenged for the first time.

By 1915, the standards of production which had been accepted almost universally in 1875 seemed outmoded. Although pictorial realism still dominated the popular theatre, it had been undermined by a host of experiments. Through all of the experiments ran a common theme: the need for unified production, a strong director, and artistic integrity, so that the theatre might once more assume the role it had played in ancient Greece as a source of insight and a place of communion. Although the war interrupted developments, it provoked reassessments, out of which new convictions and renewed vigor came in the postwar years.

THE
THEATRE
BETWEEN
THE WARS

*T*he period between the two World Wars witnessed a succession of artistic movements, most of which passed quickly after contributing to the spirit of experimentation and eclecticism which characterized the era. Despite similarities, the theatre in each country developed along individual lines determined by artistic, social, political, and economic influences. After a period of recovery following the First World War, the theatre began to shrink again under the impact of worldwide economic crises and political upheavals. During the Second World War, its vitality reached the lowest point in modern times.

German Theatre and Drama, 1915–45

The German theatre continued without interruption during the First World War and, unlike its English, French, and American counterparts, did not turn primarily to popular entertainment. When Germany became a democracy at the end of the war, the former "royal" theatres were re-christened "state" theatres, although there were few changes in organization or policy, for they continued to offer seasons composed of varied plays performed by permanent companies. After 1920, as economic conditions worsened, nonsubsidized groups found it increasingly difficult to survive and the long-run hit largely superseded the repertory system except in the state theatres.

Of the prewar figures, Max Reinhardt remained the most important. While continuing his management of the Deutsches Theater and the Kammerspiele, he also acquired the Grosses Schauspielhaus, remodeled from the Circus Schumann, where between 1919 and 1922 he presented a series of monumental productions, most notably the *Oresteia, Julius Caesar,* and *Danton's Death.* The venture ultimately failed, perhaps because the theatre's great size discouraged subtlety, and the compromises demanded by the combined open and picture-frame stages were never entirely satisfactory.

Between 1922 and 1924, Reinhardt moved his headquarters to Austria, where he had annually produced von Hofmannsthal's *Everyman* and *The Great Theatre of the World* at the Salzburg Festival since its founding in 1920. In 1922 he became director of Vienna's Theater in dem Redouten-saal, converted from an Imperial ballroom of the 1740's, where against a background of screens he presented plays and operas of the 18th century. The intimacy of this theatre contrasted markedly with the immensity of the Grosses Schauspielhaus. Although he retained and extended his Austrian enterprises, in 1924 Reinhardt returned to Berlin where he continued his manifold activities until Hitler's rise to power forced him to flee to America in 1933. Between 1905 and 1933 Reinhardt had personally directed 136 plays, while his many experiments with production styles and theatre architecture had exerted a pervasive influence on the German stage. In the United States, Reinhardt directed a few plays and films, but never fully adjusted to his new situation.

While Reinhardt's postwar activities were essentially continuations of practices which he had begun before 1914, the major new force was to be Expressionism, which began to emerge around 1910. In painting Expres-

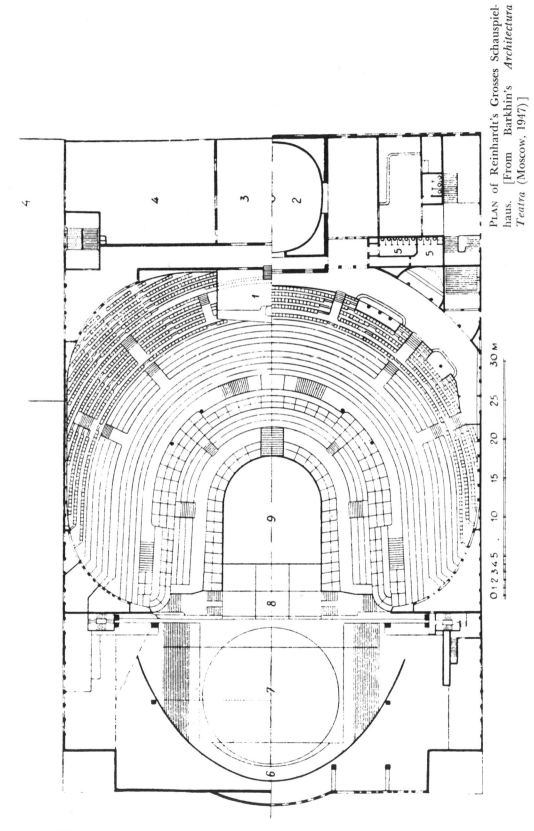

PLAN of Reinhardt's Grosses Schauspielhaus. [From Barkhin's *Architectura
Teatra* (Moscow, 1947)]

0 1 2 3 4 5   10   15   20   25   30 M

REINHARDT'S PRODUCTION of *Oedipus Rex* at the Grosses Schauspielhaus. [From *The Theatre* (1920)]

sionism took its inspiration from Van Gogh and Gauguin, while in drama the plays of Strindberg and Wedekind were its models. Soon the Sturm-bühne, an offshoot of the magazine *Der Sturm,* was presenting special matinees of "Expressionist drama in Expressionist style." The movement first gained wide recognition through the plays of Reinhard Sorge (1892–1916), whose *The Beggar* (1912) depicts a world unwilling to profit from the message of a poet-seer, and Walter Hasenclever (1890–1940), whose *The Son* (1914) argued that children are justified in killing parents who stand in the way of free expression. Because he used many of the same techniques, Karl Sternheim (1878–1943), although not strictly an Expressionist, also called attention to the movement through a series of satirical plays presented between 1908 and 1922 under the general title, "Portraits of Bourgeois Heroes." Among these the most famous is *The Underpants,* which depicts the upheaval wrought by a woman's loss of her underpants as the Prince emerges from church.

Since almost any departure from realism came to be labeled "Expressionism," the movement is difficult to define. Nevertheless, its basic premises may be outlined. An anthropomorphic view of existence led Expressionists to project human emotions and attitudes into all objects, and to seek truth in man's spiritual qualities rather than in external appearances. Expressionists opposed Realism and Naturalism on the grounds that they focused attention upon surface details and implied that the observable phenomena of contemporary materialistic and mechanistic society represent fixed truths. The Expressionists argued that external reality is alterable and should be changed until it harmonizes with man's spiritual nature, the only significant source of value. Many Expressionists sought merely to focus attention upon these inner qualities, but others took a more militant view and worked to transform social and political conditions so that they would no longer mechanize and distort man's spirit and prevent his attainment of happiness.

Since the Expressionists' "truth" existed primarily within the subjective realm, they had to seek new artistic means to express it. Distorted line, exaggerated shape, abnormal coloring, mechanical movement, and telegraphic speech were devices commonly used to lead audiences beyond surface appearances. Often everything was shown through the eyes of the protagonist, whose view might alter emphases and impose drastic interpretations upon the events. Most Expressionist plays were structurally episodic, their unity deriving from a central idea or argument, often one suggesting the possibility of a future Utopia.

The major Expressionist dramatists were Kaiser and Toller. Georg Kaiser (1878–1945) began his playwriting career in 1911 and established his reputation with *From Morn to Midnight* (1916), in which a machine-age Everyman searches for meaning in life, only to become a martyr to greed and callousness. *Gas I* (1918), while showing an unsuccessful attempt to achieve an ideal society, appears optimistic about the future, but *Gas II* (1920) seems to abandon all hope for human advancement. Ernst Toller (1893–1939) wrote his first play, *Transfiguration* (1918), while serving a prison term for antiwar activities. His most influential work was to be *Man and the Masses* (1921), the story of an idealistic revolutionary who fails in her attempt to lead workers to a better life. The play ends on an optimistic note, but Toller, like Kaiser, was to become increasingly disillusioned, and his last important work, *Hurrah, We Live* (1927), is a bitter story about a revolutionary who returns from prison to find that all his old comrades have settled into comfortable positions.

Other Expressionist playwrights include Fritz von Unruh (1885–   ), with *One Race* (1918) and *Room* (1920); Paul Kornfeld (1889–1944), with *The Seduction* (1916) and *Heaven and Hell* (1919); Anton Wildgans (1881–1932), with *Poverty* (1914) and *Love* (1916); Reinhard Goering (1887–1936), with *Sea-Battle* (1918); and Hans Chlumberg (1897–1930), with *Miracle at Verdun* (1930). As the hopes for a new social order raised by the peace conference at the end of the war gradually gave way to pessimism and bitterness, Expressionism declined sharply and by 1925 had lost its vitality. Although its techniques were adopted by other movements, its basic outlook was rejected.

Between 1915 and 1925, Expressionism also became a major style of production, especially as applied by Jessner and Fehling. Leopold Jessner (1878–1948) had worked in Hamburg and Königsberg before becoming director of the Berlin State Theatre in 1919. Here he won international fame for his imaginative use of flights of steps (*Jessnertreppen*) as the major scenic device and compositional element in his productions. His major designers, Emil Pirchan and Cesar Klein, discarded representational scenery for stylized pieces which, along with costumes and lighting, were

JESSNER'S PRODUCTION of Blut's *Empörung des Lucius* at
the Berlin State Theatre. Setting by Emil Pirchan. Note the
steps and levels for which Jessner was famous. [From
Theatre Arts (1924)]

selected primarily for their emotional and symbolic qualities. Jessner's
production of *Richard III* is typical of his approach; in it, the blood-red
costumes and light used at the peak of Richard's power dissolved into
white costumes and light as Richmond's forces came to the fore. Despite
his fame as an "Expressionist" director, Jessner's repertory was composed
primarily of classics. In 1933, he emigrated to the United States.

Unlike Jessner, Jürgen Fehling (1890–1968) made his reputation with
Expressionist drama, beginning with Toller's *Man and the Masses* at
Berlin's Volksbühne in 1921. Fehling sought to arouse intense emotional
response in spectators. In his productions, bankers foxtrotted after hearing
of a mine disaster; condemned revolutionaries performed a dance to the
accompaniment of a concertina; choral voices came out of a void; figures
were silhouetted against a yellow cyclorama. Fehling's range of devices was
greater than Jessner's, for he varied his approach with each play. Fehling
remained in Germany during Hitler's regime, serving as director of the
Berlin State Theatre.

As Expressionism declined, a more militant approach, eventually to be
called "Epic Theatre," arose. Its first major practitioner, Erwin Piscator
(1893–1966), founded the Proletarian Theatre in 1920, and after working
at the Central Theatre from 1921 to 1924 was appointed director of the
Volksbühne, where he sought to create a "proletarian drama," as opposed
to merely producing standard plays for a working-class audience. His re-

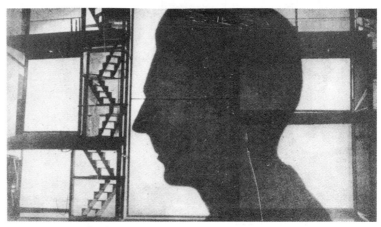

PISCATOR'S SETTING for Toller's *Hurrah,*
We Live. [From *Theatre Arts* (1932)]

shaping of texts into propaganda pieces aroused such controversy that he resigned in 1927 to found the Piscator Theatre. Here between 1927 and 1930 he experimented with the techniques later associated with Epic Theatre. For Toller's *Hurrah, We Live,* a reworking of Alexei Tolstoy's *Rasputin,* and an adaptation of Jaroslav Hacek's novel, *The Good Soldier Schweik,* Piscator used filmed sequences, cartoons, treadmills, segmented settings, and other devices to draw strong parallels between the dramatic events and real situations, thus arguing the need for social and political reforms. After Piscator was forced to close his theatre, he went to America, where until 1951 he taught at the New School for Social Research and staged a number of plays in New York and elsewhere.

Despite Piscator's pioneering work, "Epic Theatre" is now associated primarily with Bertolt Brecht (1898–1956), the movement's major theoretician and dramatist. Brecht entered the theater as a director in Munich and later worked for Reinhardt in Berlin. As a playwright, he experimented with Dadaism and Expressionism in such early plays as *Baal* (1918) and *Drums in the Night* (1919) before arriving at his more characteristic style with *A Man's a Man* (1924–26). His first major success came with *The Three-Penny Opera* (1928), with music by Kurt Weill; under Brecht's direction and with settings by Caspar Neher (1897–1962), it ran for 400 performances. In 1933, Brecht went into exile, during which he wrote most of his major works: *The Private Life of the Master Race* (1935–38), 28 scenes demonstrating Nazi inhumanity; *Mother Courage* (1937), emphasizing both the endurance and the brutalization of a woman during the Thirty Years' War; *Galileo* (1938–39); *The Good Woman of Setzuan* (1938–40), *Herr Puntila* ((1940–41), *The Resistible Rise of Arturo Ui* (1941), and *The Caucasian Chalk Circle* (1944–45), Brecht's last major play. Because of his exile, Brecht's works remained unproduced

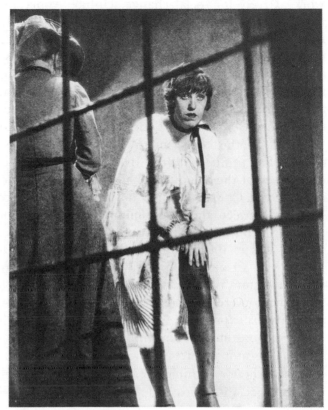

LOTTE LENYA in the original production
of Brecht's *Three Penny Opera.* [From
Theatre Arts (1936)]

until he returned to Germany in 1947, since when they have been an
increasingly pervasive influence on the theatre throughout the world.

Although Brecht's plays have gained a devoted audience, his theory
probably has been even more widely disseminated. Brecht called his
approach "Epic" in order to indicate its broad sweep and its mixture of
narrative and dramatic techniques. He wished to assign the spectator an
active role in the theatre by making him watch critically rather than pas-
sively. Consequently, he arrived at the concept of "alienation" (*verfrem-
dungseffekt*), or the making of stage events sufficiently strange that the
spectator will ask questions about them. To create this thoughtful contemplation and to prevent the spectator from confusing the stage events with
real life, Brecht wanted the mechanics of the theatre to be seen; visible
light sources, on-stage musicians, projections, the interlarding of dramatic
episodes with songs and narrative passages—these and other devices called
attention to the theatricality of the experience and created the alienation
effect required to achieve critical contemplation. Brecht hoped in this way
to lead the audience to apply what they saw in the theatre to real life and to

work actively for social change. Unlike Appia and Craig, Brecht did not believe that all of the theatrical elements should be synthesized into a master work with a unified effect. Rather, he suggested, each art should make its own comment upon the story. He also rejected Stanislavsky's approach to acting and advised performers to think of their roles "in the third person" so that they might comment upon the characters' motivations and actions. Brecht's theories have been subjected to many conflicting interpretations, but they have stimulated directors throughout the world.

Still another experiment of the 1920's—the Bauhaus—was to exert considerable influence after 1945. In 1919, Walter Gropius (1883–1969) established at the Staatliches Bauhaus in Weimar a School of Fine Arts and of Arts and Crafts in which he attempted to break down the traditional barriers between the artist and the craftsman and to unite architecture, painting, sculpture, and other arts into a communal expression. A studio theatre was established under the direction of Oskar Schlemmer (1888–1943), who set out to explore "the autonomous laws of the stage, removed from all naturalistic imitation." Various elements (color, space, form, light, movement) were abstracted and investigated to discover their possibilities as means of expression. Much of this work paralleled trends in painting. Perhaps more important, Gropius designed a "Synthetic" or "Total" theatre for Piscator in 1926. Although never built, its design has continued to influence theatre architecture. Gropius' theatre permitted varied audience-performer relationships and production approaches. It could be used as a

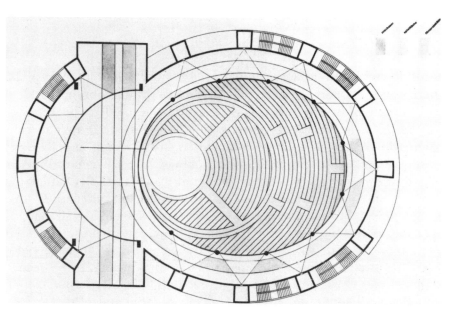

GROPIUS' "TOTAL THEATRE." Note that a portion of the seating can be revolved to form an arena stage; note also the projectors and ramps surrounding the auditorium. [From Barkhin, *Architectura Teatra* (Moscow, 1947)]

conventional picture-frame stage or, by manipulating portions of the auditorium mounted on revolving platforms, as a thrust stage or as an arena stage. Sloping ramps surrounding the auditorium also could serve as acting areas, while scenery could be projected onto screens spaced around the periphery of the auditorium and overhead to place the audience in the midst of the scene. In its imaginative use of space, Gropius' theatre has never been surpassed. When the Bauhaus was closed in 1933, its members emigrated to other countries. Their influence upon modern design and architecture is now so pervasive that its source is seldom fully recognized.

With the exception of Brecht, few dramatists of stature emerged in Germany after the decline of Expressionism. Among the best were Friedrich Wolf (1888–1953), best known for *Sailors of Cattaro* (1930); Carl Zuckmayer (1896–), remembered primarily for *The Captain from Koepenick* (1930), a satire on Prussian militarism; Franz Werfel (1890–1945), whose *Goat Song* (1921) points to the monster which always lurks beneath the civilized facade, and whose *The Eternal Road* (1935) recounts the history of the Jews; and Ferdinand Bruckner (1891–1958), noted especially for his historical plays, such as *Elizabeth of England* (1930) and *Heroic Comedy* (1948), a story of Mme. de Staël and Napoleon.

With the advent of Hitler in 1933, most of the important dramatists and theatrical workers emigrated, but such writers as Hans Johst (1890–) responded to the call for patriotic dramas. Johst's *Schlageter* (1934) won him the presidency of two important literary societies. Although the Nazis encouraged propaganda plays and historical realism, they did not openly demand compliance. Among the directors who retained an element of independence, the most important were Heinz Hilpert (1890–1967), who succeeded Reinhardt as head of the Deutsches Theater from 1933 to 1945, Karlheinz Martin (1886–1948), Berthold Viertel (1885–1953), and Jürgen Fehling. Perhaps the best of the designers were Traugott Müller, Rochus Gliese, Cesar Klein, Caspar Neher, Wilhelm Reinking, and Karl Gröning. For the most part, however, the German theatre between 1933 and 1945 was subordinated to political demands.

Theatre and Drama in Russia, 1917–45

The Russian Revolution of 1917 brought a sharp break with the political past but the new leaders did not demand conformity to an official policy until after 1927. Thus, during the first ten years of the Soviet regime the arts were permitted considerable freedom to experiment with new forms.

The Communists viewed the theatre as a national treasure, formerly reserved for the middle and upper classes, to be made available to the proletariat. It was also considered a major tool of instruction and, as such, was placed under the authority of the Commissar of Education, Anatole Lunacharsky (1875–1932). Not only was attendance at professional productions encouraged, but amateur groups were organized among peasants, workers, and soldiers. By 1926, there were about 20,000 dramatic clubs among the peasants alone. Between 1918 and 1922, amateurs also figured prominently in the many mass spectacles which recreated major events of the Revolution. The most famous of these was *The Taking of the Winter Palace,* staged in 1919 by Evreinov on the site of the actual event with a cast of about 8,000 soldiers, sailors, and workers.

The new regime proceeded slowly in its nationalization of the theatre. By 1922–23, only 33 percent of the theatre plants belonged to the state. By 1925–26, the percentage had increased to 63, but the process was not to be completed until 1936. Similarly, it was long before theatrical personnel were subjected to political domination.

Many of the most enthusiastic supporters of the Revolution were members of the *avant-garde,* who saw in the new regime the opportunity to break with the past and to create new theatrical forms. Of this faction, Meyerhold soon emerged as the leader. In 1920 he was appointed head of the theatre section in the Commissariat of Education, a position which made him nominal head of the theatre in Russia. At the same time, he continued his own work as a director, staging *The Dawn* (written in 1898 by the Belgian Symbolist, Émile Verhaeren) as a Soviet propaganda piece, in which real news bulletins were read from the stage and a public meeting was held with the audience taking part. When this production was denounced by the Central Committee of the Communist Party as foreign to the needs of the proletariat, Meyerhold resigned his government post. After working as an independent producer between 1921 and 1923, he was given a theatre bearing his name and appointed head of the state's workshop for directors. This series of events is indicative of the power of the *avant-garde* even in the face of official disapproval.

Between 1921 and 1930, Meyerhold perfected techniques with which he had experimented before the Revolution. He now developed more conscious and systematic methods, to which he applied such terms as "biomechanics," "constructivism," and "theatricalism." Biomechanics referred primarily to Meyerhold's approach to acting, intended to create a style appropriate to the machine age. His performers were trained in gymnastics, circus movement, and ballet in order to make them as efficient as machines in carrying out "an assignment received from the outside." In Meyerhold's productions, actors did not sit and converse but acted out responses kinetically through dance or acrobatic movements. "Constructivism" was a term taken over from visual art, where it had first been applied about 1912 to sculpture composed of intersecting planes and masses without representational content. Similarly, Meyerhold frequently arranged nonrepresentational platforms, ramps, turning wheels, trapezes and other objects to create a "machine for acting." The use of such "constructions" was motivated by Meyerhold's wish to make his productions frankly "theatrical" so that the audience could be led to apply the theatrical experience to the world outside. In serving this purpose, Meyerhold believed that the director was justified in adapting and changing scripts in any way he thought necessary.

MEYERHOLD'S ADAPTATION of *The Inspector General* (1926).

The most famous of Meyerhold's productions was Gogol's *The Inspector General*, presented in 1926. Meyerhold transferred the scene to a large city, reshaped all of the characters and invented several new ones. Costumes, scenery, and properties were based on stylized 19th century motifs, and the action was accompanied by period music. The most striking scene was that in which Meyerhold arranged 15 doors around the stage, from each of which an official emerged simultaneously to offer the Inspector a bribe.

Next to Meyerhold, the most influential Russian director of the 1920's was Tairov, who continued the methods he had introduced before the war. Following the Revolution, Lunacharsky had divided theatres into two groups: the well-established or "academic" theatres, which the government subsidized and allowed relative autonomy; and the unproven theatres, which were permitted to exist but given little encouragement. Thus, the government favored pre-Revolutionary groups, a practice bitterly opposed by Meyerhold. Under this scheme, the Kamerny Theatre was classified as an "academic" theatre. Until 1924, Tairov took little notice of the Revolu-

601

tion, producing such works as Wilde's *Salomé,* Scribe's *Adrienne Lecouvreur,* and Racine's *Phèdre* in the style he had always followed. Unlike most producers of the period, who clothed actors in uniform-like garments similar to those worn by the spectators, Tairov sought to lift audiences above the drabness of everyday life. After 1924, Tairov occasionally produced Russian classical and contemporary plays, but his theatre remained the principal link with the West. In addition to its predominantly Western repertory, the troupe also toured in Western Europe in 1923, 1928, and 1929. When Tairov turned to contemporary Russian works, he often ran into difficulties. In 1929 his production of Mikhail Levidov's *Plot of the Equals,* a play about the degeneration of the French Revolution into the Reign of Terror, was removed after one performance. Thereafter, Tairov's influence declined.

Another important innovator in these early years was Eugene Vakhtangov (1883–1922), who had become head of the First Studio of the Moscow Art Theatre when Sullerzhitsky died in 1916. Vakhtangov's reputation rests primarily upon four productions: Maeterlinck's *The Miracle of Saint Anthony* (performed by the Third Studio of the Moscow Art Theatre in 1921); Strindberg's *Erik XIV* (given at the First Studio in 1921); Ansky's *The Dybbuk* (performed by the Habimah Theatre in 1922); and Gozzi's *Turandot* (produced at the Third Studio in 1922).

Vakhtangov began as a faithful follower of Stanislavsky, but his

VAKHTANGOV'S PRODUCTION of *Turandot*
(1922); setting by Nivinsky.

strength came from his effective blending of the Moscow Art Theatre's realistic approach with Meyerhold's theatricalism. From Stanislavsky he preserved the emphasis upon concentration and the exploration of each character's biography and of hidden meanings; to this he added a heightened and stylized use of movement and design not unlike that of the German Expressionists. In *Erik XIV*, for example, which was conceived as a death knell for monarchy, all of the courtiers and bureaucrats were played as automatons while the proletariat was treated realistically. Vakhtangov's greatest achievement came with *Turandot*, throughout which the actors seemed to be improvising effortlessly. This production was retained in the repertory as a memorial to Vakhtangov, who died before it opened. Because he worked with several student groups and trained so many actors, Vakhtangov's influence was considerable. His approach was continued by such associates and students as Yuri Zavadsky (1894–), Boris Shchukin (1894–1939), Reuben Simonov (1899–), Boris Zakhava (1896–), Nikolai Akimov (1901–), and Alexander Popov (1892–). Most of these men were to be important leaders into the 1960's. In the post-Stalinist era, Vakhtangov's methods were to offer the most acceptable alternative to Soviet Realism.

In 1924, the First Studio became an independent organization, the Second Moscow Art Theatre, headed by Mikhail Chekhov (1891–1955), a nephew of Anton Chekhov. Entering the Moscow Art Theatre in 1910, Chekhov soon found the Stanislavsky method inadequate and later worked closely with Vakhtangov, winning considerable fame for his portrayal of Erik XIV. Chekhov thought that Stanislavsky's system restricted the actor to copying nature instead of emphasizing what might be. Thus, he came to stress inspiration above analysis as the actor's primary tool. His conceptions were always somewhat mystical, however, and in 1927 seventeen of his associates resigned from the troupe and published a denunciation. Chekhov then left Russia and settled in the United States, where he ran an acting school for many years and published *To the Actor*. The Second Moscow Art Theatre was dissolved in 1936.

Although the innovators of the 1920's attracted most attention, the conservative groups, notably the Maly Theatre in Moscow and the Alexandrinsky Theatre in Leningrad, were favored by political leaders and most of the public. Meyerhold disliked the Maly Theatre's realistic productions so much that in 1921 he recommended that the troupe be liquidated. In response, Alexander Yuzhin, the Maly's director, launched an attack on "formalism" which began a struggle not to be resolved until the 1930's.

Between 1917 and 1925, the Moscow Art Theatre played only a minor role in Russian theatrical life. It mounted only two new productions and its troupe was decimated in 1919 by the defection of several actors to the West. In 1922, it was granted permission to tour abroad, and in 1923–24 performed in America to universal praise. When the company returned to

Russia in 1924, it was at its lowest ebb. Its studios were alienated, and the company was so depleted that Stanislavsky had to add 87 new performers. Now the process of rebuilding began. In 1926, it achieved its first postwar success with Ostrovsky's *The Burning Heart,* and in 1927 presented Vsevelod Ivanov's *Armored Train 14–69,* its first important Soviet play. From this time, the company's fortunes steadily improved.

Around 1927, the Soviet attitude toward the theatre also began to change. After Lenin died in 1924, Stalin had gradually gathered power into his hands and in 1928 began his campaign to industrialize Russia and to collectivize farming. Concessions formerly granted dissident elements were withdrawn and the central government extended its power over all aspects of Soviet life. In 1927, a training program to equip party members to manage theatres was initiated and "artistic councils" within each theatre were given considerable power over repertory, style, and policy. Nevertheless, attacks on nonconformists in the theatre came primarily from the Russian Association of Proletarian Writers (RAPP), a radical group which sought to abolish everything not deriving directly from the proletariat. Its violence sufficiently alienated party leaders that it was disbanded in 1932 and replaced by the Union of Soviet Writers, headed by Gorky. At first, greater freedom seemed to be in store, but in 1934 "Socialist Realism" was declared the proper style for all art, and pressure began to be exerted to discourage "formalism." In 1936, all theatres were placed under the Central Direction of Theatres, and after 1938 the "stabilization" of companies made it almost impossible for workers to change jobs without specific government approval.

The new policies meant the gradual suppression of the *avant-garde* troupes and greater prestige for the Maly, Alexandrinsky (now renamed the State Academic Pushkin Theatre), and the Moscow Art Theatre, which after 1932 was called "the House of Gorky." The non-realistic groups attempted to adapt to the new demands. Tairov began to alternate Soviet plays with productions in his older style. In 1933, he won considerable praise for his staging of Vishnevsky's *The Optimistic Tragedy,* but by 1937 he was so out of favor that his company was merged for a time with that of the Realistic Theatre. Reopening in 1939, the Kamerny gained approval for some productions but was closed again during the war years. Meyerhold adopted a style usually called "impressionistic," exemplified in his productions of Dumas' *Camille* in 1934 and Tchaikovsky's *Queen of Spades* in 1935. In neither did he alter the text or use biomechanics; both were given lavish, if somewhat stylized, decor and both were popular successes. Nevertheless, Meyerhold's completely nonpolitical interpretations displeased officials even more than his formalism, and in 1938 his theatre was closed. In 1939, he made his last official appearance; in a speech to the First All Union Congress of Directors he admitted errors, but added: "The pitiful and wretched thing called socialist realism has nothing in common with art.

. . . Where once there were the best theatres in the world . . . in hunting formalism, you have eliminated art." Shortly afterward he was arrested and disappeared.

Despite these repressions, stylization received official approval when it was used to convey clear political messages. The most significant experiments of the 1930's were those of Nikolai Okhlopkov (1900–) at the Realistic Theatre. Originating as the Fourth Studio of the Moscow Art Theatre in 1921, the Realistic Theatre attained independent status in 1927. Okhlopkov, who had worked with both Meyerhold and Tairov, was appointed its director in 1932. He eliminated the platform stage and placed all action in the auditorium. Although he often used a central playing area, Okhlopkov also staged scenes around the periphery of the auditorium or on a bridge overhead. Realistic set pieces might be placed almost anywhere, and sound effects from many directions made the audience feel at the center of events. Okhlopkov preferred to work with dramatizations of novels, and all of his productions were "cinematic" in their rapid cutting from one scene to another. But while his selection of plays was acceptable, his production approach was considered too anarchic. For a time his theatre was merged with Tairov's, but eventually he was sent to Rostov for several years. Returning to Moscow in 1943, he became one of the most important directors of the postwar period. Yuri Zavadsky's career followed a similar path. After Vakhtangov's death he had operated a studio for a time, and in 1932 was appointed director of the Red Army Central Theatre. Here he did several fine productions, but in 1935, after refusing to merge his studio with the larger troupe, he was exiled to the provinces until 1939. Zavadsky was succeeded at the Red Army Central Theatre by Alexei Popov, who was more responsive to official demands.

Considering the uncertainties of the early years and the political pressures of the 1930's, it is not surprising that few significant playwrights emerged. Gorky was the only pre-Revolutionary author who prospered, and he wrote only two new plays, *Yegor Bulichev and the Others* (1932) and *Dostigayev and Others* (1933). In the years immediately following the Revolution, leadership passed to the Futurists, militant enemies of old forms and strong advocates of a utilitarian art suited to the needs of a machine age. The major playwright of the movement was Vladimir Mayakovsky (1894–1930), a close friend of Meyerhold, who staged all of his plays. Mayakovsky's *Mystery-Bouffe* (1918) parodied the Bible and ended with the proletariat entering the promised land, while *The Bedbug* (1929) and *The Bathhouse* (1930) satirized Soviet bureaucracy. His last two plays were received so adversely that Mayakovsky committed suicide in 1930.

Most Soviet plays were either farces or melodramas upholding the Revolution and denouncing its opposers. Among the best of the early dramatists were Vsevelod Ivanov (1895–), with *Armored Train 14–69* (1927); Michael Bulgakov (1891–1936), with *The Days of the Turbins*

A PRODUCTION at Okhlopkov's Realistic Theatre in 1932. Note the two levels and the placement of the audience.

(1925); and Constantin Trenyov (1884–1945), with *Lyubov Yarovaya* (1926). Trenev's play was the most popular of the early Soviet works, probably because it combined humor, melodrama, and sentiment. Of the later writers, the best were Nikolai Pogodin (1900–), with *Aristocrats* (1934), *The Man with the Gun* (1937), and *Kremlin Chimes* (1942); Alexander Afinogenov (1904–1941), with *Far Taiga* (1935) and *On the*

MAYAKOVSKY's *The Bedbug* as produced by Meyerhold in 1929.

SCENE from Trenyov's *Lyubov Yarovaya,* as presented at the Maly Theatre, Moscow, in 1926.

Eve (1941); Alexander Korneichuk (1905–   ), with *Truth* (1937) and *The Front* (1942); and Vsevolod Vishnevsky (1900–1951), with *The Optimistic Tragedy* (1932) and *At the Walls of Leningrad* (1941).

By the beginning of the Second World War, the Russian theatre had been subjugated to political pressures. Nevertheless, no country in the world took its theatre more seriously as a medium of ideas and as an integral part of society.

Italian Theatre and Drama, 1915–45

Many of the early Soviet artists had been members of the Futurist movement, launched in Italy in 1909 by the poet Tommaso Marinetti (1876–1944). In his manifestos, Marinetti declared both Realism and Romanticism outmoded since neither could meet the needs of a machine age. Unlike the Expressionists, who tended to blame all evils upon the mechanization of modern life, the Futurists glorified the machine and advocated that art eliminate all nonfunctional details so that it might become as efficient as a machine. In Futurist painting, girders, levers, and gears were prominent, while in literature, polished lines of verse were replaced by staccato passages. Speed, power, and utility were the ideals. The most famous Futurist theatrical productions were those staged at the Piccolo Teatro in Rome in 1918 and at the Théâtre de Pantomime Futuriste in Paris in 1927. The major Italian practitioner of Futurism was Enrico Prampolini (1894–1956), director of the Teatro Magnetico in Rome, who sought to explore the limits of the stage conceived as a cube. The ultimate significance of Futurism is difficult to assess, since it merged with a number of other non-realistic movements of the time.

A FUTURIST PANTOMIME, *The Merchant of Hearts,* staged by Enrico Prampolini at the Théâtre de Pantomime Futuriste, Paris, in 1927. [From Moussinac, *New Movement in the Theatre*]

During the First World War, a new school of writing, usually called "the theatre of the grotesque," appeared in Italy. Its name was derived from *The Mask and the Face* (1916), "a grotesque in three acts," by Luigi Chiarelli (1884–1947). Turning upon the contrast between public and private role-playing, this comedy tells the story of a man who, after confessing the murder of his wife because he thought her unfaithful, is tried and acquitted, although in actuality she is merely locked up at home. Of the many other writers who exploited this ironical vein, the best was probably Pier Maria Rosso di San Secondo (1887–), with *Marionettes, What Passion!* (1918) and *The Sleeping Beauty* (1919).

Luigi Pirandello (1867–1936) was by far the greatest Italian playwright of the period. After winning fame with his novels and short stories, Pirandello turned to playwriting in 1910 and after 1915 devoted himself increasingly to the theatre. In 1925, he founded the Art Theatre in Rome, where he presented many significant Italian and foreign plays. Here he was assisted by Marta Abba (1906–), who played leading roles, and a company which included Ruggero Ruggeri, one of Italy's most respected actors.

Pirandello's plays, of which the best are *Right You Are—If You Think You Are* (1916), *Six Characters in Search of an Author* (1921), *Henry IV*

(1922), *Naked* (1922), *Each in His Own Way* (1924), *Tonight We Improvise* (1930), and *As You Desire Me* (1930), usually turn upon a question of fact which cannot be resolved because each character has his own version of the truth. Thus, Pirandello raises doubts about the validity of the scientific approach to truth—the direct observation of reality. He seems to suggest that "truth" is necessarily personal and subjective. As one of the first dramatists to develop this theme, Pirandello was a precursor of a major strain in postwar drama.

Perhaps the most experimental troupe in Italy between the wars was that at the Teatro degli Indipendenti, directed from 1922 to 1931 by Anton Guilio Bragaglia (1890–) in cooperation with Virgilio Marchi (1895–1960), Italy's foremost designer of the period. Another outstanding troupe was established at the Sala Azzura in Milan by Gualtiero Tumiati (1876–). For the most part, however, the Italian theatre was made up of touring companies playing the latest hits. A step toward improvement was taken in 1936 with the formation of the Academy of Dramatic Art in Rome under the direction of Silvio D'Amico. Here the principles of Stanislavsky, Copeau, and Reinhardt were taught. The coming of the war interrupted the Academy's work, however, and its impact was not to be felt until after 1945.

Theatre and Drama in Spain, 1915–45

In the years between 1915 and 1945, Spain's popular playwrights continued to be Benavente, the Quinteros, and Martínez Sierra. There was little chance for freedom of expression, for Spain became a virtual dictatorship following the First World War. Nevertheless, between 1917 and 1925 Martínez Sierra was able to introduce many fine European plays and new production methods at his Teatro Eslava.

The most significant native drama of the postwar years was written by Unamuno and Valle-Inclán. Miguel de Unamuno (1864–1936), one of Spain's most respected philosophers, first expressed his theory of drama in *The Tragic Sense of Life* (1913). His declaration that tragedy stems from a conflict between man's desire for immortality and skepticism about its possibility was to contribute much to Existentialist drama following the Second World War. Because of censorship, Unamuno's plays, such as *Fedra* (1917) and *Dream Shadows* (1931), were not widely produced until after 1950. Similarly, the plays of Ramón del Valle-Inclán (1869–1936), perhaps because of their similarity to Absurdist drama, have only recently come to the fore. Valle-Inclán, noted primarily as a novelist, wrote several verse plays, satirical dramas, and farces, of which the best is probably *The Farce of the True Spanish Queen* (1920), a biting satire on the reign of Isabel II.

A new spirit began to enter Spanish literature with the "Generation of '27," a group which blossomed especially after censorship was eased under the second Republic, proclaimed in 1931. Of the new dramatists, the most significant were Lorca and Casona. Federico García Lorca (1899–1936) wrote his first play, *The Butterfly's Crime,* in 1920. After its failure, he retired to Granada, where he cultivated his interests in Symbolism, Surrealism, music, painting, and Spanish folklore, and wrote a number of puppet plays. After his *Mariana Pineda* was performed in Barcelona in 1927 by Margarita Xirgu (1888–   ), one of Spain's outstanding actresses, Lorca resumed an active interest in the theatre. Between 1930 and 1936, he wrote most of his major works, notably *The Shoemaker's Prodigious Wife* (1930), *Blood Wedding* (1933), *Yerma* (1934), and *The House of Bernarda Alba* (1935). Blending poetic imagery with primitive passions, these plays are usually considered the finest Spanish works since the Golden Age. Much of Lorca's writing was stimulated by his experience with La Barraca, a theatre group composed of university students and subsidized by the government under its program to bring cultural events to the people. Formed in 1932, La Barraca played Golden Age dramas to rural audiences, and it was the enthusiastic response of these unsophisticated spectators that influenced Lorca to turn to similar themes of love and honor.

In many ways, the career of Alejandro Casona (1903–1966) paralleled that of Lorca. Between 1931 and 1936, he too directed a government-sponsored troupe, The People's Theatre, which toured Spanish villages. Casona's troupe played primarily short, humorous plays, but like Lorca, Casona was inspired by his experiences to write for this audience. *The Siren Washed Ashore* (1934) and *The Devil Again* (1935) show that blend of realism and fantasy for which Casona was to be noted. In all his works an air of optimism suggests that human problems can be solved.

The Civil War of 1936 brought profound changes. Lorca was killed and Casona emigrated to Argentina. Until 1939 the theatre served primarily as an instrument of propaganda for both sides of the conflict, while the victory of Franco's forces was followed by severe censorship. The plays of Lorca, Casona, and Unamuno were forbidden, and the Spanish theatre entered another period of isolation.

Theatre and Drama in France, 1915–45

The First World War severely curtailed theatrical activities in France. Practically all able-bodied actors were inducted and others spent much of their time performing for the armed forces. The Parisian companies were so depleted that even the Comédie Française had to fill out casts with students from the Conservatoire. The wartime mood turned the theatre toward popular entertainment, a direction which continued to dominate the "Boulevard theatres" after the war. Of the Boulevard producers, the most successful was probably Sacha Guitry (1885–1957), author of about 150 plays, most of which he produced, directed, and starred in.

At the opposite extreme, a series of revolts against tradition—Fauvism, Cubism, Orphism, Futurism, Rayonnism, Suprematism, Constructivism, Dadaism, and Surrealism—helped to break the hold of Realism and to turn attention to new forms. During the war many artists and political dissenters sought refuge in Switzerland, where Dadaism, the most extreme of the revolts, was launched in 1917 by Tristan Tzara (1896–1963). The name, Dada (or "hobbyhorse"), chosen because of its meaninglessness, is indicative of the essentially negative approach of the movement, which sought primarily to show the uselessness of all previous endeavors, including literature itself. Although a few theatrical performances were given, little was gained beyond notoriety.

Dadaism was succeeded by Surrealism, which took a relatively positive approach. The Surrealists drew their inspiration in literature from the works of Jarry and Apollinaire. Guillaume Apollinaire (1880–1918), friend to almost all *avant-garde* writers and painters after 1900 and the principal spokesman for Cubism, influenced Surrealism largely through his play, *The Breasts of Tiresias* (1903, revised and produced in 1917), subtitled a "drame surréaliste." Purporting to be a plea for the repopulation of France, the play concerns Thérèse, who after releasing her breasts (balloons, which float away) is transformed into Tiresias, soon the parent of 40,049 children. This work exemplifies many of Apollinaire's theories; he rejected everyday logic and suggested that comedy, tragedy, burlesque, fantasy, acrobatics, and declamation should be mingled with music, dance, color, and light to create a new form of expression.

André Breton (1896–1966) gradually assumed leadership of the Surrealists and issued the movement's first "manifesto" in 1924. Freud's considerable influence upon Breton is evident in his definition of Surrealism as "pure psychic automatism, by which is intended to express, verbally, in writing, or by other means, the real process of thought. Thought's dictation, in the absence of all control exercised by the reason and outside all esthetic or moral preoccupation." Thus, the subconscious mind in a dreamlike state represented for Breton the basis of artistic truth. After his conversion to Communism in 1926, Breton sought to make Surrealism more militant, and his second manifesto (1930) denounced many of the movement's former members. Thereafter, Surrealism declined, although its crowning achievement did not come until 1938, when an international exhibition of painting demonstrated the movement's considerable accomplishments.

Surrealism's impact on the theatre was essentially indirect. The most effective uses of its techniques were made by Jean Cocteau (1892–1963), who began his theatrical work with *Parade* (1917), a ballet staged by the Ballets Russes, and *The Ox on the Roof* (1920), a pantomime performed by the Fratellini family of circus clowns. His finest plays, *Antigone* (1922), *Orpheus* (1926), and *The Infernal Machine* (1934), based on the Oedipus legend, are reworkings of myths. Cocteau's power came in part from the manner in which he juxtaposed the familiar with the legendary. For example, in *Orpheus* the protagonists are a modern young married couple, but the introduction of a mysterious glazier and a horse who delivers messages evokes a sense of mystery and significance, by means of which the ancient myth is given contemporary relevance. Although Cocteau never escaped the charge of charlatanism, he was a source of inspiration to other artists throughout his life.

Many of the new movements in the visual arts came into the theatre through the Ballets Russes, which commissioned settings from Picasso, Matisse, Juan Gris, Marie Laurencin, and Braque. The Ballets Suédois, which played in Paris between 1920 and 1925 under the direction of Rolf de Maré (1888–1964), also commissioned settings from Léger, de Chirico, and Picabia. This company extended the traditional conceptions of ballet as well through such works as Cocteau's *The Married Couple of the Eiffel Tower* (1921), in which dialogue was spoken by phonographs.

Of all the *avant-garde* figures between the wars, Antonin Artaud (1896–1948) was to be the most important. Associated with the theatre from 1921, Artaud had worked with Lugné-Poë, Dullin, and Pitoëff before founding the Théâtre Alfred Jarry in 1927 in association with Roger Vitrac. Devoted entirely to non-realistic drama, this theatre lasted only two seasons. Artaud's significant contributions were to be made after 1931, when the stimulation of a Balinese dance troupe at the Colonial Exposition in Paris motivated him to formulate his theory of the theatre, published in 1938 as *The Theatre and Its Double*.

Artaud divided men into two groups: the primitive and the civilized. He argued that because the theatre of the Western world has been dominated entirely by the second group, it has been increasingly devoted to the logical depiction of sociological or psychological problems; a theatre of "words," it seeks merely to solve a conflict or elucidate a character. Artaud stated that the "true" theatre, the Eastern (for which that of the Western world is only a "double"), is based upon prelogical, nonverbal, and incantatory experience. To replace the Western pattern, Artaud called for a "theatre of cruelty," which would disrupt the spectators' logically-controlled equilibrium and free their subconscious minds so that they might glimpse once more the mysterious sources of existence. He wished to create a theatre of magic and myth which would ruthlessly expose man's inner anxieties so that their expulsion might allow him to commune more deeply, both with himself and his fellow beings.

Artaud believed that reforms must begin with the *mise-en-scène,* in which he included all visual and aural elements. The production itself was to become the work of art for which the verbal text served merely as a pattern of incantation. By insisting that all theatrical elements play a significant role, Artaud sought to arrive at "total theatre" rather than an embellished verbal text. In many ways, Artaud's theories were extensions of Craig's. Both had the same basic attitudes about the various theatrical elements, but Craig merely sought to create a kind of ideal beauty, whereas Artaud wished to expand man's consciousness. Consequently, as Craig has become increasingly remote from contemporary preoccupations, Artaud has appeared increasingly relevant.

Somewhere between the commercial and *avant-garde* figures were Gémier, Hébertot, and Copeau. Firmin Gémier (1869–1933) began his acting career with Antoine in 1892 and later worked with groups ranging from the Théâtre de l'Oeuvre to melodrama troupes. Perhaps for this reason, Gémier was to follow an eclectic approach not unlike that of Reinhardt. From 1906 until 1922 he served as director of the Théâtre Antoine, and from 1922 until 1930 as director of the Odéon. Under Gémier, the Odéon became almost an *avant-garde* theatre, in part because his designer, René Fuerst, drew upon practically all of the recent movements. Despite Gémier's fine work as a director, his significance probably lies in his continuing attempts to bring the theatre to all the people.

The desire to make cultural activities available to the common man had led in the 1890's to the Volksbühnes of Germany and the less ambitious "people's theatres" of France. In 1903, Romain Rolland's *The Theatre of the People* outlined a program under which local groups would perform plays for their fellow citizens as in Greek times. Attracted by this

GÉMIER'S PRODUCTION of *Oedipe, Roi de Thebes* at the Cirque d'Hiver in 1919.
[From *L'Éclair* (1919)]

movement, Gémier sought to make the best professional productions available to provincial audiences through his Théâtre Ambulant, which between 1911 and 1914 toured through France with a tent theatre. In 1920, Gémier persuaded the government to create the Théâtre National Populaire. Given only a token subsidy, Gémier had to rely on other companies to contribute occasional productions to the TNP. Although it never became a significant force during Gémier's lifetime, the TNP was to become one of France's finest theatres after the Second World War. Gémier's interests in a popular theatre also led him into other experiments. In 1919 he took over the Cirque d'Hiver, where he staged *Oedipus* and a nativity play, *La Grande Pastorale*. In this and other ways, Gémier's work in France paralleled that of Reinhardt in Germany.

Jacques Hébertot (1886–) exerted his primary influence as an entrepreneur. In his three contiguous theatres, the Théâtre des Champs-Elysées, the Comédie des Champs-Elysées, and the Studio des Champs-Elysées, he employed the most imaginative directors of his age. Furthermore, he imported such companies as the Moscow Art Theatre, the Kamerny, and others. Thus, Hébertot made the best of both domestic and foreign theatre available to the Parisian public.

The most pervasive influence on the theatre between the wars was exerted by Jacques Copeau, who in 1919 reopened the Vieux Colombier

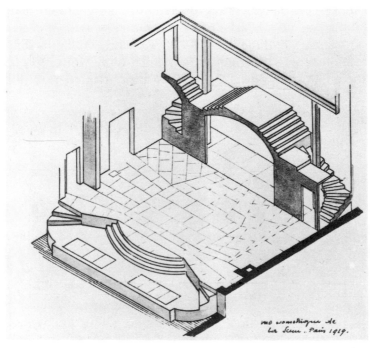

ISOMETRIC PLAN of Copeau's Vieux Colombier, 1919. [From Moussinac, *New Movement in the Theatre*]

and rededicated himself to the ideals he had set forth before the war. Unlike Gémier, Copeau thought it impossible to maintain high standards while appealing to the masses. Consequently, he was often accused of snobbism and of treating the theatre as a religion. Eventually, Copeau found it difficult to reconcile his standards with a full schedule of public performances; in 1924 he left Paris to open a school in Burgundy, where he hoped to perfect his ideas.

THE STAGE at the Vieux Colombier in use. Note that the basic structure is only partially disguised. [From Moussinac, *New Movement in the Theatre*]

Although Copeau performed for only five years, his ideals were to be continued by four other producers—Jouvet, Dullin, Pitoëff, and Baty—who dominated the Parisian theatre until the Second World War. In 1927, they formed an alliance, commonly called the Cartel des Quatre, under which they agreed to counsel each other, to share publicity, and to negotiate jointly with theatrical unions.

Louis Jouvet (1887–1951) began his career in Rouché's Théâtre des Arts, where he met Copeau, for whom he acted minor roles in 1913–14. Accompanying Copeau to New York in 1917, he remained with him until 1922 when Hébertot employed him as a director. After achieving a major success with Romains' *Dr. Knock* in 1923, Jouvet formed his own company in 1924, taking into it many members of Copeau's recently disbanded troupe. Jouvet did not prosper, however, until 1928, when he began his collaboration with Giraudoux. In 1934, he moved his company to the Théâtre de l'Athenée, a boulevard house, where he remained until 1941, after which he went into voluntary exile until 1945. Jouvet, like Copeau, put primary emphasis upon the text. Above all, he respected language and its nuances. He demanded lucid analysis and careful attention to detail from his actors. In the early years, he designed his own scenery, which was always tasteful without being innovative. At the l'Athenée, he usually worked with Christian Berard (1902–1949), one of the finest designers of the period.

Charles Dullin (1885–1949) had played at many minor theatres before joining Rouché and then Copeau. After returning to Paris in 1919, he worked for Gémier before establishing his own theatre, l'Atelier, in 1922. He remained in this small, out-of-the-way theatre until 1939. Dullin was extremely eclectic, presenting works ranging from the Greeks to the present and from tragedy to farce. Through painstaking analysis of the text, he sought to let each play dictate the proper approach to it. His aim was to capture the "inner poetry" through honesty and unity. He refused to do any play which he thought depended upon machinery or upon a director's

BÉRARD'S SETTING for Jouvet's production in 1937 of Molière's *School for Wives*. [From *Décor de Théâtre dans le Monde depuis 1935*]

tricks. Nevertheless, he put considerable emphasis upon visual design and employed some of the best artists of his time: Louis Touchagues, Lucien Coutaud, Georges Valmier, Jean-Victor Hugo, Michel Duran, and André Barsacq. Dullin's perennial hope of attracting a wider audience led him in 1941 to become director of the Théâtre Sarah Bernhardt, where he struggled along until 1947. His last years were spent in Geneva as director of the theatre section of the Maison des Arts. Dullin's impact on the theatre came in part through his school, in which such significant later figures as Barrault and Vilar received their early training.

616

André Barsacq's setting for Dullin's production of *Volpone*, 1929. [From *Décor de Théâtre dans le Monde depuis 1935*]

Georges Pitoëff (1884–1939) had performed widely in his native Russia before emigrating to Switzerland in 1914. He and his wife, Ludmilla (1896–1951), who had studied at the Conservatoire, came to Paris in 1922 and worked for Hébertot until 1925, after which they formed their own company and played in a number of Parisian theatres and toured abroad. Pitoëff was noted for his knowledge of foreign drama, of which he was the principal producer in France. As a director, Pitoëff placed primary emphasis upon the text. For him, the most powerful element was perhaps rhythm, which he sought to find and project for each character and scene. He designed his own scenery, which ranged stylistically from the abstract to the realistically pictorial. Characteristically, however, he used a few indispensable set pieces which he invested with symbolic significance. Of all the members of the Cartel, Pitoëff was probably the most versatile and experimental.

Gaston Baty (1882–1951) was the only member of the Cartel who was not an actor and who did not place primary emphasis upon the text. He began his career under Gémier in 1919, managed the Studio des Champs-Elysées for Hébertot from 1924 to 1928, and then settled in the Théâtre Montparnasse in 1930. After 1935, Baty became interested in marionettes, as a result of which his productions became increasingly stylized. Through much of his career, Baty was assisted by Marguerite Jamois (1903–1964),

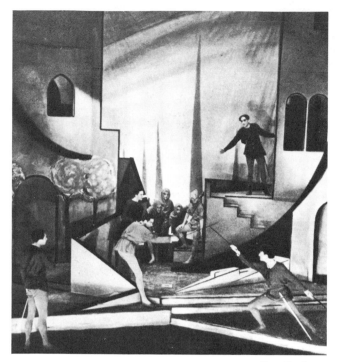

PITOËFF'S PRODUCTION of *Romeo and Juliet*. [From *Theatre Arts* (1935)]

who starred in many of his productions and directed others. To Baty, the director was the major theatrical artist. In his productions a mysterious and poetic world, created by the skillful manipulation of mood, seemed to lurk behind the surface. His emphasis upon costumes, scenery, properties, music, and lighting was sometimes criticized, but he was also called the "magician of the *mise-en-scéne.*"

The influence of Copeau was reenforced in the 1930's by several new groups. In 1930, students from Copeau's school formed the Compagnie des Quinze under the direction of Michel Saint-Denis (1897–), Copeau's nephew. From 1931 to 1933, they played at the Vieux Colombier. After the company disbanded, Saint-Denis opened the Theatre Studio in London, which, in combination with his directing work at the Old Vic and else-where, served to carry Copeau's influence into the British theatre. Léon Chancerel (1886–), another of Copeau's students, worked primarily with student groups in schools and universities and with children's theatre. His Compagnie des Comédiens-Routiers (1929–1939) played primarily for Boy Scout groups, while his Théâtre de l'Oncle Sébastien (1935–1939) presented plays for children.

Three other directors, Barsacq, Dasté, and Jacquemont, were also to be of considerable importance. André Barsacq (1909–) had studied at the

BATY'S PRODUCTION of his own adaptation of *Madame Bovary* (1936). The actors are Lucien Nat and Marguerite Jamois. [From *Theatre Arts* (1936)]

School of Decorative Arts and with Dullin before becoming one of Paris' leading scene designers. In 1937, he joined with Dasté and Jacquemont to form the Compagnie des Quatre Saisons, but left in 1940 to assume control of the Atelier when Dullin relinquished it. Barsacq has continued to direct that theatre, maintaining Dullin's high standards. Jean Dasté (1904–), Copeau's son-in-law and pupil, was a member of the Compagnie des Quinze before joining the Compagnie des Quatre Saisons. In 1940, he went with Barsacq to the Atelier, where he was one of the theatre's principal directors. Maurice Jacquemont (1910–) was trained by Chancerel and had worked with several companies before the formation of the Compagnie des Quatre Saisons, with which he continued until 1942. In 1944 he became head of the Studio des Champs-Elysées, a position he was to hold until 1960.

Copeau returned to a more active role in the theatre during the 1930's. In addition to directing both in Paris and abroad, he was associated with the Comédie Française after 1936 and served as its director in 1939–40 until dismissed by the Vichy government. Under Emile Fabré's direction between 1915 and 1936, the Comédie Française had steadily declined, in large part because of the low subsidy and political interference. After 1936, the new director, Édouard Bourdet, was able to make many improvements. Not only was the subsidy doubled, but Bourdet imported Copeau, Dullin, Jouvet, and Baty to direct several revivals. For the first time, each play's director was listed on the Comédie Française's programs. By the time the war began, the prestige of the company was fully revived. In spite of the company's conservative nature before 1936, it included some of the best actors in France: Béatrix Dussane (1888–), Berthe Bovy (1888–), André Brunot (1879–), Charles Grandval (1882–1943), Pierre Fresnay (1897–), Marie Bell (1900–), and Madeleine Renaud (1903–).

Although France produced few truly outstanding playwrights between the wars, a number achieved considerable renown. Henri-René Lenormand (1882–1951) was one of the first French writers to emphasize the subconscious mind through such works as *Time is a Dream* (1919) and *The Eater of Dreams* (1922). Henri Ghéon (1875–1944) sought to revive religious drama and for many years toured with his Compagnons de Notre-Dame. Of his approximately 100 plays, the best known are *The Poor Under the Stairs* (1921) and *Christmas in the Market Place* (1935). André Obey (1892–) was associated with the Compagnie des Quinze, which produced his first plays, *Noah* and *The Rape of Lucrece* in 1931. Perhaps his best work is found in *Man of Ashes* (1949), a retelling of the Don Juan Story. Armand Salacrou (1899–) was one of the most versatile dramatists of the period, ranging through surrealist fantasies, light comedy, drama, and historical drama. He came to public attention with *Patchouli* (1927), and did his best work with *The World is Round* (1935), a history in miniature of the struggle between the flesh and the spirit.

Of the satirical writers, the best were Jules Romains (1885–), whose *Doctor Knock, or the Triumph of Medicine* (1923) shows the exploitation of man's anxieties about his health, and Marcel Pagnol (1895–), whose *The Merchants of Glory* (1925) satirizes the business schemes built around the war dead, and *Topaze* (1928), the story of a schoolmaster who prospers only after he abandons his principles. Pagnol is now better known for his romantic trilogy about Marseilles waterfront life, *Marius* (1929), *Fanny* (1931), and *César* (1937). Surrealistic farce was exploited by Fernand Crommelynck (1888–), whose *The Magnificent Cuckold* (1921) tells of a man who, upon becoming suspicious of his wife's fidelity, insists on testing it endlessly but never to his satisfaction; and Roger Vitrac (1901–), who derided all traditional values in *Victor, or Children in Power* (1928) and *The Secret Hawker* (1936). Vitrac's reputation has grown considerably since 1963, when *Roger* was revived in Paris to critical acclaim. Marcel Achard (1901–) excelled in stylized romantic comedy, notably *Voulez-Vous Jouer avec Moâ?* (1923), *Jean de la Lune* (1929), and *The Pirate* (1938), in which, typically, a devoted lover subdues the frivolity of a coquette. The most bitter plays of the period were written by Steve Passeur (1899–), who delighted in reversing the normal pattern of relationships. In his most famous play, *The Woman Buys* (1930), a woman buys a husband and subjects him to a daily round of torment until they hate each other.

The plays of the Belgian dramatist Michel de Ghelderode (1898–1962) resemble those of Apollinaire and Cocteau, while his theories of the theatre are not unlike those of Artaud. His scorn for traditional dramaturgy is shown in the labels he applied to his works: "tragic farce," "burlesque mystery," and "tragedy for the music hall." Most of his plays show the failure of a world devoid of faith. Of his many dramas, the best known are *Escurial* (1927), *Chronicles of Hell* (1929), *Pantagleize* (1929), and *Hop, Signor* (1938). Since 1949, when he came to the attention of the Absurdists, Ghelderode's reputation has steadily risen.

Probably the most important French dramatist between the wars was Jean Giraudoux (1882–1944), a novelist and member of the Foreign Service, who in 1928 began his theatrical career with a dramatization of his novel *Siegfried*. In Jouvet, Giraudoux found his ideal interpreter and for

JOUVET'S PRODUCTION of Giraudoux's *The Trojan War Shall Not Take Place.* Jouvet is seen at the right. [From *Theatre Arts* (1936)]

him he wrote most of his important works: *Amphitryon 38* (1929), *Judith* (1931), *The Trojan War Shall Not Take Place* (1935), and *The Mad-woman of Chaillot* (1945). Giraudoux often took his subjects from familiar sources but gave them novel interpretations, for he delighted in pointing out the simple in the complex and the surprising in the familiar. All of his works are characterized by a precise intellectual stance, richly poetic diction, gentle irony, and freedom from clichés. Through them all runs a faith in man, who is considered a failure only when he will not be guided by love.

621

Giraudoux's position of preeminence was to be assumed after the war by Jean Anouilh (1910–), who began as Jouvet's secretary and turned to writing in 1932 under Giraudoux's inspiration. His first success came in 1937 with *Traveller Without Baggage*, presented by Pitoëff. Most of Anouilh's later works, such as *Carnival of Thieves* (1938), *Rendezvous in Senlis* (1941), and *Antigone* (1943), were produced by Barsacq. Anouilh has divided his plays into the serious, or "black" pieces, and the comic, or "red" pieces. In the former, typically a young, idealistic, and uncompromising hero is able to maintain his integrity only by choosing death. *Antigone* is perhaps the best-known example. In the "red" plays, although the characters are in many ways similar, a fairy-tale atmosphere permits a happier resolution. Anouilh was to be one of France's most prolific postwar writers.

With the coming of war in 1939 and the surrender of Paris to the Nazis, theatrical activities were seriously curtailed. Most of the major figures went into exile, while those that remained worked under constant surveillance. For the most part, the theatre was reduced to politically inoffensive plays or popular entertainments.

English Theatre and Drama, 1915–45

The First World War brought major changes to the English theatre. With it, the actor-manager system virtually disappeared, to be replaced by the commercial producer and the long-run. During the war, popular entertainment dominated the stage. Tree's theatre, for example, the home of Shakespeare since 1900, was now given over to *Chu Chin Chow*, a musical version of *Ali Baba and the Forty Thieves*. It ran for 2238 performances.

Probably the most significant occurrence of the war years was the emergence of the "Old Vic" as the principal producer of English classics. Built in 1818 as the Royal Coburg and later renamed the Royal Victoria, the Old Vic was taken over in 1880 by Emma Cons, a social reformer, who converted it into a "temperance Music Hall." In 1898, Miss Cons' niece, Lilian Baylis (1874–1937), became manager of the theatre and began to present operas. It was not until 1914, however, that Shakespearean plays were added. During the war years, the repertory was under the direction of Ben Greet (1857–1936), who, in the tradition of Frank Benson, had long been performing Shakespearean works for both English and American audiences.

After the war, Greet was succeeded by Robert Atkins (1886–) from

1920 to 1925, Andrew Leigh (1887–1957) until 1929, and Harcourt Williams (1880–) until 1934. In 1931, the Old Vic acquired the Sadler's Wells Theatre, and a ballet company was formed under the direction of Ninette de Valois (Edris Stannis, 1898–), who had been trained in the Diaghilev company and later established her own school. Between 1931 and 1935, the opera and ballet company and the dramatic company alternated between the Old Vic and Sadler's Wells every two weeks. When this arrangement became too cumbersome, drama was confined to the Old Vic, and opera and ballet to Sadler's Wells. The Sadler's Wells Ballet Company was to become the finest in England, and was rechristened the Royal Ballet after the Second World War.

When Miss Baylis died in 1937, it was feared that the Old Vic would close, but Tyrone Guthrie (1900–) was appointed administrator and operated it with distinction until 1945. Guthrie had made his debut as an actor in 1924, but had soon turned to directing. His first London production came in 1931, but his finest prewar work was done with the Old Vic. As a director, Guthrie was noted for his novel interpretations of standard works (sometimes considered merely bizarre by critics), and the restless

TYRONE GUTHRIE'S PRODUCTION of *Twelfth Night* at the Old Vic in 1933. [From *Theatre Arts* (1933)]

and vital quality of movement. By 1939, the Old Vic was the most respected troupe in England. With its own theatre, a permanent company, and a policy of producing the finest plays at reasonable prices, it set a standard for the entire country.

Several other producers in London helped to raise the level of performance between the wars. Among these, the most important were the Lyric Theatre, the Gate Theatre, and the Mercury Theatre. The Lyric Theatre, Hammersmith, one of the many houses built in the suburbs during the heyday of music halls, had fallen upon hard times when Nigel Playfair (1874–1934) leased it in 1918. Although Playfair presented many kinds of plays, his reputation rests upon his productions of Restoration and 18th century works, most notably *The Beggar's Opera* (which opened in 1920 for a run of 1463 performances), *The Way of the World* (1924), *The Rivals* (1925), *The Beaux' Stratagem* (1927), and *Love in a Village* (1928). Most of his productions were decorative, gay, stylized caricatures. For a time, the Lyric was the most fashionable theatre in London, but as Playfair's approach hardened into a formula, popularity declined, and in 1932 the company was dissolved. The Lyric was noted above all for its sense of style, first established by Claud Lovat Fraser (1890–1921), whose sensitive use of color and period motifs profoundly influenced others.

FARQUHAR's *The Beaux' Stratagem* at the Lyric Theatre, Hammersmith. Edith Evans appears as Mrs. Sullen. [From *Theatre Arts* (1930)]

The Gate Theatre was opened in 1925 by Peter Godfrey, a former circus clown and Shakespearean actor. Unable to secure a license for the only hall he could afford, Godfrey ran his theatre as a private club. In nine years, he produced over 350 plays. His most characteristic productions were of Expressionist plays or those with a psychoanalytic bias. Using set pieces against black drapes, unusual lighting effects, and stylized acting techniques, Godfrey was the principal exponent of Expressionism in London. In 1934, the Gate Theatre passed to Norman Marshall (1901–   ), who presented many works forbidden by the censor. He also did much to reestablish the intimate revue, which had declined since the 1920's. The theatre closed in 1940.

The Mercury Theatre was established in 1931 as the Ballet Club and was licensed as a public theatre in 1933 to Ashley Dukes (1885–1959), who emphasized poetic drama at a time when commercial managers were uninterested in it. Closely associated with Dukes was E. Martin Browne (1900–   ), who continued the theatre into the 1940's.

Of the several important groups outside of London, perhaps the best was the Birmingham Repertory Company, which, under Barry Jackson's direction between 1913 and 1935, produced about 400 plays ranging through the entire history of drama. Between 1922 and 1934, Jackson also presented 42 plays in London, many remarkably successful despite their departure from commercial formulas. Through his productions of *Hamlet* (1925), *Macbeth* (1928), and *Taming of the Shrew* (1928), Jackson began the vogue for playing Shakespeare in modern dress. When Jackson transferred his theatre to the City of Birmingham in 1935, it became England's first civic theatre.

Jackson also founded the Malvern Festival in 1929, the beginning of the summer festival movement. Operated primarily by the Birmingham Repertory Company until 1939, the Malvern Festival had no clear policy, some seasons being devoted to plays of a particular era, others to plays by specific authors. All, however, were of high quality. The festival was discontinued between 1939 and 1949.

Two other provincial troupes—the Cambridge Festival Theatre and the Oxford Repertory Company—were outstanding. The Cambridge Festival Theatre was established by Terence Gray (1895–   ) in 1926 with the avowed purpose of undermining realistic acting and production, a policy that was followed consistently. The theatre had no curtain, proscenium arch, or orchestra pit. Scenery normally consisted of ramps or other constructions set against a cyclorama, upon which patterns of light were projected. The actors' movement was often described as "choreographic" and was always highly stylized. Gray thought the text an excuse for a director's improvisations. He performed *Romeo and Juliet* in flamenco costumes; put characters in *Twelfth Night* on roller skates; and had the Judge in *The Merchant of Venice* play with a yo-yo. Gray's productions

Gammer Gurton's Needle at the Malvern
Festival. Setting by Paul Shelving. [From
Theatre Arts (1933)]

generated much controversy but had little immediate result, although
Guthrie has said that they were a major influence upon his work. The
theatre closed in 1933.

The Oxford Repertory Company, headed by J. B. Fagan (1873–1933)
from 1923 to 1929, presented 21 plays a year drawn from many countries
and periods. The schedule meant that productions were often rough, but

TERENCE GRAY'S PRODUCTION of *The Famous History of
King Henry VIII* at the Festival Theatre, Cambridge, 1931.
[From Moussinac, *New Movement in the Theatre*]

all had vitality and clear interpretations. Little scenery was used, for the theatre had only a small stage fronted by a large apron, upon which most of the action transpired. The importance of this company rests in part upon the many young actors, most notably Tyrone Guthrie, John Gielgud, Raymond Massey, Flora Robson, and Glen Byam Shaw, who received their first major experience under Fagan.

The Stratford-on-Avon seasons of Shakespeare's plays also gained in prestige after they resumed in 1919. Until 1934, most of the plays were directed by W. Bridges-Adams (1889–), who worked under adverse conditions. There were no shop or storage facilities, the Festival Committee controlled policy, and six plays were opened on six successive evenings. After the old theatre burned in 1926, the company played in a motion picture house until the present building was completed in 1932. Although the new auditorium was satisfactory, the stage was a conventional picture-frame structure; its sliding platform stages could not move entirely out of sight and the elevator stages only sank eight feet. Such blunders have required several remodelings. Bridges-Adams resigned in 1934 and was succeeded until 1942 by B. Iden Payne (1881–), whose productions were in the style of Poel, using an Elizabethan structure and Elizabethan costumes. Other directors, most notably Theodore Kommissarzhevsky, brought novel conceptions to the plays. Kommissarzhevsky's production of *The Merchant of Venice* utilized *commedia dell'arte* conventions and his *The Merry Wives of Windsor* was given a Viennese background. London critics largely ignored the Stratford company, which did not achieve its current critical stature until after the Second World War.

The little theatre movement burgeoned in England after the First World War. The British Drama League, founded in 1919 and headed by Geoffrey Whitworth (1883–1951) until 1948, organized conferences, sent out costumes and properties, aided in play selection, and held annual festivals of plays. Although many of these groups did excellent work, none equaled the quality achieved by Nugent Monck (1877–) at the Madder-market Theatre in Norwich, noted throughout England for its high level of performance.

During this period many performers of high merit appeared. Of the actresses, the best were probably Sybil Thorndike (1882–) and Edith Evans (1888–). Miss Thorndike began her career in Ben Greet's company and after 1914 acted often with the Old Vic troupe. She was especially noted in the 1920's for her portrayal of Shaw's Saint Joan, although her performances ranged from Greek tragedy to modern comedy. Miss Evans began her career with Poel and gained fame as Millamant in the Lyric Theatre's production of *The Way of the World*. She also appeared frequently with the Old Vic, at the Malvern Festival, and in many London commercial theatres. Other outstanding actresses included Lilian Braithwaite (1873–1948), Marie Tempest (1864–1942), Flora Robson (1902–),

Gertrude Lawrence (1898–1952), and Peggy Ashcroft (1907–), who would be of greater significance after 1945.

Of the actors, the most important was John Gielgud (1904–), who made his debut in 1921 and won major acclaim with Hamlet in 1934. He soon became one of England's major directors as well. In 1937–38, he leased the Queen's Theatre, assembled a company which included Peggy Ashcroft, Michael Redgrave, and Alec Guinness, and produced a repertory of classics. By the time the war began, Gielgud was accepted as England's finest actor. Other outstanding performers included Cedric Hardwicke (1893–1964), who worked closely with Barry Jackson after 1922, Donald Wolfit (1902–), who played at the Old Vic, Stratford, and with his own company, and Maurice Evans (1901–), who played for Terence Gray and the Old Vic before emigrating to America in 1935. A number of young men, who would be of greater importance after the war, also established their promise: Laurence Olivier (1907–), who had played with the Birmingham Repertory Company, Gielgud, and the Old Vic, Michael Redgrave (1908–), on the stage after 1934, Ralph Richardson (1902–), Alec Guinness (1914–), who made his debut in 1934, Anthony Quayle (1913–), on the stage after 1931, and Glen Byam Shaw (1904–), who played with the Oxford Repertory Company and Gielgud.

Few major dramatists emerged between the wars, although a number of older ones, such as Shaw, Barrie, Galsworthy, Pinero, and Ervine, continued to write. During the 1920's, three authors—Maugham, Lonsdale, and Coward—excelled in sophisticated comedy. Somerset Maugham (1874–1965) wrote his first play in 1904 and until 1933 was one of England's most prolific playwrights. His major achievement came with his comedies of manners, *Our Betters* (1917), *The Circle* (1921), *The Constant Wife* (1927), and *The Breadwinner* (1930), in which sardonic humor and unusual personal outlooks never descended into trite happy endings. Often compared with Maugham, Frederick Lonsdale (1881–1954) drew a wide following with his amusing situations and effective dialogue in *The Last of Mrs. Cheyney* (1925), *On Approval* (1927), and *The High Road* (1929). Noel Coward (1899–) captured the spirit of the postwar era with such works as *Fallen Angels* (1925), *Hay Fever* (1925), *Bitter Sweet* (1929), *Private Lives* (1930), and *Design for Living* (1932), in which unconventional behavior was combined with sophisticated wit.

Of the serious writers, J. B. Priestley (1894–) gained the greatest prestige. He began his dramatic career in 1932 with *Dangerous Corner* and went on to *Time and the Conways* (1937) and *An Inspector Calls* (1946). Although he wrote many kinds of plays, Priestley is most noted for his compression or distortion of time to illuminate characters and ideas. Of the sentimental and melodramatic school, Emlyn Williams (1905–) was perhaps the most successful. After writing two sensational plays, *A Murder has Been Arranged* (1930) and *Night Must Fall* (1935), he presented *The*

LAURENCE OLIVIER, Edith Evans and John Gielgud in Gielgud's production of *Romeo and Juliet*. [From *Theatre Arts* (1936)]

Corn is Green (1938), a sentimental story about a Welsh teacher and her star pupil.

This period also brought several attempts to revive poetic drama. Gordon Bottomley (1874–1948) wrote *King Lear's Wife* (1915), *Britain's Daughters* (1922), and *Laodice and Danae* (1930), and W. H. Auden (1907–) and Christopher Isherwood (1904–) collaborated on *The Dog Beneath the Skin* (1935) and *The Ascent of F6* (1936). The most lasting achievement was that of T. S. Eliot (1888–1965) with *Murder in the Cathedral* (1935), the story of Thomas à Becket's martyrdom. Eliot went on to write *The Family Reunion* (1939) and, after the war, several other verse plays. In general, however, the attempt to revive poetic drama was ineffective, primarily because of shortcomings in the plays rather than because of any opposition to poetry.

The revue was one of the most popular theatrical forms between the wars. C. B. Cochran (1873–1951), its most famous producer, began his work with "initimate revues" in 1914 and then turned to large-scale, lavish productions between 1918 and 1931. André Charlot (1882–) also presented many revues between 1916 and 1923, bringing Beatrice Lillie (1898–) to fame. The intimate revue was revived at the Gate Theatre in the 1930's, especially through the writing of Herbert Farjeon (1887–1945) and the performances of Hermione Gingold (1897–).

By far the most important Irish dramatist between the wars was Sean O'Casey (1884–1964), who turned attention away from folk and legendary subject matter to the urban life of his time. After three realistic works, *The Shadow of a Gunman* (1923), *Juno and the Paycock* (1924), and *The Plough and the Stars* (1926), O'Casey adopted Expressionistic techniques in such works as *The Silver Tassie* (1928), *Within the Gates* (1934), *Red Roses for Me* (1943), and *Purple Dust* (1945). His change of style precipitated a break with the Abbey Theatre in 1928, after which O'Casey lived in England. O'Casey's works have been more widely read than produced, largely because, in spite of many powerful scenes, the dramatic action is sometimes obscure. Nevertheless, his characterizations, vivid use of language, and human compassion make him one of the finest writers of modern times.

With the coming of the war in 1939, the English theatre was soon at a virtual standstill. At the height of the German blitz, only one theatre remained open in London. The Old Vic retreated to the provinces, Donald Wolfit organized lunch-time programs, and a few others attempted to keep the theatre alive, but for the most part English theatrical life was almost completely disrupted.

American Theatre and Drama, 1915–45

New trends in the theatre were slow in arriving in America, and few were naturalized until after 1915. Mrs. Fiske had won grudging acceptance of Ibsen's plays after 1900, and Arnold Daly (1875–1927) had played a two-month repertory of Shaw's works in 1905. A few short-lived and ineffectual "independent theatres," such as the Criterion Independent Theatre (1897–1900) in New York and the New Theatre (1906–1907) in Chicago, had been attempted.

Much of the impetus for change came from nonprofessional groups. Around 1912, several "little theatres" were established in emulation of the independent theatres of Europe. Among the most important of these were the Toy Theatre, opened by Mrs. Lyman Gale in Boston in 1912; the Chicago Little Theatre, formed by Maurice Brown in 1912; the Neighborhood Playhouse, established in New York by Irene and Alice Lewisohn in 1915; the Washington Square Players, formed in New York in 1915; the Provincetown Players, organized in Provincetown, Massachusetts, in 1915; and the Detroit Arts and Crafts Theatre, opened in 1916. By 1917 there were at least 50 of these groups. For the most part they depended upon unpaid volunteers for personnel and upon subscribers for financial support; most produced a series of plays each year, using techniques already widely accepted in Europe. The little theatre movement made its greatest contributions between 1912 and 1920 by preparing audiences to accept the new drama and production methods.

After 1920, the little theatres began to be indistinguishable from community theatres. Originating like its European counterpart in attempts to revive the spirit of ancient Greece, the community drama movement had begun in America around 1900. Its most ardent supporter was Percy Mackaye (1875–1956), whose *The Civic Theatre* (1912) and *Community Drama* (1917) outlined a program and whose outdoor pageants provided texts designed to involve several thousand participants. Interest in mass spectacles soon declined, however, and after 1920 most local groups turned to the performance of recent Broadway hits. By 1925, nearly 2000 community or little theatre companies were registered with the Drama League of America, an organization which encouraged local interest in drama. The number has continued to grow.

Drama programs also began to be introduced into colleges and universities. Although plays had been produced by students since the 17th century, no courses in theatre were offered until 1903, when George Pierce Baker (1866–1935) began to teach playwriting at Radcliffe College. Later opened to Harvard University students, the course was enlarged in 1913 to include a workshop for the production of plays. Baker attracted many of America's most talented young men, including Eugene O'Neill, S. N. Behrman, and Robert Edmund Jones, and instilled in them high standards as well as helping them to acquire skills. In 1925, Baker moved to Yale University where he established a drama department which was to provide professional training for many later theatre workers. In 1914 at the Carnegie Institute of Technology, Thomas Wood Stevens (1880–1942) instituted the country's first degree-granting program in theatre, and in 1918 Frederick Koch (1877–1944), founded the influential Carolina Playmakers. Many other programs soon followed. By 1945, theatre education was an accepted part of most American universities.

In the years following 1910, the "new stagecraft," as the European trends were called in America, began to find its way into the commercial theatre. Winthrop Ames (1871–1937), who had gone to Europe in 1907 to study new developments there, was employed in 1909 to manage the New Theatre in New York, an ambitious nonprofit repertory company. The large theatre soon proved both financially and artistically unsatisfactory. Ames then built the Little Theatre, seating only 300, where in the years preceding the First World War he presented a number of plays in the new style. In 1912, he imported Reinhardt's production of *Sumurun,* which also aroused much interest in European ideas.

In 1912, the Boston Opera Company hired Joseph Urban (1872–1933), a well-established Viennese designer of the new school, to mount its productions. Urban later worked in New York, where he was famous for the fresh coloring and simplicity of his settings. In 1915, the New Stage Society invited Harley Granville-Barker to direct a series of plays for its members. For Barker's production of *The Man who Married a Dumb Wife*, Robert Edmond Jones (1887–1954) provided settings usually considered the first native expression of the "new stagecraft." Jones was one of several young men, including Lee Simonson and Sam Hume, who had studied in Europe between 1912 and 1915 and had been impressed by the changing theatrical trends. In 1914, Hume arranged an exhibit of Continental scene design which was shown in New York, Detroit, Chicago, and Cleveland. Hume later was associated with the Detroit Arts and Crafts Theatre; here his associate, Sheldon Cheney (1886–) in 1916 launched *Theatre Arts Magazine,* which until 1948 was to be the principal disseminator of new ideas in America. Visits of the Abbey Theatre in 1911, the Ballets Russes in 1916, and Copeau's troupe from 1917 to 1919 also helped to stimulate interest in foreign movements.

ROBERT EDMOND JONES' DESIGN for Granville
Barker's production of *The Man Who Married
a Dumb Wife,* 1915. [From *The Theatre* (1915)]

Nevertheless, when the war ended in 1918 the American theatre was only beginning to be aware of European practices. The triumph of the new ideal owes most to the Provincetown Players, the Theatre Guild, and to Arthur Hopkins. After presenting a few programs on Cape Cod, the Provincetown Players moved to New York in 1916. In its early years, the company concentrated upon plays by American playwrights and by 1925 had presented 93 plays by 47 authors. After 1923, the group split into two branches. One continued the older practices, while the other, under Eugene O'Neill, Robert Edmond Jones, and Kenneth Macgowan, performed foreign and period plays along with the noncommercial works of O'Neill and others. Although it succumbed to financial pressures in 1929, the Provincetown Players had served an important role as an experimental theatre both for new plays and for new production techniques.

In 1918, the Washington Square Players became the Theatre Guild, a fully professional company, with the avowed purpose of presenting plays of merit not likely to interest commercial managers. After an uncertain beginning in 1919, it soon became America's most respected theatre, presenting a number of plays each year to an audience of subscribers. In 1928 it began to send out road companies as well. The Guild was governed by a Board of Directors, and usually maintained a nucleus of actors. During some years, a full company was employed by the season. The Guild adopted an eclectic approach to staging; its principal director, Philip Moeller (1880–1958) and designer, Lee Simonson (1888–1967), drew upon almost all of the European movements. During the 1930's the company gradually curtailed its activities, and by the time of the Second World War was merely another commercial producer investing in long-run hits.

In 1918 Arthur Hopkins (1878–1950) began a series of productions which were to mark him as the most adventurous of New York's commercial producers. Working with Robert Edmond Jones, Hopkins presented plays by Tolstoy, Ibsen, Gorky, Shakespeare, O'Neill, and others. In 1921, his production of *Macbeth* created a sensation with its expressionistic use of arches which tilted ever more precariously as the action moved toward its resolution and in 1922, *Hamlet*, starring John Barrymore (1882–1942), was declared one of the best productions of the century. After Hopkins and the Guild demonstrated the commercial viability of the "new stagecraft," it was gradually adopted by others and by 1930 had become the standard approach.

The "new stagecraft" was primarily a visual movement, for the total effect of most productions might best be described as "simplified realism." In addition to the work of Jones and Simonson, the major influence on scene design was Norman Bel Geddes (1893–1958), a visionary not unlike Appia. Geddes' plan for staging Dante's *The Divine Comedy* on a series of terraces (published in 1921) is still considered one of the most brilliant conceptions of any American designer. His penchant for steps, platforms and imaginative lighting is also seen in his productions of *Hamlet* (1931) and Werfel's *The Eternal Road* (1936), in which the platforms soared to a height of 50 feet. Other important designers included Cleon Throckmorton (1897–1965), Mordecai Gorelik (1899–), Boris Aronson (1900–), Aline Bernstein (1882—1955), Howard Bay (1912–), Donald Oenslager (1902), and Jo Mielziner (1901–), who was to be America's most prolific and respected designer after 1945. While all did not follow the same style, they shared a respect for simplicity and a desire to capture the spirit of a text.

ROBERT EDMOND JONES' SETTING for the banquet scene in *Macbeth,* Arthur Hopkins' production in 1921. Note the three masks suspended above the stage. [From *Theatre Arts* (1921)]

Continental influence continued to be felt in the 1920's through a series of visitors: the Moscow Art Theatre toured America in 1923–24; Reinhardt presented *The Miracle* (with designs by Geddes) in 1924 and staged a season of plays in 1927–28; and Copeau directed *The Brothers Karamazov* for the Theatre Guild in 1927. Two of Stanislavsky's actors, Richard Boleslavsky (1889–1937) and Maria Ouspenskaya (1881–1949), were induced to remain in America to run the American Laboratory Theatre between 1923 and 1930. Here the Stanislavsky system was taught in a version later popularized by Boleslavsky's book *Acting, the First Six Lessons* (1933). Among the more than 500 students who studied at the American Laboratory Theatre were Stella Adler, Lee Strasberg, and Harold Clurman.

Between 1925 and 1940 several groups tried to escape from the commercial pattern. From 1925 to 1930, Walter Hampden (1879–1955) revived the actor-manager system with his repertory company. Although the depression forced him to give up his theatre in New York, Hampden continued to tour with his troupe for many years. Between 1926 and 1933, Eva Le Gallienne (1899–) managed the Civic Repertory Theatre, produced 34 plays and built up a subscription list of 50,000. Despite its excellent repertory and wide following, the company was always in debt and could not survive the depression.

The most distinguished troupe of the 1930's was the Group Theatre,

NORMAN BEL GEDDES' PROJECT for staging
Dante's *The Divine Comedy*. [Courtesy
Hoblitzelle *Theatre Arts Library*, Uni-
versity of Texas]

launched in 1931 by Lee Strasberg (1901–   ), Harold Clurman (1901–   ),
and Cheryl Crawford (1902–   ) on the model of the Moscow Art Theatre,
whose methods and ensemble approach it emulated. With a company including Stella Adler (1904–   ), Morris Carnovsky (1898–   ), and Elia
Kazan (1909–   ), it presented plays by Paul Green, Maxwell Anderson,
Sidney Kingsley, Irwin Shaw, William Saroyan, and others, although its
reputation rests primarily upon its productions of Clifford Odets' dramas.
Success ultimately destroyed the troupe, for its actors and playwrights were
lured away as they established their worth. In 1941 the company was disbanded. Its influence has continued, however, through the work of many
former members, several of whom were instrumental in popularizing the
Stanislavsky system in America.

The depression motivated the creation of a unique experiment, the
Federal Theatre Project, which was established in 1935 to combat unem-
ployment. Headed by Hallie Flanagan Davis (1890–   ), at its peak it
employed 10,000 persons in 40 states. About 1000 productions of all types
were mounted, 65 percent of which were free. In spite of its diversity, it is
now remembered primarily for developing the "Living Newspaper," a
cinematic form which integrated factual data with dramatic vignettes. Each
script centered around a problem: *Triple-A Plowed Under* (1936) dealt
with agriculture, *Power* (1937) with rural electrification, and *One-Third
of a Nation* (1938) with slum housing. Most of the plays had as a central

HOWARD BAY'S SETTING for the living newspaper,
One Third of a Nation (1938) at the Federal
Theatre. [From *Theatre Arts* (1938)]

character the "little man" who, upon raising questions about a current
problem, was led through its background, human consequences, and possible solutions. Much of the dialogue was taken from speeches, newspaper
stories, or other documents. Many of the techniques were borrowed from
Epic Theatre. The political tone of many works eventually alienated
Congress, which in 1939 refused to appropriate funds for its continuance.

Macbeth as directed by Orson Welles at the
Federal Theatre. Setting by Nat Karson. [From
Theatre Arts (1936)]

The Federal Theatre motivated the formation of the Mercury Theatre in 1937, when Orson Welles (1915–   ) and John Houseman (1902–   ) decided to present Marc Blitzstein's *The Cradle Will Rock* after it was withdrawn from production by the Federal Theatre. Welles had already established a reputation as an actor with his portrayal of Doctor Faustus and as an imaginative producer with *Macbeth,* which he set in Haiti and performed with an all-Negro cast. Between 1937 and 1939, the Mercury Theatre presented works by Büchner, Dekker, Shaw, and Shakespeare. Its greatest success came with *Julius Caesar,* played as a comment upon Fascism.

The depression also gave impetus to the "workers theatre" movement, which had begun in 1926 with the Worker's Drama League. In 1932 a national organization was formed, later called the New Theatre League. Most of the member groups were amateur, but in 1933, a fully professional organization, the Theatre Union, was formed in New York and provided leadership for the entire movement. After the failure of the Theatre Union in 1937, the League declined and by 1942 had virtually ceased to exist. For the most part, the workers' theatres presented socialistic propaganda plays designed to arouse protest.

As the depression deepened, it became increasingly difficult for playwrights to get unusual works produced. Largely for this reason, the Playwrights' Company was created in 1938 by Maxwell Anderson, Elmer Rice, Sidney Howard, Robert E. Sherwood, and S. N. Berhman. In addition to their own plays, they also presented works by other authors. The Playwrights' Company was to be a major producing organization until 1960.

These dissident groups had little effect upon the basic pattern of the commercial theatre. The length of runs steadily increased, reaching a peak with *Tobacco Road* (1933), which played for seven years. The number of new productions also grew each season until 1927–28, when about 300 plays were mounted, but rapidly declined after 1930, having fallen to 80 by 1939–40. Theatrical production was complicated in these years by the emergence of powerful labor unions. The stagehands' union, the National Alliance of Theatrical Stage Employees, had achieved full recognition during the season of 1910–11, and in 1918 the United Scenic Artists was formed. Actors Equity Association, founded in 1912, was recognized in 1919; it became a "closed shop" in 1924 and was able to establish a minimum-wage scale in 1933. The Dramatists' Guild, formed in 1912, became the bargaining agent for all playwrights in 1926. As each group bettered working conditions, it also demanded considerably higher pay for its members and contributed to the economic problems of the theatre. Despite all difficulties, a number of producers and directors were able to maintain high standards. Among the producers, the best were Gilbert Miller (1884–   ), Jed Harris (1900–   ), John Golden (1874–1955), William A. Brady (1863–1950), and Sam Harris (1872–1941). Among the directors, the most outstanding were Guthrie McClintic (1893–1961),

Worthington Minor (1900–), Herman Shumlin (1896–), Brock Pemberton (1885–1950), and George Abbott (1887–).

Between 1915 and 1945, American dramatists began to command international respect for the first time. Few were members of any particular movement, but most shared a dislike for romantic melodrama with realistic trappings. Only one American dramatist—O'Neill—achieved genuine stature. Eugene O'Neill (1888–1953), son of James O'Neill, turned to playwriting around 1912, attended Professor Baker's playwriting classes for a time, and in 1915 had his first works presented by the Provincetown Players. This group continued to encourage him through the 1920's by performing those works rejected by commercial producers. His first full-length play, *Beyond the Horizon,* brought him to Broadway in 1920. After 1934, although he continued to write, no new works were performed until 1946.

O'Neill wrote about 25 full-length plays of uneven quality. Many were artistic failures, and even the best often suggest that more was intended than achieved. Nevertheless, his protagonists' search for some significance in life gives the plays a tone of high seriousness. O'Neill also experimented with many novel theatrical devices and dramatic techniques. In *The Great God Brown* (1926), *Lazarus Laughed* (1926), and *Days Without End* (1934) he made use of masks; in *Strange Interlude* (1928) he employed lengthy asides to express the characters' inner thoughts; in *Mourning Becomes Electra* (1931) he gained scope by adopting the trilogy form. O'Neill also ranged through many styles. The devices of expressionism were adopted for *The Hairy Ape* (1922) and *The Great God Brown,* those of symbolism for *The Fountain* (1922) and to a lesser extent for almost all the plays; those of realism for *Beyond the Horizon, Anna Christie* (1921), and *Desire Under the Elms* (1924). O'Neill's strength lay in complex characterization, strong dramatic situation, and seriousness of purpose.

Probably O'Neill's greatest rival was Maxwell Anderson (1888–1959), who after achieving renown for his anti-romantic war play, *What Price Glory?* (1924), turned to blank verse drama in *Elizabeth the Queen* (1930), *Mary of Scotland* (1933), *Winterset* (1935), and other plays. Although dramatically effective, Anderson's plays offered few new insights, being merely skillful retellings of familiar stories. Other serious playwrights included Elmer Rice (1892–1967) with *The Adding Machine* (1923), an expressionistic drama about the dehumanization of man, and *Street Scene* (1929), a naturalistic play set in the New York slums; Sidney Howard (1891–1939), with *They Knew What They Wanted* (1924), an anti-romantic comedy about three people who get their wishes by accepting compromises, *The Silver Cord* (1926), about a mother's attempt to retain her control over her newly-married son, and *Yellow Jack* (1934), a semi-documentary play about the fight to control yellow fever; Paul Green (1894–), with his tragedies, *In Abraham's Bosom* (1926) and *The*

House of Connolly (1931), and the expressionistic antiwar comedy, *Johnny Johnson* (1936); Sidney Kingsley (1906–), with *Men in White* (1933), dealing with the medical profession, and *Dead End* (1935), a naturalistic play of slum life; and Lillian Hellman (1905–), with moral fables, *The Children's Hour* (1934) and *The Little Foxes* (1938), a story of rapacious greed among the rising industrialists of the new South around 1900.

The comedy of manners was well represented by Philip Barry (1896–1949) with *Paris Bound* (1927) and *The Philadelphia Story* (1939), both treating divorce among the upper classes; S. N. Behrman (1893–), with *Biography* (1932), *Rain from Heaven* (1934), and *End of Summer* (1936), all of which contrast tolerance with inhumanity; and John van Druten (1902–1957), with *There's Always Juliet* (1931) and *The Voice of the Turtle* (1943), sophisticated stories of sex and love. Among the writers of farce, the best was George S. Kaufman (1889–1961), who worked with a number of collaborators, most successfully with Moss Hart (1904–1961) on *You Can't Take it With You* (1936) and *The Man Who Came to Dinner* (1940). William Saroyan (1900–) glorified the simple life in such plays as *My Heart's in the Highlands* (1939), *The Time of Your Life* (1939), and *The Beautiful People* (1941), all of which depict eccentric characters living on the fringes of society who find beauty and redemption.

The drama of social consciousness was most persistently practiced by John Howard Lawson (1895–), whose *Roger Bloomer* (1923), *Processional* (1925), *Internationale* (1928), and *Marching Song* (1937) were experimental in form and militantly propagandistic in theme. Clifford Odets (1906–1963) followed something of the opposite development, for his early plays, *Waiting for Lefty* (1935) and *Awake and Sing* (1935) call for group action, while his later works, *Paradise Lost* (1935) and *Golden Boy* (1937), take a more complex view of social conditions. Essentially a chronicler of family relationships, Odets' strength lay in his ability to create believable characters struggling to achieve more than life will give them.

Two of the finest dramatists of the 1930's were Sherwood and Wilder. Robert E. Sherwood (1896–1955), in *The Petrified Forest* (1935) created an allegorical cross section of American life, in *Idiot's Delight* (1936) depicted through melodramatic farce the horrors of war and the spiritual bankruptcy which gives rise to it, and in *Abe Lincoln in Illinois* (1938) sought to remind Americans of the high ideals upon which their country had been founded. Thornton Wilder's (1897–) reputation was created primarily by two plays, *Our Town* (1938), which seeks to point out the eternal patterns of human experience behind seeming progress, and *The Skin of Our Teeth* (1943), a testimonial to man's ability to survive all disasters. Wilder's frank theatricality and simplicity has won him a wide following both at home and abroad.

Much popular entertainment between the wars took the form of

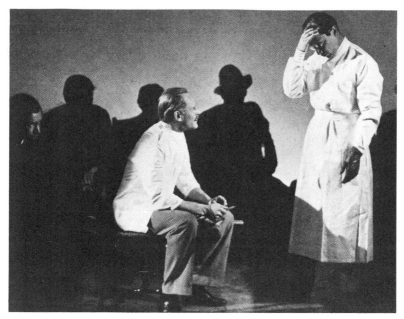

SCENE FROM Odets' *Waiting for Lefty* (1935) at the Group Theatre. [Courtesy of the Theatre Collection, The New York Public Library at Lincoln Center. Astor, Lenox and Tilden Foundations]

musical comedy and revues. Every year between 1907 and 1931, Florenz Ziegfeld (1869–1932) mounted a new edition of the *Ziegfeld Follies,* each more lavish than the last. Musical comedy, long merely the excuse for presenting beautiful chorus girls, began to move in a new direction after 1928, when Jerome Kern and Oscar Hammerstein II placed the major emphasis in *Showboat* upon a coherent story. This new direction reached its culmination in Richard Rodgers' and Oscar Hammerstein's *Oklahoma* (1943), in which music, story, dance, and setting were fully integrated to tell a semiserious story. With the triumph of the new approach, the old type of musical largely disappeared.

Of America's many outstanding performers, only a few can be mentioned: Jane Cowl (1884–1950), on the stage from 1903 but most famous for her portrayals of Juliet, Cleopatra, and the heroines of van Druten and Sherwood; Pauline Lord (1890–1950), especially remembered for her performances in *Anna Christie* and *They Knew What They Wanted;* Laurette Taylor (1884–1946), one of the most versatile actresses of her day, whose last major appearance was made as Amanda in Williams' *The Glass Menagerie;* Ina Claire (1895–), who appeared in many *Ziegfeld's Follies* before playing the heroines of Behrman's comedies; Helen Hayes (1900–), noted especially for her appearances in Barrie's plays, Anderson's *Mary of Scotland,* and Housman's *Victoria Regina;* Katherine Cornell (1898–), who gave outstanding portrayals in *Candida, The Three Sisters,*

The Barretts of Wimpole Street, and many other plays; Lynne Fontanne (1887?–), an English actress, who came to America in 1910 and whose later career was tied up with that of her husband, Alfred Lunt (1893–), with whom she appeared in *The Guardsman, Reunion in Vienna, Amphitryon 38,* and many other works.

The Second World War, like the first, interrupted the theatre's normal patterns. Energies were turned to building morale and providing diversion. The war also raised serious doubts about a world which had created such horrors as the Nazi extermination camps and such destructive weapons as the atomic bomb. Out of the questioning would come new experiments in theatre and drama.

THE THEATRE
SINCE THE
SECOND
WORLD WAR

*T*he period since the Second World War may be divided roughly into two parts: one, extending to about 1955, during which prewar theatrical practices continued to dominate; and a second, beginning about 1955, during which new ideas slowly reshaped the old. Of the many influences on the postwar theatre, three were most important: Artaud and the French Absurdists; Brecht and the German "documentary" dramatists; "happenings" and other attempts to destroy institutionalized theatre. Almost everywhere the primacy of language was questioned and nonverbal elements were exalted; communion through suprarational means was emphasized over rational discourse. But, if the old approaches were altered, they were not destroyed. Out of the conflict came a new vitality which rejuvenated the theatre.

642

French Theatre and Drama Since 1945

During the war years, the theatre in Paris was relatively prosperous. Productions were numerous and well attended, although with the exceptions of those by Dullin, Baty, Barsacq, and the Comédie Française, few were outstanding. The end of the war brought many stresses, as production costs rose and films and television drained away audiences. The new government, attempting to play a more decisive role than its predecessors, took steps to aid the theatre. In 1946, the Ministry of Arts and Letters began to subsidize productions of selected new plays and a few new companies; an annual competition was also inaugurated among the new troupes for the best production and direction. The state theatres also were reorganized. The Opéra and Opéra-Comique were placed under a single management, and the Comédie Française and Odéon were merged, the Odéon now being called the Salle Luxembourg and the main house the Salle Richelieu. At first, the Salle Luxembourg was restricted to new or recent plays, but as this scheme proved impractical, both branches came to present similar repertories. When Pierre Dux (1908–   ), Administrator of the Comédie Française from 1944 to 1947, instituted new regulations designed to reduce his actors' film appearances and other outside commitments, many of the leading *sociétaires,* including Jean-Louis Barrault, Madeleine Renaud, Marie Bell, Renée Faure, and Aimé Clairond, resigned. As a result, the troupe lost much of its strength, and, although it slowly rebuilt under the administration of Pierre-Aimé Touchard (between 1947 and 1953) and Pierre Descaves (between 1953 and 1959), its prestige suffered seriously.

The government also encouraged decentralization of the theatre, which by 1945 was restricted almost entirely to Paris. Consequently, in 1947 subsidized regional Dramatic Centers began to be established. The first, the Centre Dramatique de l'Est, based at Strasbourg, was placed under the direction of Andre Clavé (succeeded in 1953 by Michel Saint-Denis and in 1958 by Hubert Gignoux), and a second was opened almost immediately at St. Étienne under Jean Dasté. In 1949, Le Grenier, a troupe which had been performing since 1945 under the direction of Maurice Sarrazin, was designated the Dramatic Center for Toulouse, and in the same year a fourth center was established at Rennes, under Hubert Gignoux (succeeded in 1958 by Guy Parigot). Since then other centers have been inaugurated at Aix-en-Provence (1952), Tourcoing (1960), and Bourges (1963). In addition to performing in its home theatre, each troupe makes several annual tours to towns in its region. Decentralization has also been aided by the establishment of municipal cultural centers, many of which include theatrical troupes. In areas served by neither a Dramatic Center nor a municipal troupe, the government subsidizes touring companies. Both national and local authorities have aided the many dramatic festivals founded since 1945, most notably at Avignon (since 1947) and Aix-en-Provence (since 1948). In 1967, more than 50 festivals were held.

Paris continues to be the principal theatrical center, nevertheless, and the boulevard theatres, with their long-run policy are the typical organizations. The most influential theatres, however, have departed from this pattern. For a few years after the war, three members of the Cartel continued their work. Dullin remained in Paris until 1947, Baty until 1951, and Jouvet from 1945 until his death in 1951. By 1952, all of the members of the Cartel were dead. Of the younger prewar leaders, André Barsacq (at the Atelier since 1940) and Maurice Jacquemont (at the Studio des Champs-Elysées until 1960) were probably the most important. To this group should be added Marcel Herrand and Jean Marchat, who, after acting with Pitoëff's company, had formed the Rideau de Paris in the 1930's. Upon Pitoëff's death in 1939, they took over his Théâtre aux Mathurins. Until 1952, they presented there excellent productions of foreign works, as well as many new French plays.

The major leaders in the postwar years were to be Barrault and Vilar. Jean-Louis Barrault (1910–), after studying with Dullin and working with Artaud and the pantomimist Étienne Decroux, had attained an enviable reputation as an actor in both the theatre and films before the war began. In 1940, he became a *sociétaire* at the Comédie Française, where in 1943 his production of Claudel's *The Satin Slipper* was the first important example of what has come to be called "total theatre." Claudel's play, written between 1919 and 1924, had previously been considered unplayable because of its length and complexity, for the events span a century and occur in Spain, Italy, Africa, America, and at sea. At one point, the hemispheres converse, and at another the earth is represented as one bead on a rosary. A drama of love and salvation, *The Satin Slipper* was shaped by Barrault into a theatrical experience of such a high order that it was long to influence other directors. Although Barrault was later to refine his ideas, in 1943 he had already formulated his basic outlook. He has declared that the text of a play is like an iceberg, since only about one-eighth is visible. It is the director's task to complete the playwright's text by revealing the hidden portions through his imaginative use of all the theatre's resources. Barrault has arrived at a synthesis of Copeau's and Artaud's approaches.

In 1946, after resigning from the Comédie Française, Barrault (with Madeleine Renaud, whom he had married in 1936) formed the Compagnie Madeleine Renaud-Jean-Louis Barrault. With such major actors as Jean Desailly, André Brunot, Jacques Dacqmine, Edwige Feuillère, and Pierre Brasseur, Barrault produced about 40 plays ranging from the *Oresteia* to contemporary *avant-garde* works before he gave up his Théâtre Marigny in 1956.

JEAN-LOUIS BARRAULT'S PRODUCTION of Claudel's *Christophe Colomb* at the Théâtre Marigny (1953). [Photograph by Agence de Presse Bernand]

Jean Vilar (1912–   ), a fellow student of Barrault at Dullin's school, was much slower in achieving recognition, and had worked in a number of companies before being employed to organize the festival at Avignon in 1947. His work there and his fine performances in Paris (most notably as Pirandello's Henry IV in Barsacq's production) led in 1951 to his appointment as director of the Théâtre National Populaire, then on the verge of collapse. He assembled a company which included Maria Casarès, Georges Wilson, and Daniel Sorano, and was most fortunate in attracting Gérard Philipe (1922–1959), who, after a brief career in the theatre, had been one of France's major film stars. Although not immediately successful, by 1954 the TNP was one of the most popular troupes in France. Vilar's productions always placed major emphasis upon the actor, reenforced by costume and lighting. Scenery was usually restricted to platforms or a few set pieces. Vilar was the first producer to achieve wide popularity with the approach advocated by the Cartel (whose following had always been limited). Although the TNP's principal home was at the Palais de Chaillot in Paris, it also played at the Avignon Festival and toured throughout France. It soon commanded greater popular support there than any of the other state troupes, all of which played exclusively in Paris.

The work of Barrault and Vilar was recognized in the reorganization of the state theatres under General de Gaulle. In 1959, André Malraux, the new Minister of Cultural Affairs, took the Salle Luxembourg from the Comédie Francaise, renamed it the Théâtre de France and assigned it to the Renaud-Barrault troupe, which had had no fixed home since 1956. The

VILAR'S PRODUCTION of Marivaux's *Le Triomphe de l'Amour* at the TNP (1956). [Setting by Léon Gischia. Photograph by Agence de Presse Bernand]

TNP was raised to a status equal to that of the other state theatres and given an increased subsidy. Malraux made it clear that he expected all of the subsidized troupes to justify the support given them by the state. Perhaps as a result, the Comédie Française (under the administration of Maurice Escande since 1959) has introduced many new works into its repertory and has increasingly turned to *avant-garde* directors and designers to stage its productions. Although still essentially a continuer of past traditions, the troupe has regained much of its former prestige. The Théâtre de France has tended to set standards by its skillful blending of the old and the new and through its adventurous programming and production techniques. In 1963, Vilar resigned as director of the TNP, although he continued to manage the Avignon Festival and to work as an actor and director elsewhere. He was succeeded by Georges Wilson (1921–), who continued Vilar's policies. In 1966, both the Théâtre de France and the TNP acquired small theatres for more intimate and experimental productions.

Many changes in the postwar theatre were intimately connected with experiments in dramaturgy, most notably those of the Absurdists. This movement did not come to the fore until the 1950's, however, and much of the major writing of the postwar period was to come from dramatists well known before 1940. Among these, the most prolific has been Jean Anouilh, with such works as *Invitation to the Chateau* (1947), *Waltz of the Torea-*

dors (1952), *The Lark* (1953), *Becket* (1960), *The Grab Fair* (1962), and many others. In these plays Anouilh has continued to explore the problem of maintaining integrity in a world based upon compromises. Other pre-war dramatists who have made important contributions since 1945 include Marcel Achard, with *Patate* (1957) and *Eugene the Mysterious* (1964), and Armand Salacrou, with *Nights of Wrath* (1946), *Boulevard Durand* (1960), and *Like the Thistles* (1964).

Of the new dramatists, the most respected has been Henry de Montherlant (1896–   ), whose novels had won a wide following before the war. Although he had written a few minor plays, Montherlant's first produced work was *The Dead Queen* (1942), directed by Barrault at the Comédie Française. Its success led him to write *The Master of Santiago* (1948), *Port-Royal* (1954), *The Cardinal of Spain* (1960), and *The Civil War* (1964). Montherlant's gift for dialogue is undisputed, but his moral and religious views, the heart of his plays, have invariably led to heated debates.

Perhaps the best of the popular playwrights of the postwar period have been Roussin, Aymé, and Marceau. The plays of André Roussin (1911–   ), such as *The Little Hut* (1947), *Hélène* (1952), and *The Locomotive* (1966), have much in common with those of Achard, for they too treat unusual love stories with sophisticated verve. Marcel Aymé (1902–67), a novelist, turned to playwriting in 1948, since when he has written such comedies as *Clérambard* (1950), *Louisiana* (1961), *The Minotaur* (1963), and *The Convention Belzebir* (1966), in which far-fetched premises are explored for their comic and satirical possibilities. Félicien Marceau (1913–   ) achieved his first success with *The Egg* (1956) and went on to write *The Good Soup* (1959), *The Proof by Four* (1964), and *One Day I Discovered the Truth* (1967). All involve protagonists who seek to attain happiness through decidedly unconventional means, sometimes successfully and sometimes not. Despite unusual premises, Marceau's observations on life are sufficiently universal to attract a wide popular audience.

The enormous influence of postwar French drama, however, has come from Existentialist and Absurdist plays. Following the war, Existentialism as a philosophical outlook attracted considerable attention, especially through the essays and plays of Jean-Paul Sartre (1905–   ). A philosopher and novelist, Sartre turned to drama in 1943 with *The Flies,* and went on to write *No Exit* (1944), *Dirty Hands* (1948), *The Devil and the Good Lord* (1951), and *The Condemned of Altona* (1959). All illustrate Sartre's Existentialist views. Denying the existence of God, fixed standards of conduct, and verifiable moral codes, Sartre argues that each man must choose his own values and live by them regardless of prevailing standards, for to conform unquestioningly to the conventions established by others is the immoral response of a robot rather than the responsible act of a true being. Sartre's plays show characters faced with choices which require them

647

to reassess their outlooks and to forge new personal standards. In the uncertainty which followed the war, Sartre attracted a wide following, for he cast doubt upon the conformism which had made possible the Nazi atrocities. Sartre sought to make each individual responsible for his own actions and to place personal morality above social and political loyalties.

The work of Albert Camus (1913–1960) was to be of equal importance. Before turning to drama, Camus had been a theatre worker in his native Algeria, a journalist, and the editor of a clandestine newspaper during the German occupation of France. His dramatic output was small: *Cross-Purposes* (1944), *Caligula* (performed 1945), *State of Siege* (1948), *The Just* (1949), and a few adaptations. His major influence on the theatre came from his essay, "The Myth of Sisyphus" (1943), in which his definition of the "absurd" was to supply the name for the later Absurdist drama. In this essay Camus argues that the human condition is absurd because of the gap between man's hopes and the irrational universe into which he has been born. For Camus, the only remedy lies in each man's search for a set of standards (admittedly without any objective basis) which will allow him to bring order out of this chaos. Although Camus denied being an Existentialist, his conclusions were similar to those of Sartre; together, they supplied the philosophical background for the Absurdist movement which began to emerge around 1950.

Although Sartre and Camus reject rationalistic views of the universe, their plays retain the traditional dramatic forms. Since they begin with the assumption that the world is irrational and then go on to create order out of chaos, their works have clear dramatic actions. On the other hand, the Absurdists, while for the most part accepting Sartre's philosophical outlook, tend to concentrate upon the irrationality of human experience without suggesting any path beyond. By employing a succession of episodes unified merely by theme or mood instead of a cause-to-effect arrangement, they arrive at a structure paralleling the chaos which is their usual dramatic subject. The sense of absurdity is heightened by the juxtaposition of incongruous events producing seriocomic and ironical effects. Because they view language as the major rationalistic tool, the Absurdists have sought to demonstrate its inadequacy and to subordinate it to nonverbal devices. Of the Absurdists, four—Adamov, Ionesco, Beckett, and Genet—have been most important.

Arthur Adamov (1908–   ), born in Russia and educated in Switzerland, was early attracted to Surrealism, a movement which has influenced all Absurdist drama. Turning to playwriting in 1947, Adamov's first work was produced in 1950. The early plays, such as *The Invasion* (1950), *The Parody* (1952), and *All Against All* (1953), show a seriocomically cruel world of moral destruction and personal anxieties. Adamov's later works became progressively more socially oriented, especially after 1956, when he denounced his earlier work and adopted a Brechtian form. His new outlook is reflected in *Paolo Paoli* (1957), a farcical commentary upon the materialism and hypocrisy which preceded the First World War, and *Spring '71* (1960), which idealizes the men who created the Paris Commune in 1871.

Eugène Ionesco (1912–), a Roumanian by birth, has been a more consistent exponent of the Absurdist view. His first work, *The Bald Soprano* (1949, performed 1950), is labeled an "anti-play" to indicate a rebellion against conventional drama. The early works, which include *The Lesson* (1950) and *The Chairs* (1952), attracted little attention at first, but steadily grew in reputation after 1953. These plays, as well as *Amedée* (1954) and *The New Tenant* (1957), are mainly negative, for they concentrate upon the clichés of language and thought, the dominance of materialism, and the irrationality of values. Later works, such as *The Killer* (1959), *Rhinoceros* (1960), *The Aerial Pedestrian* (1963), and *Hunger and Thirst* (1966), have taken a somewhat more positive view by showing protagonists who hold out against conformity, although they cannot offer any rational basis for their actions.

SETTING by Jacques Noël for Ionesco's *The Aeriel Pedestrian* at the Théâtre de France (1963). [Photograph by Pic]

While Adamov and Ionesco have emphasized personal and social relationships, Samuel Beckett (1906–) has been concerned with man's place in the whole scheme of existence. Irish by birth, Beckett first went to Paris in the 1920's and settled there permanently in 1938. At first a novelist, he turned to dramatic writing with *Waiting for Godot* (1953), the first real success of the Absurdist movement and the beginning of popular awareness of Absurdism. None of Beckett's later plays, such as *Endgame* (1957), *Happy Days* (1961), and *Back and Forth* (1966), have equaled the popularity of *Waiting for Godot*. Beckett's characters, spiritual derelicts, are usually isolated in time and space; they torture and console each other and themselves, raise questions which cannot be answered, and struggle on in a world which seems to be disintegrating around them. Probably more than any other writer, Beckett expressed the postwar doubts about man's capacity to understand and control his world.

Jean Genet (1910–) spent much of his life in prison, a background that figures prominently in much of his writing. His first plays, *The Maids* (presented by Jouvet in 1947) and *Deathwatch* (produced by Herrand in 1949) were at first unsuccessful, and his reputation was to be made with *The Balcony* (1956), *The Blacks* (1959), and *The Screens* (1961, not produced in France until 1966). Genet's plays rebel against organized society and suggest that deviation is essential if man is to achieve integrity. They also imply that nothing has meaning without its opposite—law and crime, religion and sin, love and hate—and that deviant behavior is as valuable as the accepted virtues. Genet, viewing all systems of value as entirely arbitrary, transforms life into a series of ceremonies and rituals which give an air of stability and importance to otherwise nonsensical behavior.

With these authors should be included many others of lesser influence,

MADELEINE RENAUD in Genet's *The Screens,* Théâtre de France (1966). [Photograph by Pic]

650

such as Jacques Audiberti (1899–1965), whose *Quoat-Quoat* (1946), *The Black Feast* (1948), *The Landlady* (1960), and *The Sentry-Box* (1965) stress the power of evil and of sex over human affairs; Georges Schéhadé (1910–), whose *Evening of Proverbs* (1954), *Tale of Vasco* (1956), and *The Journey* (1961) are often reminiscent of Giraudoux's work in their combination of fantasy, precise language, and love for humanity; Jean Tardieu, who has concentrated upon one-act "chamber" plays, such as *The Information Window* (1955) and *The ABC of Our Life* (1959), treating man's enslavement to social conventions; and François Billetdoux (1927–), whose *How Goes the World, Môssieu? It Turns, Môssieu* (1964) seeks to embody the human condition in what its author has called "a Western metaphysics."

Most of the Absurdist drama was first produced in small, out-of-the-way theatres by adventurous young men, many of them heavily influenced by Artaud and later to be among France's most respected directors. Of these perhaps the most important was Roger Blin (1907–), a disciple of Artaud, who, after working with Dullin and Barrault, was closely associated with the Absurdist movement after 1949. He is especially noted for his staging of Beckett's plays. Other important directors include André Reybaz (1922–), who introduced Audiberti, Ghelderode, and Ionesco to Parisian audiences, and worked with a number of *avant-garde* theatres before becoming director of the Dramatic Center at Tourcoing in 1960; Georges Vitaly (1917–), who worked with Reybaz before founding the Théâtre LaBruyère in 1953; Jean-Marie Serreau (1915–), a pupil of Dullin who directed the first productions of Adamov's plays before opening the Théâtre de Babylone with Blin in 1952 and going on to direct at many other theatres; Jacques Fabbri (1925–), who worked with Vitaly and Reybaz before forming his own company, with which he has won special renown for his staging of farces; and Antoine Bourseiller (1930–), who won the prize for new directors in 1960 and served as director of the Studio des Champs-Elysées from 1963 to 1966, when he was appointed director of the Dramatic Center at Aix-en-Provence. To this group should be added Nicolas Bataille (1926–), Marcel Cuvelier (1924–), Michel de Ré (1925–), Jacques Polieri (1928–), and Jacques Mauclair (1919–). Beginning as members of the *avant-garde,* most of these directors now work regularly with such established troupes as the Comédie Française and the Théâtre de France.

Of recent directors, two—Planchon and Béjart—have gained most respect. Roger Planchon (1931–) had attracted considerable attention as a director of classics in Parisian theatres before establishing his own company at Villeurbanne, a working-class suburb of Lyons, in 1957. Later designated a Dramatic Center, Planchon's Théâtre de la Cité differs from others in not touring, although free bus service is provided for theatregoers from outlying areas. The repertory is very wide, but Planchon's reshaping of plays to

PLANCHON'S PRODUCTION of *Dead Souls,* adapted by Adamov
(1960). Théâtre de la Cité, Villeurbanne. [Setting by René
Allio. Photograph by Pic]

give them social significance has led to much controversy. Working closely
with René Allio (1921–   ), his principal designer, Planchon has evolved a
production style considerably influenced by Brecht. Seminaturalistic set
pieces are usually placed before a stylized permanent background which
comments upon the historical and social milieu of the drama. Planchon's
social consciousness has attracted a number of authors, such as Adamov; his
company's appearances in Paris, at the Avignon Festival, and elsewhere
have won him a devoted following.

Maurice Béjart (1927–   ) made his reputation in dance. Believing
that dance is an elementary and primitive language capable of communi-
cating with a popular audience if properly used, Béjart has sought to revive
its prestige. After struggling along in Paris and elsewhere, in 1959 he was
appointed director of the Twentieth Century Ballet Company in Brussels.
Although essentially a choreographer, Béjart has also directed operas and
plays. Such productions as *The Damnation of Faust* at the Paris Opera in
1963 and *The Temptation of Saint Anthony* at the Théâtre de France in
1967 have attracted wide attention. With his deep understanding of movement and highly developed visual sense, Béjart has created "total theatre"
of a high order.

By 1967, many young directors and playwrights were turning away
from the established theatre to present their works in cafes, art centers, and
elsewhere. Furthermore, some of the more dedicated and adventurous

MAURICE BÉJART's PRODUCTION of Berlioz' *The Damnation of Faust* at the Paris Opéra (1964). [Photograph by Pic]

653

directors had begun to open theatres in the suburbs of Paris where the theatre was previously unknown. Although the French theatre has by no means solved all of its many problems, it is now much more broadly based than in 1945 and is actively seeking still other ways to reach a wider audience.

German Theatre and Drama Since 1945

When Germany surrendered in 1944, all theatres were closed for a time but soon reopened under the surveillance of occupation forces. Since 1945, the German theatre has steadily grown and is now one of the most stable in the world. Although Germany has been divided since 1945, the theatre in the two areas shares many common characteristics. In both, the system of state-supported resident companies has been continued. In 1965, there were 175 professional theatres in West Germany, of which 120 were publicly owned, and in East Germany there were about 135 companies, all of which performed in state-owned theatres. Almost every city has a dramatic company and an opera and ballet troupe of good quality. All of the subsidized troupes in a single town are under one manager (or Intendant), appointed by the city or state, and all share a staff of directors and designers. A "dramaturg" advises the companies on the choice of plays and other artistic matters.

Among the outstanding directors of the postwar period have been Boleslaw Barlog, Fritz Kortner, Willi Schmidt, Wolfgang Langhoff, Wolfgang Heinz, and Benno Bessen in Berlin; Harry Buchwitz in Frankfort-on-Main; Gustav Gründgens and Oscar Fritz Schuh in Hamburg; Karlheinz Stroux in Düsseldorf; Heinz Hilpert in Göttingen; Rudolf Sellner in Darmstadt and Berlin; Günther Rennert in Munich; Hans Schalla in Bochum; and Karl Kayser in Leipzig. In 1951, Erwin Piscator returned to Germany, where he directed for numerous troupes, as well as being manager of the Freie Volksbühne in West Berlin until his death in 1966. Of the designers, the most influential have been Caspar Neher (1897–1962) and Teo Otto (1904–68), but Max Fritzsche, Karl Gröning, Helmut Jürgens, Wilhelm Reinking, Rudolf Heinrich, and Karl von Appen have also done outstanding work.

Although more than 100 theatre buildings were destroyed during the war, a phenomenal rebuilding program since 1950 has replaced most of them. In the new buildings, sight lines have been considerably improved, boxes have been eliminated, and the number of balconies reduced. The prewar emphasis upon complex stage machinery has continued. For example, the Schiller Theater, opened in West Berlin in 1951, has a revolving stage, elevators, and rolling platform stages. Most of the theatres are of the conventional proscenium-arch type. A few small theatres intended as second houses are more flexible, but there has been little experimentation with spatial relationships.

In addition to permanent resident troupes, festivals have been of considerable importance in postwar Germany. The most famous is still the Bayreuth Festival (revived in 1951 under the direction of Wieland Wagner until his death in 1966, and then under Wolfgang Wagner). After the war, Wagner's operas were performed for the first time at Bayreuth with simple scenic investiture much like that advocated by Appia, instead of the historical realism which had been used since Wagner's time. Bitterly opposed by traditionalists, the new methods have won approval from others.

WIELAND WAGNER'S PRODUCTION of *Tannhäuser* at Bayreuth, 1954. [From *Décor de Théâtre dans le monde depuis 1935*]

Of all the German companies, two in East Berlin—the Berliner Ensemble and the Komische Oper—have achieved the greatest renown. The work of the Berliner Ensemble is bound up with Brecht's late career. After he returned to Europe in 1947, Brecht's plays rapidly found their way into the repertories of most German troupes and his theory was soon known throughout the world. His fame was confirmed through the work of the Berliner Ensemble. Opened in 1949 with *Mother Courage,* the Berliner

Ensemble for a time shared the Deutsches Theater with another troupe. In 1954, it was given the Theater-am-Schiffbauerdamm, the house in which Brecht's *Threepenny Opera* was first produced in 1928. With its appearances in Paris in 1954 and 1955, the Berliner Ensemble became internationally famous and has since been considered one of the world's finest troupes. After Brecht's death in 1956, the company continued under the direction of Helene Weigel (1900–), Brecht's wife, who had been its director from the beginning. Brecht's methods were also retained by the company's principal directors, Manfred Wekwerth, Joachim Tenschert, and Erich Engel.

Much of the Berliner Ensemble's achievement stems from its long and careful rehearsals, sometimes extending over five months. When each production is ready, a *Modellbuch* containing 600–800 action photographs

THE BERLINER ENSEMBLE'S PRODUCTION of Brecht's *The Caucasian Chalk Circle*. Setting by Karl von Appen. [From *Décor de Théâtre dans le monde depuis 1935*]

is made. The published Modellbuchs have influenced many producers who have never seen the company perform. The Berliner Ensemble has done much to establish the validity of Brecht's theories, while the humanitarian and social emphases of his plays have suggested an alternative to the Absurdists (who have tended to dramatize personal anxieties). On the other hand, since Brecht uses non-realistic devices and, like the Absurdists, emphasizes irony and humor, the two influences have sometimes merged.

The Komische Oper was founded in 1947 by Walter Felsenstein (1901–), who established the company's style, a highly selective realism. Through lengthy and rigorous rehearsals and complete control over every artistic element, Felsenstein's productions contrast sharply with those usually seen in opera houses. The Komische Oper has become one of East Germany's most popular theatres. Its appearances elsewhere have won it a reputation only slightly below that of the Berliner Ensemble.

WALTER FELSENSTEIN'S PRODUCTION of Mozart's *The Magic Flute* at the Komische Oper (1954). Setting by Rudolf Heinrich. [Courtesy *World Theatre*]

In Austria, the pattern of postwar reconstruction paralleled that in Germany. By the mid-1960's there were 36 theatres in Austria, 20 of which were located in Vienna. Of these, four were state theatres, the Staatsoper and the Volksoper for opera, the Burgtheater and the Akademietheater for drama, while the Theater-in-der-Josefstadt and the Volkstheater were subsidized by the city of Vienna. The festival at Salzburg, reopened in 1946, has also resumed its position as one of the finest in the world.

If Germany and Austria have rebuilt one of the best systems of subsidized theatres in the world, they have been less successful in developing significant new dramatists, for until the late 1950's the major German dramatist was Brecht, all of whose major works were written before 1946. Zuckmayer returned to Germany, but his *The Devil's General* (produced in 1948), depicting the inhumanity of the Nazi hierarchy, and *The Cold Light* (1956) never equaled the popularity of his prewar satire, *The Captain from Koepenick*. Wolfgang Borchert (1921–1947) won fame with one play, *Outside the Gate* (1946), concerning a soldier returning from the war, and Fritz Hochwalder (1911–) found a wide audience at home with *The Holy Experiment* (1943), *The Fugitive* (1945), and *The Public Prosecutor* (1954), all of which pose questions of individual responsibility

657

and public guilt, but he never won a following outside of German-speaking territories.

The major drama in German during the 1950's was written by two Swiss playwrights, Frisch and Duerrenmatt, both of whom were encouraged by Kurt Hirschfeld and Oskar Walterlin of the Zurich Theatre, one of the best in Europe during the Nazi regime because so many refugees settled in Switzerland. Max Frisch (1911–) was trained as an architect but turned to writing around 1946. His reputation rests primarily upon *The Chinese Wall* (1946), *Biedermann and the Firebugs* (1958), and *Andorra* (1961), all of which treat questions of guilt. In each, the past is reviewed and the characters construct elaborate rationalizations for their actions; none is really willing to accept responsibility. Although it is clear that Frisch longs for a world of integrity, he seems to suggest that it is unattainable because men do not learn from their mistakes.

Friedrich Duerrenmatt (1921–) began writing plays in 1947. Of his many works, the most successful have been *The Visit* (1956) and *The Physicists* (1962). Like Frisch, Duerrenmatt is concerned with moral questions, which he suggests will not be solved satisfactorily because man is so readily corrupted by promises of power or wealth. His sardonic outlook has produced grim and forceful tragicomedies.

In the late 1950's, new German writers with considerable promise began to appear. Of these, Weiss and Kipphardt are perhaps the best. Peter

DUERRENMATT's *The Physicists* at the Kammer-spiele, Munich (1962). Directed by Hans Schweikart. [Courtesy *World Theatre*]

Weiss (1916–) spent the war years in Sweden and had been a painter and filmmaker before turning to playwriting. He achieved worldwide fame with *The Persecution and Assassination of Jean-Paul Marat as Performed by the Inmates of the Asylum of Charenton under the Direction of the Marquis de Sade* (1959), a work which contrasts de Sade's anarchistic views with Marat's dream of a superior social order. Set in the framework of a play performed by the inmates of an insane asylum, *Marat/Sade* has offered a great challenge to directors because of the problems posed by the essentially episodic plot, the large number of characters, and the central importance of mood and tone. After writing *Marat/Sade,* Weiss turned to documentary drama with *The Investigation* (1965), put together from testimony given during the official inquiry into the Auschwitz extermination camp. Weiss has stated that the traditional theatre is outmoded and must be replaced either by the "documentary" or the "happening." He has chosen the documentary.

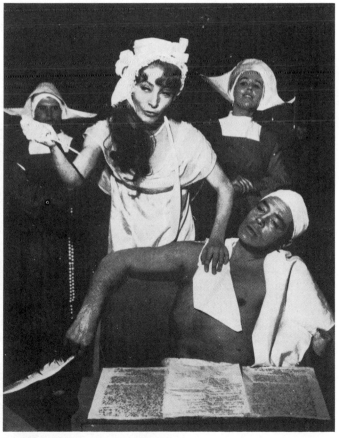

Weiss' *Marat/Sade* at the Schiller Theater, Berlin (1964).
Directed by Konrad Swinarski; designed by Peter Weiss.
[Photograph by Heinz Köster]

Heinar Kipphardt (1922–) has also moved toward the documentary. After writing *Mr. Szmil's Chairs* (1960) and *The General's Dog* (1961), he composed *The Oppenheimer Case* (1964), the dialogue of which is taken from the U.S. Senate investigations into the loyalty of J. Robert Oppenheimer. *Joel Brand* (1965) revolves about the middleman who sought to convince the Allied powers that Adolf Eichmann was serious in his proposal to exchange one million Hungarian Jews for 10,000 trucks. Rolf Hochhuth (1931–) also used actual events in *The Deputy* (1963), in which his placing the blame for the fate of European Jews on Pope Pius XII has caused bitter controversy throughout the world.

Because the majority of significant postwar German drama has dealt with questions of guilt related to larger political and social issues, it differs considerably in tone from the French Absurdist drama, which has attracted few German exponents. Of those who have written in the Absurdist vein, probably the best is Gunter Grass (1927–), with such plays as *The Wicked Cooks* (1957), in which rival factions seek to discover the recipe of a soup, apparently symbolizing significant human experience, so that it can be reproduced according to a formula. More recently Grass has turned in the direction pointed by Weiss with *Marat/Sade*. In *The Plebeians Rehearse the Revolt* (1966) Grass sets the rise of the East Berlin workers in the framework of a rehearsal of Brecht's *Coriolanus*, a device which allows him to comment upon the present by drawing parallels with the past.

Thus, while Germany has established a strong postwar theatre, it is still struggling to produce a significant new drama. Nevertheless, through the work of Brecht and other socially conscious writers, the German theatre has been a major influence on postwar developments.

American Theatre and Drama Since 1945

After 1945 the most influential figures in the American theatre were probably the director Elia Kazan and the designer Jo Mielziner, for through their joint work on such plays as Williams' *A Streetcar Named Desire* (1947) and Miller's *Death of a Salesman* (1949), they established the productional approach which was to dominate until about 1960. Under Mielziner's influence, stage settings turned away from realism, although they retained clearly representational features. This "theatricalized realism" was essentially an extension of the new stagecraft of the 1920's. On the other hand, acting moved increasingly toward psychological truth as found in the characters' inner motivations. It was an extension of the Group Theatre's approach as taught at the Actors' Studio.

Jo Mielziner's setting for Miller's *Death of a Salesman* (1949). [From *Décor de Théâtre dans le monde depuis 1935*]

Founded in 1947 by Lee Strasberg, Elia Kazan, and Cheryl Crawford, the Actors' Studio was designed to permit selected actors to work and develop according to the Stanislavsky System. Marlon Brando (1924–   ), with his characterization of the inarticulate, uneducated, and supremely self-confident Stanley Kowalski of *A Streetcar Named Desire*, came to epitomize in the popular mind the Actors' Studio style. The novelty of serious acting based upon substandard speech, untidy dress, and boorish behavior captured the public imagination and began a vogue for this approach. It also, probably quite mistakenly, created an image of the Actors' Studio as merely encouraging actors to explore their own psyches while ignoring the skills needed for projecting a characterization. Although much of the criticism is clearly exaggerated, Strasberg did place primary emphasis upon "inner truth" as the basis of good acting, and much of the Studio's training was determined by this goal. In 1956, the Studio began a program to assist playwrights; in 1960 it added a workshop for directors. By the 1960's, however, the influence of the Actors' Studio had begun to decline as interest turned toward non-realistic and period drama, for which the Studio's approach seemed too limited. Nevertheless, it has remained a powerful force.

After the war, the theatre was seriously threatened by the rapid development of television. In 1948 there were only 48 stations, but by 1958 there were 512 and over 50 million television sets. The free entertainment provided by the new medium came at just the time when production costs in the theatre were rapidly increasing. Between 1944 and 1966 the price of tickets more than doubled, and the costs of mounting a show increased at a still faster rate. Under these circumstances, producers tended to seek vehicles with broad appeal, and to avoid both plays and production styles which might offend or confuse spectators.

The Broadway theatre continued the decline which had begun before the war. It reached the lowest point in the season of 1949–50, when only 59 new productions were mounted, but then slowly climbed to about 70, a number which cannot be greatly increased until the number of theatres (about 30 since the mid-1950's) is increased. In the late 1940's, the reduction of the American theatre to a small number of Broadway productions served to motivate several attempts to diversify the theatre.

One of the most important efforts was to be the off-Broadway movement. By playing in out-of-the-way theatres or improvised auditoriums, production costs could be cut considerably, and works which would not appeal to a mass audience could be played for more restricted groups. Although the main force of the movement was to be felt during the 1950's, it had actually begun much earlier. In 1943, the city of New York acquired the Mecca Temple on 55th Street and converted it into the City Center, where opera, musical comedy, ballet, and drama were played for limited engagements at moderate prices. Under the general direction of Jean Dalrymple (1910–), the City Center was to build enviable ballet and opera troupes before moving to Lincoln Center in 1966. In 1946–47, Eva Le Gallienne, Margaret Webster, and Cheryl Crawford established the American Repertory Company (modeled on Miss Le Gallienne's earlier Civic Repertory Company), which performed a season of six plays before being forced to close.

The more typical off-Broadway groups, however, were begun by relatively unknown directors. The first to attract attention was New Stages, a group founded in 1947 by David Heilweil, who in 1950 also opened an arena theatre in the ballroom of the midtown Edison Hotel. The major upturn in prestige came in 1952, when the Circle-in-the-Square presented Williams' *Summer and Smoke,* a failure on Broadway, to high critical praise. Soon off-Broadway was viewed as a workable alternative to Broadway's commercialism. By 1955–56, there were more than 90 off-Broadway groups, and it was these which gave the first performances in New York of works by such authors as Brecht, Ionesco, and Genet.

Although the off-Broadway theatres continue to be a significant force, since 1960 their importance has declined for several reasons. Their ticket prices have gradually risen as the original concessions made by unions have been withdrawn. Furthermore, as audiences have become more familiar with new dramatic and production styles, works of the kind formerly restricted to off-Broadway groups have been performed by commercial producers. Thus, the original distinctions between Broadway and off-

Broadway have tended to disappear. Of the off-Broadway groups, three— Circle-in-the-Square, the Phoenix Theatre, and the Living Theatre—were of special importance.

The Circle-in-the-Square was opened in 1951 in a former nightclub. Under the direction of José Quintero (1924–) and Theodore Mann (1924–), the Circle-in-the-Square established the reputations of Jason Robards, Jr. (1922–), Geraldine Page (1925–), George C. Scott (1927–), and Colleen Dewhurst. In 1956, its success with O'Neill's *The Iceman Cometh,* a failure on Broadway, led to a renaissance of interest in O'Neill's work and brought Quintero to Broadway as a director. Although the group has lost some of its vitality of the 1950's, it has continued to do fine work.

The Phoenix Theatre was opened in 1953 by Norris Houghton (1909–) and T. Edward Hambleton (1911–) in an out-of-the-way but fully-equipped conventional theatre. Presenting plays of merit at low prices, performed by established stars, the Phoenix combined characteristics of the typical Broadway and off-Broadway theatres. In 1958 a permanent acting company, under the direction of Stuart Vaughan (1925–), was formed to present a series of plays each season. In 1964, a liaison was begun with the Association of Producing Artists (APA), a permanent repertory company formed in 1960 by Ellis Rabb (1930–). Intending to move to a new theatre, Houghton and Hambleton gave up the Phoenix in 1964; when their plans failed to materialize, they were left without a home. Since that time, the APA has performed at various Broadway theatres and is now probably the most respected repertory company in America.

Although both performed *avant-garde* works, neither the Circle-in-the-Square nor the Phoenix-APA departed markedly from traditional theatrical methods. The Living Theatre, on the other hand, had as one of its major goals a search for new methods suitable to new plays. Founded by Judith Malina (1926–) and her husband Julian Beck (1925–), the Living Theatre moved often after its founding in 1948, and did not win widespread recognition until its production of Gelber's *The Connection* in 1959. In 1961 it won the Paris Critics' Circle Award as the finest acting company at that year's international festival. After gaining additional fame with its productions of Brecht's *In the Jungle of Cities* and Brown's *The Brig,* the Living Theatre was forceably closed for failure to pay taxes and rent. In 1964, the troupe moved to Europe, where it has led a nomadic existence, arousing both enthusiasm and indignation with its productions of *Frankenstein,* a program of short works entitled *Mysteries and Smaller Pieces,* and Genet's *The Maids.* During its years in New York, the Living Theatre experimented with ways of involving the audience more directly in the theatrical experience. Many of the productions sought to convince spectators that they were watching real events rather than actors recreating a fictional text. Various actor-audience spatial relationships were used, and

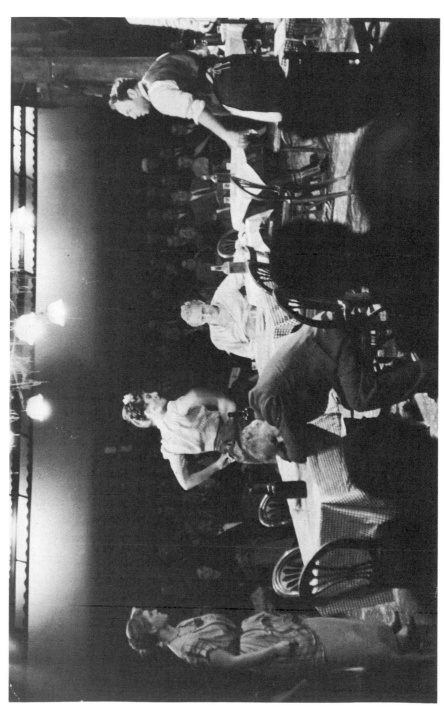

O'Neill's *The Iceman Cometh* at the Circle-in-the-Square (1956). Directed by José Quintero. [Photograph by Jerry Dantzic]

sound, music, and mood were manipulated to increase the audience's sense of active participation. Although quality varied considerably, the distinction between the Living Theatre and the typical Broadway production was both evident and intentional.

As off-Broadway lost much of its adventurousness around 1960, a new movement, usually called "off-off-Broadway," began. By the mid-1960's dozens of new groups were working in makeshift quarters, out-of-doors, or even in subways. Many charged no admission but took up collections and divided the receipts among the performers; some played merely for themselves and made no attempt to attract audiences. In performance style the groups ran the gamut from stark realism to improvised free-associational fantasy.

The off-off-Broadway movement is usually dated from 1958, when Joe Cino began to present new plays for one or two week runs at his Caffee Cino, a coffee house. Until his death in 1967 Cino was one of the major producers of new works. In 1962, Ellen Stewart opened the Cafe LaMama, which, after many difficulties over fire regulations, was converted into a private organization, the LaMama Experimental Theatre Club. Here the playwright makes most of the decisions about how his work will be presented. By 1967, the Club had produced plays by about 130 dramatists. Since 1965, Miss Stewart has toured Europe each summer with a troupe. In 1961, the Judson Memorial Church established the Judson Poets' Theatre under the artistic direction of Al Carmines, who chooses the plays and oversees productions. Performances are free, although a collection is taken up. Perhaps because of the greater selectivity and closer supervision, the Judson Poets' Theatre has been the best of the off-off-Broadway groups. In 1964 at St. Mark's Church-in-the-Bouwerie, Theatre Genesis was formed under the direction of Ralph Cook. Its aim has been to give the playwright complete freedom to express his ideas. Although not a theatre in the usual sense, the most influential of off-off-Broadway groups has been the Open Theatre, a workshop where actors, directors, and playwrights meet several times a week to work together. Founded in 1963 by Joseph Chaikin, a former actor with the Living Theatre, the Open Theatre seeks to develop new dramatic forms, and acting and directing styles suited to them. Here productions slowly take shape as cooperative endeavors. Out of the Open Theatre have come such works as van Itallie's *America Hurrah,* one of the most provocative plays of the 1966–67 season.

Both the off-Broadway and the off-off-Broadway movements are related to attempts to decentralize the American theatre. In 1935, the American National Theatre and Academy (ANTA) was chartered by Congress to stimulate the rejuvenation of the theatre outside of New York and to form an academy to train personnel. Because of lack of funds, little was accomplished, although ANTA continues to be the principal American center for collecting and exchanging information about the theatre. After the war, the attempt to found regional theatres was given its first important impetus by Margo Jones (1913–1955), who successfully established an arena theatre in Dallas in 1947.

Other pioneering groups include the Alley Theatre, founded in Houston in 1947 by Nina Vance; the Arena Stage, opened in Washington in 1949 by Edward Mangum and Zelda Finchandler; and the Actors' Workshop, begun in 1952 in San Francisco by Jules Irving and Herbert Blau. Most of the groups struggled along with semiprofessional personnel while gradually building audiences. The regional theatre movement was considerably strengthened by two events: the Ford Foundation's decision in 1959 to give financial support to those resident companies which had demonstrated strength and Tyrone Guthrie's decision to found a theatre in Minneapolis (opened in 1963 as the Tyrone Guthrie Theatre), since the example of a major director seeking a home removed from the New York theatre gave the movement much-needed prestige. The favorable publicity received by Minneapolis motivated many other cities to build art centers and to establish resident theatre companies. Although many cities merely erected buildings and failed to supply financial support for companies, an important step was taken. By 1967, there were 35 resident companies outside New York. Practically all of the regional theatres are organized as repertory companies which produce a season of varied plays for limited runs. Thus, as well as decentralizing the theatre, they also serve to diversify the repertory. Most have also been adventurous in their

INTERIOR of the Tyrone Guthrie Theatre, Minneapolis. [Courtesy Minnesota Theatre Company]

theatre buildings, using arena, open, or flexible stages to bring the audience and performer into closer contact.

The repertory movement has also reached New York, where the Lincoln Center for the Performing Arts established a repertory company in 1963 under the direction of Elia Kazan. The troupe had little success, however, and Kazan was succeeded in 1964 by Herbert Blau (who resigned in 1967) and Jules Irving. Although the company is still struggling to solve its problems, some progress has been made. Other groups in New York have also sought to diversify the theatre. In 1954 Joseph Papp established the New York Shakespeare Festival, which since 1957 has played in Central Park, where a municipally-owned, open-air theatre was constructed in 1962. The free performances attract many persons who would not ordinarily go to the theatre. In 1967 Papp established a permanent repertory company and training school to extend his work. In 1955 the American Shakespeare Festival Theatre was opened in Stratford, Connecticut, where an annual 15-week season of Shakespeare's plays is given and a training school operated.

The concern for a more diversified theatre is also reflected in the establishment of liaisons between university drama programs and professional companies. The Tyrone Guthrie Theatre works closely with the University of Minnesota, and the APA with the University of Michigan; New York University has established a professional training program; Yale University has extended its program by adding a resident professional company. The increased concern for the arts was also reflected by the passage in 1965 of the first federal legislation designed to assist them. Under its provisions, the National Council on the Arts was established. Headed by Roger Stevens, a former Broadway producer, the Council has had limited funds, but has sought to encourage worthwhile projects and to stimulate local support for the arts. It is difficult to predict the outcome of this program, for continuing federal funds are not assured. Nevertheless, a significant precedent for governmental aid has been established.

America has produced few significant dramatists since 1945, although for a time new vigor seemed assured by Williams and Miller. Tennessee Williams (1912–) came to the fore with *The Glass Menagerie* (1945) and rapidly confirmed his promise with *A Streetcar Named Desire* (1947), *The Rose Tattoo* (1951), and *Cat on a Hot Tin Roof* (1954). Since the mid-1950's he has been accused of repeating himself in such works as *Sweet Bird of Youth* (1959), *Night of the Iguana* (1961), and *Slapstick Tragedy* (1966). Williams' strength lies in his ability to create interesting characters caught in violent situations as they seek to recover a past more satisfying than the vulgar and materialistic present. As the dramatic action progresses, the protagonist is gradually forced to abandon his illusions, often after physical or moral degradation at the hands of callous and vicious characters. Williams' sensational situations have often obscured his moral concern for the survival of love and beauty in a materialistic world.

Arthur Miller (1916–) achieved his first success with *All My Sons* (1947), an Ibsenesque play about a manufacturer of airplane engines who has put profit above the safety of wartime pilots. Miller's reputation now rests primarily upon *Death of a Salesman* (1949), *The Crucible* (1953), and *A View from the Bridge* (1955). His later works, *After the Fall* (1964) and *Incident at Vichy* (1964), achieved little success. Miller has been most concerned with the social and moral implications of choices made by characters rooted in particular environments. Thus, he has often been called a "social dramatist." *Death of a Salesman* is now considered one of America's most significant plays, because it dramatizes so successfully the conflict in the American consciousness between the desire for material success and for adventure and happiness.

The postwar theatre gained considerably in stature with the return of O'Neill's plays to the repertory following the success of *The Iceman Cometh* in 1956. *A Long Day's Journey into Night* (produced 1957) was one of the most impressive plays of the 1950's, and other of O'Neill's works were performed to critical acclaim. Although he declined in power, Maxwell Anderson continued to write such plays as *Joan of Lorraine* (1946), *Anne of the Thousand Days* (1948), and *The Golden Six* (1958). Clifford Odets regained some of his former strength with *The Country Girl* (1950) and *The Flowering Peach* (1954); William Saroyan returned with *The Cave Dwellers* (1957), Lillian Hellman with *The Autumn Garden* (1951) and *Toys in the Attic* (1960), S. N. Behrman with *The Cold Wind and the Warm* (1959) and *But for Whom Charlie* (1962), and Thornton Wilder with *The Matchmaker* (1954). With the exception of O'Neill, however, none added substantially to his prewar reputation.

Although a number of new authors appeared, few lived up to their initial promises. William Inge (1913–) gained a considerable following with such works as *Come Back, Little Sheba* (1950), *Picnic* (1953), *Bus Stop* (1955), and *The Dark at the Top of the Stairs* (1957), but his work now seems essentially a more naive version of Williams'. Other dramatists include Robert Anderson (1917–) with *Tea and Sympathy* (1953) and *You Know I Can't Hear You When the Water's Running* (1966); Arthur Laurents (1918–), with *Home of the Brave* (1948) and *A Clearing in the Woods* (1957); Paddy Chayefsky (1923–) with *The Tenth Man* (1959) and *Gideon* (1961); and Neil Simon (1927–) with *Come Blow Your Horn* (1961), *Barefoot in the Park* (1963), and *The Odd Couple* (1965).

Musical drama continued one of the most popular of forms. For the most part, successful works have been adapted from well-known novels, plays, or stories. Rodgers and Hammerstein, with *Carousel* (1945), *South Pacific* (1949), and *The King and I* (1951), established the pattern which has been followed by others, such as Alan Jay Lerner and Frederick Loewe with *Brigadoon* (1947) and *My Fair Lady* (1956); Frank Loesser with

Guys and Dolls (1950) and *Most Happy Fella* (1956) ; and Jerry Herman with *Hello, Dolly* (1964) and *Mame* (1966). For a time it appeared that a musical drama of greater depth might develop. Gian Carlo Menotti (1911–) won a considerable following on Broadway with his operas, *The Medium* (1947) and *The Consul* (1950), but his later works proved less successful. Marc Blitzstein turned Hellman's *The Little Foxes* into an opera, *Regina,* and Leonard Bernstein collaborated with Miss Hellman on *Candide* (1956), a musical play based upon Voltaire's novel, and with Arthur Laurents on *West Side Story* (1957), an adaptation of *Romeo and Juliet* to the world of New York's juvenile gangs. Despite the prestige gained by these pieces, the musical has continued to be aimed at the mass audience.

By the late 1950's, American drama seemed to be at a standstill, for the earlier promise had been dissipated and no new dramatists of significance had appeared. Several off-Broadway writers seemed to offer the greatest hope, but of these only one, Albee, lived up to expectations. Edward Albee (1928–) first came to public attention in 1960 with his one-act play, *The Zoo Story,* which with *The Sand Box* (1959) and *The American Dream* (1961), resembled French Absurdist drama. His longer works, *Who's Afraid of Virginia Woolf?* (1962), *Tiny Alice* (1964), and *A Delicate Balance* (1966), however, have few marks of Absurdism. Albee has demonstrated a considerable gift for characterization, striking situation, and literate dialogue. On the other hand, he sometimes fails to mesh dramatic action with dramatic idea, with the result that his intentions are not always clear. Nevertheless, Albee continues to be the American dramatist with the greatest potential.

Among the other off-Broadway dramatists, the most important has been Jack Gelber (1932–), largely because of *The Connection* (1959), in which the action is presented as an improvisation by drug addicts while waiting for a "connection" to bring them a "fix." The play sought to break down the barriers between audience and performer, both through its style of presentation and by pointing to the conclusion that everyone is waiting for a "fix" of some kind. The off-off-Broadway theatre has also introduced many promising new playwrights, but none has yet proven his stature. Jean Claude van Itallie, with *America Hurrah* (1966), and Megan Terry, with *Viet Rock* (1966), have attracted the most favorable attention.

One of the most distinctive developments of the postwar era has been the "happening," which takes its name from Allan Kaprow's *Eighteen Happenings in Six Parts* (1959). Although its exponents, among whom are Claes Oldenburg, Robert Watts, and George Brecht, have not always agreed upon the basic components, some of the premises which underlie the happening appear to be: (1) the creator consumes his product rather than making art objects for others; (2) all those present participate, for performers and audience are synonymous; (3) since only a restricted number can be involved, a happening cannot become a mass-oriented art; (4) a true happening can occur only once, since the activity rather than the completed work is the end. The happening is essentially a nonverbal art. There are no rehearsals (although there may be lengthy preparations, or a plan of action), no professional performers, and no auditorium or stage in the usual sense. Essentially, the happening aims to break down the barriers between art and life and to destroy institutionalized theatre. Although many persons, including some former exponents, have expressed doubt about their value, "happenings" indicate the growing impatience with traditional forms.

Postwar Experiments in Poland and Czechoslovakia

Since the late 1950's, other significant experiments have been undertaken in Poland and Czechoslovakia. In recent years, the Polish Theatre Laboratory, founded in 1959 by Jerzy Grotowski, has aroused worldwide interest because of its approach to actor training. Grotowski has stated that he seeks a "poor theatre," one without the resources of the well-endowed groups, so that he can concentrate upon that which is truly essential in the theatrical experience. He sees in the actor the basic element of the theatre, and he has sought to train his performers so that they can transform themselves as needed in full view of the audience without resorting to costume and makeup. The actor is taught to depend upon his own resources and to give himself fully to the performance. Grotowski has worked primarily with well-known dramas of the past, for he is concerned with the archetypal patterns of human experience which can make both performers and audience confront themselves during the dramatic experience. Grotowski stages his plays in a large room which can be rearranged to meet the needs of each play. Every conceivable audience-performer spatial relationship has been used, for one of the aims is to involve the audience in the action.

Probably the best director in Poland is Erwin Axer, director of the Contemporary Theatre, although he has attracted less attention than Grotowski because his approach is more eclectic. Poland has also produced one of the most popular of recent European dramatists, Slawomir Mrozek (1930–). *Tango,* a parable about modern life in which a young man uses force to bring order to his family's chaotic life, only to be destroyed himself, has played to enthusiastic audiences throughout Europe.

Czechoslovakian interest in staging is symbolized by a unique organization, the Prague Institute of Scenography, founded in 1957 to provide training in the history, theory, and technique of stage production and to

AXIOMETRIC VIEW of Grotowski's arrangement of the audi-
ence-performer relationship for Slowacki's *Kordian* (1962).
Black figures represent actors, white figures spectators.
[Courtesy *World Theatre*]

SETTING by Josef Svoboda for *Their Day* by Josef Topol at
the National Theatre, Prague (1959). Note the use of projections on screens of varying sizes. [Photograph copyrighted
by Jaromir Svoboda]

671

experiment with new approaches. In addition, Josef Svoboda (1920–   ) is now probably the most respected designer in the world. Extremely eclectic, Svoboda has ranged through almost every style and has experimented constantly with new materials, techniques, and combinations of media. In 1958 he introduced the "Laterna Magika," a synthesis of projected film, stereophonic sound, live actors, and music. Unfortunately the Laterna Magika has been made a tourist attraction, and its potentialities are yet to be fully explored. Nevertheless, it is symptomatic of the postwar attempts to break down old barriers. Svoboda maintains a studio (comparable to a research organization with its permanent staff of architects and electronic engineers) where the potentialities of new devices are explored. He also designs many of the productions seen in Prague.

Czechoslovakia has a number of small experimental theatre groups. Perhaps the best is The Balustrade, run by Jan Grossman. Its resident dramatist, Vaclav Havel, is becoming well known in Europe through such plays as *The Garden Party* (1963) and *The Memorandum* (1965), satires in the Absurdist vein on bureaucracy.

English Theatre and Drama Since 1945

Following the war, the English commercial theatre developed along lines reminiscent of America's Theatrical Syndicate. In 1942 Prince Littler, owner of several provincial theatres, acquired the Stoll Theatre Corporation and began to form alliances with several other theatre owners and producers. By 1947 "The Group" controlled 75 percent of the theatres in England and owned the majority of shares in H. M. Tennant, Ltd., London's largest producing organization. "The Group" then demanded 30 to 40 percent of the gross weekly earnings of a play as a condition for leasing its theatres and reserved the right to close any play which fell below a specified weekly income.

Under these circumstances, it is not surprising that postwar English drama was innocuous. The leading dramatist was Terence Rattigan (1911–   ), who began to write plays in 1933, achieved his first popular success with *French Without Tears* (1936), and after the war turned to more serious subjects in *The Winslow Boy* (1946), *The Browning Version* (1948), and *Separate Tables* (1955). Although Rattigan created compelling situations and interesting characters, the "drawing room" atmosphere of his plays perpetuated conservative traditions.

The commercial theatre also took poetic drama under its wing for a time during the 1950's, after E. Martin Browne had generated considerable response through his work at the Mercury Theatre. Browne's production of

A Phoenix Too Frequent (1946) called attention to Christopher Fry and led to John Gielgud's production of *The Lady's Not for Burning* (1949), which established Fry's reputation and revived interest in poetic drama. Fry (1907–) went on to write *Venus Observed* (1949), *The Dark is Light Enough* (1954), *Curtmantle* (1961), and several adaptations. T. S. Eliot also returned to playwriting with *The Cocktail Party* (1949), which enjoyed a considerable popular success following its production at the Edinburgh Festival, and went on to write *The Confidential Clerk* (1953) and *The Elder Statesman* (1958). By 1955 interest in poetic drama was on the wane, for it too had come to seem merely an old formula dressed in poetic dialogue.

Between 1944 and 1956, the Old Vic and the Shakespeare Festival Theatre commanded greatest respect. The Old Vic troupe spent the war years in the provinces; when it returned to London in 1944, it played at the New Theatre, for its own building had been bombed. The management now passed from Tyrone Guthrie to Laurence Olivier, Ralph Richardson, and John Burrell, under whom the Old Vic was one of the leading companies of the world until about 1948. As the major actors developed outside interests, the troupe began to weaken, and in 1949 Hugh Hunt (1911–), who had served as director of the Bristol Old Vic since its formation in 1947, became its head. In 1950 the company returned to its own theatre, now repaired, and in 1953 the management was assumed by Michael Benthall, who assembled a fine company including John Neville (1925–), Barbara Jefford (1930–), and Paul Rogers (1917–). Although it continued to do fine work, the Old Vic never regained the glory of the early postwar years.

The Stratford-on-Avon company was strengthened by several reforms made by Barry Jackson, head of the theatre between 1946 and 1948. The company became a self-contained producing organization with its own technical staff providing costumes and scenery; storage space was added and the stage was remodeled. Jackson also gained control over the entire festival so that its activities could be coordinated, and enlivened the troupe by the addition of such vital young directors and actors as Peter Brook (1925–) and Paul Scofield (1922–). Between 1948 and 1956 the management was assumed by Anthony Quayle (1913–), who was joined in 1953 by Glen Byam Shaw. Such outstanding actors as Gielgud, Olivier, Redgrave, and Peggy Ashcroft appeared often, and in 1951 the number of productions given annually was reduced to permit more careful preparation. As the prestige of the Old Vic declined, that of the Stratford company rose.

Repertory seasons were also sponsored occasionally by commercial managers. With the backing of H. M. Tennant, John Gielgud presented a notable series of plays at the Haymarket in 1944–45, and from 1945 to 1956 the Lyric Theatre, Hammersmith, housed some outstanding revivals which were later sent on tour. Despite much fine acting, however, by 1956 the English theatre seemed merely to be looking toward the past. Many critics considered it doomed. Then, in 1956, a revolution began which soon transformed the English theatre.

The change can be attributed largely to two producing organizations, the English Stage Company and the Theatre Workshop, and to the dramatists with whom they worked. The English Stage Company was founded in 1956 under the direction of George Devine (1910–65), who began his career as an actor in 1932, taught at Michel Saint-Denis' London Theatre Studio from 1936 to 1939, and directed the Young Vic Company after the war. When Devine took over the Royal Court Theatre, once the home of Granville-Barker's troupe, he intended to emphasize new English plays and foreign works not yet seen in England. Failing to uncover a backlog of unproduced English dramas, Devine placed a notice in *The Stage* which induced John Osborne (1929–) to submit *Look Back in Anger*. The production of Osborne's play in 1956 marks the turning point in postwar British theatre.

Osborne's break with the past is not to be found in his dramaturgy, for *Look Back in Anger* is straightforwardly realistic, but in his attack upon class distinctions and upon the complacency and inertia of all classes. Its protagonist, Jimmy Porter, soon became a symbol of all the "angry young men." Osborne's next play, *The Entertainer* (1957), deviated from realism

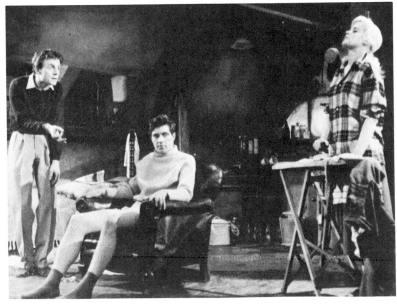

OSBORNE's *Look Back in Anger* at the Royal Court Theatre (1956). Directed by Tony Richardson. The actors are Kenneth Haigh, Alan Bates, and Mary Ure. [Photograph by Houston Rogers]

by interlarding music-hall numbers among conventionally presented scenes. Starring Olivier as a decaying entertainer, it too achieved considerable success. After the failure of *The World of Paul Slickey* (1959), Osborne turned to historical subjects in *Luther* (1961) and *A Patriot for Me* (1965), a play about an Austrian officer whose career is ruined because of his homosexuality. Although Osborne has departed considerably from his early approach, most critics believe that he has failed to develop significantly.

The English Stage Company also brought forward a number of other writers, the most important of which are N. F. Simpson (1919–), Ann Jellicoe (1928–), and John Arden (1930–). Simpson attracted considerable attention with his Absurdist play, *The Resounding Tinkle* (1956), but his later works, such as *The Form* (1961) and *The Cresta Run* (1965), have added little to his reputation. Miss Jellicoe, after arousing mixed response with her *The Sport of My Mad Mother* (1956), achieved a great success with *The Knack* (1961), an entertaining, somewhat disjointed story of the struggle between two young men, one too-naive and the other too-experienced, over a girl. In *Shelley* (1965) she presents a semi-documentary account of the poet's life. While the future of both Simpson and Jellicoe is difficult to predict, John Arden seems likely to continue one of England's most prolific playwrights. Since his *Waters of Babylon* was presented at the Royal Court in 1956, Arden has written a great number of plays, of which the most important are *Live Like Pigs* (1958), *Sergeant Musgrave's Dance* (1959), *The Happy Haven* (1960), *The Workhouse Donkey* (1960), and *Armstrong's Last Goodnight* (1964). Sometimes accused of being too literary because of his figurative language, Arden has treated many significant subjects—war, politics, old age—but his failure to take a clear stand on them has often resulted in unclear dramatic action. Nevertheless, Arden's reputation continues to grow.

Although the English Stage Company is important primarily for introducing new plays, it also presented a wide range of older drama. Like many of its predecessors, the troupe was weakened by success, for its playwrights, with the exception of Osborne, were wooed away by commercial managers. Since Devine's retirement in 1965, the company has been under the direction of William Gaskill.

The Theatre Workshop was founded in 1945 by a group of young people dissatisfied with the commercial theatre on both artistic and social grounds. Joan Littlewood soon became its leader. Having no financial resources, the company toured England and the Continent before settling in 1953 in a London suburb, Stratford, a working class district. It did its most important work between 1955, when it gained international recognition through an appearance at the world festival in Paris, and 1961, when Miss Littlewood resigned.

Two playwrights, Behan and Delaney, were especially associated with the Theatre Workshop. Brendan Behan's (1923–1964) first play, *The Quare Fellow*, written in 1945, was presented by the Theatre Workshop in 1956. A mixture of the comic and serious, it shows a cross section of prison life on the eve of a prisoner's execution. Similarly, *The Hostage* (1958) is built around varying attitudes toward the impending death of an I.R.A. agent and the hostage who is to be killed in reprisal. Many diversions (songs, dances, and character vignettes) enliven the play. Shelagh Delaney's (1939–   ) *A Taste of Honey* (1958) is the story of a young girl and her slatternly mother set against a closely observed background. The charge that Miss Littlewood had a strong hand in reshaping the plays of both Behan and Delaney is supported in part by the failure of both to produce additional significant work.

The Theatre Workshop is also noted for its production style, heavily influenced by Brecht and perhaps best exemplified in *Oh, What A Lovely War* (1963), a biting satire on the First World War. As the director of more than 150 of its productions, Miss Littlewood was responsible for establishing the company's approach. She sought to rid the theatre of its formality and to make it a place which spectators would feel as free to visit as a fun palace or a penny arcade. Her strong social consciousness led her to combine didacticism with earthy entertainment and to reinterpret the classics in startling ways. Several of the troupe's successful productions were moved to commercial theatres, and this practice so weakened the company that Miss Littlewood eventually resigned. After spending some years in Tunisia and India, she returned to England in 1967 and resumed her directing career, staging *Mrs. Wilson's Diary* for the Workshop.

Several other new English playwrights also appeared during the late 1950's. Of these, the most important were Pinter and Wesker. Harold Pinter (1930–   ), after beginning his career as an actor, turned to playwriting with *The Room* (1957). Later works include *The Dumb Waiter* (1957), *The Birthday Party* (1958), *The Caretaker* (1960), and *The Homecoming* (1965). Most of Pinter's plays occur in a single room, where the characters represent a cross section of humanity or of attitudes toward some central idea. Although the dialogue often seems a rendering of overheard conversations, it creates a nightmarish effect because the bases of anxieties or deeds are left unexplored. Pinter's early plays, which he called "comedies of menace," resemble those of the French Absurdists. Since 1959 he has been more concerned with the problems of characters seeking to live together, and his method has become more direct, although the ambiguities persist.

Arnold Wesker (1932–   ) has been England's most socially conscious dramatist. *The Kitchen* (1958) depicts a cross section of society in the microcosm of a restaurant's kitchen, while his series of connected works, *Chicken Soup with Barley* (1958), *Roots* (1959), and *I'm Talking about*

Jerusalem (1960), traces the changing social attitudes of an East London Jewish family. *Chips With Everything* (1962) is an indictment of the class system against which the protagonist unsuccessfully rebels. In 1962, Wesker became president of Center 42, a working class art movement, to which he has since devoted his time.

Of the many other dramatists, those who have attracted most attention are John Whiting (1915–63), with *A Penny for a Song* (1951) and *Marching Song* (1954), plays which puzzled audiences when first presented but which are now finding favor; Bernard Kops (1928–), with *Hamlet of Stepney Green* (1956), a retelling of Shakespeare's play in a modern setting, and *Enter Solly Gold* (1962), a comedy about a Jewish trickster; Alun Owen (1926–), whose typical works, *The Rough and Ready Lot* and *Winter Love,* treat relationships among various working class groups in Liverpool; Henry Livings (1929–), whose fantastic farces, such as *Stop It Whoever You Are* (1961) and *Eh?* (1964), satirize modern life; and Peter Shaffer (1926–), perhaps the most versatile of the writers, whose work ranges from the realistic *Five Finger Exercise* (1958) to a treatment of the conquest of Peru, *The Royal Hunt of the Sun* (1964), to Absurdist comedies, *The Private Ear* and *The Public Eye* (1962) and *Black Comedy* (1965). Much recent British drama has involved violent or shocking situations, exemplified in Fred Watson's *Infanticide in the House of Fred Ginger* (1962), in which juvenile delinquents kill a baby, and Frank Marcus' *The Killing of Sister George* (1965), in which an aging Lesbian is destroyed. This work has made the often fine plays of such playwrights as Graham Greene (1904–), with *The Living Room* (1953), *The Potting Shed* (1957), and *The Complaisant Lover* (1959), and Robert Bolt (1924–), with *The Flowering Cherry* (1957), *A Man for All Seasons* (1960), and *The Thwarting of Baron Bolligrew* (1966), appear somewhat old-fashioned.

The new spirit which entered the English Theatre in 1956 soon affected the established troupes, In 1960 Peter Hall (1931–) was named head of the Stratford-on-Avon troupe, and in 1962 Peter Brook and Michel Saint-Denis joined the management. Hall set out to remedy some of the company's drawbacks. Since the Stratford theatre was open only six months each year, it had been difficult to retain outstanding actors. Since Hall acquired the Aldwych Theatre in London in 1960, the company has operated year-round. A number of prominent actors, such as Peggy Ashcroft, Paul Scofield, Eric Porter (1928–), and Dorothy Tutin (1930–), and promising younger performers, such as Ian Holm, Roy Dotrice, and David Warner, were placed under long-term contracts. A training program was established under the direction of Michel Saint-Denis, and a policy of presenting recent and *avant-garde* works was followed by Peter Brook. Thus, in addition to performing Shakespeare's plays, the Royal Shakespeare

King Lear at the Royal Shakespeare Theatre at Stratford-upon-Avon (1962). Directed by Peter Brook. The production starred Paul Scofield as Lear, Alec McCowen as the Fool, and Irene Worth as Goneril. [Reproduced by permission of the governors of the Royal Shakespeare Theatre]

Company (a title which it was granted in 1961) has produced works by Pinter, Brecht, Gorki, Gogol, and others. One of its greatest successes was Brook's production of Weiss' *Marat/Sade*. Brook, whose approach incorporates much of Artaud's theory, has become England's most influential director and the Royal Shakespeare Company one of the major *avant-garde* troupes of the world.

Although the Old Vic regained some of its former glory under the direction of Michael Elliott (1930–), notably with such productions as Franco Zeffirelli's *Romeo and Juliet,* it was disbanded in 1963. In the same year it was replaced by the National Theatre, under the direction of Laurence Olivier. Agitation for the foundation of an English national theatre can be traced back to the 18th century, but no significant progress was made until after the Second World War. In 1949, Parliament appropriated money for a building as soon as a satisfactory plan was approved, and in 1951 the Queen laid a foundation stone. No further action was taken, however, until the London County Council agreed to share the expenses of a national troupe. The Old Vic's theatre was then acquired to serve as the troupe's home until a new building was readied.

Under Olivier, the National Theatre has rapidly become one of the most prestigious in the world. An extremely wide range of plays and styles has been attempted, for Olivier commissions the best directors and designers to work in their own way. Such major English directors as George

Franco Zeffirelli's production of *Romeo and Juliet* at the Old Vic in 1960. [From *Scene Design Throughout the World Since 1950*]

Devine, John Dexter, William Gaskill, and Peter Wood, such foreign directors as Franco Zeffirelli and Jacques Charon, and such designers as Sean Kenny, René Allio, and Josef Svoboda have enlivened the repertory. The acting company includes some of England's finest actors: Maggie Smith, Robert Stephens, Joan Plowright, Michael Redgrave, Rosemary Harris, Albert Finney, Frank Finlay, Celia Johnson, Joyce Redman, Derek Jacobi, and others. In cooperation with the Royal Court Theatre, the National Theatre has established an actors' training program under the direction of William Gaskill. Commercial producers now complain that the National Theatre and the Royal Shakespeare Company, by placing major actors under contract, have made it difficult for them to cast their plays with stars.

Much of the new status of the English theatre has been made possible by a change in attitude toward subsidies. Until the Second World War, no direct governmental aid had ever been given the arts. Then, in 1940, the Council for the Encouragement of Music and the Arts (CEMA) was given 50,000 pounds to assist in wartime work. In 1945, CEMA became the Arts Council, an independent organization financed by government funds, which decides how the support will be distributed. It has never had much money (in the 1960's it had only about one million dollars annually for drama), but it has used it to encourage organizations which seem capable of providing leadership. In 1948, Parliament also authorized local govern-

679

THE NATIONAL THEATRE'S PRODUCTION of Strindberg's *The Dance of Death* (1967). The actors are Geraldine McEwan, Robert Stephens, and Laurence Olivier. [Photograph by Dominic Photography]

ments to allot a percentage of their revenues to support the arts. As a result, several resident troupes now receive subsidies from muncipalities. The London County Council has been especially generous with such organizations as the National Theatre, the Royal Shakespeare Company, the English Stage Company, and the Royal Covent Garden Opera and Ballet companies.

The strength of the English theatre derives in part from local resident companies, of which there are now more than 50, most of which perform a mixed repertory of classics and recent works. Festivals also enliven the picture. The Edinburgh Festival (founded in 1947) and the Chichester Festival (begun in 1962) are probably the best, but others, such as those at Malvern, Glyndebourne, Canterbury, and Aldeburgh, also do excellent work. Thus, from a position of relative obscurity in 1956, the English theatre has become one of the finest in the world. It has attained this position, not by following any one approach, but by assimilating practically all of the postwar developments.

Italian Theatre and Drama Since 1945

For the most part, Italy has continued prewar patterns, for touring productions still dominate. Among these itinerant groups, three have been especially outstanding. The Compagnia Proclemer-Albertazzi has now been touring for many years and has established its actor-directors, Anna Proclemer and Giorgio Albertazzi, as Italy's most famous acting team. The Compagnia deLullo-Falk-Valli-Albani, a cooperative venture of Giorgio deLullo (leading man and director), Rosella Falk (leading lady), Romolo Valli, and Elsa Albani (outstanding character actors), in operation since 1955, has become the best of the itinerant troupes. Vittorio Gassman, Italy's finest classical actor, has sought to bring outstanding plays to the people with a series of ambitious undertakings, all now disbanded.

In addition to these touring companies, there were in 1967 ten resident theatres in Italy, each subsidized by city and state governments. Of these, the companies at Milan, Genoa, Turin, and Rome have gained the most prestige. The Teatro Piccolo in Milan, founded in 1947 by Giorgio Strehler (1921–) and Paolo Grassi (1919–), is a self-contained organization with a permanent troupe of 20 to 30 actors and a training school. Strehler has directed about three-fourths of the plays but has invited well-known foreign directors to stage others. His production style is heavily influenced by Brecht. The Teatro Stabile in Genoa, founded in 1952, is directed by Luigi Squarzina (1922–), noted especially for his productions of Strindberg's plays. The Teatro Stabile in Turin, founded in 1955, is headed by Gianfranco de Bosio. In 1967 it employed 102 actors distributed among four companies, two in Turin and two on tour. The Teatro Piccolo in Rome, directed by Orazio Costa (1911–), a pupil of Copeau, is noted for its extremely eclectic repertory.

Three independent directors—Visconti, Bene, and Zeffirelli—have also won widespread fame. Luchino Visconti (1906–), one of the initiators of the neo-realism which has characterized postwar Italian films, has directed many plays and operas between his film assignments. Carmelo Bene has achieved considerable notoriety as a director of *avant-garde* productions, in which he has also starred. Franco Zeffirelli (1923–), after beginning his career as a designer, turned to directing in 1953, although he has continued to design settings for his own productions, which typically combine novel interpretations of plays with neo-realistic visual details. Since 1958, he has been an international figure, working frequently in England, America, France, and elsewhere.

The Italian playwright's position remains as difficult as it was a

VITTORIO GASSMAN in his own production of
Alfieri's *Oreste* (1957). Setting by Gianni Poli-
dori. [Courtesy *World Theatre*]

century ago, for there is still no spoken language which is both intelligible
and realistic. Thus, the theatre remains essentially regional in its focus.
Occasionally a dramatist attracts a national following, but only one, Betti,
has achieved international stature in the postwar years. Ugo Betti (1892–
1953) began writing plays in 1927, but his reputation rests primarily upon
his late works, *Corruption in the Palace of Justice* (1948), *The Queen and
the Rebels* (1951), and *The Burnt Flower Bed* (1953). All of Betti's plays
are concerned with crises of conscience, especially among those who have
gained influence through bureaucratic means. His preoccupation with guilt
and power struck a responsive chord in the postwar consciousness.

Two other dramatists, Fabbri and de Filippo, have won lesser international recognition. Diego Fabbri (1911–) has upheld the teachings of
the church through dramas of traditional form. Of his plays, *Christ on
Trial* (1955), showing the difficulties created by Christ's presence in the
world, is probably the best known. Eduardo de Filippo (1900–) began

GOLDONI's *Servant of Two Masters* at the Piccolo Teatro, Milan. Directed by Giorgio Strehler; setting by Ezio Frigerio. [From *Scene Design Throughout the World Since 1950*]

writing around 1930. Although set in Naples and written in the Neapolitan dialect, his plays achieve universality because they show characters struggling to survive in the face of poverty, disease, and strained family relationships. They mingle the serious, comic, and pathetic with closely observed local detail. Among his best works are *Naples' Millionaires* (1946), *Filumena* (1955), *Saturday, Sunday, and Monday* (1959), and *The Boss* (1960). De Filippo, also a fine actor, worked for many years with his brother, Peppino de Felippo (1903–), one of Italy's most popular performers.

Spanish Theatre and Drama Since 1945

Because Spain has remained isolated since the end of its civil war in 1939, few of its playwrights have achieved recognition elsewhere. Of the new writers, the best are Sotelo, Buero Vallejo, Sastre, Olmo, Mihura, and Paso. Joaquín Calvo Sotelo (1905–) has continued the realistic tradition with such works as *Plaza de Oriente* (1947), *The Visitor Who Didn't Ring the Bell* (1950), and *The Power* (1965). *The Wall* (1954), dealing with a man's difficulties with his family when he decides to give up his wrongfully acquired wealth, created more debate in Spain than any play since Echegaray's Ibsenesque plays in the late 19th century. Antonio Buero Vallejo

(1916–) set the tone for many new writers with *The Story of a Stairway* (1949), a play which shows the failure of illusions in four families who live in the same apartment house. Buero Vallejo's later works range in style from realism to symbolism, and in subject matter from the historical to the contemporary. Alfonso Sastre's works, such as *Death Squad* (1953), *In the Net* (1961), and *Anna Kleiber* (1962), all of which are filled with indignation at social and political corruption, are widely known in Spain but seldom produced. Similarly, Lauro Olmo has had difficulty with censorship. *The Shirt* (1961) deals with the plight of the worker who must go abroad because he cannot earn a living at home, and *The Decoration* (1965), in treating the conflicting ideologies within a family, reflects the divisions within Spain itself. Miguel Mihura (1909–), with such plays as *Sublime Decision* (1955) and *Maribel and the Extraordinary Family* (1959), has been the most popular writer of comedy, while Alfonso Paso (1926–) seems the author destined to replace Benavente as a prolific purveyor of popular entertainment. Beginning his writing career in 1952, Paso now turns out as many as ten plays a year. Among his most popular works are *The Poor Little Thing* (1957), *The Girl's Wedding* (1960), and *Dear Professor* (1965).

A gradual relaxation of tensions in Spain has brought some decrease in censorship. Between 1949 and 1956 the works of such foreign authors as Williams, Wilder, O'Neill, Claudel, Anouilh, and Montherlant were introduced into the repertory. Further relaxations in the late 1950's returned the works of Lorca and Casona to the repertory and increased interest in Valle-Inclán and Unamuno. Nevertheless, since playwrights and producers must still be wary, the Spanish theatre remains a cautious institution.

Madrid now has about 20 theatres, most of which give two complete programs each evening. As a result, two-act plays have become increasingly common. Of the national theatres, the Teatro Espagñol is devoted to Spanish and foreign classics, while the Teatro María Guerrero produces recent Spanish and foreign plays. In 1965 a National Experimental Theatre was established to try out unusual plays and production techniques. Although Spain has taken some steps toward ending its isolation, its theatre remains conservative.

Russian Theatre and Drama Since 1945

During the war years the Russian theatre was devoted primarily to building morale. Since governmental supervision was considerably relaxed, many thought that the end of the war would bring still greater freedom. Instead, restrictions even more severe than those of the 1930's were im-

VALLE-INCLÁN's *Divine Words* at the Teatro
Bellas Artes, Madrid (1961). Directed by José
Tamayo. [Courtesy *World Theatre*]

posed in 1946, and in 1948 all subsidies, except those granted to a few
favored theatres, were stopped. The loss of governmental financial support
was a severe blow, since of Russia's 950 theatres, 450 had been destroyed
during the war. By 1953 only about 250 were left.

Artistic restrictions were imposed by making Socialist Realism the only
acceptable style and the Moscow Art Theatre's methods standard. Political
control was strengthened in 1949 when party-appointed Administrative
Directors were placed in complete charge of each theatre. Most Western
plays were removed from the repertory, and new Russian works were
expected to uphold governmental policy. A large number of plays, such as
Anatoly Safronov's *The Muscovite Character* (1949), show the reeducation
of persons who have stood in the way of party goals, while Constantin
Simonov's *Alien Shadow* (1949) and Nikolai Pogodin's *The Missouri
Waltz* (1950) are typical of the numerous anti-American plays. Other postwar drama, such as Vsevelod Vishnevsky's *1919—The Unforgettable Year*

(1949) and A. Stein's *Prologue* (1952), glorify Stalin's role in the development of Communism.

Following Stalin's death in 1953 many changes occurred. Although periods of freedom and restrictions have alternated, in general there has been a steady relaxation of the former rules, especially since Khrushchev's denunciation of Stalin in 1956. Censorship in the sense of prior judgment is no longer practiced, although many pressures are still exerted on drama, most notably through the governing boards of theatres. Realism remains the dominant style and didacticism the dominant aim, but neither is enforced and both have steadily declined in popularity. In new plays, romantic or family situations are more frequently treated, as in Pogodin's *Sonnet of Petrarch* (1957), while the theme of vindication from unjust charges, typified by Alexander Volodin's *Factory Girl* (1957), has become common. The conflict between generations, exemplified in Victor Rozov's *The Unequal Struggle* (1960), has also become a popular subject.

The traditional Soviet liking for loosely-organized, novelistic plays has been catered to in the 1960's with dramatizations of such novels as Sholokhov's *The Soil Upturned,* Dostoevsky's *The Idiot,* and Gorky's *The Barbarians.* Anti-American plays have largely disappeared from the repertory, while many previously banned Russian plays are now popular. The penchant for reshaping classics to bring out propagandistic themes has lessened considerably, and many Western plays have been introduced into the theatres. The first production of a play by Brecht was given in 1960, and works by Williams, Miller, Osborne, and others have been seen with some regularity since that time. With the exception of Ionesco's *Rhinoceros,* however, few Absurdist dramas have been presented.

The changes have meant a loss of prestige for the Moscow Art Theatre, which nevertheless remains at the head of its profession in terms of subsidies, salaries, and other governmental favors. Under the direction of Mikhail Kedrov (1893–), the Moscow Art Theatre now has a company of about 140 actors. In addition to a training school, it also has three studios, one named for Stanislavsky, one for Nemirovich-Danchenko, and a third called the Experimental Studio, established in 1965 to develop a "socially committed theatre on heroic themes." Despite its official position, the Moscow Art Theatre is now regarded by the public as something of a museum. Similarly, the Maly Theatre in Moscow has retained a privileged position only slightly lower than that of the Moscow Art Theatre. Before 1956 it performed classics almost exclusively, but now presents a wide repertory under the direction of Mikhail Tsarev (1903–), a former student of Meyerhold.

Other theatres have gained in prestige. Some changes can be attributed to the abandonment in 1956 of the fixed pay scales and ranks and the prohibitions against changing companies which had hampered actors since the 1930's. Other changes can be attributed to shifts in taste. Of the older theatres, the Vakhtangov, under the direction of Reuben Simonov, is probably the most popular, for Vakhtangov's methods have provided the most acceptable alternative to Socialist Realism. The Theatre of Satire, under Valentin Pluchek, has also grown in esteem since it created a sensation in 1954 with productions of Mayakovsky's *The Bedbug* and *The Bathhouse* in a style not unlike Meyerhold's.

At the Mayakovsky Theatre (formerly the Theatre of the Revolution), Nikolai Okhlopkov has returned to his prewar experimentation with performer-audience relationships. In the late 1950's he restaged Pogodin's *Aristocrats,* with the audience surrounding the playing area as in his productions of the 1930's. The most famous of Okhlopkov's postwar productions is probably *Hamlet* (1954), in which the setting was divided into compartments and the whole action treated as Hamlet's attempt to escape from a prison-like world. Two other prewar directors, Yuri Zavadsky at the Mossoviet Theatre and Alexei Popov at the Central Theatre of the Soviet Army, continue to be important.

OKHLOPKOV'S PRODUCTION of *Hamlet* at the Mayakovsky Theatre, Moscow, 1954. [From *Teatr* (1958)]

Two new theatres in Moscow, however, have created the greatest excitement in recent years. Founded in 1957 by Oleg Yefremov and other former students of the Moscow Art Theatre, the Contemporary Theatre (the first new troupe since the 1930's) was granted a theatre of its own in 1961. Its productional approach has not been revolutionary, for it is essentially that of the Moscow Art Theatre with less emphasis upon the scenic background; rather, its popularity stems from its repertory of vital contemporary plays, such as those of Rozov, Brecht, and Osborne. It has also presented the satires of Evgeny Schwarz (1897–1958), such as *The Naked King* (based on *The Emperor's New Clothes*) and *The Dragon* (based on the Lancelot legends), long banned because they use legendary materials to comment upon modern life.

YEFREMOV'S PRODUCTION of Aksenov's *Always on Sale* at the Contemporary Theatre, Moscow, 1966. [From *Teatr* (1967)]

The second new troupe, the Moscow Theatre of Drama and Comedy (commonly called the Taganka Theatre after the suburb in which it is located), was founded in 1964 by Yuri Lyubimov, formerly a teacher at the Vakhtangov Theatre's training school. So far, Lyubimov has depended heavily upon Brecht for his repertory, but he also created a sensation in 1965 with a dramatization of John Reed's *Ten Days That Shook the World*. So far, Lyubimov is the only Russian director devoted to "total theatre"; thus, his approach is the most distinctive in Russia.

In Leningrad, the Pushkin Theatre occupies a position comparable to that of the Moscow Art Theatre in Moscow and its prestige has suffered similarly. The most admired theatre in Leningrad is the Gorky Theatre, since 1956 under the direction of Georgi Tovstogonov (1915–   ), noted for giving classics contemporary significance. Using realistic set pieces, he often dispenses with walls, ceilings, and similar details, and employs such cinematic techniques as moving the action forward on platforms for "close-up" effects. At the Leningrad Comedy Theatre, Nikolai Akimov (1901–   ), who serves as both director and designer, also maintains high standards. Despite his fine work, Akimov's official position is probably reflected by the theatre in which he works, a large room over a grocery.

Since the end of the Stalin era, the visual style of the Russian theatre has altered radically. Rather than representing each place in detail, it is now more common to use one fixed background representative of a play's overall mood and to alternate small realistic set pieces in front of it. Among the best of recent designers are Alexander Tychler, Nisson Chifrine, Evgeny Kovalenko, Alexander Vassiliev, Yuri Pimenov, B. R. Erdman, I. G. Sumbatashvili, and M. S. Saryan.

A SETTING by Nisson Chifrine for a dramatization of a novel by Sholokhov at the Theatre of the Red Army, Moscow, 1957. [From *Scene Design Throughout the World Since 1950*]

The Russian theatre has grown steadily since 1953 to the present 500 professional troupes. Although many new buildings have been constructed since the war, numerous companies still perform in makeshift quarters. All house repertory companies which alternate the eight to twenty-eight plays which they have prepared. About 100 professional troupes play exclusively for children or young people. Although few groups now receive direct subsidies, the theatre is prosperous, for it occupies a firm place in Russian life.

International Developments

At the end of the Second World War, international cooperation was sought in every aspect of life. The formation of the United Nations was followed by many other organizations designed to promote international understanding. The International Theatre Institute (ITI), was founded in

1947 under the auspices of the United Nations Educational, Scientific, and Cultural Organization (UNESCO), which provided it with a yearly subsidy. Since 1950, the ITI has published *World Theatre,* a periodical designed to disseminate information. Now including more than 40 member centers, the ITI holds frequent international meetings, and since 1954 has sponsored an annual festival in Paris, the Théâtre des Nations, presently under the direction of Jean-Louis Barrault. Other organizations have also promoted the exchange of ideas. Among these are the International Association of Theatre Technicians, the International Association of Theatre Critics, and the International Institute of Theatre Research.

International cooperation has also encouraged the development of the theatre throughout the world, for newly created nations have sought to display their national culture to advantage. Theatres have appeared in parts of the world that formerly had few or none. In geographical scope, the theatre is now more extensive than at any time in the past.

The future of the theatre cannot be predicted. As in the past, it will probably assimilate the recent trends, which in their turn will soon appear outmoded. The theatre will survive so long as it continues to welcome the new and preserve the best of the old.

BIBLIOGRAPHY

*T*his bibliography lists those books that are either the most authoritative or the most representative of major points of view. Except in rare cases, they are in English. Notes have been introduced occasionally for clarity. Additional works may be discovered easily by consulting the following bibliographical aids:

Baker, Blanch M. *Theatre and Allied Arts*. New York, 1952.
Brockett, Oscar G., Becker, Samuel, and Bryant, Donald. *A Bibliographical Guide to Research in Speech and Dramatic Art*. Chicago, 1963.
Dramatic Index [1909–1949]. Boston, 1910–1950.
Revue d'Histoire du Théâtre [1948–present]. This quarterly journal lists in each issue publications throughout the world.

General Works

Altman, George *et al. Theatre Pictoral; A History of World Theatre as Recorded in Drawings, Paintings, Engravings, and Photographs*. Berkeley, 1953.
Bowman, Walter P. and Ball, Robert H. *Theatre Language; A Dictionary of Terms in English of the Drama and Stage from Medieval to Modern Times*. New York, 1961.
Clark, Barrett H. (ed.) *European Theories of the Drama*. Newly revised by Henry Popkin. New York, 1965.
Duerr, Edwin. *The Length and Depth of Acting*. New York, 1962.
Gassner, John. *Masters of the Drama*. 3d ed. New York, 1954.
Hartnoll, Phyllis (ed.) . *The Oxford Companion to the Theatre*, 2d ed. London, 1957.
Kindermann, Heinz. *Theatergeschichte Europas*. Salzburg, 1957–.
Laver, James. *Drama, Its Costume and Decor*. London, 1951.

BIBLIOGRAPHY

Mantzius, Karl. *A History of Theatrical Art in Ancient and Modern Times*. 6 vols. London, 1903–1921.

Nagler, Alois M. *Sources of Theatrical History*. New York, 1952.

Nicoll, Allardyce. *The Development of the Theatre*. 5th ed. London, 1966.

———. *World Drama from Aeschylus to Anouilh*. London, 1949.

Southern, Richard. *The Seven Ages of the Theatre*. New York, 1961.

Stuart, Donald C. *The Development of Dramatic Art*. New York, 1928.

Wimsatt, William K. and Brooks, Cleanth. *Literary Criticism; A Short History*. New York, 1957.

Chapter I: The Origins of the Theatre

"Arts, Human Behavior, and Africa," *African Studies Bulletin*, V (May 1962), 1–70.

Brown, Ivor. *The First Player; The Origin of Drama*. New York, 1928.

Breasted, James H. *The Development of Religion and Thought in Ancient Egypt*. New York, 1912.

Frankfort, Henri. *Kingship and the Gods*. Chicago, 1948.

Gaster, Theodor. *Thespis; Ritual, Myth and Drama in the Ancient Near East*. New York, 1950.

Havemeyer, Loomis. *The Drama of Savage Peoples*. New Haven, 1916.

Herskovits, Melville. "Dramatic Expression among Primitive Peoples," *Yale Review*, XXXIII (1944), 683–698.

Ridgeway, William. *The Drama and Dramatic Dances of Non-European Races*. Cambridge, 1915.

Chapter II: Theatre and Drama in Ancient Greece

Allen, James T. *Greek Acting in the Fifth Century*, Berkeley, 1916.

———. *The Greek Theatre of the Fifth Century before Christ*. Berkeley, 1920.

Arnott, Peter D. *Greek Scenic Conventions in the Fifth Century, B.C.* Oxford, 1962.

Bieber, Margarete. *The History of the Greek and Roman Theater*. 2d ed. Princeton, N.J., 1961.

Cornford, Francis M. *The Origin of Attic Comedy*. London, 1914.

Flickinger, R. C. *The Greek Theatre and Its Drama*. London, 1914.

Greene, William C. *Moira; Fate, Good, and Evil in Greek Thought*. Cambridge, Mass., 1944.

Hamilton, Edith. *The Greek Way*. New York, 1952.

Harsh, Philip W. *A Handbook of Classical Drama*. Stanford, Calif., 1944.

Kitto, H. D. F. *Greek Tragedy*. 2d ed. London, 1950.

Jaeger, Werner. *Paideia; The Ideals of Greek Culture*. Tr. by Gilbert Highet. 3 vols. New York, 1939–1944.

Lever, Katherine. *The Art of Greek Comedy*. London, 1956.

Murray, Gilbert. *Euripides and His Age*. New York, 1913.

Nicoll, Allardyce. *Masks, Mimes, and Miracles*. New York, 1931.

Pickard-Cambridge, A. W. *Dithyramb, Tragedy, and Comedy*. 2d ed. rev. by T. B. L. Webster. Oxford, 1962.

———. *The Dramatic Festivals of Athens.* Oxford, 1953.

———. *The Theatre of Dionysus in Athens.* Oxford, 1946.

Rees, Kelley. *The Rule of Three Actors in the Classical Greek Drama.* Chicago, 1908.

Webster, T. B. L. *Greek Theatre Production.* London, 1956.

Chapter III: Roman Theatre and Drama

Allen, James T. *Stage Antiquities of the Greeks and Romans and Their Influence.* New York, 1927.

Beare, William. *The Roman Stage; A Short History of Latin Drama in the Time of the Republic.* 2d ed. London, 1955.

Bieber, Margarete. See under Chapter II.

Duckworth, George E. *The Nature of Roman Comedy.* Princeton, N.J., 1952.

Hamilton, Edith. *The Roman Way.* New York, 1932.

Hanson, J. A. *Roman Theater-Temples.* Princeton, N.J., 1959.

Harsh, Philip W. See under Chapter II.

Lucas, Frank L. *Seneca and Elizabethan Tragedy.* Cambridge, 1922.

Nicoll, Allardyce. See under Chapter II.

Norwood, Gilbert. *Plautus and Terence.* New York, 1932.

Chapter IV: Theatre and Drama in the Middle Ages

Chambers, E. K. *The Mediaeval Stage.* 2 vols. Oxford, 1903.

Cohen, Gustave. *Histoire de la Mise-en-scène dans le Théâtre Religieux Français du Moyen Age.* Paris, 1926.

———. *Le Livre de Conduite du Régisseur et le Compte des Déspenses pour le Mystère de la Passion, joué a Mons en 1501. . . .* Paris, 1925.

Craik, Thomas W. *The Tudor Interlude; Stage, Costume, and Acting.* Leicester, 1958.

Evans, Marshall B. *The Passion Play of Lucerne.* New York, 1943.

Farnham, Willard. *The Medieval Heritage of Elizabethan Tragedy.* Berkeley, 1936.

Frank, Grace. *The Medieval French Drama.* Oxford, 1954.

Gardiner, Harold C. *Mysteries' End; An Investigation of the Last Days of the Medieval Religious Stage.* New Haven, Conn., 1946.

Hardison, O. B. *Christian Rite and Christian Drama in the Middle Ages; Essays in the Origin and Early History of Modern Drama.* Baltimore, 1965.

Hunningher, Benjamin. *The Origin of the Theater.* New York, 1961.

Nicoll, Allardyce. See under Chapter II.

Salter, F. M. *Medieval Drama in Chester.* Toronto, 1955.

Southern, Richard. *The Medieval Theatre in the Round.* London, 1957.

Stratman, Carl J. *Bibliography of Medieval Drama.* Berkeley, 1954.

Stuart, D. C. *Stage Decoration in France in the Middle Ages.* New York, 1910.

Weiner, Albert B. *Philippe de Mezieres' Description of the "Festum Praesentationis Beatae Mariae."* Translated from the Latin and Introduced by an Essay on the Birth of Modern Acting. New Haven, Conn., 1958.

Wickham, Glynne. *Early English Stages, 1300–1660.* 2 vols. New York, 1959–1962.

Williams, Arnold. *The Drama of Medieval England.* East Lansing, Mich., 1961.

Young, Karl. *The Drama of the Medieval Church.* 2 vols. Oxford, 1933.

BIBLIOGRAPHY

Chapter V: The Italian Renaissance

Bjurstrom, Per. *Giacomo Torelli and Baroque Stage Design*. Stockholm, 1961.

Burckhardt, Jakob C. *The Civilization of the Renaissance in Italy*. 3d ed. New York, 1950.

Campbell, Lily Bess. *Scenes and Machines on the English Stage during the Renaissance*. Cambridge, 1923.

Duchartre, Pierre L. *The Italian Comedy; The Improvisation, Scenarios, Lives, Attributes, Portraits and Masks of the Illustrious Characters of the Commedia dell'Arte*. Tr. by R. T. Weaver. London, 1929.

Hathaway, Baxter. *The Age of Criticism; The Late Renaissance in Italy*. Ithaca, New York, 1962.

Herrick, Marvin. *Italian Comedy in the Renaissance*. Urbana, 1960.

————. *Tragicomedy; Its Origin and Development in Italy, France, and England*. Urbana, Ill., 1955.

Hewitt, Barnard (ed.). *The Renaissance Stage; Documents of Serlio, Sabbattini, and Furttenbach*. Coral Gables, Fla., 1958.

Kennard, Joseph. *The Italian Theatre*. 2 vols. New York, 1932.

Kernodle, George. *From Art to Theatre; Form and Convention in the Renaissance*. Chicago, 1943.

Lea, Kathleen M. *Italian Popular Comedy; A Study of the Commedia dell'Arte, 1560–1620*. 2 vols. Oxford, 1934.

Nicoll, Allardyce. See under Chapter II.

————. *Stuart Masques and the Renaissance Stage*. London, 1937.

Schwartz, Isidore A. *The Commedia dell'Arte and Its Influence on French Comedy in the Seventeenth Century*. Paris, 1933.

Smith, Winifred. *The Commedia dell'Arte*. New York, 1912.

Springarn, Joel E. *A History of Literary Criticism in the Renaissance*. 2d ed. New York, 1908.

Symonds, John A. *The Renaissance in Italy*. 7 vols. London, 1909–1937.

Vasari, Giorgio. *Vasari's Lives of the Artists*. Paris, 1927.

Vitruvius. *The Ten Books of Architecture*. Tr. by M. H. Morgan. Cambridge, Mass., 1914.

Weinberg, Bernard. *A History of Literary Criticism in the Italian Renaissance*. 2 vols. Chicago, 1961.

Whites, John. *The Birth and Rebirth of Pictorial Space*. London, 1957.

Worsthorne, S. T. *Venetian Opera in the 17th Century*. Oxford, 1954.

Chapter VI: The English Theatre from 1558–1642

Adams, John C. *The Globe Playhouse: Its Design and Equipment*. 2d ed. New York, 1961.

Adams, Joseph Q. *Shakespearean Playhouses; A History of English Theatres from the Beginnings to the Restoration*. Boston, 1917.

Baldwin, T. W. *The Organization and Personnel of the Shakespearean Company*. Princeton, N.J., 1927.

Beckerman, Bernard. *Shakespeare at the Globe, 1599–1609.* New York, 1962.

Bentley, Gerald E. *The Jacobean and Caroline Stage.* 5 vols. Oxford, 1941–1956.

————. *Shakespeare: A Biographical Handbook.* New Haven, Conn., 1961.

Boas, Frederick S. *An Introduction to Stuart Drama.* London, 1946.

Brooke, C. F. T. *The Tudor Drama; A History of English National Drama to the Retirement of Shakespeare.* Boston, 1911.

Campbell, Lily Bess. See under Chapter V.

Chambers, W. K. *The Elizabethan Stage.* 4 vols. London, 1923.

————. *A Short Life of Shakespeare.* Oxford, 1933.

DeBank, Cecile. *Shakespearean Stage Production: Then and Now.* New York, 1953.

Ebisch, Walther and Schucking, L. L. *A Shakespeare Bibliography.* Oxford, 1931. Supplement, 1935.

Ellis-Fermor, Una. *The Jacobean Drama; An Interpretation.* 3d ed. London, 1953.

Gildersleeve, Virginia. *Government Regulations of the Elizabethan Drama.* New York, 1908.

Harrison, George B. *Shakespeare's Tragedies.* London, 1951.

Hodges, C. W. *The Globe Restored.* London, 1953.

Hotson, Leslie. *Shakespeare's Wooden O.* New York, 1960.

Joseph, Bertram. *Elizabethan Acting.* London, 1951.

Lawrence, W. J. *The Elizabethan Playhouse and Other Studies.* 2 vols. Stratford-on-Avon, 1912–1913.

————. *Pre-Restoration Stage Studies.* Cambridge, Mass., 1927.

Nagler, A. M. *Shakespeare's Stage.* New Haven, Conn., 1958.

Nicoll, Allardyce. See under Chapter V.

Parrott, Thomas M. *Shakespearean Comedy.* New York, 1949.

———— and Ball, Robert H. *A Short View of Elizabethan Drama.* New York, 1958.

Ralli, A. J. *A History of Shakespearean Criticism.* 2 vols. London, 1932.

Reynolds, George F. *The Staging of Elizabethan Plays at the Red Bull Theatre, 1605–1625.* New York, 1940.

Rosen, William. *Shakespeare and the Craft of Tragedy.* Cambridge, Mass., 1960.

Rossiter, A. P. *English Drama from Early Times to the Elizabethans; Its Background, Origins, and Developments.* New York, 1950.

"Shakespeare: An Annotated Bibliography," *Shakespeare Quarterly* (1924–present). [*SQ* was originally called *The Shakespeare Association Bulletin.*] Annual bibliography of writings about Shakespeare.

Shakespeare Survey: An Annual Survey of Shakespearean Study and Production. Cambridge, 1948—.

Smith, Irwin. *Shakespeare's Blackfriars Playhouse: Its History and Its Design.* New York, 1964.

Sprague, A. C. *Shakespearean Players and Performances.* Cambridge, Mass., 1953.

Welsford, Enid. *The Court Masque.* Cambridge, 1927.

Wickham, Glynne. See under Chapter IV.

Chapter VII: The Spanish Theatre from 1500 to 1700

Brenan, Gerald. *The Literature of the Spanish People.* 2d ed. New York, 1953.

Crawford, J. P. W. *Spanish Drama before Lope de Vega.* Rev. ed. Philadelphia, 1937.

Rennert, Hugo A. *The Life of Lope de Vega.* Philadelphia, 1904.

————. *The Spanish Stage in the Time of Lope de Vega.* New York, 1909.

BIBLIOGRAPHY

Shergold, N. D. *A History of the Spanish Stage from Medieval Times until the End of the 17th Century*. Oxford, 1967.

Shoemaker, William H. *The Multiple Stage in Spain during the Fifteenth and Sixteenth Centuries*. Princeton, N.J., 1935.

Williams, Ronald B. *The Staging of Plays in the Spanish Peninsula Prior to 1555*. Iowa City, 1935.

Chapter VIII: The Theatre in France from 1548 until 1700

Bjurstrom, Per. See under Chapter V.

Deierkauf-Holsboer, Wilma. *Histoire de la Mise-en-scène dans le Théâtre Français de 1600 à 1657*. Paris, 1933.

Hubert, Judd D. *Molière and the Comedy of Intellect*. Berkeley, 1962.

Lancaster, H. C. *A History of French Dramatic Literature in the Seventeenth Century*. 5 vols. in 9. Baltimore, 1929–1942.

Lawrenson, T. E. *The French Stage in the XVIIth Century: A Study in the Advent of the Italian Order*. Manchester, 1957.

Lockert, Lacy. *Studies in French Classical Tragedy*. Nashville, 1958.

Lough, John. *Paris Theatre Audiences in the Seventeenth and Eighteenth Centuries*. London, 1957.

Mahelot, Laurent. *La Memoire de Mahelot, Laurent et d'autres Décorateurs de l'Hôtel de Bourgogne et de la Comédie Française au XVIIe siècle*. Ed. by H. C. Lancaster. Paris, 1920.

Palmer, John. *Molière*. New York, 1930.

Tilley, A. A. *Molière*. Cambridge, 1936.

Turnell, Martin. *The Classical Moment; Studies in Corneille, Molière, and Racine*. New York, 1948.

Vinaver, Eugene. *Racine and Poetic Tragedy*. Tr. by P. M. Jones. Manchester, 1955.

Wiley, W. L. *The Early Public Theatre in France*. Cambridge, Mass., 1960.

Wright, C. H. C. *French Classicism*. Cambridge, Mass., 1920.

Chapter IX: The English Theatre, 1642–1790

Bernbaum, Ernest. *The Drama of Sensibility; A Sketch of the History of Sentimental Comedy and Domestic Tragedy, 1696–1780*. Cambridge, Mass., 1915.

Boas, Frederick. *An Introduction to Eighteenth Century Drama, 1700–1780*. New York, 1953.

Burnim, Kalmin. *David Garrick, Director*. Pittsburgh, 1961.

Campbell, Lily B. "A History of Costuming on the English Stage between 1660 and 1823," *University of Wisconsin Studies in Language and Literature*, II (1918), 187–223.

Cibber, Colley. *An Apology for the Life of Mr. Colley Cibber*. London, 1740. Reprinted many times.

Dobrée, Bonamy. *Restoration Comedy, 1660–1720*. Oxford, 1924.

———. *Restoration Tragedy, 1660–1720*. Oxford, 1929.

Downer, Alan S. "Nature to Advantage Dressed: Eighteenth Century Acting," *PMLA* (1943), 1002–1037.

"English Literature, 1660–1800; A Current Bibliography," *Philological Quarterly* (1926–present) . Annual list of publications.

Fitzgerald, Percy H. *The Sheridans.* 2 vols. London, 1886.

Hotson, Leslie. *The Commonwealth and Restoration Stage.* Cambridge, Mass., 1928.

Joseph, Bertram. *The Tragic Actor.* New York, 1959.

Krutch, Joseph W. *Comedy and Conscience after the Restoration.* New York, 1949.

The London Stage, 1660–1800. Carbondale, Illinois, 1960—. Not yet completed.

Lynch, James J. *Box, Pit and Gallery; Stage and Society in Johnson's London.* Berkeley, 1953.

Nicoll, Allardyce. *History of English Drama, 1660–1900.* 6 vols. London, 1955–1959.

Odell, G. G. D. *Shakespeare from Betterton to Irving.* 2 vols. New York, 1920.

Palmer, J. L. *The Comedy of Manners.* London, 1913.

Rosenfeld, Sybil. *Strolling Players and Drama in the Provinces, 1660–1765.* Cambridge, 1939.

Southern, Richard. *The Georgian Playhouse.* London, 1948.

———. *Changeable Scenery; Its Origin and Development in the British Theatre.* London, 1952.

Summers, Montague. *The Playhouse of Pepys.* London, 1935.

———. *The Restoration Theatre.* London, 1934.

Thaler, Alwin. *Shakespeare to Sheridan.* Cambridge, Mass., 1922.

Chapter X: Italy and France in the 18th Century

Bjurstrom, Per. See under Chapter V.

Borgerhoff, Elbert. *The Evolution of Liberal Theory and Practice in the French Theatre, 1680–1757.* Princeton, N.J., 1936.

Brenner, C. D. *The Theatre Italien: Its Repertory, 1716–1793, with a Historical Introduction.* Berkeley, 1961.

Goldoni, Carlo. *Memoirs of Carlo Goldoni.* Tr. by John Black. New York, 1926.

Gozzi, Carlo. *The Memoirs of Count Carlo Gozzi.* Tr. by J. A. Symonds. 2 vols. London, 1890.

Green, Frederick C. *Minuet: Critical Survey of French and English Literary Ideas in the 18th Century.* New York, 1935.

Hawkins, Frederick. *The French Stage in the Eighteenth Century.* 2 vols. London, 1888.

Jourdain, Eleanor F. *Dramatic Theory and Practice in France, 1690–1808.* New York, 1921.

Kennard, J. S. See under Chapter V.

Lancaster, H. C. *French Tragedy in the Reign of Louis XVI and the Early Years of the French Revolution, 1774–1792.* Baltimore, 1953.

———. *French Tragedy in the Time of Louis XV and Voltaire, 1715–1774.* Baltimore, 1950.

———. *Sunset: A History of Parisian Drama in the Last Years of Louis XIV, 1701–1715.* Baltimore, 1945.

Lough, John. See under Chapter VIII.

Mayor, A. H. *The Bibiena Family.* New York, 1945.

———. *Giovanni Battista Piranesi.* New York, 1952.

Melcher, Edith. *Stage Realism in France Between Diderot and Antoine.* Bryn Mawr, Penn., 1928.

BIBLIOGRAPHY

Scholz, Janos. *Baroque and Romantic Stage Design.* New York, 1950.
Theatrical Designs from the Baroque through Neo-Classicism. 3 vols. New York, 1940.
Viale Ferrero, Mercedes. *La Scenografia del '700 e i Fratelli Galliari.* Turin, 1963.

Chapter XI: Theatre in Northern and Eastern Europe
During the 18th Century

Aiken-Sneath, Betsy. *Comedy in Germany in the First Half of the 18th Century.* Oxford, 1936.
Beijer, Agne. *Court Theatres of Drottningholm and Gripsholm.* Tr. by G. L. Frolich. Malmo, 1944.
Bredsdorff, Elias *et al. An Introduction to Scandinavian Literature from the Earliest Times to Our Day.* Copenhagen, 1951.
Bruford, Walter H. *Culture and Society in Classical Weimar, 1775–1806.* Cambridge, 1962.
———. *Germany in the Eighteenth Century: The Social Background of the Literary Revival.* Cambridge, 1935.
———. *Theatre, Drama and Audience in Goethe's Germany.* London, 1957.
Gregor, Joseph. *The Russian Theatre.* London, 1930.
Heitner, R. R. *German Tragedy in the Age of Enlightenment, 1724–1768.* Berkeley, 1963.
Pascal, Roy. *The German Sturm und Drang.* Manchester, 1953.
Peacock, Ronald. *Goethe's Major Plays; An Essay.* New York, 1959.
Robertson, J. G. *The Life and Work of Goethe, 1749–1832.* London, 1932.
Slonim, Marc. *Russian Theatre from the Empire to the Soviets.* Cleveland, 1961.
Thomas, Richard R. *The Classical Ideal in German Literature, 1755–1805.* Cambridge, 1939.
Varneke, B. V. *History of the Russian Theatre; Seventeenth through Nineteenth Century.* Tr. by Boris Brasol. New York, 1951.
Willoughby, Leonard A. *The Classical Age of German Literature, 1749–1832.* London, 1926.

Chapter XII: France, Italy, and Spain in the 19th Century

Allévy, Marie Antoinette. *La Mise-en-scène en France dans la première moitié du dix-neuvieme siécle.* Paris, 1938.
Arvin, Neil E. *Eugène Scribe and the French Theatre, 1815–60.* Cambridge, Mass., 1924.
Carlson, Marvin. *The Theatre of the French Revolution.* Ithaca, New York, 1966.
Cook, John A. *Neo-Classic Drama in Spain; Theory and Practice.* Dallas, 1959.
George, A. J. *The Development of French Romanticism.* Syracuse, N.Y., 1955.
Kennard, Joseph S. See under Chapter V.
Lacey, Alexander. *Pixérécourt and the French Romantic Drama.* Toronto, 1928.
Matthews, Brander. *French Dramatists of the Nineteenth Century.* 5th ed. New York, 1914.
———. *The Theatres of Paris.* New York, 1880.
Melcher, Edith. See under Chapter X.

Moynet, Georges. *La Machinerie Théâtrale; Trucs et Decors.* Paris, 1893.

Peers, E. A. *A History of the Romantic Movement in Spain.* 2 vols. Cambridge, 1940.

Weinberg, Bernard. *French Realism: The Critical Reaction, 1830–70.* Chicago, 1937.

Chapter XIII: The Theatre in Germany and Russia in the 19th Century

Abrams, M. H. *The Mirror and the Lamp: Romantic Theory and the Critical Tradition.* New York, 1953.

Gregor, Joseph. See under Chapter XI.

Grube, Max. *The Story of the Meiningen.* Translated by Ann Marie Koller. Coral Gables, Florida, 1963.

Kauffmann, F. W. *German Dramatists of the Nineteenth Century.* Los Angeles, 1940.

Klenze, Camillo von. *From Goethe to Hauptmann.* New York, 1926.

Marstersteig, M. *Das Deutsches Theater im neunzehnten Jahrhundert.* 2d ed. Leipzig, 1924.

Pollak, Gustav. *Franz Grillparzer and the Austrian Drama.* New York, 1907.

Slonim, Marc. ee under Chapter XI.

Stein, Jack M. *Richard Wagner and the Synthesis of the Arts.* Detroit, 1960.

Varneke, B. V. See under Chapter XI.

Wagner, Richard. *Opera and Drama.* Tr. by Edwin Evans. London, 1913.

Walzel, Oskar F. *German Romanticism.* New York, 1932.

Wellek, René. *A History of Modern Literary Criticism.* 2 vols. New Haven, Conn., 1955.

Willoughby, Leonard A. *The Romantic Movement in Germany.* New York, 1930.

Witowski, Georg. *The German Drama of the 19th Century.* New York, 1909.

Chapter XIV: The English Theatre of the 19th Century

Bancroft, Marie Effie. *The Bancrofts.* New York, 1909.

Cole, J. W. *The Life and Theatrical Times of Charles Kean.* London, 1859.

Coleman, John. *Memoirs of Samuel Phelps.* London, 1886.

Disher, Maurice. *Blood and Thunder; Mid-Victorian Melodrama and Its Origins.* London, 1949.

Downer, Alan S. "Players and the Painted Stage: Nineteenth Century Acting," *PMLA,* LXI (1946), 522–576.

Fitzgerald, Percy. *The World Behind the Scenes.* London, 1881.

Joseph, Bertram. See under Chapter IX.

Macready, William Charles. *Macready's Reminiscences.* New York, 1875.

Nicoll, Allardyce. See under Chapter IX.

Odell, G. C. D. See under Chapter IX.

Planché, J. R. *The Recollections and Reflections of James Robinson Planché.* 2 vols. London, 1872.

"The Romantic Movement: A Current Selective and Critical Bibliography," *English Literary History* (1937–49), *Philological Quarterly* (1950–present). An annual list of publications.

Rowell, George. *The Victorian Theatre.* London, 1956.

BIBLIOGRAPHY

Sachs, Edwin O. and Woodrow, E. A. E. *Modern Opera Houses and Theatres.* 3 vols. London, 1897–1898.

Southern, Richard. See under Chapter IX.

Vardac, A. N. *Stage to Screen; Theatrical Method from Garrick to Griffith.* Cambridge, Mass., 1949.

"Victorian Bibliography for [1932—]," *Modern Philology,* XXX (1932–1933)–LIV (1956–1957); *Victorian Studies,* I (1957–1958) —.

Waitzkin, Leo. *The Witch of Wych Street; A Study of the Theatrical Reforms of Madame Vestris.* Cambridge, 1933.

Watson, Ernest B. *Sheridan to Robertson; A Study of the 19th Century London Stage.* Cambridge, 1926.

Chapter XV: The American Theatre to 1915

Belasco, David. *Theatre Through Its Stage Door.* New York, 1919.

Bernheim, A. L. *The Business of the Theatre.* New York, 1932.

Carson, W. G. B. *The Theatre on the Frontier.* Chicago, 1932.

———. *Managers in Distress.* St. Louis, 1949.

Coad, O. S. and Mims, Edwin, Jr. *The American Stage* (Vol. XIV of *The Pageant of America*). New Haven, Conn., 1929.

Dunlap, William. *History of the American Theatre.* New York, 1832.

Felheim, Marvin. *The Theatre of Augustin Daly: An Account of the Late Nineteenth Century Stage.* Cambridge, Mass., 1956.

Frohman, Daniel and Marcosson, I. T. *Charles Frohman, Manager and Man.* New York, 1916.

Hewitt, Barnard. *Theatre USA, 1668–1957.* New York, 1959.

Hughes, Glenn. *A History of the American Theatre, 1700–1950.* New York, 1951.

Mammen, Edward W. *The Old Stock Company School of Acting.* Boston, 1945.

Matthews, Brander and Hutton, Laurence. *Actors and Actresses of Great Britain and the United States from the Days of David Garrick to the Present Time.* 5 vols. New York, 1886.

Moody, Richard. *America Takes the Stage; Romanticism in American Drama and Theatre, 1750–1900.* Bloomington, Indiana, 1955.

Moses, Montrose J. and Brown, John M. *The American Theatre as Seen by Its Critics, 1752–1934.* New York, 1934.

Odell, G. C. D. *Annals of the New York Stage.* 15 vols. New York, 1927–1949.

Quinn, Arthur H. *A History of the American Drama from the Beginning to the Civil War.* 2d ed. New York, 1943.

———. *A History of the American Drama from the Civil War to the Present Day.* 2d ed. New York, 1949.

Seilhamer, George O. *History of the American Theatre* [1749–1797]. 3 vols. Philadelphia, 1888–1891.

Stratman, C. J. *Bibliography of the American Theatre, Excluding New York City.* Chicago, 1965.

Wilson, Garff B. *A History of American Acting.* Bloomington, Ind., 1966.

Wright, Richardson. *Revels in Jamaica, 1682–1838.* New York, 1937.

BIBLIOGRAPHY

Chapter XVI: The Theatre of the Orient

Arlington, Lewis C. *The Chinese Drama from the Earliest Times until Today*. Shanghai, 1930.

Bowers, Faubion. *Japanese Theatre*. New York, 1952.

Brandon, J. R. *Theatre in Southeast Asia*. Cambridge, Mass., 1967.

Ernst, Earle. *The Kabuki Theatre*. New York, 1956.

Gargi, Balwant. *Theatre in India*. New York, 1962.

Gupta, Chandra B. *The Indian Theatre*. Benares, 1954.

Haar, Francis. *Japanese Theatre in Highlight; A Pictorial Commentary*, Tokyo, 1952.

Hironaga, Shuzaburo. *Bunraku, Japan's Unique Puppet Theatre*. Tokyo, 1964.

Kawatake, Shigetoshi. *An Illustrated History of Japanese Theatre Arts*. Tokyo, 1956.

Kincaid, Zoe. *Kabuki, the Popular Stage of Japan*. London, 1935.

Mangkunagoro VII. *On the Wayang Kulit and Its Symbolic and Mystical Elements*. Ithaca, New York, 1957.

Mathur, Jagdesh. *Drama in Rural India*. New York, 1964.

O'Neill, P. G. *A Guide to No*. Tokyo, 1953.

Scott, A. C. *The Classical Theatre of China*. New York, 1957.

Zucker, Adolf E. *The Chinese Theatre*. Boston, 1925.

Chapter XVII: The Modern Theatre, 1875–1915

Antoine, André. *Memories of the Théâtre Libre*. Tr. Marvin Carlson. Coral Gables, Fla., 1964.

Appia, Adolphe. *The Work of Living Art and Man Is the Measure of All Things*. Coral Gables, Fla., 1960.

Bablet, Denis. *Esthétique Générale du Décor de Théâtre de 1870 à 1914*. Paris, 1965.

Bentley, Eric. *The Playwright as Thinker; A Study of Drama in Modern Times*. New York, 1946.

Bourgeois, Maurice. *J. M. Synge and the Irish Theatre*. New York, 1965.

Brustein, Robert. *The Theatre of Revolt*. New York, 1964.

Byrne, Dawson. *The Story of Ireland's National Theatre: The Abbey*. Dublin, 1929.

Carter, Lawson A. *Zola and the Theatre*. New Haven, Conn., 1963.

Cole, Toby and Chinoy, Helen K. (eds.) *Directing the Play; A Source Book of Stagecraft*. Indianapolis, 1953.

Cole, Toby (ed.). *Playwrights on Playwriting; The Meaning and Making of Modern Drama from Ibsen to Ionesco*. New York, 1961.

Cornell, Kenneth. *The Symbolist Movement*. New Haven, Conn., 1951.

Craig, Edward Gordon. *On the Art of the Theatre*. 2d ed. Boston, 1924.

Dahlstrom, C. E. W. L. *Strindberg's Dramatic Expressionism*. Vol. VII of University of Michigan Publications. Language and Literature. Ann Arbor, 1930.

Fuchs, Georg. *Revolution in the Theatre*. Trans. C. C. Kuhn. Ithaca, N.Y., 1959.

Garten, H. F. *Modern German Drama*. New York, 1959.

Gassner, John. *Form and Idea in the Modern Theatre*. New York, 1956.

———. *The Theatre in Our Times; A Survey of the Men, Materials and Movements in the Modern Theatre*. New York, 1954.

BIBLIOGRAPHY

Gorchakov, Nikolai A. *The Theatre in Soviet Russia.* Tr. by Edgar Lehman. New York, 1957.

Gorelik, Mordecai. *New Theatres for Old.* New York, 1940.

Lehmann, Andrew G. *The Symbolist Aesthetic in France, 1885–1895.* Oxford, 1950.

Lumley, Fredrick. *Trends in Twentieth Century Drama; A Survey Since Ibsen and Shaw.* 2d ed. London, 1960.

MacCarthy, Desmond. *The Court Theatre, 1904–07.* London, 1907.

Miller, Anna Irene. *The Independent Theatre in Europe, 1887 to the Present.* New York, 1931.

Newmark, Maxim. *Otto Brahm: The Man and the Critic.* New York, 1938.

Northam, John. *Ibsen's Dramatic Method; A Study of the Prose Dramas.* London, 1953.

Sayler, Oliver M. (ed.) . *Max Reinhardt and His Theatre.* New York, 1926.

Slonim, Marc. See Chapter XI.

Sondel, Bess S. *Zola's Naturalistic Theory with Particular Reference to the Drama.* Chicago, 1939.

Stanislavsky, Konstantin. *An Actor Prepares.* Tr. Elizabeth R. Hapgood. New York, 1936.

———. *Building a Character.* Tr. E. R. Hapgood. New York, 1949.

———. *My Life in Art.* Tr. J. J. Robbins. Boston, 1938.

———. *Creating a Role.* Tr. E. R. Hapgood, New York, 1961.

Waxman, S. M. *Antoine and the Théâtre Libre.* Cambridge, Mass., 1926.

Wellek, René. *A History of Modern Criticism, 1750–1950.* Vols. 3 and 4. New York, 1965.

Williams, Raymond. *Drama from Ibsen to Eliot.* London, 1952.

Zucker, A. E. *Ibsen, the Master Builder.* New York, 1929.

Chapter XVIII: The Theatre Between the Wars

Artaud, Antonin. *The Theatre and Its Double.* Tr. by Mary C. Richards. New York, 1958.

Balakian, Anna E. *Surrealism.* New York, 1959.

Bentley, Eric. See Chapter XVII.

Bishop, G. W. *Barry Jackson and The London Theatre.* London, 1933.

Boleslavsky, Richard. *Acting; The First Six Lessons.* New York, 1933.

Brecht, Bertolt. *Brecht on Theatre.* Tr. John Willett. New York, 1964.

Breton, André. *What Is Surrealism?* London, 1936.

Brustein, Robert. See Chapter XVII.

Carter, Huntly. *The New Spirit in the European Theatre, 1914–1924.* New York, 1926.

Cheney, Sheldon. *The New Movement in the Theatre.* New York, 1914.

———. *Stage Decoration.* New York, 1928.

Chekhov, Michael. *To the Actor on the Technique of Acting.* New York, 1953.

Clurman, Harold. *The Fervent Years; The Story of the Group Theatre in the Thirties.* New York, 1957.

Cole, Toby. See Chapter XVII.

Davis, Hallie Flanagan. *Arena.* New York, 1940.

Donoghue. *The Third Voice: Modern British and American Verse Drama.* Princeton, N.J., 1959.

Downer, Alan S. *Fifty Years of American Drama, 1900–1950.* Chicago, 1951.

Esslin, Martin. *Brecht; The Man and His Work.* Garden City, N.Y., 1960.

Fowlie, Wallace. *Age of Surrealism.* Bloomington, Ind., 1960.

Frank, Waldo. *The Art of the Vieux-Colombier*. New York, 1918.

Fuerst, Walter R. and Hume, Samuel J. *Twentieth Century Stage Decoration*. 2 vols. London, 1928.

Garten, H. F. See Chapter XVII.

Gielgud, John. *Early Stages*. New York, 1939.

Gorchakov, Nikolai. See Chapter XVII.

———. *The Vakhtangov School of Stage Art*, Moscow, n.d.

Gorelik, Mordecai. See Chapter XVII.

Houghton, Norris. *Moscow Rehearsals; An Account of Methods of Production in the Soviet Theatre*. New York, 1936.

Knapp, Bettina. *Louis Jouvet, Man of the Theatre*. New York, 1958.

Krutch, Joseph W. *The American Drama since 1918*. Rev. ed. New York, 1957.

Lumley, Frederick. See Chapter XVII.

MacClintock, Lander. *The Age of Pirandello*. Bloomington, Ind., 1951.

Marshall, Norman. *The Other Theatre*. London, 1947.

Macgowan, Kenneth and Jones, Robert E. *Continental Stagecraft*. New York, 1922.

Mackay, Constance D. *The Little Theatre in the United States*. New York, 1917.

Moderwell, Hiram K. *The Theatre of To-day*. New York, 1925.

Moussinac, Leon. *The New Movement in the Theatre; A Survey of Recent Developments in Europe and America*. London, 1931.

Quinn, Arthur H. See Chapter XV.

Rabkin, Gerald. *Drama and Commitment: Politics in the American Theatre of the Thirties*. Bloomington, Ind., 1964.

Samuel, Richard and Thomas, R. H. *Expressionism in German Life, Literature and the Theatre* (1910–1924). Cambridge, 1939.

Schlemmer, Oscar *et al. The Theatre of the Bauhaus*. Middletown, Conn., 1961.

Slonim, Marc. See Chapter XI.

Smith, Cecil. *Musical Comedy in America*. New York, 1950.

Sokel, Walter H. *The Writer in Extremis: Expressionism in Twentieth Century German Literature*. Stanford, Calif., 1959.

Theatre Arts. 32 vols. Detroit and New York, 1916–1948.

Wellek, René. See Chapter XVII.

Willett, John. *The Theatre of Bertolt Brecht*. New York, 1959.

Williams, Raymond. See Chapter XVII.

Chapter XIX: The Theatre Since the Second World War

Barrault, Jean-Louis. *The Theatre of Jean-Louis Barrault*. Tr. J. Chiari. New York, 1961.

Benedikt, Michael and Wellwarth, George. *Modern French Theatre; The Avant-Garde, Dada, and Surrealism*. New York, 1964.

Bentley, Eric. *In Search of Theatre*. New York, 1953.

Bowers, Faubion. *Broadway, USSR; Theatre, Ballet and Entertainment in Russia Today*. New York, 1959.

Brecht, Bertolt. See Chapter XVIII.

Brustein, Robert. See Chapter XVII.

Chiari, Joseph. *The Contemporary French Theatre; the Flight from Naturalism*. London, 1958.

Cole, Toby. See Chapter XVII.

BIBLIOGRAPHY

Donoghue, Denis. See Chapter XVIII.

Downer, Alan. *Recent American Drama*. Minneapolis, 1961.

Esslin, Martin. See Chapter XVIII.

———. *The Theatre of the Absurd*. Garden City, N.Y., 1961.

Fowlie, Wallace. *Dionysus in Paris: A Guide to Contemporary French Theatre*. 1960.

Garten, H. F. See Chapter XVII.

Gassner, John. *Directions in Modern Theatre and Drama*. New York, 1965.

———. *Theatre at the Crossroads; Plays and Playwrights of Mid-Century American Stage*. New York, 1960.

Gorchakov, Nikolai. See Chapter XVII.

Grossvogel, David I. *The Self-Conscious Stage in Modern French Drama*. New York, 1958.

Guicharnaud, Jacques. *Modern French Theatre from Giraudoux to Beckett*. New Haven, Conn., 1961.

Hainaux, René (ed.). *Stage Design Throughout the World Since 1935*. New York, 1956.

———. *Stage Design Throughout the World Since 1950*. New York, 1964.

Houghton, Norris. *Return Engagement: A Postscript to "Moscow Rehearsals."* New York, 1962.

Kirby, Michael. *Happenings*. New York, 1965.

Lumley, Frederick. See Chapter XVII.

Popkin, Henry. *The New British Drama*. New York, 1964.

Price, Julia. *The Off-Broadway Theatre*. New York, 1962.

Saint-Denis, Michel. *Theatre, the Rediscovery of Style*. New York, 1960.

Slonim, Marc. See Chapter XI.

Strasberg, Lee. *Strasberg at the Actor's Studio*. New York, 1965.

Styan, J. L. *The Dark Comedy; The Development of Modern Comic Tragedy*. Cambridge, 1962.

Taylor, John R. *Anger and After; A Guide to the New British Drama*. London, 1962.

The Tulane Drama Review. Carleton, Minn., New Orleans, and New York, 1957—.

Weales, Gerald. *American Drama since World War II*. New York, 1962.

Wellwarth, George E. *The Theatre of Protest and Paradox: Development in the Avant-Garde Drama*. New York, 1964.

Willett, John. See Chapter XVIII.

World Theatre. Paris, 1950—.

INDEX

INDEX

706

INDEX

INDEX

INDEX

INDEX

INDEX

INDEX

INDEX

INDEX

INDEX

INDEX

INDEX

INDEX

INDEX

INDEX

INDEX

INDEX